DOCTRINES AND DISCIPLINE OF THE METHODIST CHURCH

DOCTRINES

AND

DISCIPLINE

OF

The Methodist Church

1964

> THE METHODIST EPISCOPAL CHURCH
> THE METHODIST EPISCOPAL CHURCH, SOUTH
> THE METHODIST PROTESTANT CHURCH

THE METHODIST PUBLISHING HOUSE
NASHVILLE, TENNESSEE

The book editor, the secretary of the General Conference, and the publisher of The Methodist Church shall be charged with editing the *Discipline*. The editors in the exercise of their judgment shall have authority to make such changes in phraseology as may be necessary to harmonize legislation without changing its substance.

The editors are instructed to include as Part IX of the *Discipline* the contents of Section I, entitled "The General Services of the Church," from *The Book of Worship for Church and Home*, as adopted by the 1964 General Conference; and the editors are further instructed to include in the Appendix the same chapters as in the 1960 *Discipline*, except as otherwise specifically ordered by the 1964 General Conference.

—*Journal of the General Conference*, 1964

EMORY STEVENS BUCKE
BOOK EDITOR

LEON T. MOORE
SECRETARY OF THE GENERAL CONFERENCE

LOVICK PIERCE
PUBLISHER

GORDON B. DUNCAN
ASSISTANT BOOK EDITOR

PRINTED IN THE UNITED STATES OF AMERICA

287.6
n59do
964
c.2

CONTENTS

Note: The basic unit in the Discipline is the paragraph (¶), rather than page, chapter, section, etc. The paragraphs are numbered in order through the entire volume, but with many numbers skipped, in order to allow for future enactments, and to fit into the following plan:

If a paragraph is divided into numbered parts, each is called a subparagraph (§). When a paragraph number is followed by a subparagraph number, the symbol § is replaced by a period, so that the two numbers appear in the form of a single decimal number. For example, ¶ 4.3 means paragraph 4, subparagraph 3.

PART I
THE CONSTITUTION
¶¶ 1-98

PART II
THE LOCAL CHURCH
¶¶ 101-296

PART III
THE MINISTRY
¶¶ 301-446

CONTENTS

CONTENTS

CONTENTS

Episcopal Greetings

THE METHODIST DISCIPLINE is a growth rather than a purposive creation. The founders of Methodism did not work with a set plan, as to details. They dealt with conditions as these arose. The "class meeting," a distinctive feature of the movement, began as an instrument for the collection of funds. It soon revealed its fitness for religious nurture and took that work as its chief aim. The use of laymen as preachers came at first against Wesley's will, but it was continued because it seemed to be the one effective way of dealing with actual situations. Open-air preaching, always admitted as a "cross" by Mr. Wesley, came partly because the churches were closed to Methodist preachers, and partly because the people who most needed to be helped would not come to regular services in the sanctuaries. Even conferences gained their origin from the actual need of bringing workers together for consultation and inspiration.

This process of growth showed itself clearly as the church increased. Conference work was carried on by the asking of what were called "Minute Questions." These were not perfunctory and artificial. They dealt with the effective ways of presenting the deeper phases and duties of religious experience. As new forms of work were developed, new questions were added to the conference list.

In such a process of adjustment, the DISCIPLINE became a record of the successive stages of spiritual insight attained by Methodists under the grace of Christ. We have therefore expected that the DISCIPLINE would be administered, not merely as a legal document, but as a revelation of the Holy Spirit working in and through our people. We reverently insist that a fundamental aim of Methodism is to make her organization an instrument for the development of spiritual life. We do not regard the machinery as sacred in life itself, but we do regard as very sacred the souls for whom the church lives and works.

1

We do now express the faith and hope that the prayerful observance of the spiritual intent of the DISCIPLINE may be to the people called Methodists a veritable means of grace.

For this reason we wish that this publication might be found in every Methodist home, and the more so because it contains the Articles of Religion which are held more or less by all the Reformed churches of the world. Thus we remain your very affectionate brethren and pastors, who earnestly commend you to Christ.

THE COUNCIL OF BISHOPS

LLOYD C. WICKE
President

PRINCE A. TAYLOR, JR.
President Designate

ROY H. SHORT
Secretary

METHODIST BISHOPS

*A List Compiled for the Committee on the
Discipline of the Council of Bishops
by J. Tremayne Copplestone*

NAME	CONSECRATED	NAME	CONSECRATED
Thomas Coke	1784	Gilbert Haven	1872
Francis Asbury	1784	Jesse T. Peck	1872
Richard Whatcoat	1800	Edward G. Andrews	1872
William McKendree	1808	Henry W. Warren	1880
Enoch George	1816	Cyrus D. Foss	1880
Robert R. Roberts	1816	John F. Hurst	1880
Joshua Soule	1824	Erastus O. Haven	1880
Elijah Hedding	1824	Alpheus W. Wilson	1882
James O. Andrew	1832	Linus Parker	1882
John Emory	1832	John C. Granbery	1882
Beverly Waugh	1836	Robert K. Hargrove	1882
Thomas A. Morris	1836	William X. Ninde	1884
Leonidas L. Hamline	1844	John M. Walden	1884
Edmund S. Janes	1844	Willard F. Mallalieu	1884
William Capers	1846	Charles H. Fowler	1884
Robert Paine	1846	William Taylor	1884
Henry B. Bascom	1850	William W. Duncan	1886
Levi Scott	1852	Charles B. Galloway	1886
Matthew Simpson	1852	Eugene R. Hendrix	1886
Osmon C. Baker	1852	Joseph S. Key	1886
Edward R. Ames	1852	John H. Vincent	1888
George F. Pierce	1854	James N. FitzGerald	1888
John Early	1854	Isaac W. Joyce	1888
Hubbard H. Kavanaugh	1854	John P. Newman	1888
Francis Burns	1858	Daniel A. Goodsell	1888
Davis W. Clark	1864	James M. Thoburn	1888
Edward Thompson	1864	Atticus G. Haygood	1890
Calvin Kingsley	1864	Oscar P. Fitzgerald	1890
William M. Wightman	1866	Charles C. McCabe	1896
Enoch M. Marvin	1866	Joseph C. Hartzell	1896
David S. Doggett	1866	Earl Cranston	1896
Holland N. McTyeire	1866	Warren A. Candler	1898
John W. Roberts	1866	Henry C. Morrison	1898
John C. Keener	1870	David H. Moore	1900
Thomas Bowman	1872	John W. Hamilton	1900
William L. Harris	1872	Edwin W. Parker	1900
Randolph S. Foster	1872	Frank W. Warne	1900
Isaac W. Wiley	1872	A. Coke Smith	1902
Stephen M. Merrill	1872	E. Embree Hoss	1902

3

NAME	CONSECRATED	NAME	CONSECRATED
Joseph F. Berry	1904	James Cannon, Jr.	1918
Henry Spellmeyer	1904	Lauress J. Birney	1920
William F. McDowell	1904	Frederick B. Fisher	1920
James W. Bashford	1904	Ernest L. Waldorf	1920
William Burt	1904	Charles E. Locke	1920
Luther B. Wilson	1904	Ernest G. Richardson	1920
Thomas B. Neely	1904	Charles W. Burns	1920
Isaiah B. Scott	1904	Anton Bast	1920
William F. Oldham	1904	Edgar Blake	1920
John E. Robinson	1904	George H. Bickley	1920
Merriman C. Harris	1904	Frederick T. Keeney	1920
John J. Tigert	1906	H. Lester Smith	1920
Seth Ward	1906	Charles L. Mead	1920
James Atkins	1906	Robert E. Jones	1920
William F. Anderson	1908	Matthew W. Clair	1920
John L. Nuelsen	1908	William B. Beauchamp	1922
William A. Quayle	1908	James E. Dickey	1922
Charles W. Smith	1908	Sam R. Hay	1922
Wilson S. Lewis	1908	Hoyt M. Dobbs	1922
Edwin H. Hughes	1908	Hiram A. Boaz	1922
Robert McIntyre	1908	George A. Miller	1924
Frank M. Bristol	1908	Titus Lowe	1924
Collins Denny	1910	George R. Grose	1924
John C. Kilgo	1910	Brenton T. Badley	1924
William B. Murrah	1910	Wallace E. Brown	1924
Walter R. Lambuth	1910	Raymond J. Wade	1928
Richard G. Waterhouse	1910	James C. Baker	1928
Edwin D. Mouzon	1910	Edwin F. Lee	1928
James H. McCoy	1910	John Gowdy	1930
Homer C. Stuntz	1912	Chih P'ing Wang	1930
Theodore S. Henderson	1912	Arthur J. Moore	1930
William O. Shepard	1912	Paul B. Kern	1930
Naphtali Luccock	1912	A. Frank Smith	1930
Francis J. McConnell	1912	Jashwant R. Chitambar	1931
Frederick D. Leete	1912	Juan E. Gattinoni	1932
Richard J. Cooke	1912	J. Ralph Magee	1932
Wilbur P. Thirkield	1912	Ralph S. Cushman	1932
John W. Robinson	1912	J. Waskom Pickett	1936
William P. Eveland	1912	Wilbur E. Hammaker	1936
Herbert Welch	1916	Charles W. Flint	1936
Thomas Nicholson	1916	G. Bromley Oxnam	1936
Adna W. Leonard	1916	Alexander P. Shaw	1936
Matthew S. Hughes	1916	John M. Springer	1936
Charles B. Mitchell	1916	Roberto Elphick	1936
Franklin Hamilton	1916	F. H. Otto Melle	1936
Alexander P. Camphor	1916	Ralph A. Ward	1937
Eben S. Johnson	1916	Ivan Lee Holt	1938
John M. Moore	1918	William W. Peele	1938
William F. McMurry	1918	Clare Purcell	1938
Urban V. W. Darlington	1918	Charles C. Selecman	1938
Horace M. Du Bose	1918	John L. Decell	1938
William N. Ainsworth	1918	William C. Martin	1938

NAME	CONSECRATED	NAME	CONSECRATED
William T. Watkins	1938	H. Bascom Watts	1952
James H. Straughn	1939	John W. Branscomb	...1952
John C. Broomfield	1939	A. Raymond Grant	...1952
William A. C. Hughes	...1940	Julio M. Sabanes	1952
Lorenzo H. King	1940	Friedrich Wunderlich	...1953
Bruce R. Baxter	1940	Odd Hagen	1953
Shot K. Mondol	1941	Ferdinand Sigg	1954
Clement D. Rockey	1941	Prince A. Taylor, Jr.	...1956
Enrique C. Balloch	1941	Eugene M. Frank	...1956
Z. T. Kaung	1941	Nolan B. Harmon	1956
W. Y. Chen	1941	Bachman G. Hodge	...1956
Carleton Lacy	1941	Hobart B. Amstutz	...1956
Fred P. Corson	1944	Ralph E. Dodge	1956
W. Earl Ledden	1944	Mangal Singh	1956
Lewis O. Hartman	1944	Gabriel Sundaram	...1956
Newell S. Booth	1944	Charles F. Golden	...1960
Schuyler E. Garth	1944	Noah W. Moore, Jr.	1960
Charles W. Brashares	...1944	Marquis L. Harris	1960
Paul N. Garber	1944	Ralph T. Alton	1960
Costen J. Harrell	1944	Edwin R. Garrison	1960
Paul E. Martin	1944	T. Otto Nall	1960
W. Angie Smith	1944	Fred G. Holloway	1960
Edward W. Kelly	1944	James K. Mathews	...1960
Robert N. Brooks	1944	W. Vernon Middleton	...1960
Willis J. King	1944	W. Ralph Ward	1960
Arthur F. Wesley	1944	Oliver E. Slater	1960
John A. Subhan	1945	William K. Pope	1960
Dionisio D. Alejandro	...1946	Paul V. Galloway	1960
Theodor Arvidson	1946	Aubrey G. Walton	1960
J. W. E. Sommer	1946	Kenneth W. Copeland	...1960
Lloyd C. Wicke	1948	James W. Henley	...1960
John W. Lord	1948	Walter C. Gum	1960
J. W. E. Bowen	1948	Paul A. Hardin, Jr.	1960
Dana Dawson	1948	John O. Smith	1960
Marvin A. Franklin	...1948	Everett W. Palmer	1960
Roy H. Short	1948	B. Foster Stockwell	...1960
Richard C. Raines	1948	Pedro Zóttele	1962
Marshall R. Reed	1948	James S. Thomas	1964
H. Clifford Northcott	...1948	W. McFerrin Stowe	...1964
Hazen G. Werner	1948	R. Marvin Stuart	...1964
Glenn R. Phillips	1948	Dwight E. Loder	1964
Gerald H. Kennedy	1948	Thomas M. Pryor	1964
Donald H. Tippett	1948	Francis E. Kearns	1964
José L. Valencia	1948	Lance Webb	1964
Sante Uberto Barbieri	...1949	W. Kenneth Goodson	...1964
Raymond L. Archer	...1950	Edward J. Pendergrass	.1964
Edgar A. Love	1952	H. Ellis Finger, Jr.	1964
Matthew W. Clair, Jr.	...1952	Earl G. Hunt, Jr.	1964
D. Stanley Coors	1952	Robert F. Lundy	1964
Edwin E. Voigt	1952	Escrivão A. Zunguze	...1964
F. Gerald Ensley	1952	John Wesley Shungu	...1964
Frederick B. Newell	1952	Harry P. Andreassen	...1964

5

Historical Statement

The Methodist Church is a church of Christ in which "the pure Word of God is preached, and the Sacraments duly administered." This church is a great Protestant body, though it did not come directly out of the Reformation but had its origin within the Church of England. Its founder was John Wesley, a clergyman of that church, as was his father before him. His mother, Susanna Wesley, was a woman of zeal, devotion, and strength of character who was perhaps the greatest single human influence in Wesley's life.

Nurtured in this devout home, educated at Oxford University, the young John Wesley, like a second Paul, sought in vain for religious satisfaction by the strict observance of the rules of religion and the ordinances of the church. The turning point in his life came when, at a prayer meeting in Aldersgate Street, London, on May 24, 1738, he learned what Paul had discovered, that it is not by rules and laws, nor by our own efforts at self-perfection, but by faith in God's mercy as it comes to us in Christ, that man may enter upon life and peace.

The gospel which Wesley thus found for himself he began to proclaim to others, first to companions who sought his counsel, including his brother Charles, then in widening circles that took him throughout the British Isles. His message had a double emphasis, which has remained with Methodism to this day. First was the gospel of God's grace, offered to all men and equal to every human need. Second was the moral ideal which this gospel presents to men. The Bible, he declared, knows no salvation which is not salvation from sin. He called men to holiness of life, and this holiness, he insisted, is "social holiness," the love and service of their fellow men. Methodism meant "Christianity in earnest." The General Rules which are still found in our Discipline are the directions which Wesley gave to his followers to enable them to test the sincerity of their purpose and to guide them in this life.

Wesley did not plan to found a new church. In his work he simply followed, like Paul, the clear call of God, first to preach the gospel to the needy who were not being reached by the Established Church and its clergy, second to take care of those who were won to the Christian life. Step by step he was led on until Methodism became a great and transforming movement in the life of England. He gathered his people in groups, in classes and societies. He appointed leaders. He found men who were ready to carry the gospel to the masses, speaking on the streets, in the open fields, and in private homes. These men were not ordained ministers but lay preachers, or "local preachers," as they were called. He appointed these men, assigned them to various fields of labor, and supervised their work. Once a year he called them together for a conference, just as Methodist preachers meet in their Annual Conference sessions today.

Wesley thus united in extraordinary fashion three notable activities, in all of which he excelled. One was evangelism; "The world is my parish," he declared. His preachers went to the people; they did not wait for the people to come to them, and he himself knew the highways and byways of England as did no other man of his day. The second was organization and administration, by which he conserved the fruits of this preaching and extended its influence. The third was his appreciation of education and his use of the printed page. He made the press a servant of the Church and was the father of the mass circulation of inexpensive books, pamphlets, and periodicals.

From England Methodism spread to Ireland and then to America. In 1766 Philip Embury, a lay preacher from Ireland, began to preach in the city of New York. At about the same time Robert Strawbridge, another lay preacher from Ireland, settled in Frederick County, Maryland, and began the work there. In 1769 Wesley sent Richard Boardman and Joseph Pilmore to America, and two years later Francis Asbury, who became the great leader of American Methodism.

Methodism was especially adapted to American life. These itinerant preachers served the people under conditions where a settled ministry was not feasible. They sought out the scattered homes, followed the tide of migration as it moved west, preached the gospel, organized societies, established "preaching places," and formed these into "circuits." Thus by the close of the American Revolution the Methodists numbered some fifteen thousand members and eighty preachers.

In the beginning Wesley had thought of his fellows not as constituting a church but simply as forming so many societies. The preachers were not ordained, and the members were supposed to receive the Sacraments in the Anglican Church. But the Anglican clergy in America were few and far between. The Revolution had severed America from England, and Methodism to all intents and purposes had become an independent church. Wesley responded to appeals for help from America by asking the Bishop of London to ordain some of his preachers. Failing in this, he himself ordained two men and set aside Dr. Thomas Coke, who was a presbyter of the Church of England, to be a superintendent, "to preside over the flock of Christ" in America. Coke was directed to ordain Francis Asbury as a second superintendent.

At the Christmas Conference, which met in Baltimore December 24, 1784, some sixty preachers, with Dr. Coke and his companions, organized the Methodist Episcopal Church in America. Wesley had sent over *The Sunday Service*, a simplified form of the English Book of Common Prayer, with the Articles of Religion reduced in number. This book they adopted, adding to the articles one which recognized the independence of the new nation.

Our present Articles of Religion come from this book and unite us with the historic faith of Christendom. Our Ritual, too, though it has been modified, has this as its source. However, the forms for public worship taken from the Book of Common Prayer were not adapted to the freer religious life of American Methodism and never entered into common use. Instead, Methodism created a book of its own, its Discipline. This contains today the Articles of Religion, Wesley's General Rules, the Ritual and other forms of worship, and a large section which deals with the ministry, the various church organizations, and the rules governing the life and work of the church.

In the history of Methodism two notable divisions occurred. In 1828 a group of earnest and godly persons, largely moved by an insistence on lay representation, separated and became the Methodist Protestant Church. In 1844 there was another division, the cause being construed by some as the question of slavery, by others as a constitutional issue over the powers of the General Conference versus the episcopacy. After years of negotiation a Plan of Union was agreed upon; and on May 10, 1939, The Methodist Episcopal Church, The Methodist Episcopal Church, South, and The Methodist Protestant Church united to form The Methodist Church.

The Methodist Church believes today, as Methodism has from the first, that the only infallible proof of a true church of Christ is its ability to seek and to save the lost, to disseminate the Pentecostal spirit and life, to spread scriptural holiness, and to transform all peoples and nations through the gospel of Christ. The sole object of the rules, regulations, and usages of The Methodist Church is to aid the church in fulfilling its divine commission. United Methodism thanks God for the new life and strength which have come with reunion, while realizing the new obligations which this brings. At the same time it rejoices in the fact that it is a part of the one Church of our Lord and shares in a common task. Its spirit is still expressed in Wesley's word: "I desire to have a league, offensive and defensive, with every soldier of Christ. We have not only one faith, one hope, one Lord, but are directly engaged in one warfare."

THE DECLARATION OF UNION

WHEREAS, The Methodist Episcopal Church, The Methodist Episcopal Church, South, and The Methodist Protestant Church did through their respective General Conferences appoint Commissions on Interdenominational Relations and Church Union; and

WHEREAS, These Commissions acting jointly did produce, propose, and present to the three Churches a Plan of Union; and

WHEREAS, These three Churches, each acting separately for and in its own behalf, did by more than the constitutional majorities endorse and adopt this Plan of Union, in accord with their respective constitutions and disciplines, and did effect the full consummation of union in accordance with the Plan of Union; and

WHEREAS, These three Churches in adopting this Plan of Union did authorize and provide for a Uniting Conference with certain powers and duties as therein set forth; and

WHEREAS, The Uniting Conference duly authorized and legally chosen in accordance with the Plan of Union is now in session in the city of Kansas City, Missouri:

Now, THEREFORE, We, the members of the Uniting Conference, the legal and authorized representatives of The Methodist Episcopal Church, The Methodist Episcopal Church, South, and The Methodist Protestant Church, in session here assembled on this the 10th day of May, 1939, do solemnly in the presence of God and before all the world make and publish the following Declarations of fact and principle:

I

The Methodist Episcopal Church, The Methodist Episcopal Church, South, and The Methodist Protestant Church are and shall be one United Church.

II

The Plan of Union as adopted is and shall be the constitution of this United Church, and of its three constituent bodies.

III

The Methodist Episcopal Church, The Methodist Episcopal Church, South, and The Methodist Protestant Church had their common origin in the organization of the Methodist Episcopal Church in America in 1784, A.D., and have ever held, adhered to and preserved a common belief, spirit and purpose, as expressed in their common Articles of Religion.

IV

The Methodist Episcopal Church, The Methodist Episcopal Church, South, and The Methodist Protestant Church, in adopting the name "The Methodist Church" for the United Church, do not and will not surrender any right, interest or title in and to these respective names, which, by long and honored use and association, have become dear to the ministry and membership of the three uniting Churches and have become enshrined in their history and records.

V

The Methodist Church is the ecclesiastical and lawful successor of the three uniting Churches, in and through which the three Churches as one United Church shall continue to live and have their existence, continue their institutions, and hold and enjoy their property, exercise and perform their several trusts under and in accord with the Plan of Union and Discipline of the United Church; and such trusts or corporate bodies as exist in the constituent Churches shall be continued as long as legally necessary.

VI

To The Methodist Church thus established we do now solemnly declare our allegiance, and upon all its life and service we do reverently invoke the blessing of Almighty God. Amen.

[Unanimously adopted by the Uniting Conference, Kansas City, Missouri, May 10, 1939.]

PART I

THE CONSTITUTION
THE ARTICLES OF RELIGION
THE GENERAL RULES

THE CONSTITUTION OF THE
METHODIST CHURCH

Plan of Union of The Methodist Episcopal Church, The Methodist Episcopal Church, South, The Methodist Protestant Church

TRANSMITTAL

WE, the Commissions on Interdenominational Relations and Church Union of The Methodist Episcopal Church, The Methodist Episcopal Church, South, and The Methodist Protestant Church, holding that these churches are essentially one in origin, in belief, in spirit, and in purpose, and desiring that this essential unity be made actual in organization and administration in the United States of America and throughout the world, do hereby propose and transmit to our respective General Conferences the following Plan of Union and recommend to the three churches its adoption by the processes which they respectively require.

DIVISION ONE

¶ **1.** *Article I. Declaration of Union.*—The Methodist Episcopal Church, The Methodist Episcopal Church, South, and The Methodist Protestant Church shall be united in one church.

¶ **2.** *Art. II. Name.*—The name of the church shall be The Methodist Church.

¶ **3.** *Art. III. Articles of Religion.*—The Articles of Religion shall be those historically held in common by the three uniting churches. (*See* ¶¶ 61-85.)

DIVISION TWO. CONFERENCES

¶ **4.** 1. There shall be a General Conference for the entire church with such powers, duties, and privileges as are hereinafter set forth.[1]

2. There shall be Jurisdictional Conferences for the church in the United States of America, with such powers, duties, and privileges as are hereinafter set forth.[2]

3. There shall be Central Conferences for the church outside the United States of America, with such powers, duties, and privileges as are hereinafter set forth.

4. There shall be Annual Conferences as the fundamental bodies in the church, with such powers, duties, and privileges as are hereinafter set forth.

Section I. General Conference

¶ **5.** *Article I.*—The General Conference shall be composed of not less than 600 nor more than 800 delegates, one half of whom shall be ministers and one half lay members, to be elected by the Annual Conferences.[3]

¶ **6.** *Art. II.*—The General Conference shall meet in the month of April or May once in four years, beginning with such year and at such place as shall be fixed by the Uniting Conference, and thereafter at such time and in such place as shall be determined by the General Conference or by its duly authorized committees.

¶ **7.** *Art. III.*—The General Conference shall fix the ratio of representation in the General, Jurisdictional, and Central Conferences from the Annual Conferences, with the total ministerial membership in the Annual Conference as a basis; provided that each Annual Conference shall be entitled to at least one ministerial and one lay delegate in the General Conference and also in the Jurisdictional or Central Conference.[4]

---

[1] *See* Judicial Council Decision 7.
[2] *See* Judicial Council Decision 128.
[3] *See* Amendment XI (¶ 47).
[4] *See* Amendment VII (¶ 47).

¶ 8. *Art. IV.*—The General Conference shall have full legislative power over all matters distinctively connectional,[5] and in the exercise of said powers shall have authority as follows:

1. To define and fix the conditions, privileges, and duties of church membership.

2. To define and fix the qualifications and duties of elders, deacons, supply preachers, local preachers, exhorters,[6] and deaconesses.[7]

3. To define and fix the powers and duties of Annual Conferences, Mission Conferences,[8] and Missions, and of District, Quarterly, and Church Conferences.[9]

4. To provide for the organization, promotion, and administration of the work of the church outside the United States of America.[10]

5. To define and fix the powers, duties, and privileges of the episcopacy, to adopt a plan for the support of the bishops, to provide a uniform rule for their superannuation, and to provide for the discontinuance of a bishop because of inefficiency or unacceptability.[11]

6. To provide and revise the Hymnal and Ritual of the church and to regulate all matters relating to the form and mode of worship, subject to the limitations of the first Restrictive Rule.

7. To provide a judicial system and a method of judicial procedure for the church, except as herein otherwise prescribed.

8. To initiate and to direct all connectional enterprises of the church, such as publishing, evangelistic, educational, missionary, and benevolent, and to provide boards for their promotion and administration.[12]

9. To determine and provide for raising the funds

---

[5] *See* Judicial Council Decisions 7, 83-85, 96, 147, 196.
[6] Exhorters in the legislative parts of the Discipline are called lay speakers.
[7] *See* Judicial Council Decisions 7, 58, 155, 204.
[8] Mission Conferences beginning with Amendment IV of the Constitution and in the legislative parts of the Discipline are called Provisional Annual Conferences.
[9] *See* Judicial Council Decisions 7, 74, 105, 145, 146.
[10] *See* Judicial Council Decisions, 84, 182, 215.
[11] *See* Judicial Council Decisions 35, 68, 83, 84.
[12] *See* Judicial Council Decisions 183, 196, 214.

necessary to carry on the connectional work of the church.[13]

10. To fix a uniform basis upon which bishops shall be elected by the Jurisdictional Conferences and to determine the number of bishops that may be elected by Central Conferences.[14]

11. To select its presiding officers from the bishops, through a committee; provided that the bishops shall select from their own number the president of the opening session.[15]

12. To change the number and the boundaries of Jurisdictional Conferences upon the consent of a majority of the Annual Conferences in each Jurisdictional Conference involved.[16]

13. To establish such commissions for the general work of the church as may be deemed advisable.

14. To enact such other legislation as may be necessary, subject to the limitations and restrictions of the Constitution of the church.[17]

Sec. II. Restrictive Rules

¶ 9. 1. The General Conference shall not revoke, alter, or change our Articles of Religion, or establish any new standards or rules of doctrine contrary to our present existing and established standards of doctrine.[18]

2. The General Conference shall not change or alter any part or rule of our government so as to do away episcopacy or destroy the plan of our itinerant general superintendency.

3. The General Conference shall not do away the privileges of our ministers or preachers of trial by a committee and of an appeal; neither shall it do away the privileges of our members of trial before the church, or by a committee, and of an appeal.

4. The General Conference shall not revoke or change the General Rules of the United Societies.

---

[13] *See* Judicial Council Decisions 30, 196.
[14] *See* Judicial Council Decisions 84, 182.
[15] *See* Judicial Council Decision 126.
[16] *See* Judicial Council Decisions 32, 56, 215.
[17] *See* Judicial Council Decisions 58, 84, 147, 215.
[18] *See* Judicial Council Decisions 86, 142, 176.

5. The General Conference shall not appropriate the produce of the Publishing House, the Book Concern, or the Chartered Fund to any purpose other than for the benefit of the traveling, supernumerary, superannuated, and worn-out preachers, their wives, widows, and children.

Sec. III. Amendments

¶ 10. 1. Amendments to the Constitution may originate in either the General Conference or an Annual Conference.

2. Amendments to the Constitution shall be made upon a two-thirds majority of the General Conference present and voting and a two-thirds majority of all the members of the several Annual Conferences present and voting, except in the case of the first Restrictive Rule, which shall require a three-fourths majority of all the members of the Annual Conferences present and voting. The vote, after being completed, shall be canvassed by the Council of Bishops, and the amendment voted upon shall become effective upon their announcement of its having received the required majority.[19]

3. A Jurisdictional Conference may by a majority vote propose changes in the Constitution of the church, and such proposed changes shall be submitted to the next General Conference. If the General Conference adopt the measure by a two-thirds vote, it shall be submitted to the Annual Conferences according to the provision for amendments.

Sec. IV. Jurisdictional Conferences

¶ 11. *Article I.*—The Jurisdictional Conferences shall be composed of as many representatives from the Annual Conferences as shall be determined by a uniform basis established by the General Conference.

¶ 12. *Art. II.*—All Jurisdictional Conferences shall have the same status and the same privileges of action within the limits fixed by the Constitution. The ratio of repre-

---

[19] *See* Judicial Council Decisions 132, 154.

sentation of the Annual Conferences in the General Conference shall be the same for all Jurisdictional Conferences.

¶ 13. *Art. III.*—The General Conference shall fix the basis of representation in the Jurisdictional Conferences; provided that the Jurisdictional Conferences shall be composed of an equal number of ministerial and lay delegates, the ministerial to be elected by the ministerial members of the Annual Conferences and the lay delegates by the lay members.[20]

¶ 14. *Art. IV.*—Each Jurisdictional Conference shall meet within the twelve months succeeding the meeting of the General Conference at such time and place as shall have been determined by the preceding Jurisdictional Conference, or by its properly constituted committee. The first meeting of each Jurisdictional Conference after the General Conference shall be called by the Council of Bishops at a date fixed by them and at a place selected by a committee on entertainment appointed by them.

¶ 15. *Art. V.*—The Jurisdictional Conferences shall have the following powers and duties and such others as may be conferred by the General Conference:[21]

1. To promote the evangelistic, educational, missionary, and benevolent interests of the church, and to provide for interests and institutions within their boundaries.[22]

2. To elect bishops and to co-operate in carrying out such plans for their support as may be determined by the General Conference.

3. To establish and constitute Jurisdictional Conference boards as auxiliary to the general boards of the church as the need may appear, and to choose their representatives on the general boards in such manner as the General Conference may determine.[23]

4. To determine the boundaries of their Annual Conferences; provided that there shall be no Annual Conference with a membership of fewer than fifty ministers

---

[20] *See* Amendment IV (¶ 47), adopted following Judicial Council Decision 5.
[21] *See* Judicial Council Decision 84.
[22] *See* Judicial Council Decision 67.
[23] *See* Judicial Council Decision 183.

in full connection, except by the consent of the General Conference.[24]

5. To make rules and regulations for the administration of the work of the church within the jurisdiction, subject to such powers as have been or shall be vested in the General Conference.[25]

6. To appoint a Committee on Appeals to hear and determine the appeal of a traveling preacher of that jurisdiction from the decision of a trial committee.

Sec. V. Central Conferences

¶ 16. *Article I.*—There shall be Central Conferences for the work of the church outside the United States of America with such duties, powers, and privileges as are hereinafter set forth. The number and boundaries of the Central Conferences shall be determined by the Uniting Conference. Subsequently the General Conference shall have authority to change the number and boundaries of Central Conferences. The Central Conferences shall have the duties, powers, and privileges hereinafter set forth.

¶ 17. *Art. II.*—The Central Conferences shall be composed of as many delegates as shall be determined by a basis established by the General Conference. The delegates shall be ministerial and lay in equal numbers, the ministerial delegates to be elected by the ministerial members and the lay delegates to be elected by the lay members of the Annual Conferences.[26]

¶ 18. *Art. III.*—The Central Conferences shall meet within the year succeeding the meeting of the General Conference at such times and places as shall have been determined by the preceding respective Central Conferences or by commissions appointed by them, or by the General Conference. The date and place of the first meeting succeeding the first General Conference shall be fixed by the bishops of the respective Central Conferences, or in such manner as shall be determined by the General Conference.

¶ 19. *Art. IV.*—The Central Conferences shall have the

---

[24] *See* Judicial Council Decisions 28, 85.
[25] *See* Judicial Council Decision 67.
[26] *See* Amendment II (¶ 47), adopted following Judicial Council Decision 6.

following powers and duties and such others as may be conferred by the General Conference:

1. To promote the evangelistic, educational, missionary, and benevolent interests and institutions of the church within their own boundaries.

2. To elect the bishops for the respective Central Conferences in number as may be determined from time to time, upon a basis fixed by the General Conference, and to co-operate in carrying out such plans for the support of their bishops as may be determined by the General Conference.

3. To establish and constitute such Central Conference boards as may be required and to elect their administrative officers.[27]

4. To determine the boundaries of the Annual Conferences within their respective areas.

5. To make such rules and regulations for the administration of the work within their boundaries as the conditions in the respective areas may require, subject to the powers that have been or shall be vested in the General Conference.[28]

6. To appoint a Committee on Appeals to hear and determine the appeal of a traveling preacher of that Central Conference from the decision of a Committee on Trial.

Sec. VI. Episcopal Administration in Central Conferences

¶ **20. 1.** The bishops of the Central Conferences shall be elected and inducted into office by their respective Central Conferences.

2. The bishops of the Central Conferences shall have membership in the Council of Bishops with vote limited to matters relating to their respective Central Conferences.[29]

3. The bishops of the Central Conferences shall preside in the sessions of their respective Central Conferences.

4. The bishops of each Central Conference shall arrange the plan of episcopal visitation within their Central Conference.

5. The Council of Bishops may assign one of their num-

---

[27] *See* Judicial Council Decision 69.
[28] *See* Judicial Council Decisions 69, 121, 142, 147, 155.
[29] *See* Amendment VI (¶ 47).

ber to visit any Central Conference. When so assigned the bishop shall be recognized as an accredited representative of the general church; and when requested by a majority of the bishops of a Central Conference may exercise therein the functions of the episcopacy.

Sec. VII. Annual Conferences

¶ 21. *Article I.*—The Annual Conference shall be composed of all the traveling preachers in full connection with it, together with a lay member elected by each pastoral charge. The lay members shall be at least twenty-one (21) years of age and shall have been for the four years next preceding their election members of one of the constituent churches forming this union, or of The Methodist Church.[30]

¶ 22. *Art. II.*—The Annual Conference is the basic body in the church, and as such shall have reserved to it the right to vote on all constitutional amendments, on the election of ministerial and lay delegates to the General and the Jurisdictional or Central Conferences, on all matters relating to the character and conference relations of its ministerial members, and on the ordination of ministers, and such other rights as have not been delegated to the General Conference under the Constitution, with the exception that the lay members may not vote on matters of ordination, character, and conference relations of ministers. It shall discharge such duties and exercise such powers as the General Conference under the Constitution may determine.[31]

¶ 23. *Art. III.*—The Annual Conference shall elect ministerial and lay delegates to the General Conference and to its Jurisdictional or Central Conference in the manner provided in this section, Articles IV and V, at the session preceding the General Conference. The persons first elected up to the number determined by the ratio for representation in the General Conference shall be representatives in that body. Additional delegates shall be

[30] *See* Amendment X (¶ 47) ; *see also* Judicial Council Decisions 24, 36, 42, 87, 112, 113, 129, 131, 136, 159, 195.
[31] *See* Judicial Council Decisions 5-7, 38, 42, 43, 67, 72, 74-76, 78, 79, 98, 105, 115, 119, 123, 129, 132, 136, 179, 192.

elected to complete the number determined by the ratio for representation in the Jurisdictional or Central Conference, who, together with those first elected as above, shall be delegates in the Jurisdictional or Central Conference. The additional delegates to the Jurisdictional or Central Conference shall in the order of their election be the reserve delegates to the General Conference. The Annual Conference shall also elect reserve ministerial and lay delegates to the Jurisdictional or Central Conference as it may deem desirable.[32]

¶ 24. *Art. IV.*—The ministerial delegates to the General Conference and to the Jurisdictional or Central Conference shall be elected by the ministerial members of the Annual Conference, provided that such delegates shall have been traveling preachers in the constituent churches forming this union, or in The Methodist Church, for at least four years next preceding their election and are in full connection with the Annual Conference[33] electing them when elected and at the time of holding the General and Jurisdictional or Central Conferences.

¶ 25. *Art. V.*—The lay delegates to the General Conference and to the Jurisdictional or Central Conference shall be elected by the lay members of the Annual Conference; provided that such delegates be at least twenty-five (25) years of age and shall have been members of the constituent churches forming this union, or of The Methodist Church, for at least four years next preceding their election, and are members thereof within the Annual Conference electing them at the time of holding the General and Jurisdictional or Central Conferences.[34]

Sec. VIII. Boundaries

¶ 26. *Article I.*—The Methodist Church in the United States of America shall have Jurisdictional Conferences made up as follows:

Northeastern—Maine, New Hampshire, Vermont, Massachusetts, Rhode Island, New York, Connecticut, Penn-

---

[32] *See* Judicial Council Decision 76.
[33] *See* Amendment VIII (¶ 47) ; *see also* Judicial Council Decisions 1, 76, 88, 124, 162.
[34] *See* Amendment III (¶ 47) ; *see also* Judicial Council Decisions 76, 124, 174.

sylvania, New Jersey, Maryland, West Virginia, Delaware, District of Columbia, Puerto Rico.

Southeastern—Virginia, North Carolina, South Carolina, Georgia, Florida, Alabama, Tennessee, Kentucky, Mississippi, Cuba.[35]

Central—The Negro Annual Conferences, the Negro Mission Conferences and Missions in the United States of America.[36]

North Central—Ohio, Indiana, Illinois, Michigan, Wisconsin, Minnesota, Iowa, North Dakota, South Dakota.

South Central—Missouri, Arkansas, Louisiana, Nebraska, Kansas, Oklahoma, Texas, New Mexico.

Western—Washington, Idaho, Oregon, California, Nevada, Utah, Arizona, Montana, Wyoming, Colorado, Alaska, Hawaiian Islands.[37]

¶ **27.** *Art. II.*—The work of the church outside the United States of America may be formed into Central Conferences, the number and boundaries of which shall be determined by the Uniting Conference, the General Conference having authority subsequently to make changes in the number and boundaries.

¶ **28.** *Art. III.*—Changes in the number, names, and boundaries of the Jurisdictional Conferences may be effected by the General Conference upon the consent of a majority of the Annual Conferences of each of the Jurisdictional Conferences involved.[38]

¶ **29.** *Art. IV.*—Changes in the number, names, and boundaries of the Annual Conferences may be effected by the Jurisdictional Conferences in the United States of America and by the Central Conferences outside the United States of America, according to the provisions under the respective powers of the Jurisdictional and the Central Conferences.[39]

Sec. IX. District Conferences

¶ **30.** *Article I.*—There may be organized in an Annual

---

[35] *See* Judicial Council Decision 215.
[36] *See* Judicial Council Decision 128.
[37] *See* Amendment IX (¶ 47).
[38] *See* Amendment IX (¶ 47); *see also* Judicial Council Decisions 55, 56, 85, 215.
[39] *See* Judicial Council Decisions 28, 85.

Conference, District Conferences composed of such persons and invested with such powers as the General Conference may determine.

Sec. X. Quarterly Conferences

¶ **31.** *Article I.*—There shall be organized in each pastoral charge a Quarterly Conference composed of such persons and invested with such powers as the General Conference shall provide.[40]

¶ **32.** *Art. II.—Election of Church Officers.*—Unless the General Conference shall order otherwise, the officers of the church or churches constituting a pastoral charge shall be elected by the Quarterly Conference or by the members of said church or churches at a meeting called for that purpose, as may be arranged by the Quarterly Conference, unless the election is otherwise required by local church charters or state laws.

Sec. XI. Church Conferences

¶ **33.** There may be a Church Conference in each church, having such powers and duties as the General Conference may prescribe.

DIVISION THREE. EPISCOPACY

¶ **34.** *Article I.*—There shall be an episcopacy in The Methodist Church of like plan, powers, privileges, and duties as now exist in The Methodist Episcopal Church and The Methodist Episcopal Church, South.[41]

¶ **35.** *Art. II.*—The bishops shall be elected by the respective Jurisdictional and Central Conferences and ordained or consecrated in the historic manner of episcopal Methodism at such time and place as may be fixed by the General Conference.[42]

¶ **36.** *Art. III.*—There shall be a Council of Bishops composed of all the bishops of all the Jurisdictional and Central Conferences. The council shall meet at least once a year and plan for the general oversight and pro-

---

[40] *See* Judicial Council Decision 93.
[41] *See* Judicial Council Decisions 4, 57, 127.
[42] *See* Amendment I (¶ 47) ; *see also* Judicial Council Decision 21.

motion of the temporal and spiritual interests of the
entire church and for carrying into effect the rules, regulations, and responsibilities prescribed and enjoined by
the General Conference, and in accord with the provisions
set forth in this Plan of Union.

¶ 37. *Art. IV.*—The bishops of each Jurisdictional and
Central Conference shall arrange the plan of episcopal
supervision of the Annual Conferences, Mission Conferences, and Missions within their respective territories.[43]

¶ 38. *Art. V.*—The bishops shall have residential and
presidential supervision in the Jurisdictional Conferences
in which they are elected. A bishop may be transferred
from one jurisdiction to another jurisdiction for presidential and residential supervision by the Council of
Bishops when such transfer is requested by the Jurisdictional Conference to which such proposed transfer is to
be made.

A bishop may be assigned by the Council of Bishops
for presidential service or other temporary service, not
to exceed a year, in another jurisdiction than that which
elected him, provided request is made by a majority of
the bishops in the jurisdiction of the proposed service.

In the case of an emergency in any jurisdiction through
the death or disability of its bishops the Council of
Bishops may assign one or more bishops from other
jurisdictions to the work of the said jurisdiction with the
consent of a majority of the bishops of that jurisdiction.[44]

¶ 39. *Art. VI.*—The bishops of The Methodist Episcopal
Church and of The Methodist Episcopal Church, South,
at the time union is consummated, shall be bishops of
The Methodist Church.[45]

The delegates from the Annual Conferences of The
Methodist Protestant Church in the Uniting Conference
shall have the authority and power to elect to the office
of bishop two ministers of their church who, upon ordination or consecration at the Uniting Conference by the
bishops of the other two churches, shall become effective
bishops of The Methodist Church.

---

[43] *See* Judicial Council Decisions 48, 57.
[44] *See* Judicial Council Decision 84.
[45] *See* Judicial Council Decision 84.

The effective bishops shall be assigned for service to the various Jurisdictional Conferences by the Uniting Conference.

¶ **40.** *Art. VII.*—A bishop presiding over a District, Annual, or Jurisdictional Conference shall decide all questions of law coming before him in the regular business of a session; provided that such questions be presented in writing and that his decisions be recorded in the journal of the conference.

Such an episcopal decision shall not be authoritative except for the pending case until it shall have been passed upon by the Judicial Council. Each bishop shall report in writing annually all his decisions of law, with a syllabus of the same, to the Judicial Council, which shall affirm, modify, or reverse them.[46]

¶ **41.** *Art. VIII.*—The bishops of the several Jurisdictional Conferences shall preside in the sessions of their respective Jurisdictional Conferences.

DIVISION FOUR. THE JUDICIARY

¶ **42.** *Article I.*—There shall be a Judicial Council. The General Conference shall determine the number and qualifications of its members, their terms of office, and the method of election and the filling of vacancies.[47]

¶ **43.** *Art. II.*—The Judicial Council shall have authority:

1. To determine the constitutionality of any act of the General Conference upon an appeal of a majority of the Council of Bishops, or one fifth of the members of the General Conference; and to determine the constitutionality of any act of a Jurisdictional or Central Conference upon an appeal of a majority of the bishops of that Jurisdictional or Central Conference or upon the appeal of one fifth of the members of that Jurisdictional or Central Conference.[48]

2. To hear and determine any appeal from a bishop's decision on a question of law made in the Annual or District Conference when said appeal has been made by

---

[46] *See* Judicial Council Decisions 64, 189.
[47] *See* Judicial Council Decision 62.
[48] *See* Judicial Council Decisions 177, 193.

one fifth of that conference present and voting.[49]

3. To pass upon decisions of law made by bishops in Annual or District Conferences.[50]

4. To hear and determine the legality of any action taken therein by any General Conference board or Jurisdictional or Central Conference board or body, upon appeal by one third of the members thereof, or upon request of the Council of Bishops or a majority of the bishops of a Jurisdictional or a Central Conference.

5. To have such other duties and powers as may be conferred upon it by the General Conference.

6. To provide its own methods of organization and procedure.

¶ 44. *Art. III.*—All decisions of the Judicial Council shall be final. However, when the Judicial Council shall declare any act of the General Conference unconstitutional, that decision shall be reported back to that General Conference immediately.

PROCEDURE—UNITING CONFERENCE

¶ 45. *Article I.*—There shall be a Uniting Conference composed of 900 delegates, of whom 400 shall be from The Methodist Episcopal Church, 400 from The Methodist Episcopal Church, South, and 100 from The Methodist Protestant Church, chosen in such manner as may be determined by the respective General Conferences; provided that the ministerial and lay members shall be in equal numbers.

Art. II.—The Uniting Conference shall be held within twelve months after the final approval and adoption of this Plan of Union by the three churches, at the call of the bishops of the two churches and the president of the General Conference of The Methodist Protestant Church, and at a date fixed by them and at a place selected by a Joint Commission on Entertainment of five persons from each of the three churches, this commission to be appointed by the bishops of the two churches and the president of The Methodist Protestant General Conference.

Art. III.—The expenses of the Uniting Conference shall

---

[49] *See* Judicial Council Decisions 66, 153.
[50] *See* Judicial Council Decision 153.

be borne by the three churches in proportion to their respective representation.

Art. IV.—The duties and powers of the Uniting Conference, subject to the provisions of this Plan of Union, shall be:

1. To harmonize and combine the rules and regulations as found in the Disciplines of the three churches relating to membership, the conferences, the ministry, judicial administration, and temporal economy.

2. To harmonize and combine the Rituals of the three churches.

3. To provide for the unification, co-ordination, and correlation of the connectional missionary, educational, and benevolent boards and societies of the three churches.

4. To provide for the unification, co-ordination, and correlation of the publishing interests of the three churches.

5. To provide a plan for the control and safeguarding of all permanent funds and other property interests of the three churches and the interests of those persons and causes for which these funds were established.

Art. V.—In order to facilitate the work of the Uniting Conference, the three General Conferences at the sessions wherein this Plan of Union is approved shall continue their Commissions on Union with such changes in personnel as they may desire, and authorize the Joint Commission thus formed to make special preparation for the Uniting Conference by the appointment of proper committees to deal with: (*a*) membership, conferences, ministry, judicial administration, and temporal economy; (*b*) Rituals; (*c*) connectional boards and societies; (*d*) publishing interests; (*e*) permanent and pension funds; and (*f*) such other matters as imperatively call for advance consideration.

Art. VI.—All Annual Conferences of the three churches shall retain their existing status until by the action of the Uniting Conference it shall be determined otherwise.

Art. VII.—The legislative power of the Uniting Conference shall be confined to harmonizing and combining provisions now existing in the Disciplines of the three churches, or one or more of these churches.

Art. VIII.—The boundaries and composition of the Annual Conferences within the several Jurisdictional Conferences as made up in this Plan of Union shall be adjusted at the time of meeting of the Uniting Conference by the delegates from the Annual Conferences within the respective jurisdictions, sitting apart for that purpose during the period of the Uniting Conference; provided that in the case of those Annual Conferences that may be divided by the Jurisdictional Conference lines, their delegates shall allocate themselves to the respective Jurisdictional Conferences upon the basis of church membership of their conferences in the respective jurisdictions.

Art. IX.—The Uniting Conference shall fix the basis of representation of the Annual Conferences in the first General Conference and in the Jurisdictional and Central Conferences.

Art. X.—Pending the meeting of the Uniting Conference each of the three uniting churches shall be governed by the rules and regulations of its own Discipline.

RECOMMENDATIONS

¶ 46. I. The General Conference is authorized to extend to the autonomous Methodist churches outside the United States of America formerly connected with our bodies an invitation to enter into conference with us with respect to such relationship with The Methodist Church as may seem mutually desirable.

II. The co-operative relationships which already exist between any of these three Methodist bodies and churches in foreign fields not covered by other provisions herein shall be continued as may seem mutually advantageous.

III. The world-wide character of Methodism shall be recognized by participation in the Ecumenical Methodist Conference [51] and by the appointment of a commission to assist in bringing all Methodist bodies throughout the world into more intimate and effective relationship.

IV. We recommend that financial support of the Colored Methodist Episcopal Church [52] be continued by those jurisdictional divisions with which said church is

---

[51] The name of this organization was changed to World Methodist Council on September 7, 1951.
[52] The name of this church was changed to Christian Methodist Episcopal Church on May 17, 1954.

historically related, and to such an extent as those jurisdictions may deem wise.

¶ 47.   DIVISION FIVE. AMENDMENTS

[The date following each amendment is the date on which it
became effective by announcement of the Council of Bishops (*see*
¶ 10.2).—EDITORS.]

Amendment I

Amend [Division Three, Article II (¶ 35), line 3] . . . *by
striking out the words* ordained or, *so that the new paragraph will
read:*

Art. II.—The bishops shall be elected by the respective
Jurisdictional and Central Conferences and consecrated
in the historic manner of episcopal Methodism at such
time and place as may be fixed by the General Conference.[53] (December 15, 1943.)

Amendment II

Amend . . . *by adding* . . . *the words* or Mission Conferences, *so
that* [Division Two, Section V, Article II (¶ 17)] *shall read:*

Art. II.—The Central Conferences shall be composed of
as many delegates as shall be determined by a basis
established by the General Conference. The delegates shall
be ministerial and lay in equal numbers, the ministerial
delegates to be elected by the ministerial members and
the lay delegates to be elected by the lay members of the
Annual Conferences or Mission Conferences.[54] (December
15, 1943.)

Amendment III

[*Amend*] *by changing the age to* twenty-one (21) *instead of*
twenty-five (25) *as it now is* [in Division Two, Section VII,
Article V (¶ 25), line 5], *so that the paragraph will read as follows:*

Art. V.—The lay delegates to the General Conference
and to the Jurisdictional or Central Conferences shall be
elected by the lay members of the Annual Conference;

---

[53] *See* Judicial Council Decision 21.
[54] Mission Conferences in later amendments to the Constitution and in the legislative parts of the Discipline are called
Provisional Annual Conferences.

provided that such delegates be at least twenty-one (21) years of age and shall have been members of the constituent churches forming this union, or of The Methodist Church, for at least four years next preceding their election, and are members thereof within the Annual Conference electing them at the time of holding the General and Jurisdictional or Central Conferences.[55] (January 10, 1952.)

Amendment *IV*

[In Division Two, Section IV, Article III (¶ 13), line 6], *after the words* Annual Conferences *add the words* and the Provisional Annual Conferences. *The paragraph as amended will read:*

Art. III.—The General Conference shall fix the basis of representation in the Jurisdictional Conferences; provided that the Jurisdictional Conferences shall be composed of an equal number of ministerial and lay delegates, the ministerial to be elected by the ministerial members of the Annual Conferences and the Provisional Annual Conferences and the lay delegates by the lay members. (January 10, 1952.)

Amendment *V*

[This amendment was adopted by the General Conference of 1948 but failed of ratification by the requisite number of members of the several Annual Conferences. The same revision was adopted by the General Conference of 1952 as Amendment VI and, as indicated below, was ratified.—EDITORS.]

Amendment *VI*

Amend [Division Two, Section VI (¶ 20.2)] *by deleting the words* limited to matter relating to their respective Central Conferences, . . . *so that the paragraph when amended will read as follows:*

2. The bishops of the Central Conferences shall have membership in the Council of Bishops with vote.[56] (April 19, 1956.)

Amendment *VII*

Amend [Division Two, Section I, Article III (¶ 7)] . . . *so that the paragraph as amended will read as follows:*

---

[55] *See* Judicial Council Decisions 76, 124, 174.
[56] *See* Judicial Council Decision 164.

Art. III.—The General Conference shall fix the ratio of representation in the General, Jurisdictional, and Central Conferences from the Annual Conferences and the Provisional Annual Conferences, with the total ministerial membership in the Annual Conference or the Provisional Annual Conference as a basis; provided that each Annual Conference or Provisional Annual Conference, except for the Provisional Annual Conferences of a Central Conference or a Provisional Central Conference, shall be entitled to at least one ministerial and one lay delegate in the General Conference and also in the Jurisdictional or Central Conference.[57] (April 19, 1956.)

Amendment VIII

Amend [Division Two, Section VII, Article IV (¶ 24)] . . . so that the paragraph when amended will read as follows:

Art. IV.—The ministerial delegates to the General Conference and to the Jurisdictional or Central Conference shall be elected by the ministerial members of the Annual Conference or Provisional Annual Conference; provided that such delegates shall have been traveling preachers in the constituent churches forming this union, or in The Methodist Church, for at least four years next preceding their election and are in full connection with the Annual Conference or Provisional Annual Conference electing them when elected and at the time of holding the General and Jurisdictional or Central Conferences.[58] (April 19, 1956.)

Amendment IX

The Constitution of The Methodist Church shall be amended by adding a new article, to be known as Article V of Division Two, Section VIII, and to read as follows:

Art. V.—1. A local church may be transferred from one Annual Conference to another in which it is geographically located upon approval by a two-thirds vote of those present and voting in each of the following:

a) The Quarterly Conference of the local church.

---

[57] *See* Judicial Council Decision 154.
[58] *See* Judicial Council Decisions 1, 76, 88, 124, 154, 162.

b) A Church Conference of the local church.

c) Each of the two Annual Conferences involved.

The vote shall be certified by the secretaries of the specified conferences to the bishops having supervision of the Annual Conferences involved, and upon their announcement of the required majorities the transfer shall immediately be effective.

2. An Annual Conference may be transferred from one jurisdiction to another upon approval by:

a) The Annual Conference desiring transfer, by a two-thirds majority of those present and voting. The secretary of the conference shall certify the vote to the College of Bishops of the jurisdiction of which the conference has been a part.

b) The remainder of the jurisdiction from which transfer is to be made, by a two-thirds majority of the total of Annual Conference members present and voting. The vote shall be taken in the other Annual Conferences of the jurisdiction and certified by their secretaries to the College of Bishops, which shall determine whether two thirds of the total vote in the jurisdiction is favorable.

c) The jurisdiction to which transfer is to be made, by a two-thirds majority of the total of Annual Conference members present and voting. The vote shall be taken in the various Annual Conferences of the jurisdiction and certified by their secretaries to the College of Bishops, which shall determine whether two thirds of the total vote in the jurisdiction is favorable.

Upon announcement by the two Colleges of Bishops of the required majorities the transfer shall immediately be effective.

3. The vote on approval of transfer under either § 1 or § 2 shall be taken by each Annual Conference at its first session after the matter is submitted to it.

4. Transfers under the provisions of this article shall not be governed or restricted by other provisions of this Constitution relating to change of boundaries of conferences.

5. Whenever twenty-five per cent of the local-church membership of the Central Jurisdiction have been transferred by this process to another jurisdiction or jurisdic-

tions, the bishop of the area from which the largest number have been transferred shall be transferred to the jurisdiction which has received the largest number by such transfer, and the representation of the Central Jurisdiction on the boards and agencies of the church shall thereafter be proportionately reduced.

Article I of Division Two, Section VIII [¶ 26] of the Constitution of The Methodist Church shall be amended by adding at the end thereof a new paragraph as follows:

Abolition of the Central Jurisdiction.—The Central Jurisdiction shall be abolished when all of the Annual Conferences now comprising it have been transferred to other jurisdictions in accordance with the voluntary procedure of Article V of this section. Each remaining bishop of the Central Jurisdiction shall thereupon be transferred to the jurisdiction to which the majority of the membership of his area have been transferred, and the Central Jurisdiction shall then be dissolved.[59] (April 8, 1958.)

Amendment X

[Division Two, Section VII, Article I (¶ 21)] *shall be amended by inserting . . . after the first sentence* [a sentence as below, so that the paragraph] *as amended, will read:*

Article I.—The Annual Conference shall be composed of all the traveling preachers in full connection with it, together with a lay member elected by each pastoral charge. Each pastoral charge served by more than one minister in full connection shall be entitled to two lay members. The lay members shall be at least twenty-one (21) years of age and shall have been for the four years next preceding their election members of one of the constituent churches forming this union, or of The Methodist Church.[60] (April 8, 1958.)

Amendment XI

Amend [Division Two, Section I, Article I (¶ 5)] *by deleting the numeral* 800 *in line two, and substituting therefor the numeral* 900, *so that* [the paragraph], *as amended, will read:*

[59] *See* Judicial Council Decisions, 169, 211.
[60] *See* Judicial Council Decisions 24, 36, 42, 87, 112, 113, 129, 131, 136, 159, 186, 195.

Article I.—The General Conference shall be composed of not less than 600 or more than 900 delegates, one half of whom shall be ministers and one half lay members, to be elected by the Annual Conferences. (April 8, 1958.)

¶ 48.   AMENDMENTS PENDING RATIFICATION

[The General Conference of 1964 approved and referred to the members of the several Annual Conferences for ratification the constitutional amendments below.—EDITORS.]

1. *Delete the present ¶ 14 (Division II, Sec. IV, Art. IV of the Constitution) . . . and substitute for it:*

Art. IV.—Each Jurisdictional Conference shall meet at the time determined by the Council of Bishops or its delegated committee, each Jurisdictional Conference convening on the same date as the others and at a place selected by the Jurisdictional Committee on Entertainment, appointed by its College of Bishops unless such a committee has been appointed by the preceding Jurisdictional Conference.

2. *Amend ¶ 38 (Division III, Art. V of the Constitution), the first subparagraph . . . so that when amended it shall read as follows:*

Art. V.—The bishops shall have residential and presidential supervision in the Jurisdictional Conferences in which they are elected or to which they are transferred. Bishops may be transferred from one jurisdiction to another jurisdiction for presidential and residential supervision under the following conditions: (1) The transfer of bishops may be on either of two bases: (*a*) a jurisdiction which receives a bishop by transfer from another jurisdiction may transfer to that jurisdiction or to a third jurisdiction one of its own bishops eligible for transfer, so that the number transferred in by each jurisdiction shall be balanced by the number transferred out, or (*b*) a jurisdiction may receive a bishop from another jurisdiction and not transfer out a member of its own College of Bishops. (2) No bishop shall be transferred unless he shall have given his specific consent. (3) No bishop shall be eligible for transfer until he has served one quadrennium in, or under assignment by, the jurisdiction which elected him to the episcopacy. (4) All such transfers shall require approval by a majority vote of the members, present and voting, of the Jurisdictional Conferences which are involved after consideration by the Committees on Episcopacy. After the above procedures have been followed, the transferring bishop shall become a member of the receiving College of Bishops and shall be subject to residential assignment by that Jurisdictional Conference. Conditions (2), (3), and (4) above shall not apply in the case of the transfer of a bishop from the Central Jurisdiction in connection with the transfer of one or more Annual Conferences of that jurisdiction under Amendment IX.

3. *Amend Amendment X* [¶ 47, amending Division Two, Section VII, Article I (¶ 21)]. . . . *As amended the* [first sentence] *will read:*

Article I.—The Annual Conference shall be composed of all the traveling preachers in full connection with it, together with a lay member elected by each pastoral charge, the president of the Conference Woman's Society of Christian Service, and the conference lay leader.

4. *Amend Amendment X* [¶ 47, amending Division Two, Section VII, Article I (¶ 21)]. . . . *As amended the* [last two sentences] *will read:*

. . . Each pastoral charge served by more than one minister in full connection shall be entitled to as many lay members as there are effective full-time ministers in full connection. The lay members shall be at least twenty-one (21) years of age and shall have been for the four years next preceding their election members of The Methodist Church.

5. *Amend the Constitution by deleting from Amendment IX* . . . *the entire* [sub] *paragraph* 5 ["Whenever twenty-five per cent of the local-church membership . . . thereafter be proportionately reduced."] *and from the last paragraph* [the addition to ¶ 26] *the final sentence* ["Each remaining bishop . . . and the Central Jurisdiction shall then be dissolved."].

THE ARTICLES OF RELIGION

I. *Of Faith in the Holy Trinity*

¶ **61.** There is but one living and true God, everlasting, without body or parts, of infinite power, wisdom, and goodness; the maker and preserver of all things, visible and invisible. And in unity of this Godhead there are three persons, of one substance, power, and eternity—the Father, the Son, and the Holy Ghost.

II. *Of the Word, or Son of God, who was made very Man*

¶ **62.** The Son, who is the Word of the Father, the very and eternal God, of one substance with the Father, took man's nature in the womb of the blessed Virgin; so that two whole and perfect natures, that is to say, the Godhead and Manhood, were joined together in one person, never to be divided; whereof is one Christ, very God and very Man, who truly suffered, was crucified, dead, and buried, to reconcile his Father to us, and to be a sacrifice, not only for original guilt, but also for the actual sins of man.

III. *Of the Resurrection of Christ*

¶ **63.** Christ did truly rise again from the dead, and took again his body, with all things appertaining to the perfection of man's nature, wherewith he ascended into heaven, and there sitteth until he return to judge all men at the last day.

IV. *Of the Holy Ghost*

¶ **64.** The Holy Ghost, proceeding from the Father and the Son, is of one substance, majesty, and glory with the Father and the Son, very and eternal God.

V. *Of the Sufficiency of the Holy Scriptures for Salvation*

¶ **65.** The Holy Scriptures contain all things necessary to salvation; so that whatsoever is not read therein, nor may be proved thereby, is not to be required of any man that it should be believed as an article of faith, or be thought requisite or necessary to salvation. In the name of the Holy Scriptures we do understand those canonical books of the Old and New Testament of whose authority was never any doubt in the Church. The names of the canonical books are:

Genesis, Exodus, Leviticus, Numbers, Deuteronomy, Joshua, Judges, Ruth, The First Book of Samuel, The Second Book of Samuel, The First Book of Kings, The Second Book of Kings, The First Book of Chronicles, The Second Book of Chronicles, The Book of Ezra, The Book of Nehemiah, The Book of Esther, The Book of Job, The Psalms, The Proverbs, Ecclesiastes or the Preacher, Cantica or Song of Solomon, Four Prophets the Greater, Twelve Prophets the Less.

All the books of the New Testament, as they are commonly received, we do receive and account canonical.

VI. *Of the Old Testament*

¶ **66.** The Old Testament is not contrary to the New; for both in the Old and New Testament everlasting life is offered to mankind by Christ, who is the only Mediator between God and man, being both God and Man. Wherefore they are not to be heard who feign that the old fathers did look only for transitory promises. Although the law given from God by Moses as touching ceremonies and rites doth not bind Christians, nor ought the civil precepts thereof of necessity be received in any commonwealth; yet notwithstanding, no Christian whatsoever is free from the obedience of the commandments which are called moral.

VII. *Of Original or Birth Sin*

¶ **67.** Original sin standeth not in the following of Adam (as the Pelagians do vainly talk), but it is the corruption of the nature of every man, that naturally is engendered of the offspring of Adam, whereby man is very far gone from original righteousness, and of his own nature inclined to evil, and that continually.

VIII. *Of Free Will*

¶ **68.** The condition of man after the fall of Adam is such that he cannot turn and prepare himself, by his own natural strength and works, to faith, and calling upon God; wherefore we have no power to do good works, pleasant and acceptable to God, without the grace of God by Christ preventing us, that we may have a good will, and working with us, when we have that good will.

IX. *Of the Justification of Man*

¶ **69.** We are accounted righteous before God only for the merit of our Lord and Saviour Jesus Christ, by faith, and not for our own works or deservings. Wherefore, that we are justified by faith only is a most wholesome doctrine, and very full of comfort.

X. *Of Good Works*

¶ **70.** Although good works, which are the fruits of faith, and follow after justification, cannot put away our sins, and endure the severity of God's judgment; yet are they pleasing and acceptable to God in Christ, and spring out of a true and lively faith, insomuch that by them a lively faith may be as evidently known as a tree is discerned by its fruit.

XI. *Of Works of Supererogation*

¶ **71.** Voluntary works—besides, over and above God's commandments—which are called works of supererogation, cannot be taught without arrogancy and impiety. For by them men do declare that they do not only render unto God as much as they are bound to do, but that they do more for his sake than of bounden duty is required; whereas Christ saith plainly: When ye have done all that is commanded of you, say, We are unprofitable servants.

XII. *Of Sin after Justification*

¶ **72.** Not every sin willingly committed after justification is the sin against the Holy Spirit, and unpardonable. Wherefore, the grant of repentance is not to be denied to such as fall into sin after justification: after we have received the Holy Spirit, we may depart from grace given, and fall into sin, and, by the grace of God, rise again and amend our lives. And therefore they are to be condemned who say they can no more sin as long as they live here; or deny the place of forgiveness to such as truly repent.

XIII. *Of the Church*

¶ **73.** The visible Church of Christ is a congregation of faithful men in which the pure Word of God is preached, and the Sacraments duly administered according to Christ's ordinance, in all those things that of necessity are requisite to the same.

XIV. *Of Purgatory*

¶ **74.** The Romish doctrine concerning purgatory, pardon, worshiping, and adoration, as well of images as of relics, and also invocation of saints, is a fond thing, vainly invented, and grounded upon no warrant of Scripture, but repugnant to the Word of God.

XV. *Of Speaking in the Congregation in such a Tongue as the People Understand*

¶ 75. It is a thing plainly repugnant to the Word of God, and the custom of the primitive Church, to have public prayer in the church, or to administer the Sacraments, in a tongue not understood by the people.

XVI. *Of the Sacraments*

¶ 76. Sacraments ordained of Christ are not only badges or tokens of Christian men's profession, but rather they are certain signs of grace, and God's good will toward us, by which he doth work invisibly in us, and doth not only quicken, but also strengthen and confirm, our faith in him.

There are two Sacraments ordained of Christ our Lord in the Gospel; that is to say, Baptism and the Supper of the Lord.

Those five commonly called sacraments, that is to say, confirmation, penance, orders, matrimony, and extreme unction, are not to be counted for Sacraments of the Gospel; being such as have partly grown out of the *corrupt* following of the apostles, and partly are states of life allowed in the Scriptures, but yet have not the like nature of Baptism and the Lord's Supper, because they have not any visible sign or ceremony ordained of God.

The Sacraments were not ordained of Christ to be gazed upon, or to be carried about; but that we should duly use them. And in such only as worthily receive the same they have a wholesome effect or operation; but they that receive them unworthily, purchase to themselves condemnation, as St. Paul saith, I Cor. 11:29.

XVII. *Of Baptism*

¶ 77. Baptism is not only a sign of profession and mark

of difference whereby Christians are distinguished from others that are not baptized; but it is also a sign of regeneration or the new birth. The baptism of young children is to be retained in the church.[61]

XVIII. *Of the Lord's Supper*

¶ 78. The Supper of the Lord is not only a sign of the love that Christians ought to have among themselves one to another, but rather is a sacrament of our redemption by Christ's death; insomuch that, to such as rightly, worthily, and with faith receive the same, the bread which we break is a partaking of the body of Christ; and likewise the cup of blessing is a partaking of the blood of Christ.

Transubstantiation, or the change of the substance of bread and wine in the Supper of our Lord, cannot be proved by Holy Writ, but is repugnant to the plain words of Scripture, overthroweth the nature of a sacrament, and hath given occasion to many superstitions.

The body of Christ is given, taken, and eaten in the Supper, only after a heavenly and spiritual manner. And the means whereby the body of Christ is received and eaten in the Supper is faith.

The Sacrament of the Lord's Supper was not by Christ's ordinance reserved, carried about, lifted up, or worshiped.

XIX. *Of Both Kinds*

¶ 79. The cup of the Lord is not to be denied to the lay people; for both the parts of the Lord's Supper, by Christ's ordinance and commandment, ought to be administered to all Christians alike.

XX. *Of the One Oblation of Christ, finished upon the Cross*

¶ 80. The offering of Christ, once made, is that perfect redemption, propitiation, and satisfaction for all the sins of the whole world, both original and actual; and there is none other satisfaction for sin but that alone. Wherefore the sacrifice of masses, in the which it is commonly

[61] *See* Judicial Council Decision 142.

said that the priest doth offer Christ for the quick and the dead, to have remission of pain or guilt, is a blasphemous fable and dangerous deceit.

XXI. *Of the Marriage of Ministers*

¶ 81. The ministers of Christ are not commanded by God's law either to vow the estate of single life, or to abstain from marriage; therefore it is lawful for them, as for all other Christians, to marry at their own discretion, as they shall judge the same to serve best to godliness.

XXII. *Of the Rites and Ceremonies of Churches*

¶ 82. It is not necessary that rites and ceremonies should in all places be the same, or exactly alike; for they have been always different, and may be changed according to the diversity of countries, times, and men's manners, so that nothing be ordained against God's Word. Whosoever, through his private judgment, willingly and purposely doth openly break the rites and ceremonies of the church to which he belongeth, which are not repugnant to the Word of God, and are ordained and approved by common authority, ought to be rebuked openly (that others may fear to do the like), as one that offendeth against the common order of the church, and woundeth the consciences of weak brethren.

Every particular church may ordain, change, or abolish rites and ceremonies, so that all things may be done to edification.

XXIII. *Of the Rulers of the United States of America*

¶ 83. The President, the Congress, the general assemblies, the governors, and the councils of state *as the delegates of the people*, are the rulers of the United States of America, according to the division of power made to them by the Constitution of the United States and by the constitutions of their respective states. And the said states are a sovereign and independent nation, and ought not to be subject to any foreign jurisdiction.

XXIV. *Of Christian Men's Goods*

¶ 84. The riches and goods of Christians are not common, as touching the right, title, and possession of the same, as some do falsely boast. Notwithstanding, every man ought, of such things as he possesseth, liberally to give alms to the poor, according to his ability.

XXV. *Of a Christian Man's Oath*

¶ 85. As we confess that vain and rash swearing is forbidden Christian men by our Lord Jesus Christ and James his apostle; so we judge that the Christian religion doth not prohibit, but that a man may swear when the magistrate requireth, in a cause of faith and charity, so it be done according to the prophet's teaching, in justice, judgment, and truth.

The following Article from the Methodist Protestant Discipline is placed here by the United Conference. It was not one of the Articles of Religion voted upon by the three churches.

Of Sanctification

¶ 86. Sanctification is that renewal of our fallen nature by the Holy Ghost, received through faith in Jesus Christ, whose blood of atonement cleanseth from all sin; whereby we are not only delivered from the guilt of sin, but are washed from its pollution, saved from its power, and are enabled, through grace, to love God with all our hearts and to walk in his holy commandments blameless.

The following provision was adopted by the Uniting Conference. This statement seeks to interpret to our churches in foreign lands Article XXIII of the Articles of Religion. It is a legislative enactment but is not a part of the Constitution. (*See* Judicial Council Decisions 41, 176.)

Of the Duty of Christians to the Civil Authority

¶ 87. It is the duty of all Christians, and especially of all Christian ministers, to observe and obey the laws and commands of the governing or supreme authority of the country of which they are citizens or subjects or in which they reside, and to use all laudable means to encourage and enjoin obedience to the powers that be.

THE GENERAL RULES

The Nature, Design, and General Rules of Our United Societies

¶ 91. In the latter end of the year 1739 eight or ten persons who appeared to be deeply convicted of sin, and earnestly groaning for redemption, came to Mr. Wesley in London. They desired, as did two or three more the next day, that he would spend some time with them in prayer, and advise them how to flee from the wrath to come, which they saw continually hanging over their heads. That he might have more time for this great work, he appointed a day when they might all come together, which from thenceforward they did every week, namely, on Thursday in the evening. To these, and as many more as desired to join with them (for their number increased daily), he gave those advices from time to time which he judged most needful for them, and they always concluded their meeting with prayer suited to their several necessities.

¶ 92. This was the rise of the **United Society,** first in Europe, and then in America. Such a society is no other than *"a company of men having the form and seeking the power of godliness, united in order to pray together, to receive the word of exhortation, and to watch over one another in love, that they may help each other to work out their salvation."*

¶ 93. That it may the more easily be discerned whether they are indeed working out their own salvation, each society is divided into smaller companies, called **classes,** according to their respective places of abode. There are about twelve persons in a class, one of whom is styled the **leader.** It is his duty,

1. To see each person in his class once a week at least, in order: (1) to inquire how his soul prospers; (2) to advise, reprove, comfort, or exhort, as occasion may require; (3) to receive what he is willing to give toward the relief of the preachers, church, and poor.

2. To meet the ministers and the stewards of the society once a week, in order: (1) to inform the minister

of any that are sick, or of any that walk disorderly and will not be reproved; (2) to pay the stewards what he has received of his class in the week preceding.

¶ **94.** There is only one condition previously required of those who desire admission into these societies—"a desire to flee from the wrath to come, and to be saved from their sins." But wherever this is really fixed in the soul it will be shown by its fruits.

¶ **95.** It is therefore expected of all who continue therein that they shall continue to evidence their desire of salvation,

First: By doing no harm, by avoiding evil of every kind, especially that which is most generally practiced, such as:

The taking of the name of God in vain.

The profaning the day of the Lord, either by doing ordinary work therein or by buying or selling.

Drunkenness, buying or selling spirituous liquors, or drinking them, unless in cases of extreme necessity.

Slaveholding; buying or selling slaves.

Fighting, quarreling, brawling, brother going to law with brother; returning evil for evil, or railing for railing; the using of many words in buying or selling.

The buying or selling goods that have not paid the duty.

The giving or taking of things on usury—that is, unlawful interest.

Uncharitable or unprofitable conversation; particularly speaking evil of magistrates or ministers.

Doing to others as we would not they should do unto us.

Doing what we know is not for the glory of God, as:

The putting on of gold and costly apparel.

The taking of such diversions as cannot be used in the name of the Lord Jesus.

The singing those songs, or reading those books, which do not tend to the knowledge or love of God.

Softness and needless self-indulgence.

Laying up treasure upon earth.

Borrowing without a probability of paying; or taking up goods without a probability of paying for them.

¶ **96.** It is expected of all who continue in these so-cities that they shall continue to evidence their desire of salvation.

Second: By doing good; by being in every kind merci-ful after their power; as they have opportunity, doing good of every possible sort, and, as far as possible, to all men:

To their bodies, of the ability which God giveth, by giving food to the hungry, by clothing the naked, by visiting or helping them that are sick or in prison;

To their souls, by instructing, reproving, or exhorting all we have any intercourse with; trampling under foot that enthusiastic doctrine, that "we are not to do good unless *our hearts be free to it.*"

By doing good, especially to them that are of the house-hold of faith or groaning so to be; employing them preferably to others; buying one of another; helping each other in business; and so much the more because the world will love its own and them *only.*

By all possible diligence and frugality, that the gospel be not blamed.

By running with patience the race which is set before them, denying themselves, and taking up their cross daily; submitting to bear the reproach of Christ, to be as the filth and offscouring of the world; and looking that men should say all manner of evil of them *falsely*, for the Lord's sake.

¶ **97.** It is expected of all who desire to continue in these societies that they shall continue to evidence their desire of salvation,

Third: By attending upon all the ordinances of God; such are:

The public worship of God.

The ministry of the Word, either read or expounded.

The Supper of the Lord.

Family and private prayer.

Searching the Scriptures.

Fasting or abstinence.

¶ **98.** These are the General Rules of our societies; all of which we are taught of God to observe, even in his written Word, which is the only rule, and the sufficient rule, both of our faith and practice. And all these we know his Spirit writes on truly awakened hearts. If there be any among us who observes them not, who habitually breaks any of them, let it be known unto them who watch over that soul as they who must give an account. We will admonish him of the error of his ways. We will bear with him for a season. But, if then he repent not, he hath no more place among us. We have delivered our own souls.

PART II

THE LOCAL CHURCH

CHAPTER I

THE PASTORAL CHARGE

¶ 101. The visible Church of Christ is a congregation of faithful men in which the pure Word of God is preached, and the Sacraments duly administered according to Christ's ordinance, in all those things that of necessity are requisite to the same. (Article of Religion XIII, ¶ 73.)

¶ 102. The **local church** is a connectional society of persons who have professed their faith in Christ, have been baptized, have assumed the vows of membership in The Methodist Church, and are associated in fellowship as a local Methodist church in order that they may hear the Word of God, receive the Sacraments, and carry forward the work which Christ has committed to his Church. Such a society of believers, being within The Methodist Church and subject to its Discipline, is also an inherent part of the Church Universal, which is composed of all who accept Jesus Christ as Lord and Savior, and which in the Apostles' Creed we declare to be the holy catholic Church.[1]

¶ 103. In order that each local church may be an effective connectional unit in The Methodist Church, it shall be the duty of all district superintendents and pastors to organize and administer the charges and churches committed to their care in accordance with the plan hereinafter set forth.

¶ 104. Each local church shall have a definite membership and evangelistic responsibility. It shall be held ac-

---

[1] *See* Judicial Council Decision 86.

countable for its present members, wherever they live, and for persons who choose it as their church, wherever they live. (*See* ¶ 1482.)

¶ **105. 1. A pastoral charge** shall consist of one or more churches which are organized under, and subject to, the Discipline of The Methodist Church, with a single pastoral-charge Quarterly Conference, and to which a minister is or may be duly appointed or appointable as preacher in charge.

2. A pastoral charge of two or more churches is a **circuit.**

3. A **parish** shall be identified as an area of service with the membership and constituency of one or more local churches having a co-ordinated program and organization to fulfill a ministry directed to all the people of the area. It may include local churches of other denominations.

Chapter II

CHURCH MEMBERSHIP

¶ **106. 1.** The Methodist Church is a part of the Church Universal (¶ 102). Therefore all persons, without regard to race, color, national origin, or economic condition, shall be eligible to attend its worship services, to participate in its programs, and, when they take the appropriate vows (¶ 107), to be admitted into its membership in any local church in the connection.

2. The membership of a local Methodist church shall consist of all persons who have been received into its fellowship on profession of their faith (¶¶ 107-9), by transfer from some other church (¶¶ 110-11) or by restoration (¶¶ 124, 127.5, 977), and whose membership has not been terminated by death, transfer (¶¶ 121-22), withdrawal (¶¶ 123-24), expulsion (¶ 974), or action of the Quarterly Conference (¶ 127.5).

3. A member of a local Methodist church is a member of The Methodist Church anywhere in the connection (¶ 102).

49

4. All persons received into the fellowship of The Methodist Church shall, by the grace of God, fulfill their membership vows through an active expression of their faith, as exhorted in the General Rules (¶¶ 95-97), bringing their gifts and services into conformity with the redemptive will of God and witnessing for Jesus Christ in all areas of life.

SECTION I.   **Admission into the Church**

¶ 107. All persons seeking to be saved from their sins and sincerely desiring to be Christian in faith and practice are proper candidates for membership in The Methodist Church. When such persons offer themselves for membership, it shall be the duty of the pastor, or of proper persons appointed by him, to instruct them in the meaning of the Christian faith and the history, organization, and teaching of The Methodist Church; to explain to them the baptismal and membership vows (¶¶ 1713-14); and to lead them to commit themselves to Jesus Christ as Lord and Savior. When they shall have given proof of the genuineness of their faith in Christ and of their desire to assume the obligations and become faithful members of The Methodist Church, after the completion of a reasonable period of training, and after the rite of Baptism has been administered to those who have not been previously baptized, he shall bring them before the congregation, administer the vows (¶ 1714) and receive them into the fellowship of the Church, and duly enroll them as members.

¶ 108. 1. A duly authorized minister of The Methodist Church while serving as chaplain of any organization, institution, or military unit, or as a Wesley Foundation director, or while otherwise present where a local church is not available, may receive a person into the membership of The Methodist Church when such person shall have given proof of the genuineness of his faith in Christ and of his desire to assume the obligations and become a faithful member of the Church. After the vows of membership have been administered (¶ 1714), such minister shall issue a statement of membership to the local church of the choice of the person concerned, and the pastor thereof on receiving such statement shall duly enroll him as a member.

2. When a person in military service or member of the family of such person is baptized and/or received into the church by a chaplain and has no local church to which the membership and records may be sent, the chaplain shall send the name, address, and related facts to the General Board of Evangelism for recording on the general roll of military service personnel and families (¶ 1474.3).

¶ 109. Any candidate for church membership who for good reason is unable to appear before the congregation may, at the discretion of the pastor and with the approval of the Official Board, be received elsewhere in accordance with the Ritual of The Methodist Church (¶ 1714); *provided* that in the event of a clear emergency the pastor may receive such person without the approval of the board, in which case he shall report his action to the board at its next meeting.

¶ 110. A person who is a member of The Methodist Church may have his membership transferred from one local church to another by a proper certificate of transfer.

¶ 111. A member in good standing in any Christian denomination who has been baptized and who desires to unite with The Methodist Church may be received into membership by a proper certificate of transfer from his former church, or by his own declaration of Christian faith, and upon affirming his willingness to be loyal to The Methodist Church, and after he and the members of the church have entered into solemn covenant with one another as provided in the Ritual (¶ 1714).

Sec. II.   **Children and the Church**

¶ 114. 1. Because the redeeming love of God, revealed in Jesus Christ, extends to all persons, and because Jesus explicitly included the children in his kingdom, the pastor of each charge shall earnestly exhort all Christian parents or guardians to present their children to the Lord

51

in Baptism at an early age.[2] Before Baptism is administered, he shall diligently instruct the parents or guardians regarding the meaning of this Sacrament and the vows which they assume. It is expected of parents or guardians who present their children for Baptism that they shall use all diligence in bringing them up in conformity to the Word of God. It is desired that one or both parents or guardians shall be members of a Christian church or that sponsors who are members shall assume the baptismal vows. They shall be admonished of this obligation and earnestly exhorted to faithfulness therein. At the time of Baptism they shall be informed that the church, with its church-school program, will aid them in the Christian nurture of their children.

2. The pastor of the church shall, at the time of administering the Sacrament of Baptism, furnish the parents or guardians of the child who is baptized with a **certificate of Baptism,** which shall also clearly state that the child is now enrolled as a preparatory member in The Methodist Church.

3. The pastor shall keep and transmit to his successor an accurate register of the names of all baptized children in his charge, including both those who have been baptized there and those who have been baptized elsewhere. This shall constitute the preparatory membership roll of the church (¶ 132). It shall give the full name of the child, the date of birth, the date and place of Baptism, and the names of the parents or guardians and their place of residence.

4. All baptized children under the care of a Methodist church shall be retained as preparatory members in the church until this status is terminated by: reception into full membership, after a proper course of training, both in the church school and in the pastor's class (*see* § 5 *below*); transfer to another Methodist church by the rules of ¶¶ 119-121; transfer to a church of another evangelical denomination (¶ 122); death; withdrawal ¶¶ 123-24); or transfer to the constituency roll of the church (¶ 132) at the age of sixteen. The preparatory member-

---

[2] *See* Judicial Council Decision 142.

ship roll shall be balanced each year by adding and subtracting the names received and removed during the year, using the forms provided for this purpose.

5. It shall be the duty of the pastor, the parents or guardians, and the officers and teachers of the church school to lead the children of the church to an understanding of the Christian faith, to an appreciation of the privileges and obligations of church membership, and to a personal commitment to Jesus Christ as Lord and Savior, and to guide them in the use of the means of grace in living the Christian life. The pastor shall, at least annually, organize the children who have arrived at the age of decision into classes of instruction for church membership, using materials produced by The Methodist Church. Whenever children so trained in a course of study approved by The Methodist Church shall give evidence of their own Christian faith and purpose and of understanding the privileges and obligations of church membership, they may be received into full membership in the church according to the provisions of ¶ 107.

SEC. III. **Youth**

¶ **115.** It is strongly recommended that each local church offer, for senior high school youth who are members of the church, an advanced class of instruction in the meaning of the Christian life and church membership. It is further recommended that this course, taught by the pastor, emphasize Methodist doctrines and the nature and mission of the Church, leading to continued growth in the knowledge and grace of our Lord Jesus Christ.

SEC. IV. **Affiliate and Associate Membership**

¶ **116.** A member of The Methodist Church, residing for an extended period in a city or community at a distance from his home church, may on his request be enrolled as an **affiliate member** of a Methodist church located in the vicinity of his temporary residence. His home pastor shall be notified of his affiliate membership. Such membership shall entitle him to the fellowship of that church, to its pastoral care and oversight, and to participation in its activities, including the holding of office, except as otherwise provided (*see* ¶¶ 138.3, 144, 153.3, 207.4), but he shall be counted and reported only as a member of his home church. A member of another denomination may become an affiliate member under the same conditions.

¶ **117.** Associate membership may be authorized by a Central Conference (¶ 562).

SEC. V.   **Transfer and Termination of Membership**

¶ **118.** Membership in a local church may be terminated by death, transfer (¶¶ 121-22), withdrawal (¶¶ 123-24), expulsion (¶ 974), or action of the Quarterly Conference (¶ 127.5). It shall be the duty of the pastor of the charge or of the membership secretary to keep an accurate record of all terminations of membership and to report to each Quarterly Conference the names of all persons whose membership has been terminated since the conference preceding, in each instance indicating the reason for such termination.

¶ **119.** If a member of a Methodist church shall change his place of residence to another community, so far removed from his home church that he cannot participate regularly in its worship and activity, he shall be encouraged to transfer his membership to a Methodist church in the community of his newly established residence. As soon as his pastor is reliably informed of his change of residence, actual or contemplated, it shall be the pastor's duty and obligation to assist him to establish himself in the fellowship of a church in the community of his future home, and to send to a Methodist pastor in such community, or to the district superintendent, or (if neither is known) to the General Board of Evangelism, a letter of notification, giving the latest known address of the person or persons concerned and requesting local pastoral oversight. The above procedure is based on the recognition that absentee membership is not good for the individual or the church, and that it is essential that we recognize that the care of souls and the building up of the whole church is more important than retaining membership in a particular congregation, whether for sentiment or other reasons.

¶ **120.** When a pastor discovers a member of The Methodist Church residing in his community whose membership is in a church so far removed from his place of residence that he cannot participate regularly in its worship and activity, it shall be his duty and obligation to give pastoral oversight to such person, and to persuade him, if possible, to transfer his membership to a Methodist church in the community where he resides.

¶ **121.** When a pastor shall receive from another pastor of a Methodist church, or from the person concerned, a request for a **certificate of transfer** for a member of his church, he shall issue the same in the following form, and shall make proper entry on his church roll of the transfer of such person, and his membership shall thereby be transferred:

This is to certify that A.B. who resides at _____ has been a member of the _____ Methodist Church in _____. On request his (her) membership is hereby transferred to the _____ Methodist Church in _____, and he (she) is affectionately commended to its care and fellowship. Notice of this certificate of transfer has been sent to the person above named.

_____, Pastor

Date _____   *Address _____*

The original certificate shall be accompanied by a blank for the acknowledgment of the same in the following form:

The certificate of transfer of the membership of A.B. from the _____ Methodist Church in _____ to the _____ Methodist Church is hereby acknowledged. He (she) has been duly received into our fellowship and recorded as a member in this church.

_____, Pastor

Date _____   *Address _____*

Notice shall be sent to the person whose membership is thus being transferred in the following form:

This day I have issued a certificate of transfer of your membership to the _____ *Methodist Church in* _____, *commending you to its care and fellowship. In your new relationship we bid you Godspeed.*

_____, *Pastor*

Date _____   *Address* _____

The certificate of transfer shall be sent directly to the pastor of the Methodist church to which the certificate is issued, or to the district superintendent if there is no pastor. On receipt of such certificate of transfer, the pastor or the district superintendent receiving the same shall record on the membership roll of the church the name of the person thus transferred, and the person shall be a member thereof; whereupon the pastor or district superintendent shall certify to the pastor issuing the certificate that the name appearing on said certificate has been duly entered on the membership roll of the receiving church.

¶ 122. A pastor upon receiving a request from a member of his church to transfer to a church of another denomination, or upon receiving such request from a pastor or duly authorized official of another denomination, shall (with the approval of the member) issue a certificate of transfer and shall properly record the transfer of such person on the membership roll of the local church; and his membership shall thereby be terminated. For the transfer of a member of The Methodist Church to a church of another denomination forms similar to those described in ¶ 121 shall be used, with the substitution of the name of the other denomination for the word "Methodist" in appropriate places in those forms.

¶ 123. If a pastor is informed that a member of his church has, without notice, united with a church of another denomination, he shall make diligent inquiry; and if the report is confirmed, he shall enter "Withdrawn" after the person's name on the membership roll, and shall report the same to the next Quarterly Conference.

¶ 124. If a member proposes to withdraw from The Methodist Church, he shall communicate his purpose in writing to the pastor of the local church in which his membership is held. On receiving such notice of withdrawal, the pastor shall properly record the fact of withdrawal on the membership roll. If requested, the pastor shall give a statement of withdrawal to such member. Such person, on his written request, may be restored to membership on recommendation of the pastor and by vote of the Quarterly Conference.

Sec. VI. **Care of Church Members**

¶ 126. The local church shall endeavor to enlist each member in activities for spiritual growth and in participation in the services of the church and its organizations. It shall be the duty of the pastor and of the Commission on Membership and Evangelism, by regular visitation, care, and spiritual oversight, to provide necessary activities and opportunities for spiritual growth through individual and family worship, and to aid continually the members to keep their vows to uphold the church by attendance, prayers, gifts, and service. The church has a moral and spiritual obligation to nurture its non-participating and indifferent members into renewed wholeness.

¶ 127. While primary responsibility and initiative rests with each individual member faithfully to perform the vows of membership which he has solemnly assumed, if he should be neglectful of that responsibility, these procedures shall be followed:

1. If a member residing in the community is negligent of his vows, or absents himself from the worship of the church, the pastor and the membership secretary shall report his name to the special committee created by the Commission on Membership and Evangelism for reclaiming the negligent (¶ 222.4b), which committee shall do all in its power to re-enlist him in the active fellowship of the church. It shall visit him and make clear to him that, while his name is on the roll of his particular local church, he is a member of The Methodist Church as a whole, and that, since he is not attending the church where his name is enrolled, he is requested to agree in writing to do one of three things: (a) renew his vows and become a regular worshiper in the church where his

name is recorded; (*b*) request transfer to another Methodist church where he will be a regular worshiper; or (*c*) arrange transfer to a particular local church of another denomination. If the member refuses to agree in writing to any of the available alternatives over a period of three years, his name may be removed by the procedure of § 5 below.

2. If a member whose address is known is residing outside the community and is not participating in the worship or activity of the church, the directives of ¶ 119 shall be followed each year until he joins another church or requests in writing that his name be removed from the membership roll; *provided,* however that if after three years the committee has not been able to relate him to the church at his new place of residence, his name may be removed by the procedure of § 5 below.

3. If the address of a member is no longer known to the pastor, the membership secretary, and the Commission on Membership and Evangelism, they shall make every effort to locate him, including listing his name in the church bulletin, circularizing it throughout the parish, and reading it from the pulpit. If he can be located, the directives of either § 1 or § 2 above shall be followed; but if after three years of such efforts his address is still unknown, his name may be removed from the membership roll by the procedure of § 5 below.

4. The pastor, the membership secretary, and the Commission on Membership and Evangelism shall review annually the membership rolls of the church and shall see that they are complete and accurate. They shall report their findings to the fourth Quarterly Conference, including the names of the members whose addresses are unknown.

5. If the directives of § 1, § 2, or § 3 above have been followed for the specified number of years without success, the member's name may be removed from the membership roll by vote of the Quarterly Conference on recommendation of the pastor and the Commission on Membership and Evangelism, each name being considered individually. On the roll there shall be entered after his

name: "Removed by order of the Quarterly Conference"; and if the action is on the basis of § 3, there shall be added: "Reason: address unknown." The membership of the person shall thereby be terminated, and the record thereof shall be retained; *provided* that at his request he may be restored to membership by recommendation of the pastor; and *provided*, further, that should a transfer of his membership be requested, the pastor may restore him to membership for this purpose and issue the certificate of transfer.[3]

6. Recognizing that the Church has a continuing moral and spiritual obligation to nurture all persons, even those whose names have been removed from the membership roll as provided in § 5, it is recommended that the names so removed be inscribed on a **roll of names removed by Quarterly Conference action.** It shall then become the responsibility of the pastor and/or the Commission on Membership and Evangelism at least once a year to correct this roll by removing the names of persons who have: (*a*) been restored to membership in the local church (§ 5); (*b*) been restored to membership and transferred to another Methodist church (§ 5); (*c*) joined a church of another denomination; (*d*) moved beyond the geographical area of the local church; (*e*) deceased. After the record has been brought up to date, it is recommended that the pastor and/or the commission contact those whose names remain, either in person or by other means, in the most effective and practical manner, with the aid of materials and procedures made available by the General Board of Evangelism. The names and addresses of those who have moved outside the local church's area should be sent to local churches in their new communities, that those churches may visit and minister to them (¶ 104).

¶ **128.** If a local church is discontinued, the pastor shall transfer the members to such other local churches as they may select. If any do not so select, the district superintendent shall select another Methodist church and transfer their membership thereto. (*See* ¶¶ 188, 354.)

---

[3] Amended in 1964 following Judicial Council Decision 207.

SEC. VII.　**Membership Records and Reports**

¶ 130. The pastor shall report to each Quarterly Conference the names of persons received into the membership of the church or churches of the pastoral charge since the Quarterly Conference preceding, and the names of persons whose membership in the church or churches of the pastoral charge has been terminated during the same period, indicating in the case of each how he was received or how his membership was terminated.

¶ 131. The basic membership records in each local church shall consist of: (1) a permanent church register, and (2) a card index or loose-leaf book.

1. The **permanent church register** shall be a bound volume of durable material, prepared by The Methodist Publishing House at a reasonable price, in the form approved by the Council on World Service and Finance (¶ 1107). Space shall be provided for a record of members showing the full name of each, how each was admitted into the church, the date, by whom received, and how the membership of each was terminated, with the date. Space shall also be provided for recording marriages, baptisms, deaths, pastoral terms, and such other matters as may be essential to a permanent record of the church's membership and ministry, as may be determined by the Council on World Service and Finance. The names shall be recorded chronologically as each person is received into the fellowship of that church, and without reference to alphabetical order. Each name shall be numbered, in regular numerical order, and the number of each shall appear on the corresponding card or page in the card index or loose-leaf membership roll. This provision is for the purpose of ensuring facility in locating any name on the permanent church register.

2. The **card index or loose-leaf membership record** shall be kept on a form approved by the Council on World Service and Finance (¶ 1107), or on other forms that include the items approved by the said council. Space shall be provided for the name and address, how and when received, and such other information as may be determined by the committee. This record of member-

ship shall be filed in alphabetical order, and shall show the number appearing opposite each name on the permanent register so that such name may be promptly located. The pastor shall report annually to the Annual Conference the total membership of his charge as shown on his membership records.

¶ **132.** The pastor or membership secretary shall also keep a **constituency roll** containing the names and addresses of such persons as are not members of the church concerned, including unbaptized children and church-school members not yet members of the church, for whom the local church has pastoral responsibility; and a **preparatory membership roll** containing the names of all baptized children in the church who have not been received into full membership (¶ 114.3). Such other membership rolls, including an **affiliate membership roll** (¶ 116), shall be maintained as may be judged necessary for proper pastoral care and the general work of the church. (*See also* ¶ 127.6.)

¶ **133.** The Quarterly Conference shall elect a **membership secretary,** whose duty shall be, under the direction of the pastor, to keep accurate records of all membership rolls as provided in ¶¶ 131-32, and to report monthly to the Official Board through the Commission on Membership and Evangelism. (*See* ¶ 209.)

CHAPTER III

THE QUARTERLY CONFERENCE

SECTION I.   **General Provisions**

¶ **137.** Within the pastoral charge (¶ 105) the **Quarterly Conference** is the basic body of control uniting it to connectional Methodism, and through the Quarterly Conference the pastoral charge functions in its relationship thereto.[4] The Quarterly Conference shall therefore be

---

[4] *See* Judicial Council Decision 130.

organized in every pastoral charge, as provided in the
Constitution (¶¶ 31-32). The membership thereof, and its
authority, powers, duties, and responsibilities shall be as
hereinafter set forth.

¶ **138.** The following shall constitute the membership
of the Quarterly Conference, in so far as the offices and
relationships exist within the pastoral charge.

1. The pastor and the associate pastor or pastors; the
retired and supernumerary ministers residing in that
place who elect to hold membership therein; *provided* that
each such person may be a member of one Quarterly Conference only; traveling preachers who, because they are
assigned to special work, have been attached to the
Quarterly Conference concerned by appointment of the
bishop (¶ 432).

2. The local preachers holding their membership in the
pastoral charge, and deaconesses appointed to labor therein
or holding their membership in the charge while on leave
of absence.

3. The stewards, elective and ex officio (¶¶ 208-9), and
the trustees of the church, or churches, in the pastoral
charge (¶ 159); *provided*, however, that all lay members
of the Quarterly Conference shall be members of a local
church within the charge, except as provided in ¶ 562,
and all except the president of the Methodist Youth Fellowship or the president of the Youth Council shall be not
less than eighteen years of age.

¶ **139.** The district superintendent or an elder designated by him shall preside. The district superintendent
shall fix the time for the meeting of the Quarterly Conference, but the conference may appoint the place; *provided* that should necessity arise the district superintendent and the pastor may change the place of meeting. A
special session of the Quarterly Conference may be called
by the district superintendent or by the pastor with the
written consent of the district superintendent. Quarterly
Conferences for two or more pastoral charges may be held
at the same time and place, as the district superintendent
may determine. (For provisions regarding notice of meetings *see* ¶¶ 154, 168, 170-72, 180.)

¶ **140.** There shall be held for each pastoral charge a

first and fourth Quarterly Conference. The second and third Quarterly Conferences may be held at the discretion of the district superintendent. A **recording steward** shall be elected annually, who shall keep an accurate and permanent record of the proceedings and shall be the custodian of all records and reports, and who with the presiding officer shall sign the minutes.

¶ **141.** The Quarterly Conference, after a period of worship, shall transact the business committed to it by the Discipline,[5] following the order indicated on the form bearing the title "Minutes of the Quarterly Conference" approved by the Council on World Service and Finance (¶ 1107) and published by The Methodist Publishing House. The district superintendent is required in so far as possible to keep his record of each Quarterly Conference on this official form. It shall also be his duty to see that other Quarterly Conference and church records and reports are written on our approved forms. If the observance of the order of business as provided in these forms seems likely to protract a session beyond a reasonable limit, the presiding officer may, with the approval of the Quarterly Conference, select the more important matters and bring them forward.

¶ **142.** To the Quarterly Conference are committed the following powers and duties:

1. To have general oversight of the Official Board, which is the administrative body of the Quarterly Conference in each local church. (*See* ¶¶ 206-16.)

2. To receive reports from the pastor (¶ 352.22), from church officers, and from the commissions, committees, and societies of the church or churches of the pastoral charge as the Quarterly Conference may require.

3. To elect the officers of the church or churches constituting the pastoral charge (¶ 32), unless otherwise provided, in harmony with the provisions of the Constitution of The Methodist Church, and to constitute the required and optional commissions for each local church (¶¶ 144, 219) and such committees as may be determined by the Quarterly Conference (¶ 145).

---

[5] *See* Judicial Council Decision 102.

4. In cases where the Discipline permits more than one course of action in the administration and work of a pastoral charge, to determine what course shall be taken. (*See* ¶¶ 157, 176, 197-200.)

5. To recommend proper persons for license to preach and for the office of deaconess, and to certify lay speakers (¶ 146).

6. To fix the salary of the pastor or pastors (¶¶ 145.2, 148, 215.2).

7. To determine annually the amount accepted by the charge for world service and conference benevolences (¶ 147).

8. Such other powers and duties as have been or may be duly committed to it.

Sec. II.   Elections

¶ **143.** The Quarterly Conference, preferably the fourth, shall elect annually, to serve from the beginning of the ensuing conference year, except as specified below, the following officers for the pastoral charge on nomination of the Committee on Nominations, or on nomination of the pastor if there is no such committee (¶¶ 142.3, 145.1), unless otherwise provided in the Discipline; or it shall authorize the Annual Church Conference to elect such officers, in which case it shall issue a call for an Annual Church Conference for that purpose (¶¶ 32, 197-200); *provided* that in no case shall the privilege of making nominations from the floor be denied.

1. The elective stewards of the church or churches of the pastoral charge (¶¶ 207-11).

2. The church lay leader or leaders, and associate church lay leader or leaders if desired (¶ 288).

3. The district steward and reserve district steward; *provided* that the Committee on Nominations or the pastor shall confer with the district superintendent before any nomination is made (¶¶ 797, 802).

4. The lay member or members of the Annual Conference, annually or quadrennially, as the Annual Conference may direct, and one or more reserve members. If the charge's lay representative to the Annual Conference shall

cease to be a member of the charge or shall for any reason fail to serve, a reserve member in the order of his election shall serve in his place.[6] At the option of the Annual Conference, the lay member or members thus elected shall serve beginning with the next session of the Annual Conference following election.

5. Elective members of the District Conference, if any (¶ 687).

6. The chairmen of the commissions and committees (¶¶ 144, 145, 219).

7. The church-school superintendent or superintendents (¶¶ 246.1, 248.3).

8. The membership cultivation superintendent and division superintendents of each church school, on nomination of its church-school superintendent-elect with the approval of the pastor in consultation with the minister or director of Christian education (¶ 246.1).

9. A director of Christian education, or educational assistant, if desired, on nomination of the pastor with the concurrence of the Commission on Education and the Committee on Pastoral Relations or the Committee on Lay Personnel (¶¶ 246-47). For appointment of a minister to such position *see* ¶ 247.1.

10. A director of music, or music assistant, if desired, on nomination of the pastor with the concurrence of the Commission on Worship (¶ 276) or Music Committee (¶ 278.4), the Commission on Education, and the Committee on Lay Personnel (¶ 247.2). For appointment of a minister of music *see* ¶ 247.2.

11. A church business manager, if desired, on nomination of the pastor with the concurrence of the Official Board (¶¶ 212.2, 269).

12. The secretary or secretaries of stewardship (¶¶ 262-63), the church treasurer or treasurers (¶ 268), and, if desired, a financial secretary or secretaries (¶ 269).

13. The communion steward or stewards, whose duty it shall be to provide the elements of Holy Communion, under the direction of the pastor, and properly to arrange the communion table.

---

[6] *See* Judicial Council Decision 109.

14. The hospitals and homes steward or stewards, who shall be selected from among the elective stewards of § 1 above (¶ 278.3).

15. The membership secretary or secretaries (¶¶ 133, 221.1).

16. The recording steward (¶ 140).

17. The secretary or secretaries of Christian vocations (¶ 145.9).

18. The trier of appeals (¶ 1056).

19. Such other officers of the church, or churches, as may be called for by the General, Jurisdictional, Annual, or District Conference, or as shall be determined by the Quarterly Conference; *provided* that all such shall be in harmony with the provisions of the Discipline.

Note: For the election of trustees *see* ¶¶ 157-61, 183.

¶ **144.** The Quarterly Conference shall elect annually from the membership of the church or churches in the charge (except as provided in ¶ 562), on nomination of the Committee on Nominations, or of the pastor if there is no such committee, the commissions specified in ¶ 219; *provided* that in pastoral charges of more than one church the commissions shall be nominated by the Official Board of each church respectively with the concurrence of the pastor (or, if the board fails to make such nominations, they shall be made by the pastor); or it may authorize the Annual Church Conference to elect the commissions, in which case it shall authorize a call for an Annual Church Conference for that purpose (¶¶ 32, 197-200); *provided* that in no case shall the privilege of making nominations from the floor be denied. Unless otherwise provided (*see* ¶¶ 221, 274) the elected membership of each commission shall be not fewer than three, and as many additional members as the Quarterly Conference may determine; *provided* that in a small church, if the Quarterly Conference finds it necessary, each commission may be composed of the elected chairman (¶ 143.6) and the available ex officio members. Each commission shall work under the authority and direction of the Official Board, the duties of each being hereinafter defined and set forth (¶¶ 220-77). Such commissions shall be elected at the fourth Quarterly Conference of the pastoral charge, and shall serve from

the beginning of the ensuing conference year. Should the
Quarterly Conference fail to elect the commissions, the
Official Board shall elect them and report to the district
superintendent. The chairmen of all commissions shall be
nominated and elected in the same manner and at the
same time as the members of the commissions (¶ 143.6).

¶ **145.** The Quarterly Conference shall select from the
committees designated hereunder such as it determines
to be necessary to the work of the Quarterly Conference,
the chairmen and members of the same to be nominated
by the Committee on Nominations (or by the pastor if
there is no such committee), unless otherwise provided
in the Discipline, and elected by the Quarterly Conference;
or it may authorize the Annual Church Conference to
elect them together with the commissions as provided in
¶ 144.

1. The **Committee on Nominations,** of which the pastor
shall be chairman, which shall nominate to the Quarterly
Conference or to the Annual Church Conference such officers and members of Quarterly Conference commissions
and committees as the law of the church requires or as
the Quarterly Conference may determine as necessary to
its work (¶¶ 143-45); *provided* that all the elective members of the Committee on Nominations shall be nominated
from the floor; and *provided,* further, that to secure experience and stability the membership may be divided
into three classes, one of which shall be elected each year
for a three-year term.

2. The **Committee on Pastoral Relations,** which shall
consist of not fewer than three nor more than nine persons; *provided* that in a circuit each church shall have
at least one representative. Its primary function is to aid
the pastor in making his ministry most effective by being
available for counsel, keeping him advised concerning
conditions within the congregation as they affect relations
between pastor and people, and keeping the people informed concerning the nature and function of the pastoral
office. When the pastor is to be absent, the committee shall
co-operate with him to secure suitable supply ministers for
preaching and other pastoral service during his absence.
It shall consult with him about adequate provision for

his salary, housing, and travel and other expenses related to his duties, and recommend to the Commission or Commissions on Stewardship and Finance and the Official Board or Boards the amounts agreed on. After conferring with him, it may arrange with the Official Board or Boards for the necessary time and for financial assistance for his attendance at such schools or institutes as may serve his intellectual and spiritual growth. Since a responsibility of the committee is to be at all times sensitive to the relationship between pastor and people, should it become evident to the committee that the best interests of the charge and pastor will be served by a change of pastors, it shall confer with him and furnish him with this information. It shall co-operate with the pastor, the district superintendent, and the bishop in arranging for a change of pastors. The committee shall be amenable to the Quarterly Conference, and its relation to the district superintendent and bishop shall be advisory only.

3. The **Committee on Lay Personnel,** of which the pastor or a person designated by him shall be chairman, which shall be responsible for establishing and maintaining personnel policy for all lay employees, and other employees not within the jurisdiction of the Committee on Pastoral Relations, in keeping with highest standards of Christian practice. This committee shall make provision for range of compensation, working hours, vacation schedule, and sick leave. It shall, after study, recommend other lay employee benefits such as the retirement plan of the Lay Employees Pension Fund (¶ 1658) or other plans in addition to the Federal Social Security provisions; life insurance; health and hospitalization insurance; and disability insurance to compensate employees unable to work because of illness or injury. It should be the aim of this committee to insure for employees of the church rights and considerations at least no less than those representative of enlightened and Christian policies now commonly practiced by secular institutions. This committee shall be amenable to the Quarterly Conference.

4. The **Committee on Records and History,** which shall be responsible for assisting the pastor to see that all

church and Quarterly Conference records are kept on the official record blanks provided by The Methodist Publishing House under the direction of the Council on World Service and Finance (¶ 1107). This committee shall examine the Quarterly Conference records annually after the fourth Quarterly Conference and shall report the results of its examination to the first Quarterly Conference of the ensuing year. The committee, with the pastor, shall be responsible for preparing, where it does not already exist, and after the Quarterly Conference has approved such an undertaking, a history of the local church or churches from the time of organization, and provide for preserving the same in permanent form. At the close of each conference year it may add to this record facts concerning important activities and achievements of the church and its organizations. It shall see that any and all minute or record books no longer in current use are deposited with the recording steward, and shall co-operate with him in providing a permanent place for the safekeeping of the Quarterly Conference records and all other historical material belonging to the church. It shall co-operate with the Historical Society of the Annual Conference by sharing historical information and materials pertaining to the local church.

5. The **Committee on Co-operation,** which shall be responsible for co-operation with other churches and constructive agencies and groups in the community; *provided* that in each instance such co-operation shall have been approved by the Quarterly Conference or the Official Board.

6. The **Committee on Policy,** which, after a careful survey of the work and needs of the pastoral charge, shall make recommendations concerning its improvement or extension; *provided* that the pastor shall nominate this committee and shall be its chairman. On charges of more than one church, each church shall have at least one member on this committee, and as far as practicable each of the commissions shall be represented thereon.

7. The **Parsonage Committee,** which, with the approval of the trustees, shall provide an adequate and comfortable residence for the pastor and maintain the proper upkeep

and furnishing of the same; *provided* that on charges of only one church this committee shall be named by the Official Board, in which event it shall be responsible to the board (¶ 278.5).

8. The **Committee on Apportionments** (if the pastoral charge is a circuit), which shall recommend to the Quarterly Conference for its action and determination a proper schedule of apportionments among the churches of the pastoral charge of salaries, benevolences, and other items properly apportioned to the charge, or assumed by it. Each church in the pastoral charge shall have representation on this committee.

9. The **Committee on Christian Vocations,** which shall be composed of the pastor, the secretary of Christian vocations (¶ 143.17), who shall be the chairman, the superintendents or representatives of the Youth and Adult Divisions and a representative selected by the Methodist Youth Fellowship, the hospitals and homes steward, and a representative each from the Commission on Missions, the Woman's Society of Christian Service, and Methodist Men. It shall co-operate with the district secretary of Christian vocations (¶ 696) and the Conference Commission on Christian Vocations (¶ 676). The duty of this committee shall be to see that the philosophy of Christian vocation and the opportunities and challenge of church vocations are regularly presented to the youth and adults of the church, to advise interested young people and adults of the necessary qualifications for all church vocations, and to give encouragement and guidance to candidates for the pastoral ministry and other church-related vocations, working with and through the appropriate commissions of the local church. The committee shall report regularly to the Official Board and shall report to the Conference Commission on Christian Vocations on cultivation and prospects for church vocations.

In a small church the secretary of Christian vocations may serve for the committee by working with appropriate groups in the local church.

10. The **Committee on Wills and Legacies,** which shall keep before Methodist people and any others, by such means as the committee may determine, the desirability

of leaving bequests to the local church, or to other causes and institutions of The Methodist Church. The committee shall seek legal counsel to the end that bequests may be made in proper legal form. It shall report the name and address of its chairman to the General Board of Lay Activities so the board may provide suggested methods, materials, and procedures. In a small church the duty of this committee may be assigned to the Commission on Stewardship and Finance.

11. The **Farm and Home Committee,** composed of both men and women, which shall have the responsibility of assisting young couples to become established on the land and in small businesses inherent in the economy of the community, for the purpose of maintaining and strengthening the church community.

12. Any other committees which the Quarterly Conference may determine to be necessary to its work, provided the same are in harmony with the provisions of the Discipline.

SEC. III.   **Sundry Duties**

¶ **146.** The Quarterly Conference shall recommend or certify proper persons, as follows:

1. It shall, on application for issuance or renewal of a license to preach by a proper person, whose membership is within the charge, recommend such person to the District Committee on Ministerial Qualifications (¶ 695), if in the judgment of the Quarterly Conference his gifts, graces, and potential usefulness warrant such action. Such person shall conform with all the provisions of the Discipline (¶¶ 306-7). The vote to recommend shall be taken by written, secret ballot, and the recommendation shall be signed by the presiding officer.

2. It shall recommend and send to the Annual Conference Deaconess Board credentials for young women who may become candidates for the office of deaconess. (*See* ¶ 1250.1.)

3. It shall certify proper persons to serve as lay speakers, and inquire annually into the gifts, labors, and usefulness of lay speakers on the circuit, station, or mission, as specified in ¶ 293.

¶ **147.** The Quarterly Conference shall determine the amount accepted annually by the charge for world service and conference benevolences by the following procedure: As soon as practicable after the session of the Annual Conference, each district superintendent shall notify each pastoral charge in his district what amounts have been apportioned to it for world service and conference benevolences (¶¶ 795-96). It shall be the responsibility of the pastor and the respective church lay leaders to present to a meeting of each local church in the pastoral charge a statement of the apportionments for world service and conference benevolences, explaining the causes supported by each of these funds, and their place in the total program of the church. Such presentation to each local church shall be made before the Quarterly Conference of the pastoral charge shall set the amount of its acceptances. The first or second Quarterly Conference may accept, increase, or decrease the amount apportioned for world service and conference benevolences (¶ 142.7). The amount voted by the Quarterly Conference shall be the amount assumed by the pastoral charge for this cause. Should the amount contributed during the year for world service and conference benevolences exceed the charge's acceptance, the entire amount so contributed shall be remitted in regular order to the conference treasurer before the end of the conference year (¶ 267.6). The district superintendent shall also notify each pastoral charge of all other amounts properly apportioned to it. The apportionments to the pastoral charge for the General Administration Fund, for the Episcopal Fund, for district superintendents, for conference claimants, and for the minimum salary fund are not subject to change or alteration by the Quarterly Conference or by the local church.

¶ **148.** The Quarterly Conference shall fix the salary and other remuneration of the pastor, or pastors, after the following procedure: At the session of the Quarterly Conference next preceding the regular annual session of the Annual Conference, on recommendation of the Official Board or Boards and after consultation with the pastor (*see* ¶¶ 145.2, 215.2, 266.2), the conference shall set the minimum salary of the pastor for the ensuing conference year.[7] In a pastoral charge of more than one church the amount apportioned to each church shall be recorded in the minutes of the Quarterly Conference. The pastor's salary thus agreed on shall not include the traveling and moving expenses of a new appointee to the pastoral charge. These expenses, when provided for, shall be classified as current expenses and so reported in the pastor's report to the Annual Conference. (*See also* ¶ 829.)

¶ 149. 1. Annually at the fall meeting of the Quarterly Conference the pastor shall answer the following questions, and the answers thereto shall be transmitted to the executive secretary of the Conference Board of Education, or, if there is no executive secretary, to the president thereof: (*a*) Who are the young people of this pastoral charge who are members of the junior class in high school? (*b*) Who are the young people of this pastoral charge who are members of the second year in junior college? (*c*) Has a list of their names been sent to the admissions officers of the Methodist college or colleges related to the Annual Conference for their information? (*d*) Who are the young people now in colleges, universities, and schools of nursing? What is being done by the local church to extend and maintain its ministry to them? Who of these are recruits for life service in a church vocation, and in what educational institutions are they enrolled? (*e*) What young people from this pastoral charge are now in theological schools, and in what school is each enrolled? (*f*) What young people from this pastoral charge are in the armed services, and what is being done to extend and maintain the church's ministry to them?

2. Annually at the first Quarterly Conference the following questions shall be asked: (*a*) How many persons have been received into the fellowship of the church on this pastoral charge during the past conference year? (*b*) How many persons will this pastoral charge set as a minimum number to be received on profession of faith this conference year, and what means will it adopt to win

---

[7] *See* Judicial Council Decision 213.

them? (c) What program has been adopted for assimilating new members into the life of the church, and training them in Christian living and activity? (d) How many persons signed Commitment Day cards, pledging themselves to abstinence from the use of beverage alcohol? (e) How many supplemental or renewal commitments? (f) What are the plans for pressing the work in the area of alcohol problems this coming year?

3. At each Quarterly Conference the district superintendent shall ask the pastor to answer the following questions: (a) What general Advance specials (¶ 758) and conference Advance specials (¶ 759) have been assumed by the church or churches of this pastoral charge, and in what amount? (b) What amounts have been collected on them during this conference year, and what amounts have been remitted to the conference treasurer? (c) What is the report concerning the observance of the One Great Hour of Sharing (¶ 760)?

4. At each Quarterly Conference the following questions shall be asked: Who are certified as lay speakers? Have their names and addresses been forwarded to the conference lay leader?

¶ 150. In addition to the duties and responsibilities hereinbefore mentioned, the Quarterly Conference shall be charged with the following:

1. Through the Official Board as its administrative agent to supervise and promote the financial interests of the charge, including the support of the ministry, the payment of world service and conference benevolences, and prompt discharge of financial obligations for the building, repair, and general physical maintenance of the church houses and parsonage of the charge.

2. To promote all the spiritual as well as temporal interests of the church—evangelistic, educational, missionary, and benevolent.

3. To receive reports of the work of the pastor, other officers, and all the organizations of the church or churches of the pastoral charge, as the Quarterly Conference may determine.

4. To fix the place of the next session of the Quarterly Conference. (See ¶ 139.)

5. Such duties and responsibilities as the General Conference may from time to time commit to it.

SEC. IV. Authority Regarding Church Property

¶ 151. In a pastoral charge (¶ 105.1) consisting of one local church, the Quarterly Conference as constituted in ¶ 138 shall be vested with authority and power in matters relative to the real and personal property of the local church concerned as set forth in ¶¶ 156-94.

¶ 152. In a pastoral charge (¶ 105.1) consisting of two or more local churches, a **Church Quarterly Conference** shall be organized in each local church therein, and such Church Quarterly Conference shall be vested with authority and power in matters relating to the real and personal property of the local church concerned as set forth in ¶¶ 156-94.

¶ 153. The following shall constitute the membership of the Church Quarterly Conference, insofar as the offices and relationships exist within the local church, these members being the same persons who are members of the pastoral-charge Quarterly Conference from the local church concerned:

1. The pastor and associate pastor or pastors; the retired and supernumerary preachers residing in that place who elect to hold membership therein; traveling preachers who, because they are assigned to special work, have been attached to the Quarterly Conference of the pastoral charge, and who are affiliated with the said local church.

2. The local preachers holding their membership in the local church and deaconesses appointed to labor therein.

3. The stewards of the local church, elective and ex officio, and the trustees of the local church; *provided*, however, that all lay members of the Church Quarterly Conference shall be members of the said local church, except as provided in ¶ 562, and all except the president of the Methodist Youth Fellowship or the president of the Youth Council shall be not less than eighteen years of age.

¶ 154. The district superintendent or an elder designated by him shall preside. The district superintendent

shall fix the time and place of meeting. At his discretion
he may call the respective Church Quarterly Conferences
to meet at the same time and place as the Quarterly Conference of the pastoral charge to which the said local
churches are attached; in which case he shall adjourn the
Quarterly Conference of the pastoral charge, and shall
call to order the respective Church Quarterly Conferences
for the transaction of business specifically committed to
them, each Church Quarterly Conference sitting as a separate and distinct entity. Or the district superintendent
may call a Church Quarterly Conference to meet at such
other time and place as he may designate; *provided* that at
least ten days' notice shall be given of such meeting. The
actions of all Church Quarterly Conferences shall be recorded in spaces included in the "Minutes of the Quarterly Conference" (¶ 141) of the pastoral charge. This
is for the purpose of permanent record only, and the
Quarterly Conference of the said pastoral charge shall
have no voice in the decisions of the Church Quarterly
Conference of any local church attached to it in matters
specifically committed to the said Church Quarterly Conference.

SEC. V.   **The Method of Organizing a Local Church**

¶ 155. 1. A new local church or mission shall be established only with the consent of the bishop in charge and
his Cabinet, and with due consideration of the Conference
Board of Missions long-range and short-range program of
home missions and church extension (¶ 1299.1, .5). The
bishop shall designate the district within whose bounds
the church shall be organized, and the district superintendent of that district shall be the agent in charge of the
project. He shall recommend to the District Board of
Church Location and Building (¶¶ 721-24) the site for
the proposed new congregation. If there is a city or district missionary society (¶¶ 1225-27), that body shall also
be asked to approve the site (*See* ¶ 1234.)

2. The district superintendent shall call the persons
interested in the proposed church to meet at an appointed
time and place, or he may by written authorization designate any pastor in his district to call such a meeting.

3. The district superintendent, or the pastor holding authority from him, shall preside, and shall appoint a secretary to keep a record of the meeting. Following a period of worship opportunity shall be given those in attendance to present themselves for membership by proper certificates of transfer. Pastors issuing such certificates to a church not yet organized shall describe therein the proposed new church to which it is issued—as, for instance, "the proposed new church on Boston Avenue."

4. Opportunity shall also be given persons desiring to become members on profession of their faith in Christ to present themselves for membership. When the presiding minister is satisfied as to the genuineness of their faith and purpose (¶ 107), they shall be received into the membership of the church in accordance with the prescribed form (¶¶ 1713-14).

5. A list shall be made of all the persons received into the membership of the proposed church, by transfer and on profession. Those persons in the membership eighteen years of age and over shall be members of the constituting Church Conference, and each shall be entitled to vote.

6. The constituting Church Conference shall then be called to order, and it shall proceed to choose the elective stewards of the church (¶ 143.1), on nomination of a committee on nominations. Such committee shall be appointed by the presiding minister or elected on nomination from the floor as the conference may determine. In either case the presiding minister shall be chairman. When the elective stewards have been chosen in proper number (¶ 208), the presiding minister shall declare the church properly constituted.

7. He shall then adjourn the Church Conference and call to order the Quarterly Conference of the pastoral charge. The membership of said Quarterly Conference shall be the newly elected stewards and any others entitled to membership under the provisions of the Discipline (¶ 138). The Quarterly Conference shall then elect such officers of the church as the Discipline requires, including trustees of church property (¶¶ 159-60), and shall set up commissions and committees as provided in the Discipline (¶¶ 144-45). When such officers have been

duly elected and the proper commissions and committees constituted, the church is duly organized, and from this point its work shall proceed as described in the Discipline; *provided* that when a newly organized church is attached to a circuit, the pastoral-charge Quarterly Conference shall not be held until such time as representatives from all the churches of the charge can be properly assembled for that purpose.

8. The Quarterly Conference may take action, at its discretion, authorizing and directing the newly elected trustees to incorporate the newly organized church in accordance with local laws and the provisions of the Discipline.

9. For the presentation of a certificate of organization from the Annual Conference *see* ¶ 642.

CHAPTER IV

CHURCH PROPERTY

¶ **156.** All provisions of the Discipline relating to property, both real and personal, and relating to the formation and operation of any corporation, are conditioned upon their being in conformity with the local laws; and in the event of conflict therewith, the local laws shall prevail;[8] *provided*, however, that this requirement shall not be construed to give the consent of The Methodist Church to deprivation of its property without due process of law, or to the regulation of its affairs by state statute where such regulation violates the constitutional guarantee of freedom of religion and separation of church and state or violates the right of the church to maintain connectional structure; and *provided*, further, that the services of worship of every local Methodist church shall be open to all persons without regard to race, color, or national origin.

---

[8] *See* Judicial Council Decision 93.

SECTION I.   Authority of the Quarterly Conference

¶ 157. In a pastoral charge consisting of one local church, the Quarterly Conference, constituted as set forth in ¶ 138, shall be vested with power and authority as hereinafter set forth in connection with the property, both real and personal, of the said local church, namely:

1. If it so elects, to direct the Board of Trustees to incorporate the local church, expressly subject, however, to the Discipline of The Methodist Church (¶¶ 176-78), and in accordance with the pertinent local laws, and in such manner as will fully protect and exempt from any and all legal liability the individual officials and members, jointly and severally, of the local church, and the Quarterly, Annual, Jurisdictional, and General Conferences of The Methodist Church, and each of them, for and on account of the debts and other obligations, of every kind and description, of the local church.

2. To direct the Board of Trustees with respect to the purchase, sale, mortgage, incumbrance, construction, repairing, remodeling, and maintenance of any and all property of the local church. (See ¶ 165.)

3. To direct the Board of Trustees with respect to the acceptance or rejection of any and all conveyances, grants, gifts, donations, legacies, bequests, or devises, absolute or in trust, for the use and benefit of the local church, and to require the administration of any such trust in accordance with the terms and provisions thereof and of the local laws appertaining thereto. (See ¶ 165.)

4. To elect the trustees of the local church, unless otherwise provided (¶ 32), in harmony with the provisions of the Discipline.[9]

5. To do any and all things necessary to exercise such other powers and duties relating to the property, real and personal, of the local church concerned as may be committed to it by the Discipline.[10]

¶ 158. In a pastoral charge consisting of two or more local churches, a Church Quarterly Conference, consti-

---

[9] See Judicial Council Decision 130.
[10] See Judicial Council Decision 103.

tuted and organized under the Discipline of The Methodist Church as set forth in ¶¶ 153-54, in each local church therein, shall be vested with authority and power in matters relating to the real and personal property of the local church concerned. Such Church Quarterly Conference shall elect the Board of Trustees of such local church in number and manner described in ¶¶ 159-61; and the duties of such trustees, duly elected, shall be the same as and identical with the duties described in ¶¶ 162-66. The duties, authority, and power vested in the Church Quarterly Conference, in so far as they relate to the property, real and personal, of the local church concerned, are the same as and identical with the authority and power vested in the Quarterly Conference of a pastoral charge of one local church as set forth in ¶¶ 157 and 167-94; and the authority, power, and limitations therein set forth shall be applicable to the Church Quarterly Conference as fully and to the same extent as if incorporated herein. The effect of the provisions for a Church Quarterly Conference is to give to each local church in a pastoral charge of two or more churches, rather than to the pastoral-charge Quarterly Conference, supervision over and control of its own property, subject to the limitations prescribed in the Discipline with regard to local-church property.

Sec. II.　　　　**The Church Board of Trustees**

¶ 159. In each local church there shall be a **Board of Trustees** consisting of not fewer than three nor more than nine persons, each of whom shall be not less than twenty-one years of age, and at least two thirds of whom shall be members of The Methodist Church.

¶ 160. The members of the Board of Trustees shall be divided into three classes; and each class shall, as nearly as possible, consist of an equal number of members. At the fourth or final meeting of the Quarterly Conference for the Annual Conference year, on nomination by the Committee on Nominations (¶ 145.1), of which the pastor shall be chairman (or if the committee fails to nominate, on nomination of the pastor), or from the floor, it shall elect, to take office at the beginning of the ensuing conference year, to serve for a term of three years or until their successors have been duly elected and qualified, the required number of trustees to succeed those of the class whose terms then expire; *provided*, however, that nothing herein shall be construed to prevent the election of a trustee to succeed himself.[11] Or, if so ordered by the Quarterly Conference, the Board of Trustees shall be elected by a Church Conference as provided in ¶¶ 32, 196-98.

¶ 161. Any vacancy in the Board of Trustees may be filled until the next annual election, as hereinbefore provided, by the Quarterly Conference in any regular or special session on nomination by the Committee on Nominations, or by the pastor; *provided* that the privilege of making nominations from the floor shall not be denied.

¶ 162. 1. Within thirty days after the beginning of the ensuing conference year the Board of Trustees shall convene at a time and place designated by the president, or by the vice-president in the event that the president is not re-elected a trustee, or, because of his absence or disability, is unable to act, for the purpose of electing officers of the said board for the ensuing year and transacting any other business properly brought before it.

2. The Board of Trustees shall elect from the membership thereof, to hold office for a term of one year or until their successors shall be elected, a president, vice-president, secretary, and, if need requires, treasurer; *provided*, however, that the president and vice-president shall not be members of the same class; and *provided*, further, that the offices of secretary and treasurer may be held by the same person. The duties of each officer shall be the same as generally connected with the office held and which are usually and commonly discharged by the holder thereof. The Quarterly Conference may, if it is necessary to conform to the local laws, substitute the designations "chairman" and "vice-chairman" for and in place of "president" and "vice-president."

3. Where necessity requires, as a result of the in-

---

[11] *See* Judicial Council Decisions 102, 130.

corporation of a local church, the corporation directors, in addition to electing officers as provided in this paragraph shall ratify and confirm, by appropriate action, and if necessary elect, as officers of the corporation the treasurer or treasurers, as the case may be, elected by the Quarterly Conference in accordance with the provisions of ¶¶ 143.12 and 268, whose duties and responsibilities shall be as therein set forth. If more than one account is maintained in the name of the corporation in any financial institution or institutions, each such account, and the treasurer thereof, shall be appropriately designated.

¶ 163. The Board of Trustees shall meet at the call of the pastor or of its president,[12] at such times and places as shall be designated in a notice which shall be mailed to each trustee at least five days prior to the appointed time of the meeting. Waiver of notice may be used as a means to validate meetings legally where the five-day notice is impracticable.

¶ 164. The Board of Trustees shall have such authority, powers, duties, and responsibilities as shall be vested in it by the provisions of the Discipline, and it shall be subject to the directions of, and be responsible to, the Quarterly Conference,[13] and make a written report to the fourth or last Quarterly Conference, in which shall be included the following:

1. The legal description and the reasonable valuation of each parcel of real estate owned by the church.

2. The specific name of the grantee in each deed of conveyance of real estate to the local church.

3. An inventory and the reasonable valuation of all personal property owned by the local church.

4. The amount of income received from any income-producing property and a detailed list of expenditures in connection therewith.

5. The amount received during the year for building, rebuilding, remodeling, and improving real estate, and an itemized statement of expenditures.

---

[12] *See* Judicial Council Decision 102.
[13] *See* Judicial Council Decision 103.

6. Outstanding capital debts and how contracted.

7. Detailed statement of the insurance carried on each parcel of real estate, indicating whether restricted by co-insurance or other limiting conditions, and whether adequate insurance is carried.

8. The name of the custodian of all legal papers of the local church, and where they are kept.

9. A detailed list of all trusts in which the local church is the beneficiary, specifying where and how the funds are invested and in what manner the income therefrom is expended or applied.

¶ 165. Subject to the direction of the Quarterly Conference as hereinbefore provided, the Board of Trustees shall receive and administer all bequests made to the local church; shall receive and administer all trusts; shall invest all trust funds of the local church in conformity with law of the country, state, or like political unit in which the local church is located; and shall have the supervision, oversight, and care of all real property owned by the local church and of all property and equipment acquired directly by the local church or by any society, board, class, commission, or similar organization connected therewith; *provided* that the Board of Trustees shall not violate the rights of any local-church organization elsewhere granted in the Discipline; *provided*, further, that the Board of Trustees shall not prevent or interfere with the pastor in the use of any of the said property (¶ 174) for religious services or other proper meetings or purposes recognized by the law, usages, and customs of The Methodist Church, or permit the use of said property for religious or other meetings without the consent of the pastor, or in his absence the consent of the district superintendent; and *provided*, further, that the Quarterly Conference may assign certain of these duties to a Building Committee as set forth in ¶ 180. (*See also* ¶ 278.5, .6.)

¶ 166. 1. "Trustee," "trustees," and "Board of Trustees," as used herein or elsewhere in the Discipline, shall be construed to be synonymous with "director," "directors," and "Board of Directors" applied to corporations.

2. "Local laws" shall be construed to mean the laws

of the country, state, or other like political unit within the geographical bounds of which the church property is located.

3. Trustees or other members of a local church shall not be required to guarantee personally any loan made to the church by any board created by or under the authority of the General Conference.

4. Should a trustee of a local church or a director of an incorporated local church refuse to execute properly a legal instrument relating to any property of the church, when duly directed so to do by the Quarterly Conference (¶¶ 157-58), and when all legal requirements have been satisfied with reference to such execution, the said Quarterly Conference may by majority vote declare his membership on the Board of Trustees or Board of Directors vacated, and elect his successor for the unexpired term.

Sec. III.　　　　　**Acquisition of Property**

¶ 167. If the local laws do not prescribe that title to property, both real and personal, shall be otherwise taken and held, in which event the provisions thereof shall take precedence and shall be observed and the provisions hereof subordinated thereto, the title to all real property now owned or hereafter acquired by an **unincorporated local church,** and any organization, board, commission, society, or similar body connected therewith, shall be held by and/or conveyed and transferred to its duly elected trustees, who shall be named in the written instrument conveying or transferring title, and their successors in office and their assigns, as the Board of Trustees of such local church (naming it and the individual trustees), in trust, nevertheless, for the use and benefit of such local church and of The Methodist Church. Every instrument of conveyance of real estate shall contain the appropriate trust clause, as hereinafter set forth in ¶ 174.

¶ 168. Prior to the purchase by an unincorporated local church of any real estate a resolution authorizing such action shall be passed at a meeting of the Quarterly Conference, by a majority vote of its members present and voting, at a regular meeting or a special meeting of the Quarterly Conference called for that purpose;

provided, however, that not less than ten days' notice of such meeting and the proposed action shall have been given from the pulpit or in the weekly bulletin of the church; and *provided*, further, that written consent to such action shall be given by the pastor and the district superintendent. (*See* ¶ 180.)

¶ 169. If the local laws do not prescribe that title to real property of an **incorporated local church** shall be otherwise taken and held, in which event the provisions thereof shall take precedence and shall be observed, and the provisions hereof subordinated thereto, the title to all property, both real and personal, now owned or hereafter acquired by an incorporated local church, and any organization, board, commission, society, or similar body connected therewith, shall be held by and/or conveyed to the corporate body in its corporate name, in trust, nevertheless, for the use and benefit of such local church and of The Methodist Church. Every instrument of conveyance of real estate shall contain the appropriate trust clause, as hereinafter set forth in ¶ 174.

¶ 170. Prior to the purchase by a local-church corporation of any real estate, a resolution authorizing such action shall be passed by the Quarterly Conference in corporate session, or such other corporate body as the local laws may require, with the members thereof acting in their capacity as members of the corporate body, by a majority vote of those present and voting, at any regular or special meeting called for that purpose; *provided* that not less than ten days' notice of such meeting and the proposed action shall have been given from the pulpit or in the weekly bulletin of the local church; and *provided*, further, that written consent to such action shall be given by the pastor and the district superintendent; and *provided*, further, that all such transactions shall have the approval of the Quarterly Conference. (*See* ¶ 180.)

SEC. IV.   **Sale, Transfer, and Mortgage of Property**

¶ 171. Any real property owned by, or in which an **unincorporated local church** has any interest, may be sold, transferred, or mortgaged subject to the following procedure and conditions:

1. Notice of the proposed action and the date and time of the regular or special meeting of the Quarterly Conference at which it is to be considered shall be given at least ten days prior thereto (except as local laws may otherwise provide) from the pulpit of the church or in its weekly bulletin.

2. A resolution authorizing the proposed action shall be passed by a <u>majority vote</u> of the Quarterly Conference members present and voting and by a <u>majority vote</u> of the members of said church present and voting at a special meeting called to consider such action.

3. The written consent of the pastor of the local church and the district superintendent to the proposed action shall be necessary and shall be affixed to the instrument of sale, transfer, or mortgage.

4. The resolution authorizing such proposed action shall direct that any contract, deed, bill of sale, mortgage, or other necessary written instrument be executed by and on behalf of the local church by any two of the officers of its Board of Trustees, who thereupon shall be duly authorized to carry out the direction of the Quarterly Conference; and any written instrument so executed shall be binding and effective as the action of the local church. (*See* ¶ 173.)

¶ **172.** Any real property owned by, or in which an **incorporated local church** has any interest, may be sold, transferred, or mortgaged subject to the following procedure and conditions:

1. Notice of the proposed action and the date and time of the regular or special meeting of the members of the corporate body, i.e., members of the Quarterly Conference, at which it is to be considered, shall be given at least ten days prior thereto (except as local laws may otherwise provide) from the pulpit of the church or in its weekly bulletin.

2. <u>A resolution authorizing the proposed action shall be passed by a majority vote of the members of the corporate body present and voting at any regular or special meeting thereof called to consider such action,</u>

86

and by a majority vote of the members of said church present and voting at a special meeting called to consider such action; *provided* that for the sale of property which was conveyed to the church to be sold and its proceeds used for a specific purpose a vote of the members of said church shall not be required.

3. The written consent of the pastor of the local church and the district superintendent to the proposed action shall be necessary and shall be affixed to the instrument of sale, conveyance, transfer, or mortgage.

4. The resolution authorizing such proposed action shall direct and authorize the corporation's Board of Directors to take all necessary steps to carry out the action so authorized, and to cause to be executed, as hereinafter provided, any necessary contract, deed, bill of sale, mortgage, or other written instrument.

5. The Board of Directors at any regular or special meeting shall take such action and adopt such resolutions as may be necessary or required by the local laws.

6. Any required contract, deed, bill of sale, mortgage, or other written instrument necessary to carry out the action so authorized shall be executed in the name of the corporation by any two of its officers, and any written instrument so executed shall be binding and effective as the action of the corporation. (*See* ¶ 173.)

¶ 173. 1. No real property on which a church building or parsonage is located shall be mortgaged to provide for the current (or budget) expense of a local church, nor shall the principal proceeds of a sale of any such property be so used. This provision shall apply alike to unincorporated and incorporated local churches.

2. A local church, whether or not incorporated, on complying with the provisions of ¶ 171 or ¶ 172, may mortgage its unencumbered real property as security for a loan to be made to a Conference Board of Missions, or a city or district missionary society; *provided* that the proceeds of such loan shall be used only for aiding in the construction of a new church.

SEC. V.   **Trust Clauses and Release Therefrom**

¶ 174. 1. Except in conveyances from governmental

agencies or subdivisions [14] which require that the real property so conveyed shall revert to the grantor if and when its use as a place of divine worship has been terminated, all written instruments of conveyance by which premises are held or hereafter acquired, for use as a place of divine worship for members of The Methodist Church or for other church activities, shall contain the following trust clause:

In trust, that said premises shall be used, kept, and maintained as a place of divine worship of the Methodist ministry and members of The Methodist Church; subject to the Discipline, usage, and ministerial appointments of said church as from time to time authorized and declared by the General Conference and by the Annual Conference within whose bounds the said premises are situated. This provision is solely for the benefit of the grantee, and the grantor reserves no right or interest in said premises. [15]

2. All written instruments by which premises are held or hereafter acquired as a parsonage for the use and occupancy of the ministers of The Methodist Church shall contain the following trust clause:

In trust, that such premises shall be held, kept, and maintained as a place of residence for the use and occupancy of the ministers of The Methodist Church who may from time to time be entitled to occupy the same by appointment; subject to the Discipline and usage of said church, as from time to time authorized and declared by the General Conference and by the Annual Conference within whose bounds the said premises are situated. This provision is solely for the benefit of the grantee, and the grantor reserves no right or interest in said premises.

3. However, the absence of the trust clause stipulated in § 1 or § 2 of this paragraph in deeds and conveyances previously executed shall in no way exclude a local church from or relieve it of its Methodist connectional

---

[14] *See* Judicial Council Decision 107.
[15] *See* Judicial Council Decision 135.

responsibilities. Nor shall it absolve a local congregation or Board of Trustees of its responsibility to The Methodist Church provided that the intent and desire of the founders and/or the later congregations and Boards of Trustees is shown by any or all of the following indications: (*a*) the conveyance of the property to the trustees of the local Methodist church or any of its predecessors; (*b*) the use of the name, customs, and polity of The Methodist Church in such a way as to be thus known to the community as a part of this denomination; (*c*) the acceptance of the pastorate of ministers appointed by a bishop of The Methodist Church or employed by the superintendent of the district in which it is located.

¶ 175. Real property acquired by a conveyance containing either or both of the foregoing trust clauses (¶ 174) may be sold in conformity with the provisions of the Discipline of The Methodist Church (¶¶ 171-73) when its use as a church building or parsonage, as the case may be, has been or is intended to be terminated; and when such real estate is sold or mortgaged in accordance with the provisions of the Discipline of The Methodist Church, the written acknowledged consent of the proper district superintendent representing The Methodist Church to the action taken shall constitute a release and discharge of the real property so sold and conveyed from either or both of the foregoing trust clauses; or, in the event of the execution of a mortgage, such consent of the district superintendent shall constitute a formal recognition of the priority of such mortgage lien and the subordination of the foregoing trust provisions thereof; and no bona fide purchaser or mortgagee relying upon the foregoing record shall be charged with any responsibility with respect to the disposition by such local church of the proceeds of any such sale or mortgage; but the Board of Trustees receiving such proceeds shall manage, control, disburse, and expend the same in conformity to the order and direction of the Quarterly Conference, subject to the provisions of the Discipline of The Methodist Church with respect thereto.

SEC. VI.　　**Incorporation of Local Churches**

¶ **176.** When so authorized and directed by its Quarterly Conference, the Board of Trustees of a local church shall immediately take and perform any and all necessary steps and actions to incorporate the local church under and in conformity with the laws of the country, state, or like political unit in which it is located. The necessary articles to be filed with the proper governmental officials to secure a charter, and any and all amendments thereto that at any time may be contemplated shall be submitted to the district superintendent having jurisdiction for his written approval as to the conformity of the same with the provisions of the Discipline of The Methodist Church, and shall contain the following provisions:

1. The corporation shall support the doctrine, and it, and all its property, both real and personal, shall be subject to the laws, usages, and ministerial appointments of The Methodist Church as are now or shall be from time to time established, made, and declared by the lawful authority of the said church.

2. The Board of Directors of the corporation shall be the Board of Trustees of the local church elected and organized as prescribed in the Discipline of The Methodist Church.

3. The corporation shall have the power to acquire and hold title in fee simple, in trust, or otherwise, to both real and personal property and to improve, incumber, sell, convey and dispose of all such property in conformity with the Discipline of The Methodist Church.

4. Subject to the provisions of the Discipline, the corporation shall have the power to erect and maintain buildings for the worship of God, for training in Christian faith and conduct, and for Christian social intercourse, and to acquire or build and maintain residences for the use and occupancy of its ministers.

5. The by-laws of the corporation shall include the Discipline of The Methodist Church as from time to time enacted, authorized, and declared by its General Conference; and no other by-law shall be adopted inconsistent with the provisions of the Discipline.

6. The members of the corporation shall be the members of the Quarterly Conference, or such other body of the local church as the local laws may permit or require.

7. If, for any reason, the corporation shall cease to exist as a legal entity and its charter shall expire or be terminated, the title to all its property, both real and personal, shall be vested in the trustees of the Annual Conference, if the Annual Conference itself is unincorporated, in the same manner as it holds title to any other real estate, or in the Annual Conference in its corporate name if it is incorporated; and all such property shall be held in trust for the benefit of the local church.

8. Such provisions as may be required by the local laws.

¶ **177.** The provisions of ¶¶ 159-66 hereof, entitled "The Church Board of Trustees," shall be applicable to all corporations formed hereunder as fully and to the same extent as if set forth and incorporated herein; *provided*, however, that "trustee," "trustees," and "Board of Trustees" shall be construed to be synonymous with "director," "directors," and "Board of Directors," as applied to corporations.

¶ **178.** In the event that the title to any property, real or personal, of a local church shall vest in the trustees of the Annual Conference or in its corporate body as a result of the corporation ceasing to exist, then, and in that event the Board of Trustees of the Annual Conference, if the Annual Conference itself is unincorporated, or the Board of Directors of its corporate body, shall be and is hereby authorized and directed, at the request of the Quarterly Conference of the local church and without any action by the Annual Conference, to reconvey the title to the local-church property in such manner as shall be requested by the Quarterly Conference with the approval of the district superintendent.

SEC. VII.   **Building, Purchasing, Remodeling**

¶ **180.** Any local church planning to build or purchase a new church or educational building or a parsonage, or to remodel such a building if the cost will exceed ten per cent of its value, shall take the following steps:

1. It shall secure the written consent of the pastor and the district superintendent.

2. It shall secure approval of the proposed site by the District Board of Church Location and Building, as provided in ¶ 722.

3. Its Quarterly Conference (¶¶ 157-58) shall authorize the project at a regular or called meeting, not less than ten days' notice (except as local laws may otherwise provide) of such meeting and the proposed action having been given from the pulpit or in the weekly bulletin, and shall appoint a **Building Committee** of not fewer than three members of the local church to serve in the development of the project as hereinafter set forth; *provided* that the Quarterly Conference may commit to its Board of Trustees the duties of a Building Committee as here described.

4. The Building Committee shall:

a) Estimate carefully the building facilities needed to house the church's program of worship, education, and fellowship and/or to provide a residence for present and future pastors and their families.

b) Ascertain the cost of property to be purchased.

c) Develop preliminary architectural plans, complying with local building and fire codes (*see also* ¶ 182) which shall clearly outline the location on the site of all proposed present and future construction. (For provisions for architectural advisory service *see* ¶¶ 1246.2, 1248, 1401.1.)

d) Secure an estimate of the cost of the proposed construction.

e) Develop a financial plan for defraying the total cost, including an estimate of the amount the membership can contribute in cash and pledges and the amount the local church can borrow if necessary.

5. The Building Committee shall submit to the District Board of Church Location and Building, for its consideration and approval, a statement of the need for the proposed facilities, and the architectural plans and financial estimates and plans specified in § 4 above, as provided in ¶ 723.1.

6. The pastor, with the written consent of the district

superintendent, shall call a Church Conference (¶ 196), giving not less than ten days' notice (except as local laws may otherwise provide) of the meeting and the proposed action from the pulpit or in the weekly bulletin. At this conference the Building Committee shall submit, for approval by the membership, its recommendations for the proposed building project, including the data specified in §§ 4-5 above.

7. After approval of the preliminary plans and estimates as provided in §§ 4-6 above the Building Committee shall develop detailed plans and specifications and secure a reliable and detailed estimate of cost, and shall present these for approval to the Quarterly Conference and to the District Board of Church Location and Building, which shall study the data and report its conclusions as provided in ¶ 723.2.

8. The local church shall acquire a fee simple title to the lot or lots on which the building is to be erected, by deed of conveyance, executed as provided in this chapter (¶¶ 167-70 174), and shall pay the purchase price thereof in full before beginning construction.

9. If a loan is needed, the local church shall comply with the provisions of ¶¶ 171-72.

10. The local church shall not enter into a building contract or, if using a plan for volunteer labor, incur obligations for materials until it has cash on hand, pledges payable during the construction period, and (if needed) a loan or written commitment therefor which will assure prompt payment of all contractual obligations and other accounts when due. (*See also* ¶ 271.)

¶ 181. On acquisition or completion of any church building, parsonage, or other church unit a service of consecration may be held. Before any church building, parsonage, or other church unit is formally dedicated, all indebtedness against the same shall be discharged.

¶ 182. In all new church building plans, and in all major remodeling plans, adequate provisions should be made to facilitate entrance, seating, exit, and the use of facilities for persons with physical disabilities.

Sec. VIII. **Circuit and Joint Boards of Trustees**

¶ **183.** In the event that a circuit (¶ 105.2) shall own or acquire a parsonage for the use of the pastor appointed to serve the local churches comprising such circuit or shall own or acquire any other real estate for any common use of its churches, the Quarterly Conference of the pastoral charge may elect a **Circuit Board of Trustees,** to be composed of not fewer than three nor more than nine members, all of whom shall be not less than twenty-one years of age; *provided*, however, that each local church in the circuit shall have at least one representative on the board. The members of the Circuit Board of Trustees shall be divided into three classes, and each class shall, as nearly as possible, consist of an equal number of members. Nominations shall be made by the Quarterly Conference Committee on Nominations (or, if the committee fails to nominate, by the pastor). At the first election under the provisions hereof, one class shall be elected for a term of one year, one class for a term of two years, and one class for a term of three years; and thereafter, at the fourth or final meeting of the circuit Quarterly Conference for the Annual Conference year, it shall elect, to take office at the beginning of the ensuing conference year to serve for a term of three years or until their successors have been elected and qualified, the required number of trustees to succeed those of the class whose terms then expire; *provided*, however, that nothing herein shall be construed to prevent the election of a trustee to succeed himself. The provisions of ¶¶ 157 and 161-64 shall be applicable to the Circuit Board of Trustees to the same extent as if incorporated herein.

¶ **184.** When two or more local churches compose a single pastoral charge having a parsonage, and one or more thereof is separated from such charge and established as a pastoral charge, or united with another pastoral charge which does not own a parsonage, each such local church shall be entitled to receive its just share of the then reasonable value of the parsonage in which it has invested funds; and the amount of such value and just share shall be determined by a committee of three persons, appointed by the district superintendent, who shall be members of The Methodist Church but not of any of the interested local churches. Such committee shall hear all interested parties, and shall take into account the investment of any church in any such property before arriving at a final determination. From any such determination there is reserved to each of the interested churches the right of appeal to the next succeeding Annual Conference, the decision of which shall be final and binding. Any sum received as or from such share shall not be applied to current expense or current budget.

SEC. IX.   **Sundry Provisions**

¶ 185. In static and declining population areas churches of fifty members or less shall study, under the leadership of the district superintendent, the District Advisory Committee, if any, and the Conference Commission on Town and Country Work, their potential in the area to determine whether or not they shall continue to develop programs as organized churches or give special attention to relocation or merger with other congregations.

¶ 186. Two or more local churches may merge and become a single church by pursuing the following procedure:

1. The merger must be proposed by the Quarterly Conference of each of the merging churches by a resolution stating the terms and conditions of the proposed merger.

2. The plan of the merger as proposed by the Quarterly Conference of each of the merging churches must be approved by a majority vote of a Church Conference in accordance with the requirements of ¶ 196.

3. The merger must be approved by the superintendent or superintendents of the district or districts in which the merging churches are located.

4. The requirements of any and all laws of the state or states in which the merging churches are located affecting or relating to the merger of such churches must be complied with; and, in any case where there is a conflict between such laws and the procedure outlined in the Discipline, said laws shall prevail and the procedure outlined in the Discipline shall be modified to the extent necessary to eliminate such conflict.

¶ **187.** When two or more local churches are united, merged, or consolidated, the Quarterly Conferences of the constituent churches shall respectively take action to consummate legally the same, and direct the respective Boards of Trustees with respect to the transfer or disposition of the property, real and personal, as the local laws and the Discipline may require.

¶ **188.** 1. With the consent of the presiding bishop and of a majority of the district superintendents and of the District Board of Church Location and Building (¶¶ 721-24) of the district in which the action is contemplated, the Annual Conference may declare any local church within its bounds discontinued or abandoned. It shall be the duty of its Board of Trustees (¶ 190) to make such disposition of the property thereof as the Annual Conference shall direct; and if no such lawful trustees remain, or if for any reason said trustees fail to make such disposition, then it shall be the duty of the trustees of the Annual Conference to sell or dispose of said property in accordance with the direction of the Annual Conference; and it shall be the duty of the trustees thus effecting sale to remove, in so far as reasonably possible, all Christian and church insignia and symbols from such property. In the event of loss, damage to, or destruction of such local church property, the trustees of the Annual Conference are authorized to collect and receipt for any insurance payable on account thereof, as the duly and legally authorized representative of such local church.[16]

2. All the deeds, records, and other official and legal papers of a Methodist church that is declared to be abandoned or otherwise discontinued shall be collected by the district superintendent in whose district said church was located and shall be deposited for permanent safekeeping with the secretary of the Annual Conference. The conference may subsequently authorize that such records be deposited for safekeeping with its Historical Society.

---

[16] *See* Judicial Council Decision 138.

3. Any gift, legacy, devise, annuity, or other benefit to a pastoral charge or local church that accrues or becomes available after said charge or church has been discontinued or abandoned shall become the property of the trustees of the Annual Conference within whose jurisdiction the said discontinued or abandoned church was located.

4. When a church property has been abandoned by its membership and no abandonment action has been taken by the Annual Conference, and circumstances make immediate action necessary, the Annual Conference trustees may take control of the property, with the consent of the presiding bishop and the District Board of Church Location and Building of the district in which the property is located. And in the event of the sale or lease of said property the trustees of the Annual Conference shall recommend to the Annual Conference at its next session the disposition of the proceeds derived from such sale or lease.[17]

¶ 189. 1. With the consent of the presiding bishop and of a majority of the district superintendents and of the District Board of Church Location and Building, and at the request of the Quarterly Conference, or of a meeting of the membership of the church, where required by local law, and in accordance with the said law, the Annual Conference may instruct and direct the Board of Trustees of a local church to deed church property to a federated church.

2. With the consent of the presiding bishop and of a majority of the district superintendents and of the District Board of Church Location and Building, and at the request of the Quarterly Conference, or of a meeting of the membership of the church, where required by local law, and in accordance with said law, the Annual Conference may instruct and direct the Board of Trustees of a local church to deed church property to another evangelical de-

[17] *See* Judicial Council Decision 143.

97

nomination under an allocation, exchange of property, or comity agreement; *provided* that such agreement shall have been committed to writing and signed and approved by the duly qualified and authorized representatives of both parties concerned.

¶ **190.** The Quarterly Conference and the trustees or Board of Trustees of a local church shall fully comply with the instructions of the Annual Conference issued under the provisions of ¶¶ 188-89; and in the event of failure or refusal so to do, the trustees of the Annual Conference shall be vested with full power and authority to convey such property, and to carry out the instructions of the Annual Conference with regard to the disposal of the proceeds thereof.

¶ **194.** The provisions herein written concerning the organization and administration of the local church, including the procedure for acquiring, holding, and transferring real property, shall not be mandatory in Central Conferences, Provisional Central Conferences, Provisional Annual Conferences, or Missions; and in such instances the legislation in ¶¶ 541-616 shall apply.

CHAPTER V

THE CHURCH CONFERENCE

¶ **196.** There may be a **Church Conference** of any local church, composed of the members of such church who are eighteen years of age or over; *provided*, however, that the president of the Methodist Youth Fellowship or the president of the Youth Council shall be a member without age restriction except where local laws require otherwise. It may be called by the pastor or the Quarterly Conference or the district superintendent; *provided* that not less than ten days' notice (except as local laws may otherwise provide) of such meeting and its main purpose shall be given to the members of the church in writing or from the pulpit or in the weekly bulletin. The pastor, district superintendent, or church lay leader may be its chairman. The conference shall elect a secretary, whose minutes shall be reviewed by the Committee on Records and made a part of the Quarterly Conference records. The conference may review the work of the church and adopt plans for the promotion of various phases of the church's work, subject to the limitations of the Discipline. (For special matters requiring action by a Church Conference *see* ¶¶ 47 ix, 155.5-.7, 171.2, 172.2, 180.6, 189, 532, 680.)

¶ **197.** The Quarterly Conference may authorize and constitute in any pastoral charge an **Annual Church Conference** in conjunction with the fourth Quarterly Conference. It shall be composed of the members of the church or churches of the charge who are eighteen years of age or older; *provided*, however, that the president of the Methodist Youth Fellowship or the president of the Youth Council of each church shall be a member without age restriction except where local laws require otherwise. The district superintendent shall preside, or in his absence the pastor with the written consent of the district superintendent shall preside. The recording steward shall be the secretary of the meeting, or in his absence a secretary pro tem may be elected. The minutes shall be recorded in the records of the Quarterly Conference.

¶ **198.** An Annual Church Conference thus authorized by the Quarterly Conference may review the work of the year, and receive the reports of the officers, committees, and organizations of the charge as arranged in the order of business of the fourth Quarterly Conference. The Annual Church Conference may also, when such authority has been specifically granted it by the Quarterly Conference of the pastoral charge, elect such officers of the charge as would otherwise be elected by the Quarterly Conference (¶¶ 32, 143-45, 160).

¶ **199.** The Quarterly Conference of a circuit, with the consent of the district superintendent, may authorize and constitute such an Annual Church Conference in any church of the circuit, subject to such additional qualifications as the district superintendent may specify.

¶ **200.** If matters presented in the Annual Church Conference are restricted to the action of the Quarterly Conference, only members of the Quarterly Conference may vote thereon.

Chapter VI

THE OFFICIAL BOARD

Section I: **General Provisions**

¶ **206.** In every church of every pastoral charge there shall be an administrative body called the **Official Board,** hereinafter designated as the board; and it shall be the duty of the pastor and district superintendent to see that such organization is set up in every church as hereinafter set forth. The board shall be responsible to the Quarterly Conference, and shall report regularly to the sessions of the conference as its work and the occasion may require, and as the conference may request.[18]

¶ **207.** The board shall be constituted of the following persons:

1. The pastor of the local church and duly appointed associate pastor or pastors, if any, and deaconesses, if any.

2. The stewards of the local church, duly elected (¶ 208).

3. The ex officio stewards of the local church (¶ 209).

4. The trustees of the local church (¶ 159), except such as may not be members of The Methodist Church.

All lay members of the board shall be members of the local Methodist church, except as provided in ¶ 562; and in nominating and electing persons to such membership the utmost care shall be taken that only morally disciplined persons shall be so nominated, with special reference to total abstinence from alcoholic beverages.[19]

¶ **208.** Stewards shall be persons of genuine Christian character who love the church and are competent to ad-

---

[18] *See* Judicial Council Decision 103.
[19] *See* Judicial Council Decision 147.

minister its affairs. The **elective stewards** shall be not less than eighteen years of age and shall be elected annually as set forth in ¶ 143. Stewards-elect shall take office at the beginning of the conference year following their election; *provided* that in cases where a steward is elected to fill a vacancy in the board he shall take office immediately after election. Vacancies may be filled by the Quarterly Conference, in regular or special session; under no circumstances shall stewards be elected by the Official Board. Each local church shall be entitled to not fewer than three or more than thirty-five stewards, exclusive of ex officio and honorary stewards; *provided* that in churches of more than five hundred members one steward may be elected for each thirty additional members.

¶ **209.** The following officers, if members or associate members (¶ 562) of the local church, shall be **ex officio stewards** during their respective terms of office, and shall exercise all the rights and privileges which belong to a steward in The Methodist Church: the church lay leader, the church business manager, the director of Christian education or the educational assistant, the church-school superintendent, the chairmen of all commissions, the secretary of stewardship, the lay member and the first reserve lay member of the Annual Conference, the president of the Woman's Society of Christian Service, the president of Methodist Men, the church treasurer or treasurers, the financial secretary, the membership secretary, the president of the Young Adult Fellowship, and the president of the Methodist Youth Fellowship, or the president of the Youth Council if more than one fellowship is organized.

¶ **210.** With the approval of the Quarterly Conference, any church or charge may provide for rotation in the office of elective stewards. In the event such rotation in office is proposed, a resolution shall be presented to the Quarterly Conference, for its action and determination, setting forth in detail the plan and the method proposed.

¶ **211.** In each church the Quarterly Conference may make provision for the recognition of the faithful service of those stewards on the board who have reached the age of seventy-two, or who may have become physically incapacitated, by electing them honorary stewards. An honorary steward shall be entitled to all the privileges of a steward, except the right to vote.

¶ 212. 1. The board shall be organized annually by the election of a chairman (preferably a lay member), a vice-chairman, and a recording secretary. These officers shall be elected by the members of the board on the nomination of a Committee on Nominations. (See ¶ 278.1.) Additional nominations may be made from the floor.

2. If a church business manager is desired, the board shall counsel with the pastor on his nomination to the Quarterly Conference. (See ¶¶ 143.11, 269.)

¶ 213. To the board is committed the administration of the affairs of the local church, both spiritual and temporal, as hereinafter set forth, subject to the authority of the Quarterly Conference as set forth in ¶ 206. The board shall meet monthly at a time determined by the board. Special meetings may be ordered by the board, or called by the chairman or by the pastor or by a majority of the membership of the board.

¶ 214. The board shall not deny or take from any organization in the local church a right or power granted it by the Discipline.

¶ 215. It shall be the duty of the board:

1. As the administrative agency of the Quarterly Conference, to promote and to have general administrative oversight of the work of the local church, both spiritual and temporal, under the direction of the pastor, including the receiving of reports from all the organizations of the church.

2. After consultation with the Committee on Pastoral Relations (¶ 145.2), or with the pastor if there is no such committee, and after careful consideration of all matters pertaining to his efficiency, to recommend to the Quarterly Conference, at the session next preceding the Annual Conference, the salary and expense allowances of the pastor, and of the associate pastor or pastors, if any (¶ 148); and to make ample provision for the other financial needs of the church (¶ 261).

3. To promote through an educational program interest

in all the benevolent causes authorized by the General, Jurisdictional, Annual, and District Conferences, and to see that the fourth Sunday of each month is observed as **World Service Sunday**, for the purpose of supporting world service and conference benevolences, co-ordinating the same with the observance in the church school.

4. In co-operation with the pastor and the church lay leader, to promote the program of lay activities (¶¶ 286-93), in harmony with the plan and program of the General Board of Lay Activities.

5. To arrange for a program of visitation of the entire constituency of the church, particularly strangers in the community and members of the congregation who may be ill or in distress. (*See* ¶ 222.2, .4c.)

6. Under the direction of the pastor, in co-operation with the commissions to plan and as needed to approve the program and work of the local church; to promote the spiritual and temporal interests of the local church; to discharge faithfully any and all duties and responsibilities committed to it by the Quarterly Conference or by the law of the church; to take such action as it may determine to be for the well-being and progress of the local church; *provided* that all such actions shall be in harmony with the provisions of the Discipline.

7. To develop in the members of the congregation a feeling of responsibility in the establishment of new churches and church schools; and, when specifically authorized by the district superintendent and the District Board of Church Location and Building, to organize and sponsor new churches and/or church schools needed in the community, with the co-operation of the local church commissions. (*See* ¶¶ 155, 222.4f, 233.6, 251, 257.8.)

¶ **216.** Before the close of the conference year the board shall devote at least one full meeting to the development of the total program of the local church for the succeeding year, based on the program elements provided by the commissions and other groups within the church. It shall be the responsibility of the pastor and the chairman to arrange for this meeting and to insure that the commissions and other groups make advance preparation for it. This planning shall be reviewed early

in the new year and revised as needed, giving consideration to the goals and objectives adopted by the Annual
Conference session insofar as they relate to the local
church.

Sec. II.   **Commissions**

¶ **219. 1.** No local church, however small, is adequately
and effectively organized unless there is set up a minimum
structure for participating in five of the major concerns
of the Church Universal—evangelism, education, missions,
stewardship, and Christian social concerns. To the Official
Board, in co-operation with the pastor, is especially committed the promotion and administration of these phases
of the church's life and ministry. It shall be the duty of
the board to give continuous leadership and oversight
therein, through five commissions, duly constituted, whose
respective duties are hereinafter defined (¶¶ 220-75): (1)
the Commission on Membership and Evangelism; (2) the
Commission on Education; (3) the Commission on Missions; (4) the Commission on Stewardship and Finance;
(5) the Commission on Christian Social Concerns; *provided* that, when desired, a Commission on Worship
(¶¶ 276-77) may also be constituted for the promotion and
supervision of this concern of the church. Each commission shall be elected by the Quarterly Conference (¶ 144),
or by the board if the Quarterly Conference fails to do so,
and shall be auxiliary to the board. The pastor and the
church lay leader or an associate church lay leader
(¶¶ 143.2, 288) shall be ex officio members of each commission.

2. To develop a unified church program, each commission (except as provided for a small church in § 4 below)
shall include a representative elected by each other commission not otherwise represented among its membership.

3. Interim vacancies in the commissions shall be filled
in the same manner as those vacating office were chosen,
except that vacancies in offices originally elected by the
Quarterly Conference or Annual Church Conference may
be filled by the Official Board.

4. In a small church, if the Quarterly Conference finds

it necessary, each commission may be composed of the elected chairman (¶ 143.6) and the available ex officio members.

5. The several local-church commissions of a circuit or parish may be organized into circuit or parish commissions.

6. The Official Board may also organize such committees (¶ 278) as are needed to effect a broad coverage of the manifold interests of the church.

Sec. III.   The Commission on Membership and Evangelism

¶ 220. In each local church there shall be a **Commission on Membership and Evangelism** (¶¶ 144, 219), which shall be auxiliary to the General, Jurisdictional, and Annual Conference Boards of Evangelism, and the District Committee on Evangelism. It shall be the duty of this commission to seek out the unsaved and the unchurched in the community, and to exercise all diligence that they may be led into a saving knowledge of Jesus Christ and into the fellowship of the church. It shall also be the duty of the commission to seek out the inactive and negligent members of the local church, and to use all laudable means to restore them to active participation in the church's life and fellowship.

¶ 221. 1. The Commission on Membership and Evangelism shall be composed of the chairman, pastor, minister or director of evangelism if any, church lay leader or associate church lay leader, membership secretary, secretary of spiritual life of the Woman's Society of Christian Service, membership cultivation superintendent of the church school, a representative of Methodist Men, chairman of Christian witness of the Methodist Youth Fellowship, such members of the District Committee on Evangelism (¶¶ 1481-83) as have membership in the local church, not fewer than six and as many more members at large elected in accordance with ¶ 144 as the Quarterly Conference shall determine, and the representatives of other commissions specified in ¶ 219.2; *provided* that in a small church these provisions may be modified as stated in ¶ 219.4; and *provided*, further, that all members of the commission shall be members of The Methodist Church, except as provided in ¶ 562.

2. At the beginning of each conference year the chairman shall call together the members for organization. The commission shall elect a vice-chairman, secretary, and such other officers and committees as it may determine.

3. The commission shall outline its program and estimate its anticipated financial needs, including evangelistic and devotional literature and materials essential to carrying on its total responsibilities as outlined in ¶ 222, and present, through its chairman and the representative from the Commission on Stewardship and Finance, a request for the necessary funds prior to the preparation of the annual budget (¶ 266).

4. The commission shall meet monthly in order to review and plan its work and receive reports. The chairman shall make a monthly report to the Official Board covering progress of the commission's work for the preceding month and plans for the future.

5. The pastor of a circuit may organize the several local-church commissions into a single commission, as provided in ¶ 219.5, in which case its work shall be projected on a charge-wide basis.

¶ 222. The Commission on Membership and Evangelism, in co-operation with the pastor, shall promote the total program of evangelism within the church and its community. In doing this, it shall engage in creative study and planning for a comprehensive program that will meet the needs of the church and community. It shall consider that its duty and aim is to bring all men without regard to race or color into living, active fellowship with God through Jesus Christ as divine Savior and through the regenerating power of the Holy Spirit; to gather them into the fellowship of the Church; to lead them to express their Christian discipleship in every area of human life that the kingdom of God may be realized (¶ 1464).

Committed to the commission are the following specific duties:

1. To take a religious census of the community periodically, if possible with the co-operation of the other churches in the community; to seek the co-operation of

the church school, the Woman's Society of Christian Service, and other church organizations in making a responsibility list of persons from these and other sources who should be won to Christ and his Church; and by every means possible to cultivate these prospective members and get them related to and participating in the local church and its organizations.

2. To arrange for the visitation of strangers and constituents in the community.

a) To promote organized visitation evangelism during one or more periods each year, to confront these persons with Christ and challenge them to commitment, and to transfer the unrelated Methodists in the local community whose memberships are elsewhere.

b) To encourage such groups as The Twelve, the Fisherman's Club, Fellowship of Evangelism, or kindred organizations, and to co-operate with them in their work.

c) To recommend to the Quarterly Conference a minimum goal of persons to be received during the year on profession of faith, and to work diligently toward the attainment of the same.

3. To promote attendance upon the public worship of God (¶ 97) and, through friendly visitation, distribution of literature, and other means, to lead indifferent members to active participation in the life and work of the church.

a) To promote the use of the recommended special days, weeks, and seasons for evangelistic purposes.

b) To use all laudable means to create an evangelistic spirit within the membership and, under the leadership of the pastor, to assist in planning and promoting special evangelistic preaching services at least annually.

c) To distribute evangelistic and devotional literature, and use all means for acquainting the community with the church and its program.

4. *a*) In close co-operation with the pastor and in line with the general program of The Methodist Church, to create and promote a local program and lead the local church in the **Period of Spiritual Enrichment,** beginning the Sunday preceding Ash Wednesday, for the deepening of the spiritual life of all church members and for pre-

paring and sending forth dedicated disciples to be witnesses to Christ and his Church. In this period, Ash Wednesday, the World Day of Prayer, and other high points of the pre-Easter season shall be used to the best advantage.

b) To create a special committee whose duty shall be to do all in its power to re-enlist in the active fellowship of the church all members who are negligent in attending worship or in participating in the church's life and work.

c) To arrange for the visitation of those members of the congregation who may be ill or in distress.

d) To assist the pastor, when requested, in training classes for church membership.

e) To develop an adequate program for assimilating new members into the life and work of the church and its organizations.

f) To co-operate with the Commission on Education and the Commission on Missions in organizing new church schools and new churches. (*See* ¶¶ 155, 215.7, 233.6, 251, 257.8.)

5. *a*) To initiate and develop prayer groups, missions, retreats, vigils, and prayer fellowships.

b) To encourage private and family worship, and to promote the reading of the Holy Scriptures and the use of *The Upper Room* and other devotional literature.

6. With the membership secretary (¶ 133) to review, at least annually, preferably early in the year, the membership rolls of the church; to use these rolls as a basis for the program of spiritual visitation; to entreat and encourage all members to be faithful; to assist the pastor in urging those who have moved permanently from the community to join a Methodist church in their new community (¶ 119); and to make recommendations to the fourth Quarterly Conference after the provisions of ¶ 127 have been faithfully performed by the pastor and the commission.

¶ **223.** 1. If a **minister of evangelism** is desired, the Quarterly Conference shall request through the district superintendent that the bishop appoint one, and shall fix his salary (¶ 148).

2. If the employment of a layman as **director of evangelism** is desired, the pastor, with the concurrence of the commission, shall recommend a proper person to the Official Board, which shall have the power to employ him, fix his salary, and terminate his service.

3. The minister or director of evangelism shall be administratively responsible to the pastor and, in co-operation with the pastor and the chairman of the commission, shall guide the evangelistic program of the church.

Sec. IV.   **The Commission on Education**

¶ 231. In order that a local church may be so organized and administered as to provide effectively for the Christian education of its entire constituency, there shall be a **Commission on Education** in each local church (¶¶ 144, 219). It shall be auxiliary to the Annual Conference and Jurisdictional Boards of Education and to the Division of the Local Church of the General Board of Education. In a small church the Commission on Education and the Workers' Conference (¶ 249) may function as one body except in the election of the officers and teachers of the church school.

¶ 232. 1. The persons holding the following offices are members of the Commission on Education: the chairman (¶ 143.6), pastor or pastors and church lay leader or associate church lay leader (¶ 219.1), church-school superintendent, division superintendents, membership cultivation superintendent, director or minister of Christian education (or educational assistant), director or minister of music, church-school secretary, literature secretary, and secretary of stewardship. The Woman's Society of Christian Service and Methodist Men shall each elect one representative to the commission, and the Methodist Youth Fellowship shall elect two. In addition there shall be not fewer than three and as many more members at large elected in accordance with ¶ 144 as the Quarterly Conference shall determine, chosen for special competency in the educational work of the church, and also the representatives of other commissions specified in ¶ 219.2. *Provided*, however, that in a small church the foregoing provisions may be modified as stated in ¶ 219.4.

2. At the beginning of each conference year the chairman shall call together the members for organization. The commission shall elect a vice-chairman, secretary, and such other officers and committees as are suggested in the commission manual or as the commission may determine.

¶ **233.** The functions and duties of the Commission on Education shall be as follows:

1. It shall determine the policies for the church school as a whole and its parts, and shall give general direction to all the educational work of the church; *provided* that the educational program of the church shall be open to all persons without regard to race, color, nationality, or class.

2. It shall study the educational needs of the church and shall provide for the organization, guidance, supervision, and, as needed, modification of the church school and of its three divisions with their departments, classes, and groups.

3. It shall be responsible for counseling with officers and teachers regarding the curriculum materials used by the classes and departments of the church school, and shall see that they are appropriate for each class and group, and that they are selected from the curriculum materials approved by the Curriculum Committee of the General Board of Education, and are ordered under the supervision of the commission. It shall be responsible for supervising the selection and use of music and hymnbooks in the church school, in harmony with the standards of the General Board of Education, and for the integration of children's and youth choirs into the Christian education program for children and youth. It shall also be responsible for supervising the selection and use of audio-visual materials in the church school and the training of officers, teachers, and other workers in their use, and shall see that all audio-visual materials used in the church school are in harmony with the standards of the General Board of Education.

4. In order that the statistical records of church schools in The Methodist Church may be reliable and uniform, it shall follow the standards of membership, attendance, and maintenance of the roll which are established by the

General Board of Education, and shall use the forms and record books prepared by the board.

5. Along with other official bodies in the local church, it shall encourage and maintain opportunities for initiative and expression on the part of youth as well as opportunity for adult counsel.

6. It shall co-operate with the Official Board and the other commissions of the church in organizing and sponsoring new churches and church schools, as outlined in the commission manual. (*See* ¶¶ 155, 215.7, 251.)

7. It shall perform the following other duties:

a) Enlist and train the necessary officers, counselors, teachers, and other leaders.

b) Elect certain officers and teachers as required by ¶ 246, fill vacancies in these positions, and, on the recommendation of the pastor or the church-school superintendent, remove any officer or teacher for unsatisfactory service, habitual neglect, or improper conduct; *provided* that any officer elected or confirmed by the Quarterly Conference shall be removed from office only by the Quarterly Conference on recommendation of the pastor.

c) Plan the work of the church school by holding regular meetings of the commission and of all church-school workers, together and by divisions and departments. (*See* ¶ 249.)

d) Provide for the proper observance of the special days and occasions in the church year, giving particular attention to the special days that are authorized by the General Conference for observance in the church school. (*See* ¶¶ 250, 296.)

e) Provide study groups in marriage and Christian homemaking for parents and young people. (*See* ¶ 234.)

f) Provide education concerning the significance of Christian higher education and information about our church-related institutions of higher learning, Wesley Foundations, and other student activities; recommend support of these interests to the Commission on Stewardship and Finance; and encourage the observance of relevant special days in the church year. To further these interests the commission may have a Committee on Christian Higher Education.

g) Plan the financial program of the church school (including the requesting of funds, if needed, through the Commission on Stewardship and Finance), budgeting all church-school funds and giving careful supervision to expenditures.

h) Allocate space for departments and classes and control the equipment provided for the use of the church school.

i) Provide for the full utilization of the materials interpreting and leading up to church membership which are a part of the church-school curriculum of Methodism, and, when requested by the pastor, assist in training classes for church membership.

j) Provide guidance for local-church programs of camping. (*See* ¶ 1401.4.)

k) Be responsible for the guidance and supervision of all children- and youth-serving organizations meeting under the auspices of the church.

l) Co-operate in the development of the total church program as provided in ¶ 216.

¶ **234.** The Commission on Education may organize a **Committee on Family Life,** composed of the division superintendents and two other members of the Commission on Education, one representative each of the Woman's Society of Christian Service, the Methodist Youth Fellowship, the Young Adult Fellowship, Methodist Men, and the Commission on Membership and Evangelism, and others chosen because of their special skill and concern for the Christian family, which shall recommend to the commission plans for the family life education program in the local church and assist in carrying out the recommendations of the General Conference concerning family life (¶ 1821). This committee shall be responsible to the commission and shall report to its regular meetings. In a small church the commission may elect an individual **director of the family life program** instead of a committee.

¶ **235.** The Commission on Education may, in co-operation with the other commissions, organize an **Intercommission Audio-Visual Committee,** composed of at least one representative from each commission and in addition one each from the Council of Children's Workers and the Woman's Society of Christian Service. This committee shall counsel all the commissions in the selection, purchase, and use of audio-visual materials and equipment, and in the evaluation and use of radio and television programs related to the program of the church; and it shall serve as the contact group for the Television, Radio, and Film Commission. It shall be responsible for presenting to the Commission on Stewardship and Finance the plans for supporting the Television-Radio Ministry Fund and a recommendation for this to be included in the local-church benevolence budget. It shall develop a library of audio-visual materials (which may be a part of a general church library) and train the librarian responsible for its supervision. It shall report to the Commission on Education and the Official Board. When it is impractical to have a representative committee, an **audio-visual counselor** may be appointed by the Commission on Education after consultation with the other interested commissions. He shall then be responsible for the duties indicated in this paragraph.

¶ **236.** The Commission on Education may elect a **Committee on Fellowship and Recreational Life,** composed of representatives of each division and such other members as may be desired, which shall recommend to the commission plans for a comprehensive program of recreation. In a small church the commission may elect an individual **director of recreation** instead of a committee.

¶ **241.** In each local church there shall be a **church school** for the purpose of discharging the church's responsibility for instructing and guiding its entire constituency in Christian faith and living. The church school shall provide for education in the Holy Scriptures, the Christian religion, and the Christian Church (leading to commitment to Christ and to church membership) through worship, fellowship, study, and service. Its program shall include evangelism, stewardship, missions, social action, recreation, and other activities.

¶ **242.** The Commission on Education shall organize and administer the church school in harmony with the provisions of the Discipline and in accordance with standards and procedures as set forth in the manuals for church schools of various types and sizes, which manuals shall be prepared by the Division of the Local Church of the General Board of Education under the authority of the General Conference.

¶ **243.** The church school includes for all ages (1) Sunday school, (2) the Methodist Sunday Evening Fellowship, (3) weekday activities, and (4) home and extension service. Within these four parts of the church school there may be: classes and study groups; extended and additional sessions for children; Sunday evening and weekday meetings of children, youth, and adults; classes in preparation for church membership; children's and youth choirs; nursery home roll; nursery schools and kindergartens (¶ 245); children, youth, and adult home members and extension members; vacation church school; camping for children, youth, and adults; leadership education agencies; parent study groups; fellowship groups; and other activities appropriate to the Christian education of the people. When one becomes a member of any one of these groups in the church school, he thereby becomes a member of the church school. The membership roll of the church school shall be kept current in accordance with the suggested procedures of the General Board of Education. Records and reports to Quarterly and Annual Conferences shall be made in keeping with these provisions.

¶ **244.** 1. The church school shall be organized in three divisions: **Children's Division,** from birth through eleven years; **Youth Division** (Methodist Youth Fellowship), from twelve through twenty-one years; **Adult Division,** twenty-two years and over; *provided*, however, that if desired there may be two divisions for children—namely, **Younger Children's Division** and **Elementary Division**— and that older young people approaching adulthood shall be grouped in either the Youth Division or the Adult Division on the basis of their maturity, interests, needs, and social grouping in the community; and *provided*, further, that the General Board of Education may, at its discretion, modify these age provisions. In small churches each division may be composed of one or more classes. In larger churches each division may be divided into departments with classes in each department.

2. In the organization of the church school there may be councils appropriate to each age group.

3. The Commission on Education shall follow the manual issued by the Division of the Local Church of the General Board of Education describing the organization of schools of various sizes. (*See* ¶ 242.)

4. Classes, departments, and divisions shall develop their work in harmony with the Disciplinary provisions and with the standards established by the Conference and General Boards of Education. Each department and division shall include in its total program Sunday morning, Sunday evening, and such other meetings and activities as may be determined by the Commission on Education for the Christian education of the children, youth, and adults of the church; *provided* that the results shall be a unified or correlated program of work.

5. The youth of The Methodist Church between the ages of twelve and twenty-one inclusive who belong to any group for, or organizational unit of, youth in the church, shall be members of the Youth Division and thereby members of the **Methodist Youth Fellowship.** These provisions shall include college students who are related to the local church through activities which the Commission on Education shall provide. In churches at college campuses these plans shall be worked out co-operatively with the campus-related Methodist student organization.

6. Children- and youth-serving agencies shall be included in the church school provided their program is a part of the program of the church school and is under the direction of the Commission on Education and the pastor. (*See* ¶ 233.7*k*.)

7. The Woman's Society of Christian Service and the Commission on Education shall co-operate in the missionary education of children and youth.

8. The secretaries of children's work and of youth work of the Woman's Society of Christian Service shall be

members of the division councils for the age groups concerned.

9. The church lay leader, the presidents of the Woman's Society of Christian Service and of Methodist Men, the chairman of the Commission on Missions, and the leaders of such other adult groups as the Commission on Education may determine shall be members of the Adult Division Council.

¶ **245.** When the needs of the children and the facilities and resources of the local church warrant it, the Commission on Education, on recommendation of the superintendent of the Children's Division (or Younger Children's Division) and the pastor, and with the approval of the Official Board, may provide for a **through-the-week nursery school and/or kindergarten** as a part of the church school. In such case the commission shall be responsible for:

1. Determining the policies, program, and curriculum, and the conditions under which children may be enrolled.

2. Electing the teachers.

3. Providing for the physical safety of the children in accordance with local laws.

4. Recommending to the Commission on Stewardship and Finance a budget of financial needs, including teachers' salaries, materials, and equipment.

5. Determining a schedule of payments by parents for such service to their children.

6. Receiving regular reports of the school from its director and keeping permanent records of its work, leadership, and finances.

¶ **246.** Great care shall be exercised in the selection of teachers, officers, and other workers in the church school. They shall be elected annually in the following manner:

1. The Quarterly Conference shall elect, as provided in ¶ 143, to serve from the beginning of the ensuing conference year: (a) the church-school superintendent (¶¶ 143.7, 248.3); (b) a membership cultivation superintendent and three or four division superintendents (¶¶ 143.8, 244.1); (c) a director of Christian education, or educational assistant, if desired (¶¶ 143.9, 247.1). Interim

vacancies shall be filled by the Commission on Education, the pastor concurring, subject to confirmation by the next Quarterly Conference.

2. Each class or group concerned shall elect, preferably prior to the beginning of the conference year, or as need may arise: (*a*) youth officers in the Youth Division; (*b*) officers in the Adult Division; and (*c*) the teachers of adult classes, which teachers shall be selected from a list of names submitted by the Commission on Education.

3. The Commission on Education shall elect, preferably prior to the beginning of the conference year, or as need may arise, all teachers, officers, and workers not otherwise provided for, on nomination of the church-school superintendent (or superintendent-elect if elected and not yet in office) with the approval of the pastor, the director or minister of Christian education, and the division superintendents (or superintendents-elect if elected and not yet in office). (*See* ¶ 233.7*b*.)

¶ 247. 1. On nomination of the pastor, with the concurrence of the Commission on Education and the Committee on Pastoral Relations or the Committee on Lay Personnel, the Quarterly Conference may employ, or may annually request the bishop to appoint, a **director or minister of Christian education** or an educational assistant, who in co-operation with the pastor and the church-school superintendent shall guide the educational program of the local church in accordance with ¶ 233 and with the standards of the General Board of Education (¶ 1396). He shall be administratively responsible to the pastor. Provided he is certified as described in ¶ 1451, his title shall be minister of Christian education if he is an ordained ministerial member of an Annual Conference, or director of Christian education if he is a layman. In case he is not certified, his title shall be educational assistant (¶ 1451). Two or more churches may join in using the services of such a person.

2. On nomination of the pastor, with the concurrence of the Commission on Worship (¶ 276) or Music Committee (¶ 278.4), the Commission on Education, and the Committee on Lay Personnel or the Committee on Pastoral Relations, the Quarterly Conference may employ, or

may annually request the bishop to appoint, a **director or minister of music,** or a music assistant, who shall direct the total music program of the local church in accordance with the standards of the General Board of Education (¶ 1396) and of the General Commission on Worship (¶ 1569.2). He shall be administratively responsible to the pastor. Provided he is certified as described in ¶ 1451, his title shall be minister of music if he is an ordained ministerial member of an Annual Conference, or director of music if he is a layman. In case he is not certified, his title may be music assistant (¶ 1451).

3. Lay employee benefits in keeping with the recommendations of ¶ 145.3 are recommended for laymen in the above offices.

¶ **248.** In the educational work of the church the following relationships shall be observed:

1. The Christian education program of the local church school shall be the program set up and authorized by the Annual Conference Board of Education and the Division of the Local Church of the General Board of Education.

2. In the program of work herein outlined the pastor is, as elsewhere in all the work of the pastoral charge, the preacher in charge, and is responsible for the total educational program of the local church. Nothing in this plan is to be construed as interfering with his authority and responsibility.

3. The **church-school superintendent** is the administrative officer of the church school. It shall be his duty to co-operate with the pastor and with the director or minister of Christian education, if any, to stimulate, encourage, and help the other officers and teachers and to plan with them for the work of the school as a whole and in all its parts. He shall carry out the policies of the Commission on Education.

4. Under the direction of the Commission on Education the church school shall engage in co-operative enterprises with other Methodist church schools in the same district, and with schools of other communions, looking toward community betterment and community service and other Christian activities.

5. The Christian education of church-school members calls for curriculums which are graded and adapted to the needs of the pupils. The curriculums shall be based on sound educational principles and the universal gospel of the living Christ. Methodist connectionalism requires curriculums which contain the present Methodist traditions, purposes, programs, and movements. Each church school shall provide instruction in the curriculums approved by the Curriculum Committee of the General Board of Education of The Methodist Church.

¶ 249. To provide opportunity for fellowship, study, and discussion of the educational work of the church, there shall be held quarterly a general meeting of all the officers, teachers, and leaders in the church school to be known as the **Workers' Conference.** The chairman shall be the church-school superintendent, who, with the pastor, and the director or minister of Christian education, if any, shall be responsible for planning the program of the Workers' Conference. There may also be meetings of the officers and teachers of departments in those church schools that are organized by departments.

¶ 250. The following special days shall be observed:

1. In order that the members of the church school may be informed concerning the world-wide service program of Methodism and share in its support, the fourth Sunday in each month shall be observed in the church school as **World Service Sunday.** An offering shall be taken in the school for world service and conference benevolences. This offering shall be sent with other offerings of the local church for this cause to the Annual Conference treasurer. The amount raised annually in the church school for world service and conference benevolences shall be reported by the pastor and recorded in a column so designated in the statistical reports of the Annual Conference.

2. The first Sunday of **Christian Education Week,** or some other day designated by the Annual Conference, shall be observed in each local church as **Christian Education Sunday** for the purpose of emphasizing the importance of Christian education and for receiving an offering for the Conference Board of Education for the program of its local church division. The funds raised on

this day shall be remitted as may be determined by the Annual Conference. These funds shall be recorded in a column in the pastor's report to the Annual Conference, but shall not be charged to the share of the Conference Board of Education in the conference apportioned benevolences.[20]

3. **Race Relations Sunday** shall be observed in every local church on the second Sunday in February each year. This shall be the occasion for reviewing the work of The Methodist Church in the founding and support of Negro schools. It shall also be an occasion for creating better relations among all races and particularly informing our people concerning the contributions and needs of Negro colleges. An offering shall be received for the benefit of Negro colleges related to the Board of Education, which may be a part of, or in addition to, such sums as may already be included in local-church or Annual Conference budgets. Due recognition shall be given to the historic responsibility of the former Methodist Episcopal Church, South, for aid to the Christian Methodist Episcopal Church.

4. **Methodist Student Day** shall be observed annually in every local church, preferably the second Sunday in June. If not on that date, it shall be observed on some other Sunday designated by the Annual Conference or the Commission on Education of the local church. On this day emphasis shall be given to the work of higher education in church-related institutions. An offering shall be received for the support of National Methodist Scholarships and the Student Loan Fund for Methodist students.

5. Each local church shall observe **National Family Week** from the first to the second Sunday of May. It shall be the purpose of this week to focus attention on the importance of religious living. Ministers are urged to preach on the importance of Christian teaching in the home and the need for close co-operation between the church school and home and the use of religious literature in the home. Opportunity shall be given for parents to dedicate themselves to the teaching of religion in the

---

[20] *See* Judicial Council Decision 188.

home by precept and example. Because of the close relationship of the church school and the home in the teaching of children, youth, and adults, the promotion of the observance of National Family Week shall be the responsibility of the Division of the Local Church of the General Board of Education in co-operation with other boards and agencies of the church. The sole purpose of this observance shall be to strengthen family life in keeping with the resolution of the General Conference concerning the Christian family (¶ 1821). Therefore a special offering should not be taken in connection with National Family Week.

6. The first Sunday of National Family Week, or some other day selected by the Annual Conference, may be designated as **Children's Day,** for the purpose of emphasizing the responsibility of the church for our children, the same to be observed without a church-wide offering. The program for such a day shall be the concern of the Division of the Local Church of the General Board of Education and the Boards of Education of the various Annual Conferences.

¶ **251.** In a community where there is need of a Methodist church school, one may be organized with the written consent of the district superintendent. The church school, when organized, shall be under the direction of the Commission on Education of the church organizing it; or, if organized independent of a local church, it shall be under the direction and supervision of the district superintendent.

Sec. V.   **The Commission on Missions**

¶ **256.** There shall be organized in each local church a **Commission on Missions,** composed of not fewer than three and as many more members elected in accordance with ¶ 144 as the Quarterly Conference may determine, and in addition the following ex officio and representative members: the pastor or pastors; the church lay leader or an associate church lay leader; the church-school superintendent; the hospitals and homes steward; two youth members, one of whom shall be the chairman of

Christian outreach of the Methodist Youth Fellowship; the secretary of missionary education of the Woman's Society of Christian Service; and the representatives of other commissions specified in ¶ 219.2; *provided* that in a small church these provisions may be modified as stated in ¶ 219.4. It shall be auxiliary to the General Board of Missions and to the Jurisdictional and Annual Conference Boards of Missions and shall co-operate with these agencies in their plans and programs for missionary education and cultivation. At the beginning of each conference year the chairman (¶ 143.6) shall call together the members for organization. The commission shall elect a vice-chairman, secretary, and such other officers and committees as it may determine.

¶ **257.** It shall be the duty of the Commission on Missions as the central planning group for missionary education and cultivation:

1. To provide for the diffusion of missionary information, the distribution of missionary literature, the circulation of *World Outlook*, and the use of missionary audiovisual materials in the church.

2. To plan for a church-wide school of missions for children, youth, and adults in co-operation with the Woman's Society of Christian Service, the other commissions, and other agencies, using materials produced or approved by the Joint Section of Education and Cultivation. In the case of materials for children and youth, they shall also be approved by the Interboard Committee on Missionary Education.

3. To co-operate with other agencies in the survey and study of the needs of the community, and to recommend to the Quarterly Conference plans whereby the local church may undertake missionary projects for the purpose of Christianizing the total life of its own community.

4. To study the program of the General Board of Missions and recommend to the Quarterly Conference and the Official Board such approved projects—district, conference, and world—as should be supported by the local church.

5. To co-operate with the pastor, Woman's Society of Christian Service, Commission on Education, and other or-

ganizations and agencies in the local church in all plans for the development of the missionary life and spirit of the local church, especially in programs and offerings for missions on fourth Sundays, plans for raising funds for world service and conference benevolences, and the support of missionary specials by individuals, organizations, and the whole church.

6. To confer with the Commission on Stewardship and Finance and recommend to it the projects and amounts to be included in the budget of the local church for benevolent causes; to co-operate with the pastor and the Commission on Stewardship and Finance in plans for raising the church's obligation for world service and conference benevolences; and to plan for proper observance of World Service Sunday (¶¶ 215.3, 250.1, 296.1a).

7. To co-operate with the pastor and the Commission on Stewardship and Finance in an effort to insure an effective every-member visitation each year, with emphasis on stewardship and missions.

8. To co-operate with the Official Board and the other commissions in organizing and sponsoring new churches and church schools. (See ¶¶ 155, 215.7, 251.)

9. To represent the work of the Methodist Committee for Overseas Relief in the local church and encourage support of its projects.

10. To inform the whole local church, youth and adults alike, of the qualifications and current needs for missionary personnel, and to present the challenge of missionary service to the people.

11. To lead the local church in the observance of the One Great Hour of Sharing, and to interpret the Crusade scholarship program in the local church.

12. To prepare each year an operating budget for the commission and present it to the Commission on Stewardship and Finance, so that sufficient funds can be included in the annual budget (¶ 266) to enable it to do the work assigned by the Discipline.

13. To co-operate in the development of the total program of the church as provided in ¶ 216.

Sec. VI. **The Commission on Stewardship and Finance**

¶ **261.** It shall be the responsibility of the Official Board to make proper and adequate provision for the financial needs of the church, including ministerial support (i.e., for the pastor or pastors, district superintendent, conference claimants, and bishops), approved items of local expense, world service and conference benevolences, other items apportioned the church by the proper authority, and all obligations assumed by the local church.

¶ **262.** 1. There shall be in every local church a **Commission on Stewardship and Finance,** which shall, under the authority and direction of the Official Board, promote and cultivate Christian stewardship and administer the financial program of the church. It shall be auxiliary to the General, Jurisdictional, Annual Conference, and District Boards of Lay Activities.

2. The commission shall be composed of the chairman (¶ 143.6), pastor or pastors and church lay leader or associate church lay leader (¶ 219.1), secretary of stewardship, chairman of the Official Board, financial secretary or church business manager, church treasurer or treasurers, one representative each of the Woman's Society of Christian Service, Methodist Men, and the Methodist Youth Fellowship, not fewer than three and as many more members at large elected in accordance with ¶ 144 as the Quarterly Conference shall determine, and the representatives of other commissions specified in ¶ 219.2, *provided* that in a small church these provisions may be modified as stated in ¶ 219.4.

3. At the beginning of each conference year the chairman shall call together the members for organization. The commission shall elect a vice-chairman, a secretary, and such other officers and committees as are suggested in the commission manual or as the commission may determine.

4. The commission shall co-operate in the development of the total church program as provided in ¶ 216.

5. It is recommended that there be two committees to function as part of the commission, the Committee on

Finance and the Committee on Stewardship, and that the secretary of stewardship be chairman of the latter.

¶ 263. In the cultivation and promotion of Christian stewardship the **secretary of stewardship** (¶ 143.12), formerly called director of stewardship, shall develop a program of stewardship education which in turn shall be presented to the total commission for review, revision, and adoption. After such adoption the secretary and the Committee on Stewardship shall carry out the program in harmony with the directives prepared by the General Board of Lay Activities in accordance with ¶ 1512.

¶ 264. Inasmuch as the Discipline of our church clearly designates tithing as the minimum standard of giving for Methodists, it shall be the duty of every local church to carry on a program of education in the field of the stewardship of possessions with an emphasis on tithing. It shall be the duty of the secretary of stewardship, in consultation with the pastor and the chairman of the commission, to plan and recommend the details of this program of stewardship emphasis. This program should be implemented by an intensive emphasis in stewardship education and sustained by a year-round program of stewardship cultivation. It should be in the planning of every local church to give members an opportunity annually to make commitments to tithing. This program shall be auxiliary to the stewardship program as sponsored by the General Board of Lay Activities.

¶ 266. 1. The commission shall each year set up a **budget** for the local church and submit it to the Official Board for review and final decision. The commissions and committees whose work is related to program and budget shall have opportunity to make recommendations, which shall be reviewed and co-ordinated by the program committee of the every-member visitation (¶ 267.1) and by the commission before presentation to the board.

2. In setting up the budget each year the commission shall confer with:

a) The Committee on Pastoral Relations (¶ 145.2), or the pastor if there is no such committee, in order to make adequate provision for the pastor's salary (¶¶ 142.6,

148), and for his housing and travel and other expenses related to his duties.

b) The Commission on Missions, to the end that adequate provision shall be made for the benevolence causes of the church: world service and conference benevolences (through recommendation to the Quarterly Conference as described in ¶ 147), Advance specials, and conference and district projects of a missionary and church-extension nature.

c) The Commission on Education and the Commission on Missions, concerning the budget for the Television-Radio Ministry Fund.

3. It is recommended that the local-church expense and benevolence causes be set up separately, and that both causes be presented to the membership.

4. If a budget plan is used which combines local-church expense and benevolences in one system of pledging and contributing, the Commissions on Missions, Education, and Stewardship and Finance shall seriously study the ratio of the proposed acceptance for world service and conference benevolences to the amount appropriated for local-church expense and recommend a fair share for the benevolences. As there is a substantial increase in the pledging and giving of the people, conscientious care shall be taken that the benevolences receive an increase proportionate to the increase in local-church expense.

5. When causes are combined in the budget, the budgetary responsibilities of the Commission on Education and the church school, as stated in ¶ 233.7*g*, shall not be contravened.

¶ 267. When the program of the church has been developed as provided in ¶ 216 and the annual budget has been approved by the board, the commission shall, under the direction of the board, proceed to insure an income sufficient to cover the same, and shall administer the funds received according to the following plan, with such adaptations and adjustments as the board may determine:

1. There shall be an annual every-member visitation, by which all members of the local church shall be given an opportunity to make their individual pledges to the support of the church. Every member of a local church is

obligated to support the entire program of the church. Pledges should be, as far as practicable, on a weekly basis, and in proportion to one's income.

2. Should the probable income appear insufficient to meet the annual budget, steps shall be taken at the beginning of the year to provide for the deficit.

3. All payments on pledges shall be credited to the donors, and a proper account shall be kept of each subscriber and contributor.

4. Funds received shall be deposited promptly in a bank approved by the board, and the account therein shall be in the name of the local church.

5. Funds received shall be disbursed as the board directs, and to the objects for which they are contributed.

6. Contributions designated for specific causes and objects shall be promptly forwarded according to the intent of the donor, and shall not be used, even temporarily, for any other purpose.

7. When the budget of the local church has been approved, additional appropriations or items shall not be added thereto without the consent of the Official Board; and payments to no cause or item in the budget shall exceed the budget allowance except by order of the board.

8. As far as practicable, and under the direction of the commission, the treasurer shall prorate the income received each month among the respective items and causes represented in the budget, according to the proportional share of each; *provided* that the pastor's salary shall be excepted and given priority claim.

9. Report shall be made by the financial secretary and the treasurer or treasurers to the board each month, and to the Quarterly Conference when requested, of all receipts and disbursements, and of unpaid obligations against the budget.

10. It shall be the continuing duty of the commission to inform the congregation of the financial needs of the church.

¶ **268.** The church treasurer or treasurers (¶ 143.12) shall receive and disburse all money contributed to causes represented in the local-church budget, and such other funds and contributions as the Official Board may determine; or the Quarterly Conference may elect a treasurer to receive and disburse funds and contributions for local expense and a benevolence treasurer to receive and disburse funds and contributions for benevolences and similar causes, in every case under the supervision and direction of the Official Board. The treasurer shall remit each month to the conference treasurer all world service and conference benevolence funds then on hand. (*See* ¶ 147.)

¶ **269.** If a financial secretary is elected (¶ 143.12), he shall receive the contributions to the local church, keeping records of the contributors and their payments as provided in ¶ 267.3, and disburse them promptly to the treasurer or treasurers. If a financial secretary is not elected, the treasurer or treasurers shall assume these responsibilities; *provided*, however, that they may be assumed by a church business manager (¶¶ 143.11, 212.2) if deemed desirable by the pastor and the Official Board.

¶ **270.** The commission shall make provision for an annual audit of the records of the financial officers of the local church and all its organizations, and shall report to the Quarterly Conference.

¶ **271.** No local church shall engage as a fund-raising agent any person or organization not in the employ of the Board of Missions, or of some other General, Jurisdictional, or Annual Conference agency, without first obtaining the written consent of the district superintendent.

¶ **272.** No lottery, raffle, or other game of chance shall be used in raising money for any purpose.

SEC. VII.   **The Commission on Christian Social Concerns**

¶ **274.** 1. A **Commission on Christian Social Concerns** shall be constituted by the Quarterly Conference, as provided in ¶¶ 144, 219, composed of four or more members elected by the Quarterly Conference. In addition the pastor, church lay leader or associate church lay leader, secretary of Christian social relations of the Woman's Society of Christian Service, a representative of Methodist Men, chairman of Christian citizenship of the Methodist Youth Fellowship, and hospitals and homes steward shall be ex officio members; preferably no one of these shall serve as chairman. There shall also be representatives of other commissions as provided in ¶ 219.2. *Provided*, however, that in a small church the foregoing provisions may be modified as stated in ¶ 219.4.

2. In addition to the chairman elected by the Quarterly Conference (¶ 143.6) the commission may elect a vice-chairman, a secretary, and such other officers as may be necessary.

3. The commission shall develop and promote programs and study and action projects in the following areas of Christian social concern: alcohol problems and general welfare, peace and world order, and human relations and economic affairs. To this end it may divide its membership into three committees of approximately equal size, patterned after the divisions of the general board (¶¶ 1535-41).

¶ 275. 1. The commission shall provide for the observance of **World Order Sunday,** which shall be observed annually in each local church on the Sunday established by the proper department of the National Council of Churches (¶ 296.2*f*).

2. The commission shall, in co-operation with the pastor, promote in the local church the observance of **Commitment Day** on the second Sunday in November (¶¶ 296.2*g*, 1536).

3. The commission shall join with the pastor and the Commission on Education in sponsoring **Race Relations Sunday** (¶¶ 250.3, 296.1*b*).

SEC. VIII.   The Commission on Worship

¶ **276.** 1. A **Commission on Worship** may be constituted by the Quarterly Conference (¶ 219.1), which shall be auxiliary to the General, Jurisdictional, and Annual Conference Commissions on Worship. In such case the work of all committees of the Quarterly Conference and the Official Board concerned with any part of the worship services of the church—such as the Music Committee, the communion stewards, the Committee on Ushers, and others—shall be consolidated under the Commission on Worship, and shall be carried on by the commission as a whole or by its committees.

2. The commission shall be composed of three or more members elected by the Quarterly Conference (¶ 144), who shall be persons qualified by interest, training, and competence to serve the church in the field of worship, and in addition the pastor, who may be chairman, the church lay leader or an associate church lay leader (¶ 219.1), and the representatives of other commissions specified in ¶ 219.2; *provided* that in a small church these provisions may be modified as stated in ¶ 219.4. The chairman or representatives of any committee whose work has direct relationship to the place and conduct of public worship may, by vote of the Official Board, be added as ex officio members.

¶ **277.** The duties of the Commission on Worship shall be:

1. To aid in interpreting the meaning, purpose, and practice of worship, and to promote the highest standards for the conduct of worship, by encouraging: (*a*) the widest possible participation in the services of the church; (*b*) the study by individuals and groups of manuals and other helps in the art of worship; and (*c*) the use of *The Book of Worship for Church and Home* and *The Methodist Hymnal* in the church and in the home.

2. To encourage the use of suitable music in public worship and at weddings, funerals, and all other occasions; to advise the Official Board in providing proper leadership in music and the fine arts; to provide for the maintenance and care of musical instruments, music libraries, and related equipment.

3. To arrange for the care of all furnishings and appointments for the conduct of worship, and, under the direction of the pastor, to prepare the Lord's Table for Holy Communion.

4. To recruit a sufficient number of persons to serve as ushers, and to encourage the training of ushers so that, in carrying out the functions of this office, they will contribute to creating an appropriate setting for worship and to maintaining an atmosphere of reverence within the sanctuary.

5. To promote, in co-operation with the Board of Trustees and others concerned, a policy regarding the securing

of memorial gifts to the church, and to supervise the placing of proper memorials within the church building; to provide a suitable book in which the names of the donors, the ones memorialized, and the memorial gifts may be recorded.

SEC. IX.   **Committees**

¶ **278.** For the promoting of other interests and activities in the local church the Official Board shall create from its own membership and from the membership of the local church, except as provided in ¶ 562, such committees as it may judge necessary, exercising care that these committees do not overlap or conflict with the committees of the Quarterly Conference. At least one member of each committee shall be a member of the board. Except where the Discipline provides otherwise, each committee shall elect its officers; *provided* that the chairman of each shall be a member of the Official Board. Each committee shall be responsible to the board, and shall report to the board regularly (and to the Quarterly Conference if requested). The board may create such committees as it may determine from the following list, and may add others as may appear advisable for the proper prosecution of its work:

1. The **Committee on Nominations,** elected by the board on nomination from the floor, or by ballot without nomination, which shall nominate to the board the officers thereof, and the members of its respective committees. The right of nomination from the floor for officers and committee members shall in no case be denied. The pastor shall be chairman of the Committee on Nominations. (*See* ¶ 212.)

2. The **Committee on Good Literature,** whose duty it shall be to call attention to the publication of new books of worth in forming and building the Christian life, arrange for exhibits of books and pamphlets relating to the work of The Methodist Church, promote the observance of Universal Bible Sunday, secure subscriptions to *Together, Christian Advocate, Central Christian Advocate,* and conference and area publications, and promote the use of approved publications in the church school.

3. The **Committee on Hospitals and Homes,** of which

131

the hospitals and homes steward (¶¶ 143.14, 256, 274) shall be chairman, which shall promote, in co-operation with the General, Jurisdictional, and Annual Conference Boards of Hospitals and Homes (¶¶ 1550-62), the interests of hospitals and homes of The Methodist Church and the particular hospitals and homes for whose support they are respectively responsible. The hospitals and homes steward and/or the committee, through organized direct services, shall relate the congregation to the health and welfare needs of persons in the local parish and community and, on request of the pastor, shall have charge annually of the Golden Cross enrollment.

4. The **Music Committee,** which shall encourage the use of suitable music in the worship service of the local church and, with the approval of the board, make provision for proper music leadership; *provided* that if the responsibility of the music leader is to direct the total music program of the local church, including youth and children's choirs and assistance in the church school, his selection shall be as indicated in ¶ 247.2.

5. The **Parsonage Committee,** which shall take proper action in co-operation with the Board of Trustees (¶ 165) to provide an adequate and suitable residence for the pastor. (*See* ¶ 145.7.)

6. The **Committee on Church Property,** which, unless otherwise provided by the trustees, shall have supervision of the maintenance and upkeep of the sanctuary and other church units.

7. The **Committee on Men's Work,** which shall promote the training and active participation of men in the work of the local church, under the leadership of the General Board of Lay Activities.

8. Other committees as the board may determine.

SEC. X.   **The Woman's Society of Christian Service**

¶ 281. In every local church there shall be a **Woman's Society of Christian Service.**[21] The following is the authorized constitution for such a society.

---

[21] *See* Judicial Council Decision 138.

¶ **282.** *Article 1. Name.*—There shall be a Woman's Society of Christian Service in the local church, auxiliary to the Conference Woman's Society of Christian Service and the Board of Missions of The Methodist Church, through the Woman's Division. A **Wesleyan Service Guild,** auxiliary to the Woman's Society of Christian Service, composed of employed women, may also be organized in a local church.

Art. 2. Purpose.—The purpose of the Woman's Society of Christian Service and Wesleyan Service Guild shall be to help women grow in the knowledge and experience of God as revealed in Jesus Christ and to challenge them to respond to God's redemptive purpose in the world.

Toward the realization of this purpose the Woman's Society and Guild shall provide opportunities and resources which will help women grow in understanding and spiritual power; increase their knowledge of needs in the world; and share in the witness, service, and outreach of the Church.

The Woman's Society and Guild shall enlist workers and secure funds for the fulfillment of their responsibility in the mission of the Church at home and overseas.

Art. 3. Membership.—A woman may become a member of the Woman's Society of Christian Service by giving prayer, service, and an annual contribution of money to the total budget through membership offerings, pledges, or gifts. She shall contribute to, educate for, and promote the total program of the women of Methodism. The pastor shall be a member of the executive committee of the society.

Art. 4. Officers, Secretaries of Lines of Work, and Committees.—The local society shall elect a president, a vice-president, a recording secretary, and a treasurer. Secretaries of lines of work and the Committee on Nominations shall be elected, and other committees shall be appointed, in accordance with the plans of the Woman's Division of the Board of Missions as may be set forth in the by-laws for the local society. Where a simpler form of organization is necessary in a small church, there shall be five or more officers and secretaries of lines of work as determined by the local society.

Art. 5. Funds.—(1) All funds from whatsoever source secured by this society belong to this organization and shall be disbursed only in accordance with its constitution and by its order.[22]

(2) The total budget to be secured and administered by a Woman's Society of Christian Service in the local church shall include pledges to missions to be directed through the regular channels of finance of the society and also funds for local-church and community activities.

(3) All undesignated funds channeled to the Woman's Division of the Board of Missions shall be divided in the office of the treasurer of the division on a basis to be determined by the division. There shall be no division of such funds by the local society.

(4) Funds for local-church and community activities shall be secured and administered by the Woman's Society of Christian Service in the local church.

(5) Each society in the local church shall make an annual pledge to the total budget adopted by the conference society.

(6) Each society in the local church shall include in its budget a definite amount for a cultivation fund.

Art. 6. Meetings.—The society shall hold one or more meetings during a month for the transaction of its business and for the study of the work.

Art. 7. Amendments.—Proposed amendments to this constitution may be sent to the recording secretary of the Woman's Division of the Board of Missions at least forty days before the last annual meeting of the division in the quadrennium. Proposed amendments may also be sent directly to the General Conference.

Note: For a description of the Woman's Division of the Board of Missions and its subsidiary organizations see ¶¶ 1186, 1207, 1256-68.

SEC. XI. Lay Activities in the Local Church

¶ 286. The Official Board, in co-operation with the pastor, shall be responsible for the program of lay activities in the local church as outlined under the direction of the

---

[22] *See* Judicial Council Decision 138.

General, Jurisdictional, Annual Conference, and District Boards of Lay Activities (¶¶ 1490-1514). In the program of lay activities the pastor is, as in all the work of the pastoral charge, the preacher in charge, and is responsible for the total program of the church. Nothing in this plan is to be construed as interfering with his general authority and responsibility.

¶ 287. The program of lay activities in the local church shall include the interests and causes that have been committed to the General Board of Lay Activities by the Discipline (¶¶ 1497-99).

¶ 288. 1. There shall be **a church lay leader** in each local church, elected by the Quarterly Conference (¶ 143.2), who shall take leadership in promoting, in co-operation with the pastor and the chairman of the Official Board, the program of lay work of The Methodist Church. He may also be elected chairman of the Official Board. He shall be responsible for:

a) Becoming acquainted with the total program of The Methodist Church in order that he may counsel and work with the pastor in the execution of the program.

b) Presentation of the program of lay activities to the Official Board, for the adoption of plans necessary to carry on the program and for continued leadership to make it effective.

c) Working with the pastor in presenting benevolences to the congregation.

d) Working with the pastor in developing a program of training for the Official Board.

e) Organizing a Methodist Men club if none exists; co-operating with the officers of the existing club to help make the club more effective.

f) Working with all of the commissions of the church in developing and carrying out their programs. (*See* ¶ 219.1.)

g) Reporting to each regular session of the Official Board, and reporting annually to the fourth Quarterly Conference, and to such other sessions as requested.

h) Participating in the programs of the District and Conference Boards of Lay Activities.

2. There may be elected by the Quarterly Conference

(¶ 143.2) one or more **associate church lay leaders,** if desired. (*See* ¶ 219.1.)

¶ **289.** The pastor of a circuit, with the consent of the Official Boards of the charge, shall organize the several Official Boards into a single **Charge Board of Lay Activities,** of which one of the church lay leaders shall be elected chairman. This board shall promote the program of lay activities on a charge-wide basis and encourage harmony and Christian fellowship among the churches of the circuit, to the end that the charge may render a more effective service.

¶ **291.** The Official Board, in co-operation with the pastor and the church lay leader, shall be responsible for organizing **Methodist Men** in the local church and encouraging them to secure a charter. The purpose shall be the development of the spiritual life of the men of the church and the attainment of the following objectives:

1. To seek daily Christ's way of life; to bear witness to this way in business dealings and in social contacts; to engage in some definite Christian service.

2. To study and become familiar with The Methodist Church, its organization, and its doctrines.

3. To promote personal evangelism, especially among men and boys.

4. To develop Christian fellowship in the church, especially among laymen, by promoting Christian understanding.

5. To co-operate with the pastor, district superintendent, and bishop in promoting the program of the church.

6. To co-operate with other units of Methodist Men in the promotion of district, conference, and church-wide projects under the leadership of the General Board of Lay Activities. (*See* ¶ 1511.)

¶ **292.** In order to achieve the six objectives enumerated in ¶ 291, Methodist Men, as an organized unit in the local church, shall plan a program of activities in which the following are given consideration:

1. Co-operation with the Commission on Membership and Evangelism in a program of personal evangelism, and in assuring that every adult male member of the congregation is visited at least once each year.

2. Co-operation with the Commission on Stewardship and Finance in the cultivation of Christian stewardship and assistance in the annual every-member visitation.

3. Co-operation with the Commission on Education in a program of youth activities, such as Scouting or 4-H Club work in those communities where this need is not otherwise met.

4. Co-operation with the Commission on Missions in some worthy project as an expression of Christian outreach.

5. Co-operation with other official bodies of the church in recruiting and assisting worthy young people in securing a Christian education.

6. Co-operation with the pastor to relieve him of some of the responsibilities demanding his time so as to release him for ministering more fully to the spiritual needs of the people.

7. Co-operation with the pastor and official bodies of the church in sponsoring a program of training in churchmanship, including the organization and doctrines of The Methodist Church.

¶ 293. 1. A **lay speaker** is a member of a local church certified by his Quarterly Conference as qualified to perform the following duties, subject to the consent and direction of the pastor:

a) To serve the church in any way in which the witness of the spoken word can inspire the laity to better churchmanship and to better lives; to give assistance and support to the program emphases of the church; to assist in giving better leadership to the work of the church through a more effective vocal presentation of the attitudes and concerns of the church in all areas of life.

b) To conduct services of worship and hold meetings for prayer and exhortation whenever opportunity is afforded; *provided*, however, that when no pastor is appointed to the circuit, station, or mission, such services or meetings shall be held subject to the approval and supervision of the district superintendent.

c) To attend and present a written report to all sessions of the District and Quarterly Conferences.

2. A candidate recommended for lay speaker shall be

a person of evident Christian character, conduct, and concern; he shall have potential natural gifts and graces, a willingness to serve to improve himself in knowledge and understanding of the Bible, and a desire to grow in Christian grace.

3. To become a lay speaker the candidate shall:

a) Be recommended by the Official Board of his church.

b) Be recommended by the District Committee on Lay Speaking (¶ 1509), preferably on completion of the training course for lay speakers recommended by the General Board of Lay Activities.

c) Be certified by his Quarterly Conference, the certificate to be signed by the president thereof. It is recommended that a consecration service be held during the session of the Annual Conference, or in the district on an appropriate occasion with the bishop presiding.

4. A lay speaker shall report to the Quarterly Conference and be subject to an annual examination by it of his character, gifts, labors, and usefulness, and a renewal of certificate, to be signed by the president thereof.

Sec. XII.   **Special Days**

¶ 296. The special days to be observed by local churches are as follows:

1. Days to be observed in the church or the church school with an offering:

a) World Service Sunday—the fourth Sunday of each month (¶¶ 215.3, 250.1).

b) Race Relations Sunday—the second Sunday in February (¶¶ 250.3, 275.3).

c) One Great Hour of Sharing—on or about the fourth Sunday in Lent (¶ 760.1).

d) Methodist Student Day—the second Sunday in June (¶ 250.4).

e) World-wide Communion Sunday—the first Sunday in October (¶ 763).

f) Christian Education Sunday—the first Sunday in Christian Education Week, or other date designated by the Annual Conference (¶ 250.2).

2. Days to be observed in the church or the church school without an offering:

a) Period of Spiritual Enrichment—beginning the Sunday preceding Ash Wednesday (¶ 222.4*a*).

b) National Family Week—the first to the second Sunday of May (¶ 250.5).

c) Children's Day—the first Sunday in National Family Week (¶ 250.6).

d) Ministry Sunday—the Sunday of or preceding May 24 (Aldersgate Sunday).

e) Laymen's Day—the second Sunday in October (¶ 1499.3).

f) World Order Sunday—date set as provided in ¶ 275.1.

g) Commitment Day—the second Sunday in November (¶¶ 275.2, 1536).

h) Universal Bible Sunday—the second Sunday in December (¶ 278.2).

i) Student Recognition Day—the Sunday after Christmas.

3. Days to be observed in the church or the church school as ordered by the Jurisdictional or Annual Conference:

a) Hospitals and Homes Week, beginning with Golden Cross Enrollment Sunday (¶ 1560.1).

b) Retired Ministers Day (¶ 1610.6).

c) Rural Life Sunday—the fifth Sunday after Easter.

PART III

THE MINISTRY

CHAPTER I

THE CALL TO PREACH

¶ **301.** When a member of a local church manifests a desire to preach, it shall be the duty of his pastor to counsel with him concerning the opportunities and requirements of the ministry; and if the pastor is persuaded that he possesses gifts, graces, and promise of usefulness, he shall guide him toward qualifying.

[The following questions were first asked by John Wesley at the third conference of Methodist preachers in 1746. They have been retained ever since, in substantially the same words, as the standards by which prospective Methodist preachers are to be judged.—EDITORS.]

¶ **302.** In order that we may try those persons who profess to be moved by the Holy Spirit to preach, let the following questions be asked, namely:

1. Do they know God as a pardoning God? Have they the love of God abiding in them? Do they desire nothing but God? Are they holy in all manner of conversation?

2. Have they gifts, as well as grace, for the work? Have they a clear, sound understanding; a right judgment in the things of God; a just conception of salvation by faith? Do they speak justly, readily, clearly?

3. Have they fruit? Have any been truly convinced of sin and converted to God, and are believers edified by their preaching?

As long as these marks concur in anyone, we believe he is called of God to preach. These we receive as sufficient proof that he is moved by the Holy Spirit.

¶ 303. Women are included in all provisions of the Discipline referring to the ministry.[1]

CHAPTER II

THE LOCAL MINISTRY

SECTION I.   Local Preachers

¶ 304. 1. A **local preacher** is a lay member of The Methodist Church who has been granted a license to preach, or has been ordained, according to the laws of the church (¶¶ 306, 310, 393, 403). He continues to be a lay member of a local church.[2] His license to preach must be renewed each year (¶¶ 307, 320) unless he has been ordained.

2. An unordained local preacher has authority to preach and to conduct divine worship; *provided*, however, that his authority shall be restricted to the charge in which his membership is held or to which he is appointed.[3] For the authority conferred by ministerial orders *see* ¶¶ 392, 402.

3. A local preacher not serving a pastoral charge may assist his pastor, as requested by the pastor and under the pastor's supervision, subject to the laws of the church (¶¶ 308, 312).

4. A local preacher may serve a pastoral charge under the supervision of a district superintendent, either by temporary appointment (¶ 315.2), or by becoming an approved supply pastor (¶ 314).

5. A person must be a local preacher in order to become a candidate for the traveling ministry (¶ 321).

¶ 305. No member is authorized to preach without a license.

¶ 306. A license to preach may be issued as provided in ¶¶ 362.4, 690, 695 after the person has qualified by the following steps:

---

[1] *See* Judicial Council Decision 155.
[2] *See* Judicial Council Decision 173.
[3] *See* Judicial Council Decision 204.

1. Been graduated from an accredited high school, or its equivalent, or attained his twenty-fifth birthday.

2. Secured the recommendation of his Quarterly Conference, as provided in ¶ 146.1.

3. Applied to the district superintendent in writing.

4. Appeared before the District Committee on Ministerial Qualifications, held himself amenable to any psychological and aptitude tests it may require and provide, and supplied such other information as it may require for determining his gifts, graces, and potential usefulness.

5. Completed one fourth of the work required for the bachelor of divinity or equivalent degree in a school of theology accredited or approved by the University Senate, or passed the course of study prescribed for license to preach (¶ 1373.1), including Parts I, II, III, and IX of the Discipline. This course shall preferably be taken under the Department of Ministerial Education.

6. Agreed, for the sake of a disciplined example, and without implying moral superiority, to make a complete dedication of himself to the highest ideals of the Christian ministry with respect to purity of life in body, in mind, and in spirit, and to bear witness thereto by abstinence from all indulgences, including alcoholic beverages and tobacco, which may injure his influence.[4]

¶ 307. A license to preach shall be valid for one year. It may be renewed, as provided in ¶¶ 362.4, 690, 695, on recommendation of the person's Quarterly Conference, and on evidence that his gifts, graces, and usefulness continue to be satisfactory and that he is making regular progress in the required studies, as follows:

1. A local preacher who is enrolled as a pretheological or theological student in a school, college, university, or school of theology accredited or approved by the University Senate, or by the state accrediting agency, preparing for the traveling ministry shall present annually to the District Committee on Ministerial Qualifications a statement of his academic progress from the school he is attending. This statement shall take the place of any

---

[4] Amended in 1956 following Judicial Council Decision 100. Regarding § 6 *see also* Decisions 111, 157.

formal examination, provided his academic progress and character are satisfactory.

2. A local preacher who is not a student as defined in § 1 shall pursue the four-year course of study under the Department of Ministerial Education (¶ 1373.1; *see also* ¶ 327). Except as provided in ¶ 317.3, the course must be completed within eight years after the date of issue of the first license to preach; *provided*, however, that this shall not apply to those licensed before May 1, 1956.[5]

3. When a license to preach has lapsed, it may be reinstated only at the discretion of the District Committee on Ministerial Qualifications, when or if the candidate has completed satisfactorily the current studies for the license to preach.

Note: For special provisions regarding local preachers who are approved supply pastors *see* ¶¶ 317, 320.

¶ 308. A local preacher, ordained or unordained, who is not serving a charge under a district superintendent, shall be a member of, and amenable to, the Quarterly Conference where he resides, except as hereinafter stated. When he changes his residence, he shall procure from his pastor or district superintendent a certificate of his official standing and dismissal and shall present it to the pastor of the charge to which he has moved. If he neglects to do this, he shall not be recognized or use his office as a local preacher in the charge to which he has moved; and he shall continue to be amenable to the Quarterly Conference of the charge from which he has moved, which, if the neglect is long continued, after due notice (thirty days) may try him for persistent disobedience to the order of the church, and upon conviction thereof deprive him of his ministerial office and credentials.

¶ 309. 1. A local preacher, other than a student as defined in § 2 below, who is appointed to serve under a district superintendent as supply pastor shall procure from his pastor or district superintendent a certificate of his official standing and of dismissal, and shall present it to the Quarterly Conference of the charge to which he is appointed at its next session. His church membership

---

[5] Amended in 1956 following Judicial Council Decision 100.

shall be in that charge to which he is appointed; and he
shall be a member of, and amenable to, its Quarterly
Conference, subject to the jurisdiction of the Annual Conference.[6]

2. A local preacher who is serving as student supply
pastor while attending a college or school of theology accredited or approved by the University Senate may retain
his membership in his home church and Quarterly Conference, but in the discharge of his ministerial functions
he shall be amenable to the district superintendent under
whom he serves.

¶ 310. When a full member of an Annual Conference is
voluntarily located (¶¶ 374-76), or an ordained member on
trial is discontinued (¶ 321), he shall become a local
preacher with membership in the Quarterly Conference of
the pastoral charge where he resides.[7] When an unordained
member on trial is discontinued, a District Committee on
Ministerial Qualifications, after consultation with the
Board of Ministerial Training and Qualifications of the
Annual Conference which discontinued him, may grant
him a license to preach, which may be renewed as
provided in ¶ 307. A preacher who has been located or
discontinued shall be subject to the provisions of ¶¶ 308,
312, 362.3, and 432.8.

¶ 311. Whenever a local preacher, ordained or unordained, severs his relation with The Methodist Church,
the district superintendent shall require his license and
credentials of him, and shall file them with the secretary
of the Annual Conference.[8] (*See* ¶¶ 994-95.)

¶ 312. A local preacher not serving a pastoral charge
shall make to the Quarterly Conference and the District
Committee on Ministerial Qualifications, and to the
District Conference on request, a report of his labors,
as follows: (1) number of sermons preached; (2) number
of funerals conducted, with the names of the deceased;
(3) evangelistic, educational, and missionary work done
in co-operation with and under the direction of his pastor;

---

[6] *See* Judicial Council Decision 112.
[7] *See* Judicial Council Decisions 110, 173.
[8] *See* Judicial Council Decision 110.

(4) progress made in academic work or in the prescribed course of study; (5) miscellaneous items. If he is ordained, he shall include in his report the following: (6) number of marriages performed, with the names of persons married; (7) number of baptisms administered, with the names and birth dates of the persons baptized. He shall report items 2, 6, and 7 to the pastor for entry in the church records.[9]

Sec. II.   **Approved Supply Pastors**

¶ 314. An **approved supply pastor** is a local preacher, as defined in ¶ 304, who on recommendation of the Board of Ministerial Training and Qualifications has been approved by the Annual Conference as eligible for appointment during the ensuing year as a supply pastor of a charge. The approval shall be based on compliance with ¶¶ 306-7 (except as provided in ¶ 317.3) and 315-17 and shall expire unless renewed on the same basis at the next regular conference session. It does not guarantee an appointment but merely certifies eligibility. An appointment made thereunder may be terminated at any time during the conference year by a majority vote of the district superintendents.

¶ 315. 1. A local preacher desiring to become, or to continue as, an approved supply pastor must have his character, fitness, training, and effectiveness passed by a three-fourths majority of the District Committee on Ministerial Qualifications (¶ 695.3-.4), and by the Annual Conference after reference to and recommendation by its Board of Ministerial Training and Qualifications.

2. Between conference sessions a local preacher not on the approved supply pastors list may be appointed as a supply pastor. (*See* ¶¶ 362.3, 432.8.) If he fails to be approved at the following conference session, he cannot thereafter serve as a supply pastor until he is approved.[10]

¶ 316. 1. On recommendation of the board the conference may approve annually students of other denominations enrolled in a school of theology accredited or

---

[9] *See* Judicial Council Decision 197.
[10] *See* Judicial Council Decision 206.

approved by the University Senate to serve as supply pastors for the ensuing year under the supervision of a district superintendent.

2. On recommendation of the board the conference may also approve annually ministers in good standing in other evangelical denominations to serve as supply pastors while retaining their denominational affiliation; *provided* that they shall agree in writing to support and maintain the doctrine and polity of The Methodist Church while so serving. Their ordination credentials may be recognized as valid in The Methodist Church while they are serving therein.

¶ 317. In recommending to the conference those who have met the requirements to become approved supply pastors for the ensuing year the board shall classify them in three categories with educational requirements as hereinafter specified. Every approved supply pastor shall meet the educational requirements of his category. Any preacher who fails to meet these requirements shall not be appointed by a district superintendent. The categories shall be as follows:

1. Those eligible to be appointed as **student approved supply pastors.** These shall be enrolled as pretheological or theological students, under the definitions and requirements of ¶ 307.1 and ¶ 316.1.

2. Those eligible to be appointed as **full-time approved supply pastors.** A full-time approved supply pastor is a local preacher, ordained or unordained, (*a*) who meets the provisions of ¶¶ 306-7, 314-16; (*b*) who, unless ordained elder, has met the educational requirements by completing in the preceding year a full year's work in the ministerial course of study under the Department of Ministerial Education (¶ 1373) in a school for courses of study (*provided*, however, that in a case of emergency or unusual circumstances, on approval by the board, he may be authorized to pursue the course for the current year by correspondence); (*c*) who devotes his entire service to the church in the charge to which he is appointed; and (*d*) whose cash support per annum from all church sources is a sum equivalent to not less than the minimum salary

established by the Annual Conference for full-time approved supply pastors.[11] (*See* ¶ 1631.1.)

3. Those eligible to be appointed as **part-time approved supply pastors.** A part-time approved supply pastor is one (*a*) who does not devote his entire service to the charge to which he is appointed, (*b*) who does not receive in cash support per annum from all church sources a sum equivalent to the minimum salary established by the Annual Conference for full-time approved supply pastors, and (*c*) who completes a minimum of two books a year in the course of study, *provided* that the entire introductory studies and four-year course shall be completed in a maximum of twelve years from the time of first enrollment. A person who has met the qualifications for approval as a supply pastor may request to be classified as eligible to be appointed as a part-time approved supply pastor for the ensuing year.

¶ **318.** 1. An unordained approved supply pastor, only while serving as a regularly appointed pastor of a charge, may be permitted to administer the Sacraments of Baptism and the Lord's Supper and, if the laws of the state permit, to perform the marriage ceremony within the bounds of the charge to which he is assigned; *provided* that (*a*) he shall have completed one fourth of the work required for the bachelor of divinity or equivalent degree in a school of theology accredited or approved by the University Senate, or shall have passed the introductory studies for the ministry (¶ 1373); and (*b*) each succeeding year he shall be enrolled as a regular full-time student in a pretheological or theological course in a college, university, or school of theology accredited or approved by the University Senate or by the state accrediting agency, or shall have passed one full year of the ministerial course of study looking to full ordination. Failure to complete one full year annually shall cause suspension of this privilege. Authorization must be given in writing by the resident bishop under whom he serves after approval by the Annual Conference. In all missionary fields abroad the

---

[11] Amended in 1956 following Judicial Council Decision 91, and in 1960 following Decision 156.

conferring of such authorization shall rest with the Central Conference in which the pastor serves.[12]

2. An unordained part-time approved supply pastor (¶ 317.3) who has completed the introductory studies, and who shall have completed in the previous year one half of a full year's work in the ministerial course of study, shall be authorized, while serving as a regularly appointed pastor of a charge, to administer the Sacrament of Baptism and, if the laws of the state permit, to perform the marriage ceremony within the bounds of the charge to which he is assigned.

¶ 319. An approved supply pastor who is in charge of a pastoral appointment shall attend the sessions of the Annual Conference. (*See* ¶¶ 622, 645.)

¶ 320. When a local preacher is approved as a supply pastor, the Annual Conference alone has jurisdiction over his authority to preach. Continuance in this relation shall be equivalent to renewal of his license to preach. If at any time the conference declines to renew its approval of an unordained supply pastor, the District Committee on Ministerial Qualifications may renew his license to preach for one year; further renewal shall be subject to the provisions of ¶ 307. (*See* ¶¶ 362.3, 432.8.)

Chapter III

TRAVELING PREACHERS

Section I. **Admission of Preachers on Trial**

¶ 321. The first step into the traveling ministry of The Methodist Church is **admission on trial** into an Annual Conference. A member on trial is on probation as to his character, his preaching, and his competency as a pastor. During this period the church determines whether he is worthy of becoming a full member of the conference. A person on trial may be discontinued without any reflection on his character.[13]

---

[12] Amended in 1956 following Judicial Council Decision 91.
[13] *See* Judicial Council Decision 157.

¶ **322.** A candidate for the traveling ministry may be admitted on trial by vote of the ministerial members of an Annual Conference on recommendation of its Board of Ministerial Training and Qualifications after meeting the following conditions:

1. He must have a license to preach or have been ordained (¶ 304).

2. He must have been recommended in writing on the basis of a three-fourths majority vote of the District Conference or the District Committee on Ministerial Qualifications (¶¶ 690, 695.3-.4).

3. He must have met the educational requirements (¶¶ 323-25).

4. He must present a satisfactory certificate of good health, on the prescribed form, from a physician approved by the board. The conference may require psychological tests to provide additional information on the candidate's fitness for the ministry.

5. He must file with the board, in duplicate, on the prescribed form, satisfactory written answers to such questions as the board may ask concerning his age, health, family, religious and church experience, call to the ministry, educational record, and plans for service in the church. The following questions shall be included:

(1) Are you convinced that you should enter the ministry of the Church?

(2) Are you willing to face any sacrifices that may be involved?

(3) Are you in debt so as to interfere with your work, or have you obligations to others which will make it difficult for you to live on the salary you are to receive?

(4) If you are married, is your wife or husband in sympathy with your ministerial calling and willing to share in the sacrifices of your vocation?

(5) For the sake of a disciplined example, and without implying moral superiority, are you willing to make a complete dedication of yourself to the highest ideals of the Christian ministry with respect to purity of life in body, in mind, and in spirit, and to bear witness thereto by abstinence from all indulgences, including alcoholic

beverages and tobacco, which may injure your influence? [14]

(6) Are you willing to relate yourself in ministry to all persons without regard to race, color, or national origin, including receiving them into the membership and fellowship of the Church? (¶¶ 106.1, 1824.)

(7) Will you keep before you as the one great objective of your life the advancement of God's kingdom?

¶ **323.** A candidate for admission on trial must (1) have been graduated with a bachelor of arts or equivalent degree in liberal education in a college or university accredited or approved by the University Senate, and (2) have completed at least one fourth of the work required for a bachelor of divinity or equivalent degree in a school of theology accredited or approved by the University Senate, except under the special conditions of ¶ 325.

¶ **324.** Any Annual Conference may designate a bachelor of divinity or equivalent degree from a school of theology accredited or approved by the University Senate as the minimum educational requirement for admission on trial into that conference.

¶ **325.** Under special conditions an Annual Conference may, by a three-fourths majority vote, admit on trial a candidate who exhibits exceptional promise for the ministry in the following cases:

1. If he is a graduate with a bachelor of arts or equivalent degree in liberal education from a college not accredited by the University Senate who has completed one fourth of the work required for the bachelor of divinity or equivalent degree in a school of theology accredited or approved by the University Senate. (*See* ¶ 342.)

2. If he is a graduate with a bachelor of arts or equivalent degree in liberal education from a college accredited or approved by the University Senate, and has completed satisfactorily the introductory studies for the ministry and the first two years of the ministerial course of study (¶ 1373; *see also* ¶ 327).

3. If he is an approved supply pastor over thirty-five years of age who has (1) earned sixty semester hours of

---

[14] *See* Judicial Council Decisions 111, 157.

college credit, (2) completed the four-year ministerial course of study (¶ 1373), (3) served as an approved supply pastor in an Annual Conference for six consecutive years, and (4) been recommended by a three-fourths vote of the Cabinet and a three-fourths vote of the Board of Ministerial Training and Qualifications, written statements of such recommendations having been read to the conference before the vote is taken, setting forth the particular ways his ministry is exceptional and the special reasons he should be admitted on trial. (*See* ¶ 343.2.)

¶ 326. The Board of Ministerial Training and Qualifications shall require a transcript of credits from each applicant before recognizing any of his educational claims. In case of doubt the board may submit a transcript to the Department of Ministerial Education for evaluation.

¶ 327. A preacher who discontinues his theological education may request that the Department of Ministerial Education evaluate his theological work for credit in the ministerial course of study. He shall be exempted from any portion of the introductory studies or the four-year course for which he has already completed equivalent work in a school of theology accredited or approved by the University Senate provided the department shall have examined an official transcript thereof and certified it as equivalent.

¶ 328. While a member is on trial, the Annual Conference alone has jurisdiction over his authority to preach. His continuance on trial shall be equivalent to the renewal of his license to preach. (For discontinuance *see* ¶ 310.)

¶ 329. An unordained member on trial who is regularly appointed to a pastoral charge without an ordained colleague is subject to the provisions of ¶ 318.1.

¶ 330. A member on trial in a special appointment (¶ 432.4-.6) shall relate himself to the district superintendent in the area where his work is done, who shall give him supervision and report annually to his Board of Ministerial Training and Qualifications.

¶ 331. A member on trial who is pursuing the course of study shall do so in a school for courses of study (¶ 1373); *provided*, however, that in a case of emergency or unusual circumstances, on approval by the Board of Ministerial Training and Qualifications, he may be authorized to pursue the course for the current year by correspondence.

¶ 332. To be continued as a member on trial, the candidate shall make regular progress in his ministerial studies. In case of failure or delay, the Board of Ministerial Training and Qualifications shall investigate the circumstances and judge whether to extend the time, within the following limits: (*a*) for completing the theological course for the bachelor of divinity or equivalent degree, a total of eight years; (*b*) for completing the first two years of the ministerial course of study, a total of four years; (*c*) for completing the entire course of study, a total of six years. In a case clearly recognized as exceptional the board by a three-fourths vote may recommend an extension beyond these limits, which may be approved by a three-fourths vote of the Annual Conference; *provided*, however, that no candidate shall be continued on trial beyond the eighth regular conference session following his admission. (*See* ¶ 635.)

¶ 333. The educational standards and other requirements for admission shall be set by the Jurisdictional Conferences for the bilingual Annual and Provisional Annual Conferences within their territories, by the Central and Provisional Central Conferences for the Annual and Provisional Annual Conferences within their territories, and outside such territories by the Annual or Provisional Annual Conference itself.[15]

Sec. II.   **Admission into Full Connection**

¶ 341. A member on trial may be admitted into full connection in an Annual Conference by vote of its ministerial members, on recommendation of its Board of Ministerial Training and Qualifications,[16] provided he shall have: (*a*) served under episcopal appointment under the supervision of a district superintendent (*see* ¶ 330) satisfactorily to the board in one of the positions specified

---

[15] *See* Judicial Council Decision 187.
[16] *See* Judicial Council Decision 157.

in ¶ 432.1-.6 for at least two years since being admitted on trial; [17] (b) been previously ordained deacon (¶ 393); (c) fulfilled the educational requirements of ¶¶ 342-44; (d) satisfied the board regarding his physical, mental, and emotional health, by repeating the examination and tests described in ¶ 322.4 if so requested; (e) given satisfactory answers to the questions listed in ¶ 345.

¶ 342. A candidate for admission into full connection must have been graduated with a bachelor of divinity or equivalent degree in a school of theology accredited or approved by the University Senate, except under the special conditions of ¶ 343, and have completed the Methodist studies specified in ¶ 344. A candidate who was admitted on trial under the terms of ¶ 325.1 shall meet these requirements without exception.

¶ 343. 1. A candidate who was admitted on trial under the terms of ¶ 325.2 may meet the educational requirements for admission into full connection by completing the entire four-year ministerial course of study. (See ¶ 327.)

2. A candidate who was admitted on trial under the terms of ¶ 325.3 may meet the educational requirements for admission into full connection by completing four courses of special study by correspondence or in a school for courses of study under the direction of the Department of Ministerial Education.

3. Under conditions regarded as exceptional an Annual Conference may admit into full connection as provided in ¶ 341 a candidate otherwise qualified who, having discontinued his theological education subsequent to meeting the requirements of ¶ 323 for admission on trial, has completed all of the four-year ministerial course of study not covered by his theological work as provided in ¶ 327.

¶ 344. A candidate for admission into full connection on the basis specified in ¶ 342 shall present to the Board of Ministerial Training and Qualifications an official transcript showing a minimum of two semester or quarter hours of graduate credit (or their quantitative equiv-

---

[17] Amended in 1956 following Judicial Council Decisions 49, 122. See also Decision 152.

alent) in each of the fields of Methodist history, doctrine, and polity; *provided*, however, that a candidate unable to present such transcript may meet the requirement by undertaking a special course of study and/or examination in these fields provided and administered by the Department of Ministerial Education. (*See* ¶¶ 1375, 1379.)

Examination for Admission into Full Connection

[Here follow the questions which every Methodist preacher from the beginning has been required to answer upon becoming a full member of a conference. These questions were formulated by John Wesley and have been little changed throughout the years.—EDITORS.]

¶ 345. A preacher seeking admission into full connection in the conference shall, after solemn fasting and prayer, be asked, before the conference, the following questions, with any others which may be thought necessary, namely:

(1) Have you faith in Christ?

(2) Are you going on to perfection?

(3) Do you expect to be made perfect in love in this life?

(4) Are you earnestly striving after it?

(5) Are you resolved to devote yourself wholly to God and his work?

(6) Do you know the General Rules of our church?

(7) Will you keep them?

(8) Have you studied the doctrines of The Methodist Church?

(9) After full examination do you believe that our doctrines are in harmony with the Holy Scriptures?

(10) Will you preach and maintain them?

(11) Have you studied our form of church discipline and polity?

(12) Do you approve our church government and polity?

(13) Will you support and maintain them?

(14) Will you diligently instruct the children in every place?

(15) Will you visit from house to house?

(16) Will you recommend fasting or abstinence, both by precept and example?

(17) Are you determined to employ all your time in the work of God? [18]

(18) Are you in debt so as to embarrass you in your work?

(19) Will you observe the following directions?

(*a*) Be diligent. Never be unemployed. Never be triflingly employed. Never trifle away time; neither spend any more time at any one place than is strictly necessary.

(*b*) Be punctual. Do everything exactly at the time. And do not mend our rules, but keep them; not for wrath, but for conscience' sake.

SEC. III.   **Pastors**

¶ 351. A pastor is a preacher who, by appointment of the bishop or the district superintendent, is in charge of a station or circuit.

¶ 352. The duties of a pastor are:

1. To preach the gospel.

2. To administer the Sacraments of Baptism and the Lord's Supper and to perform the marriage ceremony, if qualified to do so under ¶ 318, ¶ 329, ¶ 392, or ¶ 402, and to bury the dead.

3. To visit from house to house in order to give pastoral guidance and oversight to the members of the church and others in need of a pastor's help.

4. To instruct candidates for membership in the church in the doctrines, rules, and regulations of the church; to receive persons into membership; to receive and dismiss members by certificate.

5. To form classes of the children, youth, and adults for instruction in the Word of God, and to perform the duties prescribed for the training of children.

6. To instruct youth in Christian ideals for marriage and family living, with special reference to the problems involved in interfaith marriages.

7. To organize and maintain church schools, Methodist Youth Fellowships, Young Adult Fellowships, Woman's Societies of Christian Service, and Methodist Men clubs.

---

[18] *See* Judicial Council Decision 82.

8. To hold or appoint prayer meetings, love feasts, and watch-night meetings, wherever advisable.

9. To have the oversight of the other preachers in his pastoral charge; and to arrange the appointments, wherever practicable, so as to give the local preachers regular employment on the Sabbath.

10. To see that class leaders are chosen, and to change them when necessary, and to examine each of them concerning his method of leading a class.

11. To administer all the provisions of the Discipline in his pastoral charge.

12. To see that the ordinances and regulations of the church are duly observed and that the General Rules are read and explained once a year in each congregation.

13. In the absence of the district superintendent and the bishop, to control the appointment of all services to be held in the churches in his charge.

14. To hold Quarterly Conferences, at the request of the district superintendent, and to serve as chairman of the Official Board, unless a chairman has been elected by the Official Board.

15. To explain the meaning and importance of the benevolences, and to urge their support by all the people in his charge.

16. To preach on the subject of missions and to nominate at the fourth Quarterly Conference, in case such nomination is not made by the Nominating Committee, a Commission on Missions and a chairman thereof for each congregation. (¶ 256.)

17. To preach on the subject of Christian education, and to urge upon parents the importance of educating their children, advising them to patronize the institutions of learning of our church.

18. To see that the people in the bounds of his charge are supplied with our church literature, including books, church-school literature, and the periodicals *Together*, *Christian Advocate*, and *Central Christian Advocate*.

19. To teach and preach on Christian stewardship, temperance, and world peace, and to promote these causes within the bounds of his charge.

20. *a*) To preach on the meaning of Christian vocation and the call and challenge of the ministry and other types of full-time church work, and to advise with youth, students, and young adults about their educational and vocational plans. (*See* ¶ 149.1)

b) To search out from among his membership and constituency young people for the ministry, to help them interpret the meaning of the call of God, to challenge them with the opportunities of the Christian ministry, to advise and assist them when they commit themselves thereto, to counsel with them and watch over them as their pastor through the course of their preparation, and to keep a careful record of all such decisions, reporting to the Annual Conference the number of such students enrolled in schools of theology accredited or approved by the University Senate.

21. To preach on the subject of the Bible and its circulation.

22. To make a written report to each Quarterly Conference on the following items:

a) The general state of the church in his charge.

b) The names of all who have been received into the church, with the method of reception indicated, and of all who have died, removed, withdrawn, or been expelled during the preceding quarter.

c) Number and condition of church schools, including Sunday-school meetings, weekday meetings of children, meetings of young people, fellowship meetings of adults, and vacation schools.

d) Number of sermons preached to children.

e) Other religious instruction conducted, with children and adults, including training classes.

f) Number of pastoral visits, and the use of the church-school roll in pastoral visitation.

g) Subscribers to our church periodicals.

h) Collections for benevolences.

i) Missions, including Woman's Societies of Christian Service, church extension, and missionary education in the church school.

j) Lay activities, including the financial system, lay

speaking, training of the Official Board or Boards, Christian stewardship, and Methodist Men.

k) Other items worthy of record.

l) Plans for future work.

23. To keep a separate membership record for each local church of his charge in which shall be noted the name, with the time and manner of reception and disposal, of every member of the church, including the names of preparatory members in a separate list. (*See* ¶¶ 131-32.)

24. To enter in the permanent official records of the church accurate information concerning all baptisms and marriages.

25. To keep and transmit to his successor two directories, the one in which the residences of all the members shall be recorded, and the other a constituency roll with like information.

26. To furnish to every person uniting with the church on profession of faith, or from preparatory membership, a certificate of membership.

27. To leave to his successor an account of his charge, including a list of subscribers to the benevolences and to our periodicals.

28. To make report to the Annual Conference of all items required for the statistics of the conference, and to deliver to the conference treasurer all moneys raised for benevolent causes, or satisfactory vouchers for the same, using the forms supplied by The Methodist Publishing House.

¶ 353. No pastor shall engage for an evangelist any person who is not a conference evangelist, a regular member of an Annual Conference, an approved supply pastor, a local preacher, or a lay speaker in good standing in The Methodist Church without first obtaining the written consent of his district superintendent.[19] (*See* ¶¶ 363, 1474.2, 1480.)

¶ 354. No pastor shall discontinue a preaching place in the interval between sessions of the Annual Conference without the consent of the Quarterly Conference and the district superintendent. (*See* ¶¶ 128, 188.)

---

[19] *See* Judicial Council Decision 204.

¶ 355. The pastor is urged to study and prepare for increasingly adequate marriage and family counseling.

1. In planning to perform the rite of matrimony the minister shall have one or more unhurried premarital conferences with the parties to be married to emphasize the spiritual values in all phases of marital and parental life. It is recommended that he use the official manual of the church. It is strongly urged that these conferences be held as early as possible before the date of the wedding.

2. The minister shall make his counsel available to those under the threat of marriage breakdown in order to explore every possibility of reconstructing the marriage.

¶ 356. In view of the seriousness with which the Scriptures and the Church regard divorce, a minister may solemnize the marriage of a divorced person only when he has satisfied himself by careful counseling that: (a) the divorced person is sufficiently aware of the factors leading to the failure of the previous marriage, (b) the divorced person is sincerely preparing to make the proposed marriage truly Christian, and (c) sufficient time has elapsed for adequate preparation and counseling.

SEC. IV.   District Superintendents

¶ 361. District superintendents are to be chosen and appointed by the bishop. (See ¶ 432.3.)

¶ 362. The duties of a district superintendent are:

1. To travel through his district, in order to preach and to oversee the spiritual and temporal affairs of the church.

2. In the absence of a bishop to have charge of all the traveling and local preachers in his district.

3. To change, receive, or appoint preachers during the intervals between conferences and in the absence of the bishop, as the Discipline directs; *provided* that he shall not appoint any preacher who has been rejected as an applicant, or who has been discontinued or located, except at his own request, unless the conference at the time of such rejection, discontinuance, or location shall grant such authority; and he shall not appoint any preacher who has previously been expelled from the ministry, or has surrendered his credentials to an Annual Conference,

unless the conference to which he surrendered his credentials, or from which he was expelled, restores his credentials, or recommends him; and he shall not appoint any local preacher who is not listed as an approved supply pastor, except between sessions of the Annual Conference, and then only until its next session.

4. To issue and renew licenses for local preachers in accordance with the action of the District Conference or District Committee on Ministerial Qualifications; and to furnish certified lists of the persons licensed and their addresses to the Department of Ministerial Education and to the secretary of the Annual Conference for insertion in the conference journal.

5. To preside, or to designate elders to preside, in the Quarterly Conferences of each pastoral charge, and to preside at the District Conference.

6. To take care that every part of the Discipline is observed in his district.

7. To see that all charters, deeds, and other conveyances of church property in his district conform to the Discipline and to the laws, usages, and forms of the county, state, territory, or country within which such property is situated.

8. To counsel with the pastors in his district in regard to their pastoral responsibilities and other matters affecting their ministry.

9. To advise and encourage local preachers, candidates for the ministry, and conference undergraduates in their studies.

10. To report the names and addresses of the church lay leaders in his district to the secretary of the Annual Conference for insertion in the conference journal; [20] to report the names and addresses of all candidates for the ministry to the Department of Ministerial Education; and to report the names and addresses of commission and committee chairmen, church-school superintendents, and church lay leaders elected by each Quarterly Conference in his district as may be requested by any general agency supplying report forms therefor.

---

[20] *See* Judicial Council Decision 146.

11. To prepare and deliver to his successor, and to the conference secretary, to be permanently recorded by him: (*a*) a list of all abandoned church properties and cemeteries within the bounds of his district; (*b*) a list of all church properties being permissively used by other religious organizations with the names of the local trustees thereof; (*c*) a list of all endowments, annuities, trust funds, investments, and unpaid legacies of which he has knowledge belonging to any pastoral charge or organization connected therewith in his district.

12. To report annually to the Annual Conference an accurate record of all financial transactions pertaining to abandoned properties.

13. To procure statistics from every charge and report them to the Annual Conference, in case the pastor should fail to make report; and to have the records of his District Conference at the Annual Conference for examination.

14. To decide all questions of law which may arise in the business of the Quarterly or District Conference, when submitted to him in writing, subject to an appeal to the president of the next Annual Conference.[21]

15. To promote all the interests of the church within the bounds of his district, in co-operation with the pastors and the Quarterly Conferences, giving particular attention to the following:

a) The cultivation of personal religion and the sharing of spiritual experience.

b) Evangelistic interest and activity among the churches and in behalf of the unevangelized.

c) Establishment of new preaching places and organization of new congregations wherever needed.

d) Missionary and social-service interests and activities, including the Woman's Societies of Christian Service, hospitals, homes, and orphanages.

e) Christian education, including the church schools, Methodist Youth Fellowships, church-related colleges, Wesley Foundations, and all other educational institutions and work. It shall be the duty of the district superin-

---

[21] *See* Judicial Council Decisions 29, 52.

tendent to bring the subject of Christian education before the Quarterly Conference of each pastoral charge. At least once a year he shall inquire into the character and effectiveness of the program of Christian education of every charge within his district. He shall co-operate with the Conference Board of Education and its executive secretary in promoting in all the churches of his district the plan of organization, the standards, and the literature provided or recommended by the General and Jurisdictional Boards of Education. He shall use the record and report forms provided by the General Board of Education for the use of district superintendents. He shall secure the names and addresses of the church-school superintendents of each charge and transmit them to the executive secretary of the Conference Board of Education on blanks furnished by the General Board of Education.

f) Christian literature, especially the circulation of our church papers and the distribution of literature and books issued by our Publishing House.

g) Lay activities, including personal evangelism, Christian stewardship, proper financial systems, temperance, social and economic justice, world peace, benevolences, and Christian life service.

h) Administration of the ordinances and Sacraments.

i) Formation of group ministries, larger parishes, or parish area plans to expedite the work of the church in larger areas.

16. To perform such other duties as the Discipline may direct. (*See Index.*)

¶ **363.** No district superintendent shall engage for an evangelist any person who is not a conference evangelist, a regular member of an Annual Conference, an approved supply pastor, a local preacher, or a lay speaker in good standing in The Methodist Church without first obtaining the written consent of his bishop.[22] (*See* ¶¶ 1474.2, 1480.)

SEC. V.   **Sabbatical Leave**

¶ **364.** Any minister who has been in the effective relation in any Annual Conference or Conferences for ten

---

[22] *See* Judicial Council Decision 204.

consecutive years from the time of his admission on trial may be granted a **sabbatical leave** by a bishop for one year without losing his relationship as an effective minister. This sabbatical leave is to be allowed for travel, study, rest, or for other justifiable reasons. Sabbatical leave granted by the bishop holding the conference must be upon the vote of the Annual Conference to which the minister belongs, after said minister has given notice to his district superintendent, and after the district superintendent has given notice to the bishop of his intention to request such sabbatical leave. A sabbatical leave shall not be granted to the same man more frequently than one year in seven.

SEC. VI.   **Supernumerary Ministers**

¶ 365. A **supernumerary minister** is one who, because of impaired health, or other equally sufficient reason, is temporarily unable to perform full work. This relation shall not be granted for more than five years in succession except by a two-thirds vote of the conference, upon recommendation of the Committee on Conference Relations,[23] and a statement of the reason for such recommendation. He may receive an appointment, or be left without one, according to the judgment of the Annual Conference of which he is a member; and he shall be subject to all limitations of the Discipline in respect to reappointment and continuance in the same charge that apply to effective ministers. In case he has no pastoral charge he shall have a seat in the Quarterly Conference, and all the privileges of membership, in the place where he resides. He shall report to the fourth Quarterly Conference, and to the pastor, all marriages performed and all baptisms administered. Should he reside outside the bounds of his Annual Conference, he shall forward to it annually a certificate similar to that required of a retired minister (¶ 370), and in case of failure to do so the Annual Conference may locate him without his consent. He shall have no claim on the conference funds except by vote of the conference.

---

[23] *See* Judicial Council Decision 105.

Sec. VII.   **Retired Ministers**

¶ 367. A **retired minister** is one who, at his own request, or by action of the Annual Conference, on recommendation of the Committee on Conference Relations, has been placed in the retired relation.[34]

¶ 368. Every clerical member of an Annual Conference whose seventy-second birthday precedes the first day of the regular session of his Annual Conference shall automatically be retired from the active ministry at said conference session.[25]

¶ 369. If any member of an Annual Conference who has attained age sixty-five or has completed forty years of full-time approved service, as defined in ¶ 1618, prior to the date of the opening session of the conference so requests, the Annual Conference may place him in the retired relation with the privilege of making an annuity claim.[26] (*See* ¶ 1617.)

¶ 370. Every retired minister who is not appointed as pastor of a charge shall have a seat in the Quarterly Conference, and all the privileges of membership in the church where he resides, except as set forth in ¶ 371. He shall report to the fourth Quarterly Conference and to the pastor all marriages performed and baptisms administered. If he resides outside the bounds of the conference, he shall forward annually to his conference a certificate of his Christian and his ministerial conduct, together with an account of the number and circumstances of his family, signed by the district superintendent or the pastor of the charge within the bounds of which he resides. Without this certificate the conference may, after due notice (thirty days) locate him without his consent.

¶ 371. In the case of a Quarterly Conference in a mission among non-English-speaking people, retired ministers of different race shall have a vote in the Quarterly Conference only when they shall have been duly elected to the same.

---

[24] *See* Judicial Council Decisions 87, 165.
[25] *See* Judicial Council Decisions 7, 15.
[26] *See* Judicial Council Decision 133.

Sec. VIII. **Termination of Annual Conference Membership**

By Voluntary Location

¶ 374. An Annual Conference may grant a member a certificate of location at his own request; *provided* that it shall first have examined his character at the conference session when the request is made and found him in good standing; and *provided*, further, that this relation shall be granted only to one who avowedly intends to discontinue regular ministerial or evangelistic work. This relation shall be certified by the president of the conference. The minister shall thereupon hold his membership, as local elder or deacon, in the Quarterly Conference of the charge where he resides, and shall be permitted to exercise ministerial functions only within the bounds of that charge, or of the charge to which he may be appointed. He shall report to the Quarterly Conference and the pastor all marriages performed, baptisms administered, and funerals conducted; and shall be held amenable for his conduct and the continuance of his ordination rights to the Annual Conference within which the Quarterly Conference membership is held.[27] (*See* ¶ 310.)

¶ 375. Whenever a member of the Annual Conference applies for a location it shall be asked: Is he indebted to the Publishing House? If it be ascertained that he is so indebted, the conference shall require him to secure said debt, if judged necessary or proper, before a location is granted.

¶ 376. A minister who has been located at his own request may be readmitted by an Annual Conference, at its discretion, upon presentation of his certificate of location and the recommendation of his District Committee on Ministerial Qualifications and of the Annual Conference from which he located.[28] (*See* ¶¶ 379, 1630.15.)

By Involuntary Location

¶ 377. Whenever it is determined by the Committee on Conference Relations that, in their judgment, a member

[27] *See* Judicial Council Decisions 110, 197.
[28] *See* Judicial Council Decisions 192, 197.

of the Annual Conference is unacceptable, inefficient, or indifferent in the work of the ministry, or that his conduct is such as to impair seriously his usefulness as a minister, or that his engagement in secular business, except as required by the ill health of himself or of his family, disqualifies him for pastoral work, they shall notify him in writing, and ask him to request location at the next session of the Annual Conference. If he refuses or neglects to locate as requested, the conference may, by count vote, on recommendation of the Committee on Conference Relations, locate him without his consent. In the case of involuntary location the authority to exercise the ministerial office shall be suspended, and the district superintendent shall require from him his credentials to be deposited with the secretary of the conference.

¶ 378. Whenever it is unanimously determined by the district superintendents that a member of the Annual Conference should be located for any of the reasons cited in ¶ 377, they shall notify him in writing of their judgment at least three months before the next session of the Annual Conference, and ask him to request location at such session under the provisions of ¶ 374. If he refuses or neglects to locate as requested, the district superintendent shall certify the fact to the Committee on Conference Relations, which committee shall proceed to recommend his immediate location without his consent. Upon such action his right to exercise the functions of the ministry shall be suspended, and the district superintendent shall require from him his credentials to be deposited with the secretary of the conference.

¶ 379. If a located person remains a member in good standing of The Methodist Church until the age of voluntary retirement fixed by the General Conference, he shall thereby retain the right to make an annuity claim, based upon his years of approved service; *provided*, however, that he shall have been readmitted by a two-thirds vote of the Annual Conference which granted him location; if it be nonexistent, then he shall apply for admission to the Annual Conference within the boundaries of which the major part of his service was rendered or its legal successor.[29] (*See* ¶¶ 376, 1630.15.)

By Surrender of the Ministerial Office

¶ 380. Any member of an Annual Conference in good standing who desires to surrender his ministerial office and withdraw from the conference may be allowed to do so by the conference at its session, in which case his credentials shall be filed with the official records of the Annual Conference of which he was a member, and his membership in the church shall be recorded in the society where he resides at the time of such surrender.

By Withdrawal

¶ 381. When a minister in good standing withdraws to unite with another church, his credentials should be surrendered to the conference, and if he shall desire it, they may be returned to him with the following inscription written plainly across their face, namely:

A. B. *has this day been honorably dismissed by the ——————— Annual Conference from the ministry of The Methodist Church.*

Dated ————— ——————, *President*

——————, *Secretary*

¶ 382. When in the interval between sessions of an Annual Conference a member thereof shall deposit with a bishop or with his district superintendent a letter of withdrawal from our ministry, or his credentials, or both, the same shall be presented to the Annual Conference at its next session for its action thereon.

SEC. IX. **Mission Traveling Preachers**

¶ 385. A **mission traveling preacher,** deacon, or elder, is one who is a member of a Mission without being a member of an Annual Conference. In the election of mission traveling deacons and elders the Mission shall require of all applicants the conditions and qualifications demanded of traveling deacons and elders by an Annual

---

[29] *See* Judicial Council Decision 197.

Conference. The duties, responsibilities, rights, and privileges of mission traveling deacons and elders shall be the same as those of traveling deacons and elders who are members of an Annual Conference; and such preachers may be transferred to an Annual Conference with the status attained in the Mission.

CHAPTER IV
MINISTERIAL ORDERS

SECTION I.   Deacons

¶ 391. A **deacon** is constituted by the election of the Annual Conference, on recommendation of the Board of Ministerial Training and Qualifications (¶ 671), and the laying on of the hands of a bishop.

¶ 392. A deacon has authority to preach, to conduct divine worship, to perform the marriage ceremony, to administer Baptism, and to assist an elder in administering the Lord's Supper; *provided* that, while serving as a regularly appointed pastor of a charge, he shall be authorized to administer the Lord's Supper under the conditions set forth in ¶ 318; and *provided*, further, that a local preacher who is ordained deacon shall be authorized to exercise ministerial functions only in the charge to which he is appointed or in which he resides.[30]

¶ 393. Preachers of the following classes are eligible for the order of deacon:

1. *Theological students* who have been admitted on trial after having met the requirements of ¶ 323 or ¶ 325.1.

2. *Members on trial in the course of study* who, after being admitted under ¶ 325.2, have been on trial for two consecutive years and have completed two years of the ministerial course of study under the supervision of the Board of Ministerial Training and Qualifications.

3. *Approved supply pastors* who have been under appointment for two consecutive years, have completed the introductory studies for the ministry and two full years of the ministerial course of study under the super-

---

[30] *See* Judicial Council Decision 204.

vision of the Board of Ministerial Training and Qualifications, and have been recommended in writing by their district superintendent and the District Committee on Ministerial Qualifications. (*See* ¶ 392.)

4. *Missionaries* who have been admitted on trial and are to be appointed by a bishop to a foreign Mission, or to a remote field in any conference, or to a church in a foreign country outside the boundary of a Mission or Annual Conference; *provided* that the presiding bishop and a majority of the district superintendents shall have recommended election to the order of deacon.

5. *Chaplains* who have been admitted on trial and in time of urgent need are to be appointed by a bishop to serve on full-time duty with the Armed Forces or other agency related to the Commission on Chaplains; *provided* that the presiding bishop and a majority of the district superintendents shall have recommended election to the order of deacon.

Sec. II.   **Elders**

¶ **401.** An **elder** is constituted by the election of the Annual Conference, on recommendation of the Board of Ministerial Training and Qualifications (¶ 671), and by the laying on of hands of a bishop and of elders.

¶ **402.** An elder has authority to preach, to conduct divine worship, to administer the Sacraments of Baptism and the Lord's Supper, and to perform the marriage ceremony; *provided*, however, that a local preacher who is ordained elder shall be authorized to exercise ministerial functions only in the charge to which he is appointed or in which he resides.[31]

¶ **403.** Preachers of the following classes are eligible for the order of elder:

1. *Theological graduates* who have been deacons for at least one year and have been received into full connection after having met the requirements of ¶ 342.

2. *Course of study graduates* who have been deacons for at least two years and have been received into full connection after having met the requirements of ¶ 343.

---

[31] *See* Judicial Council Decision 204.

3. *Missionaries* who have served under appointment as deacons for one full year, have been admitted into full connection, and are to be appointed by a bishop to a foreign Mission, or to the pastorate of a church in a foreign country outside of a Mission or Annual Conference, or to a Mission among foreign people within an English-speaking conference.

4. *Chaplains* who have been admitted into full connection and in time of urgent need are to be appointed to serve on full-time duty with the Armed Forces or other agencies related to the Commission on Chaplains.

¶ 404. When a preacher has fulfilled the requirements for ordination and has been elected to the order of deacon, but fails to receive his ordination through the absence of the bishop, his eligibility to the order of elder shall count from the time of his election to the order of deacon.

¶ 405. No persons shall be elected to elder's orders except such as are of unquestionable moral character and genuine piety, sound in the fundamental doctrine of Christianity and faithful in the discharge of gospel duties.[32]

CHAPTER V

MINISTERS FROM OTHER CHURCHES

¶ 411. Ministers coming from other evangelical churches, provided they present suitable testimonials of good standing through the Board of Ministerial Training and Qualifications, and give assurance of their faith, Christian experience, and other qualifications, and give evidence of their agreement with us in doctrine and discipline, and present a satisfactory certificate of good health on the prescribed form, from a physician approved by the Board of Ministerial Training and Qualifications, and meet the educational requirements, may be received into our ministry in the following manner:

1. The District Conference or District Committee on Ministerial Qualifications may receive them as local

---

[32] *See* Judicial Council Decision 157.

preachers not entitled to administer the Sacraments, pending the recognition of their orders by the Annual Conference.

2. The Annual Conference may recognize their orders as local deacons or elders provided their qualifications meet the educational and other requirements of the Discipline. (*See* ¶¶ 327, 393, 403.)

3. On recommendation of the District Committee on Ministerial Qualifications and the Board of Ministerial Training and Qualifications, the Annual Conference may recognize their orders and admit them into the membership of the conference, either on trial or in full connection, provided their qualifications meet the educational and other requirements of the Discipline, including the requirements in Methodist history, polity, and doctrine.[38] (*See* ¶¶ 321-45, 393, 403, 635.)

4. Ministers from other churches who can meet the educational standards required of Methodist ministers may apply through the Board of Ministerial Training and Qualifications to the Annual Conference, which may recognize their credentials and receive them on trial or into the full membership of the conference; *provided* that candidates for admission under this or the preceding item shall be required to answer satisfactorily the questions in ¶¶ 322, 345; and *provided*, further, that those from other than Methodist churches must take upon themselves our ordination vows, without the reimposition of hands.

5. The Annual Conference, on recommendation of the Conference Board of Ministerial Training and Qualifications, may also receive on equal standing preachers who are on trial in the ministry of another Methodist church, using, however, special care that before they are admitted to full membership, they shall meet all the educational and other requirements. (*See* ¶¶ 321-45, 635.)

¶ 412. The Board of Ministerial Training and Qualifications of an Annual Conference is required to ascertain from a minister seeking admission into its membership on credentials from another denomination whether or not membership in the effective relation was previously held

---

[38] Amended in 1960 following Judicial Council Decision 31.

in an Annual Conference of The Methodist Church, or one of its legal predecessors, and if so, when and under what circumstances his connection with such Annual Conference was severed.

¶ 413. A minister seeking admission into an Annual Conference on credentials from another denomination who has previously withdrawn from membership in the effective relation in an Annual Conference of The Methodist Church, or one of its legal predecessors, shall not be admitted or readmitted without the consent of the Annual Conference from which he withdrew, or its legal successor, or the Annual Conference of which the major portion of his former conference is a part.[34]

¶ 414. Whenever the orders of a minister are recognized according to the foregoing provisions, he shall be furnished with a certificate signed by the bishop according to the form:

This is to certify that the ——— Annual Conference of The Methodist Church, having examined the credentials of the Rev. A. B. as ——— [an elder or a deacon] of the ——— Church, and having received other testimonials of his graces, gifts, and usefulness, and being satisfied therewith, has this day accepted and recognized him in due form as ——— [an elder or a deacon] in The Methodist Church, entitled to exercise under its authority all the functions pertaining to that ordination, so long as his life and doctrine become the gospel of Christ.

Given under my hand and seal at ——— this ——— day of ——— in the year of our Lord ———.

———, *President*

¶ 415. When the orders of a minister of another church shall have been duly recognized, his certificate of ordination by said church shall be returned to him with the following inscription written plainly across its face:

Accredited by the ——— Annual Conference of The Methodist Church, this ——— day of ———, 19———, as the basis of new credentials.

———, *President*
———, *Secretary*

---

[34] ¶¶ 412-13 were added in 1944 following Judicial Council Decision 16.

Chapter VI

EPISCOPACY

Section I. **General Provisions**

¶ 421. The general plan of episcopal supervision, including the **Council of Bishops,** is set forth in the Constitution (¶¶ 20, 34-41, 47 i, vi, 48.2; *see also* ¶¶ 8.5, 9.2, 15.2, 19.2, 43.1-.4).

¶ 422. The Jurisdictional and Central Conferences are authorized to fix the percentage of votes necessary to elect a bishop. It is recommended that at least three fifths of those present and voting be necessary to elect.

¶ 423. The bishop or bishops elected by a Jurisdictional or Central Conference shall be consecrated at the session of the conference at which the election or elections take place, or at an adjourned session thereof, or at a time and place designated by the conference. At the consecration service the other Jurisdictional and Central Conferences and the church at large may be represented by one or more bishops appointed by the president of the Council of Bishops.[35]

¶ 424. In the case of an emergency in a Central Conference through the death or expiration of term of service or any other disability of a bishop, the Council of Bishops may assign one of its number to furnish the necessary episcopal supervision for that field.

¶ 425. The Council of Bishops may, with the consent of the bishop and with the concurrence of the standing Committee on Episcopacy of the jurisdiction involved, assign one of its number to some specific church-wide responsibility, deemed of sufficient importance to the welfare of the total church, for a period of a year. In this event he shall be released from the presidential responsibilities within his episcopal area for that term, and another bishop or bishops, active or retired, and not necessarily from the same jurisdiction, shall be designated by the Council of Bishops, on recommendation of the College of Bishops of the jurisdiction involved, to assume his presi-

[35] *See* Judicial Council Decision 61.

dential responsibilities during the interim. This assignment may be renewed for a second year by a two-thirds action of the Council of Bishops, a majority of the Committee on Episcopacy, and consent of the bishop and the College of Bishops involved. He shall continue to receive his regular stipend.

¶ **426.** A bishop who has served for not less than two quadrenniums may be granted a sabbatical leave for not more than one year for a justifiable reason other than health (for health *see* ¶ 775) if he so requests and if the College of Bishops of which he is a member, the Committee on Episcopacy of that jurisdiction, and the Council of Bishops or its executive committee approve. In this event he shall, for the period for which the leave is granted, be released from the presidential responsibilities within his episcopal area, and another bishop or bishops, active or retired and not necessarily from the same jurisdiction, shall be designated by the Council of Bishops, on recommendation of the College of Bishops of the jurisdiction involved, to assume his presidential duties during the interim. He shall continue to receive his housing allowance for the period of the leave.

¶ **427.** The Council of Bishops shall promote the evangelistic activities of the church and shall furnish such inspirational leadership as the need and opportunity may demand.

¶ **428.** The Council of Bishops, with the co-operation of the Department of Ministerial Education, may plan for annual regional seminars for the orientation and instruction of ministers newly appointed to the district superintendency.

Note: For other responsibilities of the Council of Bishops *see Index.*

¶ **429.** There shall be a **Conference of Methodist Bishops,** composed of all the bishops elected by the General, Jurisdictional, and Central Conferences, and bishops of affiliated autonomous Methodist churches, which shall meet in each quadrennium immediately prior to the General Conference, on call of the Council of Bishops. In case of an emergency a special meeting of the conference may be called by the Council of Bishops at any time during the quadrennium. The expense shall be charged to the Episcopal Fund. The travel expense of bishops from affiliated autonomous Methodist churches shall be paid on the same basis as that of the bishops of The Methodist Church.

SEC. II.   **Duties, Powers, and Limitations**
of Bishops

¶ **431.** The duties of a bishop are:

1. To oversee the spiritual and temporal affairs of the church.

2. To preside in the General, Jurisdictional, Central, and Annual Conferences.

3. To form the districts according to his judgment, after consultation with the district superintendents, and after the number of the same has been determined by vote of the Annual Conference.

4. To fix the appointments of the preachers in the Annual Conferences, Provisional Annual Conferences, and Missions, as the Discipline may direct. He may appoint an associate pastor for a charge when in his judgment such an appointment is necessary.

5. To read the appointments of deaconesses.

6. To fix, either within their own conference or within the conference where they attend school, the Quarterly Conference membership of all ministers who are appointed to attend school.

7. To transfer, with the consent of the bishop of the receiving Annual Conference, a ministerial member of one Annual Conference to another, provided the ministerial member agrees to said transfer; [36] and to send immediately to the secretaries of both conferences involved, to the registrar of the conference in which the member is being received if he is on trial, and to the clearinghouse of the General Board of Pensions, written notices of the transfer of the member, and of his standing in the course of study if he is an undergraduate.

8. To organize such Missions as shall have been authorized by the General Conference.

---

[36] *See* Judicial Council Decisions 114, 163, 216.

9. To consecrate bishops, to ordain elders and deacons, to consecrate deaconesses, and to see that the names of the persons ordained and consecrated by him be entered on the journals of the conference, and that proper credentials be furnished to these persons.

10. To travel through the connection at large.

¶ 432. The following provisions and limitations shall be observed by the bishop when fixing the appointments:

1. He shall appoint preachers to pastoral charges annually after consultation with the district superintendents; *provided* that, before the official declaration of the assignments of the preachers, he shall announce openly to the Cabinet his appointments; and *provided*, further, that before the final announcement of appointments is made the district superintendents shall consult with the pastors concerning their specific appointments except when the pastors involved have left the seat of the Annual Conference without the permission of the Annual Conference.[37] Bearing in mind the stated goals of an inclusive church, he shall seek the co-operation of the Cabinet and congregations in the appointment of pastors without regard to race or color.

2. He may make or change the appointments of preachers in the interval between sessions of the Annual Conference as necessity may require, after consultation with the district superintendents.

3. He shall choose and appoint the district superintendents annually; but within the Jurisdictional Conferences of the United States he shall not appoint any minister a district superintendent for more than six consecutive years nor for more than six years in any consecutive nine years.

4. On the request in each case of an appropriate Methodist official, agency, or institution, and after consultation with the district superintendents, he may make appointments annually to positions in or through Methodist and Methodist-related agencies.[38]

5. On the request in each case of an appropriate official, agency, or institution, and on the recommendation of the

[37] *See* Judicial Council Decision 101.
[38] *See* Judicial Council Decisions 166, 167.

district superintendents, confirmed by a two-thirds vote of the Annual Conference, he may make appointments annually to positions in non-Methodist agencies; *provided* that in no such case shall The Methodist Church incur any financial responsibility.

6. On the recommendation of the Conference Board of Evangelism, confirmed by a two-thirds vote of the Annual Conference, he may appoint an effective member of the conference as conference evangelist; *provided* that the appointee shall meet the standards set up by the General and Conference Boards of Evangelism for conference evangelists. (*See* ¶¶ 1474.2, 1480.)

7. He may appoint a preacher on trial or a member of an Annual Conference who desires to attend school to any college or school of theology accredited or approved by the University Senate.[39]

8. He shall not appoint any preacher who has been rejected as an applicant, or who has been discontinued or located, except at his own request, unless the conference, at the time of such rejection, discontinuance, or location, shall give such liberty; and he shall not appoint as a supply any preacher who has previously been expelled from the ministry or has surrendered his credentials to an Annual Conference unless the conference to which he surrendered his credentials, or from which he was expelled, restores his credentials or recommends it.

9. Every traveling preacher, unless retired, supernumerary, on sabbatical leave, or under arrest of character, must receive an appointment.

¶ 433. When a bishop judges it necessary, he may divide a circuit, station, or mission into two or more charges and appoint the pastors thereto; and he may unite two or more circuits or stations and appoint one pastor for the united congregations.

¶ 434. Bishops shall discharge such other duties as the Discipline may direct. (*See Index.*)

SEC. III.   **Retired Bishops**

¶ 435. 1. If a bishop cease from traveling at large among the people without the consent of the Jurisdiction-

[39] *See* Judicial Council Decision 152.

al Conference, he shall not thereafter exercise in any
degree the episcopal office in The Methodist Church.

2. A bishop may voluntarily resign from the episcopacy at any session of his Jurisdictional Conference. A
bishop so resigning shall surrender to the secretary of
his Jurisdictional Conference his consecration papers,
and he shall be furnished with a certificate of his resignation which shall entitle him to membership as a traveling
elder in the Annual Conference of which he was last a
member, or its successor. When he or his surviving widow
and dependent children become conference claimants, the
Episcopal Fund shall pay a pension on account of his
service as a bishop and his Annual Conference or Conferences on account of his approved service therein.

3. A bishop who by reason of impaired health is temporarily unable to perform full work may be released
by the Jurisdictional Conference from the obligation to
travel through the connection at large. He may choose
the place of his residence, and the Council of Bishops shall
be at liberty to assign him to such work as he may be
able to perform. He shall receive his support as provided
in ¶ 775.

¶ 436. 1. A bishop whose seventieth birthday precedes
the first day of the regular session of his Jurisdictional
Conference shall be released at the close of that conference from the obligation to travel through the connection
at large, and from residential supervision.[40]

2. A bishop, at any age and for any reason deemed
sufficient by his Jurisdictional Conference, may be re-

---

[40] *See* Judicial Council Decision 199. The General Conference
of 1964 adopted, effective with the Jurisdictional Conferences of
1968, the following revision of ¶ 436.1: "A bishop shall be released from the obligation to travel through the connection at
large and from residential supervision at the close of the regular
session of his Jurisdictional Conference the first day of which
next precedes his seventy-second birthday; *provided*, however,
that a bishop retired from residential and presidential responsibilities in accordance with this rule shall receive full
episcopal salary and house allowance, in lieu of retirement benefits, until he attains the mandatory retirement age for all ministers (*see* ¶ 368) if, during such period, he holds himself available for assignment by the Council of Bishops to some distinctive
responsibility without further compensation. He shall be assigned
to work with an agency of the church only on specific invitation
of that agency."

leased by that body from the obligation to travel through the connection at large, and from residential supervision.

3. A bishop who has reached the age of sixty-five years, and who for any reason deems it wise that he retire, shall notify in writing the president (or secretary, in case he is the president) of the College of Bishops and the secretary of the standing Committee on Episcopacy (¶ 526) of his jurisdiction. The college and committee shall convene in a joint meeting on the call of the president (or secretary) of the college within two months after receipt of the request to retire. If both, acting separately, approve the retirement by majority vote of those present and voting, the bishop shall be accorded the retired relation as soon as possible, but not later than two months from that date. The secretary of the Council of Bishops and the treasurer of the Episcopal Fund shall be notified. The college, in co-operation with the Council of Bishops when required by the Discipline, shall make provision for the supervision of the vacated area for the remainder of the quadrennium.

4. If one third or more of the members of the College of Bishops or of the standing Committee on Episcopacy of a jurisdiction have reason to believe that, because of health impairment, a bishop in the jurisdiction is no longer able to perform full work or render effective service, and the bishop does not wish to retire, the college and committee shall convene jointly to consider the matter. If both, acting separately, by majority vote of those present and voting, decide that it is in the best interests of the church that the bishop retire, he shall be so informed by the president (or secretary) of the college. If the bishop objects to this recommendation, he may request an examination by a panel of three doctors, not including his own physician, selected by the president (or secretary) of the college and the chairman of the committee. If he declines to take an examination, or if the doctors after such an examination recommend his retirement, he shall be retired. The bishop involved shall not be eligible to vote on any of the above items. The secretary of the Council of Bishops and the treasurer of the Episcopal Fund shall be notified of the action. The college, in co-operation with

the Council of Bishops when required by the Discipline, shall arrange for the presidential supervision of the Annual Conferences of the vacated area for the remainder of the quadrennium.

5. A bishop who has been retired under § 1, § 2, or § 3 may, on vote of the Council of Bishops, be appointed to take charge of an episcopal area, or parts of an area, in case of the death, resignation, or disability of the resident bishop or because of judicial procedure (provided the request is made by a majority of the bishops in the jurisdiction of the proposed change). This appointment shall not continue beyond the next session of his Jurisdictional Conference.

¶ 437. 1. A bishop who has been released from the obligation to travel through the connection at large in accordance with any of the foregoing provisions shall not preside thereafter over any Annual Conference, Provisional Annual Conference, or Mission, or make appointments, or preside at the Jurisdictional or Central Conference, but may take the chair temporarily in any conference if requested to do so by the bishop presiding. He may participate in the Council of Bishops, but without vote.[41] In case, however, a retired bishop shall be appointed by the Council of Bishops to take charge of a vacant episcopal area, or parts of an area, under the provisions of ¶ 436.5, he may preside over sessions of an Annual Conference, Provisional Annual Conference, or Mission, make appointments, and participate and vote in the meetings of the bishops.

2. A bishop who has been released under any of the foregoing provisions may continue to exercise all the rights and privileges which pertain to the episcopal office, except as herein otherwise provided.

¶ 438. Each Central Conference shall determine the rules for retirement of its bishops; *provided* that the age of retirement shall not exceed that fixed for bishops in the jurisdictions. In the event of retirement allowances'

---

[41] *See* Judicial Council Decisions 35, 40.

being paid from the Episcopal Fund, these rules shall be subject to the approval of the General Conference.[42]

SEC. IV.   **Bishops in Jurisdictions**

¶ 439. 1. Each jurisdiction having 500,000 church members or less shall be entitled to five bishops, and for each additional 500,000 church members or major fraction thereof shall be entitled to one additional bishop; *provided*, however, that in those jurisdictions where this requirement would result in there being an average of more than 70,000 square miles per episcopal area, such jurisdiction shall be entitled to five bishops for the first 400,000 church members or less, and for each additional 400,000 church members or two thirds thereof shall be entitled to one additional bishop; and *provided*, further, that the General Conference may authorize any Jurisdictional Conference to elect one or more bishops beyond the quota herein specified in order to provide episcopal supervision for mission fields outside the territory of a Jurisdictional Conference.[43]

2. Whenever a bishop is transferred from the Central Jurisdiction to another pursuant to the provisions of the first subparagraph of ¶ 38, the jurisdiction to which the transfer has been made shall thereupon temporarily be entitled to one more bishop and the Central Jurisdiction shall be entitled to one less bishop; the prescribed quota as otherwise provided in § 1 for the regional jurisdictions shall remain in force, and new elections shall be made only up to the limit of such quota.

3. In the event a bishop is transferred to a regional jurisdiction on the request of the Jurisdictional Conference, that conference may nevertheless elect bishops up to the limit of its regular quota whether or not the transfer becomes effective before the completion of such election.

¶ 440. Each Jurisdictional Conference may fix the episcopal residences within its jurisdiction and assign the bishops to the same. (*See* ¶ 526.) The bishops of the juris-

---

[42] Amended in 1952 following Judicial Council Decision 83.
[43] *See* Judicial Council Decisions 84, 182.

diction shall fix the boundaries of the episcopal area.[44] It is recommended that in arranging the plan of episcopal supervision the bishops not assign to a newly elected bishop the Annual Conference of which he was a member at the time of election.

SEC. V. **Bishops in Central Conferences**

¶ **441.** The Central Conferences shall elect bishops in the number determined by the General Conference, whose episcopal supervision shall be within the territory included in the Central Conference by which they have been elected, subject to such other conditions as the General Conference shall prescribe; *provided*, however, that a bishop elected by one Central Conference may exercise episcopal supervision in another Central Conference when so requested by such other Central Conference.

¶ **442.** A bishop elected by a Central Conference shall be constituted by election in a Central Conference and consecrated by the laying on of hands of three bishops, or at least one bishop and two elders.[45]

¶ **443.** A bishop elected by a Central Conference shall have, within the bounds of the Central Conference by which he is elected or within which he is administering, authority similar to that exercised by bishops elected by or administering in a Jurisdictional Conference.

¶ **444.** A bishop elected by a Central Conference shall have the status, rights, and duties within his territory of a bishop elected by or functioning in a Jurisdictional Conference. A bishop elected by a Central Conference shall have membership in the Council of Bishops and shall have the privilege of full participation with vote. (*See* ¶ 47 vi.) Attendance on the annual meetings of the Council of Bishops by bishops elected by Central Conferences shall be left to the option of the bishops in each Central Conference.[46]

¶ **445.** In a Central Conference where term episcopacy prevails, a bishop whose term of office expires prior to the time of compulsory retirement because of age, and who is

[44] *See* Judicial Council Decisions 48, 57, 84.
[45] *See* Judicial Council Decision 61.
[46] *See* Judicial Council Decisions 117, 164.

not re-elected by the Central Conference, shall be returned to membership as a traveling elder in the Annual Conference (or its successor) of which he ceased to be a member when elected bishop. His term of office shall expire at the close of the Central Conference at which his successor is elected, and he shall therefore be entitled to participate as a bishop in the consecration of his successor. The credentials of his office as bishop shall be submitted to the secretary of the Central Conference, who shall make thereon the notation that he has honorably completed the term of service for which he was elected and has ceased to be a bishop of The Methodist Church. (*See* ¶ 559.2.)

SEC. VI.   **Missionary Bishops**

¶ 446. 1. A **missionary bishop** is a bishop who has been elected for a specified foreign mission field with full episcopal powers, but with episcopal jurisdiction limited to the foreign mission field for which he was elected.[47]

2. Missionary bishops shall be included in all other provisions for the episcopacy, including relation to Jurisdictional Conferences, amenability, and provisions for support and retirement.

3. Notwithstanding the above definitions, in an emergency the Council of Bishops may assign a missionary bishop for specified service in any foreign field in consultation with the authorities, where such exist, of the Central Conference or the Provisional Central Conference concerned.

[47] *See* Judicial Council Decisions 21, 84, 127.

PART IV

THE CONFERENCES

CHAPTER I

THE GENERAL CONFERENCE

SECTION I.   Composition

¶ 501. The **General Conference** shall be composed of one ministerial member for every seventy ministerial members of each Annual Conference and one additional member for a major fraction thereof and an equal number of lay members, all of whom shall be elected by ballot and by a majority vote. The term "ministerial members" as used above shall refer to effective members of the Annual Conference and also supernumerary and retired members. Every Annual Conference shall be entitled to at least one ministerial and one lay member. The secretaries of the several Annual Conferences shall furnish certificates of election to the delegates severally, and shall send a certificate of such election to the secretary of the preceding General Conference immediately after the adjournment of said Annual Conference.

¶ 502. Members of the Council of Secretaries who are not elected members of the General Conference shall have the privilege of the floor on matters affecting the interests of their respective agencies, but without vote and at the expense of their respective agencies. If an agency by formal action shall so request, it may be represented by an associate secretary rather than by the regularly elected general or executive secretary.

¶ 503. Each Provisional Annual Conference and Mission outside the United States may designate a member to meet with the standing committees and have the privilege of the floor of the General Conference on matters affecting the interests of his conference, but without vote and without expense to the General Conference except for the per diem during its sessions.

¶ **504.** 1. The ministerial and lay delegates and reserves to the General Conference shall be elected by ballot in accordance with the provisions of the Constitution (¶¶ 23, 47 iii, viii). The Annual Conference may prescribe rules for disseminating information about potential lay delegates.

2. The ministerial and lay members may meet separately to vote for the election of delegates to the General and Jurisdictional Conferences.[1]

3. The election of delegates, by ballot, shall be held at the session of the Annual Conference immediately preceding the General Conference.[1]

4. The General Conference recommends to the Annual Conferences that the delegates to the General Conference be first elected on a separate ballot, to be followed, after all the delegates to the General Conference have been elected, by balloting for delegates to the Jurisdictional Conference as reserves to the General Conference.

SEC. II. **Rules**

¶ **505.** It is recommended that the meeting place of the General Conference be rotated among the jurisdictions, provided satisfactory arrangements can be made for entertainment, with special reference to the requirement for equality of accommodations for all races, without discrimination or segregation.

¶ **506.** When the General Conference is in session, it shall require the presence of a majority of the whole number of delegates to the General Conference to constitute a quorum for the transaction of business; but a smaller number may take a recess or adjourn from day to day in order to secure a quorum, and at the final session may approve the journal, order the record of the roll call, and adjourn *sine die.*

---

[1] *See* Judicial Council Decision **76.**

¶ **507.** The ministerial and lay members shall deliberate as one body. They shall vote as one body, but a separate vote shall be taken on any question when requested by one third of either order of delegates present and voting. In all cases of separate voting it shall require the concurrence of a majority of each order to adopt the proposed measure. However, in the case of changes in the Constitution, a vote of two thirds of the General Conference, as provided in the Constitution, shall be required.

¶ **508.** The plan of organization and rules of order of the General Conference shall be the plan of organization and rules of order as published in the journal of the preceding General Conference until they have been altered or modified by the action of the General Conference.

¶ **509.** The General Conference by a two-thirds vote of the delegates present, the Council of Bishops by a two-thirds vote, or two thirds of all the Annual Conferences by a majority vote of each conference, shall have the power to call at any time an extra session of the General Conference, to be held at such time as the Council of Bishops may choose and at such place as a committee chosen by the Council of Bishops may fix. The purpose of such extra session shall be stated in the call, and only such business shall be transacted as is in harmony with the purpose stated in the call. The General Conference thus called shall be composed of the delegates elected to the preceding General Conference, except when an Annual Conference shall prefer to have a new election.

¶ **510.** 1. Any organization, minister, or lay member of The Methodist Church may petition the General Conference by sending to the secretary a signed petition containing information indicating that the sender or senders are members of The Methodist Church.

2. It is recommended that each petition meet the following requirements: (*a*) Three copies of it shall be supplied to the secretary in time to be received by him not later than thirty days before the opening of the conference session; *provided*, however, that the secretary shall accept up to the opening day petitions from organizations and members overseas and from Annual Conferences meeting within thirty days before the General

Conference. (*b*) It shall deal with only one subject, and propose revisions within only one chapter of the Discipline. (*c*) If it is one of a series, each petition shall be written on a separate sheet. (*d*) It shall be addressed: "To the Members of the General Conference."

3. All petitions timely received shall be processed by the secretary so that they may be received by the appropriate legislative committees at their first meeting.

4. All general and specific quadrennial reports directed to the General Conference, including the reports of the Co-ordinating Council, shall be submitted to the duly elected delegates at least forty-five days prior to the opening of the conference session; and the content of said reports or sections thereof shall be submitted to the appropriate legislative committees prior to presentation on the conference floor, so that the committees may have opportunity to consider them in conjunction with related petitions.

SEC. III.   **General Conference Powers**

¶ 511. General Conference powers, and the restrictions thereon, are set forth in the Constitution (¶¶ 8-10; *see also* ¶¶ 11, 15-16, 18-19, 27, 30-33, 36, 42, 46, 47 i, ii, iv, ix).

¶ 512. 1. No person, no paper, no organization has the authority to speak officially for The Methodist Church, except only the General Conference under the Constitution.

2. Any individual Methodist called to testify before a legislative body to represent The Methodist Church shall be allowed to do so only by reading, without elaboration, the resolutions and positions adopted by the General Conference.

CHAPTER II

THE JURISDICTIONAL CONFERENCE

SECTION I.   **General Provisions**

¶ 516. All Jurisdictional Conferences shall have the same status and the same privileges of action within the limits fixed by the Constitution. (¶ 12.)

¶ **517.** The Jurisdictional Conference shall be composed of one ministerial delegate for every thirty ministerial members of each Annual Conference, or major fraction thereof, and an equal number of lay delegates; *provided* that no Annual Conference shall be denied the privilege of two delegates, one lay and one ministerial.[2]

¶ **518.** The ministerial and lay delegates and reserves to the Jurisdictional Conferences shall be elected by ballot in accordance with the provisions of the Constitution. (¶¶ 23, 47 iii, viii.)

¶ **519.** The ministers and lay delegates shall deliberate in one body.

¶ **520.** Each Jurisdictional Conference shall meet within the twelve months succeeding the meeting of the General Conference, but not earlier than six weeks after the convening of the General Conference, at such time and place as shall have been determined by the preceding Jurisdictional Conference or by its properly constituted committee.

¶ **521.** The Jurisdictional Conference shall adopt its own procedure, rules, and plan of organization. It shall take a majority of the whole number of delegates elected to make a quorum for the transaction of business. But a smaller number may take a recess or adjourn from day to day, and at the final session may approve the journal, order the record of the roll call, and adjourn *sine die.*

¶ **522.** The Jurisdictional Conference shall provide for the expenses of its sessions.

¶ **523.** 1. The Jurisdictional Conference may order a special session in such manner as it shall determine.

2. The College of Bishops of a jurisdiction by a two-thirds vote shall have authority to call a special session of the Jurisdictional Conference when necessary; *provided*, however, that if an episcopal area is left vacant by reason of death, retirement, or other cause within twenty-four months of the close of the preceding Jurisdictional Conference, the College of Bishops may by majority vote convene within three months, after giving not less than thirty days' notice, a special session of the Jurisdictional

---

[2] *See* Judicial Council Decision 125.

Conference for the purpose of electing and consecrating a bishop and of considering any other matters specified in the call; and *provided*, further, that in such case the standing Committee on Episcopacy may recommend to the conference reassignment of one or more of the previously elected bishops.

3. The delegates to a special session of the Jurisdictional Conference shall be the delegates last elected by each Annual Conference at the time of issue of the call for the special session.

4. A called session of the Jurisdictional Conference cannot transact any other business than that indicated in the call.

¶ 524. The Jurisdictional Conference shall be presided over by the bishops of the jurisdiction, except as provided in ¶ 38. In case no bishop of the jurisdiction is present, the conference may elect a president from the ministerial delegates.

¶ 525. A bishop elected by or administering in a Jurisdictional Conference shall be amenable for his conduct to his Jurisdictional Conference. Any bishop shall have the right of appeal to the Judicial Council.

¶ 526. 1. The Jurisdictional Conference shall elect a standing **Committee on Episcopacy,** to consist of one ministerial and one lay delegate from each Annual Conference, on nomination of the Annual Conference delegation.[3]

2. The committee shall review the work of the bishops, pass on their character and official administration, and report to the Jurisdictional Conference its findings for such action as the conference may deem appropriate within its constitutional warrant of power.[4]

---

[3] The General Conference of 1964 ordered that on announcement by the Council of Bishops of the adoption of the amendments to the Constitution indicated in ¶ 48.1-.2 this subparagraph should be revised to read as follows: "The Jurisdictional Conference shall have a standing **Committee on Episcopacy,** which shall continue until the close of the calendar year immediately preceding the next General Conference, to consist of one minister and one lay delegate from each Annual Conference elected by the Annual Conference delegation."

[4] The General Conference of 1964 ordered that on announcement by the Council of Bishops of the adoption of the amendments to the Constitution indicated in ¶ 48.1-.2 the following

3. The committee shall recommend the assignments of the bishops to their respective residences, for final action by the Jurisdictional Conference;[5] *provided*, however, that it shall not reach any conclusion concerning residential assignments until all elections of bishops for that session are completed, except in the case of a bishop being transferred into the jurisdiction; and *provided*, further, that no bishop shall be recommended for assignment to the same residence for more than twelve consecutive years, not counting years served before 1960. It may also make recommendations to the bishops of the jurisdiction concerning the formation of the episcopal areas. (*See* ¶ 440.)

4. The committee shall not recommend assignment of, nor shall the conference assign, a newly elected bishop to a residence within the bounds of the Annual Conference of which he was a member at the time of his election; nor shall the conference recommend that he administer the area within which his membership was most recently held. (*See* ¶ 440.)

---

should be inserted as §§ 3-4, the remaining subparagraphs being renumbered accordingly:

"3. The persons elected by their respective delegations to serve on the several Jurisdictional Committees on Episcopacy shall meet jointly at the time of the General Conference, constituting an **Interjurisdictional Committee on Episcopacy**, not later than the fifth day of the conference session, and at the time and place set for their convening by the president of the Council of Bishops, and shall elect from their number a chairman, vice-chairman, and secretary. The functions of this joint committee shall be to discuss the possibility of transfers of bishops across jurisdictional lines at the forthcoming Jurisdictional Conferences, for residential and presidential responsibilities in the ensuing quadrennium. It shall elect an executive committee consisting of the officers above named and two ministers and two laymen from each jurisdictional committee, elected by that committee, to conduct consultations with bishops and others interested in possible episcopal transfers. The executive committee shall be responsible to the interjurisdictional committee.

"4. No bishop shall be transferred across jurisdictional lines unless he has consented to such transfer and has served at least one quadrennium in, or under assignment by, the jurisdiction in which he was elected, and unless a concurrent transfer is effected into the jurisdiction from which he is transferring, or unless the Jurisdictional Conference which is receiving him has voted to waive this right. Such a transfer shall not be concluded until the Committee on Episcopacy of each jurisdiction involved has approved the plan, insofar as it affects its own jurisdiction, by majority vote of those present and voting, and the Jurisdictional Conferences, meeting concurrently, have also approved."

[5] *See* Judicial Council Decision 182.

¶ 527. The Jurisdictional Conference shall have powers and duties as described in the Constitution (¶ 15). It shall also have such other powers and duties as may be conferred by the General Conference,[6] and in the exercise thereof it shall act in all respects in harmony with the policy of The Methodist Church with respect to elimination of discrimination on the basis of race.

¶ 528. In all elections in a Jurisdictional Conference which are based on the number of church members within that jurisdiction, the number counted shall include lay members, ministerial members, and bishops assigned to that jurisdiction. (*See* ¶¶ 439, 1072.)

¶ 529. The Jurisdictional Conference shall have authority to examine and acknowledge the journals of the Annual Conferences within its bounds, and shall make such rules for the drawing up of the journals as may seem necessary.

¶ 530. 1. The Jurisdictional Conference shall keep an official **journal** of its proceedings, duly signed by the secretary and president, the same to be sent for examination to the ensuing General Conference.

2. For the sake of convenience and uniformity, the journal when printed should conform in page size and formation to the General Conference journal; and the printing should be done at the expense of the jurisdiction by The Methodist Publishing House.

SEC. II.   **Jurisdictional Boundaries**

¶ 531. The Methodist Church in the United States of America shall have Jurisdictional Conferences made up as described in the Constitution (¶ 26). For methods of changing the number, names, and boundaries of the Jurisdictional and Annual Conferences see ¶¶ 28, 29, 47 ix in the Constitution and also ¶¶ 532, 680.

¶ 532. Any local church shall be transferred from the jurisdiction of which it is part to another jurisdiction in which it is located geographically upon completion of all the following actions, regardless of the order in which taken: (*a*) approval by the membership and the Quar-

---

[6] *See* Judicial Council Decision 67.

terly Conference of said church; (*b*) approval by both the Annual Conference of which the church has been a part and the Annual Conference to which transfer is desired; (*c*) approval by a majority of the Annual Conferences and also by the Jurisdictional Conference of both the jurisdiction of which the church has been a part and the jurisdiction to which transfer is desired; and (*d*) approval by the General Conference in the form of an enabling act. Such transfer shall be effected when all of the required actions have been certified to the Council of Bishops by the secretaries of all the conferences involved, whereupon the Council of Bishops shall issue a declaration that the transfer has been duly effected.[7] (*See also* ¶ 680.)

Sec. III.   **Property**

¶ **533.** The Jurisdictional Conference shall not alienate any property or institution, or the proceeds derived from the sale or transfer of any property or institution, from The Methodist Church, nor shall the Jurisdictional Conference or any of its boards involve the General Conference boards or any other organization of the church in any financial obligation without the official approval of said board or organization.

¶ **534.** When property rights are involved by the change of boundary lines of Annual Conferences within the jurisdiction, the Jurisdictional Conference shall constitute a committee of arbitration to adjust all claims and make final settlement of the same. In the case of interjurisdictional conflicts, the said committee shall act with a like committee from each of the other jurisdictions involved to reach a proper settlement.

¶ **535.** No invested funds, fiduciary trusts, or property acquired by bequest, donation, or otherwise for specific objects within the boundaries of an Annual Conference or Conferences may be diverted to other purposes except by the consent of the Annual Conference or Conferences involved and with the consent of the Jurisdictional Conference or Conferences concerned, and civil court approval

---

[7] Adopted in 1952 following Judicial Council Decisions 28, 32, 55, 56, 85.

when necessary; *provided* that local churches possessing such funds or property shall not be required to obtain the consent of the Jurisdictional Conferences. The same rule shall apply to similar funds or properties acquired by the Jurisdictional Conferences for work specifically jurisdictional in its scope. In such cases the Jurisdictional Conference shall determine the disposition of the interests involved, subject to an appeal to the Judicial Council.

Provided, moreover, that trust funds may not be divided or diverted to other purposes than for the specific objects for which donated, even with the consent of Annual Conferences or Jurisdictional Conferences, unless the said conferences are the beneficiaries of said trust funds or control them.[8]

Chapter III

THE CENTRAL CONFERENCE

Section I.   Authorization

¶ **541.** In territory outside the United States of America, Annual Conferences, Provisional Annual Conferences, and Missions in such numbers as the General Conference by a two-thirds vote shall determine may be organized by the General Conference into Central Conferences or Provisional Central Conferences with such duties, privileges, and powers as are hereinafter set forth and as the General Conference by a two-thirds vote shall prescribe.

¶ **542.** There shall be such Central Conferences as have been authorized, or shall be hereafter authorized by the General Conference; *provided* that a Central Conference shall have at least a total of thirty ministerial and thirty lay delegates on the basis of representation as set forth in ¶ 543, except as the General Conference may fix a different number. A Central Conference now in existence may be continued with a lesser number of delegates for reasons deemed sufficient by the General Conference.

---

[8] *See* Judicial Council Decision 64.

Sec. II.   **Organization**

¶ **543.** The **Central Conference** shall be composed of ministerial and lay members in equal numbers, the ministerial elected by the ministerial members of the Annual Conference and the lay by the lay members thereof. For the first meeting their qualifications shall be the same as provided in ¶ 47 iii, viii, and the Annual Conference shall determine the manner of their choice. Thereafter, their qualifications and the manner of election shall be determined by the Central Conference itself.[9] Each Annual Conference and Provisional Annual Conference shall be entitled to at least two ministerial and two lay delegates, and no other selection of delegates shall be authorized which would provide for more than one ministerial delegate for every six ministerial members of an Annual Conference, except that a majority of the number fixed by a Central Conference as the ratio of representation shall entitle an Annual Conference to an additional ministerial delegate and to an additional lay delegate. A Mission is authorized to elect and send one of its members to the Central Conference concerned as the representative of the Mission, said representative to be accorded the privilege of sitting with the committees of the Central Conference, with the right to speak in the committees, and in the regular sessions of the Central Conference, but without the right to vote. The representative of the Mission shall have the same claim for payment of expenses as is allowed to members of the Central Conference.

¶ **544.** The first meeting of a Central Conference shall be called by the bishop or bishops in charge, at such time and place as he or they may select, to which members of the Annual Conferences, Provisional Annual Conferences, and Missions concerned shall be elected on the basis of representation in accordance with ¶ 543. The time and place of future meetings shall be determined by the Central Conference or its executive committee.

¶ **545.** Each Central Conference shall meet within the year succeeding the session of the General Conference, at such time and place as the Central Conference itself or

---

[9] *See* Judicial Council Decision 124.

its bishops may determine, with the right to hold such adjourned sessions as it may determine. The sessions of said conference shall be presided over by the bishops. In case no bishop be present, the conference shall elect a temporary president from among its own members. The bishops resident in a Central Conference, or a majority of them, with the concurrence of the executive committee or other authorized committee, shall have the authority to call an extra session of the Central Conference to be held at the time and place designated by them.

¶ 546. The Council of Bishops may assign one or more of their number to visit any Central Conference or Provisional Central Conference. When so assigned, the bishop shall be an accredited representative of the general church and, when requested by a majority of the bishops resident in that conference, may exercise therein the functions of the episcopacy. (*See also* ¶¶ 593, 604.)

¶ 547. The presiding officer of the Central Conference shall decide questions of order, subject to an appeal to the Central Conference, and he shall decide questions of law, subject to an appeal to the Judicial Council; but questions relating to the interpretation of the rules and regulations made by the Central Conference for the governing of its own session shall be decided by the Central Conference.

¶ 548. Each Central Conference within the bounds of which the Board of Missions has work shall maintain a co-operative and consultative relationship with the said board through a duly constituted executive committee, executive board, or council of co-operation; but the legal distinction between the Board of Missions and the organized church on the field shall always be kept clear.

¶ 549. The journal of the proceedings of a Central Conference, duly signed by the president and secretary, shall be sent for examination to the General Conference.

¶ 550. A Provisional Central Conference may become a Central Conference upon the fulfillment of the necessary requirements and upon the authorization of the General Conference.

SEC. III. **Central Conference Powers**

¶ **556.** To a Central Conference shall be committed for supervision and promotion, in harmony with the Discipline and interdenominational contractual agreements, the missionary, educational, evangelistic, industrial, publishing, medical, and other connectional interests of the Annual Conferences, Provisional Annual Conferences, and Missions within its territory, and such other matters as may be referred to it by said bodies, or by order of the General Conference; and it shall provide suitable organizations for such work and elect the necessary officers for the same.

¶ **557.** A Central Conference, when authorized by a specific enabling act of the General Conference, may elect one or more bishops from among the traveling elders of The Methodist Church. The number of bishops to be elected by each Central Conference shall be determined from time to time by the General Conference.[10]

¶ **558.** When a Central Conference shall have been authorized to elect bishops, such elections shall be conducted under the same general procedure as prevails in the Jurisdictional Conferences for the election of bishops. A Central Conference shall have power to fix the tenure of bishops elected by the said Central Conference; *provided* that such tenure shall not be for a term longer than that in force at the time for bishops elected by the Jurisdictional Conferences.[11]

¶ **559.** 1. A Central Conference shall participate in the General Episcopal Fund on payment of its apportionment on the same basis as that fixed for Annual Conferences in Jurisdictional Conferences. When the total estimated support, including salaries and all allowances for the bishops elected by it, and the amount that it will be able to provide on apportionment, have been determined by a Central Conference, these amounts in itemized form shall be submitted to the Council on World Service and Finance. This council after consideration of the relative cost of living in various Central Confer-

---

[10] *See* Judicial Council Decision 182.
[11] *See* Judicial Council Decisions 4, 61, 80.

ences, shall determine the amount to be paid from the General Episcopal Fund in meeting the budget, after which the treasurer of the General Episcopal Fund shall pay the amount established to the bishop concerned, or as the Central Conference may determine.

2. A minister who has served a term, or part of a term, as a bishop in a Central Conference where term episcopacy has prevailed shall, upon his retirement from the effective relation in the ministry, be paid an allowance from the General Episcopal Fund in such sum as the Council on World Service and Finance shall determine for the years during which he served as a bishop. (*See* ¶ 445.)

¶ **560. 1.** A Central Conference, in consultation with the bishops of that Central Conference, shall fix the episcopal areas and residences and make assignments to them of the bishops who are to reside in that Central Conference.[12] The bishops of a Central Conference shall arrange the plan of episcopal visitation within its bounds.

2. The secretary of a Central Conference in which one or more bishops have been chosen shall report to the secretary of the General Conference the names of the bishop or bishops and the residences to which they have been assigned by the Central Conference.

¶ **561.** A Central Conference shall have authority to elect and support general officers in all departments of the work of the church within the boundaries of the Central Conferences, but may not determine the number of bishops.

¶ **562.** A Central Conference shall have power to make such changes and adaptations as the peculiar conditions on the fields concerned require regarding the local church, ministry, special advices, worship, and temporal economy within its territory, including the authorizing of associate members to participate in the offices of the local church under such rules as it may see fit, *provided* that no action shall be taken which is contrary to the Constitution and the General Rules of The Methodist Church.[13]

---

[12] *See* Judicial Council Decision 182.
[13] Amended in 1960 following Judicial Council Decisions 121, 142, 147, 155.

¶ **563.** A Central Conference shall have the authority to change the provisions for the ordination of ministers in such way that the ordination of an elder may follow immediately upon his ordination as a deacon, provided that other conditions are fully met.

¶ **564.** A Central Conference shall fix the boundaries of the Annual Conferences, Provisional Annual Conferences, and Missions within its bounds, proposals for changes first having been submitted to the Annual Conferences concerned as prescribed in the Discipline of The Methodist Church; *provided*, however, that the number of Annual Conferences which may be organized within the bounds of a Central Conference shall first have been determined by the General Conference. No Annual Conference shall be organized with fewer than thirty-five ministerial members, except as provided by an enabling act for the quadrennium, which shall not reduce the number below twenty-five. Nor shall an Annual Conference be continued with fewer than twenty-five ministerial members, except as provided by an enabling act for the quadrennium.

¶ **565.** A Central Conference may advise its Annual Conferences and Provisional Annual Conferences to set standards of character and other qualifications for admission of lay members.

¶ **566.** A Central Conference shall have power to make changes and adaptations in procedure pertaining to the Annual, District, and Quarterly Conferences within its territory, and to add to the business of the Annual Conference supplementary questions considered desirable or necessary to meet its own needs.

¶ **567.** A Central Conference shall have authority to examine and acknowledge the journals of the Annual Conferences, Provisional Annual Conferences, and Missions located within its bounds, and to make rules for the drawing up of the journals as may seem necessary.

¶ **568.** A Central Conference may have a standing **Committee on Woman's Work.** This committee should preferably be composed of the women delegates and such other persons as the Central Conference may elect. The duty of this committee shall be to study the relation of women to the church and to devise ways and means of developing this portion of the church membership, to the end that it may assume its rightful responsibilities in the extension of the kingdom. The committee shall make recommendations to the Central Conference regarding women's organizations within its areas. A Central Conference organization may become a member of the World Federation of Methodist Women and may elect a representative on the World Council of the federation.

¶ 569. A Central Conference may organize a woman's unit, after consultation with the Committee on Woman's Work, in connection with any Annual Conference or Provisional Annual Conference within its bounds and provide a constitution and by-laws for it.

¶ 570. A Central Conference shall have authority to adopt rules of procedure governing the investigation and trial of its ministers, including bishops, and lay members of the church and to provide the necessary means and methods of carrying them into effect; *provided*, however, that the ministers shall not be deprived of the right of trial by a ministerial committee, and lay members of the church of the right of trial by a duly constituted committee of church members; and *provided*, also, that the rights of appeal shall be adequately safeguarded. (*See* ¶ 930.)

¶ 571. A Central Conference is authorized to prepare and translate simplified or adapted forms of such parts of the Ritual as it may deem necessary, such changes to require the approval of the resident bishop or bishops of the Central Conference.

¶ 572. A Central Conference shall have the power to conform the detailed rules, rites, and ceremonies for the solemnization of marriage to the statute laws of the country or countries within its jurisdiction.

¶ 573. Subject to the approval of the bishops resident therein, a Central Conference shall have the power to prescribe courses of study, including those in the vernaculars, for its ministry, both foreign and indigenous, including local preachers, lay speakers, Bible women, deaconesses, teachers both male and female, and all other workers whatsoever, ordained or lay. It shall also make rules and regulations for examinations in these courses.

¶ **574.** A Central Conference shall have authority to edit and publish a Central Conference Discipline which shall contain, in addition to the Constitution of the church, such sections from the general Discipline of The Methodist Church as may be pertinent to the entire church; and also such revised, adapted, or new sections as shall have been enacted by the Central Conference concerned, under the powers given by the General Conference, with the understanding that legislation passed by the General Conference becomes effective immediately through the entire church, except as provided in ¶ 575.

¶ **575.** In a Central Conference or Provisional Central Conference using a language other than English, legislation passed by a General Conference shall not take effect until six months after the close of that General Conference, in order to afford the necessary time to make adaptations and to publish a translation of the legislation which has been enacted, which translation shall be approved by the resident bishop or bishops of the Central Conference. This provision, however, shall not exclude the election of delegates to the General Conference by Annual Conferences within the territory of Central Conferences or Provisional Central Conferences.

¶ **576.** A Central Conference is authorized to interpret Article XXIII of the Articles of Religion so as to recognize the government or governments of the country or countries within its territory.

¶ **577.** A Central Conference shall have power to authorize the congregations in a certain state or country to form special organizations in order to receive the acknowledgment of the state or country according to the laws of that state or country. These organizations shall be empowered to represent the interests of the church to the authorities of the state or country according to the rules and principles of The Methodist Church, and they shall be required to give regular reports of their activities to their respective Annual Conferences.

¶ **578.** A Central Conference may, with the consent of

the bishops resident in that conference, enter into agreements with churches or missions of other denominations for the division of territory or of responsibility for Christian work within the territory of the Central Conference.

¶ 579. A Central Conference shall have the right to negotiate with other Protestant bodies looking toward the possibility of church union; *provided* that any proposals for church union shall be submitted to the General Conference for approval before consummation.

¶ 580. A Central Conference, where the laws of the land permit, shall have the power to organize and incorporate one or more executive committees, executive boards, or councils of co-operation, with such membership and such powers as may have been granted by the Central Conference, for the purpose of representing it in its property and legal interests and for transacting any necessary business that may arise in the interval between the sessions of the Central Conference, or that may be committed to said boards or committees by the Central Conferences.[14]

¶ 581. 1. A Central Conference, through a duly incorporated property-holding body or bodies, shall have authority to purchase, own, hold, or transfer property for and on behalf of The Methodist Church, and of all the unincorporated organizations of The Methodist Church within the territory of that Central Conference, or on behalf of other organizations of The Methodist Church which have entrusted their property to that Central Conference.

2. A Central Conference shall have authority to make the necessary rules and regulations for the holding and management of such properties; *provided*, however, (*a*) that all procedure shall be subject to the laws of the country or countries concerned; (*b*) that no transfer of property shall be made from one Annual Conference to another without the consent of the conference holding title to such property; (*c*) that the status of properties held by local trustees or other holding bodies shall be recognized.

---

[14] *See* Judicial Council Decision 69.

3. A Central Conference shall not, directly or indirectly through its incorporated property-holding body or bodies, alienate property or the proceeds of property without due consideration of its trusteeship for local churches, Annual Conferences, the Board of Missions, and other organizations, local or general, of the church.

4. A Central Conference, or any of its incorporated organizations, shall not involve the Board of Missions or any organization of the church in any financial obligation without the official approval of said board or organization. All invested funds, fiduciary trusts, or property belonging to an Annual Conference, a Provisional Annual Conference, or a Mission, or any of its institutions, acquired by bequest, donation, or otherwise, and designated for a specific use, shall be applied to the purpose for which they were designated. They shall not be diverted to any other purpose except by the consent of the conference or mission involved, and with the approval of the Central Conference concerned, and civil court action when necessary. The same rule shall apply to similar funds or properties acquired by a Central Conference for specific objects. In cases involving the diversion of trust funds and properties within the territory of a Central Conference, the Central Conference concerned shall determine the disposition of the interests involved subject to an appeal to the Judicial Court of the Central Conference.

Note: For description of the Commission on the Structure of Methodism Overseas *see* ¶ 1812.

CHAPTER IV

PROVISIONAL CENTRAL CONFERENCES

¶ **586.** Annual Conferences, Provisional Annual Conferences, and Missions outside the United States which are not included in Central Conferences or in the territory of affiliated autonomous churches, and which because of geographical, language, political, or other considerations have common interests that can best be served thereby, may be organized into **Provisional Central Conferences** as provided in ¶ 541.

¶ 587. The organization of Provisional Central Conferences shall conform to the regulations prescribed for Central Conferences (¶¶ 543-49) insofar as they are considered applicable by the bishop in charge.

¶ 588. The General Conference may grant to a Provisional Central Conference any of the powers of a Central Conference except that of electing bishops.

¶ 589. In the interval between General Conferences the Board of Missions, upon the recommendation of the bishops in charge and after consultation with the Annual Conferences, Provisional Annual Conferences, and Missions concerned, may make changes in the boundaries of a Provisional Central Conference and may grant to a Provisional Central Conference or to any of its component parts any of the powers of a Central Conference except that of electing bishops. All changes in boundaries and all grants of powers authorized by the Board of Missions shall be reported to the ensuing session of the General Conference and shall expire at the close of that session unless renewed by the General Conference.

¶ 590. An Annual Conference or a Provisional Annual Conference in the field of a Provisional Central Conference shall have the power to set standards of character and other qualifications for admission of its lay members.

¶ 591. To Annual Conferences, Provisional Annual Conferences, and Missions which are outside the United States and are not included in Central Conferences or Provisional Central Conferences, the General Conference may grant any of the powers of Central Conferences except that of electing bishops; and in the interval between General Conferences the Board of Missions may grant such powers when requested to do so by the bishop in charge and by the Annual Conference, Provisional Annual Conference, or Mission concerned.

¶ 592. The General Conference shall make provision for the episcopal supervision of work in the territory outside the United States which is not now included in Central Conferences. (*See* ¶ 1805.2, .3.)

¶ 593. The Council of Bishops may provide, if and

when necessary, for episcopal visitation of mission fields not included in Central or Provisional Central Conferences. (*See* ¶ 546.)

CHAPTER V

AFFILIATED AUTONOMOUS CHURCHES

¶ **600.** A self-governing church in whose establishment The Methodist Church has assisted and with which it is co-operating through its Board of Missions may be known as an **affiliated autonomous church.** Relations between The Methodist Church and an affiliated autonomous church shall be such as may be mutually agreed on by the two churches. The Board of Missions shall serve as the agent of The Methodist Church in conferring with affiliated autonomous churches.

¶ **601.** Contractual agreements with The Methodist Church of Mexico, The Methodist Church of Brazil, Korean Methodist Church, United Church of Christ in Japan, Church of Christ in Okinawa, and such other churches as may be added by action of the General Conference shall be continued until changed or modified by mutual agreement. The Board of Missions is authorized to harmonize and make uniform the present agreements and practices with respect to these churches by extending to each of them any provision contained in the present agreement with any one of them, if such change is desired by the affiliated autonomous church concerned and judged to be advisable by the Board of Missions.

¶ **602.** The contractual agreements between The Methodist Church and the affiliated autonomous Methodist churches include the following provisions:

1. Certificates of church membership given by ministers in one church shall be accepted by ministers in the others.

2. Ministers may be transferred between Annual and Provisional Annual Conferences of The Methodist Church and of affiliated autonomous Methodist churches, with the

approval and consent of the bishops or other appointive authorities involved.

3. Each affiliated autonomous Methodist church shall be entitled to two delegates, a minister and a layman, to the General Conference of The Methodist Church, with all the rights and privileges of delegates, including membership on committees, travel, and per diem paid from the General Administration Fund, except the right to vote. Such a church having more than seventy thousand full members shall be entitled to two additional delegates, at least one of whom shall be a woman, with the same rights and privileges.

4. The Methodist Church may be represented at the General Conference of each affiliated autonomous Methodist church by a member of the Council of Bishops and a delegate appointed by the Board of Missions, the delegate to be entitled to all the privileges of delegates except the right to vote.

¶ **603.** When an Annual or Provisional Annual Conference becomes a part of an affiliated autonomous Methodist church, the Council of Bishops may, at its discretion, transfer its members who so desire to the conferences from which they went to the mission field. If any have not previously had membership in other conferences of The Methodist Church, the Council of Bishops may, at its discretion, transfer them to conferences as it may determine.

¶ **604.** The Council of Bishops may assign one or more of its members for episcopal visitation to the affiliated autonomous churches. (*See* ¶ 1805.5, .6.)

¶ **605.** An affiliated united church shall be entitled to two delegates, a minister and a layman, to the General Conference of The Methodist Church, with all the rights and privileges of delegates, including membership on committees, travel, and per diem paid from the General Administration Fund, except the right to vote. Such a church having more than seventy thousand full members shall be entitled to two additional delegates, at least one of whom shall be a woman, with the same rights and privileges.

¶ **606.** When the requirements of an unaffiliated autonomous Methodist church for its ministry are comparable to those of The Methodist Church, ministers may be transferred between its properly constituted ministerial bodies and the Annual and Provisional Annual Conferences of The Methodist Church, with the approval and consent of the appointive authorities involved.

¶ **607.** When conferences overseas related to the General Conference of The Methodist Church desire to be autonomous, the procedures shall be as follows:

1. The conferences shall prepare a historical record, with reasons why autonomy is requested; and the Commission on the Structure of Methodism Overseas shall formally decide on the initiation of proceedings.

2. The commission and the conferences involved shall mutually agree on (*a*) the confession of faith and (*b*) the constitution of the new church. These shall be prepared with care, and shall be approved by the conferences.

3. The commission shall request from the General Conference one of the following: (*a*) if proceedings are not well advanced, an enabling act authorizing autonomy when conditions are met, as determined by a special committee representing the commission, the Council of Bishops, the Board of Missions, and the Judicial Council; or (*b*) if agreement has been reached on the confession of faith and constitution as specified in § 2 above, enabling legislation formally authorizing the autonomous status.

4. When the autonomous status has been approved by the General Conference and the provisions for it have been met, the following shall sign the proclamation of autonomy: the president of the Council of Bishops, the secretary of the General Conference, the chairman of the Commission on the Structure of Methodism Overseas, and the president of the Board of Missions.

5. After the proclamation of autonomy has been signed, a delegation appointed by the Council of Bishops shall share in a service recognizing the new church. The delegation shall consist of five members: one from the Council of Bishops, one from an area contiguous to the new

church, one nominated by the Commission on the Structure of Methodism Overseas, and two, at least one a woman, nominated by the Board of Missions.

6. Preparation of its Discipline is the responsibility of the autonomous church; if invited, the Commission on the Structure of Methodism Overseas shall provide assistance.

7. An autonomous church, Methodist or united, may become an affiliated autonomous church of The Methodist Church by mutual agreement with the Commission on the Structure of Methodism Overseas and incorporation in its Discipline of provisions in accordance with ¶¶ 600-606.

8. The Board of Missions shall work out whatever agreements are needed to provide the basis of mutual support in the area of personnel, funds, and other patterns of relationship.

CHAPTER VI

PROVISIONAL ANNUAL CONFERENCES

¶ 608. Any Mission established under the provisions of the Discipline may be constituted as a **Provisional Annual Conference** by the General Conference in consultation with the Central Conference, Provisional Central Conference, or Jurisdictional Conference within which the Mission is located; *provided* that no Provisional Annual Conference shall be organized with fewer than ten ministerial members, nor shall a Provisional Annual Conference be continued with fewer than six ministerial members.

¶ 609. A Provisional Annual Conference is authorized to exercise the powers of an Annual Conference subject to the approval of the presiding bishop;[15] and its members shall share *pro rata* in the produce of The Methodist Publishing House with members of the Annual Conferences. A Provisional Annual Conference within the terri-

---

[15] *See* Judicial Council Decisions 132, 195.

tory of a Central Conference or of a Provisional Central Conference may elect delegates to a Central Conference or Provisional Central Conference on the same basis as an Annual Conference, but may not elect delegates to a General Conference.[16]

¶ 610. The bishop having episcopal supervision of a Provisional Annual Conference in a foreign or a home mission field may appoint a representative as **superintendent,** to whom may be committed specific responsibility for the representation of the Board of Missions in its relation to the indigenous church and also in co-operation with other recognized evangelical missions. Such duties shall be exercised so as not to interfere with the work of the district superintendent. This superintendent may also be a district superintendent, provided he is a member of the said conference. He shall be responsible directly to the bishop appointed to administer the work in that episcopal area, and he shall make adequate reports of the work and needs of his field to the bishop and to the secretaries of the Board of Missions immediately concerned.

¶ 611. If there is no bishop present at an annual session of a Provisional Annual Conference, the superintendent shall preside; but if there is no superintendent present, the presidency shall be determined as in an Annual Conference.

¶ 612. Each Provisional Annual Conference or Mission at its annual session shall appoint a standing committee whose duty it shall be, with the concurrence of the president of the conference, to make an estimate of the amount necessary for the support of each pastoral charge, either in full or supplementary to the amount raised by the charge. Such estimates shall be subject to modification by the division of the Board of Missions immediately concerned.

¶ 613. A charge within a Provisional Annual Conference or Mission may receive aid from the Board of Mis-

---

[16] Amended in 1948 following Judicial Council Decision 60, but see subsequent Amendments IV, VII, VIII to the Constitution (¶ 47).

sions without having been designated by the conference at its meeting.

¶ **614.** In a Provisional Annual Conference in the home field there shall be a Conference Board of Missions constituted as in an Annual Conference, and having the same duties and powers. (*See* ¶¶ 1291-1303.)

CHAPTER VII

MISSIONS

SECTION I.   **In the Home Field**

¶ **615.** 1. A Mission shall meet annually at the time and place appointed by the bishop in charge, who shall preside. In the absence of the bishop the superintendent of the Mission shall preside. The presiding officer shall bring forward the regular business of the meeting, and arrange the work. For rules governing the administration of Missions in the home field *see* ¶ 1254, also ¶¶ 612-13.

SEC. II.   **In Foreign Fields**

¶ **616.** A foreign field outside of an Annual Conference, working under the care of the Board of Missions, not having met the requirements for the organization of a Provisional Annual Conference, may be organized into a Mission. For rules governing the administration of Missions in the foreign field *see* ¶ 1215, also ¶¶ 591-93, 612-13.

CHAPTER VIII

THE ANNUAL CONFERENCE

SECTION I.   **Composition and Character**

¶ **621.** The composition and character of the **Annual Conference** are set forth in the Constitution (¶¶ 21-23, 47 iii, viii, x; *see also* ¶ 48.3-.4).

¶ **622.** Approved supply pastors who are in charge of

pastoral appointments shall be seated in the Annual Conference session and given the privilege of speaking on any question, but without vote.[17]

¶ 623. Lay missionaries, both men and women, regularly appointed by the Board of Missions in fields outside the United States may be seated in the Annual Conference session and given the privileges of the floor without vote. By authorization of a Central Conference national lay workers may be given the same privileges.[18] (*See* ¶ 1216.2.)

¶ 624. Deaconesses serving within the bounds of an Annual Conference shall be seated in the Annual Conference session and given the privileges of the floor without vote.

Sec. II.   **Organization**

¶ 625. Annual Conferences may become severally bodies corporate, wherever practicable, under the law of the countries, states, and territories within whose bounds they are located.[19]

¶ 626. The bishops shall appoint the times for holding the Annual Conferences.

¶ 627. The Annual Conference or a committee thereof shall select the place for holding the conference; but should it become necessary for any reason to change the place of meeting, a majority of the district superintendents, with the consent of the bishop in charge, may change the place. The Annual Conference has the right and power to provide for an adjourned session. The bishop, with the concurrence of three fourths of the district superintendents, may call a special session of the Annual Conference. A special session shall be composed of the ministerial members of the Annual Conference and of the lay member or members most recently elected by each pastoral charge.

¶ 628. A bishop shall preside over the Annual Conference. In the absence of a bishop, the conference shall by ballot, without nomination or debate, elect a president

---

[17] *See* Judicial Council Decisions 112, 136.
[18] *See* Judicial Council Decision 1, 24.
[19] *See* Judicial Council Decisions 38, 108, 143.

from among the traveling elders. The president thus elected shall discharge all the duties of a bishop except ordination.

¶ 629. The Annual Conference at the first session following the General Conference or Jurisdictional or Central Conference (or, if it may desire, at the last session preceding the General Conference or Jurisdictional or Central Conference) shall elect a secretary and a statistician to serve for the succeeding quadrennium. (For the election and work of the treasurer of the Annual Conference *see* ¶¶ 792, 803-8.)

¶ 630. All members of the Annual Conference, including probationers, and all approved supply pastors shall attend the sessions of the Annual Conference, and they shall furnish to the Annual Conference such reports and in such form as the laws of the church may require.

SEC. III.   **Powers and Duties**

¶ 634. The Annual Conference may make rules to govern its own procedure; *provided* that no Annual Conference shall make any rule contrary to the Constitution or to the powers granted it by the General Conference; and *provided*, further, that in the exercise of the powers granted by the General Conference each Annual Conference shall act in all respects in harmony with the policy of The Methodist Church with respect to elimination of discrimination on the basis of race. An Annual Conference cannot financially obligate The Methodist Church or an organizational unit thereof except the Annual Conference itself.[20]

¶ 635. An Annual Conference may admit into membership only those who have met all the Disciplinary requirements for membership and only in the manner prescribed in the Discipline.[21]

¶ 636. The Annual Conference shall have power to hear complaints against its ministerial members and may try, reprove, suspend, deprive of ministerial office and cre-

---

[20] *See* Judicial Council Decisions 43, 92, 115, 119, 141, 170, 179, 180, 195, 213.
[21] *See* Judicial Council Decisions 170, 195.

dentials, expel, or acquit any against whom charges may have been preferred. The Annual Conference shall have power to locate a ministerial member for unacceptability or inefficiency.

¶ 637. The relation of a ministerial member of the Annual Conference shall not be changed until he has had an opportunity to appear either in person or through a representative before the Committee on Conference Relations (¶ 668), except as provided in ¶¶ 377-78.

¶ 638. Every transfer of a traveling preacher is conditioned on the passing of his character by the conference to which he is amenable up to the time of his transfer. The official announcement that a preacher is transferred changes his membership so that his rights and responsibilities in the conference to which he goes begin from the date of his transfer.

¶ 639. Whenever a ministerial member of an Annual Conference of the Central Jurisdiction, whether on trial or in full connection, is transferred to an Annual Conference of another jurisdiction, either in connection with the transfer under ¶ 47 ix of the pastoral charge to which he is appointed or by reason of the dissolution or merger of his Annual Conference, he shall have the same rights and obligations as the other members of the conference to which he is transferred.

¶ 640. The status of a ministerial member of the Annual Conference or of a probationer is further determined by those sections of the Discipline governing the ministry.

¶ 641. The Annual Conference shall provide adequate surety bonds for all officers handling funds of the conference and shall have the books of said officers audited annually. (*See* ¶¶ 729, 803, 807.)

¶ 642. The Annual Conference shall give recognition to any new churches that have been organized during the year and shall, through the presiding bishop and the secretary, send to each new church a **certificate of organization,** which the district superintendent shall on behalf of the conference present to the new church in an appropriate ceremony. (*See* ¶ 155.)

Sec. IV.   **The Business of the Conference**

¶ **645.** After religious services the secretary of the previous Annual Conference shall call the roll, including the roll of approved supply pastors. (*See* ¶¶ 319, 622, 630.) The conference shall complete its organization and proceed with its business.

¶ **646.** Inquiries shall be made in the open conference as to whether all the ministerial members of the conference are blameless in their life and official administration. The district superintendent may answer for all the preachers in his district in one answer, if it be desired to call the name of each and every preacher in open session, or the Committee on Conference Relations (¶ 668) may make inquiry of each district superintendent about each man in his district and make one report to the bishop and the conference in open session; *provided* that the conference may order an executive session of the ministerial members to consider questions relating to matters of ordination, character, and conference relations.[22]

¶ **647.** The Committee on Conference Relations shall be prepared to answer at the call of the bishop the questions regarding the standing of ministers in full connection, as provided in ¶ 668.

¶ **648.** At the conclusion of the examination of the standing of the ministers in the conference the presiding bishop may call to the bar of the conference the class to be admitted into full connection, and receive them into conference membership after asking the questions to be found in the Discipline. This examination of the ministers, and the passing of their characters, should be the business of one session.

¶ **649.** Since the Annual Conference includes laymen and ministers, it is suggested that one single sitting of the conference should consider reports of the year's work. After the statistical questions have been answered, let the boards and committees of the conference make their reports for discussion and adoption.[23] The special interests of the conference may also present reports of their

---

[22] *See* Judicial Council Decision 42.
[23] *See* Judicial Council Decision 123.

work, regard being given by the bishop to a proper allotment of time.

¶ **650.** It is suggested that for one or more sittings the conference give due consideration to the work of the coming year. The representatives of connectional interests and church-wide movements, as well as those charged with the responsibility for conference work and programs, should present their challenge and their objectives.

¶ **651.** The business of the Annual Conference shall be to inquire:

I. *Organization and General Business*

1. Who are elected for the quadrennium: secretary? statistician? treasurer? (¶¶ 629, 803.)

2. Is the Annual Conference incorporated? (¶ 625.)

3. *a*) What officers handling funds of the conference have been bonded, and in what amounts? (¶¶ 641, 729, 807.)

b) Have the books of said officers or persons been audited? (¶¶ 641, 729, 803, 807.)

4. Have the conference boards, commissions, and committees (¶¶ 666-79) been appointed or elected:

    a) Board of Ministerial Training and Qualifications?

    b) Committee on Conference Relations?

    c) District Committees on Ministerial Qualifications (¶ 695)?

    d) Committee of Investigation?

    e) District Boards of Church Location and Building (¶ 721)?

    f) Board of Trustees of the Annual Conference?

    g) Commission on World Service and Finance?

    h) Commission on Town and Country Work?

    i) Deaconess Board?

    j) Board of Missions?

    k) Board of Education?

    l) Board of Christian Social Concerns?

    m) Board of Lay Activities?

    n) Board of Hospitals and Homes?

    o) Board of Evangelism?

    p) Board of Pensions?

    q) Commission on Christian Vocations?

r) Conference Woman's Society of Christian Service?

s) Commission on Minimum Salaries?

t) Commission on Promotion and Cultivation?

u) Television, Radio, and Film Commission?

v) Committee on Publishing Interests?

w) Optional commissions and committees?

5. Have the secretaries, treasurers, and statisticians kept their respective records upon and according to the forms prescribed by The Methodist Church? (¶ 662.)

6. What is the report of the statistician?

7. What is the report of the treasurer?

8. What are the reports of the district superintendents as to the status of the work within their districts?

9. What is the schedule of minimum salaries for pastors? (¶ 826.)

10. What is the plan and what are the approved claims for the support of the district superintendents for the ensuing year? (¶¶ 801-2.)

11. What amount has been apportioned to the pastoral charges within the conference to be raised for the support of conference claimants? (¶¶ 1623, 1645.4.)

12. What are the apportionments to this conference:

a) For the World Service Fund?

b) For the Episcopal Fund?

c) For the General Administration Fund?

d) For the Interdenominational Co-operation Fund?

e) For the Temporary General Aid Fund?

f) For the Jurisdictional Administration Fund?

g) For the maintenance of our institutions of higher learning?

13. What is the percentage division between world service and conference benevolences for the current year: world service? conference? (¶ 795.)

14. What are the reports, recommendations, and plans of the conference agencies:

a) What is the report of the Board of Pensions, and what appropriations for conference claimants are reported and approved? (¶ 1623.)

b) What is the report of the Board of Missions of disbursements of missionary aid within the conference? (¶ 1299.)

c) What is the report of the Commission on World Service and Finance? (¶¶ 791-812.)

d) What is the report of the Commission on Christian Vocations? (¶¶ 675-77.)

e) What are the other reports?

15. What Methodist institutions or organizations are approved by the conference for annuity responsibility? (¶1618.2*c*, .9.)

16. What date is determined for Golden Cross Enrollment Sunday? (¶ 1560.1.)

17. *a*) Who is the conference lay leader? (¶ 1504.)

b) What is his report?

c) Who are the district and associate district lay leaders? (¶ 1508.)

18. What local churches have been:

a) Organized? (¶ 155.)

b) Merged? (¶¶ 186-87.)

c) Discontinued? (¶¶ 128, 188, 354.)

d) Relocated, and to what address?

e) Transferred into this conference from the Central Jurisdiction, and with what membership: this year? previously? (¶¶ 532, 680.)

II. *Pertaining to Ministerial Relations*

19. Are all the ministerial members of the conference blameless in their life and official administration?

20. Who constitute the Conference Committee of Investigation? (¶ 931.)

21. Who are the approved supply pastors:

a) Student approved supply pastors (¶¶ 317.1, 318), and in what schools are they enrolled?

b) Full-time approved supply pastors (¶¶ 317.2, 318), and what progress has each made in the course of study?

c) Part-time approved supply pastors (¶¶ 317.3, 318), and what progress has each made in the course of study?

22. What approved supply pastors are credited with annuity claim on account of full-time service during the past year? (To be answered after consultation of the Conference Board of Pensions with the district superintendents; ¶ 1631.)

23. What preachers, coming from other evangelical churches, have had their orders recognized (¶ 411.2): as local deacons? as local elders?

24. Who have been admitted from other evangelical churches as traveling preachers (¶ 411.3-.5):

a) As members on trial: deacons? elders?

b) As members in full connection: deacons? elders?

25. Who are admitted on trial:

a) With degrees from approved colleges and credits from approved schools of theology? (¶¶ 323-24.)

b) With degrees from colleges not accredited by the University Senate and credits from approved schools of theology? (¶ 325.1.)

c) With degrees from approved colleges and completion of the introductory studies for the ministry and the first two years of the course of study? (¶ 325.2.)

d) With partial college credit, completion of the four-year course of study, and six years' service as approved supply pastors? (¶ 325.3.)

26. Who are continued on trial, and what progress have they made in their ministerial studies (¶ 332):

a) As students in approved schools of theology?

b) As graduates of approved schools of theology?

c) In the four-year course of study?

d) In the four graduate courses of study? (¶ 343.2.)

27. Who on trial are discontinued?

28. Who are admitted into full connection?

29. Who have been elected deacons (¶ 393):

a) Theological students?

b) Members on trial in the course of study?

c) Approved supply pastors?

d) Missionaries?

e) Chaplains?

30. Who have been ordained deacons?

31. Who have been elected elders (¶ 403):

a) Theological graduates?

b) Course of study graduates?

c) Missionaries?

d) Chaplains?

32. Who have been ordained elders?

33. Who have been admitted or ordained to accommodate other conferences:

a) Admitted: on trial? into full connection?

b) Ordained after election by this conference: deacons? elders?

c) Ordained after election by other conferences: deacons? elders?

34. Who are readmitted: as deacons? as elders?

35. What retired members have been made effective?

36. Who have been received by transfer?

37. Who have been transferred out?

38. Who have had their conference membership terminated:

a) By voluntary location?

b) By involuntary location?

c) By withdrawal?

d) By judicial procedure (expelled)?

39. *a*) What ministerial members have died during the year: while in effective relation? while inactive by retirement or otherwise?

b) What approved supply pastors have died during the year?

c) What deaconesses have died during the year?

40. Who are the supernumerary ministers, and for what number of years consecutively has each held this relation? (¶ 365.)

41. Who are granted sabbatical leave? (¶ 364.)

42. What ministerial members have been retired: this year? previously?

43. What approved supply pastors have been retired: this year? previously?

44. Who are appointed to attend school:

a) Members on trial? (¶ 671.)

b) Members in full connection? (¶ 668.)

45. *a*) What is the number: of pastoral charges? of approved supply pastors? received on trial? received into full connection? transferred in? transferred out? received from other evangelical churches? readmitted? discontinued? withdrawn? expelled? located? deceased? of local preachers? of women under appointment? of retired ministers made effective? of retired ministers

serving as supply pastors? of district parsonages, with their total value and indebtedness thereon?

b) What is the number of ministers:

(1) On trial: as pastors? under special appointment? appointed to attend school? total?

(2) In full connection: as pastors and district superintendents? under special appointment? appointed to attend school? on sabbatical leave? total effective? retired? supernumerary?

(3) Total of all ministers?

46. What other personal notation should be made?

III. Concluding Business

47. What are the detailed objectives of this conference for the coming year?

48. Where shall the next session of the conference be held?

49. Is there any other business?

50. What changes have been made in appointments since the last conference session?

51. Where are the preachers stationed for the ensuing year?

Note: For other directions about the program of Annual Conference sessions *see* ¶¶ 1298, 1441, 1503.6, 1571.3*b*, 1610.5.

Sec. V. **Records and Archives**

¶ **656.** The Annual Conference shall keep an exact record of its proceedings (¶ 658), according to the forms provided by the General, Jurisdictional, and Central Conferences. It shall send to its Jurisdictional Conference or Central Conference a bound copy of the minutes of the quadrennium for examination, said copy to be returned to the secretary of the Annual Conference to be placed in the archives (¶ 663) of the conference. If there be no archives of the Annual Conference, then the secretary shall keep the bound copy to be handed on to his successor in office.

¶ **657.** Each Annual Conference shall send to the Council on World Service and Finance two printed or written copies of its annual journal signed by its president and secretary, one copy being for the Department of Research and the other for the Department of Records.

¶ **658.** The General Conference recommends the following divisions, in the order named, for the Annual Conference journals:

    I. Officers of Annual Conference.

   II. Boards, Commissions, Committees. Rolls of Conference Members.

  III. Daily Proceedings.

  IV. Disciplinary Questions.

   V. Appointments.

  VI. Reports.

 VII. Memoirs.

VIII. Roll of Dead, Deceased Ministerial Members.

  IX. Historical.

   X. Miscellaneous.

  XI. Pastoral Record (including the records of accepted supply pastors in such manner as the conference may determine).

 XII. Index.

¶ **659.** An Annual Conference in the United States shall include in its journal a list of the deaconesses and missionaries, ministerial and lay, active and retired, who have gone from the conference into the service of the church in mission fields.

Note: For further directions on the content of Annual Conference journals *see* ¶¶ 362.4, .10, 431.9, 786, 806, 812, 829-30, 1230, 1253.4*c*, .7, 1292.2, 1451.2, 1612.7, 1618.4, .9, 1629, 1631.6.

¶ **661.** The secretary of each Annual Conference shall keep a service record, together with the dates of birth and marriage, of all ministerial members of the Annual Conference. This record shall be available for use by the Conference Board of Pensions of that conference and any other conference supplemental organization existing under ¶ 1611, and by the General Board of Pensions.

¶ **662.** All records of secretaries, statisticians, and treasurers shall be kept according to the forms prepared by the Council on World Service and Finance, so that all statistical and financial items shall be handled alike in all conferences, and that uniformity of reporting shall be established as a church-wide policy.[24]

¶ 663. In each Annual Conference there shall be a **Historical Society,** to be appointed or elected in whatever manner the conference may decide, whose duties it shall be to preserve the records of the conference, gather all data referring to its organization, its past history, its former members, and to collect all data of interest from elderly persons and to preserve these for future generations, together with a record of current items of importance, and to keep before the minds of our people the glorious deeds of the heroes of the past. (See ¶¶ 1591-92.)

SEC. VI. **Conference Agencies**

¶ 666. The Annual Conference at the first session following the General Conference or Jurisdictional or Central Conference shall appoint or elect such quadrennial boards, commissions, or committees as shall be ordered by the General Conference or the Jurisdictional or the Central Conference of which the said Annual Conference is a part, or by the Annual Conference itself for the purpose of promoting the work of The Methodist Church within the bounds of the said Annual Conference. The powers and duties of these agencies shall be prescribed by the conference authorizing them or as defined in certain paragraphs of this Discipline. Members thereof shall hold office until their successors are elected.[25]

¶ 667. In the appointment or election of Annual Conference boards, commissions, and committees the provisions of the Discipline concerning membership requirements shall be held to be *minimum* requirements; each Annual Conference may make its agencies of such size as its work may need. Full-time approved supply pastors serving charges are eligible for election or appointment to such agencies, except those dealing with qualifications, orders, and status of ministers and supply pastors.

¶ 668. The Annual Conference, on nomination of its nominating committee, shall elect a **Committee on Con-**

---

[24] *See* Judicial Council Decision 213.
[25] *See* Judicial Council Decision 98.

ference Relations, consisting of not fewer than six traveling elders, arranged as far as practical in classes to serve three years each. It is recommended that at least one third of these shall have served on the committee during the immediate past quadrennium. The committee shall make recommendation to the conference concerning all proposed changes in the conference relation of elders in full connection, including: (*a*) changes from effective relation to retirement, the supernumerary relation, sabbatical leave, appointment as a student, and location; (*b*) return to the effective relation from another relation; and (*c*) readmission of those formerly located. The committee shall report to the conference transfers into or out of the conference, withdrawals, and other changes in conference relations.

¶ **669.** 1. Each Annual Conference at the first session following the General Conference shall elect for a term of four years a **Board of Ministerial Training and Qualifications,** consisting of not fewer than six nor more than twenty-five ministers in full connection in the conference, nominated by the presiding bishop after consultation with the chairman of the board of the previous quadrennium, or with a committee of the board, and with the Cabinet. It is recommended that the Conference Board of Education have due representation and that at least two thirds of the members be graduates of colleges and schools of theology accredited or approved by the University Senate. Vacancies shall be filled by the bishop after consultation with the chairman of the board.

2. The board shall organize by electing from its membership a chairman, a registrar, and such other officers as it may deem necessary.

3. The board shall convene at the seat and time of the Annual Conference, preferably the day before the session opens, to review and complete the work of the past year and to plan for the future.

4. The board shall select for each of the District Committees on Ministerial Qualifications an official representative, who need not reside within the district, to serve as a member of the committee.

5. The board shall work in co-operation with the Department of Ministerial Education (¶¶ 1371-77).

¶ 670. 1. The board shall seek, in co-operation with the Commission on Christian Vocations (¶¶ 675-77), with the bishop, district superintendents, pastors, and laymen of the conference, and with the Department of Ministerial Education and the Methodist schools of theology, to enlist suitable candidates for the Christian ministry. It shall seek in every way practicable to provide guidance and counsel to them in their training and preparation for the ministry, recommending colleges and schools of theology accredited or approved by the University Senate. It shall co-operate with our schools of theology by recommending from the Annual Conference students with definite ministerial promise.

2. For the purpose of making financial assistance available to students for the ministry, it is recommended that each Annual Conference and/or Jurisdictional Conference have a seminary loan fund or seminary student aid fund, under the direction of the Conference Board of Ministerial Training and Qualifications.

¶ 671. The board shall examine (a) all applicants for employment as approved supply pastors and (b) for admission on trial as to their fitness for the ministry, as provided in ¶¶ 314-18, 321-32, and shall make full inquiry as to the fitness of (c) candidates for admission into full connection. This must include an examination as to character, habits of life, conversion, call to the ministry, Christian experience, evangelistic and missionary concern, age, educational qualifications, domestic situation, co-operation with others, ability to lead a service of worship, and understanding of the Church's mission. (See ¶¶ 341-45.) The answers to the examination questions may be submitted in writing. The board shall also report recommendations concerning: (d) candidates for ordination as deacons; (e) candidates for ordination as elders; (f) those to be received from other churches; (g) those transferred into the conference who are not elders in full connection; and (h) students, not yet elders in full connection, to be appointed to attend school and assigned to a Quarterly Conference (¶¶ 431.6, 432.7).[26]

¶ **672.** 1. The board shall certify all information and recommendations concerning each candidate to the Annual Conference in duplicate. One copy of this record is to be kept by the registrar of the board, and one copy is to be mailed after each conference session to the Department of Ministerial Education.

2. In all cases involving discontinuance of membership on trial or termination of approved supply pastor status, the board shall file with the office of the resident bishop for permanent record a copy of the circumstances relating thereto.

¶ **673.** The board shall urge all members on trial to attend colleges and schools of theology related to The Methodist Church and accredited or approved by the University Senate, and shall encourage and assist them in every practicable way to complete the preparation recommended in ¶¶ 342, 344. It shall require and assist all who are not attending an approved school of theology to pursue promptly the courses of study (¶¶ 332, 343).

674. 1. The **registrar** of the board shall keep a full personnel record, including transcripts of academic credit, for all ministerial candidates within the bounds of the conference.

2. He shall keep a permanent record of the standing of the students in the course of study, and report to the conference when required. This record shall include the credits allowed students for work done in accredited schools of theology (¶ 327), in approved schools in the courses of study, and by correspondence.

3. The registrar, or some other designated officer of the board, shall keep a record of the educational history and interests of each minister serving in the conference. This material shall be furnished to the board by active ministers. Such records are the property of the conference and shall be carefully preserved.

¶ **675.** In each Annual Conference there shall be a **Commission on Christian Vocations,** composed of: a rep-

---

[26] *See* Judicial Council Decision 157.

resentative of the Cabinet; the executive secretary of the Conference Board of Education; the conference directors of youth work and of adult work; the chairman or another member of the Board of Ministerial Training and Qualifications; the secretary of missionary personnel of the Conference Woman's Society of Christian Service; one representative each from the Conference Boards of Hospitals and Homes, Missions, Lay Activities, Evangelism, Education, and Christian Social Concerns; one representative each from the Conference Deaconess Board and the state or regional Methodist Student Movement; one youth not over twenty-one years of age; and the district secretaries of Christian vocations (¶ 696). The Cabinet or the commission may appoint other members when advisable. The agency representatives shall be responsible for representing Christian vocations in their respective organizations.

¶ 676. It shall be the duty of this commission: (a) to co-operate with the Interboard Committee on Christian Vocations (¶ 1415), with the District Committees on Christian Vocations (¶ 696.2), and with the Committee on Christian Vocations in every local church (¶ 145.9); (b) to promote among youth and adults a philosophy of Christian vocation that recognizes the potential sacredness of all useful work and all opportunities for Christian life service; (c) to organize a program for presenting to youth and adults the opportunities and claims of the pastoral ministry and other church vocations; (d) to take into account the basic interests and aptitudes of interested youth and adults and inform them of the necessary preparation for specific church vocations; (e) to keep accurate and useful records of each youth who has indicated an interest in church vocations from the time of his first commitment until he is appointed to full-time work in the church, or until such time as responsibility for him is accepted by the proper conference board or commission.

¶ 677. Each Annual Conference, in whatever way it may decide, shall make adequate provision for the financial support of the work of its Commission on Christian Vocations so that the commission may be able to carry forward an effective program of promotion and guidance in the field of Christian vocations.

¶ 679. There may be in any Annual Conference a **Conference or Interboard Council,** composed of representatives of all conference boards and commissions, the bishop and his Cabinet, other administrative officers, and other agencies as the conference may determine, for the purpose of correlating the planning and promotion of the program of the church.[27]

Note: For other Annual Conference agencies *see* as follows: Committee on Camps and Conferences, ¶ 1455; Committee or Commission on Christian Higher Education, ¶ 1452; Board of Christian Social Concerns, ¶¶ 1545-48; Commission on College and University Religious Life, ¶ 1370; Deaconess Board, ¶ 1253; Distributing Committee, ¶ 1609; Board of Education, ¶¶ 1441-58; Board of Evangelism, ¶¶ 1478-80; Committee on Family Life, ¶ 1453; Board of Hospitals and Homes, ¶ 1562; Committee of Investigation, ¶¶ 923, 931-36; Board of Lay Activities, ¶¶ 1502-5; Methodist Youth Fellowship, ¶ 1458; Commission on Minimum Salaries, ¶ 826; Board of Missions, ¶¶ 1291-1303; Board of Pensions, ¶¶ 1611, 1623-37; Committee on Proportional Payment of Ministerial Support, ¶ 1611; Commission on Promotion and Cultivation, ¶ 755; Committee on Public Relations and Methodist Information, ¶ 1590; Committee on Publishing Interests, ¶ 1158; Television-Radio Ministry Fund Committee, ¶ 762.2; Television, Radio, and Film Commission, ¶ 1583; Commission on Town and Country Work, ¶ 1302; Board of Trustees, ¶ 711; Committee on Urban Work, ¶ 1301; Committee on Use of Methodist Curriculum Materials, ¶ 1454; Committee on Wills, Bequests, and Gifts, ¶ 1505; Woman's Society of Christian Service, ¶ 1266; Commission on World Service and Finance, ¶¶ 791-830; Commission on Worship, ¶ 1571.

SEC. VII.   **Transfers Under Amendment IX**

¶ 680. To clarify procedures under the constitutional provisions of ¶ 47 ix for the transfer of a local church from one Annual Conference to another and for the

---

[27] Adopted in 1956 following Judicial Council Decision 98. *See* also Decision 148.

transfer of an Annual Conference from one jurisdiction to another, the following rules are adopted: The votes required for transfer of a local church may originate in the local church or either of the Annual Conferences involved and shall be effective regardless of the order in which taken. The votes required for transfer of an Annual Conference may originate in the Annual Conference or among the Annual Conferences of either jurisdiction involved and shall be effective regardless of the order in which taken. In each case a vote of two thirds of those present and voting shall remain effective unless and until rescinded prior to the completion of the transfer by a vote of a majority of those present and voting.[28]

CHAPTER IX

THE DISTRICT CONFERENCE

¶ 686. A **District Conference** shall be held annually in each district if authorized by the Annual Conference. The district superintendent shall preside. If the district superintendent be absent, the District Conference is authorized to elect an elder to preside.

¶ 687. A District Conference shall be composed of all the preachers—traveling, including retired and supernumerary, and local—the deaconesses, the church lay leader, church-school superintendent, president of the Woman's Society of Christian Service, and president of the chartered Methodist Men club from each local church in the district, the district stewards, the district trustees, the district lay leader and associate district lay leaders, the lay member of the Annual Conference from each charge, the president of the District Woman's Society of Christian Service, the district directors of children's, youth, adult, and general church-school work, and such other persons as the Annual Conference may determine.

¶ 688. The district superintendent shall fix the date of the District Conference, but the District Conference shall fix the place. Should it become necessary to change the

---

[28] *See* Judicial Council Decision 211.

place, the district superintendent shall have authority to change it. The district superintendent may call special sessions when necessity requires.

¶ **689.** The District Conference shall inquire particularly into the condition of the several charges concerning: (1) their spiritual state (¶ 1481); (2) the missionary work of and in the district (¶¶ 1306-8); (3) the Christian education work through the church schools, including vacation schools and Methodist Youth Fellowships; (4) the women's work (¶ 1267); (5) the support of the church colleges and the attendance upon them; (6) the work done in and for the American Bible Society; (7) the lay activities, especially in behalf of benevolences and Christian stewardship, and in promoting worship in unserved sections and communities; (8) the work of and for our hospitals and homes; (9) the patronage of the church papers and our Publishing House; (10) the candidates for the ministry from the district and aid in their preparation; (11) the candidates for other forms of Christian service; (12) the support of the church, its ministry and its benevolences, and the financial systems that are being used. The District Conference shall receive for examination an annual report from the Committee on Records and History (¶ 145.4) of each Quarterly Conference.

¶ **690.** The District Conference shall vote on issuing or renewing licenses to preach, on recommendation of the District Committee on Ministerial Qualifications, and shall consider for approval the reports of this committee, as provided in ¶ 695.

¶ **691.** The District Conference may choose its own order of business, provided that all the business committed to it is transacted. The secretary duly elected shall keep an accurate record of the proceedings and submit it to the Annual Conference for examination.

¶ **695.** 1. There shall be a **District Committee on Ministerial Qualifications,** composed of the district superintendent as chairman, five other traveling preachers of the district nominated annually by him and approved by the Annual Conference, and one representative from and appointed by the Board of Ministerial Training and

Qualifications. Interim vacancies may be filled by the chairman.

2. The committee shall examine each person who applies in writing for a license to preach, or for a renewal of such license. Where there is evidence that his gifts, graces, and usefulness warrant and that he is qualified under ¶¶ 306-7, it may, on recommendation of his Quarterly Conference (¶ 146.1), recommend to the District Conference to issue or renew his license to preach; *provided,* however, that where no District Conference exists, final action may be taken by the committee; and *provided,* further, that before the ballot for licensing a person to preach is taken he shall have agreed to the condition set forth in ¶ 306.6. (*See* ¶362.4.)

3. The committee shall recommend to the Board of Ministerial Training and Qualifications of the Annual Conference suitable candidates for acceptance or continuance as approved supply pastors, for admission on trial, and for restoration of credentials.

4. The vote of the committee in all such matters shall be by individual written ballot, and a three-fourths majority vote of the committee shall be required for license or approval.

5. The committee shall report its work to the District Conference for approval where such conference exists.

6. The chairman and another representative of the committee shall meet annually with the Board of Ministerial Training and Qualifications, on call of the chairman of the board, either separately or with representatives of all the districts.

7. The committee shall designate an official spokesman, other than the chairman, to confer with the board, when so requested, about any candidate recommended to it by the committee.[29]

¶ **696.** 1. The district superintendent shall appoint a **district secretary of Christian vocations,** who shall work with the Conference Commission on Christian Vocations (¶¶ 675-77) and the Interboard Committee on Christian Vocations (¶ 1415). He shall seek to maintain contact

---

[29] Amended in 1956 following Judicial Council Decision 100.

with the Committees on Christian Vocations in the local churches (¶ 145.9) and to establish counseling and guidance programs in co-operation with the local churches and public schools.

2. If desired, a **District Committee on Christian Vocations** may be established to perform the duties described in § 1. It shall consist of the district secretary of Christian vocations, who shall serve as chairman, the district superintendent, the district directors of youth work and of adult work, the secretary of missionary personnel of the District Woman's Society of Christian Service, two laymen appointed by the district lay leader, two ministers appointed by the district superintendent, one representative each from the Methodist Youth Fellowship and the Methodist Student Movement, and the members of the Conference Commission on Christian Vocations residing within the district.

Note: For other district agencies *see* as follows: Committee on Camps and Conferences, ¶ 1461; staff of Christian education, ¶ 1460; Committee on Christian Social Concerns, ¶ 1549; Board of Church Location and Building, ¶¶ 721-25; Committee on Evangelism, ¶¶ 1481-83; Committee on Investigation, ¶¶ 957-58; Board of Lay Activities, ¶¶1506-8; Committee on Lay Speaking, ¶ 1509; Methodist Men, ¶ 1511; missionary society, ¶¶ 1225-34; Board of Stewards, ¶¶ 797, 802; Board of Trustees, ¶ 716.2; Woman's Society of Christian Service, ¶ 1267.

CHAPTER X

THE QUARTERLY CONFERENCE

The organization, powers, and duties of the Quarterly Conference are described in ¶¶ 137-55, under Part II, The Local Church.

PART V

TEMPORAL ECONOMY

CHAPTER I

CHURCH PROPERTY

SECTION I.   The Name "Methodist"

¶ 701. The word "Methodist" is not by our approval or consent to be used as, or as a part of, a trade name or trade mark or as, or as a part of, the name of any business firm or organization except by corporations or other business units created for the administration of work undertaken directly by The Methodist Church.

SEC. II. **Incorporated Trustees of The Methodist Church**

¶ 703. There shall be a board of trustees incorporated under the name of **The Board of Trustees of The Methodist Church.** This board shall be composed of three ministers and four lay persons. They shall be nominated, without reference to jurisdictional membership, by the Council of Bishops and be elected by the General Conference for a term of eight years, except as to the first such board, of which one clerical and two lay members shall be elected for a term of four years, and two clerical and two lay members shall be elected for a term of eight years, and they shall serve until their successors have been elected and qualified. Between General Conferences the Council of Bishops is designated to act on resignations and to fill vacancies in the membership of this board until the next session of the General Conference.

¶ 704. This corporation shall receive and administer new trusts and funds, and so far as may be legal be the successor in trust of "The Trustees of The Methodist

231

Episcopal Church," a corporation incorporated under the laws of the state of Ohio, and of "The Board of Trustees of The Methodist Episcopal Church, South," a corporation incorporated under the laws of the state of Tennessee, and of the "Board of Trustees of The Methodist Protestant Church," a corporation incorporated under the laws of the state of Maryland; and so far as is legal and as such successor in trust it shall be and is authorized and empowered to receive from its said predecessor corporations all trust funds and assets of every kind and character, real, personal, or mixed, held by them or any one of them; and it shall be and is authorized to administer such trusts and funds in accordance with the conditions under which they have been previously received and administered by said predecessor corporations. But nothing herein contained shall be construed to require the dissolution of the three corporations above mentioned, and they shall continue to administer such funds as may not be legally transferred to the new corporation. There shall be a correlating committee of nine members, of which three shall be appointed by each of the existing corporations. This committee shall have authority to secure a charter for the new corporation and to arrange the details for handling the trusts in accordance with their terms.[1]

¶ 705. The object and duty of this board shall be to receive, collect, and hold in trust for the benefit of The Methodist Church any and all donations, bequests, and devises of any kind or character, real or personal, that may be given, devised, bequeathed, or conveyed unto said board or to The Methodist Church as such for any benevolent, charitable, or religious purpose, and to administer the same and the income therefrom in accordance with the directions of the donor, trustor, or testator, and in the interests of the church, society, institution, or agency contemplated by such donors, trustors, or testators under the direction of the General Conference. The board shall have power, in its discretion, and on the advice of competent investment counsel, to invest, reinvest, buy, sell,

---

[1] As provided in this paragraph, The Board of Trustees of The Methodist Church was incorporated under the laws of the state of Ohio in 1940.

transfer, and convey any and all funds and properties which it may hold in trust, subject always to the terms of the legacy, devise, or donation. It shall have authority to determine the intent of the donor, trustor, or testator with respect to the use and disposition both of the corpus and of the income of each separate gift, bequest, or acquisition which it may receive; and if the terms of the gift, bequest, or other instrument involved are vague, uncertain, or impossible of literal fulfillment, it shall have authority, within its sound discretion, to determine the use or uses of each such fund which shall conform with the general purposes of the donor, trustor, or testator, provided such purposes can reasonably be determined from the terms of the gift, bequest, or other applicable instrument. If the specific or general purposes of the donor, trustor, or testator cannot be reasonably determined by the board with respect to any particular fund, such fund shall be held by the board as an undirected fund.

¶ **706.** The board may intervene and take all necessary legal steps to safeguard and protect the interests and rights of The Methodist Church anywhere, in all matters relating to property and rights to property whether arising by gift, devise, or otherwise, or where held in trust or established for the benefit of The Methodist Church or its membership; or abandoned church property, where Annual Conference trustees neglect to take necessary steps to protect the interests of the members of The Methodist Church in such property.

¶ **707.** It shall be the duty of the pastor within the bounds of whose charge any such gift, bequest, or devise is made to give prompt notice thereof to said board, which shall proceed to take such steps as are necessary and proper to conserve, protect, and administer the same. But the board may decline to receive or administer any such gift, devise, or bequest for any reason satisfactory to the board.

¶ **708.** The board shall make to each General Conference a full, true, and faithful report of its doings, of all funds, moneys, securities, and property held in trust by it, and of its receipts and disbursements during the quadrennium. The beneficiary of a fund held in trust by the board shall be entitled to a report at least annually on the condition of such fund and on the transactions affecting it. The amount of income accruing during a quadrennium from any undirected fund or funds held by the board shall be reported to the Council on World Service and Finance at least sixty days prior to the General Conference, for the recommendation prescribed in ¶ 737.13.

¶ **709.** There shall be a fund known as **The Permanent Fund** to be held and administered by the board, the principal of which shall be kept intact forever, and the interest accumulating from said fund shall be used by the board as the General Conference shall direct.

SEC. III.   **The Methodist Corporation**

¶ **710.** 1. There shall be a charitable corporation which shall hold title to certain property of The Methodist Church located in Washington, D.C., at Ward Circle at the intersection of Nebraska and Massachusetts Avenues. The objects to be carried on and promoted by **The Methodist Corporation** shall be and are exclusively for religious, charitable, scientific, literary, and educational purposes, including religious education and Christian social concerns. No part of the net earnings of the corporation shall inure to the benefit of any private shareholder or individual. The Board of Directors of this corporation shall be elected for a four-year term by the General Conference, and shall consist of (a) one bishop, one minister, and one layman from each jurisdiction, nominated by the Council of Bishops, and (b) three representatives each from the Council of Bishops, Council on World Service and Finance, Co-ordinating Council, and Board of Christian Social Concerns, nominated by these respective bodies. The bishop resident in Washington, D.C., shall be ex officio chairman. Interim vacancies may be filled by the Board of Directors.

2. The corporation shall have complete authority to develop a program for the utilization of the property, and to implement it by the sale or lease of all or any part thereof to any agency of The Methodist Church, subject to compliance with ¶ 1085, on such terms as the Board of Directors may deem appropriate to over-all utilization of

the property in the best interest of The Methodist Church and its program. The corporation is also authorized to liquidate the project in whole or in part if and when it concludes that it is not in the best interest of The Methodist Church to undertake a development or a further holding of the property. The corporation is authorized to receive and expend gifts and bequests for the development of this property. In the event of the dissolution of the corporation, its remaining assets and funds, after the payment and satisfaction of all debts, shall be conveyed, assigned, and transferred by the Board of Directors to such religious, charitable, scientific, literary, or educational organization or organizations as the General Conference of The Methodist Church shall direct. No funds or property shall be distributed among or inure to the benefit of any private shareholder or individual.

3. The carrying charges of the property shall be paid from the General Administration Fund. The corporation shall not have authority to commit the General Conference to any other financial obligation without approval of the General Conference. However, if circumstances make it appropriate to proceed with any phase of property development between sessions of the General Conference, the Council on World Service and Finance is authorized to empower the corporation to solicit funds during such quadrennium under such conditions and restrictions as the said council may deem appropriate.

4. The corporation shall report to each succeeding General Conference as long as The Methodist Church holds an interest in the property.

Sec. IV.   **Annual Conference Property**

¶ 711. 1. Each Annual Conference shall have a **Board of Trustees,** which shall be incorporated unless the conference is incorporated in its own name (¶ 625).[2] In either case the board shall consist of twelve persons, who must be at least twenty-one years of age, and of whom six shall be ministers in the effective relation in the confer-

---

[2] Amended in 1960 following Judicial Council Decision 108.

ence and six shall be members in good standing of local
churches within the bounds of the conference, and such
persons shall be the directors of the corporation. They
shall be elected by the conference for a term of three
years, except as to the first board, one third of whom
shall be elected for a term of one year, one third for a
term of two years, and one third for a term of three years,
and shall serve until their successors have been elected;
provided, however, that existing incorporated trustees of
any Annual Conference may continue unaffected by this
subsection unless and until such charter is amended.

2. The said corporation shall receive, collect, and hold
in trust for the benefit of the Annual Conference any and
all donations, bequests, and devises of any kind or character, real or personal, that may be given, devised, bequeathed, or conveyed to the said board or to the Annual
Conference as such for any benevolent, charitable, or religious purpose, and shall administer the same and the
income therefrom in accordance with the directions of
the donor, trustor, or testator, and in the interest of the
church, society, institution, or agency contemplated by
such donor, trustor, or testator, under the direction of
the Annual Conference. The board shall have power to
invest, reinvest, buy, sell, transfer, and convey any and
all funds and properties which it may hold in trust, subject always to the terms of the legacy, devise, or donation;
provided, however, that the foregoing shall not apply to
churches, colleges, camps, conference grounds, orphanages, or incorporated boards. When the use to be made of
any such donation, bequest, or devise is not otherwise
designated, the same shall be added to and become a part
of the "Permanent Fund" of the Annual Conference. Funds
committed to this board may be invested by it only in
collateral that is amply secured and after such investments have been approved by the said board or its agency
or committee charged with such investment, unless otherwise directed by the Annual Conference.[3]

3. The board may intervene and take all necessary legal
steps to safeguard and protect the interests and rights of

---

[3] *See* Judicial Council Decisions 135, 160, 178, 190.

the Annual Conference anywhere, and in all matters relating to property and rights to property whether arising by gift, devise, or otherwise, or where held in trust or established for the benefit of the Annual Conference or its membership.

4. It shall be the duty of the pastor within the bounds of whose charge any such gift, bequest, or devise is made to give prompt notice thereof to said board, which shall proceed to take such steps as are necessary and proper to conserve, protect, and administer the same; *provided*, however, that the board may decline to receive or administer any such gift, devise, or bequest for any reason satisfactory to the board. It shall also be the duty of the pastor to report annually to the Board of Trustees of his Annual Conference a list of all property, including real, personal, or mixed, within his charge belonging to or which should be under the control or jurisdiction of the said board.

5. The board shall make to each session of the Annual Conference a full, true, and faithful report of its doings, of all funds, moneys, securities, and property held in trust by it, and of its receipts and disbursements during the conference year. The beneficiary of a fund held in trust by the board shall also be entitled to a report at least annually on the condition of such fund and on the transactions affecting it.

¶ 712. When authorized by two thirds of the Annual Conferences comprising an episcopal area, an **episcopal residence** for the resident bishop may be acquired, which shall be under the management and control of, and the title to which shall be held in trust by, the trustees of the Annual Conference within which the residence is located; and the purchase price and maintenance cost thereof shall be equitably distributed by the trustees among the several conferences in the area. Any such property so acquired and held shall not be sold or disposed of except with the consent of a majority of the conferences that participate in the ownership. Should an Annual Conference contribute to the purchase of an episcopal residence and later be transferred to an area not owning one, if it shall ask payment for its equity, such claim shall not be denied.[4]

¶ **716.** 1. A **district parsonage** for the district superintendent may be acquired, when authorized by the Quarterly Conferences of two thirds of the charges in the district, or when authorized by a two-thirds vote of the District Conference, subject to the advice and approval of the District Board of Church Location and Building, as provided in ¶¶ 723-25.

2. The title of district property may be held in trust by a **District Board of Trustees** of not fewer than three nor more than nine persons of the same qualifications provided for trustees of local churches (¶ 159), who shall be nominated by the district superintendent and elected by the District Conference. Where there is no District Conference, they may be elected by the District Board of Stewards or by the Annual Conference on nomination of the district superintendent. They shall be elected for a term of one year and serve until their successors shall have been elected, and shall report annually to the District Conference or Annual Conference. If the title to the district parsonage is not held by a District Board of Trustees, the same shall be held in trust by the trustees of the Annual Conference of which such district is a part, and such trustees shall report annually to the Annual Conference. Except as the laws of the state, territory, or country prescribe otherwise, district property held in trust by a District Board of Trustees may be mortgaged or sold and conveyed by them only by authority of the District Conference or Annual Conference; or, if such property is held in trust by the trustees of the Annual Conference, it may be mortgaged or sold and conveyed by such trustees only by authority of the Annual Conference. The purchase price and maintenance cost of a district parsonage shall be equitably distributed among the charges of the district by the District Board of Stewards.

3. When district boundaries are changed by division, re-

---

[4] *See* Judicial Council Decision 194.

arrangement, or consolidation, so that a district parsonage purchased, owned, and maintained by one district is included within the bounds of another district, each such district shall be entitled to receive its just share of the then reasonable value of the parsonage in which it has invested funds; and the amount of such value and just share shall be determined by a committee of three persons, appointed by the bishop of the area, who shall not be residents of any of the said districts. The committee shall hear claims of each district regarding its interest therein before making decision. From any such determination there is reserved unto each of the interested districts the right of appeal to the next succeeding Annual Conference. Any sum received as or from such share shall be used for no other purpose than purchase or building of a parsonage in the district. The same procedure shall be followed in determining equities of a district in any other property which may be included in another district by changes in district boundaries.

SEC. VI.   **District Board of Church Location and Building**

¶ 721. There shall be in each district of an Annual Conference a **District Board of Church Location and Building** consisting of the district superintendent, three ministers, and three laymen nominated by the district superintendent and elected annually by the Annual Conference; *provided* that in a district of great geographical extent an additional board may be so elected. The board shall file a report of any actions taken with the Quarterly Conference of each local church involved, and the report so filed shall become a part of the minutes of the said conference or conferences. The board shall also make a written report to the District Conference (or, if there is no District Conference, to the district superintendent), and this report shall become a part of the records of that conference.

¶ 722. 1. The board shall investigate all proposed local-church building sites, ascertaining that such sites are properly located for the community to be served, and adequate in size to provide space for future expansion and parking facilities. (*See* ¶¶ 155.1, 180.2.)

2. If there is a Metropolitan Area Planning Commission (¶ 1227) in the district, the board shall consider its recommendations in planning a strategy for continuing the service of The Methodist Church in changing neighborhoods. If not, the board shall study the duties assigned to such a commission and seek ways to provide continuity of service in parishes where there is a change in the racial or cultural character of the residents, to the end that the resolutions of the General Conference involving such neighborhoods be given careful consideration.

¶ **723.** 1. The board shall require any local church in its district, before beginning or contracting for construction or purchase of a new church or educational building or a parsonage, or remodeling of such a building if the cost will exceed ten per cent of its value, to submit for consideration and approval a statement of the need for the proposed facilities, preliminary architectural plans, an estimate of the cost, and a financial plan for defraying such costs, as provided in ¶ 180.4-.5. Before finally approving the architectural plans it shall ascertain whether the preliminary plans have been reviewed as provided in ¶¶ 1248.4, 1401.1.

2. When the local church has secured final architectural plans and specifications and a reliable and detailed estimate of the cost of the proposed undertaking as provided in ¶ 180.7, the board shall require their submission for consideration and approval. The board shall study carefully the feasibility and financial soundness of the undertaking, and ascertain whether the financial plan will provide funds necessary to assure prompt payment of all proposed contractual obligations; and it shall report its conclusions to the church in writing.

¶ **724.** A decision of the board disapproving such purchase, building, or remodeling shall be final unless overruled by the Annual Conference, to which there is reserved unto the local church the right of appeal.

¶ **725.** The provisions of ¶¶ 723-24 shall apply to the acquisition of a district parsonage. (¶-716.1.)

Sec. VII. **Local-Church Property**

Regulations governing local-church property and the election and duties of trustees of local churches are set forth in ¶¶ 151-94 of Part II, The Local Church.

Sec. VIII. **Sundry Provisions**

¶ 728. Trustees of schools, colleges, universities, hospitals, homes, orphanages, institutes, and other institutions owned or controlled by The Methodist Church shall be at least twenty-one years of age. At all times not less than three fourths of them shall be members of The Methodist Church; and all must be nominated, confirmed, or elected by some governing body of the church, or by some body or officer thereof to which or to whom this power has been delegated by the governing body of the church; *provided* that the number of trustees of any such institution owned or controlled by any Annual Conference or Conferences required to be members of The Methodist Church may be reduced to not less than the majority by a three-fourths vote of such Annual Conference or Conferences; and *provided*, further, that when an institution is owned and operated jointly with some other denomination or organization, said requirement that three fourths of the trustees shall be members of The Methodist Church shall apply only to the portion of the trustees representing The Methodist Church.

¶ 729. All persons holding trust funds, securities, or moneys of any kind belonging to the General Conference or to Annual or Provisional Annual Conferences or to organizations under the control of the General, Annual, or Provisional Annual Conferences shall be bonded in a reliable company in such good and sufficient sum as the conference may direct. The accounts of such persons shall be audited at least annually by a recognized public or certified public accountant. (*See* ¶¶ 803, 807.) A report to an Annual Conference containing a financial statement which the Discipline requires to be audited shall not be approved until the audit is made and the financial statement is shown to be correct. Other parts of the report may be approved pending such audit.[5]

---

[5] Amended in 1956 following Judicial Council Decision 77.

¶ **730.** Whenever the law of the state, territory, or country in which is located any property of The Methodist Church, its agencies or subdivisions, or the provisions of an existing charter of a corporation organized and holding property for such purposes, require otherwise than in this chapter prescribed, such law or charter shall apply and be substituted for such of the provisions of this chapter as are in conflict with such law or charter.[6]

CHAPTER II

CHURCH FINANCE

SECTION I.   **General Statement**

¶ **731.** The work of the church requires the support of our people, and participation therein through service and gifts is a Christian duty and a means of grace. In order that all members of The Methodist Church may share in its manifold ministries at home and abroad and that the work committed to us may prosper, the financial plan which follows has been duly approved and adopted.

¶ **732.** The various causes, funds, and budgets of The Methodist Church shall be known and designated as follows: (1) **world service,** the general benevolences of The Methodist Church, approved by the General Conference and included in the world service budget; (2) **conference benevolences,** the Annual Conference benevolences and causes, approved by the conference and included in the conference benevolence budget; (3) the **world service budget,** the **general administration budget,** the **episcopal budget,** the **interdenominational co-operation budget,** the amounts approved or estimated by the General Conference for these causes respectively; (4) **conference benevolence budget,** the amounts approved for Annual Conference causes respectively, and included in one budget; (5) **world service and conference benevolence budget,** the world service apportionment to any Annual Conference plus its conference benevolence budget, included in one sum and distributed among the charges

---

[6] *See* Judicial Council Decision 93.

of the conference; (6) the **World Service Fund** (¶¶ 740-49), the **General Administration Fund** (¶¶ 765-68), the **Episcopal Fund** (¶¶ 769-77), the **Interdenominational Co-operation Fund** (¶ 778), the **Methodist Committee for Overseas Relief Fund** (¶¶ 1311-15), the **Fellowship of Suffering and Service Fund** (¶ 763), the **One Great Hour of Sharing Fund** (¶ 760), the **Television-Radio Ministry Fund** (¶ 762), the **Temporary General Aid Fund**,[7] funds received into the central treasury for these causes respectively.

SEC. II. Council on World Service and Finance

¶ **735.** The General Conference at each quadrennial session shall elect a **Council on World Service and Finance** which shall through its central office receive and disburse, in accordance with the directions hereinafter set forth, all funds raised throughout the church for: (1) the World Service Fund, including world service special gifts and Advance special gifts, (2) the General Administration Fund, (3) the Episcopal Fund, (4) the Interdenominational Co-operation Fund, (5) the Methodist Committee for Overseas Relief Fund, (6) the Fellowship of Suffering and Service Fund, (7) the One Great Hour of Sharing Fund, (8) the Television-Radio Ministry Fund, and (9) any other fund or funds as directed by the proper authority. (For the authority and responsibility of the council in nonfiscal matters *see* ¶¶ 1105-10.)

¶ **736.** The council shall be elected and organized in accordance with the provisions of ¶¶ 1101-4.

¶ **737.** The council shall have the authority and responsibility to perform the following functions:

---

[7] The General Conference of 1964 established a Temporary General Aid Fund to provide grants-in-aid to raise the level of pensions and minimum salaries in the Central Jurisdiction and the Rio Grande Annual Conference and assist the Annual Conferences in geographical jurisdictions receiving transfers from the Central Jurisdiction where major differences in annuity and minimum salary rates are involved, to be administered for pensions by the General Board of Pensions (¶ 1685) and for minimum salaries by the National Division of the Board of Missions. A part of the amount was included in the world service budget, and the Council on World Service and Finance was authorized to apportion the rest to the Annual Conferences in the United States on the basis described in ¶ 767.

1. It shall submit to each quadrennial session of the General Conference, for its action and determination, a budget of annual expense for its own operation and for the world service agencies for the ensuing quadrennium. The expenses of the council, including the expense of the central office, shall be a first claim against the World Service Fund, the General Administration Fund, the Episcopal Fund, and the Interdenominational Co-operation Fund; and the total expense shall be prorated annually to each in proportion to the amount received on the account of each during the fiscal year. Out of funds thus provided the treasurer shall pay the expenses of the council, including the expense of the central office, and shall keep a true and accurate account thereof.

2. It shall require annually, one month in advance of its annual meeting, or as is deemed necessary, statements of proposed budgets of all agencies receiving general church funds. It shall also require certified public accountant audits annually of all treasuries receiving general church funds through the central treasury. (*See* ¶ 781.) It shall review in each such agency budget the amount for administration, service, and promotion, with a view to maintaining a proper balance among the various parts of the budgets.

3. It shall withhold approval of any item or items for inclusion in the budget or budgets receiving general church funds which in its judgment represents unnecessary duplication of activities or programs within an agency or between two or more agencies. (*See* ¶¶ 784, 1093.1.)

4. It shall recommend to the General Conference, for its action and determination, a world service program outlining the general financial objectives of the church for the forthcoming quadrennium, and proposing the ratio distribution of world service funds among the participating agencies. It shall indicate the proportion of world service funds to be used for administration, service, and promotion. It shall recommend apportionments to the Annual Conferences, subject to the approval of the General Conference.

5. It shall consult with the Co-ordinating Council and

the Council of Bishops relative to the number and timing of all special days which are to be observed on a church-wide basis. After such consultation the Co-ordinating Council shall make appropriate recommendations to the General Conference. Between sessions of the General Conference the Council of Bishops and the Council on World Service and Finance may, in an emergency, authorize a financial appeal.

6. It shall have authority to employ a comptroller. It shall require all agencies receiving general church funds to follow uniform accounting classifications and procedures for reporting and to submit a yearly audit following such auditing procedures as it may specify. It shall have authority to pass on the acceptability of any auditing firm proposed by an agency for handling such yearly audit. All general agencies of the church shall observe a uniform fiscal year ending on May 31.

7. It shall review the investment policies of all agencies receiving general church funds with respect to permanent funds and shall require that Christian as well as sound economic principles in the handling of investment funds be observed.

8. After consultation with the agency, it shall perform or arrange facilities for handling the treasury functions for any general agency which is not large enough to have a full-time treasurer and the financial policies of which are not approved by the council. The cost of such service shall be charged to the agency.

9. On the request of a general agency, it shall hold and invest funds allocated to it when such funds are not intended for current expenditure by that agency. It shall also hold and invest funds for any general agency which does not have an investment program approved by the council.

10. It shall establish standardized annuity rates and formulate policies for the writing of annuities by institutions and agencies operating under the auspices of The Methodist Church.

11. It shall receive bequests and memorial gifts in the interests of world service or one or more of the world service agencies. The moneys from these sources, where

not otherwise designated, shall be invested by the council and the income therefrom distributed annually according to the world service ratio; and the local church of the testator or donor shall receive a world service special-gift voucher (¶ 746).

12. It shall administer the General Administration Fund (¶¶ 765-68), the Episcopal Fund (¶¶ 769-77), and the Interdenominational Co-operation Fund (¶ 778).

13. It shall receive from the Board of Trustees a report of the distributable income from undesignated funds held by the board (¶ 708), and shall recommend to the General Conference how such income should be distributed.

¶ **738.** The treasurer of the Council on World Service and Finance shall, not less than thirty days prior to the session of each Annual Conference, transmit to the presiding bishop thereof, to the president of the Conference Commission on World Service and Finance, and to the conference treasurer a statement of the apportionments to the conference for the World Service Fund, the General Administration Fund, the Episcopal Fund, the Interdenominational Co-operation Fund, and such other funds as may have been apportioned by the General Conference. (*See* ¶¶ 749, 767, 771, 778.) He shall keep an account of all amounts remitted to him by the conference treasurers and from other sources intended for: (1) the World Service Fund, including world service special gifts and Advance special gifts, (2) the General Administration Fund, (3) the Episcopal Fund, (4) the Interdenominational Co-operation Fund, (5) the Methodist Committee for Overseas Relief Fund, (6) the Fellowship of Suffering and Service Fund, (7) the One Great Hour of Sharing Fund, (8) the Television-Radio Ministry Fund, (9) the Temporary General Aid Fund, and (10) any other fund so directed by the proper authority, and shall disburse the same as authorized by the General Conference and directed by the council. A separate account shall be kept of each such fund, and none of them shall be drawn on for the benefit of another. The fiscal year for the council and for the several funds, boards, and agencies related to it, shall be from June 1 to May 31 inclusive.

¶ **739.** The treasurer shall report annually to the council and to the respective conference commissions as to all amounts received and disbursed during the year. He shall also make to each quadrennial session of the General Conference a full report of the financial transactions of the council for the preceding quadrennium. The treasurer shall be bonded for such an amount as may be determined by the council. The books of the treasurer shall be audited annually by a certified public accountant approved by the executive committee.

SEC. III.   **The World Service Fund**

¶ **740.** The **World Service Fund** is basic in the financial program of The Methodist Church. World service on apportionment (¶¶ 749, 795) represents the minimum needs of the general agencies of the church. Payment in full of these apportionments by local churches and Annual Conferences is the first benevolent responsibility of the church. (*See* ¶ 804.)

¶ **741.** 1. Prior to each quadrennial session of the General Conference the Council on World Service and Finance shall make a diligent and detailed study of the needs of all the general causes or authorized agencies of the church asking to be included in the world service budget.

2. The general secretary or other duly authorized representative of each agency of The Methodist Church requesting support out of the World Service Fund, and the authorized representative of any other agency for which askings are authorized by the General Conference, shall appear before the council at a designated time and place to represent the cause for which each is responsible.

¶ **742.** The Council on World Service and Finance shall make diligent effort to secure full information concerning the general benevolence and service causes of the church, in order that none may be neglected, jeopardized, or excluded. It shall study in relation to each other the proposed programs of the several agencies as presented to it (¶ 741.2) and shall withhold approval of any item or items for inclusion in the world service budget which in its judgment represents unnecessary duplication of activities or programs. Basing its judgment of needs upon the programs of the several agencies as approved by it,

the council shall recommend to the General Conference
for its action and determination the amount to be apportioned in the annual world service budget for each
authorized agency of the church. The total amount thus
designated by the council for the several agencies, when
approved by the General Conference, shall be the annual
world service budget for the ensuing quadrennium. The
council shall recommend also to the General Conference for
its action and determination a plan and schedule for the
distribution of the receipts for the world service budget
among the several agencies. During the quadrennium the
council shall have full authority to correlate the work of
the world service agencies in the interest of co-operation,
economy, and effectiveness, as these relate to the financial
interests of the church.

¶ **743.** Any general board, cause, agency, institution,
or any organization, group, officer, or individual of The
Methodist Church desiring or proposing to make a special
church-wide financial appeal during the quadrennium, or
at any time in the interim of the quadrennial sessions of
the General Conference, shall present a request for authorization to make such appeal to the Council on World
Service and Finance when the askings of the regular
agencies are presented as provided in ¶ 741.2. The council shall then report such request to the General Conference with a recommendation for its action thereon.
"Special appeal" shall be understood to mean any appeal
other than the general appeal for support of the world
service program as represented in the world service
budget. (*See* ¶ 742.) "Church-wide appeal" shall be understood to mean any appeal to the church at large, except
appeals to such special groups as alumni of an educational
institution.

¶ **744.** The world service agencies shall not solicit additional or special gifts from individual donors or special
groups, other than foundations, unless approval for such
solicitation is first secured from the Council on World
Service and Finance.

¶ **745.** Individual donors or local churches may make
special gifts to the support of any cause or project which
is a part of the work of any one of the world service

agencies. Such gifts may be sent directly to the agency concerned, or to the central treasury of the Council on World Service and Finance. They shall not apply on the benevolence apportionment of any local church, and shall not be charged against the agency or agencies receiving them in the ratio distribution of the on-apportionment benevolences. Bequests, gifts on the annuity plan, gifts to permanent funds, and gifts of property shall be classified as special gifts. (*See* ¶ 746.5.)

¶ **746.** 1. All special gifts made to or administered by a general agency, except as provided in § 5, shall be acknowledged by **special-gift vouchers.**

2. The vouchers acknowledging such gifts to world service agencies shall be entitled "world service special-gift vouchers"; *provided,* however, that vouchers for such gifts to the World and National Divisions of the Board of Missions or the Methodist Committee for Overseas Relief (except as provided in ¶ 1314) shall be entitled "Advance special-gift vouchers" (¶ 758); and *provided,* further, that vouchers for the One Great Hour of Sharing offering (¶ 760), Fellowship of Suffering and Service offerings (¶ 763), and contributions to the Television-Radio Ministry Fund (¶ 762) shall bear the respective names of these appeals.

3. All special-gift vouchers shall be credited in their respective special columns in the Annual Conference minutes. The agency or office issuing each voucher shall send at the same time a duplicate voucher to the central treasury for forwarding to the conference treasurer.

4. A world service agency or any individual or agency authorized to make a church-wide appeal for funds, not equipped to issue special-gift vouchers, shall channel all special gifts through the central treasury. Individuals soliciting such funds shall channel the money received through the central treasury or the treasurer of the appropriate agency, which shall issue the proper vouchers.

5. Bequests, gifts on the annuity plan at maturity, and gifts of real property shall be reported to the central treasury as **supplemental contributions,** and shall not be included among the promoted funds chargeable under ¶ 754.

¶ **747.** The Council on World Service and Finance shall also recommend to the General Conference the days in connection with the church-wide observance of which the taking of special offerings shall be authorized, and in the case of each shall recommend whether or not the receipts derived therefrom shall be credited to the contributing local church as a part of its world service apportionment, and charged against the claims of the agency receiving the same. All such recommendations are subject to the approval of the General Conference.

¶ **748.** The General Conference having determined the budgeted amounts and the plan and schedule of distribution to the participating boards and agencies as provided in ¶ 742, thereafter no benevolence interest shall be allowed to have a prior or preferred claim or increased ratio participation in the world service budget during the quadrennium except to meet an emergency, and then only by a three-fourths vote of those present and voting at a regular or called meeting of the Council on World Service and Finance, the Council of Bishops concurring in this action by a three-fourths vote of those present and voting; nor shall the total world service budget be changed in the interim between the quadrennial sessions of the General Conference except as required by unforeseen conditions, and then only by a three-fourths vote of those present and voting at a regular or called meeting of the council, the Council of Bishops concurring in this action by a three-fourths vote of those present and voting. No general board, cause, agency, institution, or any organization, group, officer, or individual employed by The Methodist Church or any of the authorized groups of The Methodist Church shall make a church-wide financial appeal in the interim of the quadrennial sessions of the General Conference, unless authorized as provided in ¶ 743, except with the approval of the Council on World Service and Finance and the Council of Bishops. In case of emergency the executive committee of either of these bodies may act in such matter for the body itself, but only by a three-fourths vote. (*See* ¶ 743.)

¶ **749.** The Council on World Service and Finance shall after careful study prepare an equitable schedule of apportionments by which the total world service budget (¶ 742) shall be distributed to the several Annual Conferences and shall present the same to the General Conference for its action and determination.[8] (*See* ¶ 740.)

SEC. IV. **Commission on Promotion and Cultivation**

¶ 750. 1. In order to co-ordinate the promotion of the general benevolence causes of The Methodist Church, to the end that our people may be informed about, and may adequately support, the work of the general agencies, there shall be a **Commission on Promotion and Cultivation,** which shall establish and maintain a central promotional office, operating under its authority and direction, for the purpose of promoting throughout the church the program of world service, Advance specials (¶ 758), One Great Hour of Sharing offerings (¶ 760), the Television-Radio Ministry Fund (¶ 762), the Fellowship of Suffering and Service (¶ 763), the Interdenominational Co-operation Fund, and other general benevolence causes except as otherwise directed by the General Conference. The location of the central promotional office shall be subject to the approval of the Co-ordinating Council.

2. The commission shall be elected quadrennially and shall be constituted as follows: six bishops, one from each jurisdiction, elected by the Council of Bishops; one minister and one layman from each jurisdiction, and six members at large, at least three of whom shall be laymen, nominated by the Council of Bishops and elected by the General Conference. In addition the general secretaries of the several agencies of The Methodist Church which participate in funds promoted by the commission and the general secretary of the Woman's Division of Christian Service shall be ex officio members without vote.

3. The commission shall be constituted at the beginning of each quadrennium, and its members shall serve until their successors are duly elected and qualified. Interim vacancies among members at large shall be filled by the Council of Bishops and among jurisdictional representa-

---

[8] *See* Judicial Council Decision 30.

tives shall be filled by the College of Bishops of the jurisdiction concerned.

¶ **751.** The commission shall elect quadrennially the
following officers: a president, a vice-president, a recording secretary, and a **general secretary,** who shall be its
administrative officer. The treasurer of the Council on
World Service and Finance shall be its treasurer.

¶ **752.** The general secretary, under the authority and
direction of the commission, shall co-ordinate and promote
on a church-wide basis world service and all other general benevolence causes except as otherwise directed by
the General Conference. The commission shall set the
general secretary's salary, and shall make provision for
a staff and office facilities to carry on the work of the
commission. The general secretary shall co-operate with
the general secretary of the Council on World Service and
Finance. He shall, by such plans as shall be authorized
by the commission, promote the general benevolence
causes of the church through the bishops, district superintendents, pastors, lay officials, and General, Jurisdictional, and Annual Conference boards and agencies.

¶ **753.** 1. The commission shall have the responsibility
of reviewing at least annually, and as often in addition as
may be necessary, the several and combined plans of the
general agencies for the production and distribution of all
free literature and promotional and resource periodicals
(except church-school literature) for the purpose of co-
ordinating the content, distribution, and timing of the
release of such materials. In case of inability to work out
adequate plans and procedures for co-ordinating the content, timing and distribution, the matter shall be referred
to the Co-ordinating Council.

2. The commission shall study the problems of co-
ordinating and simplifying the methods and facilities for
distribution of materials and may arrange for improved
and more efficient distribution of literature.

3. The commission shall publish a free program journal
for pastors and local-church leaders, *The Methodist Story,*
which shall present to the local church for its use the
program and promotional materials of the general agencies in a correlated manner, and shall be in lieu of gen-

eral-agency promotional periodicals (*provided* that this shall not apply to *The Methodist Woman* and *The Methodist Layman*). The editor shall be elected quadrennially by the commission after consultation with the Co-ordinating Council through a joint committee composed of the general secretary and two members of the commission, one of whom shall be a bishop, and the chairman and two other members of the council. He shall be responsible to the general secretary for ongoing publishing procedures, but shall himself be responsible for the editorial content of the journal.

4. In view of the fact that there is an inseparable relationship between education in stewardship and giving, the commission shall co-operate with the Boards of Education and of Lay Activities in a church-wide program of stewardship education, with special emphasis on the stewardship of possessions, which shall be closely related to giving to the benevolence causes which Methodists are called on to support. Stewardship of possessions shall be interpreted to mean that the tithe is the minimum standard of giving for Methodist people, and shall be promoted by providing appropriate literature for the use of churches and pastors in enlisting Methodist people as tithers. To carry on this program there shall be an **Interboard Committee on Stewardship,** composed of representatives of the three agencies, which shall meet annually or oftener as it may determine. The chairmanship shall rotate annually among the agencies as the committee may determine.

5. The commission may commit to its central promotional office any other cause or undertaking, financial or otherwise, not herein mentioned, demanding church-wide promotion or publicity; *provided* that such action shall have been previously approved by the Council of Bishops and the Council on World Service and Finance, or by their respective executive committees.

6. The commission shall report to the General Conference.

¶ **754.** The expenses of the commission, including the editing, publishing, and distribution of *The Methodist Story*, fourth-Sunday world service leaflets, and other publications or visual aids for the promoting of general benevolences authorized by the General Conference, shall be prorated monthly to the several promoted funds on the basis of receipts for each fund. The budget of the commission, as recommended by the Council on World Service and Finance and approved by the General Conference, shall be a fixed charge against the World Service Fund and a prior charge against the other promoted funds.

¶ 755. 1. In each Annual Conference there shall be constituted a **Conference Commission on Promotion and Cultivation** to promote the program of world service and other general benevolence causes in the pastoral charges of the conference in co-operation with the central promotional office of the general commission; *provided*, however, that if a Conference Council or similar body (¶ 679) serves as the promotional agency for all general benevolences approved by the conference, it shall function in lieu of a conference commission in co-operation with the central promotional office, and may form a committee for that purpose. This commission shall see that each agency provides for the proper presentation of the cause it represents to the Commission on World Service and Finance for consideration and recommendation to the conference in regular session. It shall also co-ordinate the promotion of all approved general and conference benevolence causes, and shall assign responsibility for the promotion of approved causes that do not clearly belong to an existing agency.

2. The commission shall be composed of the following members: the resident bishop and one or more members of his Cabinet chosen by the bishop; representatives, one from each district, at least half of whom shall be laymen, nominated by the bishop and his Cabinet or by the conference nominating committee and elected by the conference; and the executive secretaries of the Conference Boards of Missions and of Education, conference missionary secretary, secretary of missionary education of the Conference Woman's Society of Christian Service, conference lay leader, conference director of stewardship, and any members of the general commission residing with-

in the bounds of the conference. Additional members, with special qualifications for service on the commission, may be added on nomination by the commission and approval by the Cabinet. The presidents of the Commission on World Service and Finance, Conference Board of Missions, and Conference Woman's Society of Christian Service, the chairman of the Conference Television, Radio, and Film Commission, the conference or area director of public relations and Methodist information, and such additional officers as the bishop and Cabinet may name shall be ex officio members without vote.

3. In order to secure full participation in the support of the several benevolence causes the commission, or the Conference Council, may organize under its authority and direction a World Service Committee to promote the program of world service and conference benevolences (¶¶ 793, 795) and an Advance Committee to promote the program of the Advance—general Advance specials (¶¶ 756, 758), conference Advance specials (¶¶ 756, 759), and the One Great Hour of Sharing (¶ 760)—as these programs are developed by the respective agencies, and such other committees as it may deem necessary.

4. The budget for the commission shall be provided by the conference through its Commission on World Service and Finance.

Sec. V.   The Advance

¶ 756. For the more adequate support of the missionary program of the church, the **Advance** shall be organized and administered as hereinafter set forth, to the end that opportunity may be given each local church through its pastoral-charge Quarterly Conference to participate in such support, over and above its world service contributions, as each may determine. (*See* ¶ 149.3.) The Advance program shall include all special gifts (¶ 745) to missionary causes, which shall be designated as general Advance specials (¶ 758) or conference Advance specials (¶ 759), and One Great Hour of Sharing offerings (¶ 760).

¶ 757. 1. There shall be a **General Advance Committee,** organized under the authority and direction of the Gen-

255

eral Commission on Promotion and Cultivation. It shall consist of twelve members, representing equally all six jurisdictions, and including at least two bishops, two ministers, and two laymen, named by the commission from its membership. In addition the associate general secretaries of the World and National Divisions and Joint Commission on Education and Cultivation of the Board of Missions and the general secretaries of the Methodist Committee for Overseas Relief, the Council on World Service and Finance, and the General Commission on Promotion and Cultivation shall be ex officio members.

2. The committee shall have general oversight of the Advance program in accordance with the plan and procedure hereinafter described.

¶ **758. 1. A general Advance special** is a designated gift made by an individual, local church, organization, district, or Annual Conference to a specific project in missions or overseas relief that has been authorized by the General Advance Committee. Agencies authorized to receive funds for their projects as general Advance specials shall be the World and National Divisions of the Board of Missions and the Methodist Committee for Overseas Relief.

2. As far as practicable these specials shall be solicited for specific objects that may be visualized and described. Each such special object shall be approved by the Advance Committee (or by a committee on specials appointed by it) on recommendation of the agency concerned. An Annual Conference, local church, or individual may assume responsibility for an undesignated foreign, home, or overseas relief special, in which case the agency concerned shall determine where such special shall be allocated, shall inform the donor where his gift has been invested, and shall as far as practicable establish communication between donor and recipient. All specials authorized by the Advance Committee and solicited for special projects shall be reported in duplicate to the general secretary of the commission and to the treasurer of the Council on World Service and Finance.

3. Receipts for general Advance specials shall be remitted by the local-church treasurer to the conference

treasurer, who shall make remittance each month to the general treasurer. The general treasurer shall remit monthly to the respective participating agencies the amount received for each; *provided*, however, than when a donor church or individual so elects, remittance may be made directly to the treasurer of the agency administering such special, whereupon the agency receiving such remittance shall send to the central treasury a voucher for the central treasurer and a voucher for the conference treasurer.

4. Each participating agency shall administer the general Advance specials received by it in harmony with procedures approved by the Advance Committee, and shall report them to the Advance Committee at such intervals and in such detail as the committee may request.

5. Each participating agency shall, on receipt of a general Advance special, communicate with the donor, whether conference, local church, or individual, and as far as practicable establish communication between donor and recipient.

¶ **759.** Each Annual Conference is authorized to initiate and promote **conference Advance specials** for missionary and church-extension objects within the conference, as follows:

1. Proposed conference Advance specials shall be approved and promoted by the Conference Board of Missions.

2. Conference Advance specials may be administered by the Conference Board of Missions, or by the National Division of the General Board of Missions on request of the Annual Conference concerned.

3. An Annual Conference may undertake a conference-wide campaign for a lump sum to be applied to its missionary and church-extension needs. The funds so received shall be designated as conference Advance specials, and shall be administered by the Conference Board of Missions. Local churches shall report their respective contributions as conference Advance specials.

4. Unless the Annual Conference directs otherwise, a district within the conference may authorize and promote Advance specials for church-extension and missionary needs within the district, such funds to be administered

by a district missionary society organized for that purpose, or by a similar body set up by the District Conference. Such specials secured and administered on a district level shall be reported by each local church to the Annual Conference as conference Advance specials.

5. Annual Conference report forms shall include separate spaces designated as "Advance specials, general," and "Advance specials, conference"; and local churches shall report accordingly.

6. It is recommended that each Annual Conference or district administering conference Advance specials set aside each year ten per cent of the amount received for that purpose for aid to the weaker and more urgent situations outside the conference, and that such amount be remitted to the National Division of the General Board of Missions, to be administered by it as a general Advance special.

¶ 760. The annual observance of the **One Great Hour of Sharing** (continuing the Week of Dedication offering) shall be under the general supervision of the Commission on Promotion and Cultivation, in accordance with the following directives:

1. The One Great Hour of Sharing shall be observed annually on or about the fourth Sunday in Lent. All local churches shall be fully informed and encouraged to contribute a freewill offering in behalf of the Crusade scholarship program (¶ 1287), the overseas relief program (¶¶ 1311-15), the ministry to servicemen overseas program of The Methodist Church, and such capital funds emergency projects of the National Division of the Board of Missions as may be authorized by the commission.

2. In connection with the One Great Hour of Sharing there shall be an emphasis on the spiritual implications of Christian stewardship.

3. The participating agencies shall administer the funds in accordance with the ratios determined by the commission: the Crusade Scholarship Committee for the Crusade Scholarship Fund (¶ 1287); the Methodist Committee for Overseas Relief for the Overseas Relief Fund (¶¶ 1311-15); the World Division of the Board of

Missions for the Servicemen Overseas Fund in co-operation with the co-operative committee of the National Council of Churches; and the National Division for the capital funds emergency projects.

4. The One Great Hour of Sharing offering shall be promptly remitted by the local-church treasurer to the conference treasurer, who shall remit monthly to the general treasurer. The general treasurer shall distribute these funds to the participating agencies in accordance with the ratios determined by the commission.

5. A One Great Hour of Sharing special-gift voucher shall be issued (see ¶ 746), and a space for reporting the amount of the offering shall be included in the form for pastors' reports to the Annual Conference.

6. The expense budget for promoting the One Great Hour of Sharing shall be subject to approval annually by the commission and shall be a prior charge against receipts from these offerings.

¶ 761. The following general directives shall be observed in the promotion and administration of the Advance:

1. In the appeal and promotion of Advance specials and One Great Hour of Sharing offerings there shall be no goals or quotas, except as they may be set by the Annual Conferences for themselves.

2. The treasurer of the Council on World Service and Finance shall be treasurer of the Advance.

3. The expense of promotion for Advance specials shall be borne by the respective participating agencies in proportion to the amount received by each in Advance specials. The causes of the Advance shall be correlated with other financial appeals and shall be promoted by the central promotional office of the Commission on Promotion and Cultivation.

4. The appeal for Advance specials shall be channeled through bishops, district superintendents, and pastors, the details of the procedure to be determined by the Commission on Promotion and Cultivation in consultation with the Joint Commission on Education and Cultivation of the Board of Missions and the Advance Committee.

5. In each Annual Conference the Conference Board of

Missions, in co-operation with the General Board of Missions and the General and Conference Commissions on Promotion and Cultivation, shall promote Advance specials and One Great Hour of Sharing offerings through district missionary secretaries, conference and district missionary institutes, and other effective means as it may determine.

6. Should a clear emergency arise, any feature of the structure and administration of the Advance may be altered by the General Commission on Promotion and Cultivation on the approval of a majority of the Council of Bishops and of the Council on World Service and Finance.

Sec. VI.   **Other Special Appeals**

¶ **762.** There shall be a world service special-gift fund known as the **Television-Radio Ministry Fund,** which shall be used for the creation, distribution, and utilization of television and radio programs, and shall be administered by the Television, Radio, and Film Commission. It shall be raised as follows:

1. Promotion shall be by the central promotional office of the Commission on Promotion and Cultivation in consultation with the general secretary of the Television, Radio, and Film Commission or a special committee thereof as it may determine; and the appeal shall be channeled through the bishops, district superintendents, and pastors with the aid of the Conference Commissions on Promotion and Cultivation.

2. Each Annual Conference may appoint a **Television-Radio Ministry Fund Committee** to work on the conference and district level with the General and Conference Television, Radio, and Film Commissions in interpreting to the local churches the need for this fund. Each Conference Commission on Promotion and Cultivation may appoint within its membership a committee on the Television-Radio Ministry Fund, including the chairman of the Television, Radio, and Film Commission, to work on the conference and district levels.

3. No goals or quotas shall be given except as the Annual Conferences may determine for themselves.

4. A Television-Radio Ministry special-gift voucher shall be issued. (*See* ¶ 746.)

5. The Council on World Service and Finance is authorized to provide a space for recording contributions to this fund in the pastor's report to the Annual Conference.

6. All contributions for the fund shall be channeled through the conference treasurer to the treasurer of the Council on World Service and Finance.

7. If the Television, Radio, and Film Commission deems it desirable, the designation of special projects within the Television-Radio Ministry program may be authorized.

¶ 763. **The Fellowship of Suffering and Service** appeal shall be continued until it is deemed no longer needed, either by the General Conference or, between its sessions, by three-fourths vote of the Council of Bishops and of the Council on World Service and Finance meeting separately. Each local church shall be requested to transmit, either through its conference treasurer or directly to the treasurer of the Council on World Service and Finance, under designation of the Fellowship of Suffering and Service, all the Communion offering received on Worldwide Communion Sunday (the first Sunday in October) and a portion of the Communion offerings received at subsequent observances of the Sacrament of the Lord's Supper. A Fellowship of Suffering and Service special-gift voucher shall be issued (*see* ¶ 746), and a space for reporting the amount of the offerings shall be included in the form for the pastor's report to the Annual Conference. The treasurer of the Council on World Service and Finance is authorized to distribute these receipts on the basis of fifty per cent to the Methodist Committee for Overseas Relief and twenty-five per cent each to the Commission on Chaplains and the Commission on Camp Activities.

¶ 764. The General Commission on Promotion and Cultivation may organize special committees from its membership for the effective promotion of special days and other special appeals referred to it for promotion by the Council of Bishops and the Council on World Service and Finance.

Sec. VII.   **The General Administration Fund**

¶ **765.** The General Administration Fund shall provide for the expenses of the sessions of the General Conference, the Judicial Council, the Co-ordinating Council (¶ 1092.4), the Departments of Research, Records, and Statistics (¶ 1106) and the Transportation Office (¶ 1108) of the Council on World Service and Finance, the Committee on Family Life (¶ 1417), the Commission on Worship (¶ 1568), the Commission on Ecumenical Affairs (¶ 1575), the Commission on Public Relations and Methodist Information (¶ 1588), the Association of Methodist Historical Societies (¶ 1591), the World Methodist Council (¶ 1594), Religion in American Life (¶ 1599), such special commissions and committees as may be constituted by the General Conference (*see* ¶ 710), and such interchurch causes and other activities as may be authorized by the General Conference other than those provided for under the Interdenominational Co-operation Fund (¶778).[9] Any agency or institution requiring or desiring support from the General Administration Fund shall present its case for the same to the Council on World Service and Finance at a time and place which shall be indicated by the officers of the council. The council, having heard such requests, shall report the same to the General Conference with recommendations for its action and determination.

¶ **766.** The Council on World Service and Finance shall submit to each quadrennial session of the General Conference an annual general administration budget, including such items as in the judgment of the council should be provided for out of this fund for the ensuing quadrennium. The council shall likewise recommend to the General Conference what prior or preferred claims shall be allowed in the general administration budget, and by what plan or ratios the causes included in the budget shall share in the funds collected. The general administration budget thus submitted, including all recommendations, shall be subject to the action and determination of the General Conference.

¶ **767.** The Council on World Service and Finance shall

---

[9] *See* Judicial Council Decision 17.

apportion among the several Annual Conferences of the church the total general administration budget, as approved by the General Conference, by such ratio and percentage to the total giving (not including the payment of debts or for church buildings), as recorded in the General Minutes for the first three years of the quadrennium closing with the current session of the General Conference, as is necessary to raise the approved annual budget. The apportionments for the general administration budget shall not be subject to change or revision either by the Annual Conference or by the charge or local church.

¶ **768.** The treasurer of the Council on World Service and Finance shall disburse the funds received by him for the General Administration Fund as authorized by the General Conference and as directed by the council. Where the General Conference has not allocated definite sums to agencies receiving money from the General Administration Fund, the Council on World Service and Finance, or its executive committee, shall have authority to determine the amount to be allocated to each.

SEC. VIII. **The Episcopal Fund**

¶ **769.** The Episcopal Fund, raised separately from all other funds, shall provide for the salary and expenses of effective bishops and for the support of retired bishops and of the widows and minor children of deceased bishops. Subject to the approval of the Council on World Service and Finance, the treasurer shall have authority to borrow for the benefit of the Episcopal Fund such amounts as may be necessary for the proper execution of the orders of the General Conference.

¶ **770.** The Council on World Service and Finance shall recommend to each quadrennial session of the General Conference for its action and determination: (1) the amounts to be fixed as salaries of the effective bishops; (2) a schedule of such amounts as may be judged adequate to provide for their expense of house, office, and travel; (3) the amounts to be fixed as annual pensions for the support of retired bishops; and (4) a schedule of allowance for the widows and for the support of minor children of deceased bishops. From the facts in hand the council shall estimate the approximate total amount required annually during the ensuing quadrennium to provide for the items of episcopal support above mentioned, and shall report the same to the General Conference. This amount as finally determined shall be the estimated episcopal budget.

¶ 771. The Council on World Service and Finance shall estimate what percentage of the total salaries paid pastors and associate pastors by the entire church will yield an amount equal to the estimated episcopal budget, and shall make recommendations to the General Conference concerning the same for its action and determination. When such percentage has been approved by the General Conference, it shall be the basis of the annual apportionment to each Annual Conference for the Episcopal Fund. The apportionment to each Annual Conference shall be an amount equal to the approved percentage of the total cash salaries paid to the pastors and associate pastors serving charges under episcopal appointment or as supply pastors, as reported to the current session of the Annual Conference. This apportionment shall be distributed to the pastoral charges as the conference may determine. In every case the amount apportioned to a charge for the Episcopal Fund shall be paid in the same proportion as the charge pays its pastor.

¶ 772. The treasurer of the Council on World Service and Finance shall remit monthly to each effective bishop one twelfth of his annual salary, and also one twelfth of his house rent or maintenance, and office expenses as approved by the council. Allowances for retired bishops and for the widows and minor children of deceased bishops shall be paid to them severally in equal monthly installments.

¶ 773. The treasurer of the Council on World Service and Finance shall pay monthly the claim for the official travel of each bishop or missionary bishop, upon presentation of an itemized voucher.[10] "Official travel" of an effective bishop shall be interpreted to include all visitations to local churches within his area, and to institutions or

---

[10] *See* Judicial Council Decisions **117, 164.**

enterprises of The Methodist Church where he is called in the performance of his official duties, and such journeys outside his area as are within the meaning of "travel through the connection at large" (¶ 431.10). No part of the expense and no honoraria for any such visitations shall be accepted from local Methodist churches or enterprises or institutions of The Methodist Church, such expense being a proper claim against the Episcopal Fund; *provided* that, when a bishop who is a member of an agency of the church is called to a meeting of the same or to a meeting of a committee thereof, the expense incident to such journey shall be paid by the said agency.

Nothing in this interpretation is intended to preclude special or nonofficial engagements of a bishop, other than the oversight of the temporal and spiritual affairs of the church (¶ 431.1), such as series of lectures in educational institutions, baccalaureate addresses, and preaching missions of several days' duration, when such engagements do not interfere with his official duties; nor does it preclude the acceptance of honoraria for such services.

¶ **774.** 1. The pensions for the support of retired bishops elected by General or Jurisdictional Conferences and the surviving widows and minor dependent children of such deceased bishops shall be provided by means of a contributory reserve pension fund to be held and administered by the Council on World Service and Finance in consultation with the General Board of Pensions.

2. The amounts of the annual pensions payable to such persons shall be determined by the General Conference, on recommendation of the council.

3. Each bishop in active service shall contribute annually to the fund an amount equal to three per cent of his cash salary. The treasurer of the Episcopal Fund is authorized and instructed to withhold from each bishop's salary the amount of his required contribution and pay it to the fund.

4. Any and all benefit derived from the contributions required of a bishop shall be regarded as a part of the total amount of the pension payable to said bishop upon his retirement and to his surviving widow and minor dependent children.

5. The remainder of the cost of the reserve funding of such pensions shall be provided from the Episcopal Fund in accordance with such program and procedure as may from time to time be determined by the council with the approval of the General Conference.

6. The council is directed to proceed as rapidly as possible to convert fully the present pension program to a program of reserve funding of the pensions of bishops and of the widows and dependent minor children of deceased bishops.

¶ 775. Should any effective bishop in the interim of the quadrennial sessions of his Jurisdictional Conference be relieved by the College of Bishops of his jurisdiction from the performance of regular episcopal duties (¶ 431), on account of ill health or for any other reason, the president of the said College of Bishops shall so notify the treasurer of the Episcopal Fund. Beginning ninety days after such notification, he shall receive the regular pension allowance of a retired bishop, and such pension allowance shall continue until he resumes the regular duties of an effective bishop or until his status shall have been determined by his Jurisdictional Conference. Assignment of another bishop or bishops to perform the regular episcopal duties of a bishop so disabled or otherwise incapacitated, for a period of sixty days or more, shall be interpreted as a release of the said bishop from the performance of his regular episcopal duties.

¶ 776. Should any retired bishop, in the interim of the quadrennial sessions of his Jurisdictional Conference, be called into active service by the Council of Bishops and assigned to active episcopal duty (¶ 436.5), he shall be entitled to remuneration for such service out of the Episcopal Fund. In the event of such assignment of a retired bishop to active episcopal duty, the president of the Council of Bishops shall notify the treasurer of the Episcopal Fund, giving full information as to the nature and scope of the work assigned him. On the basis of this information the Council on World Service and Finance or its executive committee shall determine what salary remuneration and what expense allowance shall be allowed the bishop concerned during the period of his active service. The treasurer of the Episcopal Fund shall make remittance to him accordingly.

¶ **777.** In determining the schedule of allowances for the widows of deceased bishops the following rules shall apply: Each beneficiary who prior to the death of her husband had been his wife for not less than fifteen years while he was engaged in the effective ministry of The Methodist Church, whether bishop or traveling preacher, shall receive the full allowance for the widow of a deceased bishop, as ordered by the General Conference. The allowance of the widow of a deceased bishop who prior to the death of her husband had been his wife for less than fifteen years while he was an effective minister of The Methodist Church shall be determined on the basis of that fraction of fifteen years during which she was his wife while he was an effective minister of The Methodist Church, whether bishop or traveling preacher; *provided* that the Council on World Service and Finance may at its discretion increase the said allowance if special need exists, but in no instance shall the allowance of the widow of a deceased bishop exceed the full allowance as hereinbefore set forth.

SEC. IX.   **The Interdenominational Co-operation Fund**

¶ **778.** The Council on World Service and Finance shall recommend to the General Conference the sum which the church shall undertake to provide as its share of the budget of the National Council of Churches (¶ 1595), the General Commission on Chaplains and Armed Forces Personnel, and the World Council of Churches (¶ 1596). The sum approved by the General Conference for this purpose shall be the interdenominational co-operation budget. The Council on World Service and Finance shall recommend to the General Conference, for its consideration and determination, appropriate measures to be employed in order to provide the approved sum. The money contributed by the local churches, boards, or other agencies for this purpose shall be known as the Interdenominational Co-operation Fund, and shall be received and held by the treasurer of the Council on World Service and Finance and disbursed as the General Conference shall direct. Promotion shall be by the Commission on Promotion and Cultivation.

SEC. X.   **Miscellaneous**

¶ **781.** All boards and other agencies receiving financial support from the World Service Fund, the General Administration Fund, or any authorized church-wide appeal shall make to the Council on World Service and Finance audited reports of all receipts and disbursements in such detail and at such times as the council may direct. (*See* ¶ 737.2, .6; *also* ¶ 729.)

¶ **782.** During the quadrennium these agencies shall study their respective functions, programs, and internal operations and institute such improvements and economies in their work as they find to be feasible and practicable. They shall co-operate with the council in working out, in advance of these studies, the general areas to be included and methods of carrying out this objective. They shall report their accomplishments in improvements and economies at the close of each fiscal year to the council, which shall prepare from this information a combined report for the General Conference.

¶ **783.** 1. Each world service agency, so far as possible, shall adopt the following levels in agency organization:

a) **Board** or **division**—the general organization of staff responsibility.

b) **Section**—a broad subdivision of responsibility in a board or division.

c) **Department**—a specific phase of service to the field.

d) **Bureau**—a subdivision of responsibility within a department.

2. Each world service agency shall adopt the following titles for staff executives:

a) **General secretary**—head of a council, board, division, commission, joint section, or the Methodist Committee for Overseas Relief.

b) **Associate secretary**—an executive second in authority to a general secretary, who may be assigned authority to speak for the general secretary in his absence; *provided* that the title **associate general secre-**

tary may be used for an associate secretary who also has certain executive secretaries responsible to him, or who is administrative head of a division within a board which has one general secretary.

c) **Executive secretary**—head of a section or of an interboard committee.

d) **Director**—head of a department.

e) **Superintendent**—head of a bureau.

¶ **784.** In the event of any interboard disagreement on matters of policy and program involving world service funds, the Council on World Service and Finance shall act as arbiter. It shall also consider any complaints from contributors, whether individuals or organizations. If it shall discover what in its judgment is unnecessary duplication of activities or lack of correlation in the programs of the several agencies in relation to each other, it shall promptly direct the attention of the agencies involved to the situation and shall co-operate with them in correcting the same and may decline to supply from the world service treasury money to continue activities which have been held by the council to duplicate each other unnecessarily or plainly violate the principle of correlation as applied to the total benevolence program of the church. (*See* ¶ 737.3.)

¶ **785.** The Council on World Service and Finance may receive, take title to, collect, or hold, absolutely or in trust for the benefit of the World Service Fund, the General Administration Fund, the Episcopal Fund, the Interdenominational Co-operation Fund, the Methodist Committee for Overseas Relief Fund, the Fellowship of Suffering and Service Fund, the One Great Hour of Sharing Fund, the Television-Radio Ministry Fund, or the Temporary General Aid Fund of The Methodist Church, or any other fund or funds properly committed to its care, or for proper distribution among the causes supported by these funds, any and all donations, bequests, and devises of any kind or character, real or personal, that may be given, devised, bequeathed, or conveyed unto said Council on World Service and Finance, and administer the same and the income therefrom in accordance with the directions of the donor, trustor, or testator.

The Council on World Service and Finance shall also have power to invest, reinvest, buy, sell, transfer, and convey any and all funds and properties which it may hold absolutely or in trust, subject always to the terms of the legacy, devise, or donation.

¶ **786.** The Council on World Service and Finance shall recommend to each Conference Commission on World Service and Finance a uniform procedure for presenting its report to the Annual Conference and shall prepare a form for the guidance of the conference treasurer in making his annual statement in the conference journal. (*See* ¶ 806.)

Sec. XI.   **The Conference Commission on World Service and Finance**

¶ **791.** Each Annual Conference shall elect, at its session next succeeding the General Conference, a **Commission on World Service and Finance,** nominated by the district superintendents or a nominating committee, as the conference may determine, and composed of five ministers and six lay persons; *provided* that in smaller conferences the number may be reduced to not less than two ministers and three lay persons. Their term of service shall begin with the adjournment of the said conference session, and they shall serve for the quadrennium and until their successors shall have been chosen. No member or employee of any conference board and no employee, trustee, or director of any agency or institution participating in the funds of the conference benevolence budget shall be eligible for membership on the commission. Any vacancy shall be filled by action of the commission until the next conference session, at which time the Annual Conference shall fill the vacancy.

¶ **792.** The commission shall elect a president, a vice-president, and a secretary. The conference treasurer (¶ 803) shall be the treasurer of the commission. As an employee of the commission, he shall not be a member of it, but may sit with the commission and its executive committee at all sessions and have the privilege of the floor but without vote. He shall be bonded in a surety company approved by the commission, and for an amount which the commission judges to be adequate.

¶ 793. The chairman of each conference agency, or other duly authorized representative, shall have opportunity to represent the claims of his agency before the commission. The commission shall make diligent effort to secure full information regarding all conference benevolence and service causes, that none may be neglected, jeopardized, or excluded, and shall recommend to the Annual Conference for its action and determination the total amount to be apportioned for conference causes and included in the conference benevolence budget. All agencies receiving financial support from conference benevolences, or from any other authorized conference-wide appeal, shall make to the commission audited reports concerning all such receipts and the disbursements thereof in such detail and at such times as the commission may direct.[11]

¶ 794. The commission shall also recommend to the Annual Conference for its action and determination the amount or the percentage of the total sum of the conference benevolence budget which shall be apportioned to each cause included in the said budget.

¶ 795. The commission, on receiving from the treasurer of the Council on World Service and Finance a statement of the amount apportioned that Annual Conference for world service, shall combine the world service apportionment and the approved conference benevolence budget (¶ 793) in one total sum to be known as **world service and conference benevolences.** The total world service and conference benevolence budget thus established shall include a statement of the percentage for world service and the percentage for conference benevolences and shall be distributed annually among the districts or charges, by the method determined by the conference (¶ 796), and by such divisions and ratios as the conference may approve.[12] A like distribution shall be made of Jurisdictional Conference apportionments and any other apportionments that have been properly made to the Annual Conference. The

---

[11] *See* Judicial Council Decision 148.
[12] *See* Judicial Council Decision 63.

distribution of all apportionments mentioned in this paragraph shall be subject to the approval of the Annual Conference.

¶ 796. The commission shall recommend to the Annual Conference for its action and determination whether the apportionments referred to in ¶ 795 shall be made by the commission to the districts only, or to the charges of the conference. If the apportionments are made by the commission to the districts only, then the distribution to the charges of each district shall be made as provided in ¶ 797. The conference may order that the entire distribution to all the charges of the conference be made by the district superintendents.

¶ 797. Should the Annual Conference make the apportionments to the districts only, the distribution to the charges of each district shall be made by its **District Board of Stewards,** composed of the district superintendent as chairman and the district stewards elected by the several Quarterly Conferences (¶ 143.3). In that case it shall be the duty of the district superintendent to call a meeting of the board as soon as practicable after the adjournment of the Annual Conference; and the board shall make the distribution to the charges of the district, using such methods as it may determine, unless the Annual Conference shall have determined the method of distribution to the charges.

¶ 798. The commission shall include in its recommendations to the Annual Conference the amounts computed by the Conference Board of Pensions as necessary to meet the needs for annuity payments and relief. (*See* ¶ 1623.)

¶ 799. The commission shall report to the Annual Conference at each session the standard percentage approved by the General Conference for the Episcopal Fund as an apportionment to the Annual Conference, as described in ¶ 771. This apportionment shall be distributed to the pastoral charges as the conference may determine.

¶ 800. The commission, on receiving from the Council on World Service and Finance a statement of the amount apportioned to the Annual Conference for the General Administration Fund (¶ 767) and the Interdenominational Co-operation Fund (¶ 778), shall apportion the same to the several districts or charges as the conference may direct.

¶ **801.** It shall be the duty of the commission, unless otherwise provided (¶ 802), to estimate the total amount necessary to furnish a sufficient and equitable support for the district superintendents of the conference, including salary and suitable provision for dwelling, travel, and office expense. The commission shall recommend to the Annual Conference for its action and determination the amount estimated, including the salary and other allowances specified above, for each of the several district superintendents. The commission shall also recommend to the Annual Conference for its action and determination the basis and method by which the total amount shall be apportioned to the districts or charges in harmony with ¶ 822. The conference treasurer shall, as far as practicable, remit monthly to the several district superintendents the amounts due them, respectively, and with the approval of the Annual Conference the commission, or the treasurer, as the conference may determine, may borrow the funds necessary to make this possible. If an Annual Conference adopts the basic salary plan (¶ 827) for ministerial support, the support for the several district superintendents thereof shall be included therein. The amounts necessary to provide for suitable dwelling, travel, and office expense may be included in the basic salary budget or apportioned separately as the conference may determine.[13]

¶ **802.** Annual Conferences which elect to do so may provide for the support of district superintendents through the District Board of Stewards in each of the several districts. In that case the board, under the chairmanship of the district superintendent (¶ 797), shall estimate the salary and expenses of the district superintendent and shall apportion the same among the several charges of the district by the plan it shall adopt. The amount apportioned for the support of the district superintendent shall be included in the items of ministerial support (¶ 821). The board may elect a **district treasurer,** to whom the treasurer of each local church shall

---

[13] *See* Judicial Council Decision 44.

make remittances, and who shall in turn make payment to the district superintendent. In the event that no such treasurer is elected, remittances shall be made directly to the district superintendent. There shall be a settlement at least once a quarter, when proportional payments for the various items of ministerial support shall be made. (*See* ¶ 823.)

¶ 803. Each Annual Conference, on nomination of its Commission on World Service and Finance,[14] shall, at the first session of the conference after the General Conference, elect a **conference treasurer.** He shall serve for the quadrennium or until his successor shall be elected and qualify. If a vacancy should occur during the quadrennium, the commission shall fill the vacancy until the next session of the Annual Conference. The commission shall have authority and supervision over the treasurer. After consultation with the bishop in charge, it may remove him from office for cause, and fill the vacancy until the next session of the conference. The commission shall have the accounts of the conference treasurer for the conference year preceding audited by a certified public accountant within ninety days after the close of each session of the Annual Conference. (*See* ¶ 729.)

¶ 804. All amounts contributed in each local church for world service and conference benevolences shall be remitted monthly by the local-church treasurer to the conference treasurer, who shall each month divide the total amount thus received, setting aside the proper amount for world service and the proper amount for conference benevolences, according to the ratio of each established by the Annual Conference in the total world service and conference benevolence budget. He shall make monthly remittances of the share received by him for conference benevolences to the treasurers of the several agencies for conference work according to the rightful share and proportion of each. He shall remit monthly to the treasurer of the Council on World Service and Finance the total share received by him for world service. When the amount contributed during the year for world service

---

[14] *See* Judicial Council Decision 185.

and conference benevolences exceeds the amount apportioned to or accepted by the Annual Conference, the entire share contributed for world service shall be remitted in regular order to the treasurer of the Council on World Service and Finance before the end of the fiscal year. (*See* ¶ 267.6.)

¶ **805.** The conference treasurer shall remit monthly to the treasurer of the Council on World Service and Finance the amounts received and payable for the General Administration Fund, the Episcopal Fund, and the Interdenominational Co-operation Fund. He shall also transmit all amounts received for world service special gifts, Advance special gifts, the Fellowship of Suffering and Service, the One Great Hour of Sharing, the Methodist Committee for Overseas Relief, the Television-Radio Ministry Fund, the Temporary General Aid Fund, and all other general causes not otherwise directed.

¶ **806.** The conference treasurer shall make each month a full report of all general funds handled by him to the treasurer of the Council on World Service and Finance, and annually a report of all receipts, disbursements, and balances of all funds under his direction, which report shall be printed in the conference journal. The reports shall be made on forms authorized by the council (*see* ¶ 786), so that all financial items going outside the local church shall be handled alike in all districts and conferences, and uniformity of financial reporting shall be established as a church-wide policy.

¶ **807.** The commission shall provide a suitable bond for the conference treasurer and shall designate a depository or depositories for conference funds. It shall require the treasurers of all conference boards and agencies to be properly bonded in companies approved by the commission, and shall require that their books be properly audited at least annually. The commission shall recommend to the Annual Conference the amount in which the treasurers of all unincorporated boards or commissions shall be protected by fidelity insurance, and application for such fidelity bonds shall be made by the corporate body of the Annual Conference, and the costs shall be provided for out of the funds held by the unincorporated board or commission so insured. Institutions and organizations that are incorporated under the laws of the state shall secure fidelity bonds for the treasurers of their funds and shall pay the cost of the premium required. (*See* ¶ 729.)

¶ **808.** For the sake of economy and efficiency the Annual Conference may constitute the conference treasury as a depository for funds designated for any or all conference boards and agencies participating in the conference benevolences, eliminating as far as possible the necessity of a treasurer for each. In this event the conference treasurer shall keep a separate account for each such conference board or agency, enter the proper credits in each at the end of each month's business, and disburse the same on proper order from each board or agency, respectively. None of the above-designated accounts shall be drawn on for the benefit of another.

¶ **809.** The commission shall co-operate with the Council on World Service and Finance and with the General Board of Lay Activities in promoting and standardizing the financial system in the local churches of the conference.

¶ **810.** No Annual Conference board or interest, such as a school, college, university, or hospital, shall make a special conference-wide appeal to the local churches for funds without the approval of the Annual Conference, except in case of an extreme emergency, when such approval may be given by a two-thirds vote of the district superintendents and of the commission, acting jointly.

¶ **811.** When application is made to the conference for the privilege of a special conference-wide financial appeal, whether by special collections, campaigns, or otherwise, the application shall be referred to the commission before final action is taken thereon. The commission shall investigate the application and its possible relation to other obligations of the conference, and in the light of the facts make recommendations to the conference for its action and determination. Such application for privilege of a special appeal may be made directly to the commission for recommendation to the Annual Conference.

¶ **812.** The various conference agencies shall report each year to their respective Annual Conferences the salaries and other expenses allowed each secretary in their employ, and they shall be published in the conference journal.

Sec. XII. **Ministerial Support**

¶ 821. Assumption of the obligations of the itinerancy required to be made at the time of admission into the traveling connection puts upon the church the counter-obligation of providing support for the entire ministry of the church. In view of this, the claim for ministerial support in each pastoral charge shall include provision for the support of pastors, district superintendents, bishops, and conference claimants.

¶ 822. Each Annual Conference shall determine what plan and method shall be used in distributing the apportionments to its several districts and charges for the Episcopal Fund (¶ 771), for the support of district superintendents and conference claimants, and for the minimum salary fund (¶ 826), whether by percentages based on the current cash salary paid to the ministers serving pastoral charges under episcopal appointment and to supply pastors, or by some other method.[15]

¶ 823. When the apportionments for bishops, district superintendents, conference claimants, and the minimum salary fund for the several districts and charges have been determined, payments made to the same in each pastoral charge shall be exactly proportional to the amount paid on the ministerial salary or salaries. (*See* ¶¶ 771, 1624.) The treasurer or treasurers of each pastoral charge shall accordingly make proportional distribution of the funds raised in that charge for the support of the ministry, and remit monthly, if practicable, and quarterly at the latest (¶ 802), the items for bishops, district superintendents, conference claimants, and the minimum salary fund to the proper treasurer or treasurers.

¶ 824. The several Quarterly Conferences shall determine the pastors' salaries according to the provisions of ¶ 148.

¶ 825. No pastor shall be entitled to any claim for

---

[15] *See* Judicial Council Decisions 179, 208.

unpaid salary against any church or charge he has served after his pastoral connection with the church or charge has ceased.

¶ **826.** *Minimum Salaries*—1. Each Annual Conference shall adopt a schedule of minimum salaries for pastors and shall create a **Commission on Minimum Salaries** composed of ministers and laymen to administer it. The commission shall carefully study the number and extent of the needs for additional ministerial support within the conference, and the sources of income, and with the approval of the Commission on World Service and Finance shall present to the conference for adoption a schedule of minimum salaries, subject to such rules and regulations as the conference may adopt, so long as the rules do not conflict with the provisions of this legislation. The schedule may allow for differences in living conditions, number of dependents in pastor's family, and any other variants the conference may direct.

2. In so far as practicable, this schedule of minimum salaries shall be observed by the bishops and district superintendents in arranging charges and making appointments.

3. The Commission on Minimum Salaries shall present its estimate of the amount required to comply with the schedule of minimum salaries for the pastors, as adopted by the conference, to the Commission on World Service and Finance, which shall apportion the amount as an item of ministerial support to the districts or the charges as the conference may direct.[16]

4. The minimum salary fund, secured as described in § 3, shall be used to provide each pastor who receives less than the minimum salary with an additional amount sufficient to make the salary approved by the pastoral charge plus the supplemental aid or income from other sources equal to the minimum salary approved by the conference; *provided* that nothing in this paragraph shall be construed as limiting the right of an Annual Conference to set a maximum amount to be used in attaining such minimum salary in any given case.

---

[16] *See* Judicial Council Decisions 90, 179, 208.

5. The Commission on Minimum Salaries shall see that the amounts for minimum salaries are collected and disbursed.

¶ **827.** *Basic Salary Plan.*—1. An Annual Conference may by a two-thirds majority vote at any regular session adopt a **basic salary plan** for the support of its active itinerants and supply pastors who are giving their full time to the ministry of the church; *provided*, however, that it shall not institute the basic salary plan until the plan has been approved and ratified by a majority vote of the members of the Quarterly Conferences present and voting in seventy-five per cent of the pastoral charges of such conference. The district superintendents shall certify to the conference secretary the results of the votes taken in the several Quarterly Conferences.

2. The basic salary plan shall provide an established salary schedule for the support of the regular active itinerants and supply pastors giving their full time to the ministry of the church, which may allow for differences of living conditions, number of dependents in the family, and other variants. On recommendation of the Commission on World Service and Finance the basic salary schedule may be changed from time to time by a majority vote of the Annual Conference.

3. The Commission on World Service and Finance shall estimate the amount necessary to provide such ministerial support as may be required by the schedule adopted, which amount shall be distributed as an apportionment to the districts or pastoral charges by a method to be determined by the conference.

4. The amounts due from the pastoral charges on apportionment shall be paid to a conference treasury established for that purpose, and all basic salaries due shall be paid from that treasury. The basic salary provided for each minister concerned shall constitute his entire salary except as hereinafter provided.

5. Any pastoral charge which has made adequate provision for paying its apportionments for all ministerial support items in full may augment the basic support of its pastor.

6. The Commission on World Service and Finance shall

administer the basic salary plan and shall be responsible
for collecting and disbursing the funds.[17]

¶ **828.** *Sustentation Fund.*—An Annual Conference may
establish a **sustentation fund,** which shall be administered
by the Commission on World Service and Finance or
some other agency created or designed for the purpose
of providing emergency aid to the ministers of the conference who may be in special need. On recommendation
of the commission the amount needed for this purpose
may be apportioned to the pastoral charges as the conference may determine.

¶ **829.** The total of all travel, automobile, and other
expenses allowed and paid to a pastor in addition to his
salary shall be reported for insertion in the journal of
the Annual Conference, in a separate column from that
of pastor's salary and adjacent thereto.[18] These expenses
shall be distinguished from the moving expenses of a
new appointee to a pastoral charge, which shall be reported as provided in ¶ 148.

¶ **830.** Every ministerial member of an Annual Conference appointed to any other field than the pastorate or
district superintendency shall furnish annually to the
conference secretary, at the time of the conference session,
a statement of his remuneration; and the salaries or
remuneration of all ministers in special service shall be
published in the journal of the Annual Conference.

SEC. XII.   **The Local Church**

For description of the financial plan for the local
church *see* ¶¶ 261-72 under Part II, The Local Church.

---

[17] *See* Judicial Council Decisions 65, 70.
[18] Adopted in 1952 following Judicial Council Decision 51;
see also Decisions 151, 213.

Part VI

JUDICIAL ADMINISTRATION

Chapter I

THE JUDICIAL COUNCIL

¶ **901.** *Article* 1. *Members.*—The **Judicial Council** shall be composed of nine members, five of whom shall be ministers and four shall be laymen. They shall be at least forty years of age, and members of The Methodist Church. Their terms of office shall be eight years; *provided*, however, that a member of the council whose seventieth birthday precedes the first day of the regular session of a General Conference shall be released at the close of that General Conference from membership or responsibility in the council regardless of the date of expiration of his term of office.

Members of the council shall be nominated and elected in the manner following: At each quadrennial session of the General Conference, the Council of Bishops shall nominate by majority vote six times the number of ministers and six times the number of laymen to be elected at such session of the General Conference. At the same daily session at which the above nominations are announced, nominations for each class may be made from the floor, but at no other time. The names of all such nominees shall be published in the *Daily Christian Advocate*, with the name of the conference to which each belongs, for two consecutive issues immediately prior to the day of election, which shall be set by action of the General Conference at the session at which the nominations are made; and from these nominations the General Conference shall elect without discussion, by ballot and by majority vote,

281

the necessary number of each class; *provided*, however, that as a result of the election each jurisdiction and the overseas churches shall be represented on the council.[1]

Election of members shall be held at each session of the General Conference for only the number of members whose terms expire at such session.

Art. 2. Alternates.—There shall be eight alternates of each class, and their qualifications shall be the same as for membership on the Judicial Council. The term of the alternates shall be for eight years; *provided*, however, that an alternate whose seventieth birthday precedes the first day of the regular session of a General Conference shall be released at the close of that General Conference from membership or responsibility in the council regardless of the date of expiration of his term of office.

The alternates shall be elected in the manner following: From the nominees of each class remaining on the ballot after the election of the necessary number of members of the Judicial Council to be elected at sessions of the General Conference, the General Conference shall by separate ballot, without discussion and by majority vote, elect the number of alternates of each class to be elected at such session of the General Conference; *provided*, however, that as a result of the election each jurisdiction shall have at least one alternate of each class. An election shall be held at each session of the General Conference for only the number of each class whose terms expire at such session of the General Conference, or to fill vacancies. The above provisions shall apply as soon as expiration of the terms of the present alternates permits.

Art. 3. Vacancies.—If a vacancy in the membership of the Judicial Council occurs during the interim between sessions of the General Conference, it shall be filled by an alternate of the same class[2] and from the same jurisdiction as the member whom he succeeds, if there is such an alternate, and by the first elected if there is more than one. If there is no alternate of the same class and jurisdiction, the vacancy shall be filled by an alternate of the same class in order of election. The alternate filling

---

[1] *See* Judicial Council Decision 62.
[2] *See* Judicial Council Decision 94.

such vacancy shall hold office as a member of the Judicial Council for the unexpired term of the member whom he succeeds. In the event of any vacancy it shall be the duty of the president and secretary of the council to notify the alternate entitled to fill it.

In the event of the enforced absence of one or more members of the council at or during a session of the General Conference, such temporary vacancy may be filled for that session of the General Conference, or the remainder thereof, as provided above in this article; *provided*, however, that nothing in this provision shall affect the validity of any action of the council so long as a quorum is present.

Any permanent vacancy or vacancies among the alternates shall be filled by election at the next session of the General Conference to the class or respective classes in which such permanent vacancy or vacancies exist, and the person or persons so elected shall hold office during the unexpired term of the alternate whom each respectively succeeds.

If vacancies in the membership of the Judicial Council occur after exhaustion of the list of alternates, the council is authorized to fill such vacancies for the remainder of the quadrennium.

Art. 4. General.—The term of office of the members of the council and of the alternates shall expire upon the adjournment of the General Conference at which their successors are elected.

¶ **902.** Members of the council shall be ineligible for membership in the General Conference or Jurisdictional Conference or in any general or jurisdictional board or for administrative service in any connectional office.[3]

¶ **903.** The Judicial Council shall provide its own method of organization and procedure. It shall meet at the time and place of the meeting of the General Conference and shall continue in session until the adjournment of that body. It shall meet at such other times and places as it may deem necessary. Seven members shall constitute a quorum. An affirmative vote of at least six members of

[3] *See* Judicial Council Decisions 120, 196.

the council shall be necessary to declare any act of the General Conference unconstitutional. On other matters a majority vote of the entire council shall be sufficient.

¶ 904. 1. The Judicial Council shall determine the constitutionality of any act of the General Conference upon an appeal of a majority of the Council of Bishops, or one fifth of the members of the General Conference.

2. The Judicial Council shall have jurisdiction to pass upon the constitutionality of any proposed legislation when such declaratory decision is requested by the General Conference or by the Council of Bishops.[4]

¶ 905. The Judicial Council shall determine the constitutionality of any act of a Jurisdictional or a Central Conference upon an appeal of a majority of the bishops of that Jurisdictional or Central Conference, or upon the appeal of one fifth of the members of that Jurisdictional or Central Conference.

¶ 906. The Judicial Council shall hear and determine the legality of any action taken therein by any General Conference board, or Jurisdictional or Central Conference board or body, upon appeal by one third of the members thereof, or upon request of the Council of Bishops, or a majority of the bishops of the Jurisdictional or Central Conference.

¶ 907. The Judicial Council shall hear and determine the legality of any action taken therein by a General Conference board, or Jurisdictional or Central Conference board or body, on a matter affecting an Annual or a Provisional Annual Conference, upon appeal by two thirds of the members of the Annual or Provisional Annual Conference present and voting.

¶ 908. The Judicial Council shall hear and determine any appeal from a bishop's decision on a question of law made in the Annual or District Conference when said appeal has been made by one fifth of that conference present and voting.

¶ 909. The Judicial Council shall meet at least once a year and pass upon the decisions of law made by the bishops in Annual and District Conferences upon ques-

---

[4] See Judicial Council Decisions 177, 193.

tions submitted to them in writing, and reported in writing to the council with a syllabus of each case, and affirm, modify, or reverse them. Before affirmation no episcopal decision shall be authoritative except in the case pending. When the decisions are affirmed, they shall become the law of the church.

¶ **910.** The Judicial Council shall hear and determine an appeal of a bishop when taken from the decision of the Trial Court in his case.

¶ **911.** The Judicial Council shall have such other duties and powers as may be conferred upon it by the General Conference.

¶ **912.** All decisions of the Judicial Council shall be final. However, when the Judicial Council shall declare any act of the General Conference unconstitutional, that decision shall be reported back to that General Conference immediately.

¶ **913.** If it should occur that the opinion or decision of a Committee of Appeals of a Jurisdictional Conference should contravene a decision of the Committee of Appeals of another Jurisdictional Conference on a point or question of law, then:

a) Any person, conference, or organization interested therein may appeal the case to the Judicial Council on the ground of such conflict of decisions; or

b) The Committee on Appeals rendering the last of such opinions or decisions may certify the case to and file it with the Judicial Council on the ground of such conflict of decisions; or

c) The attention of the president of the Judicial Council being directed to such conflict, or alleged conflict of decisions, he may issue an order, in the nature of a writ of certiorari, directing the secretaries of the Committees of Appeals involved to certify a copy of a sufficient portion of the record to disclose the nature of the case, and the entire opinion and decision of the Committee of Appeals in each case, to the Judicial Council for its consideration at its next meeting.

The Judicial Council shall hear and determine the question of law involved, but shall not pass upon the facts in either case further than is necessary to decide the question of law involved. After deciding the question of law, the Judicial Council shall cause the same to be certified to each of the Committees of Appeals involved; and such Committees of Appeals shall take such action, if any, as may be necessary under the law as settled by the Judicial Council.

¶ **914.** When the General Conference shall have passed any act or legislation that appears to be unconstitutional or subject to more than one interpretation, or when any paragraph or paragraphs of the Discipline seem to be of doubtful meaning, or application, the Judicial Council, on petition as hereinafter provided, shall have jurisdiction to make a ruling in the nature of a **declaratory decision** as to the constitutionality, meaning, application, and effect of such act, legislation, or paragraph or paragraphs of the Discipline; and the decision of the Judicial Council thereon shall be as binding and effectual as a decision made by the Judicial Council on appeal under the law relating to appeals to the Judicial Council.[5]

The following bodies[6] in The Methodist Church are hereby authorized to make such petitions to the Judicial Council for declaratory decisions: (1) the Council of Bishops; (2) any General Conference board or body, on matters relating to or affecting the work of such board or body; (3) a majority of the bishops assigned to any jurisdiction on matters relating to or affecting jurisdictions or the work therein; (4) any Jurisdictional Conference, on matters relating to or affecting jurisdictions or Jurisdictional Conferences or the work therein; (5) any Jurisdictional Conference board or body, on matters relating to or affecting the work of such board or body; [7] (6) any Central Conference, on matters relating to or affecting Central Conferences, or the work therein; (7) any Central Conference board or body, on matters relating to or affecting the work of such board or body; (8) any Annual Conference, on matters relating to Annual Conferences or the work therein.

The Judicial Council shall determine from the facts in

[5] *See* Judicial Council Decisions 184, 189, 212.
[6] *See* Judicial Council Decision 177.
[7] *See* Judicial Council Decision 166.

connection with each such petition whether or not it has jurisdiction to hear and determine the same.[8]

¶ 915. When a declaratory decision is sought, all persons or bodies who have or claim any interest which would be affected by the declaration shall be parties to the proceeding, and the petition shall name such parties. If the council determines that other parties not named by the petition would be affected by such a decision, such additional parties shall also be added; and the petitioner or petitioners shall then be required to serve all parties so joined with a copy of the petition within fifteen days after the filing of the same with the Judicial Council. In like manner any interested party may on his or its own motion intervene and answer, plead, or interplead.

¶ 916. All parties shall have the privilege of filing briefs and arguments, and presenting evidence, under such rules as the council may adopt from time to time. If the Judicial Council deems it necessary to a complete understanding of the facts, in any proceeding in the nature of a petition for a declaratory decision, it may hear evidence (either orally in session or by affidavits filed) or statements of facts agreed upon by adverse parties, or it may designate one or more of its members to hear evidence and report the same to the Judicial Council.

¶ 917. In all other respects, except as provided herein, the proceedings before the Judicial Council in such matters shall be governed by the same rules and regulations as those under which appeals to the Judicial Council are heard.

¶ 918. The decisions of the Judicial Council on questions of law, with a summary of the facts and of the opinion, shall be filed with the secretary of the General Conference, and shall be published in the following manner:

1. Following each session of the Judicial Council the official publications of the church shall publish an official summary, prepared by the secretary of the council, of the decisions arrived at during that session.

2. The decisions of the Judicial Council rendered during

---

[8] *See* Judicial Council Decision 23.

each year shall be published in the *General Minutes* (¶ 1106).

Chapter II

TRIAL OF A BISHOP OR TRAVELING PREACHER

Section I. Offenses for Which a Bishop or Traveling Preacher or Local Preacher May Be Tried

¶ **921.** A bishop or traveling preacher or local preacher shall be liable to accusation and trial upon any of the following charges:

a) Unchristian tempers, words, or actions.

b) Disobedience to the order and discipline of the church.

c) Imprudent or unministerial conduct.

d) Habitual neglect of duties as a member or officer in the church.

e) Disseminating doctrines contrary to the Articles of Religion or other established standards of doctrine of the church.

f) Immorality or crime.

g) Maladministration in office in the church.

Sec. II. Investigation and Trial of a Bishop

¶ **922.** A bishop is amenable for his conduct to the Jurisdictional or Central Conference in which he has residential or presidential supervision, or to the Jurisdictional or Central Conference to which he is related.

¶ **923.** If a bishop shall be accused in writing of any of the offenses hereinbefore mentioned (¶ 921) in the interval between sessions of the Jurisdictional Conference, the district superintendent within whose district the offense is said to have been committed shall call the Committee of Investigation of that Annual Conference, who shall carefully inquire into the case; and if, in the judgment of the majority of them, there is reasonable ground for such accusation, they shall prepare and sign the proper charges and specifications, and send a copy of the same to the accused, and to the president of the College of Bishops of the jurisdiction in which the offense took place. The said president shall call together at some convenient place, in not less than ten nor more than fifteen days from the time he receives the charges, nine traveling elders of the said jurisdiction, and also the witnesses by whom the accusation is expected to be proved. The said president or some other bishop of the jurisdiction appointed by him shall preside at the investigation. If possible the accused shall have the right to make a statement in his own behalf and to interrogate witnesses, but shall not himself present any. If six or more of these traveling elders determine that a trial is justified, they shall order one, and they may suspend the bishop pending trial as hereinafter provided.

¶ 924. In case a trial be ordered, the president of the College of Bishops of the said jurisdiction shall within seven days from the date on which a trial is ordered fix the time and place of it, which shall be in not less than thirty or more than sixty days from the date of such order. The **Trial Court** shall be constituted as follows:

1. The bishop shall arrange for a meeting of the accused and his counsel and the counsel for the church, as early as practicable after the trial is ordered, to select the members of the Trial Court.

2. The bishop shall nominate, as proposed members of the Trial Court, thirteen traveling elders from a list made up of the Committees of Investigation of not fewer than four Annual Conferences within the jurisdiction.

3. The church and the accused each shall have the right of peremptory challenge to the number of four and of unlimited challenge for cause.

4. For each name stricken from this list of thirteen through the exercise of the right of challenge, the bishop shall add another from the eligible group until the required number of thirteen is thus selected. If necessary to complete the panel, nominations may be made from other traveling elders in the jurisdiction.

5. By a continuation of this same process four alternates shall be chosen who shall be called in the order of their election to serve.

6. Should the accused be the president of the College of Bishops of the jurisdiction, then a copy of such charges and specifications shall be sent to the secretary of the College of Bishops of that jurisdiction, who shall perform the duties hereinabove prescribed for the president, or designate another bishop of the same jurisdiction.

¶ 925. The court as thus constituted shall have full power to try the accused and by a vote of nine or more to suspend him from the exercise of the functions of his office; to depose him from his office or the ministry or both; to expel him from the church; or, in case of minor offenses, to fix a lesser penalty. Its findings shall be final, subject to appeal to the Judicial Council as hereinafter provided, and shall be reported to the Jurisdictional Conference for entry on its journal. The records of the trial, including the testimony, shall be signed by the president and secretary of the Trial Court and shall be placed in the custody of the secretary of the Jurisdictional Conference, together with all the documents in the case, for preservation with the papers of the Jurisdictional Conference, and shall be the basis of any appeal which may be taken.

¶ 926. An accusation preferred during the session of a Jurisdictional Conference shall be made directly to the Committee on Episcopacy, which shall investigate the charge, and, if it consider a trial necessary, shall report to the Jurisdictional Conference. If the Committee on Episcopacy should decide a trial necessary, it shall formulate charges and specifications, conforming them to the grade of offense involved in the accusation, and it shall appoint one or more of its members to prosecute the case. The bill of charges and specifications shall be a part of the report of the committee to the Jurisdictional Conference.

¶ 927. Every case to be tried under the process stated in the foregoing paragraph (¶ 926) shall be referred to a Trial Court which shall consist of thirteen traveling elders and a presiding officer, all of whom shall be appointed by the president in the chair or in such manner as the conference may determine. The church and the accused each shall have, in addition to the right of unlimited challenge for cause, the right of peremptory chal-

lenge to the number of four. The court as thus constituted shall have full power to try the accused and by a
two-thirds vote to suspend him from his office; to depose
him from his office or the ministry, or both; to expel
him from the church; or, in case of minor offenses, to fix
a lesser penalty. Its findings shall be final, subject to
appeal to the Judicial Council as hereinafter provided.

¶ 928. A bishop suspended or deposed shall have no
claim upon the Episcopal Fund for salary, dwelling, or
any other expenses from the date of such suspension or
deposition; but in case he is thereafter found not guilty
of the charge or charges for which he was suspended or
deposed, his claim upon the Episcopal Fund for the
period during which he was deprived of the functions of
his office shall be paid to him.

¶ 929. If an alleged offense has been committed beyond the bounds of any district, the district superintendent within the bounds of whose district the bishop
resides shall proceed as hereinbefore provided.

¶ 930. The several Central Conferences shall make
suitable rules for the investigation and trial of charges
against bishops elected by them. In the absence of such
rules the same procedure shall be followed as is provided
for the investigation and trial of bishops in Jurisdictional Conferences; *provided*, however, that an appeal
may be taken to the Judicial Council. If an accused bishop
is the only bishop in his Central Conference, the Council
of Bishops shall designate one of their number to conduct
the trial.

SEC. III. **Investigation and Trial of a Traveling Preacher**

¶ 931. Each Annual Conference at each session, upon
nomination of the presiding bishop, shall elect five elders,
men of experience and sound judgment in the affairs of
the church, who shall be known as the **Committee of
Investigation,** and five reserves chosen in like manner, to
serve in the absence or disqualification of the principals.

¶ 932. If a traveling preacher, whether on trial or in
full connection, in the interval between sessions of his conference, shall be accused of any of the offenses enumerated
in ¶ 921, his district superintendent, or the superintend-

ent of the district within the bounds of which such acts are alleged to have taken place, shall call the Committee of Investigation to inquire into the same, and, if possible, bring the accused and accuser face to face. The accused shall have the right to make a statement in his own behalf, but shall not present any witnesses. The district superintendent shall preside throughout the proceedings, and shall certify and declare the judgment of the committee.[9]

¶ **933.** If the accused is a district superintendent, the bishop in charge shall call in the superintendent of any other district or a traveling elder of the Annual Conference, who shall summon the Committee of Investigation of the Annual Conference of which the accused is a member to investigate the case, and he shall preside at the investigation.

¶ **934.** If in the judgment of a majority of the Committee of Investigation there is reasonable ground for such accusation, they shall prepare and sign the proper charges and specifications and send a copy to the accused, to the bishop in charge, to the district superintendent or the traveling elder duly appointed by the bishop in charge, and to the secretary of the Annual Conference.[10] On recommendation of the Committee of Investigation the bishop may suspend the accused from all ministerial services pending the trial.

¶ **935.** The bishop in charge, or the district superintendent or the traveling elder duly appointed by the bishop in charge, within ten days after receipt of a copy of such charges, shall appoint counsel for the church and notify the accused in writing to appear at a fixed time and place no less than seven days after service of such notice and within a reasonable time thereafter to select the members of the **Trial Court.** At the appointed time, in the presence of the accused and his counsel, if requested, and counsel for the church, thirteen effective elders shall be selected as a Trial Court. They shall be selected from a panel of twenty-one effective elders of the Annual Conference of which the accused is a member, who

---

[9] *See* Judicial Council Decision 89.
[10] *See* Judicial Council Decision 89.

have been nominated by the majority of the district superintendents of that conference. The counsel for the church
and the accused shall each have peremptory challenges to
the number of four and challenges for cause without limit.
If by reason of challenges for cause being sustained the
number is reduced below thirteen, additional elders shall
be nominated, in like manner as was the original panel, to
take the places of the numbers challenged, who likewise
shall be subject to challenge for cause. This method of procedure shall be followed until a Trial Court of thirteen
members has been selected. The presiding officer in
charge shall also fix the time and place for the trial,
notice of which shall be given in writing to the accused
by the counsel for the church seven days in advance of
the time fixed; *provided* that, with the consent of the
accused, the time of the trial may be fixed at an earlier
date. The bishop in charge, or another bishop invited by
him, or a traveling elder appointed by him, shall preside
at the trial. The presiding officer shall appoint a secretary, who shall keep a record of the proceedings and of
the testimony. The court thus constituted shall have
full power to try the accused and upon his conviction by
a vote of nine or more thereof shall have power to suspend
him from the exercise of the functions of his office; to
depose him from his office or the ministry or both; to
expel him from the church; or, in case of conviction of
minor offenses, to fix a lesser penalty. Its findings shall
be final, subject to appeal to the Committee on Appeals
of the Jurisdictional Conference or the Central Conference as the case may be. It shall make a faithful report
in writing of all its proceedings, signed by the president
and secretary of the committee, to the secretary of the
Annual Conference for permanent record, and deliver to
him therewith the bill of charges, the evidence taken, and
the decision rendered, together with all documents brought
into the trial.

¶ **936.** When accusation against a traveling preacher is
preferred during the session of an Annual Conference,
it shall be referred to the Annual Conference Committee
of Investigation, which committee shall report to the
conference whether or not a trial is deemed necessary.

The Committee of Investigation, when reporting a case for trial, shall formulate a bill of charges and specifications. The presiding bishop shall appoint some traveling elder of the conference as counsel for the church.

¶ **937.** The conference may constitute a Trial Court of thirteen effective elders to try the accused in the same manner as in ¶ 935. The Trial Court in the presence of a bishop or of a chairman whom the president of the conference shall have appointed, and one of the secretaries of the conference, shall try the case. The Trial Court thus constituted shall have full power, upon conviction of the accused by two-thirds vote thereof, to expel him from the ministry and membership of the church; to depose him from the ministry of the church; to suspend him from his office in the ministry; or to fix a lesser penalty. Its findings shall be final, subject to appeal to the Committee on Appeals of the Jurisdictional Conference. It shall make a faithful report in writing of all its proceedings, duly signed by the president and secretary of the Trial Court, to the secretary of the Annual Conference for entry on its journal, and deliver to him therewith the bill of charges and specifications, the evidence taken, and the decision rendered, with all documents brought into the trial. The Annual Conference may order the completion of such trial before the final adjournment of the session.[11]

¶ **938.** When an accused is tried and the specific charge is not sustained by the evidence, but the accused has been found guilty of imprudent or of unministerial conduct, this fact may be so declared and suitable penalty imposed by the court.

¶ **939.** Any traveling preacher residing beyond the bounds of his own conference shall be subject to the investigation prescribed in ¶¶ 931-35, under the authority of the superintendent of the district within which he resides, or within which he is employed. The Committee of Investigation shall consist of the Committee of Investigation of that conference. If he resides or is employed within the bounds of a Mission, he shall be subject

---

[11] *See* Judicial Council Decision 116.

to investigation under the authority of the superintendent of the district within which he holds his Quarterly Conference membership or of the superintendent of the Mission and the Committee of Investigation of the same. If he is the superintendent of the Mission, the bishop in charge shall appoint an elder to act in the case.

¶ **940.** An Annual Conference may entertain and try charges against its ministerial members though no investigation of them has been held, or though the investigation has not resulted in suspension.

¶ **941.** In all the foregoing cases the papers, including the record, charges, evidence, and findings, shall be transmitted to the ensuing session of the Annual Conference of which the accused is a member; on which papers, and on such other evidence as may be admitted, and also upon such other charges or specifications as may be presented, due notice of the same having been given to the accused, the case shall be determined.

¶ **942.** In cases of unchristian temper, words, or actions, the traveling preacher so offending shall be admonished by his district superintendent. If he offends again, one or more ministers are to be taken as witnesses. If he continues to offend, the district superintendent shall proceed as directed in ¶¶ 931-35.

¶ **943.** Any traveling preacher who shall hold a religious service within the bounds of a pastoral charge not his own, when requested by the preacher in charge or the district superintendent not to hold such service, shall be deemed guilty of disobedience to the order and discipline of the church; and if he shall not refrain from such conduct, he shall be liable to investigation and trial.

¶ **944.** If a traveling preacher is charged with disseminating publicly or privately doctrines which are contrary to our Articles of Religion, or to other existing and established standards of doctrine, and the minister so offending shall solemnly promise the Committee of Investigation not to disseminate such erroneous doctrines in public or private, it may waive suspension in order that the case may be laid before the next Annual Conference, which shall determine the matter.

SEC. IV. **Trial of an Approved Supply Pastor**

For the provisions regarding investigation and trial of an approved supply pastor *see* Chapter III, Section I, "Investigation and Trial of a Local Preacher," ¶¶ 957-65, also ¶ 981.

SEC. V.   **Preachers in Provisional Annual Conferences**

¶ 946. In all matters of judicial administration the rights, duties, and responsibilities of ministerial members of Missions and Provisional Annual Conferences are the same as those in Annual Conferences, and the procedure is the same.

SEC. VI.   **Maladministration**

¶ 947. Complaint against the administration of a bishop may be forwarded to the Jurisdictional or Central Conference and entertained there; *provided* that at least thirty days' notice in writing shall have been given to the accused and to the secretary of the conference. This shall not preclude earlier action as provided in ¶¶ 923-25.

¶ 948. A traveling preacher shall be answerable to his conference on a charge of maladministration, but not for error in judgment.

¶ 949. Errors of administration not connected with judicial proceedings may be presented in writing to the presiding bishop for his decision thereon; and the Annual Conference may order just and suitable remedies when the rights of ministers or members of the church have been injuriously affected by such errors.

SEC. VII. **Status of a Bishop or Traveling Preacher Deposed or Expelled**

¶ 950. In case a bishop or a traveling preacher shall have been deposed from the ministry without being expelled from the church, he shall be given a **certificate of membership in the church** signed by the president and secretary of the conference.

¶ 951. In case a bishop or a traveling preacher shall have been deposed from the ministry or expelled from the church for teaching publicly or privately doctrines contrary to our Articles of Religion, or our other established standards of doctrine, he shall not again be licensed to preach until, if a traveling preacher, he shall have satisfied the Annual Conference from which he was deposed or expelled; or, if a bishop, he shall have satisfied the Annual Conference from which he was elected bishop, and shall have promised in writing to desist wholly from disseminating such doctrine.

SEC. VIII. **Withdrawal Under Complaints or Charges**

¶ 952. When a bishop or a traveling preacher is accused of an offense under ¶ 921 and desires to withdraw from the church, the Jurisdictional or Central Conference in the case of a bishop, or the Annual Conference in the case of a traveling preacher, may permit him to withdraw; in which case the record shall be, "Withdrawn under complaints." If formal charges have been presented, he may be permitted to withdraw; in which case the record shall be "Withdrawn under charges." In either case his status shall be the same as if he had been expelled.[12]

CHAPTER III

INVESTIGATION AND TRIAL OF OTHER THAN TRAVELING PREACHERS

SECTION I. **Investigation and Trial of a Local Preacher**

¶ 957. Each District Conference at each session, upon nomination of its president, shall elect three local preachers and two reserves, of experience and sound judgment in the affairs of the church, who shall be known as the **Committee of Investigation.** The reserves shall serve in the absence or disqualification of the principals. Where no District Conference exists, the Annual Conference Committee of Investigation shall act.

¶ 958. When a local preacher, ordained or unordained, whether or not serving as an approved supply pastor,

---

[12] *See* Judicial Council Decision 104.

is accused of any of the offenses enumerated in ¶ 921, the district superintendent shall call the Committee of Investigation to meet, before which it shall be the duty of the accused to appear. If in the judgment of a majority of the Committee of Investigation there is reasonable ground for such accusation, they shall prepare and sign the proper charges and send a copy to the accused and to the district superintendent; and the accused may be suspended from all ministerial services pending trial. In all such cases at least seven days' notice shall be given the accused by the district superintendent. Such notice shall contain a full statement of the charges.

¶ 959. The district superintendent within ten days after giving notice of the charges shall select a **Trial Committee** of nine members and seven reserves, of experience and sound judgment in the affairs of the church, who shall be local preachers or, when necessary, members of the church. The reserves shall serve in the absence or disqualification of the principals. The church and the accused shall have three peremptory challenges and unlimited challenges for cause. The committee in the presence of the district superintendent or the traveling elder appointed by him, and a secretary appointed by the committee, shall have full power to consider and determine the case and by a two-thirds vote to convict the accused. They may suspend him from the functions of his office, or depose him from his office or the ministry or both, or expel him from the church. The secretary shall make a correct report in writing of all proceedings, evidence, and findings to the secretary of the District Conference and shall deliver to him all the papers in the case. Where there is no District Conference, then the Quarterly Conference of which the accused is a member shall act.

¶ 960. In case of unchristian temper, words, or actions, the local preacher so offending shall be admonished by his district superintendent. Should a second transgression take place, one or two members of the church are to be taken as witnesses. If he continues to offend, the case shall be investigated as provided in ¶¶ 958-59.

¶ 961. If on due trial a local preacher is found neglectful of his duties as a local preacher or unacceptable in his ministry, he may be deprived of his ministerial office; in which case, if he is ordained, the district superintendent shall require him to surrender his credentials that they may be returned to the Annual Conference.

¶ 962. If a local preacher shall disseminate, publicly or privately, doctrines which are contrary to our Articles of Religion, or to our other present existing and established standards of doctrine, the same procedure shall be observed as prescribed in ¶¶ 958-59.

¶ 963. A local preacher who shall hold religious services within the bounds of a pastoral charge not his own, when requested not to do so by the preacher in charge or district superintendent, shall be deemed guilty of disobedience to the order and discipline of the church and shall be brought to investigation or trial.

¶ 964. When a local elder or deacon is complained of as being so unacceptable or inefficient as to be no longer useful in his work, and the District or Quarterly Conference for that reason refuses to pass his character, the District or Quarterly Conference shall investigate the case; and if it appears that the complaint is well founded, and if he fails to give the conference satisfactory assurance that he will amend, or voluntarily surrender his credentials, the conference may depose him from the ministry. He may defend himself before the conference, in person or by representative. The president of the District or Quarterly Conference shall in this case comply with the requirements of ¶ 961.

¶ 965. In Provisional Annual Conferences or Missions in the United States, its territories, and insular possessions, the power to try local preachers shall remain with the respective District or Quarterly Conference; but local preachers so tried and convicted shall have the right of appeal to the annual session of the Provisional Annual Conference or the Mission.

Sec. II. Investigation and Trial of a Deaconess

¶ 966. When a deaconess is accused of any violation of a moral law, the district superintendent under whose supervision she works shall call a committee of three or more for investigation and preside at the investigation. This committee shall consist of one representative of the Commission on Deaconess Work and two or more members of the Annual Conference Deaconess Board of which the accused is a member. She shall appear before this committee, and, if charges are sustained, she shall be suspended from all deaconess services pending trial. This said district superintendent shall notify the bishop in charge, who within seven days of the receipt of such notice shall fix the time and date for the convening of the Trial Court. In this instance the Annual Conference Deaconess Board shall be the Trial Court. If the accused is found guilty, the Annual Conference Deaconess Board shall recommend to the Commission on Deaconess Work that she be suspended or deprived of office and credentials.

¶ 967. In case of improper temper, words, actions, or disloyalty to the rules and regulations of the administration or other organization with which she serves, the deaconess so offending shall be admonished by the president of the Annual Conference Deaconess Board. If she continues to offend, the case shall be investigated and tried as provided in ¶ 966.

¶ 968. If a deaconess shall contract debts which she is not able to pay, the president of the Annual Conference Deaconess Board shall appoint three judicious members of the Annual Conference Deaconess Board to consider her accounts, contracts, and circumstances. If, in their opinion, she has behaved dishonestly, or contracted debts without the probability of paying, the same procedure shall be followed as defined in ¶¶ 966-67.

Sec. III. Investigation and Trial of a Church Member

¶ 969. *Offenses for Which a Lay Member May Be Tried.*—A member shall be liable to accusation and trial upon any of the following charges:

a) Immorality or crime.

b) Disseminating doctrines contrary to the Articles of Religion or other established standards of doctrine of the church.

c) Disobedience to the order and discipline of the church.

d) Buying, selling, or manufacturing intoxicating liquor as a beverage; renting his property for the manufacture or sale thereof; signing a petition in favor of granting a license for the sale thereof; procuring a license for the sale of such liquors; becoming surety on the bond of any person engaged in such traffic; or persisting in the use of intoxicating liquor after private reproof and admonition by the pastor or church lay leader.

¶ **970.** In cases of neglect of duties of any kind, indulging in sinful tempers or words, "taking such diversions as cannot be used in the name of the Lord Jesus," or disobedience to the order and discipline of the church, the pastor or church lay leader shall privately admonish a member; and if there is an acknowledgment of fault and proper repentance, the person may be borne with. Failing such, or on further offense, the pastor or lay leader may take with him one or two discreet members of the church and give further reproof. If the offense be continued, the member shall be brought to trial.

¶ **971.** If a member of the church shall be accused of endeavoring to sow dissension in the church by inveighing against its doctrines or discipline, its ministers or members, or in any other manner, he shall first be reproved by the pastor or church lay leader. If he shall persist in such practice, he shall be brought to trial.

¶ **972.** *Investigation.*—If charges are made in writing to the preacher in charge against a member of the church, the preacher in charge shall call a **Committee of Investigation** composed of seven members of the church in good standing, and shall preside at the investigation. The accused and the accuser shall be brought face to face if possible, and the accused shall have right of making a statement in his own behalf and of interrogating witnesses, but shall not have the right of presenting witnesses. If the Committee of Investigation determines that a trial is justified, it shall formulate the charges and specifications and order a trial.

¶ **973.** *Trial Court.*—If a member be brought to trial, it shall be before a **Trial Court** composed of not fewer than

seven nor more than twelve members. They shall be
chosen by the Quarterly Conference by ballot. The accused
member and the person conducting the prosecution may
each challenge anyone so chosen for cause of disqualification by reason of personal interest or having formed and
expressed an opinion concerning the matter, and shall
also have three peremptory challenges. If the pastor deem
it advisable for obtaining a fair trial, the Quarterly Conference shall call a committee of like members from any
part of the district. The same right of challenge shall be
recognized. The district superintendent or a traveling
elder appointed by him shall preside at the trial.

¶ 974. *Penalties.*—If the accused shall be found guilty
by the decision of at least two thirds of the Trial Court,
they shall so declare, and the president of the Trial Court
shall at once pronounce the member to be expelled from
the church; *provided*, however, that the Trial Court may
impose a lesser penalty because of mitigating circumstances or other grounds.

¶ 975. *New Trial.*—If within sixty days after his conviction under the foregoing provisions the accused shall
make application in writing to the district superintendent
for a new trial on the ground of newly discovered evidence, and shall submit therewith a written statement
of the same, and if it shall appear that such evidence is
material to the issue involved, the district superintendent
shall grant a new trial.

¶ 976. In no case shall a new trial be granted upon
newly discovered evidence which could have been obtained for the trial by the exercise of due diligence, or
which is merely cumulative in its effect.

¶ 977. *Restoration.*—An expelled member shall have no
privileges of the society or of the Sacraments of the
church without repentance, contrition, and satisfactory
reformation according to the determination of the Quarterly Conference. In such case that body may restore the
member into full membership.

SEC. IV. **Withdrawal Under Complaints or Charges**

¶ 981. When a local preacher is accused of an offense
under ¶ 921 and desires to withdraw from the church, the

District Conference or, where there is no District Conference, the Quarterly Conference may permit him to withdraw; in which case the record shall be, "Withdrawn under complaints." If formal charges have been presented, he may be permitted to withdraw; in which case the record shall be, "Withdrawn under charges." In either case the status of the person withdrawn shall be the same as if expelled.

¶ 982. When a deaconess is accused of an offense and desires to withdraw from the church, the Annual Conference Deaconess Board may recommend to the Commission on Deaconess Work that she be permitted to withdraw, in which case the record shall be, "Withdrawn under complaints." If formal charges have been presented, such deaconess may be permitted to withdraw; in which case the record shall be, "Withdrawn under charges." In either case the status shall be the same as if the deaconess had been expelled.

¶ 983. When a member of the church is accused of an offense and desires to withdraw from the church, the Quarterly Conference may permit such member to withdraw; in which case the record shall be, "Withdrawn under complaints." If formal charges have been presented, such member may be permitted to withdraw; in which case the record shall be, "Withdrawn under charges." In either case the status shall be the same as if the member had been expelled.

Chapter IV

THE DEPRIVATION AND RESTORATION OF CREDENTIALS

Sec. I. Of the Credentials of Traveling Deacons or Elders

¶ 991. When a traveling deacon or elder is deprived of his credentials of ordination, by expulsion or otherwise, they shall be filed with the papers of his Annual Conference.

¶ 992. When a traveling deacon or elder desires to

surrender his credentials and retain his membership in
our church, he shall be permitted to do so, and to designate the local church in which he will hold membership.
The secretary of the conference to which he surrenders his
credentials shall issue to him a **certificate of membership**
in the church; *provided* that no minister shall be permitted to take such action when charges involving his
character have been made and sustained or are pending.
When his character is involved in cases where the law
permits final adjustment by the surrender of credentials,
this shall be also the surrender of membership in the
church.

¶ **993.** The Annual Conference to which credentials
were surrendered as provided in ¶¶ 991-92 may restore the
same at its discretion if no charges or complaints against
the minister had been lodged or were impending at the
time of his surrendering the said credentials; and if at
the time of his request for the restoration of the said
credentials he is a member in good standing of The
Methodist Church and shall present from his Quarterly
Conference a certificate of his character and a recommendation for the restoration of his credentials. In cases
of surrender of credentials under situations involving the
character of the minister the said credentials may be
restored only after the lapse of a period of at least two
years and upon the following conditions:

a) That the conference holding the credentials shall
be assured that there has been a complete amendment of
life upon the part of the former holder of the credentials.

b) That he shall have been readmitted on trial into
the Annual Conference from which he withdrew or admitted to another Annual Conference on trial or been
licensed as a local preacher by some District or Quarterly
Conference.

c) That the Annual Conference which has admitted
him on trial (if another than the one from which he
withdrew) or the District or Quarterly Conference which
licensed him shall present to the Annual Conference holding the credentials a certificate of his good character and
a recommendation that his credentials be restored.[13]

---

[13] *See* Judicial Council Decisions 18, 104.

SEC. II. **Of the Credentials of Local Deacons or Elders**

¶ **994.** When a local deacon or elder is deprived of his credentials of ordination, by expulsion or otherwise, the district superintendent shall require them of him, and file them with the Annual Conference in the bounds of which the local preacher resides.

¶ **995.** Should he later produce to the Annual Conference a recommendation from the District Conference for the restoration of his credentials, signed by its president and secretary, they may be restored to him.

SEC. III. **Of the Restoration of Lost Credentials**

¶ **996.** Should the credentials of any deacon or elder be destroyed or lost, the bishop who ordained him, or the bishop in whose territory he resides, upon ascertaining the necessary facts, may issue duplicate credentials.

CHAPTER V

GENERAL DIRECTIONS

SECTION I.   **Charges**

¶ **1001.** No charge shall be entertained for any alleged offense which shall not have been committed within two years immediately preceding the filing of the complaint, except in cases where there is a conviction in a civil or criminal court, and in such cases the charges must be filed within one year after the entry of the final judgment.

¶ **1002.** A charge shall not allege more than one offense; several charges against the same person, however, with the specifications under each of them, may be presented at one and the same time and may be tried together. When several charges are tried at the same time, a vote on each specification and charge must be separately taken.

¶ **1003.** Amendments may be made to a bill of charges up to the time of the opening of the trial at the discretion of the presiding officer, *provided* they relate to the form of statement only and do not change the nature of the alleged offense and do not introduce new matter of which the accused has not had due notice.

¶ **1004.** In case of improper words, tempers, and actions, a charge of slander shall not be entertained unless signed by a person alleged to have been slandered.

¶ **1005.** Charges and specifications for the trial of a bishop, traveling preacher, local preacher, deaconess, or members shall define the offense by its generic term as set forth in ¶¶ 921 and 969 and shall state in substance the facts upon which said charges are based.

Sec. II.   **Counsel**

¶ **1006.** In all cases of trial the accused shall be entitled to appear and to be represented by counsel of his own selection and to be heard in oral or written argument. Such counsel shall be one traveling elder if the accused is a bishop or a traveling preacher, or one member in good standing in The Methodist Church if the accused is a lay member.

¶ **1007.** In all cases of trial where counsel has not been provided, such counsel shall be appointed by the presiding officer. The counsel for the church and for the accused each shall be entitled to one assistant counsel of his own choosing.[14]

Sec. III.   **Notice**

¶ **1008.** All notices required or provided for in this chapter shall be in writing, signed by or on behalf of the person or body giving or required to give such notice, and shall be addressed to the person or body to whom it is required to be given. Such notices shall be served at least seven days in advance by delivering a copy thereof to the party or chief officer of the body to whom it is addressed in person or by registered mail addressed to the last known residence or address of such party. The fact of the giving of the notice shall affirmatively appear over the signature of the party required to give such notice and become a part of the record of the case.

---

[14] *See* Judicial Council Decision 116.

¶ **1009.** In all cases wherein it is provided that notice shall be given to a bishop or district superintendent and the charges or complaints are against that particular person, then such notice, in the case of a bishop, shall be given to another bishop within the same jurisdiction; in case of a district superintendent, to the bishop in charge.

Sec. IV. **Trials**

¶ **1010.** In all cases of investigation or trial, notice to appear shall be given to such witnesses as either party may name, and shall be issued in the name of the church and be signed by the presiding officer of the trial court.

¶ **1011.** It shall be the duty of a minister or a member of the church to appear and testify when summoned.

¶ **1012.** As soon as the court has convened, the accused shall be called upon by the presiding officer to plead to the charge, and his pleas shall be duly recorded. On his neglect or refusal to plead, the plea of "not guilty" shall be entered for him, and the trial shall proceed; *provided* that for sufficient cause the court may adjourn from time to time as convenience or necessity may require; and *provided*, also, that the accused shall, at all times during the trial, have liberty to be present except as hereinafter mentioned and in due time and order to produce his testimony and to make his defense.

¶ **1013.** If in any case the accused person, after due notice (seven days) has been given him, shall refuse or neglect to appear at the time and place set forth for the hearing, the investigation or trial may proceed in his absence. In all cases, sufficient time shall be allowed for the person to appear at the given place and time, and for the accused to prepare for the investigation or trial. The president of the tribunal to investigate or try the case shall decide what constitutes "sufficient time."

¶ **1014.** The court shall be a continuing body until the final disposition of the charge. If any member of the court shall be unable to attend all of the sessions, he shall not vote upon the final determination of the case, but the rest of the court may proceed to judgment. It

307

shall require a vote of two thirds or more of the original membership of the court to sustain the charges.

¶ **1015.** All objections to the regularity of the proceedings and the form and substance of charges and specifications shall be made at the first session of the trial. The presiding officer upon the filing of such objection shall, or on his own motion may, determine all such preliminary objection and may dismiss the case or in furtherance of truth and justice permit amendments to the specifications or charges not changing the general nature of the same.

¶ **1016.** Objections of any party to the proceedings shall be entered on the record.

¶ **1017.** No witness—afterward to be examined—shall be present during the examination of another witness if the opposing party objects. Witnesses shall be examined first by the party producing them, then cross-examined by the opposite party, after which any member of the court or either party may put additional questions. The presiding officer of the court shall determine all questions of relevancy and competency of evidence.

¶ **1018.** In case of investigation, trial, or appeal the presiding officer shall not deliver a charge reviewing or explaining the evidence or setting forth the merits of the case. He shall express no opinion on the law or the facts while the court is deliberating, unless the parties in interest be present. He shall remain and preside until the decision is rendered and the findings are completed, which he shall thereupon sign and certify.

Sec. V.   **Testimony**

¶ **1019.** The testimony shall be taken by a stenographer, if convenient, and reduced to writing and certified by the presiding officer and secretary. The record, including all exhibits, papers, and evidence in the case, shall be the basis of any appeal which may be taken.

¶ **1020.** A witness may not be disqualified because he is not a member of The Methodist Church.

¶ **1021.** The presiding officer of any court before which a case may be pending or the bishop in charge of an Annual Conference shall have power, whenever the necessity of the parties or of witnesses shall require, to appoint, on the application of either party, a commissioner or commissioners, either a minister or layman, or both, to examine the witnesses; *provided* that three days' notice of the time and place of taking such testimony shall have been given to the adverse party. Counsel for both parties shall be permitted to examine and cross-examine the witness or witnesses whose testimony is thus taken. The commissioners so appointed shall take such testimony in writing as may be offered by either party. The testimony properly certified by the signature of the commissioner or commissioners shall be transmitted to the presiding officer of the court before which the case is pending.

SEC. VI.   **Records**

¶ **1022.** In all investigations and trials the records shall be accurate and full; they shall include the proceedings in detail and all the evidence, taken stenographically if possible, the documents admitted, together with the charges, specifications, and findings, and shall be approved and attested by the presiding officer and secretary. In all investigations and trials the presiding officer shall appoint a secretary to keep a record of the proceedings and documents, of which records, when properly attested, the said presiding officer shall be the custodian. If no appeal is taken, the custodian shall deliver the entire record to the secretary of the conference concerned for record in its journal of the final disposition of the case.

¶ **1023.** If appeal be taken, the custodian shall deliver the entire record to the president of the proper appellate court, and after it has been used in the court it shall be returned to the secretary of the conference concerned for notation in its journal of the final disposition of the case.

¶ **1024.** The secretaries of Quarterly, District, Annual, and Jurisdictional Conferences shall be the custodians of the records of all trials occurring in their bodies respectively; and in case of appeal they shall deliver said records to the president or secretary of the proper appellate court. After the said appeal has been heard the records shall be returned to the conference from which they came.

Sec. VII.   **Appeals**

¶ **1025.** In all cases of appeal the appellant shall within thirty days give notice of appeal and at the same time shall furnish to the officer receiving such notice, and to the counsel for the church, a written statement of the grounds of his appeal, and the hearing in the appellate court shall be limited to the grounds set forth in such statement.[15]

¶ **1026.** When any appellate court shall reverse, in whole or in part, the findings of a trial court, or remand the case for a new trial, or change the penalty imposed by that court, it shall return to the Annual Conference or to the secretary of the trial court a statement of the grounds of its action.

¶ **1027.** An appeal shall not be allowed in any case in which the accused has failed or refused to be present in person or by counsel at his trial. Appeals, regularly taken, shall be heard by the proper appellate court, unless it shall appear to the said court that the appellant has forfeited his right to appeal by misconduct, such as refusal to abide by the findings of the committee of investigation or of the trial court; or by withdrawal from the church; or by failure to appear in person or by counsel to prosecute the appeal; or, prior to the final decision on appeal from his conviction, by resorting to suit in the civil courts against the complainant or any of the parties connected with the ecclesiastical court in which he was tried.[16]

¶ **1028.** The right of appeal, when once forfeited by neglect or otherwise, cannot be revived by any subsequent appellate court.

¶ **1029.** The right to take and to prosecute an appeal shall not be affected by the death of the person entitled to such right. His heirs or legal representatives may prosecute such appeal as he would be entitled to do if he were living.

[15] *See* Judicial Council Decisions 3, 144.
[16] *See* Judicial Council Decision 3.

310

¶ **1030.** The records and documents of the trial, including the evidence, and these only, shall be used in the hearing of any appeal, except as set forth in ¶¶ 947-49.

¶ **1031.** In no case shall an appeal operate as suspension of sentence. The finding of the trial court must stand until it is modified or reversed by the proper appellate court.

¶ **1032.** In all cases where an appeal is made, and admitted, by the appellate court, after the charges, findings, and evidence have been read and the arguments concluded, the parties shall withdraw, and the appellate court shall consider and decide the case. It may reverse, in whole or in part, the findings of the trial court, or it may remand the case for a new trial. It may determine what penalty, not higher than that affixed at the trial, may be imposed. If it neither reverses, in whole or in part, the judgment of the trial court, nor remands the case for a new trial, nor modifies the penalty, that judgment shall stand. The appellate court shall not reverse the judgment nor remand the case for a new trial on account of errors plainly not affecting the result.

¶ **1033.** In all cases the right to present evidence shall be exhausted when the case has been heard once on its merits in the proper court; but questions of law may be carried on appeal, step by step, to the Judicial Council.

¶ **1034.** The order of appeals on questions of law shall be as follows: From the decision of the district superintendent presiding in the Quarterly or District Conference to the bishop presiding in the Annual Conference, and from the decision of the bishop presiding in the Annual Conference to the Judicial Council; and from a Central Conference to the Judicial Council.

¶ **1035.** When an appeal is taken on a question of law, written notice of the same shall be served on the secretary of the body in which the decision has been rendered. It shall be his duty to see that an exact statement of the question submitted and the ruling of the chair thereon shall be entered on the journal. He shall then make and certify a copy of the question and ruling and transmit the same to the secretary of the body to which the appeal is taken. The secretary who thus receives said certified copy shall present the same in open conference and as soon as practicable lay it before the presiding officer for his ruling thereon; which ruling must be rendered before the final adjournment of that body, that said ruling together with the original question and ruling may be entered on the journal of that conference. The same course shall be followed in all subsequent appeals.

¶ **1036.** Errors or defects in judicial proceedings shall be duly considered when presented on appeal.

1. In regard to cases where there is an investigation under ¶¶ 932-34, but no trial is held as a result thereof, errors of law or administration committed by a district superintendent are to be corrected by the president of the next Annual Conference on request in open session, and in such event the conference may also order just and suitable remedies, if injury resulted from such errors.

2. Errors of law or defects in judicial proceedings which are discovered on appeal are to be corrected by the president of the next Annual Conference upon request in open session, and in such event the conference may also order just and suitable remedies, if injury has resulted from such errors.

SEC. VIII.   **Appeal of a Bishop**

¶ **1041.** A bishop shall have the right of appeal to the Judicial Council in case of an adverse decision by the trial court; *provided* that within thirty days after his conviction he notify the secretary of the Jurisdictional Conference in writing of his intension to appeal, unless such decision shall be rendered within thirty days prior to the meeting of such conference, in which case notice shall be given within ten days after his conviction.

¶ **1042.** A bishop elected by a Central Conference shall have the right of appeal to the Judicial Council in case of an adverse decision by the Central Conference; *provided* that within thirty days after the decision of the Central Conference he shall notify the secretary of the Central Conference in writing of his intention to appeal unless such decision shall be rendered within thirty days prior to the meeting of such conference, in which case notice shall be given within ten days after his conviction.

¶ **1043.** It shall be the duty of the secretary of the Jurisdictional or the Central Conference, on receiving notice of such appeal, to notify the secretary of the Judicial Council; and the council shall fix the time and place for the hearing of the appeal, and shall give due notice of the same to the appellant and to the secretary of the Jurisdictional or Central Conference, who in turn shall notify the counsel for the church.

SEC. IX. **Appeal of a Traveling Preacher**

¶ **1045.** Each Jurisdictional Conference, upon nomination of the College of Bishops, shall elect a **Court of Appeals** composed of nine traveling elders who have been at least six years successively members of The Methodist Church and an equal number of alternates. This court shall serve until its successors have been confirmed. This court shall have full power to hear and determine appeals of traveling preachers taken from any Annual Conference within the jurisdiction. The court shall elect its own president and secretary and shall adopt its own rules of procedure; and its decisions shall be final, except an appeal may be taken to the Judicial Council upon questions of law. (*See* ¶ 1033.)

¶ **1046.** In case of conviction in a trial court, a traveling preacher shall have the right of appeal to the Jurisdictional Court of Appeals as above constituted; *provided* that within thirty days after his conviction he shall notify the president of the conference in writing of his intention to appeal.

¶ **1047.** When notice of an appeal has been given to the president of the trial court, he shall give notice of the same to the secretary of the Court of Appeals of the Jurisdictional Conference and submit the documents in the case. The Jurisdictional Conference Court of Appeals shall give notice to the president of the conference from which the appeal is taken and to the appellant of the time and place where the appeal will be heard. Both the Annual Conference and the appellant may be represented by counsel. The president of the conference shall appoint counsel for the church.

¶ **1048.** The Court of Appeals of the Jurisdictional

Conference when acting as a court of appeals shall determine two questions only:

a) Does the evidence sustain the charge or charges?

b) Were there such errors of law as to vitiate the verdict?

These questions shall be determined by the records of the trial and the argument of counsel for the church and for the accused. The court shall in no case hear witnesses.

¶ **1049.** All necessary traveling and sustenance expense incurred by the Court of Appeals, the counsel for the church, and the counsel for the defendant, in the hearing of an appeal case coming from an Annual Conference and appearing before any Jurisdictional Court of Appeals, shall be paid out of the administration fund of the Jurisdictional Conference in which the proceedings arise.

SEC. X.　　**Appeal of a Local Preacher**

¶ **1051.** In case of conviction, a local preacher shall be allowed to appeal to the Annual Conference; *provided* that within thirty days after his conviction he shall signify in writing to the superintendent of the district his determination to appeal.

¶ **1052.** An appeal by a local preacher from a Quarterly Conference within the jurisdiction of a Mission shall be to the annual meeting of the said Mission.

SEC. XI.　　**Appeal of a Deaconess**

¶ **1053.** In case of conviction, a deaconess shall be allowed to appeal to the Commission on Deaconess Work; *provided* that within thirty days after her conviction she shall signify in writing to the district superintendent or president of the Annual Conference Deaconess Board by which she has been tried her determination to appeal to the Commission on Deaconess Work, which in full session, or by a special committee of not fewer than seven nor more than nine, shall hear the appeal; and its decision shall be the final determination of the case.

¶ **1054.** An appeal by a deaconess from an Annual Conference Deaconess Board within the jurisdiction of a

Provisional Annual Conference shall be to the Commission on Deaconess Work.

Sec. XII. Appeal of a Church Member

¶ 1056. The Quarterly Conference of each charge shall elect from among the members of the church a person of sound judgment and experience in the affairs of the church as a **trier of appeals** for members.

¶ 1057. Any member of the church against whom judgment shall have been rendered by a Trial Court may appeal to a Court of Appeal, as hereinafter constituted, by giving written notice of his desire to the district superintendent within thirty days after judgment is rendered.

¶ 1058. When thirty days' notice of appeal shall have been given, or sooner if agreed upon, the superintendent, having due regard for the wishes and rights of the appellant, shall convene a **Court of Appeal.** It shall be constituted of not fewer than seven nor more than nine triers of appeals in his district, but the trier of appeals of the charge to which the accused member belongs shall not be summoned. The district superintendent shall give not less than ten nor more than thirty days' notice to all persons concerned of the time and place at which the Court of Appeal shall assemble. The appellant shall have the right of challenge for cause of disqualification by reason of personal interest or other grounds deemed sufficient by the presiding officer, and he shall have the right of peremptory challenge of three of the panel summoned. The members of the court present and ready to proceed with the hearing shall not fall below seven, which number shall constitute a quorum. The district superintendent shall preside. The court may order a new trial or acquit the accused or impose any penalty prescribed in ¶ 974.

¶ 1059. The findings of the Court of Appeal shall be certified by the district superintendent to the pastor of the church of which the accused is a member for consistent proceedings.

¶ 1060. If the district superintendent shall find the convening of such a court to be impracticable or seriously inconvenient to the parties involved, he shall have the appeal heard by a Quarterly Conference within his district other than that of the local church. The proceedings shall be the same as provided in the foregoing paragraphs.

SEC. XIII.　　　　**Powers of Dismissal**

¶ **1065.** The various boards, committees, or commissions elected, authorized, or provided for by the General Conference shall have full power and authority to remove and dismiss in their discretion any member, officer, or employee thereof who shall be guilty of any immoral conduct or breach of trust, or who for any reason is unable to, or who fails to, perform the duties of his office, or for other misconduct which any of said boards, committees, or commissions may deem sufficient to warrant such dismissal and removal. In the event that any member, officer, or employee of such board, committee, or commission, including the Board of Publication, elected, authorized, or provided for by the General Conference, is found guilty of any crime involving moral turpitude by any federal, state, or county court or pleads guilty thereto, then and in that event, the board, committee, or commission of which he is a member, officer, or employee shall be and is hereby authorized to remove such officer, member, or employee so charged or convicted; and the place so vacated shall be filled as provided in the Discipline. The action of such board, committee, or commission in removing such member, officer, or employee in the circumstances above set forth shall be final; and such member, officer, or employee so removed shall have no further authority to participate in any way in the affairs of such board, committee, or commission.

Part VII

ADMINISTRATIVE AGENCIES

Chapter I

GENERAL PROVISIONS

¶ 1071. The **general agencies** of The Methodist Church are the regularly established councils (not including the Council of Bishops, the Judicial Council, and the Council of Secretaries), boards, commissions, and committees which have been constituted by the General Conference. Not included are boards of trustees, interagency committees, such commissions and committees as are created by the General Conference to fulfill a special function within the ensuing quadrennium, ecumenical groups on which The Methodist Church is represented, or committees related to the quadrennial sessions of the General Conference.

¶ 1072. If the membership of an agency is determined in part by the size of the church membership of the jurisdictions, the jurisdictional membership according to the latest official report preceding the General Conference, as shown in the *General Minutes*, shall be used to determine the size of the jurisdictional representation for the ensuing quadrennium. (*See* ¶ 528.)

¶ 1073. No person other than a bishop shall serve at the same time on more than one agency, and no bishop shall serve at the same time on more than three agencies (including any agency on which he serves as a liaison member from another agency); *provided*, however, that if this limitation would deprive a jurisdiction of episcopal representation on an agency, it may be suspended to the extent necessary to permit such representation; *provided*, further, that this limitation shall not apply to a division of a board, to an interagency body, or to the Commission on Chaplains, the Methodist Committee for Overseas Relief, or the Commission on Camp Activities; and *provided*,

that a bishop elected to the Council on World Service and
Finance shall not serve on any other agency during his
term on this council.

¶ **1074.** No person shall serve as president or chairman
of more than one general agency or division thereof.

¶ **1075.** No elected member of the staff of a general
agency shall be eligible for voting membership on any
general or jurisdictional agency, except where the Discipline specifically provides for such interagency representation.

¶ **1076.** No person who receives compensation for services rendered or commissions of any kind from an agency
shall be eligible for voting membership on that agency.[1]

¶ **1077.** 1. Tenure on any general agency shall be limited
to twelve consecutive years; *provided*, however, that this
limitation shall take effect from the General Conference of
1952, shall not be retroactive, and shall not affect staff
representatives of general agencies serving on other
agencies in accordance with Disciplinary requirements.
To provide a continuing membership on these agencies,
it is recommended that each nominating and electing body
give special attention to rotation of its representatives.[2]

2. If a general agency is merged with another agency,
the years served by members prior to the merger shall be
counted as part of the maximum specified in § 1.

3. If a person while serving on an agency is elected
bishop, the years which he has served prior to election
shall be counted as part of the maximum specified in § 1.

¶ **1078.** 1. No person who has passed the age of seventy
shall be nominated for, or elected to, membership on any
general agency.

2. A minister serving as a member of a general agency
who takes the retired relationship shall cease to be a
member thereof at the time of his retirement. The vacancy shall be filled in accordance with the appropriate
Disciplinary provision.

3. A general agency may, by majority written ballot,
elect as a non-voting honorary member a person who has

---

[1] *See* Judicial Council Decision 139.
[2] Amended in 1964 following Judicial Council Decisions 200,
205, 209.

previously served on it with distinction and who has passed the age of seventy; *provided*, however, that not more than one honorary member may be elected for every twenty-five regular members or major fraction thereof. An honorary member shall receive an expense allowance in the same manner as regular members.

¶ **1079.** If a minister who has been elected as a representative of a jurisdiction to a general agency is transferred to an Annual Conference in another jurisdiction, or a layman who has been so elected changes his legal residence to another jurisdiction, he shall cease to be a member of that agency at the time of his transfer or removal; *provided*, however, that this rule shall apply to a representative of the Central Jurisdiction whose local church or Annual Conference is transferred to another jurisdiction under ¶ 47 ix only if the transfer leaves the Central Jurisdiction with no representation on that agency. The vacancy shall be filled in accordance with the appropriate Disciplinary provision.

¶ **1080.** If a member of a general agency is absent from two consecutive regular meetings without a reason acceptable to the agency, he shall cease to be a member thereof. In that case he shall be so notified, and his place shall be filled in accordance with the appropriate Disciplinary provision.

¶ **1081.** If a bishop is unable to attend a meeting of an agency of which he is a member, the Council of Bishops may name an alternate representative to attend that meeting with the privilege of vote.

¶ **1082.** Unless otherwise specified, vacancies on boards and other agencies occurring during the quadrennium shall be filled as follows: an episcopal vacancy shall be filled by the Council of Bishops; a vacancy in jurisdictional representation shall be filled by the College of Bishops of that jurisdiction; a vacancy in the membership at large shall be filled by the agency itself.[3]

¶ **1083.** It shall be the policy of The Methodist Church that all administrative agencies and institutions (including hospitals, homes, and educational institutions):

---

[3] *See* Judicial Council Decision 198.

(a) recruit, employ, utilize, recompense, and promote their professional staff and other personnel without regard to race, color, or sex; and (b) fulfill their duties and responsibilities in a manner which does not involve racial segregation or discrimination.[4]

¶ **1085.** An agency proposing to acquire real estate or erect a building or enter into a lease for a term in excess of five years (or with an option to extend or renew beyond such period or to purchase the property) to house its administrative activities or related operations in the continental United States shall present its plans in the formative stage to the Co-ordinating Council for approval. If the Co-ordinating Council disapproves, the agency shall delay the project until it can be considered by the next General Conference. *Provided*, however, that nothing in the foregoing shall include the operational requirements of the Board of Publication. (*See* ¶ 1093.6.)

¶ **1086.** An agency publishing or proposing to publish and circulate any magazine or periodical for promotional purposes shall secure the approval of the Co-ordinating Council. If the Co-ordinating Council disapproves, the agency shall delay such publication and circulation until its request can be submitted to the next General Conference for determination. *Provided*, however, that the foregoing shall not be deemed to apply to the periodicals exempted in ¶ 753.3, or to church-school curriculum materials. (*See* ¶ 1093.7.)

¶ **1087.** The general agencies shall consult with the Co-ordinating Council in regard to publishing policy, as provided in ¶ 1093.9, and shall furnish such relevant information as the council may request. Each world service agency shall report semiannually to the council the itemized costs in connection with its publications. (*See also* ¶ 1144.1.)

---

[4] The General Conference of 1964 adopted, effective with the adjournment of the General Conference of 1968, the following:
"Elected staff personnel of a general agency shall be retired at the first regular meeting of the agency within the quadrennium in which the person shall become seventy-two years of age. All other staff personnel shall be retired not later than their seventieth birthday. An agency may retire its personnel at an earlier but not a later age than specified above."

Note: For provisions regarding the finances of the general agencies *see* Part V, Chapter II, Church Finance, especially ¶¶ 737, 741-48, 765, 768, 781-84.

CHAPTER II

CO-ORDINATING COUNCIL

¶ **1091.** There shall be a **Co-ordinating Council,** responsible directly to the General Conference. It shall co-ordinate the work of the general administrative agencies of The Methodist Church. Its membership shall consist of one bishop, one minister, one lay man, and one lay woman from each jurisdiction, plus one minister and one lay person for each additional million members or major fraction thereof above the first million members in a jurisdiction, all nominated by the Council of Bishops and elected by the General Conference; and two additional persons appointed by the Council of Bishops from among members of the church overseas who are in the United States at the time of the meetings of the council; *provided* that the Council of Bishops shall replace the representatives of the church overseas when they leave the United States. The term of membership shall be four years. (*See* ¶ 1077.) Members shall serve until their successors are appointed or elected. Staff members of general agencies are not eligible to membership. (*See* ¶¶ 1073, 1075.) Vacancies which occur during the quadrennium shall be filled by the College of Bishops of the appropriate jurisdiction.

¶ **1092.** 1. The Co-ordinating Council shall elect a president, a vice-president, and a recording secretary, who shall keep a permanent record of its meetings and of any decisions reached. Certified copies of the minutes shall be filed with the secretary of the General Conference and with the Council on World Service and Finance.

2. It shall convene annually, and at such other times as are necessary on call of the president or on written request of one fifth of the members. Sixteen members shall constitute a quorum.

3. All decisions shall require a majority vote of the entire membership.

4. It may incur expense necessary to the performance of its functions, subject to such budgetary control as may be specified by the General Conference. Its annual expenses shall be paid from the General Administration Fund.

¶ **1093.** The Co-ordinating Council shall have the following responsibilities:

1. On request of a general board or other agency, or of an Annual Conference, or on its own initiative, it shall review questions involving overlapping in activity or lack of co-operation among or within general agencies, and shall make recommendations to the boards or agencies involved for resolving such issues; *provided* that in a review of any such question a bishop who is a member of an agency involved shall be disqualified. In the event of noncompliance, the recommendations shall be reported to the next General Conference. A record of all recommendations shall be kept, and a report of each shall be forwarded to the Council of Bishops, the Council on World Service and Finance, and the secretary of the General Conference.

2. It shall study the general organizational structure of The Methodist Church and recommend to the General Conference such changes as it considers essential to maintain effective and economical operation. It shall study and recommend proposals for new structure which is needed, growing out of changing situations in the life of the Church and of society. It shall review changes in structure which may be proposed by the general agencies.

3. In consultation with the Council of Bishops and the Council of Secretaries it shall determine the need for a special program for any particular quadrennium and, if such is judged desirable, shall formulate the same in consultation with the Council of Bishops and the Council of Secretaries and present it to the General Conference for its action and determination.

4. It shall give leadership in long-range planning in The Methodist Church and shall arrange for representa-

tion of The Methodist Church in long-range planning activities in ecumenical bodies.

5. It shall recommend to the General Conference, after consultation with the Council of Bishops and the Council on World Service and Finance, the number and timing of all special days which are to be observed on a church-wide basis, except that the Council of Bishops and the Council on World Service and Finance may authorize a special financial appeal in an emergency.

6. It shall designate the agency which shall undertake any special study authorized by the General Conference when such agency has not been indicated by the General Conference.

7. It shall consider the plans of any general agency proposing to acquire real estate or erect a building or enter into a lease as described in ¶ 1085, and determine whether the proposed action is in the best interest of The Methodist Church. On the basis of that determination it shall approve or disapprove.

8. It shall consider the plans of any general agency to publish a promotional periodical, as provided in ¶ 1086.

9. It shall consult with the general agencies of The Methodist Church in regard to publishing policy. It shall lead in a continuing consultation with all editors of all publications and the president and publisher of The Methodist Publishing House, and shall suggest such steps as may seem advisable to minimize unnecessary duplication and overlappings of content emphasis and coverage, and where desirable to combine periodicals. It shall be responsible for reporting the results of these consultations to the General Conference. (See ¶¶ 1087, 1144.1.)

10. It shall (a) evaluate the procedures, mechanics, and effectiveness of overseas representation on, and participation in, the general agencies and the special commissions and committees of the General Conference; (b) evaluate the effectiveness of procedures utilized to advise overseas delegates of materials to be considered at the General Conference; and (c) implement, where possible, and recommend to the General Conference, where appropriate, measures to better assure full effective representa-

tion and participation of overseas members in the work of the church and the General Conference.

¶ **1095.** There shall be an **Interagency Committee on Research**, organized as follows:

1. The Co-ordinating Council shall appoint one of its members as chairman of an organizing subcommittee, which shall consist of the director of the Department of Research of the Council on World Service and Finance, the director of the Department of Research and Survey of the National Division of the Board of Missions, and two other persons, whom the above three shall name, one of whom shall be a professor engaged in social research in a Methodist school of theology.

2. The members of this subcommittee shall set the organizational meeting of the committee, and shall invite into membership with themselves persons engaged in research in the several agencies and schools of theology of The Methodist Church, and may in addition invite into membership non-agency research specialists up to a maximum of five persons.

3. The committee shall be convened by the representative of the Co-ordinating Council, and shall elect a chairman, vice-chairman, secretary, and such other officers as may be deemed necessary.

4. An annual written report of the committee shall be made to the Co-ordinating Council.

5. The necessary expense of the committee shall be subject to approval by the treasurer of, and be paid from, the General Administration Fund. The travel and other expenses of the members representing general agencies shall be borne by the groups represented.

6. The committee shall meet annually for the purpose of: (*a*) establishing standards for conducting research; (*b*) reviewing and evaluating research projects in terms of these standards; (*c*) serving in an advisory capacity to any general agency or official personnel on such matters as may properly come before such an interagency committee; (*d*) minimizing duplication and overlapping of research by two or more agencies.

7. The committee shall not itself conduct research

projects but, if requested, may recommend appropriate agencies for specific research work.

Chapter III

COUNCIL ON WORLD SERVICE AND FINANCE

¶ **1101.** There shall be a **Council on World Service and Finance,** which shall be incorporated. Its members shall be elected quadrennially by the General Conference, as follows: two bishops, nominated by the Council of Bishops; two ministers and two lay persons from each jurisdiction, nominated by the bishops of that jurisdiction; and seven members at large, at least three of whom shall be women, nominated by the Council of Bishops without reference to jurisdictions. The members, including bishops (¶ 1073), shall not be eligible to membership on, or employment by, any other general agency except The Board of Trustees of The Methodist Church. They shall serve until their successors are elected and qualified. Vacancies occurring between sessions of the General Conference shall be filled by the council, on nomination of the bishops of the jurisdiction concerned or, in the event of a vacancy among the members at large, the Council of Bishops.

¶ **1102.** The officers of the Council on World Service and Finance shall be a president, a vice-president, a recording secretary, and a general secretary, who shall also be the treasurer of the council, all of whom shall be elected by the council. They shall serve until the adjournment of the next succeeding quadrennial session of the General Conference after their election and until their successors are duly elected and qualified. The president, vice-president, and recording secretary shall be elected from the membership of the council. The general secretary shall sit with the council and its executive committee at all sessions, and shall have right to the floor without the privilege of voting. (*See* ¶ 1076.) The employed personnel of the council shall be selected by and shall work under the direction of the general secretary.

¶ **1103.** The Council on World Service and Finance shall convene annually, and at such other times as are necessary on call of the president or on written request of one fifth of the members. Sixteen members shall constitute a quorum.

¶ **1104.** There shall be an **executive committee** of the Council on World Service and Finance consisting of the officers of the council and six members to be elected annually by the council. The executive committee shall meet on call of the president or of a majority of the membership thereof, and shall act for the council and exercise its powers in the interim of the meetings of the council; but it shall not take any action contrary to or in conflict with any action or policy of the council. A copy of the minutes of each meeting of the executive committee shall be sent from the central office to each member of the council as soon after the meeting as practicable.

¶ **1105.** The Council on World Service and Finance shall have the authority and responsibility to perform the following functions:

1. Receive and disburse, in accordance with budgets approved by the General Conference, or its properly authorized agency, the general funds of the church as set forth in ¶¶ 737-39.

2. Require each world service agency to follow uniform policies and practices in the employment and remuneration of personnel, recognizing differences in local employment conditions.[5]

3. Establish titles for the employed executive staff of world service agencies, in the interest of uniformity and consistency. (*See* ¶ 783.)

4. Provide legal counsel where this is necessary in order to protect the interests of the church, and as the council deems advisable, at the request of a world service agency or of a bishop.

---

[5] The General Conference of 1964 directed the Council on World Service and Finance to report to the Council of Bishops in 1966, and to the General Conference in 1968, the results of surveys of the services and employment policies, with particular reference to racial discrimination in hiring and advancement, of all institutions and agencies of the church which received financial support from the Council on World Service and Finance.

¶ **1106.** The Council on World Service and Finance shall maintain and supervise, under the direction of its general secretary, three departments:

1. The **Department of Research,** the duties of which shall be to: (*a*) initiate, on approval of the council or its executive committee, such research as may be deemed essential, provided due care is taken not to duplicate similar research being made by other general agencies; (*b*) analyze, interpret, and evaluate the facts gathered through research, making them available to the general agencies; (*c*) maintain a research library and an index, including a listing and cataloguing of the past and current research made by or for the several agencies of the church; (*d*) maintain a roster of competent research persons who may be employed to do special research projects; and (*e*) co-operate with specialized research personnel associated with other agencies of the church (*see* ¶ 1095). The services of the department shall be available to any other official agency of the church.

2. The **Department of Records,** which shall have the function of maintaining an accurate record of the mail addresses of all bishops, ministers in the effective relation, supply pastors, including retired ministers serving charges, and conference lay leaders, and such lists of general, jurisdictional, conference, and district boards, commissions, and committees, and officers of the same, and of local-church commission chairmen, as may be deemed necessary. No use of these records shall be permitted for other than authorized bodies or officers of The Methodist Church.

3. The **Department of Statistics,** which shall have the duty of preparing the important statistics relating to The Methodist Church for the *General Minutes, The Methodist Fact Book*, and such other publications and releases as may be authorized by the Council.

The expenses of these three departments, including the printing of the *General Minutes, The Methodist Fact Book*, and such other publications and releases as may be authorized by the council, shall be borne by the General Administration Fund; *provided*, however, that where the research requested by an agency requires postage, supplies, temporary additional staff, or other necessary expense, an agreement as to the payment of this additional cost shall be entered into with the council before such service is undertaken. The number and qualifications of the regularly employed staff shall be determined by the council.

¶ **1107.** The Council on World Service and Finance shall maintain and supervise, under the direction of its general secretary, a **Committee on Official Forms and Records,** which shall have the duty of preparing and editing all official statistical blanks, record forms, and record books for use in The Methodist Church, except official records for use in the local church school and forms used by the Woman's Division of the Board of Missions. The committee shall consist of one bishop elected by the Council of Bishops and ten persons elected by the Council on World Service and Finance, as follows: one member of the council from each jurisdiction, and one conference secretary, one conference treasurer, one conference statistician, and one district superintendent. The following persons shall be consultants to this committee, ex officio without vote: a staff representative of the council, the directors of the Departments of Research and of Statistics, a representative elected by the Interagency Committee on Research, a representative of The Methodist Publishing House, and representatives of other general agencies when their programs are directly involved. All official statistical blanks, record forms, and record books required for use in The Methodist Church shall be printed and published by The Methodist Publishing House.

¶ **1108.** The Council on World Service and Finance shall maintain and supervise, under the direction of its general secretary, a department known as the **Transportation Office.** This department shall represent the church in its relation with the responsible persons or concerns operating the several modes of public transportation. The purchase of tickets and the securing of space reservations for travel shall be placed as nearly as possible on a self-supporting basis. The costs of the Transportation Office shall be a charge against the General Administration Fund.

¶ 1109. The Council on World Service and Finance shall maintain and supervise, under the direction of its general secretary, a **Convention Bureau.** The Convention Bureau shall offer its services to all general agencies of The Methodist Church.

¶ 1110. The Council on World Service and Finance shall operate, under the supervision of its general secretary, a department known as the **Shipping and Service Department.** It shall be the function of this department to maintain such addressing, packaging, mailing, and duplicating service as may be deemed necessary to provide these services for the general agencies. The general secretary shall co-operate with the general secretary of the Commission on Promotion and Cultivation in scheduling the general mailings to pastors, in the interest of proper spacing. The general secretary is authorized and directed to make equitable charges to the agencies using these services.

Chapter IV

THE METHODIST PUBLISHING HOUSE

Section I.   Objects and Organization

¶ 1121. **The Methodist Publishing House** comprises the publishing interests of The Methodist Church.

¶ 1122. The objects of The Methodist Publishing House shall be: the advancement of the cause of Christianity by disseminating religious knowledge and useful literary and scientific information in the form of books, tracts, and periodicals; the promotion of Christian education; the transaction of any and all business properly connected with the publishing, manufacturing, and distribution of books, tracts, periodicals, materials, and supplies for churches and church schools; and such other business as the General Conference may authorize and direct.

¶ 1123. The Methodist Publishing House shall be under

the direction and control of the **Board of Publication,** acting through an executive officer elected by the board, who shall be the **publisher of The Methodist Church,** and such other officers as the board may determine.

¶ **1124.** The net income from the operations of The Methodist Publishing House, after providing adequate reserves for the efficient operation of the business and allowing for reasonable growth and expansion, shall be appropriated by the Board of Publication and distributed annually to the several Annual Conferences for the persons who are and shall be conference claimants.

¶ **1125.** The net income from the operations of The Methodist Publishing House shall be appropriated to no other purpose than its own operating requirements and the conference claimants, as provided in ¶ 9.5 and ¶ 1124.

¶ **1126.** The members of the Board of Publication, and their successors in office, are declared to be the successors of the incorporators named in the charters of The Methodist Book Concern issued by the states of New York and Ohio, and in the charter of The Board of Publication of The Methodist Protestant Church issued by the state of Pennsylvania. The executive officer elected from time to time under this or any subsequent Discipline is declared to be the successor in office of the Book Agents of the Methodist Episcopal Church, South, named in the charter issued to the corporation of that name by the state of Tennessee.

¶ **1127.** Subject to the provisions of ¶ 1123, and to the continuing control and direction of the General Conference of The Methodist Church as set forth from time to time in the Discipline, the Board of Publication is authorized, empowered, and directed to cause the operations of The Methodist Publishing House to be carried on, and the objects defined in ¶ 1122 to be achieved, in such manner, through or by means of such agencies or instrumentalities, and by use of such procedures as the board may from time to time determine to be necessary, advisable, or appropriate, with full power and authority in the premises to take all such action and to do all such other acts and things as may be required or found to be advisable. In particular, and without limiting the generality of the foregoing, the board is authorized and empowered, for the purposes of this chapter:

1. To use, manage, operate, and otherwise utilize all property and assets of every kind, character, and description of four corporations—namely, The Methodist Book Concern, a corporation existing under the laws of the state of New York; The Methodist Book Concern, a corporation existing under the laws of the state of Ohio; The Board of Publication of The Methodist Protestant Church, a corporation existing under the laws of the state of Pennsylvania; and Book Agents of the Methodist Episcopal Church, South, a corporation existing under the laws of the state of Tennessee—as well as all income from such property and assets and the avails thereof, all with liability or obligation to account for such property and assets, the use thereof, the income therefrom, and avails thereof, only to the General Conference of The Methodist Church or as it shall direct.

2. To cause each of the said corporations to take all such action and to do all such things as the board may deem necessary or advisable to carry out the intent and purposes of this ¶ 1127. The governing body of each of the said corporations from time to time shall take all action which the board deems to be necessary or advisable to carry out the intent and purposes of this ¶ 1127. The board shall cause all legal obligations of said four corporations, now existing or hereafter incurred, to be met, fulfilled, and performed.

3. To continue to exercise the powers and administer the duties and responsibilities conferred on it as an agency of The Methodist Church through the corporation named **Board of Publication of The Methodist Church,** incorporated under the laws of the state of Illinois in accord with authority delegated to it by the General Conference of 1952, or through such other means and agencies as it may from time to time determine to be expedient and necessary in order to give full effect to the purposes expressed in this chapter.

¶ **1128.** 1. Under the corporate structure of Board of Publication of The Methodist Church, incorporated in the state of Illinois, and subject to the provisions of the preceding paragraphs of this chapter, the board is authorized and empowered to conduct its general operations under the name of The Methodist Publishing House.

2. The property, assets, and income of the said Illinois corporation shall be held by it, under the direction of the board, as an agency of The Methodist Church and shall at all times be subject to the control and direction of the General Conference of The Methodist Church as set forth from time to time in the Discipline.

3. In carrying out and executing its operations and functions, the Illinois corporation shall be entitled to hold, use, manage, operate, and otherwise utilize all property and assets of every kind, character, and description of each of the four corporations identified in ¶ 1127.1 (other than its corporate powers and franchises) and all income therefrom, and avails thereof, for the purposes and objects defined in this chapter.

4. The governing body of each of the five existing corporations under the direction of the board shall from time to time take all such action as the board deems necessary or advisable to carry out the intent and purposes of this paragraph and chapter.

5. The Illinois corporation shall be liable for and shall execute and satisfy all legal obligations of each of the four corporations named in ¶ 1127.1, but neither it nor the board shall have or be under any obligation to account for principal and income to any such other corporation or to otherwise report to any of them; *provided*, however, that the Illinois corporation shall return to each of the other four corporations custody and control of its real property and account to it for the net amount of any other assets received from such other corporation if and when such return or accounting shall be directed or required by the board or by any General Conference of The Methodist Church.

SEC. II.   **Board of Publication**

¶ 1129. The Board of Publication shall consist of forty-five members, of whom two shall be bishops selected by the Council of Bishops and five shall be members at large elected by the board. The remaining members shall be elected by the Jurisdictional Conferences on a ratio which will provide for an equitable distribution among the various jurisdictions, based on the memberships thereof; *provided* that no jurisdiction shall be represented by fewer than two members. Membership on the board shall be equally divided, as far as practicable, between ministers and laymen. It shall be the duty of the secretary of the General Conference to inform the various jurisdictional secretaries of the number of members to be elected from their jurisdictions, the ratio of such representation being computed on the basis of the latest official membership statistics available. In the elections it is recommended that special attention be given to rotation of representatives so that as nearly as possible one third of the membership shall be elected each quadrennium. (*See* ¶ 1077.) In case a vacancy occurs between sessions of the Jurisdictional Conference for any cause, the board shall fill the vacancy, for the unexpired term, from that jurisdiction in the representation of which the vacancy occurs, except in the case of members at large. The president of the Board of Publication of The Methodist Church, Incorporated, shall be an ex officio member of the board, without vote.

¶ 1130. The board shall meet annually. The place and time of all meetings shall be designated by the board; but if it fails to do so, then the time and place shall be designated by the chairman. Special meetings may be called by the chairman on his own initiative or by the board. Special meetings shall also be called by the chairman on written request of one third of the members of the board. At all meetings of the board a majority of the members shall constitute a quorum.

¶ 1131. The board shall keep a correct record of its proceedings and shall examine carefully into the affairs of The Methodist Publishing House and make written report thereof to the church through the General Conference.

¶ 1132. The board shall fix the salaries of the following officers: president (publisher), book editor, editors of the official church papers, editor of church-school publications, and other salaried officers provided for by this chapter.

¶ 1133. The board, at its discretion, may continue the

publication of the quarterly *Religion in Life*, with the book editor responsible for its editorial content.

¶ **1134.** The members of the board and all officers elected by it shall hold office until their successors are chosen.

¶ **1135.** The board shall elect from its membership an **executive committee,** of sixteen members, including the chairman, vice-chairman, and secretary of the board, who shall serve respectively as chairman, vice-chairman, and secretary of the executive committee. Not more than four members of the executive committee shall be from any one jurisdiction. In addition, the two bishops serving on the board shall be ex officio members with vote, and the president shall be an ex officio member without vote. Any vacancy occurring in the membership of the executive committee shall be filled by it, subject to confirmation by the board at its next meeting.

¶ **1136.** The executive committee shall have and may exercise all the powers of the board except those expressly reserved for board action by the Discipline or by the corporate charter and by-laws. It shall meet quarterly to examine the affairs under its charge and shall keep and submit to the board correct records of its proceedings. Special meetings may be called by the chairman on his own initiative, and shall be called on the written request of five members of the executive committee. A majority of the members shall constitute a quorum.

Sec. III.   **Executives**

¶ **1137.** Officers of each corporation under the direction of the board shall be elected annually in accordance with its charter and by-laws.

¶ **1138.** The executive officer elected pursuant to ¶ 1123 shall also be elected the **president** of each corporation under the direction of the board.

¶ **1139.** The board shall require written quarterly reports to the executive committee covering the current condition and operating status of the business.

¶ **1140.** The president (publisher) and the board shall have authority to extend the business of The Methodist

Publishing House in such manner as they may judge to be for the best interests of the church.

¶ **1141.** The board shall require the president and other corporate executive officers to give bond conditioned on the faithful discharge of their respective duties. It also shall authorize the execution of a blanket bond covering all staff personnel whose responsibilities justify such coverage. The amount of the bonds shall be fixed by the board, and the bonds shall be subject to the approval of the board. The premiums shall be paid by the board, and the chairman of the board shall be the custodian of the bonds.

¶ **1142.** The board shall have power to suspend, after hearing, and to remove, after hearing, the president or any of the officers created by this chapter, for misconduct or failure to perform the duties of their office.

SEC. IV.   **Book Editor**

¶ **1143.** The board shall elect quadrennially a **book editor,** who shall have joint responsibility with the publisher for approving manuscripts considered for publication. He shall edit all the books of our publication, and the quarterly *Religion in Life*. In the case of materials authorized by the Curriculum Committee in the field of Christian education which are to be edited by the editor of church-school publications he shall collaborate with that editor whenever such collaboration is necessary or desired. He shall perform such other editorial duties as may be required of him by the board. He shall not have responsibility for materials issued by other agencies of the church for program or promotional purposes.

SEC. V.   **General Church Periodicals**

¶ **1144.** 1. The board is authorized to publish a periodical for pastors, and a periodical for the family which shall be a general magazine informative and vital to the religious life of all Methodists. The board may, at its discretion, issue such editions of the official periodicals as in its judgment may be deemed advisable. In consultation with the Co-ordinating Council it shall explore ways and means of making the pages of these periodicals available to other general agencies to the extent possible, either through acceptable editorial channels or by paid insertion as the need may indicate. It shall make available to the council semiannually the operating statements of these periodicals and shall furnish such other relevant information as the council may request. (*See* ¶ 1093.9.)

2. For service in the Central Jurisdiction *Central Christian Advocate*, whose editor shall be a member of that jurisdiction, shall be continued until such time as the Co-ordinating Council, after consultation with representatives of the jurisdiction named by its College of Bishops, recommends the establishment of a *Christian Advocate* and *Together* for the whole church.

3. The **editors** of the periodicals authorized in §§ 1 and 2 shall be elected quadrennially by the board, after consultation with the Co-ordinating Council through a joint committee composed of the chairman and two other members of the council and the chairman and two other members of the board, one of whom shall be a bishop. The editors shall be responsible to the publisher for ongoing publishing procedures, but shall themselves be responsible for the editorial content of their respective publications.

4. All other details relating to the publishing and distribution of these periodicals, not specifically delegated to the editors, shall be under the direction of the publisher.

5. The board shall have power to suspend or remove, after hearing, any editor or associate editor for misconduct or failure to perform the duties of his office.

Sec. VI.   **Church-School Publications**

¶ **1145.** There shall be an **editor of church-school publications,** elected as set forth in ¶ 1429.

¶ **1146.** The editor of church-school publications shall be responsible for the preparation of all curriculum materials, as set forth in ¶ 1431.

¶ **1147.** The curriculum of the church school shall be determined by the Curriculum Committee, which shall include in its membership the editor of church-school publications, the book editor, and the publisher, as set forth in ¶ 1433.

¶ **1148.** The Board of Publication shall fix and pay the salaries of the editor of church-school publications and his assistants and shall have full financial responsibility for all other expenses connected with his work.

¶ **1149.** The publications of the General Board of Education shall be manufactured, published, and distributed through The Methodist Publishing House. In matters involving financial responsibility the final determination in every case shall lie with the Board of Publication. After consultation with the publisher, the editor of church-school publications shall prepare a complete budget for his work, including salaries of assistants and office secretaries, and travel, to be effective when approved by the Board of Publication, and shall direct its operation from year to year.

¶ **1150.** There shall be one complete co-ordinated system of literature published by The Methodist Publishing House for the entire Methodist Church. This literature is to be of such type and variety as to meet the needs of all groups of our people.

¶ **1151.** The Board of Publication and the publisher shall have authority to decline to publish any item of literature when in their judgment the cost would be greater than should be borne by The Methodist Publishing House.

¶ **1152.** The editor of church-school publications and the chairman of the Editorial Division of the General Board of Education shall have the right to sit with the Board of Publication for the consideration of matters pertaining to the joint interests of the Board of Publication and the Board of Education and shall have the privilege of the floor, without vote. (*See also* ¶ 1436.)

¶ **1153.** The provisions of this section shall not apply to the promotional materials of the Division of Higher Education or of the Division of the Local Church.

Sec. VII.   **Printing for Church Agencies**

¶ **1154.** It is recommended that the general agencies and institutions of The Methodist Church have all their printing done by The Methodist Publishing House. (*See* ¶¶ 530.2, 1107.)

SEC. VIII.   **Real Estate and Buildings**

¶ **1156.** The Methodist Publishing House shall not buy, sell, or exchange any real estate except by order of the General Conference, or, between sessions of the General Conference, by a two-thirds vote of all the members of the Board of Publication; nor shall the board authorize any new buildings or make any improvements, alterations, or repairs to existing buildings to cost in excess of $100,000, except by order of the General Conference, or, between sessions of the General Conference, by a two-thirds vote of all members of the board. In either case, such vote shall be taken at a regular or called meeting of the board; and, if at a called meeting, the purpose of this meeting shall have been stated in the call. (*See* ¶¶ 1085, 1093.7 for additional requirements and restrictions.)

¶ **1157.** The erection of a new building, or the improvement, alteration, or repair of an existing building, involving an expenditure of not more than $100,000, may be authorized by the vote of a majority of the executive committee. These provisions shall not prevent the making of investments on mortgage security or the protection of the same, or the collection of claims and adjustments. (*See* ¶¶ 1085, 1093.7, 1156 for additional requirements and restrictions.)

SEC. IX.   **Annual Conference Committee**

¶ **1158.** 1. There shall be organized in each Annual Conference a **Conference Committee on Publishing Interests,** consisting of no fewer than three nor more than five members at large. The resident bishop and the conference or area director of public relations and Methodist information shall be members ex officio. There may also be one additional person from each district, to be designated **district secretary of publishing interests.**

2. The committee shall meet at least once before or during every regular conference session, and shall act in co-operation with the Board of Publication in promoting the work of the board within the bounds of the conference.

CHAPTER V

INTERBOARD COMMISSION ON THE LOCAL CHURCH

¶ **1160.** There shall be an **Interboard Commission on the Local Church,** whose function shall be to act as the co-ordinator of the policies and activities of its boards, namely: the Board of Missions through the Joint Commission on Education and Cultivation, the National Division, and the Woman's Division, the Board of Education and its divisions, the Board of Evangelism, the Board of Lay Activities, the Board of Christian Social Concerns and its divisions, and any other general agency for which the General Conference may hereafter provide a mandatory commission in the local church.

¶ **1161.** The commission shall be composed of three bishops elected by the Council of Bishops and three members elected by each constituent board.

¶ **1162.** 1. The commission, in carrying out its function of co-ordinating the work of the boards which it represents, shall see that plans and programs relating to the local church and to higher education do not overlap or duplicate in activity and literature.

2. The commission shall serve as the agency through which its member boards, acting jointly, shall provide, as may be needed, manuals, filmstrips, and other guidance and training materials for members of Official Boards, Boards of Trustees, and Quarterly Conference committees in matters which concern the boards jointly. (*See* ¶ 1499.4.) This does not contravene the responsibility of a board to provide separate material within its own field.[6]

---

[6] The General Conference of 1964 referred to the Interboard Commission on the Local Church certain petitions which had been presented to it regarding the local church (including the structure and work of the Commission on Worship, relations with the campus ministry, and other varied matters) for study and report to the legislative Committee on the Local Church of the General Conference of 1968, with the request that in this study there be adequate involvement of laymen, pastors, district superintendents, and representatives of the General Commission on Worship.

¶ **1163.** Implementing the work of the commission there shall be a **secretarial council** consisting of the chief executives of the Board of Missions and its Joint Commission on Education and Cultivation, National Division, and Woman's Division, the Board of Education and its divisions, the Board of Evangelism, the Board of Lay Activities, and the Board of Christian Social Concerns and its divisions. It shall be the function of this council to facilitate co-operation among the boards in the creative planning of programs and in avoiding overlapping of function or duplication of activity. The chairmanship of the secretarial council shall rotate annually among the several secretaries.

¶ **1164.** 1. The commission shall set up an **Interboard Committee on Ministry to Neglected Areas,** composed of at least one representative each from the National Division and the Woman's Division of the Board of Missions, the Division of the Local Church of the Board of Education, the Board of Lay Activities, the Board of Christian Social Concerns, and the Board of Evangelism. Under the direction of the commission it shall study neglected metropolitan and rural areas and shall develop and recommend plans for (*a*) organizing new churches and church schools, (*b*) organizing and seeking support for mission churches and missions, (*c*) reviving and supporting dying and abandoned churches, (*d*) enlisting local churches and lay men and women in support of the foregoing activities with their means and services, and (*e*) taking other steps deemed appropriate to provide for ministry to such neglected areas and peoples.

2. When in the judgment of the commission such action would facilitate co-ordination among its boards, it may authorize other interboard committees and joint staff committees.

¶ **1165.** Any question of overlapping or duplication among the constituent boards which cannot be resolved by the commission, or any overlapping of function or duplication of activity between one of the constituent boards and another agency of The Methodist Church, shall be referred to the Co-ordinating Council. (*See* ¶ 1093.1.)

CHAPTER VI

BOARD OF MISSIONS

SECTION I.   **The Aim of Missions**

¶ **1176.** The supreme aim of missions is to make the Lord Jesus Christ known to all peoples in all lands as their divine Savior, to persuade them to become his disciples, and to gather these disciples into Christian churches; to enlist them in the building of the kingdom of God; to co-operate with these churches; to promote world Christian fellowship; and to bring to bear on all human life the spirit and principles of Christ.

SEC. II.   **Organization**

¶ **1177.** *Article 1. Name.*—The name of this organization shall be the **Board of Missions** of The Methodist Church, hereinafter called the board. Its objectives are religious, philanthropic, and educational. (*See* ¶ 1204.)

¶ **1178.** *Art. 2. Incorporation.*—The board shall be incorporated. Within the board there shall be three divisions—namely, the World Division, the National Division, and the Woman's Division—which shall each also be incorporated, and which shall be the corporate successors, respectively, of the Division of World Missions, the Division of National Missions, and the Woman's Division of Christian Service. The board and its divisions shall be incorporated in such state or states as the board may select. Subject to the limitations hereinafter specified, each of the incorporated divisions shall be subject to the supervision and control of the board, and shall be under the direction and control of the General Conference of The Methodist Church in all things not inconsistent with the constitution and laws of the United States and of the states of incorporation.

¶ **1179.** The board shall have control of all the work formerly controlled and administered by the following: the Board of Missions and Church Extension of The Methodist Church; the Missionary Society, the Board of Foreign Missions, the Board of Home Missions and

341

Church Extension, the Woman's Foreign Missionary Society, the Woman's Home Missionary Society, the Wesleyan Service Guild, and the Ladies' Aid Societies of the Methodist Episcopal Church; the Board of Missions, including the Woman's Missionary Society, the Woman's Board of Foreign Missions, the Woman's Board of Home Missions, and the Woman's Missionary Council, and the Board of Church Extension [7] of the Methodist Episcopal Church, South; and the Board of Missions of the Methodist Protestant Church, and such other corporations or agencies of the General Conference as do similar work; but this list shall not be construed as exclusive.

¶ **1180.** *Art. 3. Board of Managers.*—The management and disposition of the affairs of the board, the making and administration of appropriations, and all other activities shall be vested in a **Board of Managers,** which shall be composed as follows:

1. Fifteen bishops, representing all of the jurisdictions, resident in the United States, and in addition five bishops serving overseas (subject to such travel regulations as are provided in the Discipline for overseas bishops), all elected by the Council of Bishops.

2. Members elected quadrennially by the Jurisdictional Conferences as follows: one minister and three lay members, two of whom shall be women, from each jurisdiction for each 600,000 members, or major fraction thereof, in the jurisdiction; *provided* that no jurisdiction, in addition to the bishops, shall have fewer than two ministers and six lay members, four of whom shall be women and two men. In nominating and electing such members, the Jurisdictional Conference shall have as a basis for choice the following: (*a*) one minister and one lay man designated by each Annual Conference of the jurisdiction, on nomination of its Conference Board of Missions; (*b*) six additional names nominated by the College of Bishops of the jurisdiction; (*c*) twice the necessary number of lay women, designated by the Jurisdiction Woman's Society of Christian Service from three members nominated by each Conference Woman's Society of Christian Service of

---

[7] *See* Judicial Council Decision 99.

the jurisdiction. Vacancies among these members shall be filled by the bishops of the jurisdiction in which the vacancies occur *ad interim*, having regard to the various classifications of members.

3. Twenty-one lay men, at least three from each jurisdiction, elected quadrennially by the board on nomination of the Council of Bishops, to serve as members at large of the board.

4. Twenty-one women, at least three from each jurisdiction, elected quadrennially by the board on nomination of the Woman's Division, to serve as members at large of the board.

5. Six young people, divided equally according to sex—three representing the Methodist Youth Fellowship, one of whom shall be a member of the council of the National Conference thereof, and three representing the Methodist Student Movement, one of whom shall be the national chairman of the Commission on World Missions of the Church—elected quadrennially by the board on nomination of the Joint Staff on Youth and Student Work, which shall have selected the nominees as provided in ¶ 1405.2. Vacancies among these members shall be filled by the board on nomination of the joint staff.

6. The general secretary and treasurer of the board and the associate general secretaries of the three divisions and the Joint Commission on Education and Cultivation, all of whom shall be without vote.

¶ 1181. The term of office of all members whose election is provided for in ¶ 1180 shall begin, and the board shall organize, at a meeting to be held within ninety days after the adjournment of the last meeting of the several Jurisdictional Conferences held after the adjournment of the General Conference.

¶ 1182. *Art. 4. General Executive Committee.*—There shall be a **general executive committee,** which shall exercise the powers of the board *ad interim*. It shall be composed of the members of the executive committees of the divisions and the Joint Commission on Education and Cultivation (¶¶ 1184-87). The president of the board shall serve as chairman.

¶ 1183. *Art. 5. Divisions and Joint Agencies.*—The

board shall conduct its activities directly and through three divisions (namely, the World Division, the National Division, and the Woman's Division); a Joint Commission on Education and Cultivation; and a Joint Committee on Missionary Personnel.

¶ **1184.** *Art. 6. World Division.*—1. The **World Division** shall be composed of board members as follows: one half the member bishops resident in the United States and all those from overseas; one half the ministers, the lay men, the women, and the youth; and, without vote, the general secretary and treasurer of the board and the associate general secretary of the division. The division shall meet annually at the time of the meeting of the board and at such other times as it shall deem necessary.

2. There shall be an **executive committee,** which shall exercise the powers of the division *ad interim.* It shall be composed of nineteen members of the division: three bishops, four ministers, and four lay men elected by the division; and eight women elected by the Woman's Division as provided in ¶ 1186.2.

¶ **1185.** *Art. 7. National Division.*—1. The **National Division** shall be composed of board members as follows: one half the member bishops resident in the United States; one half the ministers, the lay men, the women, and the youth; and, without vote, the general secretary and treasurer of the board and the associate general secretary of the division. The division shall meet annually at the time of the meeting of the board and at such other times as it shall deem necessary.

2. There shall be an **executive committee,** which shall exercise the powers of the division *ad interim.* It shall be composed of nineteen members of the division: three bishops, four ministers, and four lay men elected by the division; and eight women elected by the Woman's Division as provided in ¶ 1186.2.

¶ **1186.** *Art. 8. Woman's Division.*—1. The **Woman's Division** shall be composed of board members as follows: one third of the member bishops resident in the United States, two ministers, two lay men, all the women, one half the youth, and, without vote, the general secretary and treasurer of the board and the associate general secretary of the division. The division shall meet annually at the time of the meeting of the board and at such other times as it shall deem necessary.

2. The Woman's Division shall elect an **executive committee**, which shall exercise the powers of the division *ad interim*. It shall be composed of nineteen members, of whom the division shall elect eight each from those who are members of the World and National Divisions to serve also on their respective executive committees (¶¶ 1184.2, 1185.2) and, from each group of eight, four to serve in addition on the executive committee of the Joint Commission on Education and Cultivation (¶ 1187.2).

¶ 1187. *Art. 9. Joint Commission on Education and Cultivation.*—1. The **Joint Commission on Education and Cultivation** shall be composed of thirty-one voting board members as follows: the chairman of the Joint Committee on Missionary Personnel; three bishops, three ministers, and three lay men each, elected by the World and National Divisions; twelve women, six each from the members of the World and National Divisions, elected by the Woman's Division; and, without vote, the general secretary and treasurer of the board and the associate general secretary of the commission.

2. There shall be an **executive committee**, which shall exercise the powers of the commission *ad interim*. It shall be composed of the chairman of the Joint Committee on Missionary Personnel and eighteen other members elected by the divisions from the membership of their executive committees as follows: one bishop, two ministers, and two lay men each, elected by the World and National Divisions; and eight women, elected by the Woman's Division as provided in ¶ 1186.2.

¶ 1188. *Art. 10. Joint Committee on Missionary Personnel.*—The **Joint Committee on Missionary Personnel** shall be composed of fourteen board members elected by the divisions as follows: one bishop, two ministers, and one lay man elected by the World Division; one bishop, one minister, and two lay men elected by the National Division; and six women, three each from the members of the World and National Divisions, elected by the Woman's Division.

¶ **1189.** *Art. 11. Financial Policies.*—1. All properties, trust funds, permanent funds, and other special funds and endowments now held and administered by the several organizations which merged into the Board of Missions in 1940 shall be carefully safeguarded and administered in the interest of those persons and causes for which said funds were established; *provided* that the properties, trust funds, and permanent and endowment funds shall be transferred to the Board of Missions or its respective divisions from merged boards and societies and departments of such boards and societies only when such transfers may be made in accordance with the laws of the states where the several boards and societies are chartered and on the recommendation of the respective divisions and the approval of such boards and societies. Funds of the three administrative divisions, and their preceding corporations and societies, which are subject to appropriation shall be appropriated only on recommendation of the respective divisions.

2. The income of the divisions of the board, exclusive of the Woman's Division (*see* ¶ 1261), shall be derived from apportionments, assessments, or askings distributed to jurisdictions, Annual Conferences, and pastoral charges by the budget-making agency of the General Conference in such manner as the General Conference may prescribe, and from church schools, gifts, donations, freewill offerings, annuities, bequests, specials, and other sources from which missionary and benevolence funds are usually derived, in harmony with the Discipline of The Methodist Church and actions of the General Conference. Cultivation for Advance specials shall be through regular channels of the church, exclusive of Woman's Societies of Christian Service and Wesleyan Service Guilds.

3. Askings shall be received from the fields, and budgets shall be prepared by the World and National Divisions in such manner as the board may prescribe, consistent with its constitution and charter; and this combined budget shall be presented to the budget-making agency of the General Conference. In the allocation of funds to the World and National Divisions the board shall recognize

the principle of equal distribution, but only in so far as this provides an equitable basis of division.

4. The board shall not appropriate for the regular maintenance of its work in any one year more money than was received by it for appropriation the previous fiscal year.

SEC. III. **Officers and Staff**

¶ 1191. *Article 1. Board.*—1. *Corporate Officers.*—The board shall elect as its corporate officers a president, four vice-presidents (the nominees being the presidents of the three divisions and the Joint Commission on Education and Cultivation), a treasurer, a recording secretary, and such other officers as it shall deem necessary. Vacancies shall be filled by the board or its executive committee. The board shall determine the powers and duties of its officers.

2. *Elected Staff.*—The board shall nominate and elect a general secretary, a treasurer, and such other staff as it shall deem necessary. The board shall determine the powers and duties of its elected staff.

¶ 1192. *Art. 2. Divisions.*—1. *Corporate Officers.*—Each division shall elect as its corporate officers a president, one or more vice-presidents, a treasurer, a recording secretary, and such other officers as it shall deem necessary. Vacancies shall be filled by the divisions or their executive committees. The divisions shall determine the powers and duties of their officers.

2. *Elected Staff.*—The board shall elect, on nomination of each division, an associate general secretary, one or more assistant general secretaries, a treasurer (who shall be called an associate treasurer of the board), and such other staff as the division shall deem necessary. Due provisions shall be given for the inclusion of overseas representatives on the staff of the World Division.

¶ 1193. *Art. 3. Joint Commission on Education and Cultivation.*—1. *Officers.*—The Joint Commission on Education and Cultivation shall elect as its officers a president, one or more vice-presidents, and such other officers as it shall deem necessary. Vacancies shall be filled by the commission or its executive committee. The commission shall determine the powers and duties of its officers.

2. *Elected Staff.*—The board shall elect, on nomination of the commission, an associate general secretary and such other staff as the commission shall deem necessary.

¶ **1194.** *Art. 4. Joint Committee on Missionary Personnel.*—1. *Officers.*—The Joint Committee on Missionary Personnel shall elect as its officers a chairman, one or more vice-chairmen, and such other officers as it shall deem necessary. Vacancies shall be filled by the committee. The committee shall determine the powers and duties of its officers.

2. *Elected Staff.*—The board shall elect, on nomination of the committee, an executive secretary and such other staff as the committee shall deem necessary.

¶ **1195.** The board and its divisions shall continue to recruit, elect and/or appoint, utilize, and promote staff members without regard to race and color.

¶ **1196.** *Art. 5. Staff Participation of Women.*—1. Of the five staff positions of principal administrative authority within the board—namely, the general secretary and the associate general secretaries of the divisions and joint commission—a minimum of two shall be occupied by women.

2. Of the staff positions of principal administrative authority within the World and National Divisions—namely, the associate general secretaries, assistant general secretaries, and associate treasurers—a minimum of one third of the total shall be occupied by women.

3. Of the total elected staff positions of the board, a minimum of forty per cent shall be occupied by women.

¶ **1197.** *Art. 6. Retirement.*—All elected staff members shall retire on reaching the retirement age fixed by the board's pension plan.

Sec. IV.   **Authority**

¶ **1200.** *Article 1. Board.*—The board shall have authority to make by-laws in harmony with the Discipline of The Methodist Church, its own Disciplinary constitution, and its charter, and to develop and carry out its functions as described in ¶ 1204; to regulate its proceedings in accordance with its constitution, charter, and by-laws; to buy, acquire, receive by gift, devise, or bequest, property, real, personal, and mixed, and to hold, sell, and dispose of property; to secure, appropriate, and administer funds for its work; to sue and be sued; to elect the necessary officers and members of its staff, remove them for cause, and fill vacancies; to elect such standing and other committees as are necessary to carry on its business; to develop and maintain such ecumenical relations as shall be necessary to carry out its responsibilities; and to administer its affairs through its respective divisions and joint agencies. The board shall be clothed with the power and shall have the right to do any and all things which shall be authorized by its charter.

¶ 1201. *Art. 2. Divisions.*—The divisions shall have authority to make by-laws in harmony with the charter and constitution of the board, and with its approval, and to develop and carry out the functions of the divisions as described in ¶¶ 1205-7; to regulate their proceedings in harmony with their by-laws; to elect such officers as are to be elected by the divisions, to remove any of them for cause, and to fill vacancies among the officers so elected; to nominate their staff for election by the board, to recommend their removal for cause, and to present nominations to the board to fill vacancies; to elect such standing and other committees as are necessary to carry on their business; to accept, train, and maintain workers; to buy and sell property; to solicit and accept contributions subject to annuity under the board's regulations; to recommend their budgets to the board; and to recommend the appropriation of their funds for the work of the joint agencies of the board. The Woman's Division shall have authority to appropriate funds for the work of the World and National Divisions and shall further have authority to organize jurisdiction, conference, district, and local-church Woman's Societies of Christian Service as auxiliary to the division and related to the program of the total board, and to recommend constitutions and by-laws for the same.

¶ 1202. *Art. 3. Joint Commission on Education and Cultivation.*—The Joint Commission on Education and Cultivation shall have authority to make by-laws in har-

mony with the charter and constitution of the board, and
with its approval, and to develop and carry out the functions of the commission as described in ¶ 1208; to regulate its proceedings in harmony with its by-laws; to
nominate its staff for election by the board, to recommend their removal for cause, and to present nominations to the board or its executive committee to fill vacancies; to elect such standing and other committees as are
necessary to carry on its business; to recommend to the
board through its divisions appropriations for its work,
and to administer such funds as are allocated to it by the
board; and to solicit Advance special funds for the work
of the World and National Divisions.

¶ 1203. *Art. 4. Joint Committee on Missionary Personnel.*—The Joint Committee on Missionary Personnel shall
have authority to recommend by-laws to the board for its
approval and to develop and carry out the functions of
the committee as described in ¶ 1209; to regulate its proceedings in harmony with its by-laws; to nominate its
staff for election by the board, to recommend their removal for cause, and to present nominations to the board
to fill vacancies; to recommend to the board through its
divisions appropriations for its work, and to administer
such funds as are allocated to it by the board.

SEC. V.   Functions

¶ 1204. *Article 1. Board.*—1. The functions of the board
shall be:

a) To help persons come to a knowledge of Jesus
Christ as Savior and Lord of individuals and society.

b) To seek, as an agency of the Christian Church, to
respond to God's action in Christ through engaging in
religious, educational, social, medical, and agricultural
work, in every part of the world, and to promote and
support all phases of missionary and church extension
activity in the United States and in other countries.

c) To aid persons to live and act as Christians in personal life and in the social order of all lands and among
all peoples.

d) To foster, strengthen, and promote missionary understanding, interest, and zeal throughout The Methodist Church.

e) Consistent with its constitution and charter, to establish, develop, expand, and have general oversight of the missionary and church-extension programs of The Methodist Church in home and foreign fields.

f) To determine the broad lines of policy and program and, through the respective divisions and joint agencies, to carry out the program.

g) To correlate and harmonize the work of the various units.

h) On recommendation of the divisions and joint agencies, to determine fields to be occupied and the nature of the work to be undertaken.

i) To secure, appropriate, and expend money for the support of all work under its care.

j) To build and maintain churches, hospitals, homes, schools, parsonages, and other institutions of Christian service, and to enlist, train, and support the workers for the same.

k) To elect, on nomination of the divisions and joint agencies, the staff of the respective divisions and joint agencies.

l) To receive and properly administer all properties and trust funds coming into the possession of the board as a board for missionary or other purposes.

m) To assist in the organization of and in the maintenance of co-operative relations with the boards, committees, and other agencies of the General Conference; also with the Jurisdictional, Central, and Annual Conference boards, committees, and other agencies; likewise with interdenominational and other missionary agencies in the home and foreign fields.

n) To develop and maintain the ecumenical relations necessary for the full discharge of the above functions.

o) To make a report of its activities during the quadrennium to the General Conference and the Jurisdictional Conferences.

2. The board and the several divisions thereof shall continue to perform their respective functions in har-

mony with the policy of The Methodist Church to eliminate discrimination based on race or color.

¶ **1205.** *Art. 2. World Division.*—The functions of the
World Division shall be:

a) To develop and administer the work of missions
outside the United States and its dependencies, including
that previously administered by the former Division of
World Missions and Department of Work in Foreign
Fields of the Woman's Division of Christian Service.

b) To formulate the policies for the world mission of
The Methodist Church.

c) To receive and administer the world service gifts
for the general missionary activities of The Methodist
Church in foreign fields.

d) To receive and administer the Advance special gifts
for world missionary work cultivated through the Joint
Commission on Education and Cultivation.

e) To receive and administer funds requested and allocated by the Woman's Division, keeping in mind the
special needs of women.

f) To present to the board for assignment to its various
fields of service missionaries who have been approved by
the Joint Committee on Missionary Personnel.

¶ **1206.** *Art. 3. National Division.*—The functions of
the National Division shall be:

a) To develop and administer the work of missions and
church extension in the United States and the Dominican
Republic, including that previously administered by the
former Division of National Missions and Department of
Work in Home Fields of the Woman's Division of Christian Service.

b) To formulate the policies for the home mission of
The Methodist Church.

c) To receive and administer the world service gifts
for the general missionary activities of The Methodist
Church in home fields.

d) To administer all donation aid, loan funds, and endowment, contributed and established for the work of
church extension, except such as may be administered by
the Jurisdictional and Annual Conferences.

e) To receive and administer the Advance special gifts

for home missionary work cultivated through the Joint Commission on Education and Cultivation.

f) To receive and administer funds requested from and allocated by the Woman's Division, keeping in mind the special needs of women.

g) To present to the board for assignment to its various fields of service missionaries and deaconesses who have been approved by the Joint Committee on Missionary Personnel.

¶ **1207.** *Art. 4. Woman's Division.*—The functions of the Woman's Division shall be:

a) To interpret the mission of Christ and his Church as stated in the purpose of the Woman's Society of Christian Service and the Wesleyan Service Guild.

b) To provide resources and opportunities for women that enrich their spiritual life and increase their knowledge and understanding of the needs of the world and their responsibility in meeting those needs.

c) To promote plans for securing funds for the support of the program of the church through the Board of Missions, with special concern for the needs and responsibilities of women.

d) To project plans specially directed toward leadership development of women through appropriate planning with the other divisions and agencies of the board.

e) To strengthen the church's challenge to women to enlist in full-time church-related vocations at home and abroad.

f) To enlist women in activities that have a moral and religious significance for the public welfare and that contribute to the establishment of a Christian social order around the world.

g) To plan with other agencies of the church and community in areas of common concern and responsibility.

h) To give visible evidence of our oneness in Christ by uniting in fellowship and service with other Christians, thereby strengthening the ecumenical witness and program of the church.

¶ **1208.** *Art. 5. Joint Commission on Education and Cultivation.*—1. The functions of the Joint Commission on

Education and Cultivation shall be:

a) To undergird with education and cultivation the total program of the Board of Missions.

b) To initiate and develop program through which individuals and groups may understand the biblical background and theological basis for the Christian world mission, the involvement of The Methodist Church in the missionary enterprise, and the possibilities for personal witness, involvement in, and support of the mission.

c) To prepare, sell, and distribute publications and audio-visual and other materials for the work of the board.

d) To co-operate with the Board of Education through the Interboard Committee on Missionary Education, with other agencies of The Methodist Church, and with interdenominational agencies in leadership development, in the preparation and distribution of missionary materials, and in other ventures.

e) To promote missionary councils, conventions, institutes, summer conferences, and other meetings throughout the church for the purpose of developing a missionary spirit, training leadership on all levels, disseminating missionary information, and acquainting the church with the plans and policies of the board.

f) To promote an annual call to prayer and self-denial.

g) To encourage an emphasis on missionary education in colleges, universities, and schools of theology.

h) To help foster an ecumenical interest and understanding throughout the church.

i) To cultivate, through regular channels of the church, exclusive of Woman's Societies of Christian Service and Wesleyan Service Guilds, the Advance special gifts for home and foreign missionary work administered by the World and National Divisions.

j) In consultation with the divisions of the Board of Missions and in co-operation with the Commission on Promotion and Cultivation and other appropriate agencies of the church, to develop and co-ordinate the plans for cultivating missionary giving; *provided*, however, that all such plans shall be subject to and in harmony with the general financial system of The Methodist Church as adopted by the General Conference.

2. In fulfilling these functions, the commission shall seek the co-operation of Jurisdictional and Annual Conferences, local churches, Woman's Societies of Christian Service and Wesleyan Service Guilds, other groups within the church, and district superintendents and pastors.

¶ 1209. *Art. 6. Joint Committee on Missionary Personnel.*—1. The functions of the Joint Committee on Missionary Personnel shall be:

a) To recommend to the board the standards and qualifications of missionary candidates for home and foreign service, including deaconesses.

b) To enlist, cultivate, train, and recommend candidates for missionary service at home and abroad and deaconess service in the United States.

c) To co-operate in the work of the Interboard Committee on Christian Vocations.

2. A person shall be constituted a missionary or deaconess of the board when he has met the requirements of the committee and has been accepted as a missionary or deaconess.

SEC. VI. **General Provisions for World Missions**

¶ 1211. *Art. 1. Committees on Co-ordination.*—1. In areas where the Board of Missions co-operates with churches in Central Conferences, the board shall request each Annual Conference or national unit to elect a **Committee on Co-ordination** of not less than nine nor more than eighteen members, with the presiding bishop or officer as chairman. Persons elected need not be members of the Annual Conference. The membership in addition to the chairman shall be composed of one third ministers, one third lay men, and one third lay women, with care being taken to insure representation of the various service areas of the work. The field correspondent and treasurer shall be ex officio members without vote. The one-third membership of the women shall be elected from a panel of names presented by a recognized women's body of the church (such as, Woman's Conference, Woman's Society of Christian Service, or Woman's Department).

2. The duties of the committee shall be:

a) To meet regularly at the call of the chairman or the executive committee, composed of the chairman, vice-chairman, and secretary.

b) To elect a vice-chairman, who shall be authorized to preside at meetings in the absence of the chairman, and a secretary, whose responsibility shall be to forward its minutes and the report of its recommendations promptly to the board.

c) To consult with the board on all matters of mutual concern.

d) To receive and transmit to the board reports from all the institutions and agencies of the church which receive aid from the board.

e) To make requests for missionary personnel as desired.

f) To prepare estimates of funds requested from the board for aid to work in the conference and for aid to institutions and other projects, except the financial requirement for missionary support, which is the direct responsibility of the board.

3. There shall be a **Subcommittee on Women's Work** of the committee, which shall deal with all the concerns of women in the church appropriate to the committee. This subcommittee shall be composed of all women members of the committee, and up to three additional members co-opted as desired. It shall be chaired by the bishop or officer of the area and shall have at least two regular meetings in the year.

¶ **1212.** In a Central Conference in which there is an executive board or council of co-operation constituted, the estimates for the maintenance and development of the work, prepared by the various Committees on Co-ordination, may be presented to the World Division after approval by such board or council. The estimates shall be presented conference by conference, and by projects within the conference.

¶ **1213.** In a Central or Provisional Central Conference where there is no executive board or council of co-operation, the estimates shall be sent direct to the World Division from the Committee on Co-ordination of each Annual or Provisional Annual Conference.

¶ **1214.** In an affiliated autonomous Methodist Church there shall be constituted, wherever desired, a council under a constitution acceptable to the board. This council shall be the agency through which the board shall co-operate with the church.

¶ **1215.** *Art. 2. Administration of a Mission.*—1. Foreign fields outside of an Annual Conference working under the care of the Board of Missions, not having met the requirements for the organization of a Provisional Annual Conference, may be organized into a **Mission.**

2. The Mission shall meet annually. It shall be composed of all regularly appointed missionaries, both lay and clerical, and mission traveling preachers, and other lay members. Each Mission shall determine the number of lay members and the mode of their appointment.

3. A bishop, or in his absence one of the superintendents chosen by ballot by the Mission, shall preside in the annual meeting. This meeting shall exercise in a general way the functions of a District Conference. It shall have power to license suitable persons to preach, and to pass on the character of preachers not members of an Annual Conference, to receive on trial mission traveling preachers, and to recommend to an Annual Conference proper persons for deacon's orders. The bishop or president shall at the annual meeting assign the missionaries and mission traveling preachers to the several charges for the ensuing year; *provided* that no missionary shall be transferred to or from a Mission without previous consultation with the board.

4. The work of a Mission shall be divided, when necessary, into districts, over each of which shall be placed a superintendent. It shall be the duty of the superintendent, in the absence of the bishop, to take general supervision of the work in his district with all its interests, and to report the state of that work and its needs to the bishop in charge and to the board.

5. For the consideration of financial and other matters relative to the policies of the board and the work of the missionaries, the missionaries of each Mission shall hold

an annual **missionaries' meeting** and report their proceedings to the board. In the absence of a bishop one of the missionaries shall be elected by ballot to preside.

¶ **1216.** *Art. 3. Missionaries.*—1. All missionaries who serve in fields outside the United States should relate themselves as directly as possible to the organized church in these fields through membership in a local church or Annual Conference.

2. In fields outside the United States the Annual Conference may seat in its session regularly appointed lay missionaries of the Board of Missions and national heads of major institutions in such numbers and with such qualifications as the Central Conference may prescribe, and give them the privileges of the floor. Special-term ordained missionaries who retain their conference relations in the United States may be granted similar privileges.[8] (*See* ¶ 623.)

¶ **1217.** *Art. 4. Missionaries Serving Other Churches.*—1. Missionaries of The Methodist Church, on action of the Board of Missions, may be assigned to serve in affiliated autonomous churches, in independent churches, in churches resulting from the union of Methodist churches and other communions, or in other evangelical denominations.

2. Such missionaries, while retaining their membership in their home local churches and Annual Conferences, and without impairing their relationship to the Board of Missions, shall, while on service in such fields, be free to accept such rights and privileges as may be offered to them by such churches.

3. The missionaries in such mission fields may be organized into mission councils under constitutions approved by the Board of Missions.

SEC. VII.　**General Provisions for National Missions**

¶ **1221.** The associate general secretary of the National Division shall communicate to the bishops such information as may be available concerning missions and the appointment of workers in their respective areas.

---

[8] Amended following Judicial Council Decisions 1, 24.

¶ **1222.** *Art. 1. Mission Responsibilities.*—The National Division shall give special study and promotion to mission work, including social welfare, education, and medical services in urban and rural areas, and in Missions and Annual and Provisional Annual Conferences. It shall organize such programs and conduct such activities as the development of the work may require, with special attention to the needs of people in transitional relationships. It shall assign staff members to develop these programs. They shall administer such appropriations as are committed to them for the work of the field to which they are assigned. They shall co-operate with other boards and agencies as their work may affect the group involved.

¶ **1224.** *Art. 2. City Work.*—The National Division shall promote missionary work in cities with a population of ten thousand or more. It shall aid in making studies in cities with special reference to the religious conditions of urban populations, the necessary location and adaptation of church buildings, and the programs required for needy and congested communities. It shall also aid in the organization and development of adequate religious centers in city territory, and may aid wherever possible in the development of co-operative procedures among the church and other agencies for the betterment of the community life of the people in the cities. All askings for missionary work in cities of ten thousand population or more shall require the review and recommendation of the division or such committee as it may designate.

¶ **1225.** *Art. 3. Missionary Societies.*—The National Division shall promote the organization of **city (metropolitan) or district missionary societies** wherever possible and practicable.

¶ **1226.** 1. Such a society may be organized in the interest of missions and church extension, under such name and control as it may determine, wherever, in the judgment of the bishop or bishops and district superintendent or superintendents concerned, it is deemed advisable. When two or more districts, conferences, episcopal areas, or jurisdictions have churches in the same city or metropolitan area, it is recommended that the society be so organized as to include all these churches.

The bishops involved shall initiate the effort to develop the society.

2. The purpose of such a society is to promote evangelization and to co-ordinate the work of the church in cities and contiguous communities. Charges in communities adjacent to a city but not attached to the city may be included in the society. All bishops, district superintendents, and superintendents of Missions or Provisional Annual Conferences having jurisdiction within the geographical territory covered by the society, and all pastors therein shall be ex officio members of the society or its board of managers. The membership shall also include adequate representation from Woman's Societies of Christian Service and governing boards of agencies related to the National Division. Each Quarterly Conference in the territory shall be entitled to at least one lay representative, and there shall be two representatives elected by the Conference Board of Missions.

¶ 1227. In a metropolitan area included within the bounds of two or more Annual Conferences, the National Division may promote, with the approval of the bishops and the conferences, the organization of a **Metropolitan Area Planning Commission,** which shall be composed of the bishops, the district superintendents involved, and a selected group of ministers, lay men, and lay women, representing Conference Boards of Missions, Committees on Urban Work, city missionary societies, and local churches, who have skills and experience enabling them to do creative planning for Methodism in the metropolitan area. The commission shall serve in an advisory capacity to Methodist leaders and organizations in the metropolitan area and shall make recommendations regarding immediate and long-term planning and strategy.

¶ 1228. The city (metropolitan) or district missionary society may include in its work the organization of church schools and the organization (but not the constituting) of churches, the aid of weak churches, the acquisition of real estate and the erection of buildings, the adaptation of downtown churches to their altered environment, the securing and holding of endowments for the society and for dependent churches, the conducting of missions among foreign-speaking and other needy peoples, the development of well-organized open-air evangelism, the maintenance of kindergartens and industrial schools, the promotion of social and settlement work, including services rendered in connection with juvenile court cases, and the support of rescue missions and of institutions for the relief of the sick and the destitute.

¶ 1229. In order to receive financial assistance from the division, the society shall meet the following conditions:

1. It shall be organized according to the Discipline.

2. It shall have an executive committee meeting at least once each quarter.

3. It shall be actively at work.

4. It shall have made a report to the division including: (a) number of ministers, deaconesses, or missionaries supported in whole or in part, amount paid to each, and kind of work in which each is engaged; (b) expenses of administration; (c) total amount raised by the society and how expended; (d) such other items as the division shall require.

5. It shall endeavor to raise annually by collections or otherwise an amount at least equal to that appropriated to it by the board, exclusive of appropriations made for work among foreign-speaking people.

¶ 1230. Each Annual Conference is directed to take such friendly interest in the societies which are wholly or partially within its bounds as shall promote their efficiency and facilitate their work, to arrange for the publication of their reports in the conference journal, and to provide a separate column in connection with the statement of the benevolence collections for the itemized report of the offerings for this work.

¶ 1231. If the society has an executive officer giving his entire time to the work, it is recommended that he be invited into consultation with the bishop and district superintendents in the consideration of the appointments that affect missions or churches administered or aided by the society.

¶ 1232. The society, after consultation with the Conference Board of Missions; shall have authority, in the territory covered by its constitution or charter, to make apportionments to the pastoral charges, and to collect and disburse moneys for all the objects contemplated in its organization. It shall report annually to the conference board.

¶ **1233.** It shall be the duty of each pastor whose charge lies within the territory of the society once each year to present its interests to his congregation, take a collection for it, or provide for the amount apportioned in the benevolence budget, and report the amount received to the Annual Conference.

¶ **1234.** It is recommended that any local church within its territory expecting to receive aid from the society for buildings or improvement be required to secure, as a condition to receiving such aid, the approval of the society with respect to location, plans, and methods of financing.

¶ **1235.** *Art. 4. Convocation on Urban Work.*—The National Division, in co-operation with the Council of Bishops and other interested groups, may promote a quadrennial **Convocation on Urban Work,** which shall be called by the Council of Bishops at such time as the council and the division may determine.

¶ **1237.** *Art. 5. Town and Country Work.*—1. The National Division shall promote, in co-operation with other boards and agencies, all phases of the work of the church in town and country territory and in places of less than ten thousand population; conduct surveys and research studies, and use the findings for more effective church work; develop a co-operative procedure among church and other agencies that seek to improve the economic, social, educational, and religious life of people in town and country areas; seek to develop co-operative procedures between Methodist churches and those of other denominations; and promote among ministers and in colleges and schools of theology a study of town and country life and effective ways and means of church and community work.

2. It shall give encouragement and support to Conference Boards of Missions, to Commissions on Town and Country Work, and to Jurisdictional Boards of Missions

in their efforts to develop more effective and constructive work in town and country communities.

3. All askings for missionary work in town and country (communities of less than ten thousand population) shall require the review and recommendation of the division or such committee as it shall designate.

4. It shall assist the district superintendents and Commissions on Town and Country Work in making surveys and developing plans for local parish and charge reorganization in town and country areas. This shall include recommendation of the type of multiple parish which seems most appropriate to the area under consideration.

5. It shall seek to aid Annual Conferences and local churches in establishing Methodist families on the land and in town and country communities through making available information concerning procedures and resources for this purpose from private, governmental, and religious agencies.

6. It shall promote the organization of district missionary societies (¶¶ 1225-34) wherever possible and practicable.

7. It shall provide for special professional church and community workers in town and country. Provision shall be made for training, assigning, and supervising church and community workers. There shall be consultation with advisory committees regarding personnel, programs, budgets, areas of need, and other matters.

¶ 1238. *Art. 6. National and Regional Conferences on Town and Country Work.*—In co-operation with the Council of Bishops and the Interboard Committee on Town and Country Work (¶ 1285) the National Division may promote and administer national or regional **Conferences on Town and Country Work,** which shall be called by the Council of Bishops at such times as the council, the division, and the interboard committee may determine.

¶ 1239. *Art. 7. Community Centers.*—The National Division shall provide the general supervision and administration of its related community centers. It shall review askings and administer appropriations for community centers. There shall be opportunities for guidance and counsel relative to administration, personnel, program, budgets, and other matters needed for the effective operation of the work. Provision shall be made for field consultation services and the development of training opportunities and materials.

¶ **1240.** *Art. 8. Social Welfare Residences and Child-Care Agencies.*—The National Division shall provide the general supervision and administration of its related child-care agencies and residences for business women. It shall review askings and administer appropriations for such residences and child-care agencies. There shall be opportunities for guidance and counsel relative to administration, personnel, program, budgets, and other matters needed for the effective operation of the work. Provision shall be made for field consultation services and the development of training opportunities and materials. A co-operative relationship shall be maintained with the Board of Hospitals and Homes (¶ 1559).

¶ **1241.** *Art. 9. Medical Work and Retirement Homes.*—The National Division shall provide the general supervision and administration of its related hospitals, medical work, and retirement homes. It shall review askings and administer appropriations for medical work, hospitals, and retirement homes. There shall be opportunities for guidance and counsel relative to administration, personnel, budgets, and other matters needed for effective service. A co-operative relationship shall be maintained with the Board of Hospitals and Homes (¶ 1559).

¶ **1242.** *Art. 10. Educational Work.*—The National Division shall make provision for the general administration and supervision of its related educational work and institutions. It shall review askings and administer appropriations for educational work and institutions. There shall be training opportunities for guidance and counsel relative to administration, personnel, curriculum, budgets, and other matters needed for the effective operation of the work. A co-operative relationship shall be maintained with the Division of Higher Education of the Board of Education (¶ 1360).

¶ **1243.** *Art. 11. Goodwill Industries.*—The National Division shall provide for the religious, educational, social, and industrial welfare of the handicapped and unfortunate. It shall promote and establish **Goodwill Industries** in various centers; shall review missionary askings and administer appropriations for Goodwill Industries; shall endorse and assist only those local Goodwill Industries which are organized and conducted according to its standards, rules, and regulations; and shall urge them to co-operate with the departments, sections, divisions, and boards of The Methodist Church, and other organizations serving the handicapped and unfortunate. The division may conduct national and regional institutes, and such other special training activities as will help to develop the specialized leadership required for the direction of Goodwill Industries.

¶ **1244.** *Art. 12. Research and Survey.*—The National Division shall conduct surveys and research studies in both cities and rural territories, giving attention to migrations of population, new and growing communities, changed neighborhoods, and religious conditions of racial and other groups. It shall co-operate with conference boards in making surveys. It may promote kindred activities on college and seminary campuses and within various areas of The Methodist Church. It may produce and circulate materials designed to aid administrators and pastors in conducting community self-studies and surveys. (*See also* ¶ 1095.)

¶ **1246.** *Art. 13. Church Extension.*—The National Division shall conduct its work of **church extension** under the following provisions and regulations:

1. It shall encourage the erection of churches in communities not already adequately supplied, and shall assist in the building of churches, parsonages, and other mission buildings where assistance is most needed.

2. It shall give special attention to church architecture. Local churches seeking financial aid from the division shall submit preliminary architectural plans to the division or such committee as it may designate for approval before final working drawings are started. (*See* ¶ 1248.)

3. It shall appropriate money for the various types of work in the field and the conduct of the work of the office. The division, its executive committee, or such other committee as it may designate shall determine what

should be donated or loaned to each applicant and shall administer all donation aid, loan funds, and endowments contributed and established for the work of church extension except such as may be administered by the Annual Conferences; and do such other business as may be legitimate and proper for it to do.

4. Aid in the form of donations in the erection, remodeling, and repairing of churches and parsonages shall be made available primarily to clearly missionary projects. Assistance in the development of other types of church property, if and when granted, shall be provided as loans. Priority shall be given to applications to provide churches for new communities.

5. All applications for aid from the division shall be made through the Conference Board of Missions. Grants shall be made by the division, its executive committee, or such other committee as it may designate, on recommendation of the appropriate committee and the secretary or secretaries.

6. In granting donations to churches and parsonages it shall require from the trustees of each aided local church an obligation which shall be a lien on the property involved for the return of the amount donated in the event that the work cease or the property be alienated from The Methodist Church; *provided* that these provisions may be waived in cases involving donations of one thousand dollars or less. Said lien may be subordinated to enable the trustees of the church involved to give a first mortgage for a loan. In case of relocation the division's investment and lien may be transferred to the new property.

7. When a donation is granted by the division where the property involved is held in trust by the Board of Trustees of the Annual Conference or by a board of trustees elected by and responsible to the General Conference, no lien shall be required by the division, provided the trustees agree, with the approval of the Annual Conference or the General Conference, that the property shall not be conveyed without protecting the claim of the division.

8. The division or its constituent corporations shall

raise and administer a loan fund and a revolving loan fund which shall be held separate from funds secured for general distribution. They shall consist of all money or other properties especially donated or bequeathed to the board or division or its constituent corporations as permanent funds, subject to annuity or otherwise, where the gift is intended to assist in the building and financing of churches and parsonages in the field of the National Division. These funds shall be used only as loans on adequate security or on such terms as may be determined by the division or such committee as it shall designate.

9. It shall co-operate with the Conference Boards of Missions in providing for consultations between city (metropolitan) and district missionary societies and District Boards of Church Location and Building in the development of standards and procedures for local-church building projects in the fields of site selection, study and approval of architectural plans, and financial programs. (See ¶ 1299.6.)

¶ 1247. *Art. 14. Finance and Field Service.*—The National Division shall provide a fund-raising service to be known as **Finance and Field Service,** the function of which shall be:

1. Raising funds for church, parsonage, and Christian educational buildings and equipment; for renovating, remodeling, and repair projects; and for other institutions and causes, such as conference pensions, schools of theology, Wesley Foundations, colleges, hospitals, homes, and community centers.

2. Raising funds for the retirement of church and other institution obligations. A nominal charge shall be made for fund-raising services.

3. Assisting and guiding churches in developing effective budget and other financial plans.

4. Providing counsel and suggesting plans for church building enterprises.

5. Providing construction supervision of mission church, parsonage, and other projects of the division.

6. Providing for consultation with district, conference, and missionary fund-raising personnel. A fund may be set up by the division to be secured from gifts and

legacies, the income of which shall be used for the support of the above functions.

¶ 1248. *Art. 15. Architecture.*—The National Division shall make provision for the fulfillment of the following purposes in its architectural work:

1. To prepare up-to-date church plans of a general nature in order to guide local churches in formulating a building program.

2. To distribute leaflets, folders, and booklets giving illustrations and descriptive material as a guide in development of wise, constructive programs for remodeling and enlarging existing buildings and planning for the erection of new ones.

3. To confer with representatives from throughout the church concerning architectural problems and building procedures.

4. To review and evaluate plans submitted by local churches and District Boards of Church Location and Building, and assist them in avoiding architectural blunders, as to both design and floor plans. (*See* ¶¶ 180, 723.)

5. To visit local churches, on request and as able, in order to furnish architectural counsel at the building site.

6. To consult with local architects who have been retained by local churches.

7. To furnish counsel in the preparation of plans for missionary projects which are constructed or supervised by the church builders on the staff of the division.

8. To consult with local churches and architects to ensure in church building plans proper facilities for physically handicapped persons.

¶ 1250. *Art. 16. Deaconess Work.*—1. The office of **deaconess** is hereby authorized in The Methodist Church. A deaconess is a woman who has been led by the Holy Spirit to devote herself to Christlike service under the direction of the Church, and who, having met the requirements prescribed by the Joint Committee on Missionary Personnel, including a period of not less than one year of probation, has been duly licensed, consecrated, and commissioned by a bishop. This office entitles a woman to serve The Methodist Church through any of its agencies in any capacity not requiring full clergy rights.

2. All deaconess work in the United States and its dependencies shall be under the supervision of the National Division. There shall be a Commission on Deaconess Work (¶ 1251), which shall be advisory to the division and make recommendations to it.

3. All deaconess work outside the United States and its dependencies shall be under the supervision of the Central Conferences or Provisional Central Conferences concerned, or the Annual Conferences where there is not a Central Conference.

4. A deaconess shall receive her appointment through the regular channels of the Commission on Deaconess Work, to be confirmed by the National Division and the Conference Deaconess Board.

5. *a*) There shall be a contributory pension plan for all deaconesses commissioned on or after July 24, 1940.

b) For deaconesses commissioned or consecrated previous to July, 1940, former agreements are continued, and the administrations with which they were connected are responsible for the pensions.

c) A deaconess employed by an agency having its own pension plan shall participate in that plan during her term of service with that agency.

6. All properties, trust funds, permanent funds, other special funds, and endowments now held and administered for deaconess work shall be carefully safeguarded and administered by the several forms of the administration in the interest of those persons and causes for which said funds were established.

7. A deaconess shall surrender her credentials when she is no longer available for an appointment in The Methodist Church.

8. A person may be reinstated as a deaconess on recommendation of the Conference Deaconess Board, the Commission on Deaconess Work, and the National Division, with approval by the Joint Committee on Missionary Personnel.

¶ 1251. *Art. 17. Commission on Deaconess Work.*—1. The **Commission on Deaconess Work** shall be composed

369

of one bishop chosen by the Council of Bishops; the president of each Jurisdiction Woman's Society of Christian Service, and two deaconesses and one minister from each jurisdiction chosen by the Jurisdiction Deaconess Association; three representatives, at least one a man, chosen by the National Division; one representative chosen by the Woman's Division; one representative each from the Boards of Pensions, Hospitals and Homes, and Education; the executive secretary of the Interboard Committee on Christian Vocations; and one staff representative of the Joint Committee on Missionary Personnel. The executive secretary of the commission shall be a member without vote.

2. The commission shall meet annually. Its officers shall be elected quadrennially.

3. The duties of the commission shall be:

a) To report and make recommendations to the National Division.

b) To make recommendations for enriching the life of deaconesses, suggesting techniques for attaining spiritual and mental maturity, physical and professional fitness, emotional stability, and social adjustment.

c) To recommend programs for the promotion and interpretation of deaconess work throughout the church so that the office of deaconess may grow into the fullness of its stature.

d) To make recommendations regarding possible new fields of service and new approaches to meet the needs of the present day.

e) To recommend methods for strengthening the Conference Deaconess Boards.

f) To recommend policies and procedures regarding deaconesses, their work, and their relationships to Conference Deaconess Boards, Jurisdiction Deaconess Associations, and other agencies.

¶ **1252.** *Art. 18. Jurisdiction Deaconess Association.*— 1. In each geographical jurisdiction there shall be a **Jurisdiction Deaconess Association.**

2. *a*) All active deaconesses working within the bounds of the geographical jurisdiction shall be members of the association.

b) All deaconesses in the retired relation shall be honorary members of the association.

c) Other members shall be the president of the Jurisdiction Woman's Society of Christian Service, the jurisdiction secretary of missionary service in home fields, and the president of each Conference Woman's Society of Christian Service living within the bounds of the geographical jurisdiction.

3. There shall be a meeting of the association held annually or biennially in connection with the Jurisdiction Woman's Society of Christian Service.

4. The association shall elect its officers.

5. There shall be an executive committee in the association.

6. The duties of the association shall be:

a) To promote deaconess work as authorized by the National Division through the Commission on Deaconess Work.

b) To arrange workers' conferences.

c) To provide opportunities for fellowship among workers in the geographical jurisdiction.

d) Other duties in harmony with the constitution, as may be set forth in by-laws.

¶ **1253.** *Art. 19. Conference Deaconess Board.*—1. In each Annual Conference there shall be a **Conference Deaconess Board.**

2. The purpose of the board shall be to create and maintian interest in deaconess work, to establish and interpret deaconess relationships to the Annual Conference, and to co-operate with the National Division through the Commission on Deaconess Work in forming policies and making recommendations regarding deaconess work.

3. The board shall be composed of all active deaconesses serving within the bounds of the conference; the members of the Cabinet; pastors of local churches employing deaconesses; four representatives of the Conference Woman's Society of Christian Service; one representative from the Commission on Christian Vocations; and one representative, not a deaconess, from the local board of managers or committee of each project within the conference where deaconesses live or are employed. Retired dea-

conesses living within the bounds of the conference shall be honorary members, having the privilege of the floor without vote.

4. The duties of the board shall be:

a) To review, evaluate, and report annually to the National Division through the Commission on Deaconess Work the standing of all deaconesses within the conference.

b) To study credentials received from Quarterly Conferences (¶ 146.2) and recommend to the Joint Committee on Missionary Personnel possible candidates for the office of deaconess.

c) To co-operate with the National Division through the Commission on Deaconess Work in the annual appointments of deaconesses. It shall submit the list of appointments to be read by the bishop presiding at the Annual Conference, and to be printed in the journal.

d) To arrange for the licensing and the consecration service of those deaconesses assigned to the conference for these purposes.

e) In co-operation with the Conference Woman's Society of Christian Service and other agencies of the church, to initiate and develop plans for the promotion of deaconess work, including an annual program on deaconess work.

f) To consider complaints and charges against deaconesses; to act as a trial court in case of trial; and to make recommendations to the National Division through the Commission on Deaconess Work.

5. The board shall meet annually and elect its officers.

6. There shall be an executive committee and other committees as are necessary for carrying out the duties of the board.

7. The board shall report annually to the Annual Conference, the Jurisdiction Deaconess Association, and the National Division through the Commission on Deaconess Work. Its report shall be printed in the journal of the Annual Conference.

¶ **1254.** *Art. 20. Administration of a Mission.*—1. In home fields outside an Annual Conference or among racial groups, work under the care of the Board of Missions not having met the requirements for the organization of a Provisional Annual Conference shall be administered by the board as a **Mission.**

2. The Mission shall meet annually, and shall be composed of all regularly appointed missionaries, both lay and clerical, and mission traveling preachers, and other lay members, the number of whom and the mode of their appointment each Mission shall determine for itself.

3. The bishop in charge of a Mission may appoint a superintendent of the Mission, or as many superintendents as may appear to him necessary or wise, for whom support has been provided. He shall determine the groups or charges over which the respective superintendents shall have supervision.

4. A bishop, or in his absence one of the superintendents chosen by ballot by the Mission, shall preside in the annual meeting. This meeting shall exercise in a general way the functions of a District Conference. It shall have power to license suitable persons to preach, and to pass on the character of preachers not members of an Annual Conference, to receive on trial mission traveling preachers, and to recommend to an Annual Conference proper persons for deacon's orders. The bishop or president shall at the annual meeting assign the missionaries and mission traveling preachers to the several charges for the ensuing year; *provided* that no missionary shall be transferred to or from a Mission without previous consultation with the board.

5. In case of a Mission using more than one language besides English, and extending over a wide geographical territory, the bishop may assemble in annual meetings the members of the Mission on a racial or geographical basis. The Mission may delegate to such subgroups the work of examining and recommending to an Annual Conference candidates for admission on trial, under such limitations as the Discipline provides.

6. Examinations of local and traveling preachers shall be held by the Mission, and certified to an Annual Conference. The Mission also shall make recommendations for reception on trial in an Annual Conference.

Sec. VIII.   **General Provisions for the
                  Woman's Division**

¶ **1256.** *Art. 1. Scope and Interests.*—The Woman's
Division shall include in its scope a relation to responsibilities formerly carried by the Woman's Foreign Missionary Society, the Woman's Home Missionary Society,
the Wesleyan Service Guild, and the Ladies' Aid Societies
of the Methodist Episcopal Church; the Board of Missions, Section of Woman's Work, the Woman's Missionary
Council, the former boards and societies (the Woman's
Missionary Society, the Woman's Board of Foreign Missions, and the Woman's Board of Home Missions) of the
Methodist Episcopal Church, South; the Woman's Convention of the Methodist Protestant Church; and the
deaconess work of the uniting churches within the United
States. All other organizations of women of similar purpose operating in the charges of the uniting churches may
come under the scope and interests of this division.

¶ **1257.** *Art. 2. Sections.*—The Woman's Division shall
be organized into three sections—namely, the Section of
Program and Education for Christian Mission, the Section of Christian Social Relations, and the Section of
Finance.

¶ **1258.** The **Section of Program and Education for
Christian Mission** shall co-ordinate, through the Joint
Committee for Program Co-ordination of the Joint Commission on Education and Cultivation and the Woman's
Division, plans and programs for Woman's Societies of
Christian Service and Wesleyan Service Guilds with the
joint commission and such other agencies as may have
channels to the local church; initiate plans and programs
for the enrichment and development of leadership and
service among women after appropriate planning with
other units of the board and in keeping with the division's function; promote, in co-operation with the Section
of Finance, plans for securing funds through the channels of the Woman's Societies of Christian Service and
Wesleyan Service Guilds to support the work of the
church at home and abroad; project plans for the organization, promotion, and cultivation of Woman's Societies

of Christian Service and Wesleyan Service Guilds, and strengthen those already established; and bring its plans and programs to the Woman's Division for recommendation to Woman's Societies of Christian Service and Wesleyan Service Guilds.

¶ 1259. The **Section of Christian Social Relations** shall create plans, provide opportunities, communicate information, and establish relationships that challenge women to follow Jesus Christ and respond to the gospel in national and international relationships, and thereby share in the fulfillment of the mission of Christ and his Church; establish and utilize liaison and service relationships with other units of the Board of Missions; unite with other agencies of the church in the co-ordination and projection of plans related to areas of common responsibility; share fully in ecumenical programs and plans that are concerned with responsibilities in the area of Christian social relations; and bring its plans and programs to the Woman's Division for recommendation to Woman's Societies of Christian Service and Wesleyan Service Guilds.

¶ 1260. The **Section of Finance** shall recommend financial policies to the division, appraise periodically the effectiveness of such policies, and recommend changes as necessary; report regularly to the division; co-operate with the Section of Program and Education for Christian Mission in promotional plans for securing funds through the channels of the Woman's Societies of Christian Service and Wesleyan Service Guilds for the support of the work of the church at home and abroad; receive requests from sections and associated divisions and agencies; and bring recommendations to the Woman's Division for appropriations in order to fulfill its responsibilities within the total amount available for the work. Such appropriations shall be recommended to the section by its Committee on Appropriations, which shall include additional Woman's Division representatives named by the other two sections, the Joint Commission on Education and Promotion, and the World and National Divisions.

¶ 1261. *Art. 3. Finances.*—The funds for the fulfillment

of the responsibilities of the Woman's Division in support of the work of the church at home and overseas shall be derived from annual pledges, special memberships, devises, bequests, annuities, special offerings, gifts, and moneys raised by special projects or collected in meetings held in the interest of the division. All funds, except those designated for local purposes, shall be forwarded through the regular channels of finance of the Woman's Societies of Christian Service to the treasurer of the division. Undesignated funds received by the Woman's Division shall be allocated by the division on recommendation of its Section of Finance to the work of the several sections of the Woman's Division and to the other divisions and agencies of the board for the fulfillment of the responsibilities of the division. Funds appropriated for the work of the other divisions and agencies of the board may be given with specific designation and a time limit after which unspent funds are to be returned to the division.

¶ 1262. *Art. 4. Assembly.*—There may be a delegated body termed the **Assembly,** which shall meet at such time and place as the division may determine. The purpose of the Assembly shall be to promote and deepen interest in the work of the Board of Missions and its units through the Woman's Division. The division shall determine the composition, functions, and power of the Assembly.

¶ 1265. *Art. 5. Constitution of the Jurisdiction Woman's Society of Christian Service:*

1. *Name.*—There shall be in each jurisdiction a **Jurisdiction Woman's Society of Christian Service** auxiliary to the General Board of Missions through the Woman's Division. This shall include the Wesleyan Service Guild for employed women.

2. *Function or Authority.*—Each jurisdiction society shall have authority to promote its work in accordance with the program and policy of the General Board of Missions through the Woman's Division. It shall also recommend to the division such plans and policies as will make the work within the jurisdiction more effective.

3. *Membership.*—The jurisdiction society shall be com-

posed of its officers and secretaries of lines of work; six delegates from each Conference Woman's Society of Christian Service within the jurisdiction, three of whom shall be conference officers or secretaries of lines of work; all the women members of the Jurisdictional Board of Missions and any members of the Woman's Division living within the jurisdiction; a representative of the Jurisdiction Deaconess Association; all the bishops of the jurisdiction; and such other persons as the society may determine.

4. *Officers, Secretaries of Lines of Work, and Committees.*—Each jurisdiction society shall elect a president, a vice-president, a recording secretary, and a treasurer. Secretaries of lines of work and the Committee on Nominations shall be elected, and the other committees appointed, in accordance with the plans of the Woman's Division as may be set forth in the by-laws for the jurisdiction society. The jurisdiction society shall confirm the election of the jurisdiction secretary of the Wesleyan Service Guild.

5. *Elections.*—Officers, secretaries of lines of work, and the Committee on Nominations shall be elected at the first meeting of the society following the meeting of the Jurisdictional Conference, for a term of four years, with the privilege of re-election for one additional term in the same office. This term of office applies to all officers and secretaries of lines of work. For an officer or secretary elected during a quadrennium the period to be served shall be considered the first term, thus giving the privilege of re-election for one additional term in the same office. Tenure on the executive committee of officers and secretaries of lines of work shall be limited to a total of three terms.

6. *Meetings.*—Each jurisdiction society shall meet annually at such time and place as it may determine; *provided* that in the year of the Assembly the annual meeting may take the form of an enlarged executive committee meeting. A majority shall constitute a quorum.

7. *Amendments.*—Proposed amendments to this constitution shall be sent to the recording secretary of the

Woman's Division at least forty days before the last annual meeting of the division in the quadrennium.

¶ **1266.** *Art. 6. Constitution of the Conference Woman's Society of Christian Service:*

1. *Name.*—In each Annual Conference there shall be organized a **Conference Woman's Society of Christian Service** auxiliary to the Jurisdiction Woman's Society of Christian Service and to the General Board of Missions through the Woman's Division. This shall include the Wesleyan Service Guild for employed women.

2. *Purpose.*—The purpose of the conference society shall be to plan and direct the work of the society within the conference in accordance with the constitution and by-laws of the division.

3. *Function or Authority.*—Each conference society shall have authority to promote its work in accordance with the program and policy of the General Board of Missions through the Woman's Division.

4. *Membership.*—The conference society shall be composed of representatives from societies in the local churches, the number to be determined by each conference society according to its requirements; such district officers and secretaries of lines of work as the conference society may determine; the conference officers and secretaries of lines of work and chairmen of standing committees; and any members of the Woman's Division and of the Jurisdiction Woman's Society of Christian Service residing within the bounds of the conference. The resident bishop shall be a member of the executive committee.

5. *Officers, Secretaries of Lines of Work, and Committees.*—The conference society shall elect a president, a vice-president, a recording secretary, and a treasurer. Secretaries of lines of work and the Committee on Nominations shall be elected, and the other conference committees appointed, in accordance with the plans of the Woman's Division as may be set forth in the by-laws for the conference society. The conference society shall confirm the election of the conference secretary of the Wesleyan Service Guild.

6. *Annual Conference Relationships.*—The president of the conference society shall be seated in the Annual

Conference, but without the right to vote unless she is otherwise a member of the conference. (*See* ¶ 48.3.)

7. *Meetings.*—There shall be an annual meeting of the society when reports shall be received from the conference officers and secretaries of lines of work, and from the districts. Officers and secretaries of lines of work shall be elected, the necessary business transacted, and pledges made for the year. There shall be a program of inspiration and information in harmony with the plans and projects of the Jurisdiction Woman's Society of Christian Service and the Woman's Division.

8. *Elections.*—*a)* At the last annual meeting of the quadrennium the society shall elect, according to the instructions in ¶ 1265.3, six women from the conference, three of whom shall be conference officers or secretaries of lines of work, for membership in the Jurisdiction Woman's Society of Christian Service.

b) At the annual meeting preceding the jurisdiction society's last annual meeting of the quadrennium the conference society shall nominate three women for membership on the General Board of Missions, the names to be sent to the jurisdiction society, according to the instructions in ¶ 1180.2c.

9. *Amendments.*—Proposed amendments to this constitution shall be sent to the recording secretary of the Woman's Division at least forty days before the last annual meeting of the division in the quadrennium.

¶ **1267.** *Art. 7. Constitution of the District Woman's Society of Christian Service:*

1. *Name.*—There shall be a **District Woman's Society of Christian Service** auxiliary to the Conference Woman's Society of Christian Service and the General Board of Missions through the Woman's Division. This shall include the Wesleyan Service Guild for employed women.

2. *Purpose.*—The purpose of the district society shall be to unite all the societies within the district in an earnest effort for the promotion of the work of the Conference Woman's Society of Christian Service.

3. *Function or Authority.*—Each district society shall have authority to promote its work in accordance with

the program and policy of the General Board of Missions through the Woman's Division.

4. *Membership.*—All members of Woman's Societies of Christian Service in the local churches of the district shall be considered members of the district society. The district superintendent shall be a member of the executive committee.

5. *Officers, Secretaries of Lines of Work, and Committees.*—The district society shall elect a president, a vice-president, a recording secretary, and a treasurer. Secretaries of lines of work and the Committee on Nominations shall be elected, and the other committees appointed, in accordance with the plans of the Woman's Division as may be set forth in the by-laws for the district society. The district society shall confirm the election of the district secretary of the Wesleyan Service Guild. The district president shall be the only district representative with vote on the conference executive committee.

6. *Meetings.*—There shall be an annual meeting of the district society, when reports shall be received from the societies in the district. Officers, secretaries of lines of work, and the Committee on Nominations shall be elected, necessary business transacted, pledges made by the societies, and a program of inspiration and information given along the lines of work of the Woman's Society of Christian Service.

7. *Amendments.*—Proposed amendments to this constitution shall be sent to the recording secretary of the Woman's Division at least forty days before the last annual meeting of the division in the quadrennium.

¶ 1268. *Art. 8. Local-Church Woman's Society of Christian Service.*—There shall be a Woman's Society of Christian Service in the local church, auxiliary to the Conference Woman's Society of Christian Service, as provided in ¶ 282 under Part II, The Local Church.

SEC. IX.   **Councils**

¶ 1271. *Art. 1. Secretarial Council.*—There shall be a **secretarial council,** composed of the general and associate general secretaries, the executive secretary of the Joint Committee on Missionary Personnel, and the treasurer and associate treasurers. The general secretary shall be its chairman and shall call such meetings as are necessary to carry on its function. It shall be advisory to the general secretary in making recommendations to the board, to the divisions, and to the joint agencies on matters which concern the board as a whole, and in preparing items of business and carrying out such arrangements for board and committee meetings as may be required.

¶ 1272. *Art. 2. Missionary Councils.*—1. There may be a **General Missionary Council,** composed of persons to be designated by the Board of Missions, on recommendation of the Joint Commission on Education and Cultivation, from the elected membership and staff personnel of the General, Jurisdictional, and Conference Boards of Missions and Woman's Societies of Christian Service. Meetings of this council may be held, at such times and places as the Joint Commission on Education and Cultivation or the council itself may determine, for the consideration of any or all matters relating to missions and church extension and for the dissemination of missionary information and inspiration throughout the church.

2. There may be a **Jurisdictional Missionary Council** held within each jurisdiction at such times and places as the Jurisdictional Board of Missions may determine in consultation with the Joint Commission on Education and Cultivation and in harmony with its plans.

SEC. X.   **Co-operation with Other Boards and Agencies**

¶ 1276. *Article 1. Authority for Work Overseas.*—Other agencies of The Methodist Church shall conduct work in foreign fields only with the consent of and in co-operation with the Board of Missions.

¶ 1277. *Art. 2. Interboard Committee on Christian Education.*—For the purpose of more effectively promoting Christian education outside the United States there shall be an **Interboard Committee on Christian Education,** composed of twenty-two members. Ten shall be from the Board of Education: the general secretary and five other staff members of the Division of the Local Church, the general secretary and one other staff member of the Editorial Division, and two members of the board. Ten shall be from the World Division of the Board of Missions: the associate or assistant general secretary, associate treasurer, six staff secretaries, and two board members, one being a woman. The other two shall be the executive secretary of the Interboard Committee on Missionary Education and the staff member responsible for Methodist Youth Fund education.

¶ **1278.** The committee, as its work requires, may nominate staff for election by the Board of Missions and confirmation by the Board of Education. The staff shall be administratively related to the Board of Missions, serving with the World Division.

¶ **1279.** 1. The committee shall meet annually and at such other times as it shall determine, and shall report its actions to the Boards of Education and of Missions at their annual meetings.

2. It shall have a budget for its work provided by the two boards. The major responsibility for the budget rests on the Board of Missions, supplemented by support from the Board of Education, in which the Methodist Youth Fund shall have a part.

¶ **1281.** *Art. 3. Interboard Committee on Missionary Education.*—For the purpose of promoting effective co-operation between the Board of Missions and the Board of Education in missionary education there shall be an **Interboard Committee on Missionary Education,** composed of the general secretaries of the three divisions of the Board of Education and five other persons appointed by that board, and an equal number from the Board of Missions, which shall consist of two secretaries each from the Joint Commission on Education and Cultivation and the three divisions. During the period between the General Conference and the organization of the new committee for the ensuing quadrennium, the members who have served on the committee during the last quadrennium shall continue to function. The committee shall provide for age-group subcommittees and such other subcommittees as may be needed. This committee and its subcommittees shall be advisory and creative in character. The promotion of plans and materials created by this committee shall be a responsibility of the Board of Education and of the Board of Missions. The committee shall have a budget provided for its work by the two boards on such ratio as they may decide. The committee shall meet annually and at such other times as it may determine.

¶ **1282.** The duties of this committee shall be:

1. To develop a unified program of missionary education for all age groups in the local church and in the colleges, universities, and schools of theology.

2. To co-operate with the Curriculum Committee of the Board of Education in providing missionary information for church-school literature and in the planning and preparation of curriculum materials on missions.

3. To co-operate in the publication of books for missionary education in the church.

4. To develop co-operative plans for the missionary education and missionary giving of children, youth (*see* ¶ 1414 for relationships to the Methodist Youth Fund and its Administrative Committee), and adults.

5. To report annually to the Board of Missions and to the Board of Education.

¶ **1283.** There shall be an **executive secretary** of the committee, who shall be elected by the Board of Education, on nomination of the committee, and shall be confirmed by the Board of Missions. He shall be the secretary for missionary education of the Board of Education with staff relationship to the Division of the Local Church. He shall likewise be the secretary for missionary education of the Board of Missions, having staff relationship to the Joint Commission on Education and Cultivation. The committee shall nominate annually to the Board of Education for election and the Board of Missions for confirmation such staff as may be needed. They shall be members of the staff of the Joint Commission on Education and Cultivation of the Board of Missions and likewise of the staff of the Division of the Local Church of the Board of Education. Staff members shall assume their responsibilities when they have been elected and confirmed by the two boards respectively.

¶ **1285.** *Art. 4. Interboard Committee on Town and*

Country Work.—1. There shall be an **Interboard Committee on Town and Country Work,** composed of six bishops composing a Committee on Town and Country Work of the Council of Bishops, whose chairman shall convene this committee early in the quadrennium, and representatives elected by agencies as follows: three from the National Division of the Board of Missions, one of whom shall be a woman; three from the Board of Education; and one each from the Board of Evangelism, the Board of Lay Activities, and the Division of Human Relations and Economic Affairs of the Board of Christian Social Concerns. In addition, staff members of the participating agencies whose specific function is town and country work shall be ex officio members. The committee may invite other persons to meet with it as consultants. Expenses of members attending meetings shall be borne by the agencies which they represent. Expenses of the consultants shall be borne by the agency extending the invitation.

2. The members shall hold office for the quadrennium and/or until their successors are chosen.

3. The functions of the committee shall be:

a) To provide a means of co-operative planning among the participating agencies for the strengthening of town and country work in The Methodist Church.

b) To plan national or regional Conferences on Town and Country Work as provided in ¶ 1238.

c) To ascertain the phases of rural work the participating agencies propose to carry on and to give assistance in correlating the programs for a full service to town and country churches.

d) To prepare a clear statement on interdenominational co-operation with regard to allocation of new fields of work and to disposition of properties through federations, union churches, exchange of fields, withdrawals, and similar forms of co-operative work.

4. The committee shall organize by electing such officers and subcommittees as may be needed, and shall determine its frequency of meetings. It shall report annually to the participating agencies and may make suggestions concerning work in town and country churches.

¶ **1286.** *Art. 5. Joint Committee on Architecture.*—There shall be a **Joint Committee on Architecture**, composed of staff personnel as follows: four staff members of the National Division of the Board of Missions, including representatives of the work of church extension and architecture; the executive secretary of the Section of Program Development, the staff member responsible for design of church-school buildings, and two others elected by the Division of the Local Church of the Board of Education. It shall have authority to prepare standards for the architecture of churches, parsonages, and religious educational buildings and to recommend them to the co-operating boards, and is authorized, under such provisions as the boards may agree on, to offer counsel in the erection of such buildings. It shall meet annually and at such other times as its work may require.

¶ **1287.** *Art. 6. Crusade Scholarship Committee.*—1. There shall be a program of **Crusade scholarships** to give financial assistance in the training of future leadership of the churches in the mission fields.

2. There shall be a **Crusade Scholarship Committee**, composed of fifteen members elected quadrennially as follows: from the Board of Missions five elected by the World Division, four elected by the National Division, four of the nine to be women representing both divisions; from the Board of Education three elected by the Division of Higher Education; from the Commission on Promotion and Cultivation three elected by the commission. Vacancies shall be filled by the agency in which they occur.

3. The committee shall elect its own officers quadrenially.

4. The committee shall be responsible for the selection of students recommended for the scholarships provided by the One Great Hour of Sharing offering and other grants made specifically for Crusade scholarships by any of the agencies represented thereon. Students coming under the World Division shall be nominated by the duly established committee of the national church, where one exists.

5. The committee shall provide for the administration of the Crusade scholarship program, including provision

of an office, approval of a budget for administration, and election of a director, who together with office staff shall be related to the Board of Missions and be included in the board's staff pension plan.

¶ **1288.** *Art. 7. Joint Commission on Co-operation and Counsel.*—1. In continuation of the historical relationship between The Methodist Church and the Christian Methodist Episcopal Church there shall be a **Joint Commission on Co-operation and Counsel.** Its purpose shall be to foster co-operation at all levels and in all places between the two communions, and to recommend and encourage those plans and services which may be undertaken better together than separately. It shall promote joint plans with and through established agencies of the two co-operating churches.

2. The commission shall be composed of thirty members, fifteen from each co-operating communion, appointed as provided in their respective Disciplines. Such appointments shall take account of the total life of the church but give major emphasis to those agencies that provide a channel of common concern and co-operative endeavor. The fifteen members of The Methodist Church shall be named by the Council of Bishops as follows: five from the Board of Missions; four from the Board of Education; and two each from the Boards of Evangelism, Christian Social Concerns, and Lay Activities. These agencies shall be responsible for expenses of their respective representatives.

3. The commission shall meet annually, or more often at the call of the officers.

4. The expenses involved in the commission's work shall be borne by the appropriate agency or agencies designated by each denomination.

5. The commission shall elect a chairman, a vice-chairman, and a secretary, biennially at the annual meeting immediately succeeding each General Conference.

Sec. XI.   **Jurisdictional Boards**

¶ **1290.** In each jurisdiction there may be a **Jurisdictional Board of Missions,** auxiliary to the general board, as the Jurisdictional Conference may determine. (*See* ¶¶ 15.3, 527.)

Sec. XII.   **Annual Conference Boards**

¶ 1291. *Art. 1. Composition and Purpose.*—The **Conference Board of Missions** shall be auxiliary to the general and jurisdictional boards and shall be composed of the following members, elected quadrennially: one or more lay members and an equal number of ministers from each district, and five members at large, nominated by the conference nominating committee and elected quadrennially by the Annual Conference; a representative of the Conference Board of Education; the chairman of Christian outreach and one other representative, eighteen years of age or younger, elected by the Conference Methodist Youth Fellowship; one student elected by the state or regional unit of the Methodist Student Movement; the conference and district missionary secretaries, the conference lay leader, the conference secretary of evangelism, the president and the secretary of missionary education of the Conference Woman's Society of Christian Service, the executive secretary and the chairman of the Commission on Town and Country Work, the presidents and full-time executives of city (metropolitan) and district missionary societies, the chairman of the Committee on Urban Work, the chairman of the Commission on Minimum Salaries, and any members of the general board residing within the bounds of the conference. The district superintendents may be members of the board, at the discretion of the Annual Conference.

¶ 1292. 1. The board shall elect its own officers, and two representatives to each city (metropolitan) or district missionary society organized within the bounds of the conference.

2. It shall hold its annual meeting at the call of the president, or any three members, on due notice. The transactions of the year shall be reported by the president to the Annual Conference, and a detailed statement of all disbursements of missionary and church-extension aid within the conference shall be printed in the conference journal.

3. It may hold a midyear meeting, at which time necessary business may be transacted and open meetings planned for a general and public discussion of all matters pertaining to home and foreign missions and church extension.

¶ 1293. The officers and three additional members elected by the board shall constitute an **executive committee.** The executive committee shall exercise the powers of the board *ad interim.*

¶ 1294. The board shall make nominations in accordance with ¶ 1180.2 for membership on the general board.

¶ 1295. The board shall co-operate with the general board in carrying out the policies and promoting all phases of the work of missions and church extension. It shall also represent the interests of the Methodist Committee for Overseas Relief and promote its projects in the conference. It shall co-operate with the Joint Commission on Education and Cultivation in developing an effective program of education and cultivation within the conference. To expedite this program there shall be created a Committee on Education and Cultivation, of which the conference missionary secretary shall be chairman and all district missionary secretaries shall be members. There shall also be on the committee at least one lay man and one lay woman elected by the board, and one district superintendent selected by the Cabinet. (*See* ¶ 1307.)

¶ 1296. *Art. 2. Secretaries.*—1. The Annual Conference, on nomination of the board in consultation with the Cabinet, may elect annually an **executive secretary** of the board, who, if he is a ministerial member of the conference, shall be appointed by the bishop. He shall be a member of the board without vote and shall perform such duties in the field of missions and church extension as may be assigned by the board. The expenses of his salary and of his office shall be included in the budget of the board.

2. The Annual Conference, on nomination of the board, shall elect annually a **conference missionary secretary,** to be publicly assigned by the bishop. A vacancy in this office during the conference year may be filled by the executive committee. This secretary shall promote the

policies and plans of the board, and be its representative in the conference.

¶ **1297.** *Art. 3. Budget.*—The promotional work of the board shall be included in the conference benevolence budget.

¶ **1298.** *Art. 4. Missions Anniversary.*—The board shall co-operate with the Annual Conference program committee in arranging for a **missions anniversary** at each conference session, in which the work of the General Board of Missions shall be presented. The president of the conference board shall have charge of such anniversary.

¶ **1299.** *Art. 5. Home Missions and Church Extension.* —In the program of home missions and church extension within the bounds of the Annual Conference the board shall act as follows:

1. After consultation with the bishops, the district superintendents, the city (metropolitan) or district missionary societies, the Metropolitan Area Planning Commission (where organized), the Committee on Urban Work, and the Commission on Town and Country Work, the board shall develop and recommend to the Annual Conference a conference-wide long-range and short-range plan for home missions and church extension within the bounds of the conference. It shall give due consideration to the missionary and church-extension needs of the several districts, placing special emphasis on the unchurched areas and the population and other community changes.

With the district superintendents it shall also give due consideration to the responsibilities and resources of the National Division in home missions work and support and in church-extension planning and assistance in the fields of survey, site selection, architecture, fund raising, and loans for new churches.

2. It shall co-ordinate and/or make such studies and surveys as are needed for the development of such a conference-wide strategy and program.

3. In order to help provide adequate financial resources for the conference-wide program of home missions and church extension the board shall at least quadrennially, in consultation with the Cabinet and, where advisable,

with city (metropolitan) or district missionary boards
or societies, provide for a survey of the missionary and
church-extension needs of the several districts, placing
special emphasis on the unchurched areas and the population and other community changes, with a view to
determining in each what should be the over-all financial
objective. From this study an adequate conference-
initiated financial program shall be formulated with a
view to meeting these needs. A priority list of projects
to be developed shall be prepared. The list and all
revisions shall be filed with the National Division.

4. On recommendation of its executive committee or
its Committee on Home Missions the board shall review
and approve or adjust the askings of the district superintendents for the mission aid program before they are
presented to the general board, keeping in mind that, in
making final decision on all askings from the several
conferences, the National Division must take into account
the comparative missionary needs of each project and
its permanent value of service to the entire church.

5. It may estimate annually the amount necessary for
the support of conference missionary work and also the
amount necessary for conference church extension, and
shall report both estimates to the Commission on World
Service and Finance of the conference. The amount raised
on these apportionments shall be administered by the
board and applied respectively to missions and to church
extension. The work of the board shall be subject to the
approval of the Annual Conference.[9] The board shall seek
to cover all unoccupied territory in the conference by
the establishment and support of missions, but missions
shall be established only with the consent of the bishop
in charge and his Cabinet, and with due consideration to
the board's quadrennial plan of survey and strategy.

6. The board, its executive committee, or its Section of
Church Extension, composed of not less than one third
of its members, shall review, approve or adjust, and
certify the applications to the National Division for
loans and donations. Through such committee or section

---

[9] *See* Judicial Council Decision 178.

it shall administer such funds as come into its possession for church extension within the conference; *provided* that it may turn over all its church-extension funds to the National Division, which shall expend them within the bounds of the conference under the direction of the conference board. It shall provide for consultation between city (metropolitan) and district missionary societies and District Boards of Church Location and Building and the National Division in the development of standards and procedures for local-church building projects in the fields of site selection, study and approval of architectural plans, and financial programs.

7. In the administration of such funds as come into its possession for church-extension purposes within the conference it shall have authority to lend or donate any part thereof, whichever in its judgment will better accomplish the desired end. When funds lent or donated are returned, it shall administer them as a portion of the total church-extension funds at its disposal. The foregoing shall not apply to conference board loan funds administered prior to the General Conference of 1948 by the Section of Church Extension of the former Division of National Missions. If, however, an Annual Conference so elects, funds lent may become a part of the conference board loan fund, to be administered by the National Division on the same terms, conditions, and policies used by the division.

¶ **1300.** *Art. 6. Committee on Research and Survey.*— The board may appoint a **Committee on Research and Survey,** which shall conduct surveys and make research studies within the bounds of the conference, and shall co-operate with the National Division in its work of research and survey.

¶ **1301.** *Art. 7. Committee on Urban Work.*—1. The board shall appoint, in consultation with the Cabinet, a **Committee on Urban Work,** composed of pastors; district superintendents; laity experienced in the fields of city church work, urban planning and renewal, health, welfare, recreation, education, industry, and labor; and representatives of such church agencies as church-extension and research committees, city (metropolitan) and district missionary societies, Boards of Lay Activities, Woman's Societies of Christian Service, and Commissions on Town and Country Work.

2. The function of the committee shall be in the area of consultation and recommendation to the board, to which it shall be amenable. It shall inform itself, the board, the Cabinet, the Annual Conference, and the National Division relative to effectiveness of urban churches and an urban church strategy needed in keeping with city planning and urban renewal. It shall co-operate with committees on research and church extension, city (metropolitan) and district missionary societies, and councils of churches in initiating studies of city churches and the needs of urban regions and in establishing mutually acceptable standards for serving urban residents.

3. The committee shall help the National Division plan and promote the quadrennial Convocation on Urban Work (¶ 1235) by: (a) sharing areas of concern, successful experiences, and resource persons; (b) nominating delegates from the conference and promoting attendance; and (c) planning and helping execute follow-up workshops and institutes within the conference.

¶ **1302.** *Art. 8. Commission on Town and Country Work.*—1. Each Annual Conference shall set up quadrennially, under the direction of the bishop and his Cabinet, a **Commission on Town and Country Work.** The members shall be: the bishop and the district superintendents; the conference missionary secretary, conference secretary of evangelism, and executive secretary of the Conference Board of Education; the president or vice-president and a representative elected by the Conference Woman's Society of Christian Service; one representative each elected by the Conference Boards of Missions, Education, Christian Social Concerns, Lay Activities, and Evangelism; one representative each elected by the Conference Methodist Youth Fellowship, Methodist Rural Fellowship, and Committee on Urban Work; such district secretaries of town and country work as have been elected by the commission (¶ 1308); the members of the Interboard Committee on Town and Country Work and the corresponding jurisdictional agency who reside within the conference; and one lay man or woman and one pastor from town or country to represent each district, and one church and community worker (if the conference has such work), nominated by the district superintendents or the conference nominating committee and elected by the conference. The conference may add to the commission membership, in accordance with ¶ 667 and its usual nominating procedures, such additional ministers and laymen especially interested in town and country work as are recommended by the commission. All special workers in the conference employed by The Methodist Church in rural communities shall be members of the commission. If a district ceases to be represented by its resident lay or ministerial member, the vacancy may be filled by the executive committee of the commission until the next conference session.

2. The commission shall work with the conference agencies and the conference in program areas of town and country responsibility. It shall conduct surveys and research studies of town and country areas within the bounds of the conference; develop co-operative procedures between the church and social and governmental agencies, and with the town and country departments of state councils of churches and with the churches of other denominations in local communities; work to improve the effectiveness of the town and country churches and pastors; recommend a program to co-ordinate the work of the participating boards and agencies in this program area; and outline a program of town and country work to be presented to the participating agencies and to the conference. In program areas of town and country work the conference agencies shall consult with the commission or its executive committee.

3. At the beginning of the quadrennium a convener designated by the bishop shall call the commission together at the first conference session, or within ninety days after the Jurisdictional Conference, for the purpose of organizing and determining its initial activities, procedures, and time of meeting. Reports of all meetings shall be furnished to the secretaries of the co-operating agencies, and an annual report of findings and recom-

mendations shall be presented to these agencies and to the conference.

4. The officers of the commission shall be a chairman, vice-chairman, recording secretary, and treasurer, all elected quadrennially. There shall be an **executive secretary**, or a promotional secretary, elected by the commission after consultation with the bishop and his Cabinet and confirmed by the conference. The executive or promotional secretary shall have responsibility for the general oversight and promotion of the work of the commission.

¶ **1303.** *Art. 9. Committee on Town and Country Work.* —The board may appoint a **Committee on Town and Country Work,** composed of the executive committee of the Commission of Town and Country Work and others as may be determined.

SEC. XIII.   **District Organization**

¶ **1306.** *Article 1. District Missionary Secretary.*—There shall be a **district missionary secretary** in each district, appointed by the district superintendent after consultation with the conference missionary secretary, and publicly assigned by the bishop. A vacancy in this office during the conference year may be filled by appointment by the district superintendent. This secretary shall work in co-operation with the district superintendent and conference missionary secretary.

¶ **1307.** *Art. 2. District Missionary Institute.*—There shall be held annually in each district a training program which may be a **district missionary institute,** workshop, missionary festival, or rally. It shall be for the purposes of informing, training, and motivating the pastors, members of Commissions on Missions, and other laymen of local churches within the whole district. The Conference Board of Missions, through its Committee on Education and Cultivation, shall project conference-wide plans for education and cultivation. The district superintendents and district missionary secretaries shall promote and conduct the program in their respective districts. They shall consult with the secretary of missionary education and the secretary of promotion of the District Woman's Society of Christian Service and the district lay leader. The Joint Commission on Education and Cultivation shall co-operate with them in furnishing recommendations and resources for the program, including current study books, literature, audio-visual aids, speakers, and methods. Plans should include adequate time and numbers of meetings to reach all churches effectively.

¶ **1308.** *Art. 3. District Secretary of Town and Country Work.*—A **district secretary of town and country work** may be elected for each district by the Conference Commission on Town and Country Work on nomination by the district superintendent after consultation with the executive committee of the commission. He shall work in close co-operation with the executive secretary of the commission in all phases of the town and country program. His chief functions shall be to expedite all program aspects in his district, to assist the district superintendent in implementing the program, and to serve as liaison between the district and conference programs. (*See* ¶ 1302.1.)

Note: For other district agencies in the field of missions, *see* ¶¶ 1225-34, district missionary societies, and ¶ 1267, District Woman's Society of Christian Service.

SEC. XIV.   **Local-Church Commissions**

For description of the organization and duties of the Commission on Missions *see* ¶¶ 256-57 under Part II, The Local Church.

CHAPTER VII

METHODIST COMMITTEE FOR OVERSEAS RELIEF

¶ **1311.** There shall be a **Methodist Committee for Overseas Relief** to minister in the spirit of Jesus Christ to persons in need without regard to their religion, race, or nationality. This committee shall be composed as follows: two persons, one lay and one ministerial or episcopal, from each jurisdiction, nominated by the College of

Bishops and elected by the Jurisdictional Conference, and six persons elected by the Board of Missions. The committee shall be empowered to co-opt not more than seven members at large. Vacancies shall be filled by the body concerned: by the College of Bishops of the jurisdiction, or by the Board of Missions, or, in the case of the co-opted members, by the committee itself. The committee is authorized to elect its own officers, to appoint subcommittees if desired, to employ such assistance as may be needed (*see* ¶ 783.2*a*), and to provide for its necessary expense of administration and promotion out of undesignated receipts. Its financial officers shall be bonded.

¶ **1312.** The committee is authorized and empowered:

1. To be the representative of The Methodist Church in the field of overseas relief, and rehabilitation for victims of disaster and of endemic circumstance; and services to refugees. These activities shall be carried on in consultation with the Board of Missions.

2. To give special attention and assistance to the national workers and the people of our Methodist churches overseas who are in need because of war or other disasters. In countries where the Board of Missions is at work, it is expected that the administration of specifically Methodist relief be through the board and the bishops in charge and, where possible, the indigenous church.

3. To co-operate with Church World Service; the Division of Interchurch Aid, Refugee, and World Service of the World Council of Churches; and other interdenominational relief agencies, as the committee may deem wise.

4. To supplement, when considered desirable, the work of other agencies ministering in the spirit of Christ to the relief of human suffering.

5. To transmit to the church appeals for help from recognized agencies, and to receive and allocate funds contributed by churches, groups, or individuals for the purposes stated in § 1; *provided* that no church-wide appeal for funds shall be made without the approval of the Council of Bishops and the Council on World Service and Finance.

¶ **1313.** In order to provide adequate means for the prosecution of this work, the committee, in addition to its receipts by voluntary gifts and by participation in the Fellowship of Suffering and Service and the One Great Hour of Sharing offerings (¶¶ 760, 763), shall be included in any church-wide appeal to meet emergencies growing out of war, internal strife, or natural disaster. Financial promotion shall be by the Commission on Promotion and Cultivation in consultation with the general secretary of the committee.

¶ 1314. Authorization is given to the committee to acknowledge gifts by its own vouchers. Such gifts, however, cannot receive credit on world service apportionments. (See ¶ 746.)

¶ 1315. If at any time during the quadrennium the Council of Bishops, the Council on World Service and Finance, and the Board of Missions decide that the specific work of the committee is no longer needed, the committee shall be discharged and its responsibilities and assets shall be assigned to such agency as those three bodies may determine.

Chapter VIII

BOARD OF EDUCATION

Section I.   Purpose

¶ 1324. Christian education has its roots in the nature of the Christian gospel itself. Jesus is frequently called Master or Teacher, and he is the authority in our church's program of Christian nurture. His Great Commission is: "Go therefore and make disciples of all nations, . . . teaching them to observe all that I have commanded you; and lo, I am with you always." The purpose of Christian education is to learn, to teach, and to use his way by which persons of all ages are related through Jesus Christ to God as Father and to all men as brothers. The divisions of the Board of Education shall develop standards consistent with this purpose and support their attainment through appropriate program and curriculum materials in Methodism's local churches, colleges, universities, and schools of theology.

Sec. II.   **Organization**

¶ **1325.** 1. There shall be a **Board of Education** of
The Methodist Church, hereinafter referred to as the
General Board of Education or the board, for the promotion of Christian education. The board shall have general
oversight of the educational interests of the church in the
United States. It may co-operate with the Board of Missions for the advancement of Christian education in other
lands.

2. The General Board of Education shall be incorporated
under the laws of whatever state the board may determine.

3. The board shall meet annually at such time and
place as it may determine, subject to the provisions of
the act of incorporation, and may hold such special meetings as may be necessary. A majority of the members of
the board shall constitute a quorum.

4. The board shall appoint such committees as may be
necessary for the proper discharge of its business. It may
adopt such by-laws for the regulation of the affairs of the
board and its divisions and committees as are not inconsistent with the act of incorporation or with General
Conference legislation.

¶ **1326.** 1. The board shall be constituted quadrennially,
and its members and all officers elected by it shall hold
office until their successors have been chosen.

2. Membership of the board shall consist of fifteen
bishops resident in the United States, representing all of
the jurisdictions, elected by the Council of Bishops, together with additional members elected as follows: each
Jurisdictional Conference shall elect to the membership
of the Board of Education on nomination of its Committee on Education one minister and one layman without regard to the number of members within the jurisdiction, and in addition one minister and one layman for
each 450,000 members or major fraction thereof within
the jurisdiction; *provided* that not more than two thereof
shall be from any one Annual Conference.

3. There shall be elected a sufficient number of members
at large without respect to jurisdictions or Annual Conferences to bring the membership to a total of ninety-one.
These shall be persons of demonstrated competence in

the field of education in the church, community, and/or higher education, elected in the following manner: seven by the General Conference on nomination of the Council of Bishops, and the remaining number by the board on nomination of its nominating committee.

4. There shall be six young people—four representing the Methodist Youth Fellowship, one of whom shall be a member of the council of the National Conference thereof, and two representing the Methodist Student Movement—elected quadrennially by the board on nomination of the Joint Staff on Youth and Student Work, which shall have selected the nominees as provided in ¶ 1405.2.

5. If any vacancy occurs in the membership of the board, it shall be filled in the following manner: in the case of a bishop or a member at large elected by the General Conference, by the Council of Bishops; in the case of a ministerial or lay representative of a jurisdiction, by the board on nomination of the College of Bishops of the jurisdiction, such member to serve until the next meeting of the Jurisdictional Conference; in the case of a youth representative, by the board on nomination of the Joint Staff on Youth and Student Work; in the case of a member at large elected by the board, by the board on nomination of its nominating committee.[10]

¶ 1327. 1. Within three months after the adjournment of the last Jurisdictional Conference to meet in that year, the elected members of the board shall be assembled by a convener, designated by the Council of Bishops, to organize in the following manner.

2. A nominating committee shall be elected, which shall be composed of one member chosen by the members from each jurisdiction and one bishop chosen by the bishops who are members of the board.

3. The nominating committee shall nominate for election by the board: (a) members of the three constituent divisions of the board—the Division of Higher Education, the Division of the Local Church, and the Editorial Division—in ratio of five, five, and two; (b) a president

---

[10] Amended in 1964 following Judicial Council Decision 198.

and a recording secretary for the board; (c) members at large as provided in ¶ 1326.3, .5.

4. The members of the divisions and the president and recording secretary of the board shall be elected from the membership of the board. The president, who shall be a presiding, not an administrative, officer, shall preside over the meetings of the board and of the executive committee. Each division shall elect a chairman, and these chairmen shall be vice-presidents of the board. The officers of the board and members of the divisions, together with the officers of each division, shall hold office for the quadrennium.

5. The general secretaries of the Division of Higher Education and the Division of the Local Church shall be elected for the quadrennium by the board from nominations made by the respective divisions. A vacancy in either office shall be filled by election by the board. The general secretary of the Editorial Division shall be elected as provided in ¶ 1429.

6. The treasurer shall be elected by the board on nomination of the executive committee.

7. No member of the board shall be a salaried officer of the board.

8. The salaries and duties of all employees of the board except in the Editorial Division shall be fixed by the board.

¶ 1328. The board is authorized to solicit and create special funds, to receive gifts and bequests, to hold properties and securities in trust, and to administer all these financial affairs in accordance with its own rules and the provisions of the Discipline.

¶ 1329. 1. The board shall conduct its work through the three administrative divisions hereinbefore named (¶ 1327.3a), each of which shall be responsible for the specific areas assigned to it by the board.

2. Each of the divisions shall elect from its members an **advisory committee**, consisting of its chairman, recording secretary, and other members to the following totals: Division of Higher Education, seven; Division of the Local Church, seven; Editorial Division, four. In addition

the president of the board shall be ex officio a member of each advisory committee.

These committees shall assist in the conduct of the work and serve as members of the executive committee of the board. (*See* ¶ 1330.1.)

3. The **general secretaries** of the divisions shall be the administrative officers of their respective divisions under such regulations as the board may make. Reports of the work of the respective divisions, including organization and budget, except the budget of the Editorial Division, shall be presented annually by them to the board. Assistants to the general secretaries of the Division of Higher Education and the Division of the Local Church shall be elected annually by the divisions on nomination of the respective general secretaries. Assistants to the general secretary of the Editorial Division shall be appointed by him and reported to the board.

4. Each of the divisions shall provide for a review of its work, pass upon recommendations of its general secretary and staff, and make recommendations to the board concerning its needs and programs.

5. The general secretaries shall attend the meetings of the board, the executive committee, and their respective divisions, participating in their deliberations, but without vote.

6. The three general secretaries shall form a **secretarial council,** which shall choose annually in rotation from its members a presiding officer, and shall meet as necessary to correlate the work of the three divisions.

¶ **1330. 1.** The **executive committee** of the board shall be composed of the president and recording secretary of the board and the members of the advisory committees of the three divisions as provided in ¶ 1329.2. A majority of the members shall constitute a quorum.

2. The executive committee shall manage the funds of the board under such regulations as the board may adopt; appoint finance and investment committees, which shall render to it detailed reports at each meeting; fix the official bond of the treasurer and of any other officers entrusted with the handling of funds; consider and ap-

prove the administrative budgets of the board and its divisions, except the Editorial Division.

3. The **treasurer** of the board shall be the custodian of all the funds of the board. He shall keep the accounts of the assets, liabilities, receipts, and disbursements of the board and of the Division of Higher Education and the Division of the Local Church. He shall pay out funds on order of the general secretaries of these divisions. He shall report annually to the board and to the executive committee as requested by it. An associate treasurer may be elected by the board on nomination of the executive committee.

4. The board may commit to the executive committee such other powers and duties as it may determine. Minutes of the executive committee shall be sent to the members of the board and submitted to the annual meeting of the board for approval. Meetings of the committee shall be held at least once each year, not including meetings held in connection with the annual meetings of the board.

¶ **1331.** All assets and liabilities existing at the time of union in the funds of the Boards of Education of the three uniting churches shall be the assets and liabilities of the corresponding divisions in the new Board of Education.

¶ **1332.** The Division of Higher Education and the Division of the Local Church shall present quadrennially to the Council on World Service and Finance a statement of the amounts required for their general expenses and for the support of their work, and the appropriations of the council shall be made to each division. The Editorial Division shall be financed as provided in ¶¶ 1148-49. In all cases the purposes for which funds are committed to the board shall be strictly observed.

¶ **1333.** The board shall have authority to make provision for co-operation with any of the general boards or other agencies of the church, or with other agencies, in matters within its field. Each Annual Conference shall determine for itself to what extent it will undertake to co-operate with other denominations or agencies in its own territory.

¶ **1334.** The Board of Education shall be the legal

successor and successor in trust of the General Board of Christian Education of the Methodist Episcopal Church, South, the Board of Education of the Methodist Episcopal Church, the Board of Education of the Methodist Protestant Church, the Board of Education for Negroes of the Methodist Episcopal Church, the Board of Sunday Schools of the Methodist Episcopal Church, and the Epworth League of the Methodist Episcopal Church; and it is authorized and empowered at any time it may deem such action to be desirable or convenient to take corporate action in the name of said corporations to surrender the charter or charters of one or several or all of said corporations (including a transfer of all of the properties of said corporations to the Board of Education if necessary or desirable), or to merge, consolidate, or affiliate such corporations, or any of them, with the Board of Education in compliance with appropriate state corporation laws, so as to accomplish as nearly as may legally be possible the end result that the Board of Education shall be the one legal entity authorized to act on behalf of the interests heretofore or hereafter in the name of one or the other of said corporations.

¶ **1335.** As a means of educating the church in regard to better race relations and the needs of Negro schools, **Race Relations Sunday** shall be observed in all the congregations. (*See* ¶ 250.3.)

SEC. III.   **Division of Higher Education**

¶ **1351.** 1. Higher education is part of both our Methodist heritage and our present task. In establishing and maintaining educational institutions and in ministering to students without respect to race or national origin the church continues its historic work of uniting knowledge and vital piety.

2. There shall be a **Division of Higher Education,** which shall represent The Methodist Church in all activities connected with secondary, higher, and ministerial education. The division shall have an advisory relationship to all educational institutions in the United States affiliated with The Methodist Church: universities, colleges, secondary schools, schools of theology, and Wesley

Foundations and similar organizations. On request it may serve in an advisory capacity to the several agencies of the church owning or administering educational institutions.

3. Its principal objectives shall be: (*a*) to develop an educational plan and purpose which shall definitely relate the educational institutions of the church to the church; (*b*) to foster within them the highest educational standards and soundest business practices; (*c*) to interpret to them their place and function in the life and work of the church; (*d*) to encourage them in their commitment to Christian standards and ideals in their teaching, policies, and practices; (*e*) to create and maintain within them an atmosphere conducive to a knowledge and understanding of the Christian message and mission; (*f*) to interpret to the membership of the church the distinctive services rendered by these educational institutions and their functions in the church and society; and (*g*) to lead the church in a program designed to assure their permanence, efficiency, academic excellence, and Christian commitment.

4. It shall operate through three constituent departments: Educational Institutions, College and University Religious Life, and Ministerial Education.

5. It shall elect, without respect to race or national origin, on nomination of the general secretary, directors for each of the departments, and such other staff members as are needed for the operation of the division.

6. It shall engage personnel, without respect to race or national origin, and appoint such commissions and committees and adopt such regulations as necessary for the discharge of its responsibilities.

¶ 1352. The specific responsibilities of the division are:

1. To devise ways and means to interpret and aid the higher education program of the church. (*See* ¶ 1356.2.)

2. To co-operate with Annual Conferences in establishing and conducting institutions of higher education in the United States in areas in which facilities for Christian higher education are not adequately provided. (*See* ¶ 1391.)

3. To maintain an advisory relationship to the schools

of theology in the planning of their educational programs and in the development of their financial support, and in developing and conducting in-service programs of education for preachers, including approved supply pastors and other local preachers.

4. To promote Christian instruction, afford opportunities for Christian service, and offer guidance in Christian vocations for students at educational institutions of The Methodist Church and for Methodist students at tax-supported and other institutions not related to The Methodist Church.[11]

5. To make use, in so far as is practicable, of the existing church organization and publications for carrying out its work of interpretation, setting up such conferences and producing such materials as will strengthen the interrelation of the church and its educational institutions.

6. To study the financial status of Methodist educational institutions, encourage the church to give them continuing and conscientious support, provide guidance and leadership in their special financial campaigns, and formulate procedures by which they can approach Methodist members and constituents for gifts and bequests.

7. To direct attention to the work and needs of educational institutions which stand in special relationship to the church at large, and to request support for them, with due recognition of the needs of schools and colleges historically operated for Negroes.

8. To furnish guidance, plans of procedure, personal leadership, and plans for special gifts to be known as **educational specials** in the promotion of the work of higher education in the Annual Conferences and in the local churches.

9. To devise methods of credit for local-church giving to educational institutions related to the division, including the listing of all such giving in appropriate columns in the statistical reports of the Annual Conference minutes.

¶ 1353. The **Department of Educational Institutions,** which term shall include universities, colleges, and sec-

[11] *See* Judicial Council Decision 175.

ondary schools, shall have primary responsibility for the work of the division as outlined in ¶¶ 1351-52 and hereafter described more specifically in ¶¶ 1354-59 in so far as the provisions thereof relate to the universities, colleges, secondary, and other schools of The Methodist Church.

¶ 1354. 1. The division shall appropriate the funds available for the support of educational institutions related to The Methodist Church, under such rules as it may adopt.

2. In making appropriations for the support of educational institutions, the division shall give due consideration to their current financial needs as shown in carefully prepared reports presented by them on forms provided. Appropriations to institutions from funds at the disposal of the division shall not debar those institutions from soliciting aid from their supporting conferences or from other sources. (*See* ¶ 1391.)

3. The division shall co-operate with the General and Annual Conferences in their efforts to provide the institutions related to them adequate financial income for the operation of accredited educational programs.

4. The division shall recommend to Jurisdictional and Annual Conference Boards of Education concerned with the appropriation of conference funds those institutions whose educational and religious aims and programs are in active accord with the policies of the church as expressed in the Discipline and through special General Conference enactments. (*See* ¶¶ 1367, 1385.)

5. The division shall have power to administer under the rules and regulations of the board any and all funds, gifts, and bequests which have been or may be committed to it; and, subject to the approval of the board, it may solicit or create special funds for its projects. The purposes for which the funds are given and accepted shall be sacredly observed.

6. The division shall take such action as is necessary to protect or recover the investment which it or an Annual Conference has made in capital funds to any institution founded, organized, developed, or assisted under the direction or with the co-operation of The

Methodist Church, should any such institution discontinue operation or move to sever or to modify its connection with the church or violate the terms of any such grant of new capital funds made by The Methodist Church.

¶ 1355. 1. The division shall, in co-operation with the University Senate, study population growth and trends and make recommendations to the Annual Conferences concerning the needs for new institutions of learning and the discontinuance, reopening, relocation, and merger of existing institutions.

2. No educational institution hereafter established or acquired shall be qualified for classification as a Methodist institution or be aided by the division unless the division shall have been consulted and shall have approved the expenditures involved in the establishment or acquisition of such institution. (*See* ¶¶ 1367, 1391.)

3. An institution receiving appropriations from the division which incurs debt obligations, bonded or otherwise, for expansion programs without first submitting its proposed plans to the division for consideration and counsel relinquishes its right to appropriations until the debt so incurred is liquidated.

¶ 1356. 1. The division, through such officers, committees, and commissions as it may deem necessary, shall provide for the co-operative study of plans for maximum correlation of the work of our educational institutions with the church's entire program of Christian education.

2. In co-operation with the Annual Conferences and the pastors and Commissions on Education of local churches, the division shall bring to the attention of our members the contribution of our educational institutions to the life and character of youth, and the place the institutions have in the preservation and propagation of Christianity. (*See* ¶¶ 233.7*f*, 352.17, 1352.1.)

¶ 1357. 1. The division shall be the agency of the board in administering institutions for **Christian education among Negroes,** except those institutions now owned by other agencies. It shall have authority to institute plans by which schools sponsored by the division may co-operate with or may unite with schools of other denominations or under independent control, provided the interests of The Methodist Church are adequately protected.

2. The division shall encourage such schools to secure adequate endowments for their support and maintenance. Whenever the division is assured that their support will be adequate and the property will be conserved and perpetuated for Christian education under the auspices and control of The Methodist Church, it may transfer the schools to boards of trustees under such conditions as the General Board of Education may prescribe, including right of reversion to the General Board of Education.

3. The division shall be responsible for promoting Race Relations Sunday. (*See* ¶¶ 250.3, 1335.)

¶ **1358.** 1. The division shall promote and administer the **Student Loan Fund,** the **National Methodist Scholarship Fund,** and other grants and bequests made to the division for the aid of students in accordance with regulations recommended by the division and adopted by the board.

2. The division shall be responsible for promoting Methodist Student Day. (*See* ¶ 250.4.)

Note: For the participation of the division in the Crusade scholarship program *see* ¶ 1287.

¶ **1359. Educational societies or foundations** created by Annual Conferences for the promotion of work in Christian higher education may be recognized as auxiliaries to the Division of Higher Education when their objects and purposes, their articles of incorporation, and their methods of administration shall have been approved by the Annual Conference within whose bounds they are incorporated. All auxiliaries thus approved may be required to make an annual report of their fiscal and administrative affairs to the division.

¶ **1360.** There shall be a **Committee on Co-operation and Counsel** of ten members, five to be appointed by the Division of Higher Education and five by the Board of Missions, nominated by the National Division, to take under consideration all matters involving educational work in institutions in which agencies of both boards may have responsibility. (*See* ¶ 1242.)

¶ **1363.** The **Department of College and University Religious Life** shall have primary responsibility for the work of the division with college and university students as outlined in ¶¶ 1351-52 and hereafter described more specifically in ¶¶ 1364-70.

¶ **1364.** In its work with students the division, in cooperation with Annual Conferences, shall have the following responsibilities:

1. To organize and maintain Wesley Foundations at tax-supported and independent institutions.

2. To assist Methodist institutions of higher education in their religious activities.[12]

3. To study the religious needs of students, provide for evangelistic work among students, and enlist suitable candidates for full-time religious vocations.

¶ **1365.** There shall be a governing body for the campus ministry in every college community where The Methodist Church is at work, as follows:

1. For each Wesley Foundation there shall be a Board of Directors as described in ¶ 1366.

2. The division shall encourage each Methodist-related college or university to establish a **Committee on Campus Religious Life,** which may serve also as a Campus-Church Relations Committee, and to state qualifications and define duties of the committee in consultation with the division.

3. For each other institution there shall be a **Campus-Church Relations Committee** nominated by a local Methodist body and elected by the Conference Board of Education.[13]

¶ **1366. 1.** A **Wesley Foundation** is the organized educational ministry through which The Methodist Church makes a unified approach to the tax-supported or independent college or university. The nature of its work shall be defined by the division.

2. A Wesley Foundation shall have a **Board of Directors** composed of members from the local campus-church community and members at large representing the interests of the Annual Conference or Conferences. They shall be

---

[12] *See* Judicial Council Decision 175.
[13] *See* Judicial Council Decision 175.

elected by the Annual Conference or Conferences on nomination of the Conference Board or Boards of Education.

3. The Board of Directors shall be responsible for the direction and administration of the foundation in accordance with the policies and standards established by the conference board or boards and the division. The foundation shall be related functionally and co-operatively, through its Board of Directors, to the Methodist local church or churches in the immediate vicinity of the college or university. The Board of Directors, when incorporated, may hold property, according to the laws of The Methodist Church and the state in which the foundation is located.[14]

¶ 1367. 1. The division shall appoint a **Commission on Standards for Wesley Foundations,** which shall be the accrediting agency for all Wesley Foundations and interdenominational campus ministry related to The Methodist Church at tax-supported and independent colleges and universities in the United States. It shall be composed of six members of the division and five persons, not members of the General Board of Education, who are actively engaged in Wesley Foundation work, and who are fitted by training and experience to establish standards and evaluate the educational, religious, and financial program of Wesley Foundations. It shall report annually to the division and to the Annual Conferences those Wesley Foundations which meet the standards it has established.[15]

2. Each Wesley Foundation or similar organization approved by the Commission on Standards and each unit seeking such approval shall submit annually to the division reports of program and financial operations.

¶ 1368. 1. In carrying out its responsibility for the operation and maintenance of religious work among Methodist students enrolled in institutions of higher education, the division through the Department of College and University Religious Life shall relate campus Christian

---

[14] Amended in 1960 concurrently with Judicial Council Decision 175.
[15] *See* Judicial Council Decisions 137, 175.

organizations on Methodist campuses, Wesley Foundations at tax-supported and independent colleges and universities, and such other organizations as may be
developed, to the intercollegiate Christian movement
known as the **Methodist Student Movement.** There shall
be such state or similar area units, regional and national,
as the division shall see fit to maintain. The department
shall publish such materials as are necessary to develop
this work.

2. Some of the purposes of the Methodist Student Movement shall be:

a) To lead all members of the college and university
community to accept the Christian faith in God according
to the Scriptures, to live as true disciples of Jesus Christ,
and to become members of Christ's Church.

b) To deepen, enrich, and mature the Christian faith
of college and university men and women through commitment to Jesus Christ and his Church, and to prepare
them for active lives of service and leadership in and
through the Church during and after their student years.

c) To witness in the campus community to the mission,
message, and life of the Church.

¶ 1369. 1. There shall be a **National Conference of the
Methodist Student Movement** for the purpose of fellowship, evaluation, and program planning in areas that
relate to the campus ministry. It shall be composed of
the presidents of Methodist student organizations of state
or similar geographical regions, the Methodist Student
Movement delegates to the National Student Christian
Federation, eleven representative students at large, a
campus minister or director from each of the seven regions, the staff of the Department of College and University Religious Life, student members of the general
boards and other agencies, and the staff responsible for
the campus ministry of other general agencies.

2. Through this conference the students shall have
free opportunity to participate creatively in planning the
church's program by making recommendations to all the
agencies of the church and by proposing student members
for nomination to the general boards as provided in

¶ 1405. The conference shall report to the division annually on its meetings and activities.

¶ 1370. 1. The Boards of Education of the Annual Conferences of a given state or similar geographical region shall create or provide for continuing at the beginning of each quadrennium a Conference or an **Interconference Commission on College and University Religious Life,** which shall co-ordinate all intercollegiate work of the Methodist Student Movement and give general oversight to the campus ministry at the institutions of higher learning in that region. It shall co-operate with the Department of College and University Religious Life in promoting its program and policies.

2. The duties of the commission shall be:

a) To evaluate the campus ministry within its region.

b) To report its evaluation to the Conference Board or Boards of Education.

c) To recommend improvements in facilities, program, finance, and personnel.

d) To approve the purchase or sale of property and the plans for any new building, including a parsonage, proposed by a Wesley Foundation, and the financial program covering the liquidation of its cost. Where deemed advisable, the commission may invite the chairman of the District Board of Church Location and Building in which the foundation making the proposal is located to serve in an advisory capacity as the commission studies the proposal and makes its recommendations.

e) To co-operate in the interpretation of the Methodist Student Movement.

3. The commission may elect a state or **regional director of the Methodist Student Movement,** whose duties and responsibilities shall be determined by the commission in co-operation with the executive secretaries of the conference boards involved and with the Department of College and University Religious Life.

Note: For provisions for correlating youth and student work *see* ¶ 1405.

¶ 1371. 1. The **Department of Ministerial Education** shall have primary responsibility for the work of the division in relation to the schools of theology and the preparation of the ministry of the church, and shall be responsible for promoting theological education in the church. It shall be composed of twelve persons, six bishops and six ministers, selected from the membership of the division. In addition the division shall select six administrators from the Methodist schools of theology to serve as advisory members of the department; *provided* that these representatives shall not participate in the allocation of appropriations for schools of theology. The division shall also select from the faculties of the schools of theology six advisory members to assist in preparing the courses of study described in ¶ 1373.

2. The division shall elect, on nomination of the general secretary, a **director of ministerial education**, who shall be responsible for that part of the program of the division concerned with the enlistment and educational preparation of candidates for the ministry. In matters pertaining to ministerial education he shall serve as liaison officer between the boards and other agencies and the schools of theology of the church.

3. The division shall elect, on nomination of the general secretary, such associate directors as are deemed necessary to assist in the program of the department.

4. The department shall be responsible for: maintenance of the educational standards for the ministry (see Part III, The Ministry, Chapters II-V, ¶¶ 304-415); development and promotion of a program of ministerial enlistment and guidance (in co-operative relationship with the Interboard Committee on Christian Vocations); the educational preparation of candidates for the ministry; relationships with the Annual Conference Boards of Ministerial Training and Qualifications (¶¶ 669-74); schools and programs of continuing education and inspiration for ministers; supervision of the courses of study as described in ¶ 1373; and interdenominational relationships that relate to the ministry, such as with the Department of the Ministry of the National Council of Churches.

¶ **1372.** The work of the department shall be supported from the general benevolences of the church. The division shall recommend to the Council on World Service and

Finance, as items apart from its own budget, the amounts of financial support which should be allocated for ministerial education. (*See* ¶ 1378.)

¶ **1373.** 1. The department shall prescribe studies required for license to preach, introductory studies, and the **four-year course of study.** It shall recommend courses of reading and also provide advanced courses of study for preachers who have finished the above courses.

2. It shall provide and administer special courses of study and examinations in Methodist history, doctrine, and polity for candidates lacking seminary credits in these fields (¶ 344).

3. It shall co-operate with the Boards of Ministerial Training and Qualifications and other conference boards in organizing, financing, and conducting **pastors' schools,** which shall be of two kinds: (*a*) short-term schools to provide programs of inspiration and instruction for all ministers; (*b*) schools which offer work in the courses of study.

4. It shall, in co-operation with the Methodist schools of theology, administer **correspondence** work in the courses of study described in § 1.

5. All work in the courses of study for candidates for the traveling ministry (¶¶ 325.2, .3, 343) and for local preachers seeking renewal of license (¶ 307.2), including approved supply pastors qualifying for appointment (¶ 317.2, .3) and for authority to administer the Sacraments (¶ 318), shall be taken under the direction of the Department of Ministerial Education either in an approved course of study school or through correspondence.

¶ **1374.** The department also may provide a program of continuing non-credit education for ministers who have satisfied the basic educational requirements, to consist of courses with study guides and a resident study program to provide on-campus periods of study for groups of invited ministers.

¶ **1375.** The department shall certify the course offerings in non-Methodist seminaries for meeting the requirements in Methodist history, doctrine, and polity specified in ¶ 344 and provide the Boards of Ministerial Training and Qualifications with a list of the courses approved. It shall consult with the Methodist schools of theology in regard to courses meeting these requirements (¶ 1379).

¶ 1376. The department shall develop and promote a program of selective enlistment and guidance of candidates for the ministry in co-operation with the Interboard Committee on Christian Vocations, the Methodist schools of theology, the Boards of Ministerial Training and Qualifications, and the bishops, district superintendents, counselors with preministerial students in the colleges and universities, and directors of Wesley Foundations. It shall also sponsor and promote conferences on the ministry in the Annual Conferences in co-operation with the Interboard Committee on Christian Vocations and the respective bishops, Conference Committees or Commissions on Christian Higher Education, Conference Boards of Education, and Boards of Ministerial Training and Qualifications.

¶ 1377. The department shall be responsible for a continuing study of the ministry, and a report of its findings shall be given to each General Conference. (*See also* ¶ 1814.)

SEC. IV.   Schools of Theology

¶ 1378. 1. The **schools of theology** of The Methodist Church are established and maintained for the education of ministers. They exist for the benefit of the whole church, and their support shall be provided by the church as a part of its general benevolent giving. (*See* ¶ 1354.2.)

2. For the purpose of providing for the better support of these schools, the Division of Higher Education, in consultation with their administrative officers, shall establish budget askings for their adequate support; and the amount necessary for such support shall be added as a separate item in the askings of the General Board of Education from the benevolence funds as determined by the authoritative body; *provided*, however, that the receiving of appropriations of such funds through the division shall not debar the schools from soliciting additional funds from the Annual and Jurisdictional Conferences as a part of the program of Christian higher education.

3. No school of theology or department of theology in a college or university shall be established without first submitting its proposed organization and classification to the University Senate for prior approval. (*See* ¶ 1391.)

¶ **1379.** Our schools of theology, in addition to preparing their students for effective service for Christ and the Church, shall acquaint them with the current programs of The Methodist Church, such as its educational, missionary, social, and other service programs, and with the organizations and terminology of the church. Each school of theology, in consultation with the Department of Ministerial Education, shall provide in its curriculum the courses in Methodist history, doctrine, and polity specified in ¶ 344. (*See also* ¶ 1375.)

¶ **1380.** The Methodist schools of theology share with the Boards of Ministerial Training and Qualifications the responsibility for the selection and education of young people for admission to the Annual Conferences.

1. It is recommended therefore that these schools, before admitting a candidate for the Methodist ministry as a divinity student, shall (*a*) inquire into his personal character and promise of usefulness in the ministry, (*b*) require satisfactory evidence of his having been licensed to preach, and (*c*) require a letter of recommendation from the Board of Ministerial Training and Qualifications of the Annual Conference in which he resides.

2. It is further recommended that, when such a candidate has been admitted, the school shall give careful attention to his progress in studies and his personal and religious development, to determine whether he should be continued in his preparation for the ministry. When a candidate's progress is adjudged to be unsatisfactory, he should not be permitted to continue. Notification of the termination of his relationship in the school shall be given by the school to the registrar of the Board of Ministerial Training and Qualifications where his Annual Conference relations are recorded.

SEC. V.   **University Senate**

¶ **1382.** The **University Senate** shall be the accrediting and standardizing agency for all the educational institutions related to The Methodist Church.

¶ 1383. 1. The senate shall be composed of twenty-one persons, not members of the General Board of Education, who are actively engaged in the work of education and are fitted by training and experience for the technical work of establishing standards and evaluating educational institutions in accordance with such standards. Eleven of these members shall be elected quadrennially by the General Board of Education, and ten shall be appointed by the Council of Bishops. Due regard shall be given to representation from the various types of institutions included in the senate's classification of educational institutions. If, in consequence of the retirement of a member from educational work or for any other cause, a vacancy occurs during the quadrennium, it shall be filled by the agency by which the retiring member was elected, at its next meeting.

2. The general secretary of the Division of Higher Education shall be the **executive secretary** of the senate. He shall convene it at the beginning of each quadrennium for organization. The senate shall elect its own officers, including a president, a vice-president, and a recording secretary, and may appoint such committees and may delegate to them such powers as are incident to its work. Thereafter it shall meet annually at such time and place as it may determine. Special meetings may be called on the written request of five members or at the discretion of the president and the executive secretary.

¶ 1384. The senate shall establish and assist in maintaining standards for the educational institutions related to The Methodist Church and shall sustain an advisory relation to the Division of Higher Education in matters of educational institutions. It shall prepare and publish annually a proper classification of all educational institutions in the United States which are related to The Methodist Church. Such classification shall comprise the official senate list of educational institutions related to the church in the United States, and on the basis of this list the division shall be governed in its work.

¶ 1385. At its discretion the senate shall **investigate**

the objectives, academic programs, educational standards, personnel, plant and equipment, business and management practices, financial program, public relations, student personnel services, religious life, and church relations of any designated educational institution claiming or adjudged to be related to The Methodist Church and shall report to the sponsoring board or agency through the Division of Higher Education decisions as to whether or not the institution is such as to justify its official recognition and continued financial support by the church.

¶ **1386.** The senate shall act as consultant and counselor on all educational matters to all educational institutions related to the church and as it deems necessary shall make to the sponsoring board or other agency of the church through the Division of Higher Education, to the Conference Boards of Education, or to other constituent bodies recommendations leading to their improvement or accreditation. Failure of any educational institution to make reasonable progress in complying with said recommendations of the senate may render the institution ineligible for further support by the Division of Higher Education, or by its related board or other agency, Annual Conference, or Conferences.

¶ **1387.** The senate as the accrediting agent for all educational institutions of the church may investigate, on its own initiative or at the written request of any general board of the church or Conference Board of Education or institutional board of trustees, the educational work of an institution related to said board, and shall report to the board concerned its recommendations as to what specific changes or improvements should be made.

¶ **1388.** After consultation with the officers of the senate, the Division of Higher Education shall provide in its annual budget, as it may deem sufficient, for the expense of the senate, except that expenses incurred by the senate on behalf of any other board of the church shall be borne by that board.

¶ **1389.** It shall be the duty of the senate to classify educational institutions in the United States related to The Methodist Church as follows:

　1. Universities

2. Colleges of liberal arts
3. Schools of theology
4. Junior colleges
5. Secondary schools
6. Other schools

The senate shall be consulted before any change in the classification of an institution is proposed.

¶ **1390.** It shall be the duty of the executive secretary of the senate to secure from each educational institution related to The Methodist Church such information as may be needed by the senate for an understanding of the status, work, and progress of the institution. This information shall be supplied on forms approved by the senate.

¶ **1391.** 1. In co-operation with the Division of Higher Education, the senate shall study population growth and trends and consider recommendations to the Annual Conferences concerning the need for new institutions of learning, and the discontinuance, reopening, relocation, and merger of existing institutions. (*See* ¶ 1355.1.)

2. Within the United States no educational institution or foundation (¶ 1359) of The Methodist Church shall hereafter be established or reopened until its plans and organization shall have been approved by the senate. No Annual or Provisional Annual Conference shall acquire or affiliate with a school, college, university, or other educational institution, through any board or society, unless the approval of the senate shall have been obtained previously and unless, in the judgment of the Division of Higher Education, there is reasonable assurance of financial support sufficient to equip and maintain the institution in the classification approved for it by the senate. (*See* ¶ 1355.2.)

Sec. VI. Division of the Local Church

¶ **1396.** The Division of the Local Church shall develop a comprehensive and unified program of Christian education which shall lead to commitment to Christ and membership in his Church and to a knowledge of the Holy Scriptures, the Christian religion, and the Christian Church. It shall provide for worship, fellowship, study, and service, including social, recreational, evangelistic, stewardship, and missionary activities, and education in the Christian way of life. It shall be responsible for forming standards and preparing programs for the organization and work of Christian education in the local church in accordance with provisions as set forth in ¶¶ 231-51, including standards for the offices of director or minister of Christian education and director or minister of music. It shall also seek ways and means of promoting the attendance of children, youth, and adults in all church-school organizations, and especially in the group known as the Sunday school, and shall establish standards defining membership and attendance in the church school and governing the maintenance of the membership roll. In co-operation with the Editorial Division it shall seek to inform the church on all phases of church-school work; shall establish and maintain standards; shall co-operate with the Curriculum Committee in determining the curriculum of the church school, including the courses of leadership education; and give direction to a comprehensive and unified program of Christian education in the local church. It shall provide for instruction concerning the significance and work of the church and the functions of its various officers and boards. In co-operation with the Television, Radio, and Film Commission it shall plan and provide education in the use of audio-visual materials.

¶ 1397. The division shall organize such departments as may be necessary for the proper promotion of Christian education of children, youth, young adults, and other adults in local churches; and for leadership education, evangelism, and missionary education in the church schools.

¶ 1398. 1. The division shall have supervision of all the training processes of the church for both lay and ministerial workers, except where these have been specifically delegated to other agencies.

2. The division shall provide programs for the training of pastors, parents, teachers, officials, and others in the work of the local church, and promote these programs through various types of training schools, correspondence work, and such other agencies as it may see fit to estab-

lish. It shall have authority also to promote and conduct educational conferences, councils, assemblies, and other meetings in the interest of church schools and Christian education of children, youth, and adults, and in the interest of an improved leadership.

¶ 1399. The division shall co-operate with other agencies in the promotion of brotherhoods, men's councils, and kindred organizations to the end that the different organizations of the church may be correlated under a unified program for aggressive Christian service.

¶ 1400. The division shall have authority to co-operate with the Jurisdictional and Annual Conference Boards of Education, the Editorial Division, and other agencies in the promotion and holding of a meeting to be known as the **Methodist Conference on Christian Education.**

¶ 1401. 1. The division shall provide guidance for local churches in equipment, arrangement, and design of church-school buildings or rooms.

2. The division shall develop, in consultation with the Department of Ministerial Education, standards governing the work of local-church directors and ministers of Christian education and concerning their certification as provided in ¶¶ 247, 1451.

3. The division shall develop standards governing the work of local-church directors and ministers of music and serve as may be possible in advancing this field of work in the church. It shall co-operate with the **National Fellowship of Methodist Musicians.**

4. The division shall prepare standards for all types of camping, including standards for camp sites and other physical aspects of camping and standards for the program, leadership, and curriculum for use in Methodist camps, including day camps. In keeping with the policy of The Methodist Church on race (¶ 1824), such standards shall contain a recommendation that all camps shall be available to all persons without regard to race or national origin.

¶ 1402. The division, with the co-operation of the Division of Higher Education where its program is concerned, shall have authority to develop, within the church, organizations of youth, nationally and in jurisdictions, conferences, districts, and subdivisions of districts; *provided*, however, that such organizations shall include all groups within a given age range within the local church.

¶ **1403.** The youth of The Methodist Church between the ages of twelve and twenty-one inclusive, except as provided in ¶ 244.1, who belong to any group for or organizational unit of youth in the church shall be members of the Youth Division, and thereby members of the **Methodist Youth Fellowship.** These provisions shall include college students who are related to the local church through activities which the Commission on Education shall provide. In churches at college campuses these plans shall be worked out co-operatively with the campus-related Methodist student organizations.

¶ **1404.** 1. The Division of the Local Church, with the co-operation of the other agencies of The Methodist Church which have an interest in youth work, is authorized to sponsor the **National Conference of the Methodist Youth Fellowship,** whose functions shall include the following:

a) To initiate and support special plans and projects at the national level which are of particular interest to youth.

b) To provide for the free expression of the convictions of Methodist youth on issues vital to them.

c) To make recommendations regarding the youth ministry of the church.

2. The membership of this conference shall consist of presidents of senior high and older youth organizations of Annual Conferences, or their duly elected representatives; the youth members of the boards and other agencies of the church; six conference directors of youth work (one from each jurisdiction, elected by the conference directors of youth work of that jurisdiction for a two-year term, the election to take place during the Methodist Conference on Christian Education); staff members of the Council on Youth Work of the Division of the Local Church; staff members of the Department of Youth Publications of the Editorial Division; and one staff member each from the Joint Commission on Education

and Cultivation of the Board of Missions, the Board of Christian Social Concerns, the Board of Evangelism, the Interboard Committee on Christian Vocations, the Board of Lay Activities, and the Commission on Chaplains.

3. The conference may meet annually and shall elect its own council, from among whom the Methodist representatives to the Central Committee of the United Christian Youth Movement shall be chosen. The treasurer of the General Board of Education shall be its treasurer. Its financial support shall be provided by the general agencies which co-operate in sponsoring it. It may adopt a constitution and by-laws governing its operations. It shall report annually on its meetings and activities to the Division of the Local Church.

4. For administrative purposes the conference (and staff, if any) shall be related to the Division of the Local Church. Any staff employed shall be recommended by the conference to the general secretary of the division for appropriate action. Such staff shall be responsible to the conference for carrying out its program.

¶ **1405.** 1. The Division of the Local Church shall be responsible for unifying youth work of The Methodist Church, and the Division of Higher Education shall be responsible for unifying student work of The Methodist Church. For the purpose of correlating youth and student work of the General Board of Education, the two divisions shall develop interstaff co-operation between their staff members responsible for youth work and for student work through a **Joint Staff on Youth and Student Work.** This joint staff shall correlate youth and student work of the board, giving particular emphasis to areas of mutual concern. It shall call together as needed the council of officers and staff advisers of the National Conference of the Methodist Youth Fellowship (¶ 1404) and of the National Conference of the Methodist Student Movement (¶ 1369), to meet jointly to review the program and activities of these organizations, discuss needs and trends in youth and student work, and correlate efforts of mutual interest and concern.

2. The joint staff shall nominate youth and student members to the general boards of the church, selecting

youth nominees from lists submitted by the National Conference of the Methodist Youth Fellowship and student nominees from lists submitted by the National Conference of the Methodist Student Movement. It shall consider ability and experience, youth age range, student status, and jurisdictional representation. Youth nominees shall be twenty years of age or younger at the time of their election.

¶ **1407.** 1. In order that church schools may be made available for those for whom The Methodist Church is responsible, the Division of the Local Church shall be authorized to project and promote plans for church-school extension throughout the church, and to contribute to the support of church schools requiring assistance in mission territory.

2. The division shall have authority to enter into agreements with Jurisdictional Boards of Education by which the jurisdictional board may promote a program of church-school extension in accordance with the policies of the general board and employ extension secretaries for work in rural and neglected areas. As part of this agreement, the jurisdictional board shall make an annual budget for the extension program, which shall be submitted, together with quarterly reports on the distribution of the funds herein provided for, to the general secretary of the division.

¶ **1408.** The division shall have the responsibility for working out, in co-operation with Jurisdictional Boards of Education, a general program and plan of organization for the furtherance within the Annual Conference of all the interests of Christian education with the supervision of which the division is charged. This shall include the holding within the conference territory of training schools, conferences, educational councils, federations, assemblies, and such other meetings in the interest of Christian education as the division may deem wise. It shall call together the officers and representatives of the jurisdictional boards for counsel regarding Annual Conference organization and program of work in the field of Christian education in the local church.

¶ **1409.** 1. The division shall have authority to receive

and administer funds, gifts, or bequests that may be committed to it for any portion of its work; and to solicit, establish, and administer any special funds that may be found necessary for the carrying out of its plans and policies.

2. The division may solicit special contributions in the church schools in its own area of work. Only such special solicitations as are approved by the Divisional Committee on the Local Church may be promoted in the church schools.

¶ 1410. The division shall, in co-operation with the Division of Higher Education, discover and give guidance to volunteers for all forms of vocational religious work, offering training courses and all other aids designed to provide vocational guidance for all young people of the church.

Sec. VII. Co-operation With Other Boards

¶ 1412. 1. There shall be an Interboard Committee on Town and Country work. (See ¶ 1285.)

2. There shall be an Interboard Committee on Christian Education. (See ¶¶ 1277-79.)

3. There shall be a Joint Committee on Architecture. (See ¶ 1286.)

4. There shall be an Interboard Committee on Stewardship. (See ¶ 753.4.)

¶ 1413. There shall be an Interboard Committee on Missionary Education for the purpose of promoting effective co-operation between the Board of Missions and the Board of Education. (See ¶¶ 1281-83.)

¶ 1414. 1. In the discharge of its responsibility for youth work in The Methodist Church the Division of the Local Church shall establish and provide for participation by local-church, District, and Conference Methodist Youth Fellowships in the **Methodist Youth Fund.** Local treasurers shall send the full amount of the Methodist Youth Fund offerings to the treasurer of the Annual Conference, by whom it shall be sent monthly to the treasurer of the General Board of Education to be directed for missions and youth work as follows: 45 per cent for missions through the World and National Divisions of the Board of Missions; 25 per cent for Christian education in mission fields to strengthen local-church work through the Annual Conferences; 15 per cent returned to the Annual Conferences for youth work therein; 15 per cent for Christian education through the Division of the Local Church. The Methodist Youth Fund shall be given recognition in a separate column in the pastor's report to the Annual Conference, but shall not receive benevolence credit.

2. There shall be an **Administrative Committee on the Methodist Youth Fund** consisting of the associate general secretaries of the three divisions and joint commission of the Board of Missions, the general secretary and the director of the Council on Youth Work of the Division of the Local Church, the executive secretary of the Interboard Committee on Missionary Education, and the staff member responsible for Methodist Youth Fund education. The committee shall meet at least once a year. It shall have responsibility for annual review of the plans for Methodist Youth Fund education and of the distribution of funds, making recommendations to the responsible agencies for necessary adjustments within the allocations set forth in § 1. It shall give special attention to creative and new developments relative to the use of the fund and to the requests of youth thereon, making provision for youth and adult workers with youth to function in advisory capacities. It shall review and recommend the annual budget to be used for Methodist Youth Fund education by the Methodist Youth Fund office and shall nominate for election by the General Board of Education and confirmation by the Board of Missions such staff as may be necessary. The office shall be lodged in the Division of the Local Church. The staff shall hold membership within this division and likewise in the Joint Commission on Education and Cultivation of the Board of Missions. The committee shall report annually to the two boards and for information annually to the Interboard Committee on Missionary Education.

3. The policies under which the Methodist Youth Fund office operates shall be those agreed on by all the agencies related thereto. Methodist Youth Fund education shall

be planned and carried out in harmony with the philosophy of missionary education expressed through the program and work of the Interboard Committee on Missionary Education and also with the philosophy of unity in the total youth program of the church. (See ¶¶ 1282, 1403.)

¶ 1415. 1. There shall be an **Interboard Committee on Christian Vocations.** Its purpose shall be to develop plans and correlate efforts for the more effective enlistment and guidance of persons in vocations in the church and its agencies, and to seek to interpret to the church through its several agencies the total field of vocation in Christian terms. It shall give leadership in developing a philosophy of Christian vocation, always stressing the potential sacredness of all useful work. It shall lead in discovering and making known the various needs of the church at home and abroad, and seek to enlist youth for Christian service through all the appropriate agencies of the church. (See ¶¶ 146, 670, 675-77, 1209, 1364, 1376, 1557.5) In over-all planning it shall cooperate with its constituent agencies (§ 2) in the development of programs so that reciprocal interests shall be maintained.

2. The committee shall be composed of six bishops, one selected by the College of Bishops of each jurisdiction; four representatives from the Board of Missions, four from the Board of Education, two from the Board of Hospitals and Homes, and one each from the Association of Methodist Theological Schools, the Board of Lay Activities, the Board of Christian Social Concerns, the Commission on Chaplains, and the Board of Evangelism, selected by their respective agencies; and the director of the Department of Ministerial Education. The committee may elect two members at large.

3. The committee shall elect from its membership an **executive committee,** consisting of its chairman, one bishop (unless the chairman is a bishop), one representative from the Department of Ministerial Education, one from the Board of Hospitals and Homes, two from the Board of Education, and two—one a woman—from the Board of Missions.

4. There shall be an **executive secretary** for the com-

mittee, elected by the General Board of Education on nomination of the committee. He shall be responsible to the committee. He shall be administratively related to the Division of the Local Church and have such staff relationships with the other participating agencies as shall be necessary to the promotion of his work.

5. The expenses of the committee shall be met by the participating agencies on such ratio as they may decide.

¶ **1417.** 1. There shall be a **General Committee on Family Life,** which shall be related administratively to the Division of the Local Church and shall co-operate with its staff for Christian family program development to promote activities of a creative nature that can be most efficiently engaged in by the boards working together, including the planning of national, regional, and area conferences on family life. (*See* ¶¶ 234, 1453.)

2. The committee shall be composed of four bishops, one of whom shall be designated chairman, three ministers, and three laymen elected by the Council of Bishops, and staff members or other representatives elected by general agencies as follows: five from the Division of the Local Church and two from the Editorial Division of the Board of Education; two from the Board of Evangelism; one each from the World and National Divisions and one staff and one board member from the Woman's Division of the Board of Missions; one from each division of the Board of Christian Social Concerns; and one each from the Board of Lay Activities, the Television, Radio, and Film Commission, the Board of Hospitals and Homes, the Commission on Chaplains, the Commission on Camp Activities, and The Methodist Publishing House. In addition three ministers and three laymen at large shall be elected by the committee.

3. The program of the committee shall be financed by the General Administration Fund according to the budget adopted by the General Conference.

¶ **1418.** A **Joint Committee on Materials for Training for Church Membership** shall be created by the Board of Education and the Board of Evangelism for the purpose of preparing materials for the training of persons for church membership. These materials shall be co-ordinated with the church-school curriculum and shall be prepared in consultation with the Curriculum Committee. They shall be for training classes of various lengths of time, that there may be ample materials for extended courses when desired. The committee shall be composed of two bishops, three pastors and three laymen (one from each jurisdiction), the general secretaries of the Division of the Local Church and of the Editorial Division of the Board of Education, the general secretary and an additional staff member of the Board of Evangelism, the book editor, the director of the Department of Ministerial Education, and five other qualified persons elected by the committee.

SEC. VIII.   **Education in the Local Church**

The program for education in the local church is described in ¶¶ 231-51, under Part II, The Local Church.

SEC. IX.   **Editorial Division**

¶ **1421.** There shall be an **Editorial Division,** which shall have responsibility for development of the curriculum materials for use in Methodist church schools (see ¶ 243). Materials shall be provided to guide in the development of a balanced, comprehensive, and unified curriculum in the local church. These materials shall be designed to provide opportunities for experience through which the influence of the Holy Spirit may lead children, youth, and adults into a maturing faith in God through commitment to Jesus Christ and his Church.

¶ **1422.** The division shall reflect through its publications and other materials the official positions of The Methodist Church and the policies of the General Board of Education. It shall give appropriate support through its publications and other materials to the world service causes and special emphases authorized by the General Conference.

¶ **1423.** The division may co-operate with the Curriculum Committee in the development for the Board of Education of theological and educational statements representative of Methodist life and thought to serve as a guide in curriculum construction. It may also formulate objectives for the curriculum of Christian education to provide for balance, sequence, and progression. The above shall be subject to the approval of the Board of Education.

¶ **1424.** The division shall issue a list of the curriculum materials that are approved by the Curriculum Committee for use in Methodist church schools. Such materials shall include the materials prepared through the Board of Education and may include materials prepared by other agencies.

¶ **1425.** The division may co-operate with other denominations through the National Council of Churches or in other ways in curriculum planning. It may develop patterns of co-operative publication wherever both the division and The Methodist Publishing House find this to be practicable and in harmony with editorial and publishing policies.

¶ **1426.** The division may co-operate in curriculum planning and construction for and by Methodist bodies overseas, through the Interboard Committee on Christian Education and with such agencies as the National Council of Churches, the World Council of Christian Education and Sunday School Association, and the World Council of Churches.

¶ **1427.** The division may co-operate with the Jurisdictional and Annual Conference Boards of Education, the Division of the Local Church, the Division of Higher Education, and other agencies in the holding of the meetings of the Methodist Conference on Christian Education. (*See* ¶ 1400.)

¶ **1428.** The division shall co-operate through its representatives in the work of the Interboard Committee on Missionary Education (¶ 1281), the Interboard Committee on Christian Education (¶ 1277), the Interboard Committee on Christian Vocations (¶ 1415), the General Committee on Family Life (¶ 1417), the Joint Committee on Materials for Training in Church Membership (¶ 1418), the National Conference of the Methodist Youth Fellowship (¶ 1404), and the Television, Radio, and Film Commission (¶ 1581.2).

¶ **1429.** The **general secretary** of the division, who

shall be the editor of church-school publications (¶¶ 1145-53), shall be elected quadrennially by the General Board of Education from nominations of a joint committee composed of the chairman and two other members of the Board of Publication and the president of the Board of Education and two members from the Editorial Division. The election of the editor shall be subject to confirmation by the Board of Publication. A vacancy in this office shall be filled by the same procedure.

¶ **1430.** The general secretary shall appoint his assistants. He shall be responsible for directing their activities and for establishing their relationships to the General Board of Education and to the Board of Publication.

¶ **1431.** The general secretary shall be responsible to the General Board of Education through the Editorial Division regarding editorial policies, content, and preparation of the church-school publications and other materials. In matters of publication and financing he shall be responsible to the Board of Publication. (*See* ¶¶ 1148-53.)

¶ **1432.** The division shall carry on its activities through a **Department of Children's Publications,** a **Department of Youth Publications, a Department of Adult Publications, a Department of General Publications,** and such other departments as it may determine.

¶ **1433.** 1. There shall be a **Curriculum Committee,** which shall determine the nature and content of the curriculum of the church school. Descriptions of this curriculum shall be recommended by the general secretary to the Editorial Division for final approval by the General Board of Education.

2. The committee shall consist of thirty voting members. Twelve members at large chosen on the basis of training and experience in Christian education, three of whom may be members of the Editorial Division, shall be elected by the board on nomination of the division after consultation with the general secretaries of the three divisions. The other members shall be the three general secretaries; the four editors of children's, youth, adult, and general publications; the three directors of the Councils of Children's, Youth, and Adult Work and

the executive secretary of the Section of Leadership Development of the Division of the Local Church; the publisher, book editor, and vice-president in charge of the Publishing Division of The Methodist Publishing House; the executive secretary of the Interboard Committee on Missionary Education; and one representative each named by the Boards of Christian Social Concerns, Lay Activities, and Evangelism.

3. Members of the staffs of the three divisions of the General Board of Education appointed by the respective general secretaries shall be consulting members of the Curriculum Committee. The executive committee of the board may elect on nomination of the general secretaries additional persons (especially from staffs of other boards and agencies) to serve as consulting members. Consulting members shall have full privileges of membership except for voting on final recommendations to the board.

¶ **1434.** In the development of formats and types of curriculum materials, the Editorial Division shall work co-operatively with the Board of Publication, which agency has final responsibility in relation to publishing and financial matters. The division shall authorize additions or changes in the list of publications to be produced, within the provisions of ¶ 1149. These materials may include a variety of formats, such as periodicals, books and booklets, graphic resources, recordings, and projected audio-visual resources.

¶ **1435.** The publications and materials of the Editorial Division shall be published, manufactured, promoted, and distributed through The Methodist Publishing House as set forth in ¶¶ 1145-53. The interpretation and promotion of these materials shall be a responsibility of the General Board of Education and the Board of Publication.

¶ **1436.** The publisher may sit with the General Board of Education for the consideration of matters pertaining to the joint interests of the Board of Education and the Board of Publication and shall have the privilege of the floor, without vote. (*See also* ¶ 1152.)

SEC. X.   **Jurisdictional Boards**

¶ **1440.** In each jurisdiction there may be a **Jurisdic-**

tional Board of Education, auxiliary to the general board, as the Jurisdictional Conference may determine. (*See* ¶¶ 15.3, 527.)

SEC. XI.   **Annual Conference Boards**

¶ **1441.** In each Annual Conference there shall be a **Conference Board of Education,** elected by the conference to promote church-school extension, the program of Christian education, and the use of church-school literature approved by the General Board of Education. Each conference shall set apart a portion of a session in which the interests of Christian education shall be adequately considered.

¶ **1442. 1.** The board shall be auxiliary to the jurisdictional board, if there be any, and to the general board, and shall co-operate with them. It shall be responsible for developing and promoting a conference program of Christian education which will provide guidance and help for all the agencies of Christian education within the bounds of the conference, such as: the Commissions on Education in local churches and the related agencies of Christian education (*see* ¶¶ 241, 243), leadership training schools, Bible conferences, camps, assemblies, institutes, and other educational agencies. It shall encourage and give help in the use of Methodist curriculum materials. It shall promote and assist all institutions of higher education related to the conference, Wesley Foundations, and the Methodist Student Movement, and shall give leadership and support to the Faculty Christian Movement.

2. The board may be incorporated under the laws of the state (or all of the states) within whose bounds the conference is located. The board may receive gifts for its work. It may hold title to property for use in its work and housing for its personnel. It shall report to each session of the conference on the legal and financial status and physical condition of all such property.

3. The board in co-operation with other conference agencies shall be responsible for developing and recommending to the Annual Conference long-range plans for the procurement of camp and conference properties in accordance with standards of camping developed by the

General Board of Education (¶ 1401.4). The development and operational policies of all camp and conference properties shall be under the direction of the conference board, or organizations delegated by it, in co-operation with other conference agencies. (*See* ¶ 1455.)

¶ **1443.** The board shall be composed of: (1) an equal number of laymen and ministers elected quadrennially, the number and manner of election to be determined by the conference; (2) three representatives of the Conference Methodist Youth Fellowship, of whom one shall be its president, one shall be the president or duly elected representative of its Older Youth Council or Committee, and the third shall be chosen by the fellowship and shall be twenty years of age or younger at the time of his selection; and one student chosen by the state or regional student organization operating within the conference territory; (3) the president of the Conference Young Adult Fellowship; (4) one certified director or minister of Christian education employed in a local church within the conference; and (5) additional members, either clerical or lay, nominated at any time during the quadrennium by the board in such numbers as it may deem advisable, for election by the conference. Vacancies in the elected membership between conference sessions may be filled by the executive committee of the board pending the action of the next conference session. Care shall be taken to elect persons who, by training and experience, are qualified for the work of the board. No salaried officer or employee of the board shall be a member. A majority of the members shall constitute a quorum. The members shall continue in office until their successors have been elected and the successor board organized.

¶ **1444.** The officers of the board shall be a president, vice-president, recording secretary, and treasurer, all of whom shall be elected by the board for the quadrennium. There shall also be an executive secretary (who may serve two or more contiguous conferences), elected by the board after consultation with the bishop and his Cabinet and confirmed by the conference; *provided* that in the filling of a vacancy which occurs between conference sessions the approval of the conference shall not be required for the interim period. The retiring board shall complete the business and make its annual report to the conference, and shall make such recommendations as it may desire to the new board.

¶ **1446.** The president shall be a presiding, not an administrative, officer. The treasurer, who shall be adequately bonded, shall receive, and receipt for, all funds of the board and disburse them by check as ordered by the board.

¶ **1447.** There shall be an **executive committee** of the board, of which the president shall be a member. The executive committee shall meet on the call of the president or of one third of the members, and shall transact all necessary business of the board *ad interim*, under such regulations as the board may adopt. Its acts shall be reported to the annual meeting of the board. The executive committee shall act as the finance committee of the board, and shall prepare a statement of its financial needs for the next year.

¶ **1448.** 1. The **executive secretary** shall have responsibility for the general oversight and promotion of all the work of the board and for the direction and supervision of its salaried and other workers, who shall report to him as may be required. He shall make a full report annually both to the board and to each of the three general secretaries of the general board.

2. The executive secretary shall give leadership and direction to the program of Christian education in the local churches, enlisting the co-operation of the district superintendents and the district directors.

3. The executive secretary shall give active co-operation to the Methodist schools, colleges, and universities within the conference; through the Interconference Commission on College and University Religious Life assist in supporting the Wesley Foundations and co-ordinating the intercollegiate program of the Methodist Student Movement within the state or region; and help to integrate the work of Christian education as undertaken by the local church and by the schools and colleges. He shall consult with this commission about the duties and relation to the

conference staff of the state or regional director of the Methodist Student Movement.

4. On nomination of the executive secretary such additional salaried and other workers as the board may deem necessary shall be elected annually by the board. The executive secretary shall consult with the responsible officers of the Conference Methodist Youth Fellowship before nominating conference directors of youth work.

5. The executive secretary shall nominate annually, after consultation with each district superintendent, the district directors, as provided in ¶ 1460.

¶ 1449. The board shall report its proceedings and policies to the Annual Conference, including the treasurer's report, showing all resources and liabilities of the board, its income and its expenditures. Immediately following the conference session it shall report to the Jurisdictional Board of Education, through its executive secretary, a summary of its acts and the names of its officers and salaried workers. It shall transmit to the jurisdictional board the names and addresses of church-school superintendents and the officers of the district and conference organizations operating under the conference board and of youth assemblies and other organizations.

¶ 1450. The president, or someone designated by him, shall present to the Commission on World Service and Finance of the conference the financial needs of the colleges and Wesley Foundations related to the conference (as determined by the board on recommendation of its Committee or Commission on Christian Higher Education), of the work of the board in its field program of Christian education in the local churches of the conference, and of other work in which the board may be engaged. In accordance with the financial plan of the church, an apportionment shall be allotted to the churches within the conference for the work of the Conference Board of Education. Other sources of income shall be gifts, returns from special days, and receipts from missionary offerings in the church school. The board shall determine the distribution of the funds thus received to each of the general interests under the care of the board.[16]

[16] See Judicial Council Decisions 188, 191.

Note: For description of the program for Christian Education Sunday, Methodist Student Day, and Race Relations Sunday *see* ¶ 250.2-.4.

¶ **1451.** 1. It shall be the duty of the board to determine whether applicants meet the standards of the general board for directors and ministers of Christian education (¶¶ 247.1, 1401.2) and directors and ministers of music (¶¶ 247.2, 1401.3), and to certify and keep a record of those who do. The board shall set up a committee or committees on these offices whose duties shall be: (*a*) to review the credentials of candidates and make recommendations to the board for certification in harmony with the said standards and (*b*) to recommend to the board plans for institutes, conferences, and other occasions for fellowship and training for directors and ministers of Christian education and educational assistants, and for directors and ministers of music and music assistants and others responsible for music in the local church. Whenever possible one or more directors or ministers of Christian education and of music shall serve on this committee. All persons certified shall furnish to the board, on blanks provided by the general board, information for purposes of annual review and approval of status.

2. A roster of certified directors and ministers of Christian education and certified directors and ministers of music shall be included in the annual report of the board and published in the conference journal. A person so certified may move to another Annual Conference and be recorded there without re-establishing status.

3. Certified directors of Christian education may be consecrated and commissioned at a conference session or other suitable time.

¶ **1452.** 1. The board shall constitute a **Conference Committee on Christian Higher Education,** composed of not fewer than eight of its members. This committee shall have specific responsibility for developing knowledge of and support for the schools, colleges, universities, schools of theology, and Wesley Foundations related to The Methodist Church and particularly those related to the conference.

2. An Annual Conference, at its discretion, may enlarge

the committee into a **Conference Commission on Christian Higher Education,** which shall include the members of the committee, the executive secretary of the board, the bishop and district superintendents, the conference lay leader, the president of the Conference Woman's Society of Christian Service, the state or regional director of the Methodist Student Movement, and up to twenty members at large elected by the committee because of their experience and ability in the field of education. The members shall be named as soon after the adjournment of the General Conference as feasible. They shall serve four years except that ex officio membership shall coincide with term of office. The commission shall elect its officers quadrennially, and they shall serve until their successors are duly elected and qualified. It may employ such staff members as are deemed necessary for its work. The Annual Conference shall make provision for its expense as the conference may determine.

3. Two or more Annual Conferences may, on recommendation of their Boards of Education, join in constituting an **Area** or **Regional Commission on Christian Higher Education,** the membership of which shall be determined by the co-operating conferences in consultation with their bishop or bishops and shall include representatives of the Conference Committees on Christian Higher Education.

4. The committee or commission shall:

a) Co-operate with the Division of Higher Education in the achievement of its objectives (¶¶ 1351-52).

b) Make provision for such conferences, training courses, and study groups as will assist in meeting its responsibility.

c) Report annually to the board and the Annual Conference on the programs of those institutions of learning and Wesley Foundations related to the conference and supported by it, including a statement concerning the capital and current financial needs of each and their program of service to The Methodist Church. (*See* ¶ 1351.)

d) Recommend annually to the board, for presentation to the Annual Conference, a minimum goal for the support of educational institutions and Wesley Foundations; or, if none are related to the conference, recommend the method of distributing to Methodist educational institutions, either directly or through the Division of Higher Education, the funds raised for higher education.[17]

¶ 1453. The board may constitute a **Conference Committee on Family Life,** composed of the executive secretary and two members of the board; the conference directors of children's, youth, and adult work; one representative each from the Conference Methodist Youth Fellowship and Young Adult Fellowship and from the Conference Boards of Lay Activities and Evangelism; the secretary of Christian social relations of the Conference Woman's Society of Christian Service; and one district superintendent elected by the Cabinet. Special resource persons may be added as the committee shall determine. Its duty shall be to study the forces which affect family life within the conference and recommend to the board program plans to strengthen family life. It shall be administratively related to the board and shall report to it annually. (*See* ¶¶ 234, 1417.)

¶ 1454. The board may constitute a **Committee on Use of Methodist Curriculum Materials,** composed of the executive secretary, the conference director of general church-school work, and one member of the board from each district. This committee shall encourage the adoption of Methodist curriculum materials by any classes, groups, or church schools not now using them.

¶ 1455. 1. On recommendation of the board, in cooperation with other conference agencies, the Annual Conference may constitute a **Conference Committee on Camps and Conferences,** composed of the executive secretary and three or more members of the board, of whom one shall be a youth and one a young adult; the conference directors of camps and conferences, children's work, youth work, adult work, and general church-school work; one or more district superintendents elected by the Cabinet; the chairmen of District Committees on Camps and Conferences (¶ 1461); a representative of

---

[17] *See* Judicial Council Decision 191.

the trustees of any camp or conference properties of the board (¶ 1442.3); one representative each from the Conference Board of Trustees and any other incorporated trustees holding title to properties used extensively in the Christian education program of camping, conferences, and related enterprises of the Annual Conference or of the districts; and a representative each from the Conference Woman's Society of Christian Service and the Conference Board of Lay Activities. Other persons may be added on the basis of qualifications to meet specific needs.

2. The committee may select, develop, and operate properties as charged by the board and authorized by the Annual Conference; develop and recommend to the board policies and long-range plans for the selection, development, and operation of campsites and facilities to meet program needs; recommend fund-raising procedures for the purchase and development of sites and facilities; and work with District Committees on Camps and Conferences as directed by the board.

¶ 1456. The board shall have authority, in co-operation with the Conference Television, Radio, and Film Commission, to provide training conferences for selected persons in the Annual Conference, district, and local church in the effective use of audio-visual materials. (*See* ¶ 1583.1.)

¶ 1457. The board shall have authority to co-operate with other conference boards in matters of common interest. It shall also have authority to co-operate with the General and Jurisdictional Boards of Education and other agencies in the holding of the Methodist Conference on Christian Education. (*See* ¶ 1400.)

Note: For the constitution of the Commission on Town and Country Work *see* ¶ 1302.

1458. In each Annual Conference there shall be an official conference youth organization known as the **Conference Methodist Youth Fellowship.** Its purpose shall be to strengthen the youth program in the local churches of the conference. It shall be under the sponsorship and the responsibility of the Conference Board of Education, to which it shall report, and of the General Board of Education. It shall co-operate with other agencies with which youth are concerned within the conference and with the National Conference of the Methodist Youth Fellowship (¶ 1404). The executive secretary of the conference board and the conference director of youth work shall be advisers to its council.

SEC. XII.　　**District Organizations**

¶ 1460. In each district the Annual Conference shall elect annually a district director of adult work, of youth work, of children's work, and of general church-school work, and such others as may be desired, who with the district superintendent shall constitute the **district staff of Christian education.** They shall be nominated by the executive secretary of the Conference Board of Education, after consultation with the district superintendent, and the nominations shall be reported to the board for confirmation and transmittal to the Annual Conference. Interim vacancies shall be filled by the executive secretary in consultation with the district superintendent. Unless otherwise stipulated by the board, the district director of general church-school work shall .serve as chairman and, in situations where separate statements are impractical, spokesman for the staff.

¶ 1461. 1. The District or Annual Conference may constitute a **District Committee on Camps and Conferences** on recommendation of the district staff of Christian education, in co-operation with other district agencies. The chairman shall be nominated and confirmed in the same manner as the district directors (¶ 1460). The committee shall include the district superintendent and other members of the district staff, at least one camp director or institute dean representing each age group actively involved in camps and conferences and related enterprises in the district, and other persons to meet specific needs.

2. Its responsibilities shall be: to co-operate with the Conference Committee on Camps and Conferences (¶ 1455) ; to make available to pastors and church-school superintendents information as to suitable locations and recommended guidance materials relating to camping, conferences, and retreats; to encourage and initiate train-

ing for such enterprises; to interpret and assist the local church in implementing standards relating to program and leadership and to the use and care of any sites or facilities used for camping, planning conferences, and retreats; and to refer to the district staff, for confirmation by the District Conference, nominations by the age-group directors of persons to serve as directors or deans of summer camps, institutes, or conferences sponsored by the district.

3. If the committee is charged with the development and/or operation of camp or conference facilities held in trust by the Conference or District Board of Trustees, there shall be added to its membership a representative from such board. The selection, development, or improvement of any such properties, or of conference- or district-owned property the title to which is vested in other incorporated boards but which is used primarily for Christian education enterprises of the district, shall be in harmony with the policies and standards of the Conference and General Boards of Education.

4. District property may be acquired for use in the program of camps and conferences when authorized by the District or Annual Conference on recommendation of the district staff of Christian education, after consultation with the Conference Board of Education and in keeping with the standards of the general board.

Chapter IX

BOARD OF EVANGELISM

Section I.   The Aim of Evangelism

¶ 1464. The aim of evangelism is to bring all men into living, active fellowship with God through Jesus Christ as divine Savior and through the regenerating power of the Holy Spirit; to gather them into the fellowship of the Church; to lead them to express their Christian discipleship in every area of human life that the kingdom of God may be realized.

Sec. II   **Incorporation**

¶ **1465.** There shall be an incorporated **General Board of Evangelism** of The Methodist Church, hereinafter called the board. It shall be incorporated under the laws of the state in which its headquarters are established by the General Conference; or the present Tennessee charter of incorporation of the Commission on Evangelism may be amended.

Sec. II   **Constitution**

¶ **1466.** *Article 1. Name and Object.*—The name of this organization shall be the General Board of Evangelism of The Methodist Church. Its objects are religious, evangelistic, designed to diffuse the blessings of the gospel of the Lord Jesus Christ by the promotion and support of all forms and phases of evangelism; to promote evangelistic intelligence, interest, and zeal throughout the membership of The Methodist Church; to promote the practice of intercession and of individual and family worship; and to stimulate the entire membership of the church in worship and in Christian service.

¶ **1467.** *Art. 2. Authority.*—The board shall have authority to regulate its own proceedings in accordance with its constitution and charter; to buy, acquire, receive by gift, devise, or bequest, property, real, personal, and mixed, and to hold, sell, and dispose of property; to secure, appropriate, and administer funds for its work; to sue and be sued; to elect the necessary officers and members of its staff, remove them for cause, and fill vacancies; to make by-laws in harmony with the Discipline of The Methodist Church and the charter of the board; and it shall have the right to do any and all things which shall be authorized by its charter; *provided* that, in cases of devises or gifts of real estate to this board in states where such devises or gifts are not valid when made to religious corporations, the board shall be empowered to name trustees for the purpose of receiving and taking title to such gifts or devises for the benefit of the board.

¶ **1468.** *Art. 3. Membership.*—The membership of the board shall be composed of six bishops, with representa-

tion from each jurisdiction, elected by the Council of
Bishops at the time of the General Conference; two ministers, one lay man, and one lay woman from each jurisdiction, elected by the Jurisdictional Conferences; the
secretary of spiritual life of the Woman's Division of the
Board of Missions; and a member of the council of the
National Conference of the Methodist Youth Fellowship, a
student representative of the National Conference of the
Methodist Student Movement, and twelve members from
the church at large, elected by the board.

¶ **1469.** *Art. 4. President.*—The president of the board
shall be a bishop elected by the board. He shall make a
report and present a program of work for the board to
the Council of Bishops for their approval at each regular
meeting of the council.

¶ **1470.** *Art. 5. Other Officers.*—The board shall elect
from its membership a vice-president, a recording secretary, and an **executive committee** of seven members, including the president of the board, the other six members
to be selected by the board, one from each jurisdiction.
A treasurer shall be elected by the board, and shall be a
member of the staff.

¶ **1471.** *Art. 6. Executive Officers.*—The board shall elect
a **general secretary** and, on nomination by the executive
committee, shall elect such other secretaries, directors,
and editors as may be needed.

¶ **1472.** *Art. 7. Financial Support.*—The financial support of the general work of the board shall be derived
from the general benevolence funds of the church, and
that of *The Upper Room* as provided for in ¶ 1485.

¶ **1473.** *Art. 8. Meetings.*—The Board shall hold an annual meeting and such other meetings as it may deem
necessary for the accomplishment of the work.

¶ **1474.** *Art. 9. Duties.*—1. The board shall give particular emphasis to the promotion of full, well-rounded, and
practical programs of evangelism on the conference, district, and local-church levels. To this end it shall give
guidance and help to the Jurisdictional Boards of Evangelism, the Conference Boards of Evangelism, the District
Committees on Evangelism, and the Commissions on
Membership and Evangelism in local churches. (*See*

¶ 119.) The board shall give guidance to the church in using the appropriate days and seasons of the Christian calendar for special evangelistic emphasis.

2. The board shall set up standards for **conference evangelists** and shall make these standards known to the church at large. It shall send copies of the standards annually to the bishops, the district superintendents, the Conference Boards of Evangelism, and the Association of Conference Evangelists. It shall provide uniform report blanks for use of the conference evangelist in reporting to the Annual Conference. It shall supervise the work of the Association of Conference Evangelists.

3. The board shall establish a **general roll of military service personnel** and families and shall be authorized to record thereon the names of persons whose certificates of membership are sent to it by Methodist chaplains. It shall be responsible for continued contact and cultivation of such service persons and their families until they have been transferred to a local church.

(For the responsibility of the board in producing and distributing literature for the cultivation of the devotional life *see* ¶ 1485.)

¶ **1475.** *Art.* 10. *Co-operation.*—The board shall co-operate with the various agencies of the church in the training of our ministers for leadership in the field of evangelism and in creating a literature to serve the cause for evangelism. (For interboard agencies on which the Board of Evangelism is represented *see* ¶¶ 1160, 1164, 1285, 1415, 1417, 1418, 1433.)

¶ **1476.** *Art.* 11. *Chaplains.*—The board and its staff shall co-operate closely with the Commission on Chaplains. It shall attempt to help Methodist chaplains in every possible way, informing them concerning all forms and phases of evangelism, including evangelistic and devotional literature. (*See also* ¶ 1474.3.)

SEC. IV. **Jurisdictional Board of Evangelism**

¶ **1477.** In each jurisdiction there may be a **Jurisdictional Board of Evangelism,** auxiliary to the general board, as the Jurisdictional Conference may determine. (*See* ¶¶ 15.3, 527.)

Sec. V. **Annual Conference Board of Evangelism**

¶ **1478.** 1. Each Annual Conference shall elect for the quadrennium a **Conference Board of Evangelism,** which shall plan and promote a program of evangelism throughout the conference. It shall give guidance to the District Committees on Evangelism and to local-church Commissions on Membership and Evangelism in carrying out their purposes and responsibilities, as outlined in ¶ 222 (*see* § 5 *below*); and it shall co-operate with the general and jurisdictional boards in promoting evangelistic plans and programs.

2. The board shall include in its membership the district superintendents, the district secretaries of evangelism, the vice-chairmen of the District Committees on Evangelism, one pastor from each district, such members of the general and jurisdictional boards as reside within the bounds of the conference, the secretary of spiritual life of the Conference Woman's Society of Christian Service, a layman nominated by the Conference Board of Lay Activities, the conference secretary of evangelism, and the chairman of Christian witness of the Conference Methodist Youth fellowship, together with a representative from any other organization that the conference desires. If the conference desires, its nominating committee may nominate additional members, one half of whom shall be ministers and one half laymen; *provided* that no salaried officer, employee, or one receiving remuneration from the board shall be a member thereof.

3. The board shall elect its own chairman, vice-chairman (who shall serve as conference director of The Twelve), recording secretary, and treasurer quadrennially together with such other officers and executive committee members as desired, and shall fill vacancies throughout the quadrennium as they occur. At the end of the quadrennium the retiring board shall complete its business and make its report to the Annual Conference and its recommendations to the new board. The new board shall organize immediately, formulate plans for an ongoing evangelism, and also make its report and recommendations to the Annual Conference.

4. The chairman shall be the presiding, not the administrative, officer of the board, and shall not be the conference secretary or director of evangelism. His duties shall be to preside over all board and executive committee meetings, to present the report of the board to the Annual Conference, and to support the evangelistic causes and programs of the conference. In co-operation with the secretary or director he shall annually present the askings of the board to the Commission on World Service and Finance (¶ 793).

5. The board shall divide itself into six standing committees, each committee to have as its major purpose the carrying out in the conference of one of the groupings of duties listed in ¶ 222.

¶ 1479. 1. Each Annual Conference, on nomination of its Board of Evangelism, shall elect annually a **conference secretary of evangelism** (except as provided in § 2), to be publicly assigned by the bishop, who shall promote the policies and program of the General, Jurisdictional, and Conference Boards of Evangelism in the Annual Conference. He shall be the administrative and executive officer of the board. It shall be his duty to lead in program planning, to implement and execute the plans and programs adopted, and to carry the leadership of evangelism throughout the conference, working closely with the board, the bishop, the district superintendents, and district secretaries of evangelism, and the District Committees on Evangelism. He shall direct the expenditure of the funds of the board, faithfully adhering to its program and financial policies.

2. The board may elect, after consultation with the bishop and his Cabinet, a full-time **conference director of evangelism,** who shall be subject to confirmation by the Annual Conference; *provided* that in filling a vacancy confirmation shall not be required for the interim period. He shall serve as the administrative and executive officer of the board, instead of a conference secretary of evangelism, and shall assume all the duties assigned to that office (*see* § 1). Additional duties shall be carefully outlined by the board, to which he shall be amenable. He

shall have no vote in board or executive committee meetings.

¶ **1480.** The board may recommend to the Annual Conference and to the bishop in charge the appointment of certain effective members of the conference as **conference evangelists;** *provided* that such persons shall meet the standards set up by the general board and the conference board for conference evangelists (¶ 1474.2).

Sec. VI. District Committee on Evangelism

¶ **1481.** 1. Each district of each Annual Conference shall provide a **District Committee on Evangelism,** which shall promote the program of evangelism as outlined by the general board and in co-operation with the Conference Board of Evangelism.

2. The committee shall include in its membership such members of the conference board as reside within the bounds of the district, the secretary of spiritual life of the District Woman's Society of Christian Service, the chairman of Christian witness or a representative elected by the District Methodist Youth Fellowship, the district lay leader or a representative elected by the District Board of Lay Activities, the district superintendent, the conference evangelists whose Quarterly Conference membership is within the district, and also at least three pastors, three lay men, three lay women, and three youth members, distributed equitably throughout the sections of the district, elected by the District Conference or, if no District Conference is held, appointed by the district superintendent.

3. The committee shall divide itself into six standing subcommittees, each to have as its major purpose the carrying out in the district of one of the groupings of duties listed in ¶ 222.

¶ **1482.** In order to reach the unchurched and the unsaved, the committee, under the leadership of the district superintendent, shall seek to work out areas of evangelistic responsibility, geographic or otherwise, in whatever manner may seem to be most feasible in each situation, so that no unsaved or unchurched person may be omitted from the responsibility of some local church. (*See* ¶ 104.)

¶ **1483.** There shall be a **district secretary of evangelism** in each district, nominated by the district superintendent and publicly assigned by the bishop, who shall be other than the conference secretary of evangelism, the chairman of the conference board, or the district superintendent. He shall be chairman of the committee, and a layman selected by the district superintendent shall be vice-chairman and shall serve as district director of The Twelve. The chairman and the vice-chairman shall work in co-operation with the district superintendent, the conference board, and the conference secretary or director of evangelism.

SEC. VII.   **Local-Church Commission**

¶ **1484.** Each local church shall have a Commission on Membership and Evangelism. (*See* ¶¶ 219-22, under Part II, The Local Church.)

SEC. VIII.   *The Upper Room*

¶ **1485.** The General Board of Evangelism is hereby instructed to assume the management and publication of *The Upper Room* and to produce and distribute such literature as that now represented by *The Upper Room* for the cultivation of the devotional life; *provided*, however, that no funds either now in hand or hereafter accumulated by *The Upper Room* or other devotional and related literature hereafter produced shall be used for the support of other features of the board's work, but all net income from the sale of such publications shall be conserved by the board for the purpose of preparing and circulating such literature; *provided*, however, that this shall not prevent the setting up of a reserve fund out of such produce as a protection against unforeseen emergencies.

Chapter X

BOARD OF LAY ACTIVITIES

SECTION I.   The General Board

¶ 1490. 1. There shall be a **General Board of Lay Activities** of The Methodist Church.

2. The purpose of the board shall be to deepen the spiritual life of the lay members of the church and to cultivate among them an increasing sense of responsibility, loyalty, and interest in Christian thinking and participation, that they may become a part of the active working force in the mission of the church at large and each local church.

¶ 1491. 1. The board shall be composed of three effective bishops, elected by the Council of Bishops; six effective ministers, one from each jurisdiction; and thirty-two lay members, twenty-seven of whom shall be distributed among the several jurisdictions on the basis of church membership; *provided* that no jurisdiction shall have fewer than two lay members. The six ministers and the twenty-seven lay members shall be elected by the Jurisdictional Conferences on nomination of their Committees on Lay Activities; *provided* that the lay members shall be selected from the present or past conference lay leaders of the several Annual Conferences in the jurisdiction. There shall be five lay members at large from within the United States, elected by the board on nomination of the Council of Bishops. There shall also be one lay member at large from outside the United States, elected by the board on nomination of the Council of Bishops. This shall be an annual election, and each man so elected shall not be eligible to succeed himself. The following shall be ex officio members: the secretary of stewardship or other national officer of the National Conference of the Methodist Youth Fellowship, the president or other national officer of the Methodist Student Movement, and the president or other national officer of the Woman's Division of the Board of Missions. Interim vacancies in the lay membership shall be filled by the board itself.

2. The headquarters of the board shall be fixed by the General Conference.

3. The board shall be duly incorporated.

¶ 1492. 1. The board shall be charged with leadership for and development of the several major areas of the work of lay activities in The Methodist Church, and shall use suitable means to promote an effective general program, to co-operate with other agencies of the church in the interest of lay activities, and to assist Jurisdictional, Annual Conference, and District Boards of Lay Activities in their programs, to the end that every available resource may be provided to help each local church carry on an effective program of lay activities.

2. The board shall develop effective methods for the program of lay activities in the local church and provide instructional and promotional materials to encourage their use. In particular it shall develop a program of sound finance for the local church, including the continual development and improvement of the annual every-member visitation program, with methods and materials for its promotion, and also the simultaneous every-member visitation program. It shall produce training and program materials for conference, district, and local-church lay leaders, and training courses and other materials for Methodist Men and lay speakers.

¶ 1493. The board shall elect a **general secretary**, who shall have general supervision of the work under the direction of the board, and who shall be subject to the authority and control of the board. On nomination of the general secretary, such other staff members as the board deems necessary shall be elected by the board. The board shall have authority to fill vacancies in offices occurring *ad interim*, including that of the general secretary.

¶ 1494. The board is authorized to solicit and create special funds, to receive gifts and bequests, to hold properties and securities in trust, and to administer all these financial affairs in accordance with its own rules and the provisions of the Discipline.

¶ 1495. The work of the board shall be considered a benevolent interest of the church, and the Council on

World Service and Finance shall include in the appropriations recommended for adoption by the General Conference such sum as may be necessary for the proper support of the board. The board shall report to the council its estimate of the amount needed annually for its work.

¶ **1496.** The board shall be organized quadrennially by the election of the six members at large, a president, a vice-president, a recording secretary, chairmen of the three sections, the general secretary, a treasurer, and such other officers as it may determine are necessary for the conduct of its business. It shall have authority to regulate its own proceedings, including the fixing of the time for its annual sessions. All officers and members of the board shall remain in office until their successors are duly elected and qualified, following which the new board shall be organized. The board shall report quadrennially to the General Conference and to the several Jurisdictional Conferences.

¶ **1497.** There shall be a **Section of Men's Work,** which shall have the following responsibilities:

1. **Methodist Men** shall be the authorized organization for the men of the church. The formation and chartering of a local unit of Methodist Men in every pastoral charge and the development of an effective, efficient organization shall be a continuing objective. (*See* ¶¶ 291-92).

2. The section shall give special consideration to (*a*) the training and the active participation of the non-affiliated men in all programs and work of the church and (*b*) correlating men's work with other lay work.

3. Recognizing that individuals grow in Christian character not only through private study and devotion but also through the stimulus that arises from interchange of ideas, purposes, and interests among individuals and groups, the section shall develop opportunities for men to grow spiritually through sharing in the execution of challenging plans and special projects designed to serve the kingdom of God. Through participation in workshops and similar activities it shall emphasize the importance of, and shall plan for participation of men in, personal evangelism, especially among men and boys, active shar-

ing through Christian social activities, and regular attendance at church services.

4. The section shall solicit the co-operation of the Jurisdictional and Annual Conference Boards of Lay Activities and other agencies in the promotion and holding each quadrennium of a **National Conference of Methodist Men.**

5. To assist in fulfilling the total mission of The Methodist Church, the section may, in co-operation with the Television, Radio, and Film Commission, promote and follow up a radio program as one of its special projects.

¶ **1498.** There shall be a **Section of Stewardship and Finance,** which shall be responsible for:

1. Setting forth and promoting concepts of Christian stewardship in The Methodist Church. It shall provide consultation for other agencies where the concepts of stewardship are being considered in literature and program. It shall use all practicable means to promote the principles of stewardship to the point where they will be understood, accepted, and practiced by all Methodists.

2. Developing a sound program of finance for the local church. In recognition that the success of every function of the local church is dependent on adequate finances, the section is charged with the responsibility to develop a suitable financial system for the local church. This shall include a continuing stewardship education, the development and constant up-dating of every-member visitation plans and methods, the provision of training and leadership guidance for simultaneous every-member visitation on a district, conference, or area basis, and direction for the every-member visitation in local churches.

3. Giving careful attention to assuring adequate support for the ministry, taking into consideration such factors as cost of living, cost of education, travel, automobile expense, and an adequate standard of living.

4. Keeping all Methodists informed of the ever-growing need for increased world service and other benevolent giving by our membership, and giving all possible encouragement to increased giving for world service and other benevolent purposes.

5. (a) Providing certified business and administrative

practices in the local church, (b) providing counsel for local-church administrators or church business managers, and (c) developing standards for in-service training and co-ordinating efforts to provide academic training and recognition.

6. Giving leadership, direction, and training to the Commission on Stewardship and Finance of the local church in matters pertaining to budget building, the raising of adequate funds for local needs and world-wide needs, and proper keeping of the financial records of the local church's work.

7. Soliciting the co-operation of the Jurisdictional and Annual Conference Boards of Lay Activities and other agencies in the promotion and holding each quadrennium of a **National Convocation on Christian Stewardship.**

8. Taking such action as may be deemed necessary to encourage Methodists to provide for their continued interest in world service, or in one or more of the world service agencies, through wills, legacies, and gifts. The section shall co-operate with local-church Committees on Wills and Legacies (¶ 145.10) and with Conference Committees on Wills, Bequests, and Gifts (¶ 1505) in such ways as may be deemed mutually helpful.

¶ **1499.** The **Section of Leadership Development and Communications** shall have the following responsibilities:

1. The section shall have the duty to develop lay leadership for the promotion of all phases of lay work. It shall assist, guide, and co-operate with conference boards in holding retreats within the bounds of the Annual Conferences for inspiration, fellowship, and information among the laymen of the conference. It shall: (a) co-operate with conference and district organizations in the training of the laity to work effectively in each phase; (b) enlist the co-operation of conference, district, and local-church lay leaders and organizations to make use of periodicals and materials furnished by the church to the laity, giving special attention to those referred to in ¶ 1492.2; (c) co-operate with other agencies in finding the greatest possible service for every person who belongs to The Methodist Church. It may establish permanent lay training centers wherever possible for the undergirding

of the lay ministry in the church and for the spiritual, educational, and theological edification of laymen in the churches. Such centers shall be established in co-operation with institutions of higher education and schools of theology of The Methodist Church after consultation with the General Board of Education, and may be established in co-operation with other denominations whenever practicable.

2. The section shall supervise the program of lay speaking and shall give leadership and direction to the development of training courses and other materials for lay speakers, and such other means to encourage the development of an adequate number of qualified lay speakers to the ends (a) that there may be no silent pulpits in Methodist churches, and (b) that laymen may be able to articulate their faith and witness within the organizational structure of the church and in groups and meetings out in the world. Lay schools of theology may be set up and scheduled in co-operation with institutions of higher education and schools of theology of The Methodist Church.

3. One Sunday each year shall be designated as **Laymen's Day,** the program to be under the direction of the General Board of Lay Activities. Laymen's Day shall be observed in each local church for the purpose of emphasizing the importance of the ministry of the laity in the life and work of the church. The official date for Laymen's Day shall be the date approved by the General Division of United Church Men of the National Council of the Churches of Christ in the United States of America as a joint observance by the constituent denominations; provided that this designation of a date shall not apply to conferences outside the United States.

4. The section shall provide a program of training for Official Boards, to help the officers and members become acquainted with their responsibilities, understand and appreciate the organization of the church, and co-ordinate the total program of the local church with the program of the church at large.

5. The section shall give leadership, direction, and training to conference, district, and local-church lay

leaders, lay members of the Annual Conference, and organizations in carrying out the purpose set forth in ¶ 1492.1.

6. The section shall provide counsel and training for the local-church Board of Trustees.

SEC. II.   **Jurisdictional Boards**

¶ **1501.** In each jurisdiction there may be a **Jurisdictional Board of Lay Activities,** auxiliary to the general board, as the Jurisdictional Conference may determine. (*See* ¶¶ 15.3, 527.)

SEC. III.   **Annual Conference Boards**

¶ **1502.** 1. There shall be in every Annual Conference a **Conference Board of Lay Activities,** composed of the conference lay leader (¶ 1504.1), who shall be chairman, the associate conference lay leaders and conference directors of program activities if any (¶ 1504.4), the district and associate district lay leaders (¶ 1508.1), the district superintendents, any members of the general and jurisdictional boards residing within the conference, and three members at large, if desired, nominated by the Cabinet in consultation with the conference lay leader and elected by the Annual Conference.

2. The board shall elect a vice-chairman, secretary, and treasurer.

3. The board may set up an **executive committee,** composed of the conference lay leader as chairman, the elected officers (§ 2), the associate conference lay leaders and conference directors of program activities if any, and the district superintendents and district lay leaders.

¶ **1503.** 1. Within the Annual Conference the board shall promote a program of lay activities as outlined in ¶¶ 1497-99, auxiliary to that of the general board. It shall be charged with leadership for and development of the several major areas of the work of lay activities in the conference, and shall use suitable means to promote an effective conference program, to co-operate with other conference agencies in the interest of lay activities, and to assist District Boards of Lay Activities in their programs, to the end that every available resource may be provided to help each local church carry on an effective program of lay activities.

2. The board shall use the training and program materials prepared by the general board for district and local-church lay leaders, and shall encourage the use of other training, instructional, and promotional materials developed and distributed by the general board. (See ¶ 1492.2.)

3. The board shall co-operate with the General and Jurisdictional Boards of Lay Activities in promoting and encouraging attendance at the National Conference of Methodist Men and the Convocation on Christian Stewardship.

4. The board shall co-operate with the other conference boards in executing their plans for larger service in the work of the church.

5. The board shall co-operate with the Committee on Wills, Bequests, and Gifts (¶ 1505) in promoting and encouraging Methodists and friends of the church to make wills and other bequests which remember the conference and general agencies and institutions as well as the local church.

6. The board shall report to the Annual Conference each year and shall hold an anniversary, or otherwise provide for an adequate representation of the work of lay activities during the session of the conference.

7. The board shall hold an annual meeting in connection with the Annual Conference session and such other meetings as may be deemed advisable by the board and on the call of the conference lay leader.

8. The board shall, during the latter part of the conference year, develop plans for carrying forward the work in the coming conference year. It shall estimate the necessary amount for the support of this work, and shall make provisions for the adequate presentation of this need to the Commission on World Service and Finance for its consideration and recommendation to the Annual Conference.

¶ 1504. 1. The **conference lay leader** shall be elected annually by the Annual Conference on nomination of the

board, which nomination shall be by ballot.[18] An interim
vacancy may be filled by the board.

2. The conference lay leader shall be seated in the
Annual Conference, but without vote unless he is otherwise a member. (*See* ¶ 48.3.)

3. As executive officer of the board the conference lay
leader shall: (*a*) take the initiative in developing quadrennial and/or annual objectives, in formulating plans,
and in assigning responsibilities for carrying out the
program of lay activities as outlined by the general
board; (*b*) confer with the bishop and correlate the
work of the board with all other activities within the
conference; (*c*) make a written report to the board at its
regular session and to the Annual Conference each year;
and (*d*) make a comprehensive report to the general
board, following the close of the conference year, which
shall include the names and correct addresses of the
district and associate district lay leaders of the several
districts.

4. If it appears advisable, the board may elect, on
nomination of the conference lay leader, one or more
associate conference lay leaders and/or conference directors of such program activities as stewardship, Methodist
Men, lay speaking, etc.

¶ **1505.** The bishop may appoint or the Annual Conference may elect, or may authorize the Conference Board
of Lay Activities to elect, a **Committee on Wills, Bequests, and Gifts,** which shall be responsible by whatever means it deems best for encouraging Methodists
and friends of the church to make wills and other bequests which remember the conference and general
agencies and institutions as well as the local church. It
shall co-operate with local-church Committees on Wills
and Legacies and with the general board program for
wills, bequests, and gifts.

SEC. IV.   **District Boards**

¶ **1506.** 1. There shall be in every district a **District
Board of Lay Activities,** composed of the district lay

---

[18] *See* Judicial Council Decision 77.

leader, who shall be chairman, the associate district lay leaders, the district director of lay speaking and other district directors of program activities if any (¶ 1508.4), the group lay leaders if any (¶ 1508.5), the district superintendent, the church lay leader of each local church, and the president of each chartered Methodist Men club.

2. The board shall elect a secretary and, if desired, a treasurer and a vice-chairman, who shall be a representative Methodist Men president or church lay leader.

3. The board shall have an **executive committee,** composed of the district lay leader as chairman, the elected officers (§ 2), the associate district lay leaders, the district director of lay speaking and other district directors of program activities if any, and the district superintendent. It shall meet at least quarterly, and shall confer with the district superintendent regarding the promotion of lay activities and the correlation of the work with all other activities within the district.

¶ **1507.** The board shall co-operate with the conference board in promoting the program of lay activities outlined under the direction of the General, Jurisdictional, and Conference Boards of Lay Activities.

¶ **1508.** 1. The **district lay leader** and the associate district lay leaders shall be elected annually by the Annual Conference on nomination of the district superintendent and the conference lay leader; *provided* that, where the conference so determines, the nominations may be made by the board. The board shall have authority to fill interim vacancies; *provided* that, where the conference so determines, the conference lay leader and the district superintendent shall have authority to fill such vacancies.

2. As the executive officer of the board the district lay leader shall: (*a*) call at least one meeting annually of all members of the board to give direction to its work; (*b*) take the initiative in developing quadrennial and/or annual objectives, in formulating plans, and in assigning responsibilities for carrying out the program of lay activities as outlined by the general and conference boards; (*c*) make a written report to each regular meeting of the board and to the District Conference; and (*d*) make a detailed report to the conference lay leader at the close

of the conference year, which shall include the names and correct addresses of the associate district lay leaders.

3. The associate district lay leaders shall co-operate with the district lay leader in the work of lay activities as the board may direct. It is recommended that each one visit every Methodist Men club within his assigned section of the district annually, and make a written report to the district lay leader quarterly.

4. The board may elect, on nomination of the district lay leader, a **district director of lay speaking** and, if desired, other district directors of program activities such as stewardship, Methodist Men, etc.

5. If the large number of churches in the district makes it advisable to distribute the work load to meet organizational needs, the board may elect, on nomination of the district lay leader, **group lay leaders** who shall work with the associate lay leaders, and whose duty it shall be to guide the church lay leaders, preferably six in number, and chapters of Methodist Men assigned to them.

¶ **1509.** There shall be a **District Committee on Lay Speaking,** composed of the district superintendent, district lay leader, and district director of lay speaking (¶ 1508.4), which shall recommend candidates for certification as lay speakers in accordance with ¶ 293.

SEC. V.   **Methodist Men**

¶ **1511.** The General Board of Lay Activities shall give special consideration to men's work, correlating it with the total program of lay activities. **Methodist Men** shall be the duly authorized organization for this purpose. The board shall have authority to promote and charter local units of Methodist Men and to affiliate with the movement other existing men's organizations in the local church. Larger units—such as county, subdistrict, metropolitan area, or district units—may be chartered by the board for the purpose of promoting units in the local churches and as a means of developing a wider fellowship of service, in co-operation with the district lay leader, district superintendent, and conference lay leader. The board shall develop such organizational and administrative procedures as are necessary to meet the needs of an expanding fellowship of Christian service. (For the program of Methodist Men in the local church *see* ¶¶ 291-92.)

Sec. VI.   **Christian Stewardship**

¶ 1512. The General Board of Lay Activities is charged with the cultivation and promotion of Christian stewardship in The Methodist Church. It shall initiate plans, develop literature, and perfect organization to utilize effectively in the work of the church and in the development of Christian character this vital doctrine of Christian faith and practice.

¶ 1513. The study, practice, and promotion of Christian stewardship are essential to the highest individual holiness as well as the fullest realization of the Church's mission. The individual Christian must know, love, and live the truth himself before he can lead others into the experience of "stewards of the manifold grace of God."

¶ 1514. God is the owner of all things. Man is a steward. God's ownership and man's stewardship ought to be acknowledged.

Stewardship is the practical expression of one's experience of God. Therefore, all one's life, all personal abilities, and all material resources constitute a gift from God, which should be used for his glory and for the welfare of mankind. This is central in Christian faith and should control and direct all one's being.

Stewardship involves both motives and methods in the production and acquisition of wealth, the service ideal in vocation and avocation, and the conservation of natural resources. It also governs motives and methods in the investment and expenditure of one's total material gains.

Christian experience demonstrates that the acknowledgment of God's ownership and man's stewardship should result in systematic, proportionate, and abundant giving. Tithing is commended as a historic and workable method attested by many Christians throughout centuries of religious custom and joyful experience.

Stewardship likewise requires the offering of oneself and the sharing of one's abilities in the work of the organized agencies of the church and community which serve Kingdom interests.

Christian stewardship inevitably expresses itself in one's daily economic experiences and in all life and service.

SEC. VII.   **Lay Activities in Local Churches**

For information on lay activities in local churches *see* Part II, The Local Church, especially the following: concerning the over-all program of lay activities, including the duties of church lay leaders and the program of Methodist Men, ¶¶ 286-93; concerning the promotion of Christian stewardship in the financial program of the local church, ¶¶ 262-64.

CHAPTER XI

BOARD OF CHRISTIAN SOCIAL CONCERNS

SECTION I.   **Purpose and Names**

¶ **1516.** Through all of its history Methodism has sought to relate the gospel which it has preached to the life of its members and to the communities in which they have lived. It has sought to follow Christ in bringing the whole of life, with its activities, possessions, and relationships, into conformity with the will of God. To lift up before the members of the church and also the secular world the Christian concern for personal, social, and civic righteousness, to analyze the issues which confront the nation and the world as well as the local community and the person, and to propose Christian lines of action, there shall be a **Board of Christian Social Concerns.** The board shall be incorporated.

¶ **1517.** Board members and executives of the board shall speak and act in the true freedom of forgiven men. Truth is possible when controversies, expected because of human differences, are conducted in Christian love. The board is expected to speak to the church its convictions, interpretations, and concerns. Recognizing the freedom of all Christian men, the board never presumes to speak for the whole church. (*See* ¶ 512.)

SEC. II.   **Organization**

¶ **1518.** *Membership.*—The Board of Christian Social Concerns, hereinafter referred to as the board or the general board, shall be composed as follows: nine bishops elected by the Council of Bishops, with representation from each jurisdiction; one minister and one lay person for each 400,000 members or major fraction thereof, *provided* that there shall be no fewer than three ministers and three laymen from each jurisdiction, elected by the Jurisdictional Conference; three young people—two representing the Methodist Youth Fellowship, one of whom shall be a member of the council of the National Conference thereof, and one representing the Methodist Student Movement—elected by the board on nomination of the Joint Staff of Youth and Student Work, which shall have selected the nominees as provided in ¶ 1405.2; the chairman of the Section of Christian Social Relations of the Woman's Division of the Board of Missions; and nine members at large elected by the board on nomination of its divisions, as provided in ¶ 1526.3. In addition, in order that there may be an established liaison relationship with certain other boards of the church, there shall be eight liaison members with privilege of the floor but without vote: two elected by the Board of Missions from its own membership, one each from the World and National Divisions; three by the Board of Education, one from each of its divisions; one by the Board of Evangelism; one by the Board of Lay Activities; and one by the Board of Hospitals and Homes. No member of the board shall be a salaried officer thereof.

¶ **1519.** *Vacancies.*—If a vacancy occurs in the board by death or resignation, it shall be filled as follows: in the case of a bishop, by the College of Bishops of the jurisdiction; in the case of a ministerial or lay representative from a jurisdiction, by the board on nomination of the College of Bishops of the jurisdiction, such member to serve until the next meeting of the Jurisdictional Confer-

ence; in the case of a youth or student member or a
member at large, as provided in ¶ 1518.

¶ **1520.** *Officers.*—The board shall elect a president,
who shall be a bishop; three vice-presidents, each of
whom shall serve as the chairman of one division; a recording secretary; a treasurer; and such other officers as
it may determine.

¶ **1521.** *Executive Committee.*—The board shall establish an **executive committee,** which shall consist of the
officers of the board and four additional members from
each of the three divisions of the board, one of whom shall
be the recording secretary of the division. This committee
shall have the power *ad interim* to fill any vacancies occurring in the field and office staff and to transact such
business as is necessary between the meetings of the
board. It shall report all of its actions for confirmation at
the next meeting of the board.

¶ **1522.** *Nominating Committee.*—A **nominating committee** of seven members shall be constituted. It shall be
composed of one member, ministerial or lay, from each
jurisdiction, chosen by the board members from that
jurisdiction, and one bishop chosen by the bishops who are
board members. The bishop shall serve as convener. This
committee shall nominate the officers of the board (¶ 1520)
and assign each member of the board, including the vice-
presidents, to one of the three divisions (¶ 1526).

¶ **1523.** *Meetings.*—1. The board shall meet for purposes of organization and other necessary actions quadrennially after the adjournment of the General Conference and not later than October 15 of that year. The
organization meeting shall be convened by the bishop
designated by the Council of Bishops for that purpose,
and he shall fix the time and place.

2. The board shall hold an annual meeting, at a time
and place to be determined by its executive committee,
and such other meetings as its work may require, and
shall enact suitable by-laws governing the activities of
the board and its employees. A majority of the membership shall constitute a quorum.

¶ **1524.** The members of the board shall constitute the
membership of its predecessor boards, namely, the Board

of Temperance of The Methodist Church and all of its
legal predecessors, the Board of World Peace of The
Methodist Church and all of its legal predecessors, and
the Board of Social and Economic Relations of The Methodist Church.

¶ **1525.** *Financial Support.*—1. The work of the board
shall be supported from the general benevolences of the
church, the amount to be determined by the General Conference, on recommendation of the Council on World
Service and Finance. The board shall present quadrennially to the council a statement of the amount required
for its general expense and for the support of each of its
divisions.

2. Either on behalf of its total work or on behalf of one
or more of its divisions, the board may solicit and create
special funds, receive gifts and bequests, hold properties
and securities in trust, and administer all these financial
affairs in accordance with its own rules and the provisions
of the Discipline (*see* ¶¶ 743, 748). Funds vested in any
of the predecessor boards shall be conserved for the exclusive use of the appropriate division of this board and
for the specific purposes for which such funds have been
given.

¶ **1526.** *Divisions.*—1. The board shall be organized into
three divisions: the Division of Alcohol Problems and
General Welfare, the Division of Peace and World Order,
and the Division of Human Relations and Economic
Affairs. The members of the board shall be assigned to
divisions by the nominating committee (¶ 1522), subject
to the approval of the board. It shall be the duty of this
committee to assign the membership, other than members
at large, to the three divisions so that the three shall as
nearly as possible be of the same size, and shall have
members from each jurisdiction and from ministerial and
lay groups in as nearly as possible equal proportion. No
member shall belong to more than one division, except
that the president of the board shall be a member ex
officio of each division.

2. Each division shall organize itself under the chairmanship of a vice-president of the board and shall elect a
recording secretary. It shall also elect three of its own

number by written ballot who, together with the chairman and recording secretary, shall constitute the executive committee of that division. The members of the divisional executive committee shall be members of the executive committee of the board.

3. Each division shall nominate for election by the board three members at large, selected on the basis of their specialized skills and knowledge relevant to the work of the division, to be members of that division and of the board. (*See* ¶ 1518.)

¶ **1527.** Each division shall meet at the same time and place as the board. A special meeting of the division may be held on the call of its chairman, or of three members of its executive committee, or of ten of its members. All such special meetings shall be chargeable to the budget of the division.

¶ **1528.** 1. The members assigned to each division shall have the responsibility of establishing policies relating to the work of that division and the conduct of its staff, subject to the approval of the board.

2. The divisions shall co-operatively carry forward the total work of the board through the Annual Conferences and districts, in the local churches, and in such other places and by such means as they may have opportunity to present the witness of Christian social concern.

¶ **1530.** *Staff.*—The board shall elect quadrennially a general secretary, three associate general secretaries, and a staff treasurer on nomination of the executive committee. Other staff personnel shall be approved by the executive committee of the board on nomination of the president and the general secretary. The executive committee of the board may, at its discretion, assign this responsibility to the executive committee of a division. The salaries and duties of all employees of the board shall be fixed by the board.

¶ **1531.** *General and Associate General Secretaries.*—1. The **general secretary** shall be an ex officio member of the board, of its executive committee, and of the executive committee of each division, without vote. He shall be the chief administrative officer of the board, responsible for the co-ordination of the total program of the board and for the general administration of the headquarters office and of such facilities and functions as serve all three divisions of the board. Under his supervision there shall be a **director of organizational administration,** who shall have charge of the service bureau, finance, and purchasing; a **director of communication and publication,** who shall edit and prepare publicity, promotional, and audio-visual materials; a **director of educational liaison,** who shall maintain close relations with, and interpret the work of the board to, the several divisions of the Board of Education; a legislative officer if the board so orders; and such other staff persons as are deemed necessary by the board.

2. Each of the **associate general secretaries** shall have primary responsibility for those Christian social concerns which are assigned to his particular division. Within this area and under the direction of the division and its executive committee he with his staff shall develop a program of research, education, and action, bringing these concerns to the attention of the denomination and all its churches and of the communities they serve. He shall be responsible, under the direction of the division and its executive committee, for the administration of the budget, including the income from trust funds allocated to his division. The three associate general secretaries shall co-operate with one another and with the general secretary to prevent undue overlapping in the work of the divisions and to avoid conflicts in scheduling of meetings and conferences.

3. The general secretary and the associate general secretaries shall be members of the Council of Secretaries (¶ 1593).

Sec. III. **Headquarters**

¶ **1534.** 1. The headquarters of the board and of its divisions shall be in Washington, D. C.

2. In addition to the general headquarters, there shall be a New York United Nations office conducted in co-operation with the Woman's Division of the Board of Missions. In the operation of this office the Division of Peace and World Order shall represent the board and

shall carry the board's responsibility for staffing and budget.

Sec. IV.   **Division of Alcohol Problems and General Welfare**

¶ **1535.** 1. It shall be the responsibility of the **Division of Alcohol Problems and General Welfare** to conduct a program of research, education, and action centering around the following Christian social concerns: alcohol problems, tobacco, drug abuse, gambling, sex and moral values and pornography, juvenile delinquency, crime and rehabilitation, mental health, medical care, problems of aging, population problems, planned parenthood, public safety, morality and mass media, community welfare policies and practices, and such other related concerns as the board may specify. For clarification of responsibility in relation to other boards, *see* ¶ 1558.

2. The work assigned to the division shall be carried forward by the associate general secretary and such other staff members as the division shall determine, subject to budget allocations. The staff shall report to the division at the time of the annual board meeting concerning the work of the past year and plans proposed for further implementation of its assigned responsibilities.

¶ **1536.** To enlist Methodists and encourage others to commit themselves to personal abstinence from alcoholic beverages and to temperate living, and to challenge church members to creative action for a sober home and social life, the second Sunday in November shall be observed each year as **Commitment Day,** to be promoted in every church with assistance by the General Board of Christian Social Concerns for that purpose. Because of the particular emphasis of the day it is suggested that no special offering be received, unless it be for the propagation of the Methodist program of temperance.

Sec. V.   **Division of Peace and World Order**

¶ **1538.** 1. It shall be the responsibility of the **Division of Peace and World Order** to conduct a program of research, education, and action centering around the following Christian social concerns: American foreign policy; United Nations and related international organizations; disarmament and nuclear weapon control; space control; foreign aid, tariffs, and trade; immigration and naturalization; military policy and conscription legislation; conscientious objectors and the draft; and such other concerns as the board may specify. The general policies shall be established by the division, subject to the approval of the board.

2. The work assigned to the division shall be carried forward by the associate general secretary and such other staff members as the division shall determine, subject to budget allocations. The staff shall report to the division at the time of the annual board meeting concerning the work of the past year and plans proposed for further implementation of its assigned responsibilities.

SEC. VI.   **Division of Human Relations
and Economic Affairs**

¶ **1541.** 1. It shall be the responsibility of the **Division of Human Relations and Economic Affairs** to conduct a program of research, education, and action centering around the following Christian social concerns: race relations; civil liberties; public policy on education; church and state relations; [19] civic responsibility; labor-management relations; agriculture; conservation; government and private economic policy and practice; technological change; unemployment; housing; and such other concerns as the board may specify. The general policies shall be established by the division, subject to the approval of the board.

2. The work assigned to the division shall be carried forward by the associate general secretary and such other staff members as the division shall determine, subject to budget allocations. The staff shall report to the division at the time of the annual board meeting concerning the

---

[19] The General Conference of 1964 adopted in principle, and referred to the General Board of Christian Social Concerns for implementation, a resolution to create for the 1964-68 quadrennium a Commission to Study Church-State Relations, to continue the study begun during the previous quadrennium and report to the legislative Committee on Christian Social Concerns of the General Conference of 1968.

work of the past year and plans proposed for further implementation of its assigned responsibilities.

SEC. VII.   **Jurisdictional Boards**

¶ 1544. In each jurisdiction there may be a **Jurisdictional Board of Christian Social Concerns,** auxiliary to the general board, as the Jurisdictional Conference may determine. (*See* ¶¶ 15.3, 527.)

SEC. VIII.   **Annual Conference Boards**

¶ 1545. Each Annual Conference shall elect, on nomination of the nominating committee of the conference, or otherwise as the conference may direct, a **Conference Board of Christian Social Concerns.** It shall have no fewer than fifteen nor more than sixty members, with an approximately equal number of laymen and ministers. The lay members shall include the chairman of Christian citizenship of the Conference Methodist Youth Fellowship, a student nominated by the state or regional unit of the Methodist Student Movement, and the secretary of Christian social relations of the Conference Woman's Society of Christian Service. The remaining lay members shall consist of an approximately equal number of men and women. All district directors of Christian social concerns and any members of the general and jurisdictional boards living within the bounds of the conference shall be ex officio members.

¶ 1546. The conference board, in co-operation with the general board, shall develop and promote programs on Christian social concerns within the bounds of the conference. To this end it may divide its membership into three committees of approximately equal size, patterned after the divisions of the general board. They shall have responsibility to co-operate with one another to advance the concerns of their respective divisions.

¶ 1547. The board shall estimate annually the amount necessary for the support of its work and report this amount to the Commission on World Service and Finance for its consideration and recommendation to the Annual Conference. The work of the board shall be considered a benevolence interest of the church within the conference.

¶ **1548.** The board may employ a person or persons to further its purposes. Two or more Annual Conferences may co-operate in developing their programs and in the employment of one or more persons.

Sec. IX. **District Committees**

¶ **1549.** The district superintendent, after consultation with the conference board, shall appoint a **district director of Christian social concerns** and, if desired, a **District Committee on Christian Social Concerns** of laymen and ministers to work with him to further the purposes of the conference board. The secretary of Christian social relations of the District Woman's Society of Christian Service shall be an ex officio member. If the Annual Conference so orders, three district directors shall be appointed, each to represent the interests of one of the divisions within the general board.

Sec. X. **Local-Church Commissions**

For the program of Christian social concerns in the local church *see* ¶¶ 274-75.

Chapter XII

BOARD OF HOSPITALS AND HOMES

Section I. **Constitution**

¶ **1550.** *Name and Purpose.*—There shall be a **Board of Hospitals and Homes** of The Methodist Church, which shall have an advisory relationship to Methodist philanthropic interests and institutions, such as hospitals, homes for the aged, homes for children, and homes for youth, located in the United States, its territories, and dependencies. This advisory relationship shall apply also to a hospital or home which is owned or supervised by any agency of The Methodist Church in the United States, its territories, or dependencies.

¶ **1551.** *Incorporation.*—The Board of Hospitals and Homes of The Methodist Church shall be duly incorporated according to the laws of Illinois. Its headquarters shall be located in the state of Illinois.

¶ **1552.** *Management.*—The management of the board shall be vested in a Board of Managers of twenty-one: two bishops, elected by the Council of Bishops; one minister and one lay member from each jurisdiction, elected by the Jurisdictional Conference, at least one of whom shall be an active administrator of an institution under the general supervision of the board; and seven members at large, elected by the board, three of whom may be active administrators of institutions under its general supervision. All of the Board of Managers shall be members of The Methodist Church. Should a vacancy occur among those elected by the jurisdictions, the College of Bishops where such vacancy occurs shall elect the person to fill the unexpired term. All other vacancies shall be filled by the electing body.

¶ **1553.** *Officers.*—1. The officers of the Board of Managers shall be a president, elected by the board from the bishops who are members, a vice-president, a recording secretary, and a treasurer. All of these officers shall be elected by the board for the quadrennium. In addition there shall be such other officers and agents as the board may from time to time determine.

2. The board may elect a **general secretary** and provide for his salary and necessary help. This secretary shall be subject to the authority and control of the board.

¶ **1554.** *Meetings.*—1. An annual meeting of the board shall be held at such time and place as the board may determine.

2. An **executive committee** of nine members shall be elected by the board, to include the officers of the board and five additional members to be elected by the board with the provision that each jurisdiction shall be represented on the committee by an elected member, the general secretary being a member of the executive committee ex officio without vote (¶ 1076). Five members of the executive committee shall constitute a quorum.

¶ **1555.** *Affiliation.*—In order that Methodist philanthropic activities may be made scientific and Christian, hospitals or homes known as institutions of The Methodist Church and maintaining Christian standards or looking to Methodist constituency for support, and not affiliated with any other board of the church, shall be expected to affiliate with the Board of Hospitals and Homes.

¶ 1556. *Financial Support.*—Since the Board of Hospitals and Homes is empowered to act only in an advisory, educational, and co-operative capacity, its support shall be derived as follows: (*a*) from gifts, devises, wills, bequests, and from administration of trust funds; and (*b*) from such share in the general benevolences of the church as the General Conference may determine.

¶ 1557. *Powers.*—1. The board may make surveys, disseminate information, suggest plans for securing funds, maintain a bureau for the purpose of securing experts in all lines of work, provide architectural data, and render assistance, other than financial assistance, in the promotion and establishment of new institutions. (*See* ¶ 1558.) It shall make appraisals and advise as to the validity and wisdom of accepting or rejecting institutions, such as hospitals and homes, to become beneficiaries in any way of the approval or support of The Methodist Church in any Annual Conference of the United States. It may suggest plans for Annual Conferences regarding their religious ministry to state and non-Methodist hospitals and homes needing such ministry.

2. The board shall formulate standards, spiritual, financial, and scientific, to protect the aims and ideals of The Methodist Church and shall encourage and assist institutions in attaining these standards.

3. The board is authorized to establish a **Certification Council,** under such rules and regulations as it may determine, to develop criteria and to implement a program for the classification and certification of institutions and agencies of philanthropic service related to The Methodist Church.

4. The board shall provide for conference boards the consultative services regarding proposed new institutions specified in ¶¶ 1562.3, 1564.

5. The board may organize a **Personnel Bureau,** under such rules and regulations as it may determine: (*a*) to

help institutions of philanthropic service in The Methodist Church to find adequately trained Christian personnel to conduct the various types of work represented by Methodist hospitals and homes; (*b*) to encourage Methodist youth who are socially minded and who are desirous of investing their lives in some form of Christian institutional work; and (*c*) to co-operate in the work of the Interboard Committee on Christian Vocations (¶ 1415.)

6. The board shall cause to be established a **code of ethics** to serve as a standard and guide for service institutions of The Methodist Church in developing Christian and scientific characteristics.

7. The board is empowered to act as trustee for the administration of bequests or endowments for institutions of the church and, as a result of said trusts, to assist designated Christian social welfare work anywhere throughout the church.

8. As an advisory, standardizing, and educational agency of The Methodist Church, the board is empowered to prepare interpretative literature which can be used in a practical manner throughout the church for Golden Cross or other appeals.

9. The Board of Managers is authorized to organize committees, set up financial accounts, assist institutions in efforts to secure funds, and perform such other functions as the normal work of the board may require.

10. The Board of Hospitals and Homes shall not be responsible, legally or morally, for the debts, contracts, or obligations, or for any other financial commitments of any character or description, created, undertaken, or assumed by any institution, agency, or interest of The Methodist Church, whether or not such institution, agency, or interest shall be approved, accepted, or recognized by the board, or shall be affiliated with the board, or whether or not the promotion or establishment of the same shall be approved, under any of the provisions of this constitution, or otherwise. No such institution, agency, or interest of The Methodist Church, and no officer or member of the Board of Managers of this board, shall have any authority whatsoever to take any action, directly or by implication, at variance with, or deviating from, the

limitation contained in the preceding sentence hereof.

¶ **1558.** *Clarification of Responsibility.*—1. In the field of Methodist health and welfare the Board of Hospitals and Homes carries primary responsibility for direct services and the Board of Christian Social Concerns carries primary responsibility for affecting public policy. Both boards carry a joint responsibility for community health and welfare planning. This clarification of responsibility shall not be interpreted as affecting the function and role of the Board of Missions.

2. The terms used in § 1 shall be understood as follows: "Direct services" includes advising and administering the operation of organized services to persons in need, whether through an institution or a local church. "Community health and welfare planning" refers to the assessing of needs for health and welfare services and the development of support for needed public and church-related services. "Affecting public policy" encompasses the representation of the church in developing public support for legislation and rules of procedure relating to public agencies in health and welfare.

¶ **1559.** *Interboard Consultation.*—There shall be a consultative interboard staff committee between the National Division of the Board of Missions and the Board of Hospitals and Homes, established by these agencies. (*See* ¶¶ 1240-41.)

Sec. II.   **Golden Cross**

¶ **1560.** 1. There shall be a **Golden Cross Society** of The Methodist Church, which shall promote the hospitals and homes work under the direction of the Board of Hospitals and Homes and shall collect moneys and afford other material assistance in providing care for the sick, older persons, children, and youth. The enrollment in the Methodist Golden Cross Society shall be held annually in order to secure interest in, and support of, hospitals and homes in every congregation in such manner and on such date as determined by the patronizing Annual Conference or Conferences. The week following **Golden Cross Enrollment Sunday** shall be known as **Hospitals and Homes Week.** Funds raised through this enrollment shall be used as directed by the Annual Conference through its Board of Hospitals and Homes, in keeping with the policies of the society.

2. The right of any Annual Conference to employ such methods for financing its philanthropic institutions as it may decide on is recognized, and the Board of Hospitals and Homes shall be available for advice and guidance.

3. There shall be a **Golden Cross Fellowship** of The Methodist Church, membership in which shall be open to all Methodists who are seeking to fulfill their Christian vocation through a life of service in one of the helping and healing occupations. It shall be auxiliary to the Board of Hospitals and Homes, and shall have as its purposes: (*a*) in co-operation with Annual Conference Commissions on Christian Vocations, the recruiting and guidance of others into the helping and healing professions as an expression of Christian vocation; (*b*) the provision of a questing fellowship which seeks to clarify and deepen the understanding of how the Christian faith relates to the healing process and how the theological dimensions of Methodist belief relate to the life of service; and (*c*) the provision of a place where lay and professional persons may exchange dialogue to the end that a better understanding of the helping and healing process in its relation to faith may be the result for both. There may be student membership in each Annual Conference chapter of the fellowship.

SEC. III.   **Jurisdictional Boards**

¶ **1561.** In each jurisdiction there may be a **Jurisdictional Board of Hospitals and Homes,** auxiliary to the general board, as the Jurisdictional Conference may determine. (*See* ¶¶ 15.3, 527.)

SEC. IV.   **Annual Conference Boards**

¶ **1562.** 1. Each Annual Conference shall promote within its bounds a **Conference Board of Hospitals and Homes,** composed as follows: (*a*) At least one ministerial and one lay member shall be elected from each district of the conference; *provided* that there shall be a minimum of four ministers and four lay members. (*b*) Any member of the general board within the conference shall be an ex officio member. (*c*) Administrators of hospitals and homes related to the conference shall be ex officio members, without vote.

2. The board shall meet at least once before or during each regular conference session and shall act in co-operation with the general board to promote the interest of the hospitals and homes within the bounds of the conference. It may aid in planning and developing a religious ministry, wherever practicable, in state and non-Methodist hospitals and homes needing such ministry. Where civil law requires the election of boards of trustees or managers by the Annual Conference, it may nominate the persons for such election.

3. The board, in co-operation with the general board, shall help lift spiritual, financial, and scientific standards in Methodist health and welfare ministries in the Annual Conference. It shall seek to strengthen the ties between affiliated hospitals and homes and the church. It shall make recommendations to the Annual Conference regarding establishment of new institutions and changes in existing institutions, as provided in ¶ 1564. In so doing, it shall use the consultative services of the general board. The architectural plans as well as charter and by-laws of any proposed new institution shall first be submitted to the general board for suggestions before they are taken to the Annual Conference for action and approval.

4. The board shall organize with a chairman, who may become a voting member of the National Association of Methodist Hospitals and Homes under the payment of the personal membership dues of the association; he shall be expected to take as much interest as possible in the program of Christian philanthropy in Methodism as represented by the association.

5. There may be an interboard committee of ten persons, composed of five representatives elected by the board and five elected by the Conference Woman's Society of Christian Service, for co-operation in matters of mutual interest.

SEC. V.   **District Directors**

¶ **1563.** In each district the district superintendent may designate one of the representatives of the district on the conference board (¶ 1562.1*a*) as **district director of hospitals and homes.**

SEC. VI.   **Local-Church Committees**

See ¶ 278.3 under Part II, The Local Church.

SEC. VII.   **Philanthropic Institutions**

¶ **1564.** No new Methodist helping and healing institution shall be established, nor shall an existing institution alter its major purpose and functions, nor add any new facility in another location, without first receiving the approval of the Annual Conference, on recommendation of the Conference Board of Hospitals and Homes, after consultation with the general board, as provided in ¶ 1562.3. This restriction shall not apply to institutions of the Board of Missions.

¶ **1565.** All hospitals and homes operated by, or under the auspices of, or related to any connectional unit of, The Methodist Church are urged to make their programs and services available to all persons regardless of race.

¶ **1566. Women's Auxiliaries** connected with the various philanthropic institutions of Methodism may be organized under, or given approval on compliance with, established standard requirements and procedures, such as the adoption of a constitution and by-laws fixing the identity, responsibility, and relationship of such organization as an auxiliary of a Methodist institution. Such an auxiliary, when so organized, and when request is made by the board of trustees of the institution which it represents, shall be granted a certificate of recognition from the Board of Hospitals and Homes.

¶ **1567.** There shall be organized a **National Association of Methodist Hospitals and Homes,** to be composed of the representatives of institutions and the presidents of juridictional and conference boards who are connected with Methodist philanthropy. This association shall have its own constitution and by-laws, shall meet in convention once a year, and shall establish its requirements for membership and have such membership dues as it may require. It shall work under the general direction of the Board of Hospitals and Homes, whose general secretary shall be an ex officio member of the association's executive committee. The aim and purpose of this association, in co-operation with the board, shall be to help lift the spiritual, scientific, and financial standards of our church hospitals and homes.

Chapter XIII

COMMISSIONS

Section I.   **Commission on Worship**

¶ **1568.** 1. There shall be a **Commission on Worship,** composed of the book editor ex officio and two bishops, one minister and one lay person from each jurisdiction, and three members from the church at large elected by the General Conference on nomination of the Council of Bishops. Vacancies during the quadrennium shall be filled by the Council of Bishops.

2. The officers of the commission shall be a chairman, a vice-chairman, and a secretary, elected quadrennially in such manner as it may determine.

3. The commission shall meet at least once a year, and at such other time as the commission and its officers shall determine.

4. The expense of the commission shall be borne by the General Administration Fund. The commission shall present a proposed budget to the Council on World Service and Finance for its consideration and action.

¶ **1569.** The functions of the commission shall be:

1. To cultivate beauty, dignity, and meaning in the worship experience of the church.

2. To encourage by means of manuals and other publications, and by seminars, workshops, and other media, good taste and practice in the conduct of worship, church music, church architecture, and the use of the arts in the church.

3. When need arises, to prepare forms of worship and to revise existing orders of worship for recommendation to the General Conference.

4. To supervise future editions of *The Book of Worship for Church and Home*, as may be authorized by the General Conference.

5. To make recommendations to the General Conference concerning future editions of *The Methodist Hymnal*.

6. To advise with any of the general agencies of the church in the publication and circulation of any orders of service and other liturgical materials bearing the imprint of The Methodist Church.

7. To advise with official publications of the church concerning material offered in the fields of worship and liturgical arts.

8. To consult with the Television, Radio, and Film Commission on matters of joint concern.

9. To encourage in our schools of theology and pastors' schools the best possible instruction in the meaning and conduct of worship.

10. To advise with those responsible for planning the program of the General Conference and other general assemblies of the church regarding the worship services on these occasions.

11. To offer suggestions and direction to the Commissions on Worship of the various conferences and of the local churches. (*See* ¶¶ 276-77, 1571.)

12. To relate The Methodist Church to the Department of Worship and the Arts of the National Council of Churches and to the Interdenominational Bureau of Architecture.

¶ 1570. It shall be the purpose of the commission to enrich and not to govern the devotional life of the church, recalling our dual heritage of liturgical and free worship, and that "it is not necessary that rites and ceremonies should in all places be the same" (¶ 82).

¶ 1571. 1. Each Annual Conference may constitute a **Conference Commission on Worship,** which shall be auxiliary to the general and jurisdictional commissions, to report each year to the conference in such manner as the conference may direct. It shall be composed of at least one ministerial and one lay member from each district. Any member of the general commission within the conference shall be an ex officio member.

2. The commission shall meet at least once before each regular conference session. It shall organize with a chairman, vice-chairman, and secretary.

3. The duties of the commission shall be to act in cooperation with the general commission:

a) To promote the interests of worship within the bounds of the conference.

b) To foster the use of the best resources for worship at conference meetings, and in all the churches of the conference.

c) To promote the use of *The Book of Worship for Church and Home* and *The Methodist Hymnal* in all the churches of the conference.

d) To plan and promote seminars and demonstrations on ways of worship and the use of hymns within the bounds of the conference.

e) To provide exhibits at the conference sessions in such fields as architecture, church appointments, etc.

f) To co-operate with the Board of Education and the National Fellowship of Methodist Musicians in promoting seminars and all other conferences on church music.

SEC. II. **Commission on Chaplains**

¶ **1572.** 1. There shall be a **Commission on Chaplains,** which shall represent The Methodist Church in the recruitment, endorsement, and general oversight of all Methodist ministers serving as chaplains in the Armed Forces, Veterans Administration, and other federal agencies; in industry; and in state and local public and private institutions, other than those of The Methodist Church. The commission shall render such other services to these chaplains as may be referred to it by the Council of Bishops.

2. The commission shall be composed of six bishops, one from each jurisdiction, and five ministers and five laymen, elected by the General Conference on nomination of the Council of Bishops. Vacancies shall be filled by the Council of Bishops. A member bishop shall serve

481

as chairman. The commission may elect advisory members, without vote, one from each department of the Armed Forces, from the Veterans Administration, and from other fields where Methodist chaplains are serving.

3. The commission is authorized to receive and disburse such share of the Fellowship of Suffering and Service offering as may be determined by the General Conference and such other funds and special gifts as are specifically given to the Commission on Chaplains.

SEC. III.   Commission on Camp Activities

¶ 1573. The Commission on Camp Activities shall be continued until it is deemed no longer needed (¶ 763). It shall consist of six bishops elected by the Council of Bishops.

SEC. IV.   Commission on Ecumenical Affairs

¶ 1575. 1. There shall be a Commission on Ecumenical Affairs composed of fifty-four members of The Methodist Church elected by the General Conference on nomination of the Council of Bishops. These shall include two each from the Boards of Missions and of Education, the General Board of the National Council of Churches, and the Assembly of the World Council of Churches; three from the Executive Committee of the World Methodist Council and two from its affiliate World Federation of Methodist Women; and three youth representatives (at least one a student); *provided* that among the foregoing there shall be not less than four bishops, three lay men, and three lay women. In addition there shall be twelve representatives from Methodist schools of theology, two from Central Conferences, and from each jurisdiction a bishop, a minister, a lay man, and a lay woman.

2. The commission shall:

a) Proclaim and work for the unity of the Church.

b) Recommend to the Council of Bishops, when requested by the council, qualified members of The Methodist Church for ecumenical councils, agencies, and meetings.

c) Analyze the relationship of The Methodist Church to the pronouncements and actions of the ecumenical councils and agencies and publicize the same; and channel materials coming from the ecumenical councils and agencies to the proper agencies of the church, and materials coming from the church and its agencies to the proper agencies of the ecumenical councils.

d) Explore, receive, study, and recommend action on proposals for union of The Methodist Church with other denominations.

e) Interpret The Methodist Church in the light of the New Testament definitions of the Church, in the light of church history, and in its relationships to the ecumenical councils, agencies, and movements.

f) Report periodically to the church, to the General Conference, and to the Council of Bishops on the participation of The Methodist Church in the various phases of the ecumenical movement.

3. In carrying out its work the commission shall give attention to ecumenical studies, the relationship of The Methodist Church to ecumenical organizations, church union, and such additional concerns as relate to ecumenical interests and responsibilities of the church.

4. When the General Conference decides that negotiations with another Christian body are in order, it shall create an ad hoc committee for such purpose, with the provision that one half its membership shall derive from the commission and one half shall be named from the church at large on the basis of special competence for the negotiations in view. Provision shall be made for the ad hoc committee in the course of its work to advise and consult with the commission.

5. The commission shall elect its president from among the bishops that constitute its membership at the beginning of each quadrennium. It shall elect vice-presidents from among its membership to preside over the business of subcommittees needful for the work of the commission.

6. The Council on World Service and Finance shall make provision for the support of the work of the commission, including provision for a general secretary and an office for the commission.

7. Vacancies in membership due to death or resigna-

tion in the interim shall be filled by the Council of Bishops.[20]

Sec. V. Interagency Commission on Cultivation, Promotion, and Publication

¶ **1576.** There shall be an **Interagency Commission on Cultivation, Promotion, and Publication,** whose function shall be to act as the co-ordinator of the policies and activities of the Commission on Promotion and Cultivation, the Television, Radio, and Film Commission, the Commission on Public Relations and Methodist Information, and the Board of Publication.

¶ **1577.** The membership of the commission shall be composed of the following representatives from its constituent agencies: four members from the Commission on Promotion and Cultivation, two from the Television, Radio, and Film Commission, one from the Commission on Public Relations and Methodist Information, and two from the Board of Publication.

¶ **1578.** The commission, in carrying out its function of co-ordinating the work of the agencies which is represents, shall see that plans and programs relating to cultivation, promotion, films, radio, television, public relations, Methodist information, and publishing do not overlap or duplicate. Any questions of overlapping or duplication which cannot be resolved by the commission shall be referred to the Co-ordinating Council. (*See* ¶ 1093.1.) When in the judgment of the commission such action would facilitate co-ordination among its agencies, it may authorize interboard staff committees.

¶ **1579.** Implementing the work of the commission there shall be a **secretarial council,** consisting of the general secretary or other representative of each constituent agency. It shall be the function of this council to facilitate co-operation among the agencies in the creative planning of their respective programs and in avoiding over-

---

[20] In establishing the Commission on Ecumenical Affairs the General Conference of 1964 directed that until its organization the former Commission on Church Union should continue with the same membership, organization, and powers, and with the right to draw on the budget established for the new commission.

lapping of function or duplication of activity. The chairmanship of the secretarial council shall rotate annually among its members.

Sec. VI. Commission on Promotion and Cultivation

For the organization and functions of the Commission on Promotion and Cultivation *see* ¶¶ 750-64, under Part V, Temporal Economy.

Sec. VII. Television, Radio, and Film Commission

¶ 1581. 1. There shall be an incorporated **Television, Radio, and Film Commission** of The Methodist Church. Its headquarters shall be in Nashville, Tennessee.

2. The membership shall consist of three bishops elected by the Council of Bishops; one minister and one layman from each jurisdiction elected by its College of Bishops; ten members of the Council of Secretaries, elected by the council, including at least one each from the Boards of Missions, Education, Evangelism, Lay Activities, and Christian Social Concerns, and the Commission on Promotion and Cultivation; and five members at large elected by the commission.

3. Officers of the commission shall be a president, vice-president, secretary, and treasurer, elected quadrennially in such manner as the commission may determine.

4. The purpose and function of the commission shall be:

a) To unify and co-ordinate the audio-visual programs of all Methodist agencies dealing with projected pictures, recordings, transcriptions, radio and television programs, and other audio-visual materials.

b) To make the studies necessary for the development of a unified and comprehensive program of resources to serve all age groups in the home, church, and community, and to represent the great causes of the church.

c) To produce and distribute such programs and materials in the area of the work of member agencies as the agencies may request and finance, and such other resources as are needed to serve the great causes of the church. In so far as practical the rental or sale of materials for Methodist use shall be handled through The Methodist Publishing House.

d) To represent The Methodist Church in the Broadcasting and Film Commission of the National Council of Churches, and any other interdenominational agencies working in the area of mass communication.

e) To provide funds for scholarships, and other training opportunities, to prepare qualified persons for full-time Christian service in this field, and to work with other Methodist agencies in providing training opportunities for ministers and lay leaders so that resources provided may be effectively used.

5. The financial support of the commission shall be determined as follows: The General Conference shall determine and provide from world service funds, on the recommendation of the Council on World Service and Finance, the budget of the commission. The budget shall include provision for necessary staff and administrative cost and such funds as may be deemed necessary to enable the commission to fulfill its stated functions. Additional contributions may be accepted from member agencies which are not supported by world service funds. (*See* ¶ 762.)

6. The General Conference, on recommendation of the Council on World Service and Finance and of the commission, shall allot such funds as it deems wise to the Broadcasting and Film Commission of the National Council of Churches. If this apportionment is included in a total church budget for the National Council of Churches, it shall be paid only after annual approval by the commission.

¶ **1582.** There may be in each jurisdiction a **Jurisdictional Television, Radio, and Film Commission** auxiliary to the general commission.

¶ **1583.** 1. There shall be a **Conference Television, Radio, and Film Commission** in each Annual Conference, which, in co-operation with the program boards, and other agencies in the conference, shall have for its purpose serving the conference in the field of mass-communication media, including radio, television, and audio-visual materials, by:

a) Promotion of the principles of good communication.

b) Promotion of the use of mass-communication methods and materials by the local churches.

c) Promotion of the Television-Radio Ministry Fund.

d) Where necessary, establishment of audio-visual libraries and assistance in training audio-visual librarians.

e) Production and distribution of programs for conference-wide use.

f) Co-operation with the Conference Board of Education and other conference agencies to provide training opportunities for leaders in the use of audio-visual methods and materials.

g) Service to other agencies of the conference, and close co-operation with the conference or area public relations office.

h) Co-operation with other agencies to organize and train local-church Intercommission Audio-Visual Committees.

i) Provision of training opportunities for leaders from local churches and conference organizations in the use of radio and television and as audio-visual librarians in the development of audio-visual libraries.

j) Co-operation with the general commission in the promotion and placement of television and radio programs within the conference.

2. The commission shall be composed of one district superintendent designated by the bishop; five persons whose experience and training qualify them for this service, elected by the conference; one representative of the Conference Commission on Promotion and Cultivation; three members of the Conference Commission on Public Relations and Methodist Information, or of such other agency as functions for the conference in this area; one representative each from the Conference Boards of Education, Missions, Evangelism, Lay Activities, and Christian Social Concerns, and from the Woman's Society of Christian Service, named by the agency; and at least three members at large, who may be elected by the commission. Any member of the general or jurisdictional commission residing within the bounds of the conference shall be an ex officio member.

3. The commission shall organize by electing a chair-

man, secretary, and treasurer, who may be the conference treasurer.

4. The commission may elect a **director,** whose duty shall be to execute the policies and program established by the commission.

5. The commission shall have a **Committee on Finance,** consisting of three members of the commission and two members at large, to promote the Television-Radio Ministry Fund in the conference, the districts, and the local churches. It shall co-operate with the general commission and the Commission on Promotion and Cultivation.

6. The commission may request funds from the conference through the Commission on World Service and Finance.

7. Where desired, the officers of the conference commissions within an episcopal area may, at the request of the bishop, function as an **Area Television, Radio, and Film Commission.**

¶ **1584.** There may be in each district a **district television, radio, and film director,** who shall be responsible for implementing the work of the commission on the district level. He shall be appointed by the district superintendent in consultation with the chairman of the conference commission. The several district directors may, on vote of the conference commission, be members of that commission.

¶ **1585.** The chairman of the Intercommission Audio-Visual Committee (¶ 235) shall be the liaison person between the local church and the Conference and General Television, Radio, and Film Commissions.

Sec. VIII. Commission on Public Relations and Methodist Information

¶ **1586.** There shall be a **Commission on Public Relations and Methodist Information,** which shall gather news of public interest concerning Methodist activities and opinion and disseminate it through the secular press, the religious press, radio, television, and other legitimate media of public information; *provided* that in its relations with the media it serves, and with the public generally, the commission may use such abbreviation of its name as it may deem appropriate. It shall be composed of nine persons, one of whom shall be a bishop, who shall act as chairman, elected by the General Conference on nomination of the Council of Bishops. Care shall be taken to nominate persons whose experience in public relations, journalism, advertising, radio and television, business, or the church particularly qualifies them for this service. Vacancies occurring between sessions of the General Conference shall be filled by the commission. Members shall hold office until the next session of the General Conference, or until their successors are elected.

¶ **1587.** The commission is authorized to employ a **general secretary,** who may be known as director, and such other persons as may be necessary to give effect to its purpose.

¶ **1588.** The expense of the commission shall be borne by the General Administration Fund. The commission shall present a proposed budget to the Council on World Service and Finance for its consideration and action.

¶ **1589.** 1. The commission shall be the official general news gathering and distributing agency for The Methodist Church and its general agencies. It may arrange with other general agencies for some persons in those organizations to represent the commission in direct release of Methodist news items to the religious and/or secular press; but agencies which supported news gathering and distribution services during the 1948-52 quadrennium shall continue to provide for their budgets.

2. The commission shall have general supervision over planning public relations and procedures for making releases throughout the church in the United States. It may encourage and work with area and conference directors of public relations, may assist in pastors' schools and conduct seminars in public relations, and may prepare instruction materials for local-church use concerning public relations.

3. The commission shall maintain co-operative relationship with the editors of all boards and other agencies and editors of area and conference periodicals.

¶ **1590.** There may be area, conference, district, and local-church Commissions or Committees on Public Relations and Methodist Information, to be constituted and organized as the respective governing bodies may determine. Such commissions or committees shall be related to the general commission.

CHAPTER XIV

ASSOCIATION OF METHODIST HISTORICAL SOCIETIES

¶ 1591. 1. *Organization and Purpose.*—*a*) The **Association of Methodist Historical Societies** shall be a federation of the Jurisdictional, Annual Conference, and other historical associations and societies of The Methodist Church. It shall be affiliated with the International Methodist Historical Society. It shall be the official historical agency of The Methodist Church.

b) Its purpose shall be to gather, preserve, and disseminate materials and facts on the history of Methodism, to co-operate with other bodies, especially the international society and the World Methodist Council, and to do any and all things necessary to the promotion and care of the historical interests of The Methodist Church. It shall maintain archives in which shall be preserved historical records and materials of every kind relating to The Methodist Church.

2. *Executive Committee.*—*a*) The activities of the association shall be directed by an **executive committee** designated quadrennially. It shall be composed of its own officers; the secretary of the Council of Bishops and two other bishops appointed by the council; the secretary of the General Conference; the president of the Methodist Librarians' Fellowship; the presidents or chairmen of the active Jurisdictional Historical Associations; the president, the executive secretary, and the treasurer of the American Section of the World Methodist Council; the editorial director of *Christian Advocate* and *Together*, the book editor, and the manager of Abingdon Press; and

eight members nominated by the previous committee and elected by the General Conference. The committee is empowered to fill interim vacancies among the eight elected members.

b) The executive committee shall meet on the call of the president and executive secretary. It shall hold an annual meeting, elect the officers, and exercise the authority usually incident to an executive body.

c) There shall be an **administrative committee** composed of the officers, which shall perform the duties and exercise the authority of the executive committee between meetings.

d) The executive and administrative committees may vote by mail on any matter. Mail polls shall be carried out by the executive secretary, who shall state clearly the propositions to be voted on and announce the results to all the members.

3. *Officers.*—*a*) There shall be a president, two or more vice-presidents, an executive secretary, and a treasurer, all elected quadrennially.

b) These officers shall perform the duties usually incident to the positions. The executive secretary shall be the executive and administrative officer and shall carry on all the work of the association, keep the records and minutes, and do the editorial work.

c) The executive committee may elect such other officers as may be needed and prescribe their duties.

4. *Finances.*—*a*) The association shall be financed by appropriations of the General Conference, the sale of literature and historical materials, and the gifts of interested individuals and groups.

b) The executive committee shall prepare an annual budget based on the expected income and shall prescribe the manner of its administration.

5. *Associate Memberships.*—The association may provide for individual subscribing memberships whereby persons who so desire may become associate members by making an annual contribution. Such members shall receive the association's quarterly magazine *Methodist His-*

tory and shall be entitled to participate in its regular affairs.

6. *Methodist Shrines.*—*a*) Twelve buildings and sites have been designated as **Methodist shrines** by the General Conference: (1) John Street Church, New York City; (2) St. George's Church, Philadelphia; (3) Barratt's Chapel, near Frederica, Delaware; (4) Robert Strawbridge's Log House, near New Windsor, Maryland; (5) the Green Hill House, Louisburg, North Carolina; (6) Saint Simons Island, Brunswick, Georgia; (7) the Edward Cox House, Bluff City, Tennessee; (8) Rehoboth Church, Union, West Virginia; (9) the Wyandot Indian Mission, Upper Sandusky, Ohio; (10) Old McKendree Chapel, Jackson, Missouri; (11) Acuff's Chapel, Highway 11-W between Blountville and Kingsport, Tennessee; (12) Old Stone Church and Cemetery, Leesburg, Virginia.

b) To qualify for designation as a Methodist shrine a building or a site must have been so linked with significant events and outstanding personalities in the origin and development of American Methodism as to have distinctive historical interest and value for the denomination as a whole, as contrasted with local or regional historical significance.

c) During each quadrennium the association shall review data submitted on behalf of churches, buildings, and sites which are nominated for designation as Methodist shrines and shall make such recommendations as it deems appropriate to the ensuing General Conference.

7. *Methodist Landmarks.*—Jurisdictional and Annual Conferences may designate buildings and sites as **Methodist landmarks.** To qualify as a Methodist landmark a building or a site should have been so related to significant events and important personalities in the origin and development of Methodism within the jurisdiction or the Annual Conference that it has peculiar historical interest and value for the jurisdiction or for the Annual Conference.

¶ **1592.** There may be a **Jurisdictional Historical As-**

sociation in each jurisdiction, auxiliary to the Association of Methodist Historical Societies, as the Jurisdictional Conference may determine.

Note: For description of the Historical Society in each Annual Conference *see* ¶ 663.

CHAPTER XV

COUNCIL OF SECRETARIES

¶ **1593.** 1. There shall be a **Council of Secretaries,** whose membership shall consist of the chief executives of the following agencies: one from the Board of Missions and one each from its divisions and Joint Commission on Education and Cultivation; one from each division of the Board of Education; one from the Board of Christian Social Concerns and one each from its divisions; one each from the Boards of Hospitals and Homes, Evangelism, Lay Activities, and Pensions; one each from the Commissions on Chaplains, Camp Activities, Ecumenical Affairs, Promotion and Cultivation, and Public Relations and Methodist Information; and one each from The Methodist Publishing House, the Council on World Service and Finance, the Television, Radio, and Film Commission, the American Bible Society, the Interboard Committee on Missionary Education, the Interboard Committee on Christian Vocations, the Methodist Committee for Overseas Relief, the Association of Methodist Historical Societies, and the American section of the World Methodist Council.

2. The council shall meet periodically to consider matters of common interest and co-operation among the several general agencies of the church. It shall consider existing and emerging conditions and needs where the co-operative services of two or more agencies are needed, and devise ways and means of meeting those needs when they fall within the Disciplinary functions of two or more general agencies. It shall seek to further co-operation between existing agencies in their regular work and in

carrying out such additional responsibilities as the General Conference may place on them. It shall report annually to the Council of Bishops and to the Council on World Service and Finance, and quadrennially to the General Conference.

CHAPTER XVI

INTERDENOMINATIONAL AGENCIES

¶ **1594.** The Methodist Church is a charter member of the **World Methodist Council.** The members of the section representing The Methodist Church shall be nominated by the Council of Bishops, due regard being given to geographical representation. Financial support of the World Methodist Council shall be channeled through the central treasury, as shall be directed by the Council on World Service and Finance.

¶ **1595. 1.** The Methodist Church is a charter member of the **National Council of the Churches of Christ in the United States of America.** It has borne its proportionate share of financial support, and through the Interdenominational Co-operation Fund is authorized and directed to continue its support. (*See* ¶ 778.)

2. The representatives of The Methodist Church to the Assembly, the General Board, and other agencies of the National Council of Churches shall be nominated by the Council of Bishops and elected by the General Conference, due regard being given to geographical representation. When representatives must be chosen or vacancies must be filled between sessions of the General Conference, the Council of Bishops is authorized and instructed to do so.

3. Methodist support of the National Council of Churches shall be channeled through the central treasury, as shall be directed by the Council on World Service and Finance, which shall give due credit for Methodist gifts and contributions to this cause, and shall include them in its annual financial report to the church. The sources of income shall include: (*a*) the National Council of Churches' share of

the Interdenominational Co-operation Fund, as determined by the General Conference; and (b) such payments by the general agencies of the church as each agency may deem its responsibility and proportionate share in the co-operative program of the council. Personal, group, or local-church gifts shall be included as a part of the ratio distribution of the Interdenominational Co-operation Fund.

¶ 1596. 1. The Methodist Church is a charter member of the **World Council of Churches.** It has borne its proportionate share of financial support, and through the Interdenominational Co-operation Fund is authorized and directed to continue its support.

2. The representatives of The Methodist Church to the Assembly and other agencies of the World Council of Churches shall be nominated by the Council of Bishops and elected by the General Conference, due regard being given to geographical representation. When representatives must be chosen or vacancies must be filled between sessions of the General Conference, the Council of Bishops is authorized and intructed to do so.

4. Methodist support of the World Council of Churches shall be channeled through the central treasury, as shall be directed by the Council on World Service and Finance, which shall give due credit for Methodist gifts and contributions received by the World Council of Churches, and shall include them in its annual financial report to the church.

¶ 1598. To encourage the wider circulation of the Holy Scriptures throughout the world, and to provide for the translation, printing, and distribution essential thereto, the **American Bible Society** shall be recognized as one of the general missionary agencies of The Methodist Church, and the Council on World Service and Finance shall make appropriate provision for participating in its support.

¶ 1599. **Religion in American Life, Incorporated,** is recognized as an interdenominational and interfaith agency through which The Methodist Church may work to direct attention to church attendance and loyalty to the Christian faith. In endorsing this program the Council of Bishops shall nominate to its board of directors five members, to be elected by the General Conference. Further, the Council on World Service and Finance shall recommend to the General Conference, for its action and determination, the amount to be included in the General Administration Fund as the Methodist share in this participation.

PART VIII

PENSIONS AND PERMANENT FUNDS

CHAPTER I

GENERAL BOARD OF PENSIONS

SECTION I.   **Organization**

¶ 1601. 1. There shall be a **General Board of Pensions** of The Methodist Church (hereafter called the board in this chapter and the general board in the remainder of Part VIII) with its principal office and place of business in Evanston, Illinois, having the general supervision and administration of the support of conference claimants of The Methodist Church. The Board of Pensions of The Methodist Church, Incorporated in Illinois, which is incorporated under the laws of the state of Illinois in that name (formerly known as "The Board of Pensions and Relief of The Methodist Episcopal Church") and The Board of Pensions of The Methodist Church, Incorporated in Maryland, which is incorporated under the laws of the state of Maryland in that name (formerly known as "The General Fund for Superannuates of The Methodist Protestant Church"), and The Board of Pensions of The Methodist Church, Incorporated in Missouri, which is incorporated under the laws of the state of Missouri in that name (formerly known as "The Board of Finance of the Methodist Episcopal Church, South") shall be continued, subject to the direction, supervision, and control of the General Board of Pensions of The Methodist Church.

2. The general supervision and administration of the pension and relief systems and plans of The Methodist

Church, subject to the direction, supervision, and control of the board, shall be conducted by and through the office of the board in Evanston, Illinois.

3. The board shall have authority to establish, maintain, and discontinue from time to time such subordinate offices as it shall deem proper and advisable.

¶ **1602.** 1. The board shall be composed of one bishop, elected by the Council of Bishops; one minister and one layman from each jurisdiction, elected by the Jurisdictional Conference on nomination of its Committee on Nominations; four ministers and four laymen, not more than two from the same jurisdiction, elected by the General Conference on nomination of the Council of Bishops; and six members at large, not more than two from the same jurisdiction, nominated and elected by the board in such manner as it shall provide in its by-laws.[1]

The ministerial membership of the board shall be limited to ministers in the effective relation.

The general secretary of the board shall be an ex officio member thereof without vote.

The terms of all members so elected shall be four years, to take effect at the annual meeting of the board following the General Conference. Members shall serve during the terms for which they are elected, or until their successors shall have been elected and qualified.

2. A vacancy in the membership shall be filled for the unexpired term by the board.

3. The members of the board shall constitute the membership of the respective boards of directors of the aforesaid three constituent corporations. The general secretary shall be an ex officio member of each without vote.

4. In all matters not specifically covered by General Conference legislation, the board shall have authority to adopt rules and policies for the administration of the support of conference claimants.

5. The annual meetings of the board and of the boards of directors of the constituent corporations shall be held at the same date and place, at which time the board shall

---

[1] Amended in 1964 following Judicial Council Decision 183. *See also* Decision 214.

review and consider responsibilities committed to its care and take such action as it deems advisable in the furtherance of the best interests of the pension program of The Methodist Church. Special meetings of the board may be called by any two of the officers named in ¶1603.1.

6. A majority of the members of the board shall constitute a quorum.

¶ **1603.** 1. The board shall elect quadrennially at its annual meeting following the General Conference a president, a vice-president, and a recording secretary, all of whom shall be members of the board, and shall also elect quadrennially a **general secretary** and one or more other secretaries for four-year terms. The treasurers of the respective corporations shall be elected by the board for terms of four years, and may be persons who are not members of the board. A vacancy in any of these offices shall be filled by the board for the remainder of the unexpired term.

2. An **executive committee** shall be elected by the board. The same committee shall also respectively be elected by, and serve as the executive committee of, each of the three constituent corporations, unless otherwise required by applicable laws of the respective states of incorporation, in which case the board shall recognize such laws and the corporations shall have power to comply therewith.

SEC. II. **Authorizations**

¶ **1604.** 1. The General Board of Pensions is authorized to adopt and further any and all plans, to undertake any and all activities, and to create, obtain, accept, receive, and administer any and all trust or other funds or property for the purpose of increasing the revenues, and of providing for, aiding in, and contributing to the support, relief, assistance, and pensioning of Methodist ministers and their families, conference claimants of The Methodist Church, and other church workers and lay employees in The Methodist Church and its constituent boards, organizations, and institutions; and to do any and all acts and things necessary and convenient in connection therewith or incident thereto; and to perform any and all other duties and functions from time to time imposed or directed by the General Conference of The Methodist Church.

2. The board is authorized to receive, hold, manage, merge, consolidate, administer, invest, and reinvest, by and through its constituent corporations, all connectional pension funds, subject to the other provisions of the Discipline, and with due regard to any and all special contracts, agreements, and laws applicable thereto. (For rules and regulations of the Ministers Reserve Pension Fund, *see* ¶¶ 1642-57; for other pension funds, *see* ¶¶ 1658-59, 1666, 1671, 1676.)

3. The board is authorized to receive, hold, manage, administer, invest, and reinvest, by and through its constituent corporations, endowment funds belonging to Annual Conferences, or other funds for the support of conference claimants to be administered for the benefit of such Annual Conferences; *provided* that at no time shall any part of the principal of the endowment funds be appropriated by the board for any purpose. The net income of such endowment funds shall be accounted for annually to the board and paid over to the Annual Conferences concerned for the benefit of their conference claimants.

4. The board, by and through its constituent corporations, is authorized and empowered to receive any gift, devise, or bequest made or intended for the benefit of disabled, superannuated, or retired ministers, widows of ministers, and the dependent children of ministers, such persons being commonly called conference claimants, of The Methodist Church (being successor to the Methodist Episcopal Church, the Methodist Episcopal Church, South, and the Methodist Protestant Church); and if the language or terms of any gift, devise, or bequest be inexact or ambiguous, the board shall dispose of or administer the same in the manner deemed most equitable according to the apparent intent of the donor as determined by the board, after careful inquiry into the circumstances in connection with the making of such gift, devise, or bequest.

5. The three constituent corporations shall, until otherwise determined by the board, continue to collect, receive,

and administer such gifts, devises, and bequests and other funds as may be specifically designated to them by donors, subject to the rules and regulations of the board with respect thereto. All undesignated gifts, devises, bequests, and donations shall be collected, received, and administered under the direction of the board.

¶ 1605. The board shall adopt ways and means to increase the endowment funds to be administered, either for the board or for the Annual Conferences, by obtaining gifts, annuities, and bequests, and also to increase the current contributions of the pastoral charges for conference claimants.

¶ 1606. The board shall share in the funds raised for the world service budget of The Methodist Church, as provided for in ¶¶ 741-42 and enabling acts.

Chapter II

PERMANENT FUNDS

¶ 1607. The **Chartered Fund** shall be administered by the General Board of Pensions for the benefit of all the Annual and Provisional Annual Conferences in The Methodist Church the boundaries of which are within the United States, its territorial and insular possessions, and Cuba, unless the General Conference shall order otherwise; and once a year the net earnings of the fund, after provision for depreciation, shall be divided equally among such Annual and Provisional Annual Conferences in accordance with the restrictive rule contained in ¶ 9.5.

¶ 1608. The General Board of Pensions shall order and direct that the income from the **General Endowment Fund for Conference Claimants** (formerly known as the General Endowment Fund for Superannuates of The Methodist Episcopal Church, South) now held by The Board of Pensions of The Methodist Church, Incorporated in Missouri, shall be distributed on account of service of conference claimants rendered in an Annual Conference of the former Methodist Episcopal Church, South, or service rendered in an Annual Conference of The Methodist Church; *provided*, however, that such distribution shall be restricted to Annual Conferences which, directly or through their predecessor Annual Conferences, participated in raising this fund, in proportion to the number of approved years of annuity responsibility of each such Annual Conference as shall be determined by the General Board of Pensions.

¶ 1609. 1. Whenever two or more Annual Conferences or Provisional Annual Conferences are to be merged, in whole or in part, there shall be elected by each conference affected a Distributing Committee of three members, and three alternates, which shall act jointly with similar committees from the other conference or conferences. The **Joint Distributing Committee** thus formed shall have power and authority: (1) to allocate the pension responsibility involved; (2) to distribute equitably the permanent funds and other pension assets of the conference or conferences affected, taking into consideration in the division to the successor conference or conferences the number of churches, ministerial conference members, and pension responsibility involved; (3) to the extent not otherwise previously provided for by the conference or conferences involved, to distribute equitably any other assets or property and any other liabilities or obligations. It shall be governed by the legal restrictions or limitations of any contract, pledge, deed, or other instrument.

2. The Joint Distributing Committee shall conduct a hearing thereon, after publication of notice thereof in two consecutive issues of *Christian Advocate* and *Together*, the last publication to be not less than thirty days preceding the hearing; and it shall have power to continue and adjourn such hearing from time to time until it is finally concluded and a final decision is rendered.

3. The committee shall be convened promptly by the general secretary of the General Board of Pensions, or by some other officer of that board appointed by him in writing, and shall elect a chairman, a vice-chairman, and a secretary from its membership. It shall prescribe the time and place of the hearing, and the secretary of the committee shall give the notice aforesaid.

4. The committee shall determine the number of years of approved service rendered in the conferences which will lose their identity in the merging of conference territory, and the findings of the committee shall be final unless definite evidence to the contrary is discovered, and the annuity payments by the continuing conference or conferences shall be made accordingly.

5. The committee shall keep complete minutes of its transactions, and a copy thereof shall be filed with the secretary of each conference involved and with the General Board of Pensions.

6. Until the committee's work shall have been completed, the corporate organization of each conference in the process of merger shall be maintained. After the committee shall have completed its work, the officers of such corporation, subject to the completion of its business, shall dissolve or merge it, being authorized to do so by the conference involved.

CHAPTER III

ANNUAL CONFERENCE ORGANIZATIONS

SECTION I.   Authorization

¶ 1610. 1. Annual Conferences, hereafter in this chapter called conferences, are authorized to establish and maintain investment funds, preachers aid societies, and organizations and funds of similar character, under such names, plans, rules, and regulations as they may determine, the income from which shall be applied to the support of conference claimants. It is recommended that each conference provide a corporation to administer its permanent funds, under some other corporate name than that used by the General Board of Pensions, the directors of which shall be elected, or otherwise designated, by the conference where permissible under the laws of the state of incorporation.

2. All distributable funds, unless otherwise ordered by the conference, shall be disbursed by the Conference

Board of Pensions, excepting only such funds as are otherwise restricted by specific provisions or limitations in gifts, devises, bequests, trusts, pledges, deeds, or other similar instruments, which restrictions and limitations shall be observed.

3. On and after June 1, 1956, it shall not be permissible for any conference or permanent-fund organization thereof, to deprive its conference claimants who are conference claimants in other conferences of the privilege of sharing in the distribution of the earned income of such permanent funds through the clearinghouse operations as provided hereinafter in ¶ 1636; *provided*, however, that a lien may be filed on the annuity of any conference claimant on account of unpaid assessments, obligations, or pledges owed to such permanent funds, in accordance with ¶ 1634.

4. Provided that no laws of the state in which it is organized or incorporated prohibit its so doing, a conference shall have power to require from its ministerial members and approved supply pastors who are appointed with annuity claim on the conference an annual contribution to either its permanent or reserve fund or for current distribution or to a preachers aid society for the benefit of its annuitants, subject to the following provisions: (1) the annual payment may be made in installments as provided by the conference; (2) the conference may fix a financial penalty for failure of the member to pay; (3) in case his membership in the conference is terminated under the provisions of the Discipline, the conference may refund the amount so paid, in whole or in part, after hearing has been given to him in case such hearing is requested; (4) the making of such payment shall not be used as the ground of contractual obligations upon the part of the conference, or as the ground of any special or additional annuity claim of a member against the conference, neither shall it prevent disallowance of his annuity claim by conference action; (5) ministers entering a conference shall not be charged an initial entry fee by any organization mentioned in § 1 of this paragraph; furthermore, the annual contribution required from a ministerial member of the conference or an approved

supply pastor shall not exceed the equivalent of three per cent of his cash salary.[2]

5. Each conference shall hold one service during its sessions, to be known as the **Conference Claimants Anniversary,** for the promotion of the interests of the conference claimants.

6. Each conference, on recommendation of its Conference Board of Pensions or one of the organizations mentioned in § 1 of this paragraph, shall select a Sunday in each year to be observed in the churches as **Retired Ministers Day,** in honor of the retired ministers, their wives, and the widows of ministers, and in recognition of the church's obligation for their support. The bishop shall request each conference in his area to insert Retired Ministers Day in its calendar, and he shall diligently promote the observance of it.

SEC. II.   **Conference Board of Pensions**

¶ **1611.** 1. There shall be organized in each Annual Conference a conference board, auxiliary to the General Board of Pensions, to be known as the **Conference Board of Pensions** (hereafter called the board in this section and the conference board in the remainder of Part VIII), which shall have charge of the interests and work of providing for the support of its conference claimants, except as otherwise provided for by the general board.

2. The board shall be composed of not less than twelve members, not indebted to or beneficiaries of conference claimants' funds of the conference, ministers in the effective relation and laymen in equal number, elected for a term of eight years and so arranged in two equal classes that one half shall be elected quadrennially; and in addition thereto any ministerial member of the conference or lay member of a church within the conference who is a member of the General Board of Pensions. A lay member of the board may or may not be a member of the Annual Conference. A vacancy in the membership of the board shall be filled by the board for the remainder of the conference year in which the vacancy occurs, and at its next

---

[2] *See* Judicial Council Decision 181.

session the conference shall fill the vacancy for the remainder of the unexpired term.

3. The members shall assume their duties at the adjournment of the conference session at which they were elected.

4. The board shall organize by electing a chairman, vice-chairman, secretary, and treasurer, who shall serve during the ensuing quadrennium, or until their successors shall have been elected and qualified. These officers shall constitute an **executive committee;** *provided*, however, that three members may be added thereto by the board. The duty of the executive committee shall be to administer the work of the board during the conference year in the interim between regular or special meetings of the board. The office of secretary may be combined with that of treasurer. The treasurer may be a person who is not a member of the board, in which case he shall not be a member of the executive committee. Calls for special meetings of the board shall be issued by the secretary on request of the chairman, or the vice-chairman, when the chairman is unable to act.

5. The board shall report to the conference the names, addresses, and years of approved service of the conference claimants, the names of those who have died during the year, the names of the dependent children of deceased ministerial members of the conference, and any other useful information, and shall show separately the amount paid to each by the conference from the annuity and necessitous funds.

6. The appropriations to the conference claimants shall be subject to the approval of the conference.

7. The board shall make a report to the General Board of Pensions immediately following the session of the conference, on forms provided for that purpose by the general board.

8. The conference shall constitute the board a committee on proportional payment of ministerial support, for the purpose of comparing the records of amounts paid on support of pastors and conference claimants by each pastoral charge, computing the proportional distribution thereof, and keeping a permanent record of defaults; or

the conference may organize a special **Committee on Proportional Payment of Ministerial Support,** which shall keep permanent records and furnish necessary information to the board regarding adjustment of annuities. (*See* ¶ 1624.)

9. The board shall administer all annuities and relief provided for the benefit of special conference claimants. (*See* ¶ 1631.)

10. The board shall investigate carefully all cases in which applications have been made by conference claimants for relief or necessitous appropriation, so as to determine equitably the amount of relief to be granted in each case.

11. The conference, on recommendation of the board, shall designate a bank or other depository for deposit of the funds held by the board.

12. The board, through the Conference Commission on World Service and Finance, shall provide a fidelity bond in suitable amount for all persons handling its funds. (*See* ¶¶ 729, 804.)

13. The board may build up a stabilization fund from the income for conference claimants in order to stabilize the annuity rate. Such stabilization fund should be at least the equivalent of twenty-five per cent of the average annual income of the board for all purposes for the five years immediately preceding. Such stabilization fund shall be held as the conference shall direct and shall be subject to the requirements of § 11 of this paragraph.

SEC. III. **Financial Policy**

¶ **1612.** The following rules shall apply to financial administration of Annual Conference pension and pension-related permanent funds:

1. Persons connected in any way with the securities, real estate, or other forms of investment sold to or purchased from such funds shall be ineligible to serve on the investment committee responsible therefor.

2. No officer or member of a conference agency handling such funds shall receive a personal commission, bonus, or remuneration in connection with the purchase or sale of securities or other properties for that agency, or shall be

eligible to obtain a loan in any amount from funds committed to the care of that agency.

3. No local church or organization thereof shall be eligible to obtain a loan in any amount from such funds.[3]

4. The principle of diversification of investments shall be observed, in order to obtain proper geographical and class distribution of investment commitments.

5. Real property may be accepted as consideration for gift annuity agreements only with the stipulation that the annuity shall not exceed the net income from the property until such property shall have been liquidated. Upon liquidation, the annuity shall be paid upon the net proceeds at the established annuity rate.

6. A conference agency handling such funds shall not offer higher rates of annuity than those listed in the annuity schedule approved by the Council on World Service and Finance. (*See* ¶ 737.10.)

7. On order of the conference, there shall be printed in its journal a list of the investments held by each agency handling such funds directly or indirectly under the control of the conference, or such list may be distributed directly to the members of the conference at their request. A copy of all such lists concerning conference claimants shall be filed annually with the General Board of Pensions.

8. The borrowing of money in any conference year by a conference corporation or organization to enable the Conference Board of Pensions to complete payment of annuities at a designated annuity rate shall be done only on authority of the conference granted by three-fourths vote of the members present and voting.

CHAPTER IV

PENSION CODE

¶ **1613.** The administration of the pensions and support of conference claimants within the Annual Conferences situated in the United States, hereafter in this

---

[3] *See* Judicial Council Decision 145.

chapter called conferences, shall be the responsibility of the General Board of Pensions, and shall be governed by the rules and regulations contained in the following **code**, and such amendments thereto as may hereafter be adopted.

¶ **1614.** *Definition of Conference Claimants.*—Retired ministers, the widows of ministers, and dependent children of deceased ministers are **conference claimants.**

¶ **1615.** *Nature of Ministerial Support.*—Assumption of the obligations of the ministry required to be made at the time of his admission to membership in an Annual Conference puts upon the church the inevitable counter-obligation of providing a comfortable support for the minister during the period of his conference membership and for his widow and dependent children after his death; but such counterobligation with reference to these benefits shall not be construed as contractual unless and until provision shall have been made therefor on an actuarial reserve basis. (*See* ¶ 821.)

¶ **1616.** *Approval of Claim.*—The Annual Conference shall be the sole judge of the admissibility and validity of annuity claims and shall be fully competent to determine all payments, disallowances, and deductions thereunder, subject to the specific regulations relating thereto contained in the Discipline.[4]

¶ **1617.** *Retirement.*—1. The Annual Conference may place any ministerial member thereof in the retired relation, with or without his consent and irrespective of his age, if such relation is recommended by the Committee on Conference Relations. (*See* ¶ 367.)[5]

2. Every ministerial member of an Annual Conference who has attained age seventy-two prior to the first day of the session of the conference shall be placed in the retired relation. (*See* ¶ 368).[6]

3. At his own request the Annual Conference may place any ministerial member thereof in the retired relation, with the privilege of making an annuity claim, if he has attained age sixty-five, or has completed forty years of

---

[4] *See* Judicial Council Decisions 171, 180, 192.
[5] *See* Judicial Council Decision 192.
[6] *See* Judicial Council Decisions 7, 15, 165.

full-time approved service, as defined in ¶ 1618, prior to the first day of the session of the conference to which said request is presented. (*See* ¶ 369.)[7]

4. Retirement with the privilege of making an annuity claim on the ground of personal disability shall be permitted only after a thorough investigation of the case by, and presentation of a medical certificate to, the Committee on Conference Relations. This certificate shall be made on a form approved by the General Board of Pensions, and shall be given by a regular medical doctor, other than the personal physician of the applicant, who has been approved by the Committee on Conference Relations. If such disability continue for more than one year, such medical certificate shall be required annually.[8]

5. If retirement takes place for other reasons than personal disability, the right to make an annuity claim from the time of retirement until the ministerial member qualifies under § 3 shall be granted on recommendation of the Committee on Conference Relations and a three-fourths vote of those present and voting in the Annual Conference; *provided*, however, that in case of emergency occurring between sessions of the conference the Conference Board of Pensions shall have authority to grant relief at its discretion.

6. When because of physical or mental incapacity a minister is forced to give up his ministerial work during the conference year, upon recommendation of the Cabinet, accompanied by a medical certificate, as set forth in § 4 of this paragraph, the Conference Board of Pensions may grant him an appropriation from an emergency fund for the remaining part of the conference year.

7. The Conference Board of Pensions, on recommendation of the Cabinet, may grant aid to a minister in the effective relation who has attained the age of voluntary retirement and has been compelled because of an emergency to relinquish his ministerial work during the conference year.

¶ 1618. *Definitions.*—1. The term **years of approved service** shall mean full-time service rendered in and to

---

[7] *See* Judicial Council Decision 150.
[8] *See* Judicial Council Decisions 149, **171.**

any appointment mentioned in § 2 of this paragraph.[9] Part-time service can be counted for annuity claim only by a three-fourths vote of those present and voting in the Annual Conference on recommendation of the Conference Board of Pensions.

2. The following years of approved service on trial or in the effective relation [10] in an Annual Conference of The Methodist Church, as defined in § 8 of this paragraph, are eligible to be counted for the purpose of determining the annuity claims payable thereon:

a) As pastor, associate or assistant pastor, or other minister in a pastoral charge.

b) As district superintendent, presiding elder, conference president, or other full-time salaried official of the conference.

c) Under special appointment to an institution, organization, or agency which in the judgment of the Annual Conference rendered to it some form of service, direct or indirect, sufficient to warrant granting an annuity from the conference funds therefor, or to a community church; *provided*, however, that such institution, organization, agency, or community church accepts and pays annually such apportionments as the conference may require in accordance with the provision set forth in ¶ 1623.7; and *provided*, furthermore, that any church-related institution, organization, agency, or community church may arrange for a pension related to such service through one of the pension funds administered by the General Board of Pensions.

d) Under the special appointment as an evangelist; *provided*, however, that if annuity responsibility be accepted by the conference therefor, such conference may require the payment of an apportionment by such evangelist in accordance with the provision in ¶ 1623.7.

e) As a student appointed to attend school, not to exceed three years; *provided*, however, that all years of appointment to attend school prior to the General Conference of

---

[9] *See* Judicial Council Decision 150.
[10] *See* Judicial Council Decision 181.

1960 are eligible to be counted for the purpose of determining the annuity claim thereon.

f) As a minister on sabbatical leave. (*See* ¶ 364.)

g) As the wife of a minister during his years of approved service. (*See* ¶ 1620.)

h) As a chaplain on full-time duty prior to December 31, 1946, in case no pension is granted for such years of service by the employing organization, institution, or agency related to the Commission on Chaplains of The Methodist Church as set forth in ¶ 1572; *provided*, however, that provision for pension on account of service rendered after December 31, 1946, as a chaplain on full-time duty shall be made by the Chaplains Pension Fund in accordance with rules and regulations to be determined jointly by the General Board of Pensions and the Commission on Chaplains.

i) In calculating fractional years of service of a conference claimant the following formula shall be used in all cases, irrespective of the time when such service was rendered, including those involved in clearinghouse operations: Any period up to one month and fourteen days shall not be counted; one month and fifteen days to four months and fourteen days shall be counted as one quarter of a year; four months and fifteen days to seven months and fourteen days shall be counted as one half of a year; seven months and fifteen days to ten months and fourteen days shall be counted as three quarters of a year; ten months and fifteen days to eleven months and twenty-nine days shall be counted as one year. Each of the above-mentioned periods shall be inclusive of all days therein.

3. The following years of service on trial or in the effective relation shall not be approved as a basis of annuity claim:

a) Years for which a pension, or any other form of compensation or "deferred salary," is received from any source other than the Annual Conference.[11]

b) A year of service rendered concurrently by a minister and his wife, whether on the same pastoral charge, or otherwise as members of an Annual Conference, or as

---

[11] *See* Judicial Council Decision 180.

approved supply pastors therein, shall be counted only as one year. A year of service rendered as an approved supply pastor by the wife of a ministerial member of the conference on a separate pastoral charge shall not be eligible for count as full-time pastoral service.

4. On recommendation of the Conference Board of Pensions and approval by the Annual Conference, special appointments shall be listed in the conference journal as follows: (1) with annuity claim (*a*) upon this Annual Conference, or (*b*) upon a general board, an institution, or an agency of The Methodist Church; (2) without annuity claim upon this Annual Conference.[12] If at any session the conference fails to make such listing, it may be done subsequently, whenever desirable, under the Disciplinary question, "What other personal notation should be made?" (¶ 651.46.)

5. The **annuity rate** shall mean the sum determined annually by the Annual Conference, payable as an annuity for each year of approved service of a retired minister rendered in The Methodist Church. The annuity rate shall be determined by the conference without restriction, but it is recommended that such rate be not less than one per cent of the average salary of the conference as hereinafter defined in § 6.

6. The **average salary** of the conference for the purposes of this annuity plan shall mean the average salary (including house rent at a valuation equivalent to twenty per cent of the cash salary in cases in which a parsonage is occupied or house rent is provided) of the ministers in the conference who are on trial or in the effective relation as pastors or district superintendents, and the full-time approved supply pastors named in answer to question 22 in the business of the Annual Conference (¶¶ 651, 1631.10), based on the salaries as published in the statistical report of the conference; *provided*, however, that the conference may request that its average salary be computed on the basis of the salaries paid all pastors and district superintendents. In computing the average salary no account shall be taken of salaries of ministers who have

---

[12] *See* Judicial Council Decision 95.

served less than one year on a pastoral charge. The average salary shall be established by the General Board of Pensions for each conference annually.

7. **Dependent child** shall mean a child of a deceased minister or a child legally adopted before the minister's retirement or death, under sixteen years of age, and dependent for his or her support. If the child is kept in a standard school, the age limit may be extended not to exceed six additional years by action of the Conference Board of Pensions. (*See* ¶ 1621.)

8. **The Methodist Church** shall mean The Methodist Church after the Uniting Conference of 1939, also any of the churches united in 1939, as they were constituted prior to 1939.

9. On recommendation of the Conference Board of Pensions, the Annual Conference shall determine the Methodist institutions and organizations related to it, service in which shall be approved for annuity responsibility of the conference; *provided*, however, that such list may be revised at any session of the conference.[13] Such list shall be printed annually in the conference journal under the Disciplinary question "What Methodist institutions or organizations are approved by the conference for annuity responsibility?" (¶ 651.15.)

¶ **1619.** *Claim of a Retired Minister.*—The annuity claim of a retired minister shall be for an amount equivalent to the total of his years of approved service multiplied by the annuity rate as defined above, irrespective of breaks in the sequence of such service; *provided*, however, that if the minister has been retired for reason of personal disability and if the years of approved service are fewer than ten, effective with the 1961 clearinghouse year, the pension shall be based on ten years of service. The clearinghouse shall allocate this additional obligation pro rata among the conferences served.

¶ **1620.** *Claim of a Widow.*—1. The annuity claim of a widow shall be for an amount equivalent to the total of her years of approved service (¶ 1618.2*g*, .3*b*) multiplied by seventy per cent of the annuity rate. The sev-

---

[13] *See* Judicial Council Decision 180.

enty per cent may be raised to seventy-five per cent at the option of the Annual Conference. The fact that a widow served as the wife of a minister of The Methodist Church until his death and, after an intervening period of widowhood, served again as the wife of another minister of The Methodist Church shall not prevent the approval of all such years of service for the purpose of computing her annuity claim. If the total years of service on which her annuity claim is based are fewer than ten, the pension shall be based on ten years of service; the clearinghouse shall allocate this additional obligation pro rata among the conferences charged with her annuity claim. If the total years of service on which her annuity claim is based are fifteen or more, the pension shall be based on the total of her husband's years of approved service and shall be charged through the clearinghouse accordingly.

2. The annuity claim of a widow of a ministerial member or of an approved supply pastor shall become effective immediately on the death of such husband; *provided*, however, that if he was himself a conference claimant or a special conference claimant at the time of his death, her annuity claim shall become effective with the date of the next payment which would have been scheduled for him if he had lived.

3. The widow of a deceased ministerial member of a conference or approved supply pastor who remarries shall have no annuity claim during such marriage until her attainment of age sixty-five, at which time her annuity claim may be reinstated; but if such subsequent marriage shall be dissolved by the husband's death or by legal process, the conference on recommendation of the Conference Board of Pensions may reinstate her annuity claim thereafter subject to the provisions of the pension code.

4. The widow of a deceased minister whose conference membership was terminated under the provisions of ¶¶ 374-82 or 935-37, 952 shall have the right to make an annuity claim on the conferences concerned based on her years of approved service; *provided*, however, that such claim must be approved, on recommendation of the Con-

ference Board of Pensions, by a two-thirds vote of those present and voting in the Annual Conference.

5. An Annual Conference, on recommendation of its Conference Board of Pensions, may by a two-thirds vote of those present and voting grant annuity and/or necessitous relief to a wife for her years of approved service without granting annuity to her husband if he has disqualified himself by some moral dereliction, mental illness, or other cause beyond the wife's control.[14]

6. The Conference Board of Pensions shall obtain annually satisfactory evidence that a widow is living and is eligible to receive annuity payments in accordance with the provisions of the pension code.

¶ 1621. *Claim of a Dependent Child.*—1. The claim of an unmarried dependent child shall be determined by multiplying the equivalent of the deceased father's years of approved service by one fourth of the annuity rate to which the retired ministers are entitled. If the total years of service on which the child's annuity claim is based are fewer than ten, effective with the 1961 clearinghouse year, the pension shall be based on ten years of service. The clearinghouse shall allocate this additional obligation pro rata among the conferences charged with the annuity claim.

2. The claim of an unmarried dependent child shall become effective immediately on the death of the father and shall cease on attainment of age sixteen. If the child is kept in a standard school, the age limit may be extended, not to exceed six additional years, by action of the Conference Board of Pensions. On recommendation of the board and approval by two thirds of those present and voting in the Annual Conference, renewed annually, a claim may be validated for a child past sixteen years of age in case of evident mental or physical incapacity to provide self-support; *provided,* however, that such mental or physical incapacity shall have become apparent prior to the attainment of age twenty-one and shall have continued thereafter; and *provided,* furthermore, that before recommending such claim the board shall require a med-

---

[14] *See* Judicial Council Decision 201.

ical certificate and may require subsequent certificates certifying the continuance of such incapacity.

3. A certificate of attendance of a dependent child at a standard school shall be obtained annually between the ages of sixteen and twenty-two by the conference board, on a form to be provided by the general board.

¶ **1622.** *Claim of a Missionary.*—1. A regularly commissioned missionary of the Board of Missions, holding membership in an Annual Conference or Provisional Annual Conference or connected with a Mission, shall be entitled to make an annuity claim on the division of the Board of Missions which provides his support.

2. A retired missionary who has been granted the retired relation in an Annual Conference abroad shall be entitled to make an annuity claim on a conference in the United States on account of years of approved service rendered therein. Such claim shall be presented to the General Board of Pensions, and payments due thereunder shall be collected from the conferences concerned and forwarded to the claimant by the general board in such manner as it may deem most expeditious and economical. In such cases the general board shall certify the years of approved service to each conference concerned.

¶ **1623.** *Apportionments.*—1. The Annual Conference, on recommendation of the Conference Board of Pensions, shall determine the annuity rate payable. The recommended standard annuity rate is a sum equivalent to one per cent of the average salary of the conference. (*See* ¶ 1618.5, .6.)

2. The Conference Board of Pensions shall compute the total amount necessary to meet the prospective annuity disbursements according to the annuity rate determined. After all amounts which will be received from other sources for the support of conference claimants have been subtracted from this total, the remaining amount necessary shall be apportioned to the several pastoral charges of the conference on such basis as the conference may from time to time determine. (*See* ¶ 822.) In case the basis of apportionment adopted is that of a percentage of the cash salaries of the ministers, where there is more than one minister serving a pastoral charge the apportion-

ment thereto shall be on the basis of all cash salaries paid to such ministers.

3. The apportionment to the pastoral charges for both regular relief and emergency appropriations for conference claimants who are in distress, or because of other special circumstances, shall be estimated by the Conference Board of Pensions.[15]

4. The Conference Commission on World Service and Finance shall include in its recommendations to the Annual Conference the amounts computed by the Conference Board of Pensions as necessary to meet the needs for annuity payments and relief. (*See* ¶ 798.)

5. The apportionment for aged and disabled supply pastors, if any, shall be combined with the apportionment for regular conference claimants.

6. The apportionment to a federated church, if and when it is served by a ministerial member or an approved supply pastor of the Annual Conference, shall be made on the same basis as the apportionments to the pastoral charges of the conference; *provided*, however, that an annual apportionment may be made to a federated church in accordance with the terms of an agreement between the Conference Board of Pensions and such federated church.[16]

7. *a*) An Annual Conference which accepts annuity responsibility in any conference year for service rendered by a member thereof under special appointment to an institution, organization, agency, or community church, as provided in ¶ 1618.2c, may make an apportionment to such institution, organization, agency, or community church served for such amount as the conference may determine; *provided*, however, that such apportionment shall not exceed an amount equivalent to twelve times the annuity rate which has been adopted for that conference year. (*See also* ¶ 1618.4, .9.)[17]

b) Until the person concerned or his widow becomes a conference claimant, moneys collected on apportionments

---

[15] Amended in 1944 following Judicial Council Decision 13.
[16] *See* Judicial Council Decision 202.
[17] *See* Judicial Council Decisions 180, 202.

made under authority of this subsection may be conserved by the Conference Board of Pensions in a special fund.

c) Such moneys shall be released for general distribution when the parties concerned become conference claimants; one twelfth of the funds accumulated, in each case, to be released annually thereafter for distribution. Moneys so conserved and distributed shall be regarded as part of the general resources for distribution by the Conference Board of Pensions.

d) If the Annual Conference shall have entered the Ministers Reserve Pension Fund and the minister under special appointment is a member of the Fund, such apportionment shall not exceed the annual contribution for a member of the Fund as hereinafter provided in ¶ 1645. (*See also* ¶ 1618.4, .9.)

¶ **1624.** *Proportional Payment.*—1. When the apportionment to the pastoral charges for the support of conference claimants and for the Ministers Reserve Pension Fund has been determined as provided in ¶¶ 822 and 1645.4, payments made thereon by each pastoral charge shall be exactly proportionate to payments made on the salary or salaries of the minister or ministers serving it. (*See* ¶ 823.)

2. The amount apportioned to each pastoral charge for the support of conference claimants and for the Ministers Reserve Pension Fund shall be paid to the conference treasurer monthly or quarterly, and the conference treasurer shall remit monthly to the treasurer or treasurers of these respective funds.

3. The treasurer of the pastoral charge shall be primarily responsible for the application of § 1 of this paragraph; but in the event of his failure to apply it, the pastor shall adjust his cash salary and the payment according to the proper ratio, as provided above, before he enters the respective amounts in his statistical report to the Annual Conference. And, on retirement, amounts in default shall be deducted from his annuity as provided in ¶ 1634.1. If such pastor is a member of the Ministers Reserve Pension Fund, the annual contribution to the service annuity credit by the conference of such member shall be reduced proportionately by the conference in any

conference year in which proportional payment, as required herein, has not been observed.

4. The Conference Board of Pensions shall render a statement annually to all ministers of the conference who have failed to observe the provisions of this paragraph, indicating the amounts in default for that and all preceding conference years. Copies thereof shall be sent to the clearinghouse of the general board, and the information contained thereon shall be recorded upon the service records of the individual ministers concerned.

5. If a retired minister fails to observe the provisions of this paragraph while serving as a supply pastor in any conference year, the amount of such default shall be deducted from his annuity during the ensuing conference year.

6. It shall not be permissible for a pastor to receive a bonus or other supplementary compensation tending to defeat proportional payment. Failure to comply with this section shall be deemed disobedience to the order and discipline of The Methodist Church. The Conference Board of Pensions may recommend to the conference that the pastor's annuity claim be disallowed for the year during which such bonus or supplementary compensation was so received.[18]

¶ 1625. *Distribution.*—1. Moneys designated for distribution to the claimants as annuities shall be distributed on the basis of years of approved service, and shall consist of:

a) The appropriation from The Methodist Publishing House.

b) The income from investments for annuity distribution held for this purpose.

c) Gifts and bequests for annuity distribution.

d) Money received from the apportionments to the pastoral charges for annuity distribution.

e) Money received from all special offerings for distribution to conference claimants.

2. Moneys designated for relief on the basis of special need and emergency relief shall consist of:

---

[18] *See* Judicial Council Decisions 51, 151.

a) The appropriation from the Chartered Fund.

b) Money received from the apportionment to the pastoral charges; *provided* that each conference shall set aside for necessitous and emergency distribution such part of its fund as it may deem necessary, but not to exceed five per cent of the total amount collected on apportionment to the pastoral charges.

3. The Conference Board of Pensions may pay annuities in quarterly or monthly installments.

4. The amount received for the support of conference claimants each year from the pastoral charges in advance of the conference sessions shall be reserved for appropriation and expenditure during the ensuing conference year; *provided*, however, that the conferences now paying on a current income basis may continue to do so temporarily, but as quickly as feasible shall change to collection of income one year in advance of payment.

¶ 1626. *Relinquishment.*—1. For a year at a time a conference claimant may voluntarily relinquish in writing his annuity claim and any amount payable thereunder; *provided* that the disposal of the relinquished amount shall be entirely under the control of the Conference Board of Pensions.

2. Any agreement made prior to retirement to relinquish at retirement a future annuity claim shall be null and void.[19]

¶ 1627. *Disallowance.*—1. Upon recommendation of a majority of the Conference Board of Pensions, after opportunity has been given for hearing the claimant's objections, which may be made in person, or by a ministerial member of an Annual Conference acting as the claimant's personal representative, the annuity claim of any conference claimant may be disallowed, in whole or in part, by three-fourths vote of the ministers of the Annual Conference, present and voting, for any of the following causes:

a) Receipt of a pension or other periodical income from an individual church, or from other sources, which may

---

[19] *See* Judicial Council Decision 187.

521

be presumed to cover and adequately compensate for certain years of service included in the claim.[20]

b) Service in a special appointment which did not confer sufficient benefit on The Methodist Church to justify apportioning the annuity cost thereof to the pastoral charges of the conference.

c) Having been found guilty of unministerial or unchristian conduct by the Disciplinary processes.

2. The following rules and procedures shall be observed in all cases of disallowance of annuity claims:

a) The secretary of the Conference Board of Pensions shall notify the conference claimant, by registered mail, at the last address known to the conference secretary, concerning the proposed disallowance not less than three months in advance of the conference session at which his case will be adjudicated.

b) The notification of the claimant shall specify the cause or causes under which the case will be cited.

c) If he or she cannot be present, the claimant shall have the right to choose a ministerial member of any Annual Conference to present his or her objections to the proposed disallowance before the Conference Board of Pensions prior to action on the case.

d) The Conference Board of Pensions shall present to the conference the proposal for disallowance in written form with a full statement of the case and a record of its vote for and against recommendation.

e) Disallowance cannot be made by general rule of the Annual Conference; each case must be heard and adjudicated separately.

3. When an annuity claim shall have been disallowed, under § 1 of this paragraph, it may be reconsidered at any subsequent annual session of the conference, upon recommendation of the Conference Board of Pensions, or by two-thirds vote of the members of the conference present and voting.

4. Disallowance can be made only by the conference where membership is held or, in the case of a widow

---

[20] *See* Judicial Council Decision 180.

or minor dependent children, the conference with which the claimant is directly connected.

¶ **1629.** *Service Records.*—1. The General Board of Pensions shall maintain complete service records of ministerial members of the Annual Conferences compiled from the answers to the Disciplinary questions as published in the conference journals and in the General Minutes of The Methodist Church.

2. Power to revise, correct, or adjust a minister's service record as it concerns his annuity lies with the Annual Conference solely. It is recommended that, prior to the revision of a member's service record, the General Board of Pensions be requested to review the relevant data and report its findings. Such revisions, corrections, and adjustments, after having been adopted by the conference concerned, shall be published in the conference journal as a personal notation in the answers to the Disciplinary questions (¶ 651.46), and notice thereof shall be sent to the general board by the conference secretary.

3. The secretary of each Annual Conference shall publish annually in the conference journal the chronological roll of ministerial members and approved supply pastors, indicating the total number of years of approved service of each; *provided*, however, that if the alphabetical roll printed in the conference journal contains the required information, a separate chronological roll shall not be mandatory. (*See* ¶ 632.)[21]

4. In the conference statistical tables there shall be provided a separate column with the caption "Conference Claimants," which shall show the amount apportioned to each charge and the amount paid.

5. The conference secretary shall have the power to require from each and every ministerial member of it a signed statement concerning the date of his birth, the date of birth of his wife, the date of their marriage, and the dates of birth of their dependent children, and to require similar data from approved supply pastors.

¶ **1630.** *General Regulations.*—1. A minister who re-

---

[21] *See* Judicial Council Decision 165.

fuses to prorate ministerial support may be brought to trial for violation of a law of the church.

2. Annuities are granted by the conference annually, including those granted on the ground of disability; the determination of what constitutes disability lies with the conference. If a member of the conference who is receiving an annuity on the ground of disability recovers sufficiently to resume ministerial work or to engage in a remunerative occupation, his annuity may be continued, reduced, or terminated by the Annual Conference on recommendation of the Conference Board of Pensions. (See ¶ 1617.4.)

3. The annuity claim of an effective minister cannot be recognized by the Conference Board of Pensions between annual sessions of the conference; he must be retired first. Provision for emergency cases may be made in accordance with ¶ 1617.5-.7.

4. A minor child of a living retired minister cannot be a conference claimant.

5. Although the conference has power to require a contribution to its funds and to fix a financial penalty for defaults, a minister cannot be brought to trial for failure to make such required contribution.

6. A conference may withhold money from a conference claimant in order to discharge his obligation for assessments voted by the conference for conference claimants.

7. A minister cannot be retired automatically by operation of a conference rule fixing an age of retirement other than that specified in the Discipline.

8. A minister cannot present his credentials to and be accepted into the ministry of another denomination and at the same time retain his standing in an Annual Conference of The Methodist Church. Such action constitutes withdrawal from our ministry. However, if a ministerial member while in good standing in an Annual Conference voluntarily withdraws from the ministry of The Methodist Church and enters the ministry of another church within one year from the date of withdrawal, on the attainment of age sixty-five and retirement from the ministry of such other church or denomination, on recommendation of the Conference Board of Pensions and a three-fourths vote

of those present and voting in the Annual Conference in which ministerial membership was last held, he may be recognized as a conference claimant and allowed an annuity claim on account of approved service in The Methodist Church.

9. A conference member cannot relinquish his annuity claim at conference time and then ask for it, or a portion of it, during the conference year.

10. An Annual Conference may not make any arrangement with a life insurance company for the purchase of annuities for the benefit of individual effective or retired ministers, or take any steps to nullify, in whole or in part, the annuity plan of The Methodist Church by making contracts with outside parties. However, group life insurance may be provided through the medium of a life insurance company.

11. Money received for the support of conference claimants shall be appropriated only for the payment of pension or relief benefits to conference claimants and the administrative costs of the pension program, except as provided in ¶ 1631.5.

12. A minister on trial or the widow and dependent children of a minister who was on trial at the time of his death may become conference claimants subject to the provisions of the pension code.

13. A widow of a retired minister who married him after his retirement or a child born of such marriage is not entitled to make an annuity claim, except as provided in ¶ 1620.1.

14. A minister in the supernumerary relation cannot make an annuity claim, but may be granted emergency relief by the Conference Board of Pensions.

15. *a*) If a located person, whether located voluntarily or involuntarily, remains a member in good standing of The Methodist Church until the attainment of age seventy-two, he shall retain the right to make an annuity claim based on his years of approved service; *provided*, however, that upon presentation of satisfactory evidence regarding his character during location he shall have been read-

mitted into the Annual Conference, or its legal successor, which granted him location. (*See* ¶¶ 374-79.) [22]

b) If a located person becomes physically or mentally disabled so as to be unable to provide self-support, on presentation of satisfactory evidence regarding his character during location, accompanied by a medical certificate in accordance with the provision in ¶ 1617.4, on joint recommendation of the Committee on Conference Relations and the Conference Board of Pensions, he may be readmitted by a three-fourths vote of the Annual Conference, or its legal successor, which granted him location, and placed in the retired relation for the purpose of making an annuity claim; *provided*, however, that such certificate of disability shall be made on a form approved by the General Board of Pensions and shall be presented annually to the conference board during such disability prior to age seventy-two.

16. In determining the annuity claim of a regular conference claimant, the years of approved service as a fulltime approved supply pastor rendered prior to admission on trial by a conference may be counted and payment made therefor at the rate for a special conference claimant. (*See* ¶ 1631.)

17. Full-time service rendered as pastor of a charge between the date of termination of membership in an Annual or Provisional Annual Conference and the date of readmission may be approved for an annuity claim on recommendation of the Conference Board of Pensions and vote of the conference.

18. If the conference provides a dwelling for the use of a conference claimant, an adjustment may be made in his annuity as determined by the conference, after recommendation by the Conference Board of Pensions.

19. Pension responsibility on account of appointment to attend school after May 7, 1960, by a member on trial or in full connection shall be allocated to the Annual Conference in which he shall thereafter first render a full year of approved service as a member in the effective relation under an appointment other than to attend school;

---

[22] *See* Judicial Council Decision 192.

provided, however, that if no such service is rendered, the responsibility shall be allocated to the conference in which membership was held at the time of appointment to attend school.

¶ **1631.** *Special Conference Claimants.*—1. An approved supply pastor who shall have qualified under ¶¶ 314-17, and who shall have rendered not less than four consecutive years of full-time approved service in one Annual Conference as pastor or assistant pastor of a charge may on retirement make an annuity claim as a **special conference claimant;** *provided*, however, that any period of less than one full year of service in any conference may not be counted; [23] and *provided*, furthermore, that years of full-time service rendered to a board, institution, or other agency of The Methodist Church may be counted when determining eligibility, but the annuity as a special conference claimant shall be based only on full-time approved service as pastor or assistant pastor of a charge. Full-time approved service for which pension credit may be given shall mean service under appointment as pastor or assistant pastor of a charge for which the cash support per annum from all church sources shall be not less than the minimum salary established by the conference for full-time approved supply pastors.

2. On recommendation of the Committee on Conference Relations an approved supply pastor who has attained age sixty-five prior to the first day of the conference session, and who has rendered the minimum number of years of approved service may request retirement, and upon retirement shall be designated a special conference claimant.

3. Every approved supply pastor who has attained age seventy-two prior to the first day of the conference session shall be retired. (*See* ¶ 368.) [24]

4. A special conference claimant (§ 1) shall be entitled to make an annuity claim, for each year of full-time approved service rendered as a regularly appointed pastor or assistant pastor, of an amount not less than seventy-five

[23] *See* Judicial Council Decision 206.
[24] *See* Judicial Council Decision 165.

per cent of the annuity rate applied to claims of regular conference claimants; *provided*, however, that any conference may apply the same annuity rate to the claims of special conference claimants as to the claims of the regular conference claimants.

5. In necessitous cases, the Conference Board of Pensions may grant relief to special conference claimants subject to the approval of the conference; *provided*, also, that relief may be granted to an approved supply pastor who has been retired by reason of age or disability prior to completion of the years of approved service required under § 1 of this paragraph for eligibility as a special conference claimant.

6. The list of special conference claimants showing their respective years of service and the payments to them shall be kept separately from the list of regular conference claimants, and shall be published in the conference journal.

7. The regulations of the general pension code, including those on proportional payment and the claims of widows and children, shall apply to the administration of funds for special conference claimants with the exceptions specified in this paragraph; *provided*, however, that all years of approved service of such claimants shall be the direct responsibility of the conference in which the service was rendered and shall not involve clearinghouse operations.

8. The sources of annuity and relief funds payable to special conference claimants shall be: (1) collections for that purpose from the pastoral charges; (2) any amounts specifically designated for that purpose coming from any source.

9. Missions within the United States may organize a Conference Board of Pensions to care for the special needs of special conference claimants with the help of the General Board of Pensions. In such cases the Mission shall establish the annuity rate to be paid annually.

10. The following questions shall be included in the business of the Annual Conference: (*a*) "What approved supply pastors are credited with annuity claim on account of full-time service during the past year? (To be answered

after consultation of the Conference Board of Pensions with the district superintendents.)" (b) "What approved supply pastors have been retired: This year? Previously?" (See ¶ 651.22, .43.)

11. The widow of an approved supply pastor whose husband died prior to completion of the years of full-time approved service required under § 1 of this paragraph may, on recommendation of the Conference Board of Pensions and a two-thirds vote of those present and voting in the Annual Conference, be granted a pension based on the approved years of her husband's service during the time that she was his wife.

¶ 1633. *Operation in Other Countries.*—The provisions in this pension code are to give guidance in the administration of pensions in the conferences of The Methodist Church outside the United States. Insofar as may be practicable, the general principles involved in the code shall be regarded and employed in such conferences until the General Conference shall order otherwise.

¶ 1634. *Liens on Annuities.*—1. Whenever a conference claimant shall be in debt to the conference or any of its organizations on account of unpaid assessments, obligations, or pledges for the benefit of conference claimants, such debt shall constitute a lien on the annuity of the person involved, and the conference shall have power to appropriate and apply his or her annuity, or any part thereof, to the payment of such debt; *provided*, however, that not more than one quarter of the annuity payable by the conference in which the debt was incurred, or one quarter of the total indebtedness, whichever is greater, shall be appropriated in any year for such purpose, and *provided*, furthermore, that such power shall not be interpreted as applying to the settlement of other debts of a conference claimant. (See ¶ 1624.)

2. *a)* A conference having a claim for unpaid assessments in connection with its funds for conference claimants against a ministerial member of another conference, shall file such claim with the clearinghouse within two years following the date of transfer from the conference having the claim;

provided, however, that this time limit shall not apply to any claim filed on or before December 31, 1957.

b) The clearinghouse shall file a copy of said claim with the Conference Board of Pensions of the conference to which the member has been transferred, shall send a copy thereof to the member concerned, and shall record the claim on his service record.

3. *a*) A conference which has filed a claim in accordance with § 2 of this paragraph may file a lien through the clearinghouse against the annuity of a conference claimant for the unpaid amount of the said claim; *provided*, however, that the said lien shall be filed within one year of the date of retirement or death of the minister concerned, whichever first occurred. Thereupon the clearinghouse shall request the conference concerned to deduct the unpaid amount of the claim from the annuity of the conference claimant against whose annuity the said lien has been filed, and to remit to the clearinghouse as soon as practicable the amounts deducted.

b) The amount of any deduction made under this subsection shall be subject to the limitations provided in § 1 of this paragraph; and, furthermore, it is hereby stipulated that interest on liens of this character, if charged, shall be computed only at simple interest. The clearinghouse shall have no responsibility for transmission of moneys collected under this subsection until such moneys have been remitted to it. No "debtor" conference shall withhold or deduct a part of the money it is required to pay to the clearinghouse with the intent of satisfying in advance any claims which the conference may desire to make under this subsection.

¶ **1635.** *Operation Through the General Board.*— 1. When authorized by the Annual Conference, the Conference Board of Pensions may deposit all or any part of the funds under its control with the general board as set forth in ¶ 1604.3.

2. The Annual Conference may authorize the general board to make the periodical payments to the conference claimants; and in such case the conference board shall prepare annually a complete schedule of the plan of distribution for the guidance of the general board in making

such payments, and shall co-operate fully with it, in order to ensure efficient and prompt service. Checks issued, as the general board may determine, under the provisions of this subsection, shall show plainly the name of the conference for which the disbursements are made.

3. The general board shall be entitled to collect an annual service fee, figured on a cost basis, for the work specified in the preceding subsection.

4. The general board shall furnish annually to the conference board a report showing full details of the transactions under § 2 of this paragraph.

¶ **1636.** *Divided Annuity Responsibility.*—1. The responsibility for annuity for years of approved service of a conference claimant shall rest with the Annual Conference in which the service was performed, or its legal successor.[25]

2. The clearinghouse system of distribution of divided annuity responsibility shall be continued. The clearinghouse figures shall be determined by the General Board of Pensions, subject to such modifications as may be necessitated by the provisions of § 1 above. The general board shall have authority to fix annually in advance the clearinghouse rate of annuity for each Annual Conference. The clearinghouse rate shall be based on a conservative estimate of the prospective income available for distribution and need not coincide with the annuity rate fixed subsequently by the conference. In the event that the conference fixes a higher rate than the clearinghouse rate, the difference shall be paid directly to all claimants within and without the conference.

3. The general board is authorized and empowered to make all the rules concerning details that may be necessary to put this paragraph into effect, and shall determine the distribution of service responsibility for each conference claimant involved in the operation of the clearinghouse.

4. The fiscal year for clearinghouse operations shall be the calendar year.

¶ **1637.** *Annuity Responsibility in Missions or Provi-*

---

[25] *See* Judicial Council Decision 203.

sional Annual Conferences.—The responsibility for the annuity on account of years of approved service in a Mission or Provisional Annual Conference within the United States shall rest jointly with (*a*) the Mission or Provisional Annual Conference concerned, (*b*) the General Board of Pensions, and (*c*) the Division of National Missions. The revenue for annuity purposes covering such service shall be provided by the aforesaid parties in accordance with such plan or plans as may be mutually agreed to by them.

CHAPTER V

MINISTERS RESERVE PENSION FUND

¶ 1642. *Establishment.*—1. A reserve pension system to be called the **Ministers Reserve Pension Fund** of The Methodist Church, hereinafter called the Fund, is hereby established. It shall be administered by the General Board of Pensions in accordance with and subject to the provisions that follow.

2. An Annual or Provisional Annual Conference, hereafter in this chapter called a conference, at any time, on its own determination, by a two-thirds vote of its membership present and voting, may enter the Fund and may actively participate therein when it accepts the conditions and fulfills the requirements herein set forth.

¶ 1643. *Definitions.*—The following definitions shall apply to the interpretation of the plan of the Fund, unless the context plainly indicates otherwise:

1. **Employer** shall mean any connectional board, organization, or institution which receives the services of a member of the Fund in either a pastoral or nonpastoral capacity, and which shall pay therefor any form of salary, compensation, or allowance.

2. **Support** of a member of the Fund shall mean:

a) The sum or sums annually received from a pastoral charge as compensation for his services, plus an amount equivalent to twenty per cent thereof, if the minister occupy a parsonage free of rent.

b) The salary of a district superintendent received from the district as compensation for his services, plus an amount equivalent to twenty per cent thereof if he occupy a district parsonage free of rent.

c) The salary or compensation received by a pastor from a federated or community church, or from a church of another denomination, plus an amount equivalent to twenty per cent thereof, if he occupy a parsonage free of rent.

d) The financial aid furnished by a missionary board, or other organization, or by the minimum salary fund of the conference.

e) The salary, compensation, or allowance received for services rendered under special episcopal appointment.

3. **Regular interest** shall mean interest, compounded annually, at a rate periodically determined by the general board on the basis of net earnings but not to exceed four per cent per annum.

4. **Service annuity** shall mean an annuity payable in monthly installments in advance during life, beginning at the date of retirement, to be provided by the Fund on the basis of allocated credits together with the regular interest accumulated thereon. (*See* ¶¶ 1645, 1653.1.)

5. **Income annuity** shall mean an annuity payable in monthly installments in advance during life, beginning at the date of retirement, to be provided by the Fund on the basis of personal contributions of the member together with the regular interest accumulated thereon.

6. **Pension** shall mean the total of the service annuity and the income annuity.

7. **Widow's pension** shall mean an annuity, payable in monthly installments in advance, to the widow of a member of the Fund who dies before attaining retirement, to be provided by the Fund on the basis of the personal contributions of the deceased member, together with the regular interest accumulated thereon, plus seventy per cent of the service annuity credits, together with the regular interest accumulated thereon.

8. **Child's annuity** shall mean an annuity payable in monthly installments in advance to a minor child of a deceased member of the Fund.

9. **Minor child** shall mean a child under twenty-two years of age.

10. The meaning of the word "child" shall be interpreted to include a child legally adopted.

11. **New entrant** shall mean a minister who shall be admitted on trial in an Annual or Provisional Annual Conference on or after the entry of such conference into the Fund, including a minister who on May 1, 1952, was on trial in a conference which prior to that date had entered the Fund. (Approved service on trial, as defined in ¶ 1618.2, rendered by a minister who became a member of the Fund prior to May 1, 1952, may be approved for annuity claim under the provision of the pension code, or under the Ministers Reserve Pension Fund as provided in ¶ 1644.5.)

12. **Previous entrant** shall mean a minister in good standing on trial or in full membership in an Annual or Provisional Annual Conference prior to the entry of such conference into the Fund.

13. **Pension code** shall mean the rules and regulations concerning pensions and relief contained in ¶¶ 1613-37 inclusive.

¶ **1644.** *Membership.*—1. The membership of the Fund shall consist of the new entrants in Annual or Provisional Annual Conferences in the United States of America, such previous entrants as are received under § 2 below, and qualified full-time approved supply pastors. Members of such conferences who have not been enrolled as members of the Fund, and who are serving under special appointment to a board, institution, organization, or a community church, without annuity claim on the conference, may be enrolled as members of the Fund for the purpose of arranging for pension coverage on account of such service with the agency covered, in accordance with the rules and regulations of the Fund, and with the consent of the General Board of Pensions.

2. Previous entrants who are members of conferences participating in the Fund may become members of the Fund by a two-thirds vote of the conference membership present and voting; *provided*, however, that accrued service obligations under the pension code shall be funded

for or by such previous entrants, in such manner and amount as shall be satisfactory to the general board.

3. A minister received by transfer into a conference on or after the date of entry of the conference into the Fund shall be classed as a new entrant while serving in such conference; *provided*, however, that members received by transfer past forty years of age shall not be accepted as members of the Fund unless an initial provision for service annuity be made by or for them in such manner and amount as shall be satisfactory to the executive officers of the general board.

4. A member of the Fund shall be classed as a new entrant while serving in any conference participating in the Fund.

5. The accrued service obligation of a conference under the pension code for a member of the Fund may be funded by such conference upon entry into the Fund in such manner and amount as shall be satisfactory to the executive officers of the general board.

6. When a member of the Fund transfers to a conference not participating in the Fund, he shall be subject to the provisions of the pension code for years served in such conference; but on subsequent entry into a conference participating in the Fund he shall resume contribution and receive credits therefrom.

¶ **1645.** *Contributions by the Conference.*—1. Each conference that hereafter enters the Fund shall contribute annually thereto an amount equivalent to not less than nine per cent of the average salary of the conference (as defined in ¶ 1618.6 of the pension code) for each qualified member of the conference who is also a member of the Fund.

2. In case of the transfer of a member of the Fund into a conference participating in the Fund the contribution required on behalf of such member shall be proportional to the number of days of service rendered such conference during the fiscal year of the Fund in which the transfer shall have been effected.

3. In case of the transfer of a member of the Fund out of a conference participating in the Fund the contribution required on behalf of such member shall be proportional

to the number of days of service rendered such conference during the fiscal year of the Fund in which the transfer shall have been effected.

4. Each conference shall determine the plan by which it shall secure the annual contribution to the Fund required in § 1 of this paragraph and shall make suitable and adequate provision therefor.

5. Each conference shall collect the contributions due the Fund, and shall have power to adjudicate all questions in connection therewith.

6. The contributions required in § 1 of this paragraph shall be made to the conference treasurer, or any other officer who may be designated by the conference, who shall transmit the same to the general board within thirty days after the conference session, together with a schedule of information showing the members covered by the payment transmitted.

7. A deficiency in the payment of the annual amount required of a conference shall reduce accordingly the service annuity credits of the members of the Fund in such conference, and also any other benefits provided by the Fund for them, unless otherwise ordered by the conference as provided in § 8.

8. In the event of the failure of a pastoral charge, district, or employer to pay, in whole or in part, the amount apportioned in any year by a conference for the purposes of the Fund, such conference shall reduce equitably the service annuity credit for such year of service of such member of the Fund serving said pastoral charge, district, or employer, and shall advise the general board and the member concerned of its action in the case.

9. It shall be the duty of the Conference Board of Pensions to instruct the newly enrolled members of the Fund concerning its rules and regulations, to co-operate with the general board in obtaining information from members as may be required by the Fund, to adjudicate matters pertaining to contributions to the Fund, and to recommend to the conference any apportionment for the Fund that may be levied on the pastoral charges.

10. When a member of a conference who is also a member of the Fund is under special appointment without

annuity claim on such conference, the organization he is serving shall contribute annually to the Fund the equivalent of the current contribution made on behalf of each qualified member of the Fund in good standing. Failure to make such contribution in any conference year shall deprive the appointee concerned of service annuity credit for that conference year.

¶ 1646. *Contributions by Members.*—1. An annual contribution, the equivalent of three per cent of the average salary of the conference (as defined in ¶ 1618.6 of the pension code), shall be paid directly to the Fund by each qualified member thereof in monthly or quarterly installments payable in advance in accordance with the schedule of payment dates as determined by the general board; *provided*, however, that if his support (as defined in ¶ 1643.2) is less than the average salary of the conference, a member may elect to contribute annually the equivalent of three per cent of such support; and *provided*, furthermore, that by vote of the conference, on recommendation of the conference board, the amounts of the annual contributions required of members of the Fund shall be withheld by the treasurers of the pastoral charges, or other organizations concerned, and remitted directly to the Fund in monthly or quarterly installments. Such contributions shall be applicable to income annuity credit only.[26]

2. In case a minister transfers into a conference participating in the Fund and, by reason of such transfer, becomes a member of the Fund, the first installment due from him shall be that which next falls due for the members of the Fund in that conference following the date of such transfer.

3. In case a member of the Fund transfers out of a conference participating in the Fund, the last installment due from him while he is a member of such conference shall be that which normally falls due before the date of such transfer.

4. In case the transfer of a member of the Fund is effected between conferences, both of which are participating in the Fund, the amounts of the quarterly installments

---

[26] Amended in 1956 following Judicial Council Decision 118.

and the dates upon which installments fall due shall be adjusted in accordance with the schedule of payment dates for such conferences as determined by the general board.

5. If a minister is required to make a contribution to the Fund, he shall not be required by the conference, or by any organization thereof related to the support of conference claimants, to make any other contribution for pension purposes. If he consents to make such other contribution, it shall be voluntary. (*See* ¶ 1610.4.)

6. In any case a minister who has previously obtained membership in the Fund, while he is a member of a conference not participating in the Fund, shall have the right to continue contributions toward the accumulations for providing income annuity.

7. *Additional Member Contributions.*—Subject to such limitations, regulations, and conditions as the general board may adopt, a member of the Fund may pay into the Fund, in addition to the required member contributions, such amounts as he may elect for the purpose of providing an income annuity or other benefits additional to the income annuity provided through his regular contributions.

¶ 1647. *Pensions.*—1. *Service Annuity.*—A member of the Fund who shall have attained age sixty-five or completed forty years of full-time approved service and who shall have been granted the retired relation shall receive thereafter, during his lifetime, a service annuity. On the death of a member of the Fund while receiving a service annuity the equivalent of seventy per cent of such annuity shall be continued to his widow, if their marriage took place before the member entered into the service annuity.

The service annuity and the seventy per cent thereof to be continued to the widow shall be the actuarial equivalent of his allocated service annuity credits together with the regular interest accumulated thereon, determined on the basis of the actual ages of the member and his wife at the time of entry into the service annuity.

If at the time of his entry into the service annuity a member is unmarried or a widower, the calculation of the amount of such service annuity shall be made on the basis of assumed equal ages for man and wife.

The service annuity shall be determined according to the tables of annuity rates for such purpose in current use by the general board.

2. *Income Annuity.*—At the same time that a member of the Fund, whether married or single, is granted a service annuity, he shall be entitled to an income annuity of a type identical with his service annuity, the amount thereof to be the actuarial equivalent of his personal contributions to the Fund together with the regular interest accumulated thereon.

The income annuity shall be determined according to the tables of annuity rates for such purpose in current use by the general board.

3. *Income Annuity Credit Guarantee Option.*—At the time of entering upon his pension, a member of the Fund may elect an option under which he shall receive a reduced pension, but with the provision that if the pension payments received by him and his widow aggregate less than his income annuity credits at the time of retirement, there shall be paid to his designated beneficiary or to his estate, as he shall have designated, an amount equivalent to the excess of such income annuity credits over such pension payments.

¶ **1648.** *Widow's Pension.*—1. If a member of the Fund dies prior to retirement, his widow shall receive a pension consisting of an income annuity which shall be the actuarial equivalent of her deceased husband's income annuity credits and a service annuity which shall be the actuarial equivalent of seventy per cent of his service annuity credits.

2. If the service annuity of a widow is less than fifteen per cent of the average salary of the conference, it shall be supplemented by a grant from the Disability and Survivor Benefit Fund sufficient to produce such an amount; *provided* that the total annual benefit from these sources shall not be less than $450. The income annuity payable under § 1 of this paragraph shall be in addition to said service annuity and grant.

¶ **1649.** *Child's Pension.*—1. Each unmarried minor

child of a deceased member of the Fund shall be granted an annuity equal to five per cent of the average salary of the conference, but not less than $150, payable until attainment of age sixteen.

2. On presentation to it annually of a satisfactory certificate of enrollment, attendance, and work done in a standard school or college, the general board shall grant an unmarried child of a deceased member of the Fund an annuity equal to ten per cent of the average salary of the conference, but not less than $300, payable from age sixteen until attainment of age twenty-two.

¶ **1650.** *Limitation of Annual Payments.*—1. If a member of the Fund dies prior to retirement, the total of the annual payments thereafter, in any year, to his widow and minor children shall not exceed seventy per cent of the average salary of the conference as defined in the pension code (¶ 1618.6).

2. If a member of the Fund dies while receiving a pension, the total of the annual payments thereafter, in any year, to his widow and children shall not exceed the annual pension which he was receiving prior to his decease.

¶ **1651.** 1. *Disability Benefits.*—*a*) An annual disability benefit shall be given to a disabled member of the Fund under age sixty-five if disability shall have been evident for a period of not less than one hundred eighty days, and the member shall have submitted to such examinations as may be required by the general board, and it shall appear from the reports that his health has failed as a result of a disease or injury, and that presumably he is totally and permanently incapacitated for both ministerial work and the support of his family. This benefit shall not exceed one third of the average salary of the conference as defined in the pension code (¶ 1618.6). At the discretion of the general board, the initial payment of the benefit may be made to cover all or any part of the waiting period of one hundred eighty days, or only the period of disability following the termination of the waiting period.

b) During the continuance of his disability, a member of the Fund shall receive an annual allocation to be applied on his service annuity credit, equivalent to the current service annuity credit in the conference of which he is a member, said allocation to be provided from the disability fund.

c) When recommended by the general board, the continuation of the above disability benefits (§§ 1*a*, 1*b*) shall be subject to the yearly approval of the member's conference.

d) During the continuance of his disability, a member of the Fund shall be exempt from the requirement to contribute to the Fund, but when his disability has been terminated and he has entered into a salaried relationship with a pastoral charge, district, or employer, he shall resume contributions to the Fund.

e) If a disabled member of the Fund recovers sufficiently to resume ministerial work or to engage in a remunerative occupation, his disability allowance may be reduced or terminated by the general board at its discretion.

f) During the continuance of his disability, the member may be required, at the discretion of the general board, while still under age sixty-five, to have a medical examination at any time by a physician appointed to act in behalf of the general board.

g) If disability continues until age sixty-five, the disability benefits shall terminate, and thereafter a disabled member of the Fund shall receive his pension, according to the provisions of ¶ 1647.

2. *Death Benefit.*—When a member of the Fund dies, a benefit may be paid in one sum out of the Contingent Fund to his widow, if any, in accordance with rules and regulations which shall be adopted by the general board.

¶ **1652.** *Refunds.*—1. On ceasing to be a member of a conference prior to retirement, a member of the Fund shall receive as a refund, in lieu of all other benefits, a sum equivalent to his accumulated income annuity credits; and a sum equivalent to his accumulated service annuity credits shall be transferred to the account of the conference or conferences which contributed them; *provided,* however, that if such member enters the ministry of another church or denomination, and allows his accumulated income annuity credits to remain in the Fund, then his accumulated income annuity credits and service annuity credits shall be applied in accordance with the provisions set forth in ¶¶ 1647-48; and *provided*, furthermore, that the exercise of this privilege shall not confer any right to make a claim on the Fund for disability or other benefits not specifically provided for in this paragraph.

2. On his ceasing to be a member of a conference after retirement, the service annuity shall cease automatically and the income annuity shall be commuted in the form of a cash settlement to be actuarially determined and made by the general board.

3. If a member of the Fund dies prior to receipt of any installment of his income annuity, and without leaving a widow or minor child or children, there shall be refunded to his estate a sum equivalent to his accumulated income annuity credits; and a sum equivalent to his accumulated service annuity credits shall be transferred to the account of the conference or conferences which contributed them.

4. If the widow of a member of the Fund remarries, the service annuity shall cease automatically, but may be reinstated on her attainment of age sixty-five or on the termination of her marital status by her husband's death or by legal process; and the income annuity shall be commuted in the form of a cash settlement to be actuarially determined and made by the general board. This shall apply to a surviving widow of a member who dies while in the retired relation, as well as to a widow of a member who dies prior to retirement.

¶ **1653.** *Funds.*—1. The annual contributions required in ¶ 1645.1, up to and including nine per cent of the average salary of the conference, shall be appropriated for the purposes of the Fund according to the following percentages:

Service Annuity Fund 70%
Disability and Survivor Benefit Fund 27%
Contingent Fund 3%

The amount of the contributions in excess of nine per cent of the average salary of the conference shall be allocated to the Service Annuity Fund.

2. The seventy per cent of the contributions of each conference for the Service Annuity Fund shall be apportioned equally among its members in the effective relation and probationers who shall be also members of the Fund, except as provided in ¶ 1645.7, .8, .10, and shall be allocated to each of them annually. The amounts so allocated together with the regular interest thereon shall be held by the general board for the service annuities described in ¶ 1647.1.

3. The twenty-seven per cent of the contributions of the conferences for the Disability and Survivor Benefit Fund shall be administered by the general board as indicated in ¶¶ 1647-51.

4. The three per cent of the contributions of the conferences for the Contingent Fund shall be administered by the general board as hereinafter provided.

5. A Contingent Fund shall be created and administered by the general board to which shall be credited:

a) The three per cent of the conference contributions provided in §§ 1, 4 of this paragraph.

b) The excess interest earnings above regular interest in any of the other funds.

d) Any resources of the Ministers Reserve Pension Fund not otherwise designated or allocated.

6. The Contingent Fund shall be used at the discretion of the general board in such ways and for such purposes as in its judgment shall best serve the interests for which the Ministers Reserve Pension Fund is created.

¶ **1654.** *Initial Reserve Fund.*—1. Each conference entering the Fund shall be required to provide an initial reserve fund for the liabilities assumed on account of new entrants. The amount of such initial reserve fund, the conditions of its actuarial calculation, and the manner of financing its liabilities shall be determined by the general board on request of the conference concerned.

2. The initial reserve fund and the earnings therefrom shall be used exclusively for the financing of the aforesaid liabilities.

¶ **1655.** *Authorization.*—1. The general board is authorized, instructed, and empowered to put the Ministers Reserve Pension Fund plan as herein set forth into operation in any conference after such conference shall have decided to enter and shall have made provision for the requisite initial reserve fund specified herein.

2. The general board is hereby authorized to act as a reserve funding agency for such conferences as may desire to transfer to it any or all of their obligations for previous entrants under the pension code at a fixed rate of annuity per year of service.

3. The general board is hereby authorized to administer the Fund and to adopt such rules and regulations as may be necessary for its efficient operation, subject to the limitation that this power shall not be exercised so as to nullify any of the provisions of the plan.

¶ **1656.** *Partial Reserve Funding.*—The general board may make provision for partial reserve funding of annuities payable under the pension code as described in ¶¶ 1613-37.

1. An Annual or Provisional Annual Conference, at any time, on its own determination, by a two-thirds vote of its membership present and voting, may actively participate in the Partial Reserve Pension Fund, hereafter in this paragraph referred to as the Fund, when it accepts the conditions and fulfills the requirements set forth.

2. *Membership.*—*a*) The membership of the Fund shall consist of the ministers who are on trial or in full connection in a conference which is actively participating in the Fund, and who are not members of the Ministers Reserve Pension Fund.

b) When a member of the Ministers Reserve Pension Fund is received by transfer into a conference participating in the Partial Reserve Pension Fund, but not in the Ministers Reserve Pension Fund, he shall be subject to the provisions of the Partial Reserve Pension Fund for the years served in such conference. (*See* ¶ 1644.3.)

3. *Contributions by the Conference.*—*a*) Each conference participating in the Fund shall contribute annually to the credit of each qualified member of the Fund such sum as it may designate, based on a percentage of the average salary of the conference (as defined in the pension code, ¶ 1618.6).

b) Each conference shall determine the plan by which

it shall secure the amount necessary to make the contributions required in § 3a and shall make suitable and adequate provision therefor.

c) A deficiency in the payment of the annual amount required of a conference shall reduce accordingly the credits of the members of the Fund in such conference.

d) The provisions in ¶ 1645.2, .3 shall determine the amount of contribution to the credit of a member of the Fund transferring into or out of a conference actively participating in the Fund.

4. *Contributions by Members.*—*a*) An annual contribution, the equivalent of three per cent of the average salary of the conference (as defined in ¶ 1618.6 of the pension code), shall be paid directly to the Fund by each qualified member thereof in monthly or quarterly installments, payable in advance in accordance with the schedule of payment dates as determined by the general board; *provided*, however, that if his support (as defined in ¶ 1643.2) is less than the average salary of the conference, a member may elect to contribute annually the equivalent of three per cent of such support; and *provided*, furthermore, that by vote of the conference, on recommendation of the conference board, the amounts of the annual contributions required of members of the Fund shall be withheld by the treasurers of the pastoral charges, or other organizations concerned, and remitted directly to the Fund in monthly or quarterly installments. Such contributions shall be applicable to income annuity credit only.

b) The provisions of ¶ 1646.2-.4 shall determine the amount and the date of payment of the contribution required of a member who transfers into or out of a conference actively participating in the Fund.

c) A member of the Fund, while he is a member of a conference not participating in the Fund, shall have the right to continue contributions toward the accumulations for providing income annuity.

5. *Additional Member Contributions.*—Subject to such limitations, regulations and conditions as the general board may adopt, a member of the Fund may pay into the Fund, in addition to the required member contribu-

tions, such amounts as he may elect for the purpose of
providing an income annuity or other benefits additional
to the income annuity provided through his regular
contributions.

6. It shall be the duty of the Conference Board of
Pensions to instruct the newly enrolled members of the
Fund concerning its rules and regulations, to co-operate
with the general board in obtaining information from
members as may be required by the Fund, to adjudicate
matters pertaining to contributions to the Fund, and
to recommend to the conference any apportionment for
the Fund that may be levied on the pastoral charges.

7. *Initial Reserve Fund.—a*) A conference participating
in the Fund may provide an **initial reserve fund** from
which there shall be allocated the annual contributions
to the credit of the members of the Fund as required in
§ 3a.

b) The amount of such initial reserve fund shall be
determined by the general board on request of the conference concerned.

c) The initial reserve fund and the earnings therefrom
shall be used exclusively in financing the aforesaid annual
contributions.

d) The general board shall determine the circumstances
under which an initial reserve fund shall be required of
a conference in order to participate in the Fund.

8. *Pensions.—a*) *Service Annuity.—*A member of the
Fund who shall have attained age sixty-five and who shall
have been granted the retired relation shall receive thereafter, during his lifetime, a service annuity. On the
death of a member of the Fund while receiving a service
annuity the equivalent of seventy per cent of such annuity
shall be continued to his widow, if their marriage took
place before the member entered into the service annuity.

The service annuity and the seventy per cent thereof
to be continued to the widow shall be the actuarial equivalent of his allocated service annuity credits together with
the regular interest accumulated thereon, determined on
the basis of the actual ages of the member and his wife at
the time of entry into the service annuity.

b) A conference participating in the Fund may regard

the service annuity based on the contributions made by such conference as a part of the annuity provided for a conference claimant by such conference under the pension code (¶¶ 1619, 1620, 1631).

c) Income Annuity.—At the same time that a member of the Fund is granted a service annuity, he shall be entitled to an income annuity of a type identical with his service annuity, the amount thereof to be the actuarial equivalent of his personal contributions to the Fund together with the regular interest accumulated thereon. The income annuity payable under the provisions of this section shall be considered as an addition to the pension normally provided under the pension code.

d) The service annuity and the income annuity shall be determined according to the tables of annuity rates for such purpose in current use by the general board.

e) Income Annuity Credit Guarantee Option.—At the time of entering upon his pension, a member of the Fund may elect an option under which he shall receive a reduced pension, but with the provision that if the pension payments received by him and his widow aggregate less than his income annuity credits at the time of retirement, there shall be paid to his designated beneficiary or to his estate, as he shall have designated, an amount equivalent to the excess of such income annuity credits over such pension payments.

9. *Widow's Pension.*—If a member of the Fund dies prior to retirement, a pension shall be paid to his widow, based on her age and provided by the total of her deceased husband's personal contributions together with the regular interest accumulated thereon, plus seventy per cent of his service annuity credits together with the regular interest accumulated thereon at the time of his death.

10. *Death Benefit.*—When a member of the Fund dies, a benefit may be paid in one sum out of the Contingent Fund to his widow, if any, in accordance with rules and regulations which shall be adopted by the general board.

11. *Refunds.*—The regulations concerning refunds as provided in ¶ 1652 shall apply in the Partial Reserve Pension Fund. Participation in this Fund does not imply any right of the participant to make a claim on the

general board for disability or other benefits not specifically provided for in this paragraph.

12. A Contingent Fund shall be created and administered by the general board for the Partial Reserve Pension Fund, to which shall be credited:

a) The excess interest earnings above regular interest credited.

c) Any resources of the Partial Reserve Pension Fund not otherwise designated or allocated.

The Contingent Fund shall be used at the discretion of the general board in such ways and for such purposes as in its judgment shall best serve the interests of the Fund.

13. The general board is hereby authorized to administer the Fund and to adopt such rules and regulations as may be necessary for its efficient operation, subject to the limitation that this power shall not be exercised so as to nullify any of the Disciplinary provisions of the plan.

¶ **1657.** The general board shall have authority to make special arrangements with conferences whereby partial reserve funding of the pensions for full-time approved supply pastors can be accomplished along lines similar to those hereinbefore described in ¶ 1656.

CHAPTER VI
LAY EMPLOYEES PENSION FUND

¶ **1658.** 1. A pension fund to be known and designated as the **Lay Employees Pension Fund** of The Methodist Church is hereby established. The fund shall be held, administered, and disbursed by the General Board of Pensions of The Methodist Church in accordance with rules and regulations which shall be adopted from time to time by the board.

2. The purpose of the Fund shall be to provide annuities for lay employees of local churches, boards, commissions, agencies, institutions, and organizations in the United States of America listed in the book of Discipline of The Methodist Church or in the directory printed in the

journal of any Annual Conference of The Methodist Church situated in the United States of America.

¶ **1659.** 1. Effective June 1, 1948, any person then resident within the United States who was then serving as a secretary of an effective bishop of The Methodist Church, or who had previously served as a secretary to an effective bishop or bishops of The Methodist Church and was then serving or thereafter shall serve in any form of employment connected with The Methodist Church, on retirement or being no longer in the employ of a bishop, board, or agency of The Methodist Church and on attainment of age sixty shall be entitled to make an annuity claim on the Episcopal Fund for the secretarial service rendered an effective bishop or bishops prior to June 1, 1948.

2. The bishops or boards or agencies respectively shall be responsible for informing their employees concerning their pension rights under this paragraph and shall notify all who are involved in providing the pension.

3. Effective June 1, 1952, the full-time lay employees of an effective bishop resident in the United States of America shall be enrolled as participating lay employees in the Lay Employees Pension Fund of The Methodist Church, in accordance with the rules and regulations of said Fund.

4. As the participating employer of such participating lay employees the bishop shall deduct the required contributions from the compensation of such participating lay employees and shall forward such amounts concurrently with the required employer's contributions to the Fund; *provided*, however, that the employer's contributions shall be paid from the allowances made by the Episcopal Fund or other sources for office expense of the bishop.

5. Effective June 1, 1952, the General Board of Pensions shall transfer the individual accounts held for secretaries, assistant secretaries, or other office employees of a bishop, together with accrued interest, to the Lay Employees Pension Fund, and thereafter such employees shall be enrolled as participating lay employees in the Lay Employees Pension Fund, as provided in § 3 of this paragraph.

Chapter VII

JOINT CONTRIBUTORY ANNUITY FUND

¶ **1666.** 1. A pension fund to be known and designated as the **Joint Contributory Annuity Fund** of The Methodist Church is hereby established. The Fund shall be held, administered, and disbursed by the General Board of Pensions of The Methodist Church in accordance with rules and regulations which shall be adopted from time to time by the board.

2. The purpose of the Fund shall be to provide pensions for ministerial members of Annual or Provisional Annual Conferences, their widows or dependent children, on account of service rendered under special appointment to an institution, organization, agency, or community church for which a pension is not otherwise provided.

Chapter VIII

CHAPLAINS PENSION FUND

¶ **1671.** A pension fund to be known and designated as the **Chaplains Pension Fund** of The Methodist Church is hereby established. The Fund shall be held, administered, and disbursed by the General Board of Pensions of The Methodist Church in accordance with rules and regulations to be determined jointly by the board and the Commission on Chaplains of The Methodist Church.

2. The purpose of the Fund shall be to provide pensions for ministerial members of Annual or Provisional Annual Conferences, their widows or dependent children, on account of approved service rendered under special appointment as chaplains on full-time duty with the Armed Forces of the United States, or with organizations, institutions, or agencies related to the Commission on Chaplains of The Methodist Church, for which a pension is not otherwise provided.

Chapter IX

STAFF PENSION FUND

¶ **1676.** 1. A pension fund to be known and designated as the **Staff Pension Fund** of The Methodist Church is hereby established. The Fund shall be held, administered, and disbursed by the General Board of Pensions of The Methodist Church in accordance with rules and regulations which shall be adopted from time to time by the board.

2. The purpose of the Fund shall be to provide annuities for ministerial members of Annual or Provisional Annual Conferences under appointment to, and lay employees of, boards, commissions, agencies, institutions, and organizations in the United States of America listed in the book of Discipline of The Methodist Church or in the directory printed in the journal of any Annual Conference of The Methodist Church situated in the United States of America.

Chapter X

HOSPITALIZATION AND MEDICAL EXPENSE PROGRAM

¶ **1681.** The General Board of Pensions of The Methodist Church is hereby authorized to establish and administer, through The Board of Pensions of The Methodist Church, Incorporated in Illinois, in accordance with the authority vested in the general board under ¶ 1601, a **Hospitalization and Medical Expense Program** for ministers of The Methodist Church, and lay employees as defined in ¶ 1658.2, and their dependents, under rules and regulations which shall be adopted from time to time by the general board.

Chapter XI

DEATH BENEFIT PROGRAM

¶ **1683.** The General Board of Pensions of The Methodist Church is hereby authorized to establish and administer, through The Board of Pensions of The Methodist Church, Incorporated in Illinois, in accordance with the authority vested in the general board under ¶¶ 1601, 1604, a **Death Benefit Program** for ministers of The Methodist Church, and lay employees as defined in ¶ 1658.2, under rules and regulations which shall be adopted from time to time by the general board.

Chapter XII

TEMPORARY GENERAL AID FUND

¶ **1685.** The General Board of Pensions is hereby authorized and directed to administer a **Temporary General Aid Fund** in consultation with the Commission on Interjurisdictional Relations or its successor as determined by the General Conference.

Chapter XIII

EPISCOPAL PENSIONS

¶ **1686.** The provisions regarding pensions for retired bishops, and for the widows and minor children of deceased bishops, are set forth in ¶¶ 774-77 under Part V, Temporal Economy.

Chapter XIV

COMMITTEE ON PENSION LEGISLATION

¶ **1699.** The General Board of Pensions shall appoint quadrennially from its membership a **Committee on Pension Legislation,** which shall consist of one bishop, and one minister and one layman from each jurisdiction, whose responsibility it shall be to study the operation of the various pension programs of The Methodist Church and to present recommendations to each succeeding General Conference.

Part IX

THE GENERAL SERVICES OF THE CHURCH

¶ 1711. THE ORDER OF WORSHIP
Brief Form

† *Let the people be in silent meditation and prayer upon entering the sanctuary. Let the service of worship begin at the time appointed.*

† *At the end of all prayers the people shall say Amen.*

PRELUDE

SCRIPTURE SENTENCES, OR CALL TO WORSHIP
† *To be said or sung.*

HYMN
† *The people standing.*

PRAYERS
† *Here the minister may use an invocation or collect and prayers of confession and the Lord's Prayer.*

PSALTER OR OTHER ACT OF PRAISE
† *To be read responsively or in unison, the people standing; then shall be said or sung the Gloria Patri.*

ANTHEM

THE SCRIPTURE LESSONS

AFFIRMATION OF FAITH
† *The people standing; then may be sung a doxology.*

Pastoral Prayer

Offertory

† *Here parish notices may be given.*

† *The minister may read Scripture sentences before the offering is received. An anthem may be sung during the receiving of the offering. Following the presentation of the offering a prayer of dedication may be said or sung.*

† *At the discretion of the minister the offertory and prayers may follow the sermon.*

Hymn

† *The people standing.*

The Sermon

Invitation to Christian Discipleship

Hymn

† *The people standing.*

Benediction

† *The people may be seated for silent prayer.*

Postlude

¶ 1712. THE ORDER OF WORSHIP
Complete Form

† *Let the people be in silent meditation and prayer upon entering the sanctuary. Let the service of worship begin at the time appointed.*

† *Scripture sentences, alternate prayers, affirmations of faith, and benedictions may be found in* The Book of Worship *and* The Methodist Hymnal.

† *At the end of all prayers the people shall say Amen.*

Prelude

Scripture Sentences, or Call to Worship

† *To be said or sung.*

HYMN

† *The people standing.*

† *If a processional, the hymn may precede the Scripture sentences.*

INVOCATION

† *By the minister, the people standing.*

Almighty God, from whom every good prayer cometh, and who pourest out on all who desire it, the spirit of grace and supplication: Deliver us, when we draw nigh to thee, from coldness of heart and wanderings of mind, that with steadfast thoughts and kindled affections, we may worship thee in spirit and in truth; through Jesus Christ our Lord. **Amen.**

CALL TO CONFESSION

† *By the minister, the people standing.*

Dearly beloved, the Scriptures move us to acknowledge and confess our sins before almighty God our heavenly Father, with a humble, lowly, penitent, and obedient heart, to the end that we may obtain forgiveness by his infinite goodness and mercy. Wherefore I pray and beseech you, as many as are here present, to accompany me with a pure heart and humble voice, unto the throne of heavenly grace.

† *Or the minister may say,*

Let us confess our sins to Almighty God.

GENERAL CONFESSION

† *To be said by all, the people seated and bowed, or kneeling.*

Almighty and most merciful Father, we have erred and strayed from thy ways like lost sheep. We have followed too much the devices and desires of our own hearts. We have offended against thy holy laws. We have left undone those things which we ought to have done, and we have done those things which we ought not to have done. But thou, O Lord, have mercy upon us. Spare thou those, O God, who confess their faults. Restore thou those who are penitent, according to thy

promises declared unto mankind in Christ Jesus our
Lord. And grant, O most merciful Father, for his sake,
that we may hereafter live a godly, righteous, and
sober life, to the glory of thy holy name. Amen.

PRAYER FOR PARDON OR WORDS OF ASSURANCE
† *By the minister.*

O Lord, we beseech thee, absolve thy people from their
offenses, that through thy bountiful goodness, we may be
delivered from the bonds of those sins which by our
frailty we have committed. Grant this, O heavenly Father,
for the sake of Jesus Christ, our blessed Lord and Savior.
Amen.

THE LORD'S PRAYER
† *To be said by all.*

Our Father, who art in heaven, hallowed be thy name.
Thy kingdom come, thy will be done on earth as it is
in heaven. Give us this day our daily bread. And forgive us our trespasses, as we forgive those who trespass against us. And lead us not into temptation, but
deliver us from evil. For thine is the kingdom, and the
power, and the glory, forever. Amen.

Minister: O Lord, open thou our lips.
People: **And our mouth shall show forth thy praise.**
Minister: Praise ye the Lord.
People: **The Lord's name be praised.**

PSALTER OR OTHER ACT OF PRAISE
† *To be read responsively or in unison, the people standing; then shall be said or sung,*

Glory be to the Father, and to the Son, and to the Holy
Ghost; as it was in the beginning, is now, and ever
shall be, world without end. Amen.

ANTHEM

THE SCRIPTURE LESSONS
† *Here shall be read two lessons, one from the Old Testament, and one from the Epistles or Gospels.*

AFFIRMATION OF FAITH
† *The people standing; then may be sung a doxology.*

> *Minister:* The Lord be with you.
> *People:* **And with thy spirit.**
> *Minister:* Let us pray.

COLLECT
† *By the minister, or the minister and people, the people seated and bowed, or kneeling.*

O Lord, our heavenly Father, almighty and everlasting God, who hast safely brought us to the beginning of this day: Defend us in the same with thy mighty power; and grant that this day we fall into no sin, neither run into any kind of danger, but that all our doings may be ordered by thy governance, to do always that which is righteous in thy sight; through Jesus Christ our Lord. **Amen.**

PASTORAL PRAYER

OFFERTORY
† *Here parish notices may be given.*

† *The minister may read Scripture sentences before the offering is received. An anthem may be sung during the receiving of the offering. Following the presentation of the offering a prayer of dedication may be said or sung.*

† *At the discretion of the minister the offertory and prayers may follow the sermon.*

HYMN
† *The people standing.*

THE SERMON

INVITATION TO CHRISTIAN DISCIPLESHIP

HYMN
† *The people standing. This may be a recessional hymn.*

BENEDICTION
† *The people may be seated for silent prayer.*

POSTLUDE

¶ 1713. The Order for the Administration of the
SACRAMENT OF BAPTISM

† *Our ministers are enjoined diligently to teach the people committed to their pastoral care the meaning and purpose of the Baptism of children and to urge them to present their children for Baptism at an early age.*

† *When youth and adults present themselves for Baptism, the minister shall take due care that they have been instructed in the meaning of Christian Baptism.*

† *This Sacrament should be administered in the church in the presence of the people in a stated hour of worship. But at the minister's discretion this Sacrament may be administered at another time and place.*

† *This Sacrament may be administered by sprinkling, pouring, or immersion.*

† *The minister shall see that the names of all baptized children are properly recorded as preparatory members on the permanent records of the church, and in each instance he shall deliver to the parents or sponsors a certificate of Baptism.*

† *Children baptized in infancy shall be reported annually in the number of preparatory members until they shall have been received into full membership in the Church or shall have attained their adulthood.*

1. CHILDREN

† *Parents or sponsors presenting a child for Baptism should be members of Christ's holy Church.*

† *The parents or sponsors, with the child to be baptized, shall stand before the minister, who, addressing the people, shall say,*

Dearly beloved, Baptism is an outward and visible sign of the grace of the Lord Jesus Christ, through which grace we become partakers of his righteousness and heirs of life eternal. Those receiving this Sacrament are thereby marked as Christian disciples, and initiated into the fellowship of Christ's holy Church. Our Lord has expressly given to little children a place among the people of God, which holy privilege must not be denied them. Remember the words of the Lord Jesus Christ, how he said, "Let the children come to me, do not hinder them; for to such belongs the kingdom of God."

† *Then the minister shall address the parents or sponsors, saying.*

Beloved, do you in presenting *this child* for holy Baptism confess your faith in our Lord and Savior Jesus Christ?

We do.

Do you therefore accept as your bounden duty and privilege to live before *this child* a life that becomes the gospel; to exercise all godly care that *he* be brought up in the Christian faith, that *he* be taught the Holy Scriptures, and that *he* learn to give reverent attendance upon the private and public worship of God?

We do.

Will you endeavor to keep *this child* under the ministry and guidance of the Church until *he* by the power of God shall accept for *himself* the gift of salvation, and be confirmed as a full and responsible member of Christ's holy Church?

We will.

† *Then the minister shall take the child in his arms, and shall say to the parents or sponsors,*

What name is given this child?

† *And then, repeating the name, though not including the surname, the minister shall baptize the child, saying,*

N., I baptize you in the name of the Father, and of the Son, and of the Holy Spirit. **Amen.**

† *Then the minister may have the people stand, and, addressing them, may say,*

Brethren of the household of faith, I commend to your love and care *this child*, whom we this day recognize as *a member* of the family of God. Will you endeavor so to live that *he* may grow in the knowledge and love of God the Father, through our Savior Jesus Christ?

✝ *Then the people shall say,*

**With God's help we will so order our lives after the
example of Christ that this child, surrounded by steadfast love, may be established in the faith, and confirmed and strengthened in the way that leads to life
eternal.**

✝ *Then the minister shall say,*

Let us pray.

O God, our heavenly Father, grant that *this child*, as *he
grows* in years, may also grow in grace and in the knowledge of the Lord Jesus Christ, and that by the restraining
and renewing influence of the Holy Spirit *he* may ever be
a true *child* of thine, serving thee faithfully all *his* days.

So guide and uphold the *parents* (*or sponsors*) of *this
child* that, by loving care, wise counsel, and holy example,
they may lead *him* into that life of faith whose strength
is righteousness and whose fruit is everlasting joy and
peace; through Jesus Christ our Lord. **Amen.**

✝ *Then the minister may give this or another blessing:*

God the Father, God the Son, and God the Holy Spirit
bless, preserve, and keep you, now and for evermore.
Amen.

2. YOUTH AND ADULTS

✝ *The person or persons to be baptized shall stand before
the minister, who, addressing the people, shall say,*

Dearly beloved, forasmuch as all men have sinned and
fallen short of the glory of God, and our Savior Christ
said, "Unless one is born of water and the Spirit, he cannot enter the kingdom of God," I beseech you to call upon
God the Father, through our Lord Jesus Christ, that of
his bounteous goodness he will grant that *this person* may
receive the forgiveness of sins, be baptized with water
and the Holy Spirit, and may be received into Christ's
holy Church, and be made *a* living *member* of the same.

Let us pray.

Almighty and everlasting God, the aid of all who need,
the helper of all who call upon thee for comfort, the life

of all who believe, and the resurrection of the dead: We call upon thee for *this* thy *servant*, that *he* coming to thy holy Baptism may receive remission of *his* sins and be filled with the Holy Spirit. Receive *him*, O Lord, as thou hast promised by thy well-beloved Son, and grant that *he* may be faithful to thee all the days of *his* life, and finally come to the eternal kingdom which thou hast promised; through Jesus Christ our Lord. **Amen.**

† *Then, addressing the person or persons to be baptized, the minister shall say,*

Well beloved, you are come here desiring to receive holy Baptism. We have prayed that God, through our Lord Jesus Christ, would grant to receive you, release you from sin, sanctify you with the Holy Spirit, and give you the kingdom of heaven, and everlasting life.

Do you truly and earnestly repent of your sins and accept Jesus Christ as your Savior?

I do.

Do you believe in God, the Father Almighty, maker of heaven and earth; and in Jesus Christ his only Son our Lord; and in the Holy Spirit, the Lord, the giver of life?

I do.

Do you desire to be baptized in this faith?

I do.

Will you then obediently keep God's holy will and commandments and walk in the same all the days of your life?

I will, by God's help.

† *Then the minister shall say,*

Let us pray.

O merciful God, grant that all sinful affections may die in *this* thy *servant*, and that all things belonging to thy Spirit may live and grow in *him*. Grant that *he* may have the power and strength to triumph over evil, may receive the fulness of thy grace, and ever remain in the number of thy faithful and beloved children; through Jesus Christ our Lord. Amen.

† *The minister, asking the name of each person to be baptized, and then repeating the same, though not including the surname, shall baptize him, saying,*

N., I baptize you in the name of the Father, and of the Son, and of the Holy Spirit. **Amen.**

† *Then the minister may have the people stand, and, addressing them, may say,*

Brethren of the household of faith, I commend to your love and care *this person*, whom we this day recognize as *a member* of the family of God. Will you endeavor so to live that *he* may grow in the knowledge and love of God the Father, through our Savior Jesus Christ?

† *Then the people shall say,*

With God's help we will so order our lives after the example of Christ that, surrounded by steadfast love, you may be established in the faith, and confirmed and strengthened in the way that leads to life eternal.

† *Then the minister may give this or another blessing:*

God the Father, God the Son, and God the Holy Spirit bless, preserve, and keep you, now and for evermore. **Amen.**

———————

¶ 1714.   The Order for
CONFIRMATION AND RECEPTION
INTO THE CHURCH

† *This service shall be conducted in the church in the presence of the people at such a time in a stated hour of worship as the minister may determine.*

† *All who are to be confirmed as members of Christ's holy Church shall have been baptized, and instructed in the doctrines and duties of the Christian faith.*

† *Those to be confirmed shall stand before the minister, who, addressing the people, shall say,*

Dearly beloved, the Church is of God, and will be preserved to the end of time, for the conduct of worship and the due administration of his Word and Sacraments, the maintenance of Christian fellowship and discipline, the edification of believers, and the conversion of the world. All, of every age and station, stand in need of the means of grace which it alone supplies.

These persons who *are* to be confirmed *have* received the Sacrament of Baptism, *have* also been instructed in the teachings of the Church, and *are* now ready to profess publicly the faith into which *they were* baptized.

† *Then the minister, addressing those who are to be confirmed, shall say,*

Do you here, in the presence of God, and of this congregation, renew the solemn promise and vow that you made, or that was made in your name, at your Baptism?

I do.

Do you confess Jesus Christ as your Lord and Savior and pledge your allegiance to his kingdom?

I do.

Do you receive and profess the Christian faith as contained in the Scriptures of the Old and New Testaments?

I do.

Do you promise according to the grace given you to live a Christian life and always remain a faithful member of Christ's holy Church?

I do.

† *Then the candidates shall kneel, and the minister, laying his hands upon the head of each severally, shall say,*

N., the Lord defend you with his heavenly grace and by his Spirit confirm you in the faith and fellowship of all true disciples of Jesus Christ. **Amen.**

† *Those confirmed shall rise, and the minister, addressing the people, may say,*

Let those persons who are members of other communions in Christ's holy Church, and who now desire to enter into the fellowship of this congregation, present themselves to be received into the membership of The Methodist Church.

† *Then those confirmed and those to be received from other communions shall stand before the minister; and he, addressing them, shall say,*

Will you be loyal to The Methodist Church, and uphold it by your prayers, your presence, your gifts and your service?

I will.

† *Then the minister may say,*

Let those persons who are members of other congregations of The Methodist Church, and who now desire to enter into the fellowship of this congregation, present themselves to be welcomed.

† *Here a lay member, selected by the Official Board, may join with the minister in offering the right hand of fellowship to all those received.*

† *Then the minister may have those received face the congregation, and, causing the people to stand, he shall address them, saying,*

Brethren I commend to your love and care *these persons* whom we this day receive into the membership of this congregation. Do all in your power to increase *their* faith, confirm *their* hope, and perfect *them* in love.

† *Whereupon the people shall say,*

We rejoice to recognize you as *members* of Christ's holy Church, and bid you welcome to this congregation of The Methodist Church. With you we renew our vows to uphold it by our prayers, our presence, our gifts, and our service.

† *Then the minister may say,*

Go forth in peace, and be of good courage; hold fast that which is good, rejoicing in the power of the Holy Spirit. And the blessing of God, Father, Son, and Holy Spirit, be with you and remain with you forever. **Amen.**

† *On any day when persons are to be received by transfer only, the minister will use only that part of the service which applies to them.*

**¶ 1715. The Order for the Administration of the
SACRAMENT OF THE LORD'S SUPPER
Or Holy Communion**

† *It shall be the duty of the pastor to administer the
Sacrament of the Lord's Supper at regularly appointed
times to the people committed to his care, remembering
the charge laid upon him at the time of his ordination:
"Be thou a faithful dispenser of the Word of God, and of
his holy Sacraments."*

† *The order for the administration of this Sacrament to
the sick, to those confined to their homes, or to others in
circumstances where the full service is impracticable,
should include the Invitation, the General Confession,
the Prayer for Pardon, the Comfortable Words, the
Prayer of Consecration, the Prayer of Humble Access,
the Words of Distribution, the Prayer of Thanksgiving,
and the Benediction.*

† *At the time of Holy Communion, the Lord's Table shall
have upon it a fair white linen cloth. The elements of
bread and wine shall be placed thereon. The pure, un-
fermented juice of the grape shall be used.*

† *It is our custom to deliver the elements into the hands
of the people while they kneel before the Lord's Table.
But at the discretion of the minister, the elements may
be served to any or to all of the people while standing,
or while seated in the pews.*

† *Upon entering the church, the people shall bow in prayer
and shall remain until the entire service is concluded.*

† *All people who intend to lead a Christian life are invited
to receive this holy Sacrament.*

† *The service may begin with a prelude.*

† *A hymn may be sung, the people standing.*

† *Or the minister may begin the service with one or more
of the following or other suitable sentences from the
Scriptures:*

Behold, I stand at the door and knock; if any one hears
my voice and opens the door, I will come in to him and
eat with him, and he with me. *Revelation 3:20*

I am the living bread which came down from heaven; if any one eats of this bread, he will live forever; and the bread which I shall give for the life of the world is my flesh. *John 6:51*

The cup of blessing which we bless, is it not a participation in the blood of Christ? The bread which we break, is it not a participation in the body of Christ? Because there is one bread, we who are many are one body, for we all partake of the one bread. *I Corinthians 10:16-17*

Beloved, let us love one another; for love is of God, and he who loves is born of God and knows God. In this the love of God was made manifest among us, that God sent his only Son into the world, so that we might live through him. *I John 4:7, 9*

Christ our Paschal Lamb is offered up for us, once for all, when he bore our sins on his body upon the cross; for he is the very Lamb of God that taketh away the sins of the world: Wherefore let us keep a joyful and holy feast with the Lord.

From I Corinthians 5:7-8; I Peter 2:24; John 1:29

What no eye has seen, nor ear heard, nor the heart of man conceived, what God has prepared for those who love him, God has revealed to us through the Spirit. For the Spirit searches everything, even the depths of God.

I Corinthians 2:9-10

† *Here the minister, facing the people, shall say,*

　　　　　The Lord be with you,

People:　　**And with thy spirit.**

Minister: Let us pray.

† *Then, kneeling or bowed, the minister and people together shall say,*

Almighty God, unto whom all hearts are open, all desires known, and from whom no secrets are hid: Cleanse the thoughts of our hearts by the inspiration of thy Holy Spirit, that we may perfectly love thee, and

worthily magnify thy holy name; through Christ our Lord. Amen.

Our Father, who art in heaven, hallowed be thy name. Thy kingdom come, thy will be done on earth as it is in heaven. Give us this day our daily bread. And forgive us our trespasses, as we forgive those who trespass against us. And lead us not into temptation, but deliver us from evil. For thine is the kingdom, and the power, and the glory, forever. Amen.

† *Then, standing, all shall sing or say,*

Glory be to God on high, and on earth peace, good will toward men. We praise thee, we bless thee, we worship thee, we glorify thee, we give thanks to thee for thy great glory: O Lord God, heavenly King, God the Father Almighty.

O Lord, the only begotten Son, Jesus Christ: O Lord God, Lamb of God, Son of the Father: that takest away the sins of the world, have mercy upon us. Thou that takest away the sins of the world, receive our prayer. Thou that sittest at the right hand of God the Father, have mercy upon us.

For thou only art holy; thou only art the Lord; thou only, O Christ, with the Holy Ghost, art most high in the glory of God the Father. Amen.

† *The minister, facing the people while they remain standing, shall say,*

Ye that do truly and earnestly repent of your sins, and are in love and charity with your neighbors, and intend to lead a new life, following the commandments of God, and walking from henceforth in his holy ways: Draw near with faith, and take this holy Sacrament to your comfort, and make your humble confession to almighty God.

† *Then the minister, kneeling and facing the Lord's Table, and all the people, kneeling or bowed, shall make together this general confession:*

Almighty God, Father of our Lord Jesus Christ, maker of all things, judge of all men: We acknowledge and bewail our manifold sins and wickedness, which we from time to time most grievously have committed, by thought, word, and deed, against thy divine majesty. We do earnestly repent, and are heartily sorry for these our misdoings; the remembrance of them is grievous unto us. Have mercy upon us, have mercy upon us, most merciful Father. For thy Son our Lord Jesus Christ's sake, forgive us all that is past; and grant that we may ever hereafter serve and please thee in newness of life, to the honor and glory of thy name; through Jesus Christ our Lord. Amen.

✝ *Then the minister shall pray, saying,*

Almighty God, our heavenly Father, who of thy great mercy hast promised forgiveness of sins to all them that with hearty repentance and true faith turn to thee: Have mercy upon us; pardon and deliver us from all our sins; confirm and strengthen us in all goodness; and bring us to everlasting life; through Jesus Christ our Lord. **Amen.**

✝ *The minister, standing and facing the people, shall say,*

Hear what comfortable words the Scriptures say to all that truly turn to the Lord:

✝ *Then the minister shall say one or more of the following sentences:*

Come to me, all who labor and are heavy-laden, and I will give you rest.   *Matthew 11:28*

God so loved the world that he gave his only Son, that whoever believes in him should not perish but have eternal life.   *John 3:16*

The saying is sure and worthy of full acceptance, that Christ Jesus came into the world to save sinners.
                    I Timothy 1:15

If we confess our sins, he is faithful and just, and will forgive our sins and cleanse us from all unrighteousness.
                    I John 1:9

If any one sins, we have an advocate with the Father, Jesus Christ the righteous; and he is the expiation for our sins, and not for ours only but also for the sins of the whole world. *From I John 2:1-2*

† *Here the minister may offer a pastoral prayer, or he may say,*

Let us pray for the whole state of Christ's Church.

† *Then may follow this prayer, the minister beginning, the people responding:*

Most merciful Father, we humbly beseech thee to receive these our prayers for the universal Church, that thou wilt confirm it in the truth of thy holy faith, inspire it with unity and concord, and extend and prosper it throughout the world.

We beseech thee also, so to guide and strengthen the witness of the Church to those in authority in all nations, that they may maintain the justice and welfare of all mankind.

Hear us, we beseech thee, O Lord.

Give grace, O heavenly Father, to all ministers of thy Church, that both by their life and doctrine they may set forth thy true and lively Word, and faithfully administer thy holy Sacraments.

And to all thy people give thy heavenly grace, that with willing heart and due reverence, they may hear and receive thy holy Word, truly serving thee in holiness and righteousness all the days of their lives.

Hear us, we beseech thee, O Lord.

And we most humbly beseech thee, of thy goodness, O Lord, to support and strengthen all those who, in this transitory life, are in trouble, sorrow, need, sickness, or any other adversity.

Hear us, we beseech thee, O Lord.

We remember with thanksgiving those who have loved and served thee in thy Church on earth, who now rest from their labors (especially those most dear to us, whom we name in our hearts before thee). Keep us in fellowship with all thy saints, and bring us at length to the joy of thy heavenly kingdom.

Grant this, O Father, for the sake of Jesus Christ, our only mediator and advocate. Amen.

† *Then shall be read the lesson(s) from the Holy Scriptures. If two lessons are read, let one be the Epistle and the other the Gospel. An anthem or a hymn may be sung after the first lesson.*

† *Here the minister and people may say the Apostles' Creed or another of the Christian affirmations of faith, the people standing.*

† *Then shall follow the sermon.*

† *Here parish notices may be given.*

† *A hymn may be sung. The minister shall uncover the elements, and shall proceed to receive the offering from the people. When the offering is presented, the people shall stand, and a prayer of dedication shall be said or sung.*

† *Where custom prevails, an offering may be left by the people at the chancel when they come forward to receive the elements.*

† *The people shall remain standing, and the minister, facing the people, shall say,*

Lift up your hearts.

People: **We lift them up unto the Lord.**

Minister: Let us give thanks unto the Lord.

People: **It is meet and right so to do.**

† *Then the minister, facing the Lord's Table, shall say,*
It is very meet, right, and our bounden duty that we should at all times and in all places give thanks unto thee, O Lord, holy Father, almighty, everlasting God.

† *Here may follow the Proper Preface,[1] or else the minister immediately shall say,*

Therefore with angels and archangels, and with all the company of heaven, we laud and magnify thy glorious name, evermore praising thee, and saying:

† *Then shall all sing or say,*

---

[1] *See ¶ 1716.*

Holy, holy, holy, Lord God of hosts: Heaven and earth are full of thy glory! Glory be to thee, O Lord most high! Amen.

† *The people shall kneel or bow; the minister, facing the Lord's Table, shall offer the Prayer of Consecration:*

Almighty God, our heavenly Father, who of thy tender mercy didst give thine only Son Jesus Christ to suffer death upon the cross for our redemption; who made there, by the one offering of himself, a full, perfect, and sufficient sacrifice for the sins of the whole world; and did institute, and in his holy gospel command us to continue, a perpetual memory of his precious death until his coming again:

Hear us, O merciful Father, we most humbly beseech thee, and grant that we, receiving these thy creatures of bread and wine, according to thy Son our Savior Jesus Christ's holy institution, in remembrance of his passion, death, and resurrection, may be partakers of the divine nature through him:

Who in the same night that he was betrayed, took bread [*here the minister may take the bread in his hands*], and when he had given thanks, he broke it, and gave it to his disciples saying, Take, eat; this is my body which is given for you; do this in remembrance of me. Likewise after supper he took the cup [*here the minister may take the cup in his hands*]; and when he had given thanks, he gave it to them, saying, Drink ye all of this; for this is my blood of the New Covenant, which is shed for you and for many, for the forgiveness of sins; do this, as oft as ye shall drink it, in remembrance of me. Amen.

† *The minister shall kneel before the Lord's Table. After a brief silence, the minister and people together shall pray, saying,*

We do not presume to come to this thy table, O merciful Lord, trusting in our own righteousness, but in thy manifold and great mercies. We are not worthy so much as to gather up the crumbs under thy table. But thou art the same Lord, whose property is always to have mercy. Grant us therefore, gracious Lord, so to partake of this Sacrament of thy Son Jesus Christ, that we may walk in newness of life, may grow into his likeness, and may evermore dwell in him, and he in us. Amen.

† *Here may be sung or said,*

O Lamb of God, that takest away the sins of the world, have mercy upon us.

O Lamb of God, that takest away the sins of the world, have mercy upon us.

O Lamb of God, that takest away the sins of the world, grant us thy peace.

† *The minister shall first receive the Holy Communion in both kinds, and then shall deliver the same to any who are assisting him. Then the minister or those assisting him shall deliver the elements in both kinds to the people.*

† *During the distribution of the elements appropriate hymns may be sung or played.*

† *When the bread is given, one or both of the following sentences shall be said:*

The body of our Lord Jesus Christ, which was given for thee, preserve thy soul and body unto everlasting life.

Take and eat this in remembrance that Christ died for thee, and feed on him in thy heart by faith with thanksgiving.

† *When the cup is given, one or both of the following sentences shall be said:*

The blood of our Lord Jesus Christ, which was shed for thee, preserve thy soul and body unto everlasting life.

Drink this in remembrance that Christ's blood was shed for thee, and be thankful.

† *When all have communed, the minister shall place upon the Lord's Table all that remains of the elements, covering the same.*

† *Then the minister, standing and facing the people, shall say,*

>The peace of the Lord be with you.

People: **And with thy spirit.**

Minister: Let us give thanks unto the Lord.

† *Then the minister, kneeling before the Lord's Table, and the people, kneeling or bowed, shall pray, saying,*

O Lord, our heavenly Father, we, thy humble servants, desire thy fatherly goodness mercifully to accept this our sacrifice of praise and thanksgiving; most humbly beseeching thee to grant, that, by the merits and death of thy Son Jesus Christ, and through faith in his blood, we and thy whole Church may obtain forgiveness of our sins, and all other benefits of his passion.

And here we offer and present unto thee, O Lord, ourselves, our souls and bodies, to be a reasonable, holy, and lively sacrifice unto thee; humbly beseeching thee that all we who are partakers of this Holy Communion may be filled with thy grace and heavenly benediction. And although we be unworthy, through our manifold sins, to offer unto thee any sacrifice, yet we beseech thee to accept this our bounden duty and service, not weighing our merits, but pardoning our offenses;

Through Jesus Christ our Lord, by whom, and with whom, in the unity of the Holy Spirit, all honor and glory be unto thee, O Father Almighty, world without end. Amen.

† *Then a hymn may be sung.*

† *Then the minister shall let the people depart with this blessing:*

The peace of God, which passeth all understanding, keep your hearts and minds in the knowledge and love of God, and of his Son Jesus Christ our Lord; and the blessing of God Almighty, the Father, the Son, and the Holy Spirit, be among you, and remain with you always. **Amen.**

† *A postlude may follow.*

¶ 1716. Proper Prefaces for Certain Days
To Precede the Sanctus in the
Order for Holy Communion

Christmas

Because thou didst give Jesus Christ, thine only Son, to be born as at this time for us; who, by the operation of the Holy Ghost, was made very man, and that without spot of sin, to make us clean from all sin. Therefore with angels, *etc.*

Epiphany

Through Jesus Christ our Lord; who, in substance of our mortal flesh, manifested forth his glory, that he might bring us out of darkness into his own glorious light. Therefore with angels, *etc.*

Easter

But chiefly are we bound to praise thee for the glorious resurrection of thy Son Jesus Christ our Lord, who by his death hath destroyed death, and by his rising to life again hath restored to us everlasting life. Therefore with angels, *etc.*

Pentecost

Through Jesus Christ our Lord; according to whose most true promise, the Holy Spirit came down as at this time from heaven, lighting upon the disciples, to teach them, and to lead them into all truth, whereby we have been brought out of darkness into the clear light and true knowledge of thee, and of thy Son Jesus Christ. Therefore with angels, *etc.*

¶ 1717.   A Brief Form of the
Order for the Administration of the
SACRAMENT OF THE LORD'S SUPPER
Or Holy Communion

† *This form for the administration of Holy Communion may be included in an order of worship, following the sermon.*

† *The minister shall uncover the elements, and shall proceed to receive the offering from the people. When the offering is presented, the people shall stand, and a prayer of dedication shall be said or sung.*

† *Where custom prevails, an offering may be left by the people at the chancel when they come forward to receive the elements.*

† *The people standing, the minister, facing the people, shall say,*

Ye that do truly and earnestly repent of your sins, and are in love and charity with your neighbors, and intend to lead a new life, following the commandments of God, and walking from henceforth in his holy ways: Draw near with faith, and take this holy Sacrament to your comfort, and make your humble confession to almighty God.

† *Then the minister, kneeling and facing the Lord's Table, and all the people, kneeling or bowed, shall make together this general confession:*

Almighty God, Father of our Lord Jesus Christ, maker of all things, judge of all men: We acknowledge and bewail our manifold sins and wickedness, which we from time to time most grievously have committed, by thought, word, and deed, against thy divine majesty. We do earnestly repent, and are heartily sorry for these our misdoings; the remembrance of them is grievous unto us. Have mercy upon us, have mercy upon us, most merciful Father. For thy Son our Lord Jesus Christ's sake, forgive us all that is past; and grant that we may ever hereafter serve and please thee in newness of life, to the honor and glory of thy name; through Jesus Christ our Lord. Amen.

† *Then the minister shall pray, saying,*

Almighty God, our heavenly Father, who of thy great mercy hast promised forgiveness of sins to all them that with hearty repentance and true faith turn to thee: Have mercy upon us; pardon and deliver us from all our sins; confirm and strengthen us in all goodness; and bring us to everlasting life; through Jesus Christ our Lord. **Amen.**

† *The minister, standing and facing the people, shall say,*
Hear what comfortable words the Scriptures say to all
that truly turn to the Lord:

† *Then the minister shall say one or more of the following
 sentences:*
Come to me, all who labor and are heavy-laden, and I will
give you rest. *Matthew 11:28*

God so loved the world that he gave his only Son, that
whoever believes in him should not perish but have
eternal life. *John 3:16*

The saying is sure and worthy of full acceptance, that
Christ Jesus came into the world to save sinners.
I Timothy 1:15

If we confess our sins, he is faithful and just, and will
forgive our sins and cleanse us from all unrighteousness.
I John 1:9

If any one sins, we have an advocate with the Father,
Jesus Christ the righteous, and he is the expiation of our
sins, and not for ours only but also for the sins of the
whole world. *From I John 2:1-2*

† *The people shall kneel or bow; the minister, facing the
 Lord's Table, shall offer the Prayer of Consecration:*
Almighty God, our heavenly Father, who of thy tender
mercy didst give thine only Son Jesus Christ to suffer
death upon the cross for our redemption; who made there,
by the one offering of himself, a full, perfect, and sufficient
sacrifice for the sins of the whole world; and did institute,
and in his holy gospel command us to continue, a perpetual memory of his precious death until his coming
again:
 Hear us, O merciful Father, we most humbly beseech
thee, and grant that we, receiving these thy creatures of
bread and wine, according to thy Son our Savior Jesus
Christ's holy institution, in remembrance of his passion,
death, and resurrection, may be partakers of the divine
nature through him:

Who in the same night that he was betrayed, took bread [*here the minister may take the bread in his hands*], and when he had given thanks, he broke it, and gave it to his disciples, saying, Take, eat; this is my body which is given for you; do this in remembrance of me. Likewise after supper he took the cup [*here the minister may take the cup in his hands*]; and when he had given thanks, he gave it to them, saying, Drink ye all of this; for this is my blood of the New Covenant, which is shed for you and for many, for the forgiveness of sins; do this, as oft as ye shall drink it, in remembrance of me. **Amen.**

† *The minister shall kneel before the Lord's Table. After a brief silence, the minister and people shall offer the following prayer:*

We do not presume to come to this thy table, O merciful Lord, trusting in our own righteousness, but in thy manifold and great mercies. We are not worthy so much as to gather up the crumbs under thy table. But thou art the same Lord, whose property is always to have mercy. Grant us therefore, gracious Lord, so to partake of this Sacrament of thy Son Jesus Christ, that we may walk in newness of life, may grow into his likeness, and may evermore dwell in him, and he in us. Amen.

† *The minister shall first receive the Holy Communion in both kinds, and then shall deliver the same to any who are assisting him. Then the minister or those assisting him shall deliver the elements in both kinds to the people.*

† *During the distribution of the elements appropriate hymns may be sung or played.*

† *When the bread is given, one or both of the following sentences shall be said:*

The body of our Lord Jesus Christ, which was given for thee, preserve thy soul and body unto everlasting life.

Take and eat this in remembrance that Christ died for thee, and feed on him in thy heart by faith with thanksgiving.

† *When the cup is given, one or both of the following sentences shall be said:*

The blood of our Lord Jesus Christ, which was shed for thee, preserve thy soul and body unto everlasting life.

Drink this in remembrance that Christ's blood was shed for thee, and be thankful.

† *When all have communed, the minister shall place upon the Lord's Table all that remains of the elements, covering the same.*

† *Then the minister, kneeling before the Lord's Table, and the people, kneeling or bowed, shall pray, saying,*

O Lord, our heavenly Father, we, thy humble servants, desire thy fatherly goodness mercifully to accept this our sacrifice of praise and thanksgiving; most humbly beseeching thee to grant, that, by the merits and death of thy Son Jesus Christ, and through faith in his blood, we and thy whole Church may obtain forgiveness of our sins, and all other benefits of his passion.

And here we offer and present unto thee, O Lord, ourselves, our souls and bodies, to be a reasonable, holy, and lively sacrifice unto thee; humbly beseeching thee that all we who are partakers of this Holy Communion may be filled with thy grace and heavenly benediction. And although we be unworthy, through our manifold sins, to offer unto thee any sacrifice, yet we beseech thee to accept this our bounden duty and service, not weighing our merits, but pardoning our offenses;

Through Jesus Christ our Lord, by whom, and with whom, in the unity of the Holy Spirit, all honor and glory be unto thee, O Father Almighty, world without end. Amen.

† *Then a hymn may be sung.*

† *Then the minister shall let the people depart with this blessing:*

The peace of God, which passeth all understanding, keep your hearts and minds in the knowledge and love of God, and of his Son Jesus Christ our Lord; and the blessing of

God Almighty, the Father, the Son, and the Holy Spirit, be among you, and remain with you always. **Amen.**

¶ 1718.   The Order for the
                SERVICE OF MARRIAGE

† *The minister is enjoined diligently to instruct those requesting his offices for their prospective marriage in the Christian significance of the holy estate into which they seek to enter.*

† *All arrangements pertaining to the service of marriage shall be made in full consultation with the minister.*

† *This service may begin with a prelude, anthem, solo, or hymn. It may include a processional and recessional and be concluded with a postlude.*

† *The congregation shall stand as the wedding procession begins.*

† *The Christian names of the bride and bridegroom may be used in place of "this man and this woman" in the first, third, and fourth paragraphs.*

† *When the Sacrament of the Lord's Supper is requested, this service should be provided at a time other than the service of marriage.*

† *At the time appointed, the persons to be married, having been qualified according to the laws of the state and the standards of the Church, standing together facing the minister, the man at the minister's left hand and the woman at the right hand, the minister shall say,*

Dearly beloved, we are gathered together here in the sight of God, and in the presence of these witnesses, to join together *this man and this woman* in holy matrimony; which is an honorable estate, instituted of God, and signifying unto us the mystical union which exists between Christ and his Church; which holy estate Christ adorned and beautified with his presence in Cana of Galilee. It is therefore not to be entered into unadvisedly, but reverently, discreetly, and in the fear of God. Into this holy estate these two persons come now to be joined. If any man can show just cause why they may not lawfully be joined together, let him now speak, or else hereafter forever hold his peace.

† *Addressing the persons to be married, the minister shall say:*

I require and charge you both, as you stand in the presence of God, before whom the secrets of all hearts are disclosed, that, having duly considered the holy covenant you are about to make, you do now declare before this company your pledge of faith, each to the other. Be well assured that if these solemn vows are kept inviolate, as God's Word demands, and if steadfastly you endeavor to do the will of your heavenly Father, God will bless your marriage, will grant you fulfillment in it, and will establish your home in peace.

† *Then shall the minister say to the man, using his Christian name,*

N., wilt thou have this woman to be thy wedded wife, to live together in the holy estate of matrimony? Wilt thou love her, comfort her, honor and keep her, in sickness and in health; and forsaking all other keep thee only unto her so long as ye both shall live?

† *The man shall answer,*

    I will.

† *Then shall the minister say to the woman, using her Christian name,*

N., wilt thou have this man to be thy wedded husband, to live together in the holy estate of matrimony? Wilt thou love him, comfort him, honor and keep him, in sickness and in health; and forsaking all other keep thee only unto him so long as ye both shall live?

† *The woman shall answer,*

    I will.

† *Then shall the minister say,*

Who giveth this woman to be married to this man?

† *The father of the woman, or whoever gives her in marriage, shall answer,*

I do.

† *Then the minister, receiving the hand of the woman from her father or other sponsor, shall cause the man with his right hand to take the woman by her right hand, and say after him,*

I, N., take thee, N., to be my wedded wife, to have and to hold, from this day forward, for better, for worse, for richer, for poorer, in sickness and in health, to love and to cherish, till death us do part, according to God's holy ordinance; and thereto I pledge thee my faith.

† *Then shall they loose their hands; and the woman, with her right hand taking the man by his right hand, shall say after the minister,*

I, N., take thee, N., to be my wedded husband, to have and to hold, from this day forward, for better, for worse, for richer, for poorer, in sickness and in health, to love and to cherish, till death us do part, according to God's holy ordinance; and thereto I pledge thee my faith.

† *Then they may give to each other rings, or the man may give to the woman a ring, in this wise: the minister taking the ring or rings, shall say,*

The wedding ring is the outward and visible sign of an inward and spiritual grace, signifying to all the uniting of this man and this woman in holy matrimony, through the Church of Jesus Christ our Lord.

† *Then the minister may say,*

Let us pray.

Bless, O Lord, the giving of these rings, that they who wear them may abide in thy peace, and continue in thy favor; through Jesus Christ our Lord. **Amen.**

† *Or, if there be but one ring, the minister may say,*

Bless, O Lord, the giving of this ring, that he who gives it and she who wears it may abide forever in thy peace, and continue in thy favor; through Jesus Christ our Lord. **Amen.**

† *The minister shall then deliver the proper ring to the man to put upon the third finger of the woman's left hand. The man, holding the ring there, shall say after the minister,*

In token and pledge of our constant faith and abiding love, with this ring I thee wed, in the name of the Father, and of the Son, and of the Holy Spirit. Amen.

† *Then, if there is a second ring, the minister shall deliver it to the woman to put upon the third finger of the man's left hand; and the woman, holding the ring there, shall say after the minister,*

In token and pledge of our constant faith and abiding love, with this ring I thee wed, in the name of the Father, and of the Son, and of the Holy Spirit. Amen.

† *Then shall the minister join their right hands together and, with his hand on their united hands, shall say,*

Forasmuch as *N.* and *N.* have consented together in holy wedlock, and have witnessed the same before God and this company, and thereto have pledged their faith each to the other and have declared the same by joining hands and by giving and receiving *rings;* I pronounce that they are husband and wife together, in the name of the Father, and of the Son, and of the Holy Spirit. Those whom God hath joined together let not man put asunder. **Amen.**

† *Then shall the minister say,*

Let us pray.

† *Then shall the husband and wife kneel; the minister shall say,*

O eternal God, creator and preserver of all mankind, giver of all spiritual grace, the author of everlasting life: Send thy blessing upon this man and this woman, whom we bless in thy name; that they may surely perform and keep the vow and covenant between them made, and may ever remain in perfect love and peace together, and live according to thy laws.

Look graciously upon them, that they may love, honor, and cherish each other, and so live together in faithfulness and patience, in wisdom and true godliness, that their home may be a haven of blessing and a place of peace; through Jesus Christ our Lord. **Amen.**

† *Then the husband and wife, still kneeling, shall join with the minister and congregation in the Lord's Prayer, saying,*

Our Father, who art in heaven, hallowed be thy name. Thy kingdom come, thy will be done on earth as it is in heaven. Give us this day our daily bread. And forgive us our trespasses, as we forgive those who trespass against us. And lead us not into temptation, but deliver us from evil. For thine is the kingdom, and the power, and the glory, forever. Amen.

† *Then the minister shall give this blessing:*

God, the Father, the Son, and the Holy Spirit, bless, preserve, and keep you; the Lord graciously with his favor look upon you, and so fill you with all spiritual benediction and love that you may so live together in this life that in the world to come you may have life everlasting. **Amen.**

¶ 1719. The Order for the
BURIAL OF THE DEAD

† *The death of a member of the church should be reported to the pastor as soon as possible, and arrangements for the funeral should be made in consultation with him.*

† *The pastor shall not accept an honorarium for this service when the deceased was a member of his parish.*

† *Funeral services of church members should be held in the sanctuary. The casket should be placed before the altar or the Lord's Table and remain closed.*

† *In the event of cremation the service may be adapted at the discretion of the minister.*

† *The service may begin and end with appropriate music selected in consultation with the minister.*

† *The minister shall begin the service by reading one or more of the following sentences; or the minister, meeting the body, and going before it, shall say one or more of the following sentences:*

Jesus said, "I am the resurrection and the life; he who believes in me, though he die, yet shall he live, and whoever lives and believes in me shall never die."

John 11:25-26

The eternal God is your dwelling place, and underneath are the everlasting arms.   *Deuteronomy 33:27a*

The Lord is my light and my salvation; whom shall I fear? The Lord is the stronghold of my life; of whom shall I be afraid?   *Psalm 27:1*

Blessed be the Lord! for he has heard the voice of my supplications. The Lord is my strength and my shield; in him my heart trusts.   *Psalm 28:6-7a*

For we know that if the earthly tent we live in is destroyed, we have a building from God, a house not made with hands, eternal in the heavens.   *II Corinthians 5:1*

† *Here a hymn may be sung, and then the minister shall say,*

Let us pray.

† *Here the minister may offer one or more of the following prayers:*

O God, the Lord of life, the conqueror of death, our help in every time of trouble, who dost not willingly grieve or afflict the children of men: Comfort us who mourn, and give us grace, in the presence of death, to worship thee, that we may have sure hope of eternal life and be enabled to put our whole trust in thy goodness and mercy; through Jesus Christ our Lord. **Amen.**

Almighty God, our Father, from whom we come, and unto whom our spirits return: Thou hast been our dwelling place in all generations. Thou art our refuge and strength, a very present help in trouble. Grant us thy blessing in this hour, and enable us so to put our trust in thee that our spirits may grow calm and our hearts be comforted. Lift our eyes beyond the shadows of earth, and help us to see the light of eternity. So may we find grace and strength for this and every time of need; through Jesus Christ our Lord. **Amen.**

O God our Father, creator of all mankind, giver and preserver of all life: We confess to thee our slowness to accept death as part of thy plan for life. We confess our reluctance to commit to thee those whom we love. Restore our faith that we may come to trust in thy care and providence; through Jesus Christ our Lord. **Amen.**[2]

O Jesus Christ our risen Lord, who in death hast gone before us: Grant us the assurance of thy presence, that we who are anxious and fearful in the face of death may confidently face the future, in the knowledge that thou hast prepared a place for all who love thee. **Amen.**[3]

† *Here one or more of the following psalms may be read by the minister, or by the minister and people responsively or in unison. If the people participate, they shall stand for the psalm and remain standing for the* Gloria Patri.

The Lord is my shepherd;
   I shall not want.
He maketh me to lie down in green pastures:
   he leadeth me beside the still waters.
He restoreth my soul:
   he leadeth me in the paths of righteousness for his
      name's sake.
Yea, though I walk through the valley of the shadow of
      death, I will fear no evil:
   for thou art with me; thy rod and thy staff they com-
      fort me.
Thou preparest a table before me in the presence of mine
      enemies:

[2] By Edwin B. Womack.
[3] By Donald R. Jessup.

thou anointest my head with oil; my cup runneth over.
Surely goodness and mercy shall follow me all the days of
  my life.
And I will dwell in the house of the Lord for ever.

Psalm 23 KJV

The Lord is my light and my salvation;
  whom shall I fear?
The Lord is the stronghold of my life;
  of whom shall I be afraid?
Though a host encamp against me,
  my heart shall not fear;
though war arise against me,
  yet I will be confident.
One thing have I asked of the Lord,
  that will I seek after;
that I may dwell in the house of the Lord
  all the days of my life
to behold the beauty of the Lord,
  and to inquire in his temple.
For he will hide me in his shelter
  in the day of trouble;
he will set me high upon a rock.
I believe that I shall see the goodness of the Lord
  in the land of the living!
Wait for the Lord;
  be strong, and let your heart take courage;
  yea, wait for the Lord.   *From Psalm 27*

Lord, thou hast been our dwelling place
  in all generations.
Before the mountains were brought forth,
  or ever thou hadst formed the earth and the world,
  from everlasting to everlasting thou art God.
For a thousand years in thy sight
  are but as yesterday when it is past,
  or as a watch in the night.
Thou dost sweep men away; they are like a dream,
  like grass which is renewed in the morning:
in the morning it flourishes and is renewed;
  in the evening it fades and withers.

So teach us to number our days
  that we may get a heart of wisdom.
Let thy work be manifest to thy servants,
  and thy glorious power to their children.
Let the favor of the Lord our God be upon us,
  and establish thou the work of our hands upon us,
  yea, the work of our hands establish thou it.

From Psalm 90

I lift up my eyes to the hills.
  From whence does my help come?
My help comes from the Lord,
  who made heaven and earth.
He will not let your foot be moved,
  he who keeps you will not slumber.
Behold, he who keeps Israel
  will neither slumber nor sleep.
The Lord is your keeper;
  the Lord is your shade
  on your right hand.
The sun shall not smite you by day,
  nor the moon by night.
The Lord will keep you from all evil;
  he will keep your life.
The Lord will keep
  your going out and your coming in
  from this time forward and for evermore. *Psalm 121*

† *Then the people shall say or sing,*

Glory be to the Father, and to the Son, and to the Holy Ghost; as it was in the beginning, is now, and ever shall be, world without end. Amen.

† *Here the congregation may confess their faith according to the Apostles' Creed or another affirmation of faith.*

† *Here one or more of the following lessons from the Scriptures shall be read:*

"Let not your hearts be troubled; believe in God, believe also in me. In my Father's house are many rooms; if it were not so, would I have told you that I go to prepare a place for you? And when I go and prepare a place for you, I will come again and will take you to myself, that

587

where I am you may be also. And you know the way
where I am going."

Thomas said to him, "Lord, we do not know where you
are going; how can we know the way?"

Jesus said to him, "I am the way, and the truth, and the
life; no one comes to the Father, but by me. If you had
known me, you would have known my Father also; hence-
forth you know him and have seen him.

"If you love me, you will keep my commandments. And
I will pray the Father, and he will give you another Counselor, to be with you for ever, even the Spirit of truth,
whom the world cannot receive, because it neither sees
him nor knows him; you know him, for he dwells with
you, and will be in you.

"Peace I leave with you; my peace I give to you; not
as the world gives do I give to you. Let not your hearts
be troubled, neither let them be afraid."

John 14:1-7, 15-17, 27

All who are led by the Spirit of God are sons of God. For
you did not receive the spirit of slavery to fall back into
fear, but you have received the spirit of sonship. When we
cry, "Abba! Father!" it is the Spirit himself bearing
witness with our spirit that we are children of God, and if
children, then heirs, heirs of God and fellow heirs with
Christ, provided we suffer with him in order that we
may also be glorified with him.

I consider that the sufferings of this present time are
not worth comparing with the glory that is to be revealed
to us.

We know that in everything God works for good with
those who love him, who are called according to his purpose.

What then shall we say to this? If God is for us, who
is against us? Who shall separate us from the love of
Christ? Shall tribulation, or distress, or persecution, or
famine, or nakedness, or peril, or sword? No, in all these
things we are more than conquerors through him who
loved us. For I am sure that neither death, nor life, nor
angels, nor principalities, nor things present, nor things to
come, nor powers, nor height, nor depth, nor anything else

in all creation, will be able to separate us from the love of God in Christ Jesus our Lord.

Romans 8:14-18, 28, 31, 35, 37-39

In fact Christ has been raised from the dead, the first fruits of those who have fallen asleep. For as by a man came death, by a man has come also the resurrection of the dead. For as in Adam all die, so also in Christ shall all be made alive.

But some one will ask, "How are the dead raised? With what kind of body do they come?" You foolish man! What you sow does not come to life unless it dies. But God gives it a body as he has chosen.

So is it with the resurrection of the dead. What is sown is perishable, what is raised is imperishable. It is sown in dishonor, it is raised in glory. It is sown in weakness, it is raised in power. It is sown a physical body, it is raised a spiritual body. If there is a physical body, there is also a spiritual body. Just as we have borne the image of the man of dust, we shall also bear the image of the man of heaven. I tell you this, brethren: flesh and blood cannot inherit the kingdom of God, nor does the perishable inherit the imperishable.

For this perishable nature must put on the imperishable, and this mortal nature must put on immortality. When the perishable puts on the imperishable, and the mortal puts on immortality, then shall come to pass the saying that is written: "Death is swallowed up in victory." "O death, where is thy victory? O death, where is thy sting?" The sting of death is sin, and the power of sin is the law. But thanks be to God, who gives us the victory through our Lord Jesus Christ.

Therefore, my beloved brethren, be steadfast, immovable, always abounding in the work of the Lord, knowing that in the Lord your labor is not in vain.

I Corinthians 15:20-22, 35-36, 38a, 42-44, 49-50, 53-58

And I saw the holy city, new Jerusalem, coming down out of heaven from God, prepared as a bride adorned for her husband; and I heard a great voice from the throne saying, "Behold, the dwelling of God is with men. He will dwell with them, and they shall be his people, and God himself will be with them; he will wipe away every tear from their eyes, and death shall be no more, neither shall there be mourning nor crying nor pain any more, for the former things have passed away."

And he who sat upon the throne said, "Behold, I make all things new." Also he said, "Write this, for these words are trustworthy and true." And he said to me, "It is done! I am the Alpha and the Omega, the beginning and the end. To the thirsty I will give water without price from the fountain of the water of life. He who conquers shall have this heritage, and I will be his God and he shall be my son."   *Revelation 21:2-7*

Then he showed me the river of the water of life, bright as crystal, flowing from the throne of God and of the Lamb through the middle of the street of the city; also, on either side of the river, the tree of life with its twelve kinds of fruit, yielding its fruit each month; and the leaves of the tree were for the healing of the nations. There shall no more be anything accursed, but the throne of God and of the Lamb shall be in it, and his servants shall worship him; they shall see his face, and his name shall be on their foreheads. And night shall be no more; they need no light of lamp or sun, for the Lord God will be their light, and they shall reign for ever and ever.
                              Revelation 22:1-5

For this reason I bow my knees before the Father, from whom every family in heaven and on earth is named, that according to the riches of his glory he may grant you to be strengthened with might through his Spirit in the inner man, and that Christ may dwell in your hearts through faith; that you, being rooted and grounded in love, may have power to comprehend with all the saints what is the breadth and length and height and depth, and to know the love of Christ which surpasses knowledge, that you may be filled with all the fulness of God.

Now to him who by the power at work within us is able to do far more abundantly than all we ask or think, to him be glory in the church and in Christ Jesus to all generations, for ever and ever. Amen.   *Ephesians 3:14-21*

† *Here may be sung a hymn or anthem.*

† *Then may follow a sermon, after which the minister may pray as he is moved, or may offer one or more of the following prayers:*

Eternal God, who committest to us the swift and solemn trust of life: Since we know not what a day may bring forth, but only that the hour for serving thee is always present, may we wake to the instant claims of thy holy will, not waiting for tomorrow, but yielding today. Consecrate with thy presence the way our feet may go; and the humblest work will shine, and the roughest places be made plain. Lift us above unrighteous anger and mistrust into faith and hope and love by a simple and steadfast reliance on thy sure will. In all things draw us to the mind of Christ, that thy lost image may be traced again, and that thou mayest own us at one with him and thee. **Amen.**

O God, who art the strength of thy saints, and who redeemest the souls of thy servants: We bless thy name for all those who have died in the Lord, and who now rest from their labors, having received the end of their faith, even the salvation of their souls. Especially we call to remembrance thy lovingkindness and thy tender mercies to this *thy servant.* For all thy goodness that withheld not *his* portion in the joys of this earthly life, and for thy guiding hand along the way of *his* pilgrimage, we give thee thanks and praise. Especially we bless thee for thy grace that kindled in *his* heart the love of thy dear name, that enabled *him* to fight the good fight, to endure unto the end, and to obtain the victory, yea, to become more than conqueror, through him that loveth us. We magnify thy holy name that, *his* trials and temptations being ended, sickness and death being passed, with all the dangers and difficulties of this mortal life, *his* spirit is at home in thy presence, with whom dwelleth eternal peace. And grant, O Lord, we beseech thee, that we who rejoice in the triumph of thy saints may profit by their example, that, becoming followers of their faith and patience, we also may enter with them into an inheritance incorruptible and undefiled, and that fadeth not away; through Jesus Christ our Lord. **Amen.**

Almighty God, the fountain of all life, who art our refuge and strength and our help in trouble: Enable us, we pray thee, to put our trust in thee, that we may obtain comfort, and find grace to help in this and every time of need; through Jesus Christ our Lord. **Amen.**

Remember thy servant, O Lord, according to the favor which thou bearest unto thy people, and grant that, increasing in knowledge and love of thee, *he* may go from strength to strength, in the life of perfect service in thy heavenly kingdom; through Jesus Christ our Lord, who liveth and reigneth with thee and the Holy Spirit ever, one God, world without end. **Amen.**

Father of spirits, we have joy at this time in all who have faithfully lived, and in all who have peacefully died. We thank thee for all fair memories and all living hopes; for the sacred ties that bind us to the unseen world; for the dear and holy dead who compass us as a cloud of witnesses, and make the distant heaven a home to our hearts. May we be followers of those who now inherit the promises; through Jesus Christ our Lord. **Amen.**

O Lord and Master, who thyself didst weep beside the grave, and art touched with the feeling of our sorrows: Fulfill now thy promise that thou wilt not leave thy people comfortless, but wilt come to them. Reveal thyself unto thy sorrowing servants, and cause them to hear thee say, I am the resurrection and the life. Help them, O Lord, to turn to thee with true discernment, and to abide in thee through living faith, that, finding now the comfort of thy presence, they may have also a sure confidence in thee for all that is to come; until the day break, and the shadows flee away. Hear us for thy great mercy's sake, O Jesus Christ our Lord. **Amen.**

O Thou who hast ordered this wondrous world, and who knowest all things in earth and heaven: So fill our hearts with trust in thee that, by night and by day, at all times and in all seasons, we may without fear commit those who are dear to us to thy never-failing love for this life and the life to come. **Amen.**

O Lord, we pray thee, give us thy strength, that we may live more bravely and faithfully for the sake of those who are no longer with us here upon earth; and grant us so to serve thee day by day that we may find eternal fellowship with them; through him who died and rose again for us all, Jesus Christ our Lord. **Amen.**

Almighty God, who art leading us through the changes of time to the rest and blessedness of eternity: Be thou near to comfort and uphold. Make us to know and feel that thy children are precious in thy sight, that they live evermore with thee, and that thy mercy endureth forever. Thankful for the life which thou hast given us for these seasons, we pray thy help now to resign it obediently unto thee. Assist us to return to the scenes of our daily life, to obey thy will with patience, and to bear our trials with fortitude and hope. And when the peace of death falls upon us, may we find our perfect rest in thee; through Jesus Christ our Lord. **Amen.**

† *For a child one or both of the following prayers may be used:*

O God, whose most dear Son did take little children into his arms and bless them: Give us grace, we beseech thee, to entrust the soul of this child to thy never-failing love and care, and bring us all to thy heavenly kingdom; through the same thy Son, Jesus Christ our Lord. **Amen.**

O God, we pray that thou wilt keep in thy tender love the life of this child whom we hold in blessed memory. Help us who continue here to serve thee with constancy, trusting in thy promise of eternal life, that hereafter we may be united with thy blessed children in glory everlasting; through Jesus Christ our Lord. **Amen.**

† *Then the minister shall give this blessing:*

The peace of God, which passeth all understanding, keep your hearts and minds in the knowledge and love of God, and of his Son Jesus Christ our Lord; and the blessing of God Almighty, the Father, the Son, and the Holy Spirit, be among you, and remain with you always. **Amen.**

✝ *At the grave, when the people are assembled, the minister shall say one or more of the following sentences:*

Our help is in the name of the Lord, who made heaven and earth.   *Psalm 124:8*

As a father pities his children, so the Lord pities those who fear him.   *Psalm 103:13*

Say to those who are of a fearful heart, "Be strong, fear not! Behold, your God will come and save you."
From Isaiah 35:4

The steadfast love of the Lord is from everlasting to everlasting upon those who fear him, and his righteousness to children's children.   *Psalm 103:17*

✝ *Then the minister may say,*

Forasmuch as the spirit of the departed has entered into the life immortal, we therefore commit *his* body to its resting place, but *his* spirit we commend to God, remembering how Jesus said upon the cross, "Father, into thy hands I commend my spirit."

✝ *Or the minister may say,*

Forasmuch as almighty God hath received unto himself the soul of our departed *brother*, we therefore tenderly commit *his* body to the ground, in the blessed hope that as *he* hath borne the image of the earthly so also *he* shall bear the image of the heavenly.

✝ *Or the minister may say,*

Forasmuch as the spirit of the departed hath returned to God who gave it, we therefore commit *his* body to the ground, earth to earth, ashes to ashes, dust to dust; looking for the general resurrection in the last day, and the life of the world to come, through our Lord Jesus Christ; at whose coming in glorious majesty to judge the world, the earth and the sea shall give up their dead; and the corruptible bodies of those who sleep in him shall be changed and made like unto his own glorious body; according to the mighty working whereby he is able to subdue all things unto himself.

† *Then may be said,*

I heard a voice from heaven, saying unto me:

Blessed are the dead who die in the Lord from hence-forth: Yea, saith the Spirit, that they may rest from their labors; and their works do follow them.

Lord, have mercy upon us.

Christ, have mercy upon us.

Lord, have mercy upon us.

† *Here the minister and people may pray, saying,*

Our Father, who art in heaven, hallowed be thy name. Thy kingdom come, thy will be done on earth as it is in heaven. Give us this day our daily bread. And for-give us our trespasses, as we forgive those who trespass against us. And lead us not into temptation, but deliver us from evil. For thine is the kingdom, and the power, and the glory, forever. Amen.

† *Then the minister may offer one or more of the follow-ing prayers:*

Almighty God, with whom do live the spirits of those who depart hence in the Lord, and with whom the souls of the faithful after death are in strength and gladness: We give thee hearty thanks for the good examples of all those thy servants who, having finished their course in faith, do now rest from their labor. And we beseech thee that we, with all those who have finished their course in faith, may have our perfect consummation and bliss in thy eternal and everlasting glory; through Jesus Christ our Lord. **Amen.**

O merciful God, the Father of our Lord Jesus Christ, who is the resurrection and the life, in whom whosoever be-lieveth shall live, though he die, and whosoever liveth and believeth in him shall not die eternally: We beseech thee, O Father, to raise us from the death of sin into the life of righteousness, that when we shall depart this life we may rest in him, and may receive that blessing which thy well-beloved Son shall pronounce to all that love and fear thee, saying, Come, ye blessed of my Father, receive the kingdom prepared for you from the foundation of the world. Grant this, we beseech thee, O merciful Father, through Jesus Christ our Mediator and Redeemer. **Amen.**

O God of infinite compassion, who art the comforter of thy children: Look down in thy tender love and pity, we beseech thee, upon thy servants. In the stillness of our hearts we entreat for them thy sustaining grace. Be thou their stay, their strength, and their shield, that trusting in thee they may know thy presence near, and in the assurance of thy love be delivered out of their distresses; through Jesus Christ our Lord. **Amen.**[4]

† *Then the minister may give one of these blessings:*

Now may the God of peace who brought again from the dead our Lord Jesus, the great shepherd of the sheep, by the blood of the eternal covenant, equip you with everything good that you may do his will, working in you that which is pleasing in his sight, through Jesus Christ; to whom be glory for ever and ever. **Amen.**

The grace of our Lord Jesus Christ and the love of God and the fellowship of the Holy Spirit be with you all. **Amen.**

¶ 1720.   The Order for the ORDINATION OF DEACONS

† *When the day appointed by the bishop is come, there shall be a sermon or exhortation declaring the duty and office of such as come to be admitted deacons, how necessary that order is in the Church of Christ, and also how the people ought to esteem them in their office; after which one of the elders shall present unto the bishop all who are to be ordained, and say,*

I present unto you *these persons* **present to be ordained** *deacons:*

---

[4] Adapted by permission from *The Book of Common Order* (1932) of the United Church of Canada.

† *Their names having been read aloud, the bishop shall say to the people,*

Brethren, *these are they* whom we purpose, God willing, this day to ordain *deacons*. For, after due examination, we find that *they are* lawfully called to this office and ministry and that *they are persons* meet for the same. But if there be any of you who knows any valid reason for which *any one of them* ought not to be received into this holy ministry, let him come forth in the name of God, and disclose what the impediment is.

† *If any impediment be alleged, the bishop shall desist from ordaining that person until he shall be found to be innocent.*

† *Then shall be read the Collect:*

Almighty God, who by thy divine providence hast appointed divers orders of ministers in thy Church, and didst inspire thine apostles to choose into the order of deacons thy first martyr, St. Stephen, with others: Mercifully behold *these* thy *servants*, now called to the like office and administration; so replenish *them* with the truth of thy doctrine, and adorn *them* with innocency of life, that by both word and good example *they* may faithfully serve thee in this office, to the glory of thy name and the edification of thy Church; through the merits of our Savior Jesus Christ, who liveth and reigneth with thee and the Holy Spirit, one God, now and forever. **Amen.**

† *Then shall be read the Epistle:*

Deacons likewise must be serious; they must hold the mystery of the faith with a clear conscience. Those who serve well as deacons gain a good standing for themselves and also great confidence in the faith which is in Christ Jesus.   *I Timothy 3:8a, 9, 13*

Look carefully then how you walk, not as unwise men but as wise, making the most of the time. Therefore do not be foolish, but understand what the will of the Lord is. Be filled with the Spirit, always and for everything giving thanks in the name of our Lord Jesus Christ to God the Father. Be subject to one another out of reverence for Christ.   *Ephesians 5:15-16a, 17, 18b, 20-21*

Finally, be strong in the Lord and in the strength of his might. Put on the whole armor of God, that you may be able to stand against the wiles of the devil. For we are not contending against flesh and blood, but against the principalities, against the powers, against the world rulers of this present darkness, against the spiritual hosts of wickedness in the heavenly places. Therefore take the whole armor of God, that you may be able to withstand in the evil day, and having done all, to stand. Stand therefore, having girded your loins with truth, and having put on the breastplate of righteousness, and having shod your feet with the equipment of the gospel of peace; above all taking the shield of faith, with which you can quench all the flaming darts of the evil one. And take the helmet of salvation, and the sword of the Spirit, which is the word of God. Pray at all times in the Spirit, with all prayer and supplication. To that end keep alert with all perseverance, making supplication for all the saints.

Ephesians 6:10-18

† *Then the bishop, in the presence of the people, shall examine every one of those to be ordained, after this manner:*

Do you trust that you are inwardly moved by the Holy Spirit to take upon you the office of the ministry in the Church of Christ, to serve God for the promoting of his glory and the edifying of his people?

I trust so.

Do you unfeignedly believe the Scriptures of the Old and New Testaments?

I do believe them.

Will you diligently read and expound the same unto the people whom you shall be appointed to serve?

I will.

It appertains to the office of a deacon to conduct divine worship and to assist the elder in the administration of the Holy Communion, to read and expound the Holy Scriptures, to instruct the youth, and to baptize. And, furthermore, it is his office to search for the needy, that they may be visited and relieved. Will you do this gladly and willingly?

I will so do, by the help of God.

Will you apply all your diligence to frame and fashion your own *lives* and the lives of your *families* according to the teachings of Christ?

I will, the Lord being my helper.

Will you reverently heed them to whom the charge over you is committed, following with a glad mind and will their godly admonitions?

I will so do.

† *Here those to be ordained shall kneel, and the bishop, laying his hands upon the head of each severally, shall say,*

Take thou authority to execute the office of a deacon in the Church of God; in the name of the Father, and of the Son, and of the Holy Spirit. **Amen.**

† *Then the bishop shall deliver to every one of them the Bible, saying,*

Take thou authority to read the Holy Scriptures in the Church of God, and to preach the Word. **Amen.**

† *Then shall be read the Gospel:*

Let your loins be girded and your lamps burning, and be like men who are waiting for their master to come home from the marriage feast, so that they may open to him at once when he comes and knocks. Blessed are those servants whom the master finds awake when he comes; truly, I say to you, he will gird himself and have them sit at table, and he will come and serve them. If he comes in the second watch, or in the third, and finds them so, blessed are those servants! *Luke 12:35-38*

† *Then the bishop shall pray, saying,*

Almighty God, giver of all good things, who of thy great goodness hast vouchsafed to accept *these* thy *servants* into the office of deacon in thy Church: Make *them*, we beseech thee, O Lord, to be modest, humble, and constant in *their* ministration, and to have a ready will to observe all spiritual discipline; that *they*, continuing ever stable and strong in thy Son Jesus Christ, may so well behave *themselves* in this office that *they* may be found worthy to be called into the higher ministry in thy Church; through thy Son our Savior Jesus Christ, to whom be glory and honor, world without end. **Amen.**

Direct us, O Lord, in all our doings, with thy most gracious favor, and further us with thy continual help, that in all our works, begun, continued, and ended in thee, we may glorify thy holy name, and finally, by thy mercy, obtain everlasting life; through Jesus Christ our Lord. **Amen.**

† *Then the bishop may give this blessing:*

The peace of God, which passeth all understanding, keep your hearts and minds in the knowledge and love of God, and of his Son Jesus Christ our Lord; and the blessing of God Almighty, the Father, the Son, and the Holy Spirit, be among you, and remain with you always. **Amen.**

¶ 1721.   The Order for the
ORDINATION OF ELDERS

† *When the day appointed by the bishop is come, there shall be a sermon or exhortation declaring the duty and office of such as come to be admitted elders, how necessary that order is in the Church of Christ, and also how the people ought to esteem them in their office; after which one of the elders shall present unto the bishop all who are to be ordained, and say,*

I present unto you *these persons* present to be ordained *elders*:

† *Their names having been read aloud, the bishop shall say to the people,*

Brethren, *these are they* whom we purpose, God willing, this day to ordain *elders*. For, after due inquiry, we find that *they are* lawfully called to this office and ministry, and that *they are persons* meet for the same. But if there be any of you who knows any valid reason for which *any one of them* ought not to be received into this holy ministry, let him come forth in the name of God, and disclose what the impediment is.

† *If any impediment be alleged, the bishop shall desist from ordaining that person until he shall be found to be innocent.*

† *Then shall be read the Collect:*

Almighty God, giver of all good things, who by thy Holy Spirit hast appointed divers orders of ministers in thy Church: Mercifully behold *these* thy *servants*, now called to the office of elder, and so replenish *them* with the truth of thy doctrine, and adorn *them* with innocency of life, that by both word and good example *they* may faithfully serve thee in this office, to the glory of thy name and the advancement of thy Church; through the merits of our Savior Jesus Christ, who liveth and reigneth with thee and the Holy Spirit, one God, world without end. **Amen.**

† *Then shall be read the Epistle and the Gospel:*

Of this gospel I was made a minister according to the gift of God's grace which was given me by the working of his power. To me, though I am the very least of all the saints, this grace was given, to preach to the Gentiles the unsearchable riches of Christ, and to make all men see what is the plan of the mystery hidden for ages in God who created all things. And his gifts were that some should be apostles, some prophets, some evangelists, some pastors and teachers, for the equipment of the saints, for the work of ministry, for building up the body of Christ, until we all attain to the unity of the faith and of the knowledge of the Son of God, to mature manhood, to the measure of the stature of the fulness of Christ.

Ephesians 3:7-9; 4:11-13

Jesus said, "I am the door; if any one enters by me, he will be saved, and will go in and out and find pasture. The thief comes only to steal and kill and destroy; I came that they may have life, and have it abundantly. I am the good shepherd. The good shepherd lays down his life for the sheep. He who is a hireling and not a shepherd, whose own the sheep are not, sees the wolf coming and leaves the sheep and flees; and the wolf snatches them and scatters them. He flees because he is a hireling and cares nothing for the sheep. I am the good shepherd; I know my own and my own know me, as the Father knows me and I know the Father; and I lay down my life for the sheep. And I have other sheep, that are not of this fold; I must bring them also, and they will heed my voice. So there shall be one flock, one shepherd."   *John 10:9-16*

† *Then the bishop shall say to the persons to be ordained elders,*

Dearly beloved, you have heard of what dignity and of how great importance is this office whereunto you are called. And now again we exhort you, in the name of our Lord Jesus Christ, that you are to be *messengers, watchmen,* and *stewards* of the Lord; to teach and to admonish, to feed and provide for the Lord's family; to seek for Christ's sheep that are dispersed abroad, and for his children who are in the midst of this evil world, that they may be saved through Christ forever.

Have always, therefore, in your remembrance how great a treasure is committed to your charge. For they unto whom you are to minister are the sheep of Christ, for whom he gave his life. The Church which you must serve is his Bride and his Body. And if it shall happen the Church, or any member thereof, do take any hurt or hindrance by reason of your negligence, you know the greatness of the fault. Wherefore see that you never cease your labor, your care, and your diligence until you have done all that lieth in you, according to your bounden duty, to bring all such as shall be committed to your charge unto perfectness in Christ.

Forasmuch, then, as your office is both of so great excellency and of so great difficulty, consider how you ought to forsake, as much as you can, all worldly cares, and be studious in learning the Scriptures, and in acquiring such knowledge and skill as may help you to declare the living Word of God.

We hope that you have weighed and pondered these things with *yourselves* long before this time, and that you have clearly determined, by God's grace, to give *yourselves* wholly to this work whereunto it has pleased God to call you. Also that you will continually pray that the Holy Spirit may assist you to order your own *lives* and the lives of your *families* after the rule and doctrine of Christ, that you may grow riper and stronger in ministry and be godly and wholesome *examples* for the people to follow.

And now, that this congregation of Christ here assembled may also understand your purpose in these things, and that this your promise may the more move you to perform your duties, you shall answer plainly to these things which we, in the name of God and his Church, shall ask of you touching the same:

Do you believe in your heart that you are truly called, according to the will of our Lord Jesus Christ, to the ministry of elders?

I do so believe.

Are you persuaded that the Holy Scriptures contain all truth required for eternal salvation through faith in Jesus Christ? And are you determined out of the same Holy Scriptures so to instruct the people committed to your charge that they may enter into eternal life?

I am so persuaded and determined, by God's grace.

Will you give faithful diligence duly to minister the doctrine of Christ, the Sacraments, and the discipline of the Church, and in the spirit of Christ to defend the Church against all doctrine contrary to God's Word?

I will so do, by the help of the Lord.

Will you be diligent in prayer, in the reading of the Holy Scriptures, and in such studies as help to the knowledge of God and of his kingdom?

I will, the Lord being my helper.

Will you apply all your diligence to frame and fashion your own *lives* and the lives of your *families* according to the teachings of Christ?

I will, the Lord being my helper.

Will you maintain and set forward, as much as lieth in you, quietness, peace, and love among all Christian people, and especially among them that shall be committed to your charge?

I will so do, the Lord being my helper.

Will you reverently heed them to whom the charge over you is committed, following with a glad mind and will their godly admonitions?

I will so do.

† *Then the bishop shall pray, saying,*

Almighty God, our heavenly Father, who hath given you a good will to do all these things, grant also unto you wisdom and power to perform the same, that he may accomplish in you the good work which he hath begun, that you may be found blameless; through Jesus Christ our Lord. **Amen.**

† *Here those to be ordained elders shall kneel. The people shall be requested to make their earnest supplications in silent prayer to God for them. Silence shall be kept for a space, after which shall be said the* Veni, Creator Spiritus, *the bishop beginning, and all others responding.*

Come, Holy Ghost, our souls inspire,
  And lighten with celestial fire.
Thou the anointing Spirit art,
  Who dost thy sevenfold gifts impart.
Thy blessed unction from above
  Is comfort, life, and fire of love.
Enable with perpetual light
  The dullness of our blinded sight.
Anoint and cheer our soilèd face
  With the abundance of thy grace.
Keep far our foes, give peace at home;
  Where thou art guide, no ill can come.
Teach us to know the Father, Son,

And thee, of both, to be but One;
That through the ages all along,
This may be our endless song:
Praise to thy eternal merit,
Father, Son, and Holy Spirit. Amen.

† *Then the bishop shall say,*
Let us pray.

Almighty God, our heavenly Father, we bless and magnify thy holy name for the gift of thy most dearly beloved Son Jesus Christ our Redeemer, and for all his apostles, prophets, evangelists, teachers, and pastors, whom he hath sent abroad into the world. For these here present whom thou hast called to the same holy office and ministry, we render unto thee our most hearty thanks. And now, O Lord, we humbly beseech thee to grant that by *these* thy *ministers,* and by those over whom *they* shall be appointed, thy holy name may be forever glorified, and thy blessed kingdom enlarged; through thy Son Jesus Christ our Lord, who liveth and reigneth with thee in the unity of the Holy Spirit, one God, world without end. **Amen.**

† *Those to be ordained still kneeling, the bishop and elders assisting shall lay their hands upon the head of each severally, the bishop saying,*

The Lord pour upon thee the Holy Spirit for the office and work of an elder in the Church of God, now committed unto thee by the authority of the Church through the imposition of our hands. And be thou a faithful dispenser of the Word of God, and of his holy Sacraments; in the name of the Father, and of the Son, and of the Holy Spirit. **Amen.**

† *Then the bishop shall deliver to every one of them the Bible, saying,*

Take thou authority as an elder in the Church to preach the Word of God, and to administer the holy Sacraments in the congregation. **Amen.**

† *Then the bishop shall pray, saying,*

Most merciful Father, we beseech thee to send upon *these* thy *servants* thy heavenly blessings, that *they* may be clothed with righteousness, and that thy Word spoken by *them* may never be spoken in vain. Grant also that we may have grace to receive what *they* shall deliver out of thy Word as the means of our salvation, and that in all our words and deeds we may seek thy glory, and the increase of thy kingdom; through Jesus Christ our Lord. **Amen.**

Direct us, O Lord, in all our doings, with thy most gracious favor, and further us with thy continual help, that in all our works, begun, continued, and ended in thee, we may glorify thy holy name, and finally, by thy mercy, obtain everlasting life; through Jesus Christ our Lord. **Amen.**

† *Then the bishop may give this blessing:*

The peace of God, which passeth all understanding, keep your hearts and minds in the knowledge and love of God, and of his Son Jesus Christ our Lord; and the blessing of God Almighty, the Father, the Son, and the Holy Spirit, be among you, and remain with you always. **Amen.**

† *If on the same day the order for deacon be given to some and that of elder to others, the deacons shall be presented first, and then the elders. The Collect shall be said and the Epistle read, immediately after which they who are to be ordained deacons shall be examined and ordained as above described. Then, the Gospel having been read, they who are to be ordained elders shall likewise be examined and ordained.*

¶ 1722.   The Order for the CONSECRATION OF BISHOPS

† *When the time appointed for the consecration of bishops is come, the service shall begin with a hymn, after which the Collect shall be read:*

Almighty God, who by thy Son Jesus Christ didst give to thy holy apostles, elders, and evangelists many excellent gifts, and didst charge them to feed thy flock: Give grace, we beseech thee, to all the ministers and pastors of thy Church, that they may diligently preach thy Word and duly administer the godly discipline thereof; and grant to the people that they may faithfully follow the same, that they may receive the crown of everlasting glory; through Jesus Christ our Lord. **Amen.**

† *Then an elder shall read the Epistle:*

And from Miletus he sent to Ephesus and called to him the elders of the church. And when they came to him, he said to them: "You yourselves know how I lived among you all the time from the first day that I set foot in Asia, serving the Lord with all humility and with tears and with trials which befell me; how I did not shrink from declaring to you anything that was profitable, and teaching you in public and from house to house, testifying both to Jews and to Greeks of repentance to God and of faith in our Lord Jesus Christ. And now, behold, I am going to Jerusalem, bound in the Spirit, not knowing what shall befall me there; except that the Holy Spirit testifies to me in every city that imprisonment and afflictions await me. But I do not account my life of any value nor as precious to myself, if only I may accomplish my course and the ministry which I received from the Lord Jesus, to testify to the gospel of the grace of God. Take heed to yourselves and to all the flock, in which the Holy Spirit has made you guardians, to feed the church of the Lord which he obtained with his own blood. I know that after my departure fierce wolves will come in among you, not sparing the flock; and from among your own selves will arise men speaking perverse things, to draw away the disciples after them. Therefore be alert, remembering that for three years I did not cease night or day to admonish every one with tears. And now I commend you to God and to the word of his grace, which is able to build you up and to give you the inheritance among all those who are sanctified." *Acts 20:17-24; 28-32*

† *Then an elder shall read the Gospel:*

When they had finished breakfast, Jesus said to Simon Peter, "Simon, son of John, do you love me more than these?" He said to him, "Yes, Lord; you know that I love you." He said to him, "Feed my lambs." A second time he said to him, "Simon, son of John, do you love me?" He said to him, "Yes, Lord; you know that I love you." He said to him, "Tend my sheep." He said to him the third time, "Simon, son of John, do you love me?" Peter was grieved because he said to him the third time, "Do you love me?" And he said to him, "Lord, you know everything; you know that I love you." Jesus said to him, "Feed my sheep."   *John 21:15-17*

And Jesus came and said to them, "All authority in heaven and on earth has been given to me. Go therefore and make disciples of all nations, baptizing them in the name of the Father and of the Son and of the Holy Spirit, teaching them to observe all that I have commanded you; and lo, I am with you always, to the close of the age."
                                        Matthew 28:18-20

† *Then each elected bishop shall be presented by two elders to the officiating bishop, the elders saying,*

We present unto you this elder chosen to be consecrated a bishop.

† *Then the bishop shall call upon the people present to pray, saying,*

Dearly beloved, it is written in the Gospel of St. Luke that our Savior Christ continued the whole night in prayer before he chose and sent forth his twelve apostles. It is also written in the Acts of the Apostles that the disciples who were at Antioch did fast and pray before they laid hands on Paul and Barnabas and sent them forth on their first mission to the Gentiles. Let us therefore, following the example of our Savior Christ and his apostles, give ourselves to prayer before we admit and send forth *this person* presented to us, to the work whereunto we trust the Holy Spirit hath called *him.*

† *Then the bishop shall pray, saying,*

Almighty God, giver of all good things, who by thy Holy Spirit has appointed divers offices in thy Church; graciously behold *this* thy *servant* now called to the office and ministry of a bishop. So replenish *him* with the truth of thy doctrine, and so adorn *him* with innocency of life, that by both word and deed *he* may faithfully serve thee in this office, to the glory of thy name and the edifying and well governing of thy Church; through the merits of our Savior Jesus Christ, who liveth and reigneth with thee and the Holy Spirit, one God, world without end. **Amen.**

† *Then the bishop shall say to the person or persons to be consecrated,*

Brother, forasmuch as the Holy Scriptures command that we should not be hasty in admitting any person to government in the Church of Christ, before you are admitted to this ministration, you will, in the fear of God, give answer to these questions:

Are you persuaded that you are truly called to this ministration, according to the will of our Lord Jesus Christ?

I am so persuaded.

Are you persuaded that the Holy Scriptures contain sufficiently all truth required for eternal salvation through faith in Jesus Christ? And are you determined out of the same Holy Scriptures so to instruct the people committed to your charge that they may enter into eternal life?

I am so persuaded and determined, by God's grace.

Will you then faithfully exercise *yourself* in the Holy Scriptures, and call upon God through study and prayer for the true understanding of the same?

I will so do, by the help of God.

Are you ready with all faithful diligence to seek and to promote the truth of Christ and to defend the Church against all doctrine contrary to God's Word?

I am ready, the Lord being my helper.

Will you live soberly, righteously, and devoutly in this present world, that you may show *yourself* in all things an example of good works unto others, to the honor and glory of God?

I will so do, the Lord being my helper.

Will you show *yourself* gentle, and be merciful for Christ's sake to poor and needy people, and to all strangers destitute of help?

I will, by the help of God.

Will you maintain and set forward, as much as lieth in you, quietness, love, and peace among all men; and faithfully exercise such discipline in the Church as shall be committed unto you?

I will so do, by the help of God.

Will you be faithful in ordaining and appointing others; and will you ever seek to deal justly and kindly with your brethren of the ministry over whom you are placed as chief pastor?

I will so do, by the help of God.

† *Then the bishop shall pray, saying,*

Almighty God, our heavenly Father, who hath given you a good will to do all these things, grant also unto you wisdom and power to perform the same, that he may accomplish in you the good work which he hath begun, that you may be found blameless; through Jesus Christ our Lord. **Amen.**

† *Then the persons to be consecrated bishops shall kneel. The people shall be requested to make their earnest supplications in silent prayer to God for them. Silence shall be kept for a space, after which shall be said the* Veni, Creator Spiritus, *the officiating bishop beginning, and all others responding.*

Come, Holy Ghost, our souls inspire,
    And lighten with celestial fire.
Thou the anointing Spirit art,
    Who dost thy sevenfold gifts impart.
Thy blessed unction from above

Is comfort, life, and fire of love.
Enable with perpetual light
The dullness of our blinded sight.
Anoint and cheer our soilèd face
With the abundance of thy grace.
Keep far our foes, give peace at home;
Where thou art guide, no ill can come.
Teach us to know the Father, Son,
And thee, of both, to be but One;
That through the ages all along,
This may be our endless song
Praise to thy eternal merit,
Father, Son, and Holy Spirit. Amen.

† *Then the bishop shall say,*

Let us pray.

Almighty and most merciful Father, who of thine infinite goodness hast given thine only and dearly beloved Son Jesus Christ to be our Redeemer, and hast made some apostles, some prophets, some evangelists, some pastors and teachers, to the edifying and making perfect of thy Church: Grant, we beseech thee, to *this* thy *servant* such grace that *he* may evermore be ready to spread abroad thy gospel, the glad tidings of reconciliation with thee, and to use the authority given *him*, not to destruction, but to salvation; not to hurt, but to help; so that as *a* wise and faithful *servant*, giving to all their portion in due season, *he* may at last be received into everlasting joy; through Jesus Christ our Lord, who, with thee and the Holy Spirit, liveth and reigneth, one God, world without end. **Amen.**

† *The persons to be consecrated still kneeling, the bishops and elders assisting shall lay their hands upon the head of each severally, the officiating bishop saying,*

The Lord pour upon thee the Holy Spirit for the office and work of a bishop in the Church of God, now committed unto thee by the authority of the Church through the imposition of our hands, in the name of the Father, and of the Son, and of the Holy Spirit. And remember that thou stir up the grace of God which is in thee; for God hath not given us the spirit of fear, but of power, and of love, and of a sound mind. **Amen.**

† *Then the bishop shall deliver to each the Bible, saying,*

Give heed unto reading, exhortation, and teaching. Think upon the things contained in this Book. Be diligent in them, that the increase coming thereby may be manifest unto all men. Take heed unto thyself and to thy teaching; for by so doing thou shalt save both thyself and them that hear thee. Be to the flock of Christ a shepherd. Hold up the weak, heal the sick, bind up the broken, bring again the outcast, seek the lost; faithfully minister discipline, but forget not mercy; that the kingdom of God may come upon the earth and, when the Chief Shepherd shall appear, that you may receive the never-fading crown of glory; through Jesus Christ our Lord. **Amen.**

† *Then the bishop shall pray, saying,*

Most merciful Father, we beseech thee to send down upon *this* thy *servant* thy heavenly blessing, and so endue *him* with thy Holy Spirit that *he*, preaching thy word, not only may be earnest to reprove, beseech, and rebuke with all patience and doctrine, but also may be to such as believe a wholesome example in word, in conversation, in love, in faith, in chastity, and in purity; that, faithfully fulfilling *his* course, at the latter day *he* may receive the crown of righteousness laid up by the Lord, the righteous judge, who liveth and reigneth with thee and the Holy Spirit, one God, world without end. **Amen.**

Direct us, O Lord, in all our doings, with thy most gracious favor, and further us with thy continual help, that in all our works, begun, continued, and ended in thee, we may glorify thy holy name, and finally, by thy mercy, obtain everlasting life; through Jesus Christ our Lord. **Amen.**

† *Then the bishop may give this blessing:*

The peace of God, which passeth all understanding, keep your hearts and minds in the knowledge and love of God, and of his Son Jesus Christ our Lord; and the blessing of God Almighty, the Father, the Son, and the Holy Spirit, be among you, and remain with you always. **Amen.**

APPENDIX

APPENDIX

Chapter I

JUDICIAL COUNCIL: RULES AND DIGESTS OF DECISIONS

¶ 1801. Rules of Practice and Procedure

1. *Officers.*—The officers of the Judicial Council shall be a president, a vice-president, and a secretary, to be elected quadrennially by a majority vote of the council; *provided* that no officer shall be elected to succeed himself in any particular office.

2. *Duties of President.*—The president shall perform all the duties incident to the office of a presiding officer of a judicial body, including the right to call the Judicial Council into session, as provided by the Discipline.

3. *Duties of the Vice-President.*—In case of absence or inability of the president, or at the request of the president, the vice-president shall preside over part or all of any session of the Judicial Council and perform all duties devolving upon the presiding officer while so presiding at such session.

4. *Duties of the Secretary.*—The secretary shall perform all duties incident to the position of secretary or clerk of a judicial body, and such other duties as shall be requested of him by the Judicial Council, among which shall be:

a) To keep a correct and complete record of all proceedings of the Judicial Council, including discussions, opinions, and all other actions taken by the council.

b) To keep the docket and perform the duties incident thereto, as hereinafter provided.

c) To furnish certified copy or copies of the record of the action of the Judicial Council, or any matter determined by it, to the party or parties interested and to such others as may have a right thereto.

d) To send to the secretary of the Council of Bishops certified copies of all decisions of the Judicial Council on questions of law, as provided in ¶ 909.

e) To notify the president of the Judicial Council immediately upon the filing of any matter submitted to the Judicial Council for determination, giving him a full and complete statement of the matter involved, together with such additional data as he may deem necessary.

5. *Docket.*—All matters of whatsoever kind and character

which may be brought before the Judicial Council for determination shall be filed in consecutive order by the secretary and shall be reported fully to the council. At the conclusion of any annual session or General Conference session of the Judicial Council, all papers, documents, and exhibits in all matters finally disposed of shall be sent by the secretary for safekeeping to the library of Drew University.

6. *Proceedings Preparatory for Hearing.—a*) When any matter is appealed to the Judicial Council for determination, the document or documents and exhibits setting forth the same shall be filed with the secretary of the Judicial Council, and entered by him upon the docket of the council. All appeals, petitions, and requests for declaratory decisions shall be certified by the secretary or other proper officer of the conference, council, board, commission, or other body seeking a determination of the Judicial Council, to which shall be attached a relevant copy or transcript of the journal or minutes of such petitioning body.

b) When a cause has been placed on the docket of the Judicial Council, the secretary thereof shall, within thirty (30) days from said date, furnish to each member of the council a copy of the document or documents and exhibits setting forth such appeal, or a careful and accurate digest thereof.

7. *Arguments.*—Interested parties may be heard in person or by others appearing for them, or both, but not more than two on the same side shall be heard except by consent of the council. Arguments shall be limited to one hour for each side; but upon request before the argument is begun, the council may allow such additional time as it may deem necessary for an adequate presentation of the issues involved.

8. *Interested Persons Not Parties May Be Heard.*—Any person or persons not parties to the record, but interested in a question of law pending before the Judicial Council may, with the consent of the council, be heard thereon before the council in session.

9. *Decisions.*—All decisions by the council shall be in writing and shall be accompanied by an opinion in which the reasons upon which it is based shall be stated with a citation of the pertinent authorities, and shall show whether or not all members of the council concur in the decision, giving the names of such members as do not concur. Any member of the council who dissents may give in writing the reasons for his dissent, which shall be entered of record.

10. *Approval and Signing of the Record.*—The record of all sessions of the Judicial Council shall be approved by the

council in session and signed by the president and attested by the secretary.

11. *No Discussions Outside Council Meetings.*—The members of the Judicial Council will not permit discussion with them in matters pending before them, or that may be referred to them for determination, save and except before the Judicial Council in session.

12. *Rules May Be Amended.*—These rules may be amended, repealed, or extended at any session of the Judicial Council by a majority vote thereof.

¶ 1802. Digests of Decisions

[These digests reproduce the official summaries prepared by the Judicial Council except that references to Disciplinary paragraphs have been edited for the convenience of readers of the present edition. Each paragraph number, if the number or the legislation itself has been changed since the date of the decision, is followed by an editorial note enclosed in square brackets, like those enclosing this explanation. The note gives the date of the edition of the Discipline used in the decision and the corresponding paragraph number in the present edition, with an indication if there has been any significant amendment. Other bracketed notes bring terminology up to date. For complete texts of the decisions see the Journals of the General Conferences of 1952 (1-87) and 1956 (88-130) and the *General Minutes* of 1960 (131-75) and 1964 (176-216), or see the volume *Decisions of the Judicial Council* (Methodist Publishing House, 1964).—EDITORS.]

1. Lay missionaries as defined in ¶ 974 [1939; now ¶ 1216.2, amended] are not eligible to vote in an Annual Conference for ministerial delegates to General Conference. April 26, 1940.

2. An appeal was taken from a bishop's rulings in an Annual Conference before Unification, which appeal passed to the Judicial Council under ¶ 1624 [1939; an interim enabling act]. This appeal involved a request for rulings asking interpretations of prior pension laws of the Methodist Episcopal Church. As the record did not show that any vested rights of the appellant were affected, the appeal was dismissed, and the bishop's rulings affirmed. April 26, 1940.

3. A member of an Annual Conference located under the provisions of the 1932 Discipline (Methodist Episcopal Church), although he may have been improperly deprived of his right to be heard when his Annual Conference was considering the report of the Conference Relations Committee on his case, but who thereafter defied the action of the conference by continuing to preach in a charge where previously appointed, thereby forfeits his right of appeal. A member may forfeit his right of appeal by contumacious treatment of the church and its authority. April 27, 1940.

4. ¶ 462 [1939; now ¶ 558], providing for election by

Central Conferences of bishops for a limited term, is constitutional. April 30, 1940.

5. That part of ¶ 492 [1939; now ¶ 609, amended] which attempts to grant to members of a Mission Conference [Provisional Annual Conference] the right to elect delegates to Jurisdictional Conferences is unconstitutional. May 2, 1940. [See ¶ 47 iv.]

6. That part of ¶ 452 [1939; now ¶ 543, amended] which attempts to grant to Mission Conferences [Provisional Annual Conferences] the right to elect delegates to Central Conferences is unconstitutional. May 3, 1940. [See ¶ 47 ii.]

7. The legislation enacted by the 1940 General Conference providing for automatic retirement of clerical members of Annual Conferences whose seventy-second birthday precedes the first day of the regular session of the Annual Conference (¶ 231 [1940; now ¶ 368]) is constitutional, as it is a general principle of constitutional construction that legislation must be upheld unless it is clearly in conflict with the Constitution interpreted as a whole. The matter of uniform regulations for retirement of ministers is a connectional matter, and as such it is a subject over which the General Conference under the Constitution has legislative power. May 5, 1940.

8. An "unstationed" minister under the provisions of the Methodist Protestant Church Discipline of 1936 is in the same relation to an Annual Conference as "located" ministers under the provisions of ¶¶ 235-39 [1940; now ¶¶ 374-79]. April 15, 1941.

9. A general rule by action of an Annual Conference as to retired ministers receiving a pension and also receiving pay as supply pastor is in conflict with the provisions of ¶ 1329 [1940; now ¶ 1627, amended] as to disallowance of claims in whole or in part, as it denies the claimant the right to make an oral or written statement to the Board of Conference Claimants [Conference Board of Pensions], and denies him the protection of the two-thirds vote of the conference prescribed in said paragraph. April 15, 1941.

10. Members of an Annual Conference Board of Lay Activities, being a board that asks for appropriations from the Annual Conference Commission on World Service and Finance, are ineligible for membership on the commission, under the provisions of ¶ 1224 and ¶ 1228 [1940; now ¶¶ 1502.1, 1503.8]. April 28, 1942.

11. In view of the inhibition by the Missouri state constitution of religious corporations except to hold title to real estate for church edifices, parsonages, and cemeteries, the trustees of an Annual Conference in Missouri may not be

incorporated, but the trustees duly elected as an unincorporated board are the proper parties to recover possession of property of abandoned churches under the provisions of ¶ 782 [1940; now ¶ 188]. April 29, 1942.

12. The decisions of a Joint Distributing Committee duly constituted under the provisions of ¶ 1312 [1939; now ¶ 1609, amended], having acted in accordance with such provisions, are binding upon the several conferences affected by merger. April 29, 1942.

13. An Annual Conference Board of Conference Claimants [Conference Board of Pensions] is not required to submit its askings for appropriations to the Annual Conference Commission on World Service and Finance under the provisions of ¶¶ 832, 834, and 835 [1940; now ¶¶ 791, 793, 794, amended] but reports its recommendations directly to the Annual Conference in accordance with ¶ 1323.2 [1940; now ¶ 1623 .3-.4, amended]. To reconcile conflicting provisions in legislative enactment, the entire legislation must be considered, and the legislative intent is to be drawn from the act as a whole. April 29, 1942.

14. Under the provisions of ¶ 1330 [1940; now ¶ 1636, amended], no liability rests on the Annual Conference of which the claimant was a member on retirement for the years of service of such claimant which he served in a Mission Conference. December 8, 1943.

15. Action of an Annual Conference in retiring ministers on age limit, under the provisions of ¶ 231 [1940; now ¶ 368], is legal, as said paragraph has been heretofore held to be constitutional. December 8, 1943.

16. An Annual Conference Committee on Conference Relations and Ministerial Qualifications [Board of Ministerial Training and Qualifications] may, under the provisions of ¶¶ 463 and 466 [1940; now ¶¶ 669-71, amended], recommend for admission a minister claiming to come from another evangelical church (¶ 311 [1940; now ¶ 411, amended, but see ¶¶ 412-13]), even though such minister had previously been a member of the same conference from which he had withdrawn; but final action thereon rests with the Annual Conference, which may accept or reject the recommendations for admission submitted by the committee. December 8, 1943.

17. The expenses which may be paid from the General Administration Fund are strictly limited by the provisions of ¶ 848 [1940; now ¶ 765, amended], and therefore the General Commission [Council] on World Service and Finance is not thereby authorized to pay expenses incurred by a Jurisdic-

tional Committee of Appeals acting under the provisions of ¶ 694 [1940; now ¶ 1045]. April 27, 1944.

18. The procedure for restoration of credentials of a traveling deacon or elder which have been surrendered, under ¶ 707 [1940; now ¶ 993, amended], requires that the steps therein outlined shall be strictly followed. April 26, 1944.

19. Under the provisions of ¶ 1309 [1940; now ¶ 1608], ministers who at time of retirement may have been members of an Annual Conference within the territory assigned to the Illinois Corporation are nevertheless entitled to annuities from the Endowment Fund for Superannuates held by the Missouri Corporation on account of the years of service formerly rendered in an Annual Conference of the Methodist Episcopal Church, South, or in an Annual Conference of the Methodist Episcopal Church in territory assigned to the Missouri Corporation. However, no claimant has any vested right or equity in such General Endowment Fund nor the income derived therefrom. April 26, 1944.

20. The widow of a former member of a conference of the Methodist Episcopal Church, who voluntarily located under the then provisions of the Discipline of that church, may not invoke the provision of that Discipline applying to involuntary locations, and therefore has no claim for a pension which the deceased located minister himself did not have. May 2, 1944.

21. As the only provision in the Constitution relating to election of bishops is that they shall be elected by the respective Jurisdictional and Central Conferences, it would be unconstitutional for the General Conference to elect missionary bishops. May 1, 1944.

22. A bishop, effective or retired, is not a member of an Annual Conference, and should not be counted in reporting total membership of the conference for voting or other purposes. May 2, 1944.

23. The provisions of the Discipline as to declaratory decisions by the Judicial Council do not confer upon the council any legislative power, and whenever there is doubt as to the meaning of any General Conference legislation, it is the duty of the General Conference itself to clarify its own enactment. May 2, 1944.

24. That part of ¶ 934 [1940; now ¶ 1216.2, amended], which provides that outside the United States of America lay missionaries may be seated in an Annual Conference "with the right to vote on all questions not ministerial or constitutional, etc.," is unconstitutional, as ¶ 21 of the Constitution strictly defines the composition and qualifications of the members of an Annual Conference. May 2, 1944.

25. ¶ 1716 [1940], under heading "Statement on Peace and War," and ¶ 1712 [1940; now ¶ 1820, amended], under the heading "Our Social Creed," contained identical provisions as to claims for exemption from military service by conscientious objectors who may be members of The Methodist Church, and although the Statement on Peace and War adopted by the 1944 General Conference is somewhat at variance with the "Statement on Peace and War," ¶ 1716, yet it did not repeal ¶ 1712; and accordingly conscientious objectors who are members of The Methodist Church still have the same protection as heretofore. May 4, 1944.

26. The determination of the meaning of the words "church members" as used in ¶ 871 [1940; now ¶ 1129, amended] is a legislative matter within the province of the General Conference, and is not a judicial matter to be settled by the Judicial Council, unless the question arises in some case legally pending before the council. May 3, 1944.

27. Under the provisions of ¶ 1619 and ¶ 1618.8 a retired minister of the Mississippi Conference, formerly a member of the Methodist Protestant Church, who originally entered the ministry of the Methodist Episcopal Church, South, but was involuntarily located, and who was subsequently received into the ministry of the Methodist Protestant Church, is entitled to have the years of service in the Methodist Episcopal Church, South, included in the number of years on which his annuity claim is based. December 4, 1944.

28. The Constitution of The Methodist Church provides that boundaries of Annual Conferences shall be determined by the respective Jurisdictional Conference, and this power may not be delegated to the Annual Conferences themselves. December 4, 1944.

29. The Board of Trustees of a local church is not such a body as would have the right to appeal directly to the Judicial Council, so that it may petition for a declaratory decision under the provisions of ¶ 914; but the questions of law involved in any such request for a declaratory decision may be acted upon by the Quarterly Conference under ¶ 362 .14 and may thus eventually become subject to review by the Judicial Council. December 4, 1944.

30. The action of the General Conference of 1944 in asking for contributions to world service determined by a percentage in excess of contributions during a particular fiscal year is within the constitutional powers of the General Conference as prescribed by ¶ 8.9, even though in a particular case it may seem to result in an unfair apportionment. December 5, 1944.

31. Ministers coming from other evangelical churches, whether proceeding under § 1, 2, or 3 of ¶ 411 [1944; now §§ 1-4, amended], are in all cases subject to the requirement of meeting "the educational standards required of Methodist ministers." December 5, 1944.

32. Under the constitutional provisions contained in ¶ 8 .12 the General Conference may change boundaries of Jurisdictional Conferences only by consent of the Annual Conferences in each Jurisdictional Conference involved. Accordingly the action of the 1944 General Conference granting permission to the Central Jurisdiction only to change boundaries of the Delaware Annual Conference, which proposed changes involved also changes in boundaries of certain Annual Conferences in the Northeastern Jurisdiction, did not grant any power to the Northeastern Jurisdictional Conference to initiate any such boundary changes. December 5, 1944.

33. The provision of ¶ 914 limits the jurisdiction of the Judicial Council as to declaratory decisions so that they do not include moot or hypothetical questions; and the same principle applies to requests for rulings by a bishop in an Annual Conference, which requests should be based upon some action taken or proposed to be taken, wherein under the specific facts in each case some doubt may have arisen as to the legality of the action taken or proposed. May 8, 1946.

34. District Conferences may license proper persons to preach and other orders under the provisions of ¶ 670 *et seq.* [1944]; but "all votes to license shall be by ballot," and the casting of a ballot by the secretary pursuant to a vote authorizing him to do so is illegal. May 8, 1946.

35. The provision of ¶ 437, in connection with retired bishops of Jurisdictional Conferences, stating that "he may participate in the Council of Bishops, but without vote," is not in conflict with the Constitution, ¶ 34, as the Constitution by ¶ 8.5 granted unto the General Conference the power to "define and fix the powers, duties, and privileges of the episcopacy." May 8, 1946.

36. As an Annual Conference has no quorum, a session of conference held in wartime abbreviated to one day, and ostensibly restricted in attendance to officers and certain committees (although it was stated that all members of the conference were entitled to be present), although irregular, was nevertheless a legal session. May 9, 1946.

37. The jurisdiction of the Judicial Council to pass on the constitutionality of an act of the General Conference is limited by ¶ 43.1, and its jurisdiction as to declaratory decisions is limited by ¶ 914 [1944; later amended], in neither

one of which paragraphs is provision made for initiating any such procedure by an Annual Conference. Accordingly the Judicial Council may not render any decision involving the constitutionality of ¶ 646 on the request, petition, or other action of an Annual Conference only. May 9, 1946.

38. In a case where an Annual Conference (as permitted by the Discipline) has been incorporated under the provisions of the statutes of the state of Kansas, and the corporation has adopted by-laws in statutory form, the corporate sessions must be called in the manner provided by the by-laws; but when the conference is once in such corporate session, it may exercise all the powers it ever possessed, including the right to amend its by-laws and its charter. May 9, 1946.

39. A resolution of the General Conference of 1944 "that in all official literature and pronouncements of The Methodist Church respecting the date of its origin, it shall date from 1784" does not involve a constitutional question, and accordingly the Judicial Council will not take jurisdiction; but at the same time the council holds that under Art. V of the Declaration of Union the present organization of The Methodist Church began in 1939. May 9, 1946.

40. The decision of the Judicial Council upholding the constitutionality of ¶ 437 as to voting by retired bishops affirmed. (See Judicial Council Decision 35.) April 23, 1947.

41. The footnote to Art. XXIII, Articles of Religion [¶ 83], held to be not a constitutional part of the Articles of Religion. It was made a footnote by legislative act only. April 24, 1947.

42. The provisions of ¶ 646 permitting an Annual Conference to "order an executive session of the ministerial members to consider questions relating to matters of ordination, character, and conference relations" held to be constitutional. April 24, 1947.

43. A standing rule of an Annual Conference, adopted according to ¶ 631 [1944; now ¶ 634], which provides that "a retired minister may not serve on a quadrennial board or commission" is not contrary to the Constitution. April 23, 1947.

44. In Annual Conferences which provide for support of district superintendents according to ¶ 788 [1944; now ¶ 801] the amount of such support (including salary and allowances) and the apportionments thereof must be recommended annually by the Annual Conference Commission on World Service and Finance, and may not be regulated by a standing rule of the conference. April 23, 1947.

45. An Annual Conference may by proper action make appropriations from conference funds to institutions or

organizations on the governing boards of which the Annual Conference is not represented by trustees, directors, or other officials. April 23, 1947.

46. The provision of ¶ 1618.2*i* as to calculating years of service of a conference claimant covers "all cases" and refers to all service of retired ministers, irrespective of whether before or after the year 1944. April 24, 1947.

47. A minister tried in the year 1941, in accordance with the provisions of the 1940 Discipline, and the judgment of the trial court affirmed by the Jurisdictional Committee of Appeals in 1942, which judgment became final under the provisions of the Discipline, may not appeal to the Judicial Council to review the case for alleged errors of law under the provisions of ¶¶ 1033 and 1045, which legislation was enacted in 1944 to cover cases decided after said paragraphs became effective; and therefore such an attempted appeal was dismissed. April 24, 1947.

48. A Jurisdictional Conference has the right under ¶ 440 to assign a bishop to the supervision of Mission Conferences and Provisional Annual Conferences, even though the geographical territory covered by such Mission and Provisional Conferences may overlap the geographical territory assigned to other bishops, as there is nothing in the Discipline that would limit the phrase "episcopal area" as used in ¶ 440 to a geographical definition. April 24, 1947.

49. The proviso in ¶ 341 [1944; later amended] as to admission into full connection in the Annual Conference of one who while a student has been regularly appointed as pastor does not eliminate the two-year trial period as required by the first part of this paragraph. May 3, 1948.

50. None of the provisions of the Pension Code, with particular reference to ¶¶ 1618, 1623, and 1624, limit an Annual Conference, in making an apportionment for conference claimants, to an amount exactly necessary to meet the disbursements for that particular year; but under the provisions of ¶ 1613.10 [1944; now ¶ 1611.13] any excess amount raised by such an apportionment may be used to create a reserve fund for future years. May 3, 1948.

51. An allowance for "travel expenses" to pastors is not to be regarded as supplementary compensation tending to defeat proportional payment under the terms of ¶ 1624, provided always that such item represents an actual expense for the purpose stated, and is not a cover-up for additional salary paid to the pastor. May 4, 1948.

52. The Quarterly Conference of a local church may not appeal to the Judicial Council, nor petition for a declaratory

decision, as it is not an "authority in the church that would have the right of appeal" under the provisions of ¶ 914. May 5, 1948.

53. The provision of ¶ 555 [1944; now ¶ 444; *see* ¶ 47 vi] giving a Central Conference bishop the right to vote in the Council of Bishops "whenever the interest of his Central Conference or the interests common to all Central Conferences are involved" is constitutional. May 6, 1948.

54. Enabling acts, adopted in 1940 and 1944, as to continuing the corporate life or operation of various corporations, boards, and other agencies of the church, where the incomplete status still continues, do not need to be re-enacted in 1948, as this legislation, unless specifically limited as to time, is in effect until repealed or amended. May 6, 1948.

55. When the procedure provided by the Constitution for making changes in Jurisdictional Conference boundaries has been complied with, the enactment of legislation by the General Conference making such boundary changes is constitutional. May 6, 1948.

56. Under the constitutional provisions contained in ¶ 8 .12 the General Conference may change the boundaries of Jurisdictional Conferences only by consent of a majority of the Annual Conferences in each jurisdiction as therein prescribed. Accordingly any legislation attempted by General Conference without complying with these provisions is invalid. May 6, 1948.

57. An amendment to ¶ 440 which would require the consent of the Jurisdictional Committee on Episcopacy for fixing boundaries of episcopal areas is unconstitutional, as this power is reserved to the bishops as a part of episcopal administration under the Constitution. May 6, 1948.

58. Under the Constitution, the General Conference has unlimited authority, *inter alia*, to define and fix the qualifications of elders and deacons; and accordingly a special act of the General Conference prescribing that in the Germany Central Conference the ordination of an elder may take the place of ordination as a deacon, and that the ordination as a deacon may be omitted, is constitutional. May 6, 1948.

59. The Judicial Council has no jurisdiction to determine constitutionality of affirmations of faith. May 7, 1948.

60. That portion of ¶ 607 [1944; later amended; *see* ¶ 47 iv, vii, viii] reading "and they (Provisional Annual Conferences) may elect one ministerial and one lay delegate to the Jurisdictional Conference" is unconstitutional. May 7, 1948.

61. A Central Conference bishop whose term of office expires and he is not re-elected is returned to membership in the

Annual Conference of which he ceased to be a member when
elected bishop. His term of office expires at the close of the
Central Conference at which his successor is elected; hence
he would be entitled to participate as a bishop in the consecration of his successor. April 29, 1949.

62. The act of the 1948 General Conference adding to ¶
901 Art. 1 the following clause: "*Provided*, however, that as a
result of the election each jurisdiction shall be represented on
the council," is constitutional. The decision is based on the
interpretation that same refers to the manner of election and
does not constitute any member of the Judicial Council as the
representative of any particular group, section, area, or jurisdiction. The Judicial Council is a judicial tribunal, and not
a representative body as such. The members are to be free
from any sectional interests and to serve the entire church.
Any other interpretation of the act in question would render
it wholly unconstitutional. April 29, 1949.

63. Designated gifts under ¶ 775 of the 1944 Discipline
(¶ 745 of the 1948 Discipline) [deleted in 1952] are subject
to the settled and established plan that contributions for the
cause of world service and conference benevolences by a
charge shall first be divided on the ratio prescribed by the
Annual Conference. Only that portion of such contributions
allocated under the conference ratio to world service can be
designated to world service projects; and only that portion
of such contributions allocated under the conference ratio to
conference benevolences can be designated to conference
benevolence projects. April 29, 1949.

64. An Annual Conference can dispose of by gift to a non-
denominational body a college owned and controlled by it
even though same has been built by private donations; *provided* that, if there should be assets belonging to the college
made in consideration of its remaining a Methodist college
under the control and management of the Annual Conference,
the disposition of such particular assets would be a matter
of property rights and controlled by civil law, over which
property rights the Judicial Council would probably have no
jurisdiction. April 29, 1949.

65. Terms and provisions set out in ¶ 807 [1948; now
¶ 827] are defined or interpreted as follows: (1) "At any
regular session" means any session of an Annual Conference
at which business is transacted. (2) "Regular active itinerants," as used in said paragraph, includes only effective members of the Annual Conference serving as pastors, and does
not include district superintendents and members of the conference serving under special appointments. (3) By "basic"

is meant the schedule of salaries to be paid pastors and supply pastors from a common treasury under any basic salary plan adopted by an Annual Conference; such salaries to be uniform, subject only to the variants allowed under said ¶ 807. Such salaries may be augmented by pastoral charges as provided in ¶ 807.3. (*See also* Judicial Council Decision 70.) April 29, 1949.

66. The Judicial Council does not have jurisdiction to review the decision of a bishop not requested or made in open session of an Annual or District Conference. April 29, 1949.

67. Under the Constitution, ¶ 15, the Jurisdictional Conference has authority "to make rules and regulations for the administration of the work of the church within the jurisdiction." The act of the South Central Jurisdictional Conference recommending that "no Annual Conference establish a conference encampment without consideration by the Conference Board of Education" is constitutional. April 29, 1949.

68. When a minister is elected and consecrated as a bishop in The Methodist Church, he ceases to be a member of an Annual Conference and is no longer subject to the Ministers Reserve Pension Plan. April 29, 1949.

69. Under the grant of powers to Central Conferences by General Conference legislation within the provisions of the Constitution, the Germany Central Conference had authority to create an administrative committee to have charge of current matters of business, and to represent that conference in legal matters arising between conference sessions. Such committee, however, shall be responsible to the Central Conference. April 26, 1950.

70. Although by the general terms of ¶ 807 [1948; now ¶ 827] district superintendents are not included in the classification of "regular active itinerants" (*see* Judicial Council Decision 65), yet in an Annual Conference which provides for support of district superintendents on recommendation of the Conference Commission on World Service and Finance (¶ 788 [1948; now ¶ 801]), if it also adopts the basic salary plan, there should be included therein the support of district superintendents. April 27, 1950.

71. Enabling acts, adopted in 1940 and in 1944, as to continuing the corporate life or operation of various corporations, boards, and other agencies of the church, where the incomplete status still continues, do not need to be re-enacted, as this legislation, unless specifically limited as to time, is in effect until repealed or amended. April 28, 1950.

72. ¶ 347 [1948; now ¶ 332, amended] applies only to the four-year course of study and does not apply to the two years'

graduate study required of members of the conference admitted by the three-fourths vote rule under ¶ 323 [1948; now ¶ 325.3]. The Annual Conference under ¶ 22 has authority to prescribe time in which these two years of graduate study must be completed. For dereliction of a member in this respect the Annual Conference could, under other provisions of the Discipline, take appropriate action. April 29, 1950.

73. An Annual Conference has the authority to instruct its Board of Conference Claimants [Conference Board of Pensions] to include supply years in computing the annuity years of a member of the conference. January 3, 1951.

74. A business session of the lay delegates to an Annual Conference would be illegal if not called for the purpose of electing lay delegates to the General and Jurisdictional Conferences. January 3, 1951.

75. The Ohio Annual Conference of The Methodist Church, now being the White Cross Hospital Association of Ohio, is the source of ultimate control of the White Cross Hospital and has the right and power at its discretion to change or amend the method of electing the trustees of the corporation; but, until the Annual Conference changes the method set forth in Art. VI of the present constitution of said White Cross Hospital Association, it is bound thereby. January 3, 1951.

76. § 2 of ¶ 502 [1948; now ¶ 504] is not unconstitutional. The following sentence in § 3 of ¶ 502, "A spring Annual Conference may elect the delegates to the General and Jurisdictional Conferences at its third regular session following the adjournment of the General Conference," is unconstitutional. November 28, 1951.

77. (1) A report to an Annual Conference, containing a financial statement which the Discipline requires to be audited, should not be approved until the audit is made and the financial statement is shown to be correct. Other parts of the report may be approved pending such audit.

(2) The Discipline does not specify the manner of presenting nominations for conference lay leader to the Annual Conference; hence oral nominations are permissible unless the Annual Conference has provided otherwise.

(3) In the Kentucky Annual Conference the nomination of the conference lay leader, to be valid, must be made by the Annual Conference Board of Lay Activities by ballot at a meeting of such board at which a majority of the members of the board are present and voting, and by a majority vote of the members of the board present and voting.

(4) The Discipline does not require that a certificate reciting the process by which the nomination was determined shall

be presented with the nomination. When the nomination of a conference lay leader is presented to the Annual Conference by a representative of the Board of Lay Activities, the regularity of same will be presumed in the absence of a showing to the contrary. November 27, 1951.

78. The Annual Conference has no authority to delegate its responsibilities and powers to Quarterly Conferences except as explicitly given that authority by the General Conference. Therefore the Pittsburgh Annual Conference had no authority to delegate to the Quarterly Conferences the power to determine whether or not the Annual Conference would adopt the [Ministers] Reserve Pension Plan. November 28, 1951.

79. The Annual Conference has no authority to delegate its responsibilities and powers to Quarterly Conferences except as explicitly given that authority by the General Conference. Therefore the Illinois Annual Conference had no authority to delegate to the Quarterly Conferences the power to determine whether or not the Annual Conference would adopt the [Ministers] Reserve Pension Plan. November 28, 1951.

80. A Central Conference bishop whose term of office expires or is terminated is returned to membership in the Annual Conference of which he was a member when elected bishop. D. D. Alejandro is bound by the 1946 action of the Central Conference under which he was elected, consecrated, and served as bishop. At the close of the 1948 session of the Philippines Central Conference he automatically became an effective member of the Philippines Annual Conference. November 27, 1951.

81. A retired minister whose pension payments from the Annual Conference were reduced during the quadrennium 1944-48 in accordance with the provisions of ¶ 1630.1, Discipline of 1944 [deleted in 1948], has no right to claim from the Board of Conference Claimants [Conference Board of Pensions] the amount of such reductions. November 28, 1951.

82. It is not necessary to adopt a fixed rule to determine the applicability of the term "full-time ministry" (¶ 343 Question 17 [1948; now ¶ 345]), as each case must be considered by the Committee on Conference Relations on the facts applicable thereto. November 28, 1951.

83. Under present provisions of the Discipline no age limit has been made for the retirement of Central Conference bishops. ¶ 436 applies only to bishops assigned to jurisdictions under the Plan of Union and those elected by Jurisdictional Conferences since Union. Under ¶ 8 the General Conference has the right to prescribe a uniform rule for the superannua-

tion of all bishops, but to date it has not exercised that power. April 26, 1952.

84. All bishops elected by a Jurisdictional Conference under ¶ 439 have the same status as any bishop assigned to a jurisdiction under the Plan of Union or who has been elected by a Jurisdictional Conference; and any bishop assigned to or elected by any Jurisdictional Conference may be assigned to any area over which the jurisdiction has been given episcopal supervision, including missions outside the territory of such jurisdiction. April 30, 1952.

85. The transfer of a local church of the Central Jurisdiction to an Annual Conference of another jurisdiction can be done only in accordance with appropriate action of the General Conference, Jurisdictional Conferences, and Annual Conferences, as provided in the Constitution. This method of making such a change can only be changed by a constitutional amendment. May 1, 1952.

86. (1) The sentence: "Such a society of believers, being within The Methodist Church and subject to its Discipline, is also an inherent part of the Church Universal, which is composed of all who accept Jesus Christ as Lord and Saviour, and which in the Apostles' Creed we declare to be the holy catholic Church," is not so clearly in violation of the First Restrictive Rule as to constitute its insertion in the proposed legislation of which it forms a part a legal matter of such a nature as to authorize the Judicial Council to take jurisdiction and render a decision as to its constitutionality.

(2) The proposal to add by legislation the words "is the creation of God and" to ¶ 101 of the report under consideration, same being Art. XIII of the Articles of Religion, does alter and change said article. It is therefore in violation of the First Restrictive Rule [¶ 9.1], and is unconstitutional. May 3, 1952.

87. There is nothing in either the Constitution or the general legislation of The Methodist Church that would deprive a retired traveling preacher of his right to vote as a full member of the Annual Conference. May 5, 1952.

88. A retired member of an Annual Conference may be elected to membership in a Central Conference if he meets the conditions required by law of all those who represent their Annual Conferences in the General or Central Conference. November 25, 1952.

89. A Committee of Investigation has authority only to inquire whether or not the accused person is guilty of committing one of the offenses enumerated in ¶ 921. Its findings must be certified and declared to the Annual Conference by

the district superintendent. If in the judgment of the committee the evidence does seem to substantiate the accusation, the committee has no alternative but to prepare and file the proper charges and specifications. November 25, 1952.

90. The provisions of ¶ 806.4 [1948; now ¶ 826.3, amended] are mandatory.

91. An unordained student pastor, who is a candidate for the traveling ministry, while serving as a regularly appointed pastor of a charge, may be authorized to administer the Sacraments of Baptism and the Lord's Supper, and, if the laws of the state permit, to perform the marriage ceremony within the bounds of his pastoral charge, provided he has passed the course of study for admission on trial; but he may be excused from advancing in the conference course of study while attending a college or seminary "approved by the authorized standardizing agency." November 25, 1952.

92. An Annual Conference may authorize a subsidiary hospital corporation to borrow up to a certain percentage of the value of its property for the purpose of its expansion program. When appraised as provided in the resolution under consideration, it cannot be held that such resolution authorized an unlimited incurring of indebtedness. November 25, 1952.

93. No quorum is necessary for a session of the Quarterly Conference, and it is legal to reduce the number of the trustees in a church from nine to three to comply with the state law. November 25, 1952.

94. Dr. L. Dorsey Spaugy, being the first in order of election of the ministerial alternates to membership upon the Judicial Council, is the lawful successor of Dr. Chas. B. Ketcham, deceased. June 25, 1953. [From the decision: "The expressions 'of each class' or 'respective classes' as used in the articles of ¶ 901 quoted above refer to ministerial and lay members or ministerial alternates or lay alternates, and not to the class or classes of any particular year or years."]

95. Special appointments listed in the Annual Conference journal in compliance with ¶ 1618.4, showing annuity responsibility, must be the special appointments of the current conference and not those of the previous conference. June 26, 1953.

96. The Discipline of The Methodist Church is a book of law, and the only official and authoritative book of law of The Methodist Church—"a body of laws pertaining to church government," regulating every phase of the life and work of The Methodist Church, including regulations relating to its temporal economy and to the ownership, use, and disposition of church property. June 26, 1953.

97. All "approved full-time supply pastors" except those who have already been ordained elders are required to obey the provisions of ¶ 320 [1952; now ¶ 317.2, amended]. June 26, 1953.

98. An Annual Conference may create a commission or "council" for the purpose of correlating and promoting the work of the various agencies of the conference but without authority over those boards, commissions, and committees whose powers and duties are defined in certain paragraphs of the Discipline. July 19, 1954.

99. General legislation giving the Division of National Missions of the Board of Missions control over the work of the Board of Church Extension of the Methodist Episcopal Church, South (a Kentucky corporation) did not give it the authority to change the residence of the secretary from Louisville, Kentucky, where it was fixed by basic law under the facts in this case. The General Conference is the only body which has power to make the change contemplated. July 19, 1954.

100. Where there is no District Conference, the District Committee on Ministerial Qualifications has sole and final authority to license local preachers, and to renew their licenses. Where there is a District Conference, the final authority for licensing local preachers and for renewing their licenses is vested in the District Conference. In either case, for the securing of a license the applicant must comply with the provisions of ¶ 304 [1952; now ¶ 306, amended]. In the matter of renewal of a license, where there is a District Conference, it is the duty of the District Committee on Ministerial Qualifications to examine the applicant and report to the District Conference whether in its opinion the "gifts, graces, and usefulness" of the applicant warrant a renewal; but the final action for such renewal shall be taken by the District Conference. July 20, 1954.

101. The word "consult" in ¶ 432.1 means an exchange of ideas between the district superintendent and the pastor concerning his appointment before the final announcement. Simultaneous releasing of the appointments before the final reading does not constitute consultation as required in ¶ 432.1. July 20, 1954.

102. (1) A second Quarterly Conference held on May 13, 1953, on a call announced to the congregation at its prayer service April 29, 1953, was regular and had the right to consider and act upon the matter of proceedings to recover from the ex-treasurer the treasurer's books and records for the previous year; and the courts will entertain suits between mem-

bers of the church as between members of society and other groups.

(2) The action of the Quarterly Conference of Inglenook First Methodist Church adding to its Board of Trustees three new members at its second Quarterly Conference was null and void.

(3) The resolution of the Quarterly Conference authorizing the trustees to employ attorneys without the fee being stipulated was within the authority of the Quarterly Conference and was legal.

(4) The meeting of the Board of Trustees not called by the chairman and participated in by three illegally elected trustees was illegal and void. July 20, 1954.

103. A steward and trustee having been church treasurer for years and having failed of re-election, and then withholding the church records and account books from his successor and from the Commission on Finance and Auditing Committee, was acting at variance to his duties as a steward and trustee, and was subject to being removed from the offices of steward and trustee by the Quarterly Conference to which he was amenable without having been previously notified of such proposed action, and without charges being preferred against him under ¶¶ 1001-5. The Board of Stewards [Official Board] and the Board of Trustees are subject to the Quarterly Conference, and so are the individual stewards and trustees; and when a steward or trustee acts contrary to his duties as such the Quarterly Conference has the inherent right and authority to vacate his offices as steward and trustee. July 20, 1954.

104. After a lapse of two years since the charges were lodged by the Investigating Committee, and when the application is accompanied by the proper recommendations, and other requirements of the Discipline have been met, no trial is necessary on the old charges in order to have a preacher's credentials restored according to ¶ 993. The Annual Conference determines for itself whether there has been complete amendment of life on the part of the applicant and what committee shall present the recommendation to the Annual Conference. July 20, 1954.

105. The words "upon recommendation of the Committee on Conference Relations" [¶ 365] do not mean that an Annual Conference cannot act contrary to its committee's recommendation if it wishes to do so. July 20, 1954.

106. There is no legislation in the 1952 Discipline of The Methodist Church dealing with pension for a resigned bishop or his widow and therefore no basis for a declaratory decision on such legislation by the Judicial Council as requested

by the executive committee of the Council on World Service and Finance. The Judicial Council therefore declines to accept jurisdiction in this instance. July 20, 1954. [*See* ¶ 435 .2 as amended in 1956.]

107. The words "or subdivisions" as they appear in the second line of ¶ 174 mean subdivisions of governmental agencies and not subdivisions of private real estate projects. July 20, 1954.

108. If the Board of Trustees of the Annual Conference are the directors of the incorporated Annual Conference and are performing the same functions and duties as those assigned to an incorporated Board of Trustees in ¶ 709 [1952; now ¶ 711, amended], that constitutes a substantial compliance with the provisions of ¶ 709, and the separate incorporation of the Board of Trustees of the Annual Conference is not necessary. July 21, 1954.

109. An Official Board or a Quarterly Conference has no authority in the law of The Methodist Church to order or instruct lay or reserve lay members to vote in any prescribed manner on issues expected to come before an Annual Conference. July 21, 1954.

110. A minister who locates voluntarily retains his relationship as a local preacher in the Quarterly Conference where he resides. His license is not subject to renewal annually. He is held amenable for his conduct and the continuance of his ordination rights to the Annual Conference in which his Quarterly Conference membership is held. He continues as a local preacher in the Quarterly Conference until such time as he voluntarily surrenders his credentials or is deprived of such by due process of trial. July 21, 1954.

111. The answer of a candidate for the traveling ministry to the question set out in ¶ 321 Question 4 [1952; now ¶ 322 .5 Question 5] as to abstinence from the use of tobacco in order to be satisfactory must be in the affirmative and without qualification. July 21, 1954.

112. An approved supply pastor represents his charge as a pastor in every respect except the right to vote. Therefore he cannot represent the charge in the dual capacity of pastor and lay member at the same time. July 29, 1955.

113. A pastoral charge consists of all the churches of a circuit, and they are entitled to elect only one lay member to an Annual Conference. July 29, 1955.

114. That part of ¶ 431.7 which requires the consent of a ministerial member of an Annual Conference before he can be transferred to another Annual Conference is constitutional. July 29, 1955.

115. While an Annual Conference has the right to fix the dates of the fiscal year on which it operates, from the legal point of view the conference year begins with the adjournment of an Annual Conference session and ends with the adjournment of the next regular session of the conference. July 29, 1955.

116. The Judicial Council has jurisdiction only on questions of law. The charges against appellant, though meager, are sufficient to inform him of the offense with which he is charged. The charges having been made during the session of the Annual Conference, the accused was triable under ¶¶ 936 and 937, and not under ¶ 935. Five days were given the accused to prepare for trial. As a matter of law that cannot be held to be insufficient time. ¶ 1006 establishes a policy that the council for the accused must be a traveling preacher. By inference the assistant counsel provided in ¶ 1007 must be a traveling preacher. The trial having been conducted substantially in accordance with the provisions of the Discipline, the judgments of the Trial Court and of the Court of Appeals are in all things affirmed. July 29, 1955.

117. A retired bishop of a Central Conference is authorized to attend meetings of the Council of Bishops with expenses paid. July 29, 1955.

118. Church treasurers cannot withhold the three per cent pension fund assessments on salaries of ministers and remit them to the pension board. Such assessments must be sent in by the ministers themselves. If the ministers should agree to such withholding and authorize the church treasurer to send same to the fund in quarterly installments, that would constitute compliance with ¶ 1646 [1952; amended in 1956]. July 29, 1955.

119. When an Annual Conference adopts a standing rule, it is bound by such rule unless same is suspended or rescinded and some other action taken. Any action in conflict with the standing rule taken without suspending or rescinding the rule is void. Therefore, the proceeds of the sale of Grace Methodist Church belong to the Conference Claimants Endowment Fund as determined by the standing rule of the Oregon Annual Conference. July 29, 1955.

120. Fred B. Noble being automatically retired from membership upon the Judicial Council at the 1956 General Conference, he would be in all respects eligible to serve as a delegate to the 1956 Jurisdictional Conference of the Southeastern Jurisdiction of The Methodist Church, which meets after the 1956 General Conference closes. The time of his election as such a delegate is immaterial, his eligibility to serve as such

delegate at the time the Jurisdictional Conference meets being the determining factor as to the validity of his election. July 30, 1955.

121. Since the Philippines Central Conference has failed to take action regarding the ordination of women, the Northwest Philippines Annual Conference has the right to ordain a woman as a local deacon. July 30, 1955.

122. The phrase "who has been appointed in the regular itinerant work on circuits or stations" in ¶ 341 [1952; amended in 1956] must be interpreted as applying only to pastoral appointments to circuits or stations. April 26, 1956.

123. An Annual Conference has the power to hear, discuss, amend, adopt, or reject reports from conference boards even though they contain material referring to persons or organizations in a derogatory manner without their having prior notice. April 26, 1956.

124. A preacher on trial in an Annual Conference cannot serve as lay delegate in a Central Conference. April 26, 1956.

125. The Tennessee Annual Conference of the Central Jurisdiction with forty-one ministerial members is entitled to only one ministerial and one lay delegate to the Jurisdictional Conference. These two are the delegates elected to the General Conference. April 26, 1956.

126. A Central Conference bishop may preside over the General Conference. April 27, 1956.

127. The General Conference has authority to authorize a Jurisdictional Conference to elect a missionary bishop. April 30, 1956.

128. The Liberia Annual Conference cannot be a part of the Central Jurisdiction. May 1, 1956.

129. An Annual Conference may grant the privileges of the floor to a minister in a sister church, but cannot grant to such minister the right to vote. May 3, 1956.

130. A Quarterly Conference may adopt a policy for the election of trustees which is subject at all times to suspension or rejection by a majority vote of the Quarterly Conference. May 3, 1956.

131. A missionary minister serving on the field shall be counted in the Annual Conference of which he is a member for General Conference representation. October 24, 1956.

132. A Provisional Annual Conference may not vote on the constitutional amendments handed down to the Annual Conferences by the 1956 General Conference. October 24, 1956.

133. The effective date of the retirement of a minister who voluntarily retires is the date of the adjournment of the

Annual Conference which approved his retirement. October 24, 1956.

134. The words "formal vote of the conference" as used in ¶ 1924 [1952; deleted in 1964] and in the amendment thereto made by the General Conference of 1956, were intended to mean the formal vote of the ministers of the conference entitled to vote under the Constitution on the question before the conference. October 24, 1956.

135. Annual Conference Boards of Trustees or other Annual Conference organizations may legally receive title to real estate which does not contain the "trust clause" as contained in ¶ 174. October 24, 1956.

136. An Annual Conference may not extend voting privileges to full-time approved supply pastors who are ordained elders and who have served charges during the past year. October 24, 1956.

137. The General Conference acted within its constitutional powers in directing the Board of Education of The Methodist Church through its Division of Educational Institutions [Division of Higher Education] to appoint a Commission on Standards for Wesley Foundations to establish standards and evaluate the educational, religious, and financial program of Wesley Foundations and report to the division the Wesley Foundations which meet the standards established by the commission and therefore qualify for financial support from the General Board of Education and the Annual Conferences. October 18, 1957.

138. The trustees of an Annual Conference can dispose of funds belonging to the Woman's Society of Christian Service of a discontinued church as directed by the Annual Conference. October 18, 1957.

139. The general provisions of ¶¶ 1101-8 [1956; now amended and expanded as ¶¶ 1071-87] are applicable only to the general administrative agencies of The Methodist Church and cannot be held to apply to a Board of Directors or Trustees of a children's home which is the property of an Annual Conference or of Annual Conferences of The Methodist Church. October 18, 1957.

140. The report of the Joint Committee on Distribution of Responsibility for Conference Claimants submitted to the 1955 session of the California-Nevada Annual Conference did not change the report of the Joint Distributing Committee of 1940. Therefore, the ruling of Bishop Tippett on this question is affirmed. October 18, 1957.

141. An Annual Conference may adopt a rule establishing a quorum for the transaction of business. October 18, 1957.

142. The enactments of the Latin America Central Conference revising ¶ 127 [1956; now ¶ 114.1] are contrary to the Constitution of The Methodist Church and may not be included in the Discipline of said conference under the provisions of ¶ 562. October 18, 1957.

143. The sale of property of an abandoned church should and must be authorized by action of an Annual Conference in session as an ecclesiastical body. October 18, 1957.

144. When an appellant fails to comply with the provision of ¶ 1025 which requires that a written statement of the grounds of appeal be furnished at the same time notice of appeal is given, the appeal must be dismissed. February 8, 1958.

145. ¶ 1612.3 is constitutional and is binding on the West Texas Conference Endowment Association, charged with the administration of the pension-related funds in its hands. February 8, 1958.

146. ¶ 362.10 is not in violation of the Constitution of The Methodist Church, and its provision for the publication of the names of local-church lay leaders in the journals of Annual Conferences is mandatory. February 8, 1958.

147. A Central Conference cannot adopt legislation which would have the effect of changing, modifying, or altering ¶ 207, relating to the qualification for membership on the Official Board of the local church. February 8, 1958.

148. An Interboard Council may serve as a budget review committee for the Annual Conference Commission on World Service and Finance.

An Annual Conference Commission on World Service and Finance may utilize the services of an Interboard Council in the preparation of its report to the Annual Conference, provided the right is reserved to every conference agency to appear before the Conference Commission on World Service and Finance for the purpose of presenting its cause to said commission. October 17, 1958.

149. A ministerial member of an Annual Conference who has been placed in the retired relation with the privilege of making an annuity claim on the ground of personal disability may not serve a church in a ministerial capacity and receive compensation for such service and at the same time draw an annuity from the Board of Pensions of an Annual Conference. October 17, 1958.

150. Full-time years of service as an approved supply pastor, prior to admission on trial by an Annual Conference, may be counted as a part of the forty years of service as a

basis for the request of any ministerial member of an Annual Conference for the retired relation. October 17, 1958.

151. The adoption of a rule by an Annual Conference authorizing Official Boards to pay in whole or in part such parsonage utilities as heat, light, gas, telephone, and water, the amount paid not to exceed the actual cost of such utilities and requiring that the amounts paid shall be reported in an appropriate column in the statistical records of the minutes is not in conflict with the provisions of ¶ 1624.6, or any other provision of the 1956 Discipline. October 17, 1958.

152. Appointment to attend school as provided for in ¶ 432.7 does not meet the requirements of ¶ 341 (a) relating to qualifications for admission into full connection in an Annual Conference. October 17, 1958.

153. When the provisions of the Discipline concerning appeals from episcopal decisions on questions of law (¶¶ 43.2 and 908), or concerning episcopal decisions of law made in response to questions properly submitted (¶¶ 40, 43.3, and 909), are not followed, the Judicial Council must decline to take jurisdiction. October 17, 1958.

154. Amendments VII and VIII to the Constitution of The Methodist Church were constitutionally adopted. October 17, 1958.

155. A Central Conference may not change General Conference legislation regarding the granting of full clergy rights for women.

A Central Conference may not refuse to accept a woman who has been given full clergy rights by an Annual Conference.

A bishop has the power to transfer a woman ministerial member of an Annual Conference to any other Annual Conference provided he has the consent of the bishop of the receiving conference, and provided the ministerial member agrees to said transfer. October 17, 1958.

156. The determination of the meaning of the words "part-time approved supply pastor" and "full-time approved supply pastor" as used in ¶ 317.2-.3 [amended in 1960] is a legislative matter within the province of the General Conference and is not a judicial matter to be determined by the Judicial Council. October 17, 1958.

157. An Annual Conference Board of Ministerial Training and Qualifications may withhold recommendation for ordination or full connection in the Annual Conference of a candidate who, in its judgment, has been unfaithful to his ministerial vows. October 17, 1959.

158. On the basis of factual data supplied him, Bishop Valencia ruled that Lingkod A. Juane had been a member of

The Methodist Church for four years prior to election as a lay member of the Philippines Annual Conference and was therefore eligible to sit as a lay member of the Philippines Annual Conference in its 1959 session. His ruling is hereby affirmed. October 17, 1959.

159. A pastoral charge served by three ministers or traveling preachers, only one of whom is in full connection with the Annual Conference within the territorial boundaries of which the pastoral charge is situated, is entitled to elect only one of its lay members to represent it as a member of such Annual Conference. October 17, 1959.

160. Funds in the Permanent Fund of an Annual Conference are disposable by that Annual Conference. October 17, 1959.

161. No decision. ["In view of (a later development) we consider the matter moot and now deem no further action on our part necessary."] October 17, 1959.

162. In determining the eligibility of a ministerial member of an Annual Conference for election as ministerial delegate to the General Conference or Central Conference under ¶ 24 of the Constitution, his years as a traveling preacher may be counted from the date of his admission on trial. October 17, 1959.

163. The petition of the Council of Bishops for a rehearing of Case No. 114 is denied. October 17, 1959.

164. Central Conference bishops have been granted full rights of membership and participation in the Council of Bishops and are entitled to attend all meetings of the Council of Bishops with expenses paid. April 30, 1960.

165. (1) A ministerial member or approved supply pastor retired under the provisions of the Discipline at age seventy-two is then automatically subject to the provisions of the Discipline relating to annuity claims.

(2) The Conference Board of Pensions may determine the number of years of service for which a minister is eligible for annuity, without formal action of the Annual Conference session. April 30, 1960.

166. (1) Southern Methodist University (including the Perkins School of Theology) is an integral agency of The Methodist Church.

(2) An effective Methodist minister who has been appointed by a bishop to the Perkins School of Theology of Southern Methodist University is performing his services in such post on an assignment or designation by the church.

(3) Effective Methodist ministers appointed by bishops to the faculty of the Perkins School of Theology of Southern

Methodist University are in the exercise of their ministry. May 2, 1960.

167. (1) An effective Methodist minister who has been appointed by a bishop to the faculty of a Methodist theological school is performing his services in such post on an assignment or designation of The Methodist Church.

(2) An effective Methodist minister who has been appointed by a bishop to the faculty of a Methodist theological school is in the exercise of his ministry in the services rendered by him at said institution. May 2, 1960.

168. Unmeritorious and untimely resubmission of appeal [of Case No. 116] declined. May 2, 1960.

169. An Annual Conference may be transferred from one jurisdiction into another under Amendment IX [without regard to the geographical boundaries of the jurisdictions involved (from the decision)]. May 2, 1960.

170. The ruling of Bishop José L. Valencia that the Northwest Philippines Annual Conference could accept the report of its Credentials Committee in unseating Benjamin Casiano, a lay member, is affirmed. May 5, 1960.

171. A ministerial member of an Annual Conference who has been placed in the retired relation with the privilege of making an annuity claim on the ground of personal disability can receive payment for "full-time" or "nearly full-time" secular employment and at the same time draw an annuity from the Conference Board of Pensions. May 5, 1960.

172. (1) A request for an explanation, or for a statement of the implications or effect of decisions of the Judicial Council, does not constitute a request for a declaratory decision under the provisions of ¶ 914 of the Discipline.

(2) The powers and duties of the General Conference and the Judicial Council are totally different and separate and apart and cannot be jointly exercised. May 5, 1960.

173. The ruling of Bishop Valencia that Ezekias G. Gacutan, a former minister who had voluntarily located, thereupon became a layman, is affirmed. May 6, 1960.

174. (1) A former minister who is now under voluntary location can be elected lay delegate to the General or Central Conference by an Annual Conference.

(2) A reserve lay member of an Annual Conference or anyone who meets the requirements set forth in ¶ 47 iii of the Constitution can be elected lay delegate to the General or Central Conference. May 6, 1960.

175. (1) Direct and final responsibility for the supervision of a local Wesley Foundation rests with a local board of directors subject only to prior authority vested in Annual

Conference Boards of Education, Interconference Commissions on Student Religious Work [College and University Religious Life], and the General Board of Education, and subject in regard to employed personnel who may be effective ministerial members of an Annual Conference to prior obligations inherent in the Methodist appointive system.

(2) Likewise direct and final responsibility for the supervision of programs of religious work (Methodist Student Movement) for Methodist students on the campuses of Methodist institutions of higher education rests solely with the Boards of Trustees of such institutions, subject only to prior and final authority vested in Annual Conferences and other constitutional bodies, and subject in regard to employed personnel who may be effective ministerial members of an Annual Conference to prior obligations inherent in the Methodist appointive system. May 6, 1960.

176. The action of the 1960 General Conference in adopting the resolution relating to the so-called sit-in demonstrations was not unconstitutional. October 27, 1960.

177. Under the existing constitutional and legislative provisions for declaratory decisions, the Judicial Council has no authority to render a declaratory decision on request of the General Conference to interpret the meaning of the language in the Constitution or the constitutionality of possible future legislation. October 28, 1960.

178. A Board of Missions (and Church Extension) of an Annual Conference of The Methodist Church may purchase and hold property. October 27, 1960.

179. An Annual Conference has no right to enact a compulsory apportionment to the ministerial members of the Annual Conference for the support of the minimum salary plan or fund of the Annual Conference. October 28, 1960.

180. An Annual Conference has authority to grant annuities on an adjusted basis to conference members related to institutions that are approved by the Annual Conference for annuity responsibility and having their own pension plans. October 28, 1960.

181. A retired minister appointed as supply pastor of a charge cannot be required to pay any portion of his salary into any fund for pensions. October 29, 1960.

182. The action of the Northeastern Jurisdictional Conference, with respect to the election of a bishop by the Africa Central Conference and the reassignment of Bishop Newell S. Booth, is unconstitutional insofar as it assumes to delegate authority to its Quadrennial Committee on Episcopacy to determine when a new bishop shall be elected for the

Africa Central Conference, and to change the assignment of Bishop Newell S. Booth to the Africa Central Conference made by the Northeastern Jurisdictional Conference and to the Elisabethville Area made by the Africa Central Conference. October 29, 1960.

183. The Constitution of The Methodist Church provides that the required number of members of a general board from a jurisdiction shall be chosen by the Jurisdictional Conference itself. Hence, the legislation of the 1960 General Conference providing for the election of such members from the respective jurisdictions to the General Board of Pensions by the General Conference is unconstitutional. February 19, 1961.

184. There is no provision in the law of the church which authorizes the Judicial Council to hear and determine a question of law or the legality of an act, legislation, or a rule of an Annual Conference upon direct application of that conference, except upon an appeal from a bishop's ruling made by one fifth of the conference present and voting. Nor is there any provision of law which authorizes the Judicial Council to render a declaratory decision as to the meaning, application, or effect of an act, legislation, or ruling of an Annual Conference at the request of the conference adopting such act, legislation, or rule. October 19, 1961.

185. An Annual Conference is limited in its election of a conference treasurer to nominees of its Commission on World Service and Finance. October 19, 1961.

186. The ruling of Bishop D. D. Alejandro that St. Paul's Church is entitled to an additional lay member in the Philippines Annual Conference is reversed. October 19, 1961.

187. The ruling of Bishop D. D. Alejandro that the readmission on trial of Miguel Fernandez in the Philippines Annual Conference was legal is reversed. October 20, 1961.

188. The Church School Rally Day [Christian Education Sunday] offering is received for the [Conference] Board of Education for the program of its local church division and may not be absorbed into the general budget of an Annual Conference Council in which all the agencies, boards, and commissions share. October 21, 1961.

189. The Judicial Council will not render a declaratory decision on a moot or academic question raised after the fact or action. October 21, 1961.

190. An Annual Conference has broad powers to direct its Board of Trustees concerning the investment of its trust funds, including the right to instruct its Board of Trustees

not to commingle the funds in its hands with other funds. October 21, 1961.

191. The Conference Board of Education has the duty to determine and present to the Commission on World Service and Finance the financial needs of the colleges and Wesley Foundations related to the conference. It also is responsible for determining the allocation and distribution of funds raised within the conference for these institutions. The Conference Commission on [Christian] Higher Education reports both to the Conference Board of Education and to the Annual Conference, provided its recommendations to the Annual Conference with regard to items for which the Conference Board of Education has responsibility are in harmony with the recommendations of the Conference Board of Education. The Conference Board of Education may modify those items in the report of the Commission on Higher Education which it has the responsibility of determining. October 21, 1961.

192. The Indiana Annual Conference acted within its legal rights in readmitting R. W. Parsley to the membership of the Annual Conference, and in determining his status and his claim to annuity. October 21, 1961.

193. Under existing constitutional and legislative provisions for declaratory decisions, the Judicial Council has no authority to render a declaratory decision at the request of a Central Conference to interpret the meaning or effect of possible future legislation of the General Conference, or to determine the powers of a Central Conference thereunder. October 11, 1962.

194. Under ¶ 712 the Central Pennsylvania Annual Conference has an equity in the Washington Area Episcopal Residence Fund. October 12, 1962.

195. Lay delegates elected to a Provisional Annual Conference to be eligible to serve as members of said conference shall be at least twenty-one years of age and shall have been for four years next preceding their election members of one of the constituent churches of the conference or of The Methodist Church. October 12, 1962.

196. A member of the Judicial Council is eligible for administrative service on the Annual Conference or district level in the positions of executive secretary of an Interboard Council, in full-time administrative service for any board or agency of an Annual Conference, or in the position of a district superintendent serving within an Annual Conference. October 12, 1962.

197. The rulings of Bishop James W. Henley regarding the status of an elder on voluntary location are affirmed with

the amendments and amplifications indicated. October 12, 1962.

198. A vacancy in a jurisdictional representation in the General Board of Education in the interim between Jurisdictional Conferences cannot be filled by either the South Central Jurisdictional Council or the General Board of Education. It shall be filled by the College of Bishops of that jurisdiction. The authority given to a Jurisdictional Conference to elect members to the General Board of Education is a grant of authority that cannot be delegated. October 12, 1962.

199. Under legislation adopted by a Central Conference that the retirement age of bishops of that Central Conference "be the same as that obtaining for bishops in the Jurisdictional Conferences of The Methodist Church in the United States," a bishop whose seventieth birthday precedes the first day of the regular session of the Central Conference is not retired or released from his obligations to travel through the connection at large and to provide residential supervision until the close of said regular session of the conference. October 11, 1963.

200. The provisions of ¶ 1104 [1960; now ¶ 1077.1, amended] do not apply to the Commission on Entertainment and Program of the General Conference. October 11, 1963.

201. A divorced wife of a former Methodist minister is not eligible for a pension which might be granted to a wife for her years of approved service. October 12, 1963.

202. The actions of the New England Annual Conference concerning annuity credit and responsibility of a federated church are in conformity with the provisions of the 1960 Discipline of The Methodist Church. October 12, 1963.

203. The ruling of Bishop Alejandro in regard to division of responsibility for the annuity claim of Rev. Candido Padilla is affirmed. October 12, 1963.

204. ¶¶ 304.2, 392, and 402 of the 1960 Discipline which limit the authority of an unordained or ordained local preacher in the exercise of his ministerial functions to the charge to which he is appointed or in which he resides are constitutional. The alleged inconsistency which is implied between ¶¶ 353 and 363, which mention no limitations on local preachers serving as evangelists, and ¶¶ 304.2, 392, and 402, which indicate limitations as noted above, does not render ¶¶ 304.2, 392, and 402 unconstitutional. May 1, 1964.

205. The provisions of ¶ 1104 [1960; now ¶ 1077.1, amended] limiting the tenure of members of any division, board, commission, or council to twelve consecutive years do

not apply to or limit the tenure of members of the General Committee on Family Life. April 29, 1964.

206. Local preachers may count their years of approved effective service only as defined by the provisions of the Discipline. May 5, 1964.

207. (1) The Quarterly Conference has sole authority to determine whether or not members may be dropped from the membership roll of a local Methodist Church.

(2) The "five-year clause" in ¶ 127 [amended in 1964] begins with the date the pastor and special committee initiate the process outlined, but in no case can it begin prior to May 7, 1960. May 1, 1964.

208. An Annual Conference has the authority under ¶ 822 to determine the plan and method to be used in distributing apportionments to its several districts and charges for the minimum salary fund required by ¶ 826, provided the plan and method is in substantial compliance with the purpose and intent of ¶ 826. May 1, 1964.

209. The provisions of ¶ 1104 [1960; now ¶ 1077.1, amended] limiting the tenure of members of any division, board, commission, or council to twelve consecutive years do not apply to or limit the tenure of members of the Methodist Committee for Overseas Relief. May 1, 1964.

210. (1) Bishop Newell Booth is available for assignment by the Northeastern Jurisdictional Conference.

(2) Said jurisdiction has the same responsibility to provide for his assignment as for any other effective bishop elected by and in connection with that jurisdiction. May 1, 1964.

211. ¶ 680 as adopted on May 1, 1964, by the General Conference of The Methodist Church is constitutional. May 2, 1964.

212. Under the Constitution and the existing legislative provisions for declaratory decisions, the authority and jurisdiction of the Judicial Council is limited to the making of rulings as to the constitutionality, meaning, application, and effect of an act or legislation passed by the General Conference or of a paragraph or paragraphs of the Discipline. May 1, 1964.

213. The action of an Annual Conference designating a percentage of the total support of its pastors as "travel and expense fund" is illegal. May 7, 1964.

214. The legislation adopted by the 1964 General Conference as set forth in ¶ 1602.1 providing for the composition of the General Board of Pensions is constitutional.

215. (1) While the Cuba Annual Conference may be removed from the Southeastern Jurisdiction by processes other

than a constitutional amendment, the word "Cuba" could be removed from the Constitution only by constitutional amendment.

(2) Only the General Conference has the power to grant autonomy to an Annual Conference, Provisional Annual Conference, Central Conference, or Provisional Central Conference. May 7, 1964.

216. The Judicial Council declines to reconsider its Decision No. 163 relating to the constitutionality of ¶ 431.7. May 7, 1964.

Chapter II

ENABLING ACTS

Note: For past enabling acts *see as follows:* Those adopted by the General Conferences of 1956 and 1960 appear in the respective Disciplines of 1956 and 1960. Those adopted by earlier General Conferences may be found in the journals of those conferences.[1]

¶ 1804. Numbers of Bishops in Central Conferences

1. The Africa Central Conference is authorized to elect not to exceed four bishops, provided that this shall supply episcopal supervision for Angola and Mozambique.

2. The China Central Conference is authorized to elect one or more bishops for China, provided that by such election there shall not be more than four effective bishops resident in that field at any one time during the quadrennium.

3. The Latin America Central Conference is authorized to elect two bishops for Latin America, provided that by such election there shall not be more than two effective bishops in that field at any one time during the quadrennium.

4. The Southern Asia Central Conference is authorized to elect one or more bishops for that Central Conference, provided that by such election there shall not be more than four effective bishops resident in that field at any one time during the quadrennium.

5. The Philippines Central Conference is authorized to elect two bishops for that Central Conference, provided that by such election there shall not be more than two effective bishops resident in the field at any one time during the quadrennium.

[1] *See* Judicial Council Decisions 54, 71.

6. The Southeastern Asia Central Conference is authorized to elect one bishop for that Central Conference.

7. If a Liberia Central Conference is organized during the quadrennium 1964-68 (¶ 1807.1), that Central Conference shall be authorized to elect one bishop.

8. Any episcopal vacancy in a Central Conference occurring during the quadrennium shall be filled as set forth in ¶ 557; *provided,* however, that the number of bishops holding residential supervision within the bounds of the respective Central Conferences shall at no time during the quadrennium exceed the numbers specified above in §§ 1-7, and one each in Central and Southern Europe, Germany, and Northern Europe.

¶ 1805. Special Provisions for Episcopal Supervision

Presidential, visitational, and residential episcopal supervision of fields outside the United States not included in Central Conferences, and in emergency situations in Central Conferences, shall be provided during the 1964-68 quadrennium as follows:

1. The Council of Bishops shall provide episcopal supervision of the work in Burma, Cuba, Sumatra, and Pakistan until such time as the Burma, Cuba, and Sumatra Annual Conferences and the Pakistan Provisional Central Conference become autonomous churches (¶ 1806).

2. The Council of Bishops shall provide episcopal supervision of the work in Liberia until such time as the Liberia Annual Conference shall become an autonomous church (¶ 1806) or a Liberia Central Conference shall be organized (¶ 1807.1).

3. The Council of Bishops shall provide episcopal supervision for the Hong Kong and Taiwan Provisional Annual Conferences, which shall be administered outside the China Central Conference for the 1964-68 quadrennium.

The Council of Bishops is hereby authorized to ask Jurisdictional or Central Conferences to provide the supervision specified in §§ 1-3 for a period not to exceed a quadrennium, if the council shall deem necessary or advisable. A Jurisdictional Conference so asked is authorized, in accordance with ¶ 439, to have during the quadrennium one bishop in addition to its membership quota, provided a mandatory retirement in 1968 will reduce the total number of bishops in the jurisdiction to the membership quota.

4. The provision in the 1960 Discipline that the Northeastern Jurisdictional Conference provide residential and

presidential supervision within the Africa Central Conference is hereby discontinued.[2]

5. The South Central Jurisdictional Conference shall provide for episcopal visitation to the Latin America Central Conference and to the affiliated autonomous churches in Latin America.

6. The Southeastern Jurisdictional Conference shall provide for episcopal visitation to the affiliated autonomous church in Cuba (¶ 1806).

Inasmuch as the territory in which is located the work for which the foregoing provides the episcopal supervision is not in any case included in the geographical boundaries for the Jurisdictional Conference which elects the bishop or bishops involved, therefore the said bishops are directed to report on the supervision of their fields to the Council of Bishops as well as to the Central Conferences to which they are related.

If during the ensuing quadrennium any emergency in episcopal supervision should arise in any of the fields covered by the foregoing provisions, the Council of Bishops shall provide the necessary episcopal supervision.

¶ 1806. Conferences Becoming Autonomous Churches

The Burma, Cuba, Liberia, and Sumatra Annual Conferences and the Pakistan Provisional Central Conference are hereby authorized to become autonomous churches when the requirements, as established by the General Conference, are met. (*See also* ¶¶ 1807.1, 1809.4.)

¶ 1807. Central and Provisional Central Conferences

1. On full compliance with all the provisions of the Discipline of 1964 relating thereto, authority is hereby given for the Liberia Annual Conference and the Pakistan Provisional Central Conference to become organized into Central Conferences during the quadrennium ending in 1968, provided that each shall have a minimum of twenty ministerial members on the basis of one delegate for each four ministerial members of the Annual Conference. (*See also* ¶ 1806.)

2. Any Central Conference already provided for in the enabling acts of this General Conference hereby is authorized to continue during the quadrennium ending in 1968 even though it may fall below the Disciplinary membership.

¶ 1808. Organization of Annual and Provisional Annual Conferences

1. On full compliance with all the provisions of the Disci-

---

[2] *See* Judicial Council Decision 182.

pline of 1964 relating thereto, authority is hereby given for the Peru and Costa Rica Provisional Annual Conferences to become organized into Annual Conferences during the quadrennium ending in 1968, provided that they shall have a minimum of twenty-five ministerial members.

2. Subject to the provisions of ¶ 608, and to the approval of the National Division of the Board of Missions, authority is hereby given to the Hawaii Mission to become a Provisional Annual Conference during the quadrennium ending in 1968. (*See also* ¶ 1810.1.)

¶ 1809. Continuation of Annual and Provisional Annual Conferences

1. Authority is hereby given the Belgium, Central West, Czechoslovakia, Denmark, East Tennessee, Idaho, Northeast Germany, Rio Grande, and Tennessee (Central Jurisdiction) Annual Conferences to continue as Annual Conferences during the quadrennium ending in 1968.

2. Authority is hereby given the Baltic and Slavic, Bulgaria, Hong Kong, Taiwan, and Sarawak Iban Provisional Annual Conferences to continue as Provisional Annual Conferences during the quadrennium ending in 1968.

3. The Northeast Germany Annual Conference may change its boundaries if necessary during the quadrennium ending in 1968.

4. Authority is hereby given the Burma, Cuba, Liberia, Sumatra, and Indus River Annual Conferences and the Karachi Provisional Annual Conference to continue as Annual and Provisional Annual Conferences during the quadrennium until such time as they become autonomous churches (¶ 1806).

5. Any Annual or Provisional Annual Conference already provided for in the enabling acts of this General Conference hereby is authorized to continue during the quadrennium ending in 1968 even though it may fall below the Disciplinary membership.

¶ 1810.   Miscellaneous Authorizations

1. Authority is hereby given to the Hawaii Mission to become a district of the Southern California–Arizona Annual Conference during the quadrennium ending in 1968, when requested by the Mission and approved by the Southern California–Arizona Annual Conference. (*See also* ¶ 1808.2.)

2. The Sumatra Annual Conference, after consultation with the East Asia Christian Conference and the National Christian Council of Indonesia, may re-open Methodist work in Java and other parts of Indonesia.

3. Transfer of the Andaman Islands from the Burma Annual Conference of the Southeastern Asia Central Conference to the Southern Asia Central Conference, as already approved by these conferences, is hereby authorized.

CHAPTER III

QUADRENNIAL COMMISSIONS

¶ 1812.   Commission on the Structure of Methodism Overseas

1. There shall be a Commission on the Structure of Methodism Overseas for the quadrennium 1964-68. Recognizing the difference in conditions that exist in various fields of the world, and the changes taking place in those fields, this commission shall continue to study the structure and supervision of The Methodist Church in its work outside of the United States and its territories, and its relationship to other church bodies, and in particular shall review the historical development, structure, and operation of Central Conferences and the legislation pertaining thereto, and shall prepare such recommendations as it considers necessary for presentation to the General Conference of 1968. All resolutions and petitions related to Central Conferences presented to the General Conference shall be referred to this commission for consideration, action, and report to the General Conference.

2. The commission shall be constituted as follows: four bishops administering in Jurisdictional Conferences, four bishops administering in Central Conferences, one minister and one layman from each Jurisdictional Conference, and one person from each Central Conference; *provided* that a Central Conference having a church membership of 200,000 or more shall have two representatives. All of these shall be nominated by the Council of Bishops and approved by the General Conference. There shall be added to the commission by the Board of Missions four persons, two men and two women. Bishops having supervision of work outside the United States and its territories and bishops of affiliated autonomous churches shall be considered consultative members of the commission and shall be called in, when available, at the time of meeting of the commission. When a representative of a Central Conference cannot be present to represent his field, the bishop or bishops of that field shall designate someone to represent it. Those members of the commission representing Central Conferences

who are not delegates to the General Conference or who are not in the United States at the time the commission will meet shall be replaced by persons who are in the United States on nomination of the bishops of the Central Conferences they represent.

3. The commission shall meet immediately following election for organization, annually at a time and place to be established by the commission or its chairman, and immediately before the General Conference of 1968.

4. The expenses of this commission shall be paid from the General Conference Expense Fund.

¶ 1813. Commission on Interjurisdictional Relations

1. The continuing program of The Methodist Church to abolish the Central Jurisdiction, promote interracial brotherhood through Christian love, and achieve a more inclusive church shall be entrusted to a quadrennial Commission on Interjurisdictional Relations. The General Conference of 1964 shall elect on nomination of the College of Bishops of each jurisdiction a commission composed of the following representatives of each jurisdiction: one bishop, one minister, and two laymen. Officers shall be elected from the ministerial or lay membership.

2. The responsibilities and authority of this commission shall be as follows:

a) To study and recommend courses of action which shall implement the use of Amendment IX (¶ 47 ix) on all levels of church structure.

b) To study the possibilities and problems inherent in the transfer of local churches, districts, Annual Conferences, and areas as provided in Amendment IX, and to give such information, guidance, and other assistance as may be possible and proper to those considering such transfer.

c) To make an immediate study of the reasons for reluctance to make use of Amendment IX, where such reluctance exists, and to bring together responsible churchmen, ministerial and lay, to expedite action.

d) Where such transfers cannot be made in either direction at present, to recommend the immediate development of a long-range program designed to create better understanding of mutual problems.

e) To give special attention and study to such matters as may impede the speedy implementation of Amendment IX, including the adjustment of ministerial requirements, pension and apportionment differentials, minimum support, church extension, and ministerial itinerancy.

f) To make progress reports to the Council of Bishops, and to the church through the church press.

g) To present an inclusive report to the General Conference of 1968 containing findings and recommendations which shall be printed and distributed to the delegates at least three months prior to the convening of the conference.

h) To work closely with the General, Jurisdictional, and Annual Conference Boards of Christian Social Concerns, with the Section of Christian Social Relations of the Woman's Division of the Board of Missions, and with all other agencies having information and facilities for expediting the use of Amendment IX and for promoting interracial brotherhood and Christian love.

3. The commission shall consider the duly elected representatives of each jurisdiction on its membership as jurisdictional commissions, and delegate to them such responsibilities as may properly and expeditiously be fulfilled by them.

4. The general commission shall make specific delegation of responsibilities, wherever possible, on local, district, conference, and area levels of church structure:

a) In co-operation with existing agencies to formulate and promote programs of education and courses of action to develop greater interracial understanding and brotherhood on all levels of church life.

b) To study the policies, programs, and activities of the church, its agencies, and related institutions with respect to the practice of interracial brotherhood.

c) To assist church extension through the establishment, wherever possible, of preaching places, and the organization of new congregations characterized by interracial brotherhood.

5. In evolving an over-all plan designed to achieve a racially inclusive fellowship at all levels of the church's life, the commission shall be specifically charged with the responsibility of working with jurisdictions and Annual Conferences through the plans and procedures as follows:

a) Joint Cabinet meetings led by resident bishops of the two jurisdictions in overlapping Annual Conferences and episcopal areas.

b) Joint meetings of Annual Conference boards and commissions for co-operative planning and action.

c) Joint planning and administration of evangelistic efforts by conference, district, and local-church groups in urban areas under the supervision of appropriate evangelistic leaders.

d) Holding of interracial pastors' schools jointly planned by the leaders of the groups involved.

e) Holding of interracial leadership training conferences, camps, and assemblies for children, youth, and adults where-ever mutually desirable, with representatives of both races involved in planning and administering the enterprises.

f) Opening of all churches for worship to all without re-gard to race or ethnic background.

g) Exchange of pulpits on special occasions and for longer periods of time when mutually desirable.

h) Invitations to local churches for reciprocal family and group visitations for worship and fellowship between different congregations.

i) Establishment of interracial commissions by the two racial groups on all levels down to the local community for discussion, joint planning, and administration of special ac-tivities for the purpose of serving the church and the commu-nity, and of developing greater interracial understanding and brotherhood.

6. To assist and enable the commission in the achievement of the foregoing objectives, each jurisdiction shall establish an advisory council, consisting of one member from each Annual Conference, with approximately an equal number of ministers and laymen, plus two bishops. The commission shall arrange for each council to meet at least once a year, either with the commission or with one or more of the other councils, to consider problems of adjustment related to transfers and mergers and to facilitate such transfers where they may be voted or impeded.

7. The commission shall be given adequate financing to carry out fully and efficiently the responsibilities assigned to it.

8. The commission shall meet before the conclusion of the 1964 General Conference.

9. If by September 1, 1967, for any reason the Central Jurisdiction shall not have been dissolved by the procedures of Amendment IX (¶ 47 ix), the commission shall draft a plan for its termination to report to the General Conference of 1968.

¶ 1814. Committee to Study the Ministry

A Committee to Study the Ministry shall be named by the Council of Bishops, to continue the study of matters pertain-ing to offices, orders of the ministry, conference relationships, and other subjects of an ecclesiological nature, and report its findings and recommendations to the church at large one year prior to the 1968 General Conference, in order that these shall be available to that conference. The commission may consult with any board or other agency of the total church, at home or abroad. An amount not to exceed $40,000 shall be made available from the General Administration Fund to cover cost of the study during the quadrennium. The committee shall consist of one pastor or district superintendent from each jurisdiction, one minister in a special appointment, one minister from the faculty of each of five schools of theology, two bishops, and two laymen. An equitable balance of theological viewpoint shall be borne in mind in the selection of the members. The committee shall be free to consult with official representatives of the Evangelical United Brethren Church.

¶ 1815. Committee to Frame an Archival Policy

The Council of Bishops shall appoint a committee, including persons from the Council of Secretaries, the Association of Methodist Historical Societies, and the Society of American Archivists, to frame a general church agency archival policy and to report to the 1968 General Conference.

CHAPTER IV

THE METHODIST SOCIAL CREED

"We instruct those in charge of publishing the Discipline to include the Social Creed, with such revisions as may be adopted from time to time, in all future editions unless other directions are received from the General Conference."—Discipline, 1940.

¶ 1820.

I. OUR HERITAGE.—The interest of The Methodist Church in social welfare springs from the gospel, and from the labors of John Wesley, who ministered to the physical, intellectual, and social needs of the people to whom he preached the gospel of personal redemption.

In our historic position we have sought to follow Christ in bringing the whole of life, with its activities, possessions, and relationships, into conformity with the will of God.

As Methodists we have an obligation to affirm our position on social and economic questions.

II. OUR THEOLOGICAL BASIS.—The Methodist Church must view the perplexing times and problems which we face today in the light of the life and teachings of Jesus. Jesus taught us to love our neighbors and seek justice for them as well as for ourselves. To be silent in the face of need, injustice, and exploitation is to deny him.

We believe that God is Father of all peoples and races, that Jesus Christ is his Son, that all men are brothers, and that each person is of infinite worth as a child of God.

We believe that "the earth is the Lord's and the fulness thereof." Our own capacities and all we possess are gifts of the Creator, and should be held and used in stewardship to him.

We believe that God in Christ is seeking to redeem all men and also society. This redemption is a continuing necessity.

We believe that the grace of God in Christ is available for redemption from individual and social sin as we seek in penitence and obedience to do his holy will.

We believe that all persons have supreme value in the sight of God, and ought to be so regarded by us. We test all institutions and practices by their effect upon persons. Since Jesus died for the redemption of all men, we believe we should live to help save man from sin and from every influence which would harm or destroy him.

III. OUR DECLARATION OF SOCIAL CONCERN.—Applying the foregoing principles, The Methodist Church declares itself as follows:

A. *The Family.*—We seek equal rights and justice for all persons; protection of the individual and the family by high standards of morality; Christian education for marriage, parenthood, and the home; adequate housing; improved marriage and divorce laws.

We believe that the church must be vitally concerned with the health and welfare needs of all people, first within the family, and, where necessary, through institutional care with high standards of scientific service and Christian dedication.

We believe that planned parenthood, practiced with respect for human life, fulfills rather than violates the will of God. It is the duty of each married couple prayerfully and responsibly to seek parenthood, avert it, or defer it, in accordance with the best expression of their Christian love. Families in all parts of the world should have available to them necessary information and medical assistance for birth control through public and private programs. This issue must be seen in reference to the pressing population problem now before the whole world.

We believe it is the plain responsibility of the family, as it is also the deep concern of the community, that the welfare of children whose mothers are employed outside the home be safeguarded. This responsibility includes provision for the protection, education, spiritual nurture, and wholesome recreation of every child, and for religious and educational programs which will secure these ends.

B. *Economic Life.*—1. *Christianity and the Economic Order.*
—With full acknowledgment of stewardship under God and
accountability to him, we stand for the acquisition of property
by moral processes and the right to private ownership thereof.
We refuse to identify Christianity with any economic system.
We are under obligation to test each aspect of every economic
order by the commands of Christ and judge its practices by
the Christian gospel. We believe that it is our duty not only
to bring Christ to the individual, but also to bring the increasingly technological society within which we live more nearly
into conformity with the teachings of Christ. We believe that a
free democratic way of life, influenced by Christian principles,
can bring to mankind a society in which liberty is preserved,
justice established, and brotherhood achieved.

We believe in the use of such opportunities for political
action as are consistent with Christian principles. We urge
Christians to view political responsibilities as an opportunity
for Christian witness and service.

2. *Responsible Use of Power.*—The Christian point of view
demands that concentrations of power in government, labor,
business, and religious organizations be used responsibly. The
task of the church in this regard is to help people in positions
of power and the organizations which they serve to achieve
and exercise a high level of social responsibility.

3. *Poverty and Unemployment.*—We believe that the economic development which makes possible material plenty for
all imposes upon us great moral responsibility, in that the
physical and spiritual development of millions of persons
throughout the world is hindered by poverty. We therefore
stand for the eradication of poverty everywhere.

We believe it is our Christian duty to provide opportunities
for education and training for people to earn a living for
themselves and their dependents, so that they may take advantage of new technology.

Lack of significant employment tends to destroy human
self-respect. We believe that employable workers must be safeguarded from enforced unemployment.

4. *Wealth.*—We recognize the perils of prosperity. Our Lord
has told us that we cannot serve God and mammon. As Christians we must examine earnestly before God our personal and
business practices, lest we adopt the standards and assump-
tions of a materialistic society. Churches and their institutions
as well as individuals own property, invest funds, and employ
labor. In these areas practices and relationships must conform
to the highest Christian standards.

5. *Working Conditions.*—We oppose all forms of social,

economic, and moral waste. We urge the protection of the worker from dangerous and unsanitary working conditions, and from occupational diseases.

We stand for reasonable hours of labor, for just wages, for a fair day's work for a fair days' wages, for just working conditions, for periods of leisure, and for an equitable division of the product of industry.

We believe special protection should be provided for women and children, as well as migrant workers and others especially vulnerable to exploitation.

6. *Social Benefits for Workers.*—We stand for public and private programs of economic security for old age, for adequate insurance covering sickness and injury to the worker, and for increased protection against those preventable conditions which produce want.

7. *The Right to Organize for Collective Bargaining.*—We stand for the right of employees and employers alike to organize for collective bargaining, protection of both in the exercise of their right, the responsibility of both to bargain in good faith, and the obligation of both to work for the public good.

8. *Town and Country Life.*—We recognize the basic significance of town and country areas in relation to population supply, natural resources, community life, and Christian culture. We believe farmers, other agriculture workers, and those displaced by mechanization should have opportunity to earn a fair income.

Methodism, because of its large town and country membership and world-wide impact, must lead in developing an adequate Christian program in rural areas everywhere. This should pertain to people in their relationship to God, to the stewardship of the soil and the conservation of all natural resources, and to family, church, and community welfare.

9. *Urban Life.*—We believe the inner city to be a mission field crying out for bold new creative ways of witness. Here is emerging a pagan generation committed to values that run counter to those of the Christ. Therefore we call our urban congregations to a deeper involvement in neighborhood life. We call the Church to come into the city for Christ's sake, there to touch all forgotten persons with his compassion.

10. *Christian Vocation.*—We believe that every employable person so far as possible should be engaged in some vocation productive of common good. Every such vocation should be viewed as a Christian calling by those who pursue it as well as by those who receive its benefits, and our daily work should

be regarded as a sphere of service to God. The creative use of leisure is also a major responsibility for the Christian.

C. *The Church and General Welfare.*—The Church is called to be a redeeming community of discerning Christian love—a fellowship of those who confess their sin, who rejoice in the love of God freely given, and who commit themselves continually to spiritual excellence in every facet of life.

1. *Alcohol Problems.*—We believe that the Christian principle of love for God and neighbor calls us to abstain from the use of alcoholic beverages and to minister to those victimized by their use. The use of beverage alcohol imperils the abundant life to which Christ calls us. This is especially true in an organized and mechanized society. Individuals and families are destroyed by its use. We join with men of good conscience who seek to overcome the social, economic, and moral waste which this indulgence has created. The Church must become a healing and redemptive fellowship for those who suffer because of beverage alcohol.

2. *Crime and Rehabilitation.*—We stand for the application of the redemptive principle in treating law offenders and for study and action directed toward the improvement of laws, correctional facilities and services, and court procedures in order to facilitate rehabilitation. For this reason we deplore capital punishment.

We do not believe an individual should be excused from his personal responsibility to society; but we recognize that crime, and in particular juvenile delinquency leading to crime, is often a result of family failure and bad social conditions. Christian citizens and churches have a special opportunity and responsibility for creating those conditions of family life and social surroundings, wholesome recreation, vocational training, personal counseling, and social adjustment by which crime may be reduced, and offenders rehabilitated and redeemed by God's grace.

3. *Gambling.*—We stand for the achievement of community and personal standards which make unnecessary the resort to petty or commercial gambling as a recreation, escape, or producer of public or charitable revenue. As an act of faith and love, Christians should abstain from all gambling, and should participate in efforts to minister to those victimized by the practice, including compulsive gamblers.

4. *Mental Health and Medical Care.*—We stand for the provision of adequate medical care for all people, with special attention being given the aging, the young, and minority and low income groups. We strongly favor the healing ministries of the Church and other private groups. We support our

government, individuals, and foundations in required research in public health ; and we support legislation to meet these needs.

We believe that adequate facilities with professionally trained staff must be made available for the emotionally ill and the mentally retarded of every community. We also believe that churches may become spiritual centers of healing through worship, pastoral concern, and volunteer service for the emotionally ill.

5. *Drug Abuse.*—We seek to overcome those social and psychological forces which lead so large a part of our society to unhealthful dependence upon tobacco, alcohol, and drugs. The illicit traffic in drugs cannot be tolerated. Society must provide through public and private facilities for the treatment, rehabilitation, and after-care of narcotic addicts and other victims of drug abuse.

6. *Sex in Christian Life.*—We believe that sexual intercourse within holy matrimony with fidelity and love is a sacred experience and constitutes a needed expression of affection. We also believe that sexual intercourse outside the bonds of matrimony is contrary to the will of God. The outrageous exploitation of the strong forces underlying sexual experience is a destructive element of our culture. It not only distorts the meaning of sex experience but constitutes a blasphemous disregard of God's purpose for men and women. A case in point is the distribution of hard-core pornographic and other sex-exploitive material. We advocate thorough educational efforts in home, church, and school designed to elevate our whole understanding of the meaning of sexual experience.

7. *Social Welfare.*—We believe that meeting human need is both a private and a community responsibility. Adequate public assistance should be made available to all persons solely on the basis of need. Every individual should provide for his own needs and share responsibility for the needs of others to the full extent of his ability, but we believe that no person in an affluent society should be demoralized because of unmet need.

D. *Human Rights.*—1. *Freedom from Discrimination.*—We stand for equal rights for all racial, cultural, and religious groups, and insist that the principles set forth in this creed apply to all alike. The right to choose a home, enter a school, secure employment, vote, and have access to public accommodations should be guaranteed to all regardless of race, culture, national origin, social class, or religion. Neither should any person be denied equal political, economic, or legal rights or opportunities because of sex.

segmentheaderTHE METHODIST SOCIAL CREED ¶ 1820

That the Church should ever refuse access to worship or membership in its fellowship to any person because of race, color, or national origin is contrary to our fundamental Christian convictions.

2. *Civil Liberties and Civil Rights.*—We stand for freedom of speech, assembly, and press and broadcasting. The fundamental responsibility in the use of these freedoms and the justification of their exercise is adherence to the truth.

We stand for the right of all individuals and groups to advocate any peaceful and constitutional method for the solution of the problems that confront society.

E. *Peace and World Order.*—We believe that Christianity cannot be nationalistic; it must be universal in its outlook and appeal. The influence of the church must always be on the side of every effort seeking to remove those conditions of heart and mind, of social, economic, and international injustice, and of ideological conflict in which wars begin.

We must actively and constantly create the conditions of peace. We stand for the promotion of understanding, reconciliation, and good will; the relief of suffering, the lifting of living standards around the world; concern for the freedom and welfare of dependent and subject persons; the removal of racial tensions; the taking of steps toward disarmament; and the support of patient negotiations.

1. *International Organization.*—We believe that the United Nations is a working center of international co-operation which provides the most hopeful avenue leading to peace and world order. The United Nations with its related agencies should be strengthened through governmental co-operation and support. This effort deserves the support of all Christians. The Church itself, as a world fellowship, makes an important contribution to the development of world order.

2. *The Christian and Military Service.*—The Methodist Church, true to the principles of the New Testament, teaches respect for properly constituted civil authority. It encourages both love of country and love of all men. Believing that government rests upon the support of its conscientious citizens, it holds within its fellowship those who sincerely differ as to the Christian's duty in regard to military service. We ask and claim exemption by legal processes from all forms of military preparation or service for all religious conscientious objectors, as for those of the historic peace churches. We recognize the right of the individual to answer the call of his government according to the dictates of his Christian conscience. We also recognize that non-violent resistance can be a valid form of Christian witness. In all of these situations members of The

663

Methodist Church have the authority and support of their church.[3]

IV. OUR MANDATE: READ, STUDY, APPLY.—We recommend that this Social Creed be presented to our congregations orally or in printed form at least once a year, and that frequent references be made to it. Every local church shall encourage the study of the Social Creed and seek to apply its principles.

CHAPTER V

MISCELLANEOUS RESOLUTIONS

¶ 1821.   The Christian Family

The wedding ritual states that marriage is "instituted of God" and therefore transcends any social and legal contract. It is God's plan not only for the procreation of the race but also for providing the highest and deepest expression of human love in which each member of the family finds fulfillment.

The modern family is struggling against great difficulties: the tensions created by the world situation, uncertainties due to the present military demands on youth, inadequate housing, uprooting of families due to unprecedented population shifts, and the coarsening influence of many mass media on the lives of children. The end result of these difficulties is evidenced by the high rate of divorce, juvenile delinquency, broken lives, and a general laxity of moral standards. It is only when the family fulfills its highest functions and is truly Christian that its members rise above these difficulties and thus aid in halting the trends threatening the home.

The home is the place where emotional weaknesses of the members of the family come to light, where children express their innate hunger to be secure, to belong, to be needed, to be recognized.

Religion and the family naturally belong together. What religion is to accomplish it can do best in the family. What the family must do, it cannot do without religion. Religion and the family are natural allies. Religion is inseparable from the family. Family life at its best is a matter of living life at the deepest level, which is a level of relationship to God.

1. *What Is the Christian Family?*—The Christian family is committed to behavior in keeping with Christian ideals for family relations, community life, and national and world

---

[3] *See* Judicial Council Decision 25.

citizenship. It is the highest achievement and expression in human relationships. In it parents so live the Christian life and practice the presence of God that children come to accept God as revealed in Jesus Christ as the great reality of life. Each member of it is accepted and respected as a person having sacred worth.

The Christian family seeks to bring every member into a living relationship to God and a total commitment to Jesus Christ. It accepts the responsibility of worship and instruction to the end of developing the total Christian life, spiritual and material, of each person. It manifests a faith in God and observes the daily discipline of Bible reading, prayer, and grace at meals. It recognizes itself as the church in the home and participates in the fellowship and activity of the organized church. Amid a materialistic culture it gives supremacy to spiritual and moral values.

2. *Religion and the Family.*—The undergirding love of God, as taught by Christian parents, by word and example, is one of the greatest sources of emotional and spiritual security for the growing life. Where the awareness of God is present, families will find opportunities for informal experience of prayer in many situations of life. The beauties of nature, the joys of comradeship, the tragedies of bereavement, the elation that comes with good fortune, the facing of common problems—all these can be shared with God in the simple words of prayer.

In addition to these moments of informal religious expression, the Christian family will provide for planned periods of worship. This will include the participation in leadership by children as well as by adults. There is no substitute for the Bible as a central aid to worship when parents read it with appreciation for the growing needs of children. We recommend the use of such resources for worship as *The Christian Home*, *The Upper Room*, *Power*, and the devotional materials in the church-school literature and other church periodicals.

3. *Marriage Relations.*—Marriage is an achievement. It doesn't just happen. It comprises a growing oneness in which emotional adjustments from time to time are affected by an understanding of right ways of living together.

a) Preparation.—It is increasingly obvious that if marriage is to succeed, there must be adequate preparation. Therefore it is recommended that the pastor accept responsibility for providing a regular course of instruction for youth on the Christian ideals of friendship, courtship, and marriage in each local church, using the available materials. In our youth assemblies, camps, and institutes qualified persons should give counsel on personal problems, social relations, and the duties and privileges of Christian marriage. Suitable books, pamphlets, and audio-visual resources should be made available for young people. It is further recommended that courses of instruction for young married couples on home building, income budgeting, child training, life adjustments, and personality needs be given by each local church.

The time has come when every person planning marriage should have the opportunity for skilled and careful counseling by ministers or staff workers who are prepared in this field. If this is to be done, pastors must be trained to guide people, through counseling, both before and after marriage.

b) Mixed Marriages.—Since research findings call attention to the importance of common cultural and religious backgrounds for successful marriages, the increase in the number of mixed marriages is a cause for concern. Young people would do well, therefore, to consider the hazards of mixed marriage before they become emotionally involved. If love seems to be leading them toward engagement, they should discuss the issues involved with their pastors.

Whenever a minister becomes aware of a contemplated mixed marriage, he should seek opportunity to counsel with the couple regarding the potential difficulties. The couple should be helped to understand the Methodist faith and way of life.

Even though mixed marriages are fraught with unusual difficulties, we recognize there are many such marriages among members of our churches. Each minister is urged, therefore, to counsel with such married couples and to make available to them all possible help in strengthening their marriages.

c) Planned Parenthood.—Parenthood is a Christian privilege and responsibility; and the highest ideals of the Christian family can be achieved when children are wanted, anticipated, and welcomed into the home. We believe that planned parenthood, practiced in Christian conscience, fulfills the will of God. In the light of the population explosion, a more responsible attitude toward family planning is called for.

d) Divorce.—Divorce is not the answer to the problems that cause it. It is symptomatic of deeper difficulties. The Church must stand ready to point out these basic problems to couples contemplating divorce, and help them to discover and, if possible, to overcome such difficulties. In addition, the Church must stand ready to depict the unhappy circumstances that are to await the divorced person. As a Christian church, and as ministers, we are obligated to aid, by counsel, persons who have experienced broken marriage, to guide them so that they may make satisfactory adjustments, and to surround them with the love and fellowship of the Church.

4. *Relationships in the Home.*—Living together within the family is a vital test of religious living. The highest qualities are found in the life and character of Jesus Christ; these must be manifest in daily family living.

If we want to help the children in our homes develop, there must be an inner acceptance of each child. He must be loved for himself with all the limitations he may possess. In each instance his importance as an individual must be recognized.

a) Parent-Child Relations.—We recognize that parents are constantly teaching in the home in unrecognized ways as well as in their conscious efforts. Parents, in co-operation with the church-school teachers, should make possible the Christian education of their children throughout the week. There is great need for parents to interpret to their children in a Christian way the present world issues and needs, the politics of national and international relationships, the efforts of the people of the world through the United Nations to do those things which make for peace and more abundant life, the complex problems created by the use of beverage alcohol and narcotics, the need for adhering to Christian moral standards amid the tensions and pressures of our present-day living.

At these points the Church and the family can support and strengthen each other in their ideals of personal conduct and social righteousness.

b) Co-operation.—We recommend that our churches co-operate with other agencies in the community that are working for the improvement of family life and for the strengthening of Christian character. The National Conference on Family Life has demonstrated one way in which church boards and agencies can work together for the promotion of Christian family living.

c) Sex Education.—Parents must assume the responsibility of interpreting to each child, before his adolescence, the facts regarding the origin of life. If properly instructed, parents are best fitted to educate their children in regard to sex; but if they have been negligent, then qualified persons in the Church should reverently teach the beautiful truths of life. We recognize that sex education is not mere information. It includes also the formation of attitudes and habits.

d) Mass Media.—There is need for parents to guide their children in learning how to evaluate in the light of the Christian faith the propaganda and behavior patterns to which they are constantly exposed through newspapers, magazines, radio, television, and movies. Through family conversations, Christian and non-Christian attitudes expressed through mass media should be identified.

e) Three-Generation Families.—In the family there must be a recognition of the older adult. Medical science is making life increasingly longer. Older adults need and should have a significant place of recognition in the family circle, and should be helped to fit into the young family.

5. *The Church and the Family.*—The Church and the family need each other. Through their support of the Church, parents teach by example its importance in the life of the nation. When they neglect the Church, they teach their children that it is of little importance in the lives of people.

a) Study Classes.—To help parents understand the importance of teaching in the home, and the best methods for guiding their children, it is recommended that local churches make provision for study classes and discussion groups on child development, family relationships, and the teaching of religion in the home, using the helpful materials provided through the regular church publications.

b) Family Worship.—There is value in all the members of the family worshiping together both in the home and in the church. It is expected that local churches will provide resources and help for the family worship experiences. Churches are encouraged to hold occasional special services at which the entire family can worship together, with the service planned for the participation of all age groups.

c) National Family Week.—It is important for the churches to focus attention on the family at frequent intervals during the year. Especially do we recommend the observance of National Family Week, as provided in ¶ 250.5, and participation in the Family Life Conference.

d) Home-Church Co-operation.—Parents and teachers are urged to meet together frequently to discuss the Christian nurture of children and ways in which they can work together for better teaching. Parents are urged to read together with their children the lesson materials provided by The Methodist Church. Teachers are urged to keep parents informed regarding the objectives of the lesson materials and to point out ways in which parents can further these objectives through home participation. Parents are urged to take an active part in teaching both at home and in the church school.

6. *Legislation.*—To protect both the individual and society from hasty marriages we favor legislation requiring a period of days or weeks between the application for a marriage license and the granting of it. This will allow sufficient time for consideration on the part of the two persons concerned. We

also favor a longer interval between application for and granting of divorce. Every state should require a reasonably high minimum age for marriage.

We recommend laws requiring a medical examination of both contracting parties, and the refusal of a license to those unfitted physically or mentally by heredity or otherwise for the responsible state of matrimony.

We look with favor upon the increasing development of family life courts, and urge that when such courts are established they employ competent staff counselors who are sensitive to the religious resources available to families in trouble.

We further favor more nearly uniform marriage and divorce laws, and request that a study of the marriage and divorce laws be made by the General Committee on Family Life.

¶ 1822. Alcohol Problems and General Welfare

Throughout its history The Methodist Church has been concerned for the general welfare of persons. We are called by Christ to provide direct relief for persons in need, through private and public resources, and to seek diligently to change those conditions in society which create human suffering. All men should have maximum opportunity for security, health, happiness, and the abundant life to which Christ calls us.

1. *Alcohol Problems.*—The Methodist Church reasserts its fundamental concern with the problems of alcohol and the conviction that its members should abstain from all use of alcoholic beverages. The use of beverage alcohol in our highly organized and mechanized society denies the abundant life, creating havoc and misery in the lives of millions. Alcoholism alone, with its five million victims, has become the nation's third largest health problem. The use of alcohol causes men to harm their neighbors, both by deed and by example. Feeding a pattern of guilty involvement and callous rationalization, it separates man from God. Therefore, the Church continues its unceasing battle against intoxicating beverages.

Thus Methodists are called by love not only to abstain, but also to seek healing and justice for the neighbor who is victimized. Concern for the alcoholic and for all those in trouble because of beverage alcohol is the clear mandate of the Christian faith.

Total abstinence is a challenge to a more disciplined life in Christ, a witness based on Christian love and concern. It is a matter of conscience and Christian responsibility.

The Methodist stand is clear. We stand for total abstinence, and urge all members to abstain. Those accepting nomination or appointment for any official leadership in The Methodist Church are expected to set a worthy example by refraining from all use of intoxicating beverages.

Abstinence is not enough. We also urge our people to join with those engaged in positive and constructive programs seeking solutions to alcohol problems. These include education in church and school, rehabilitation for alcoholics, strongest attainable legal controls, and the stimulation of sound empirical research. Christians who love God and their fellow men can do no less.

2. *Social Welfare.*—Social welfare increasingly implies the concern of all persons, organized for the welfare of all persons. Continued high levels of unemployment and pockets of poverty highlight the critical need for public and private assistance to those unable to earn an adequate livelihood.

Public programs of welfare are needed which: provide physical necessities for the destitute; respect the integrity and dignity of persons; encourage economic independence; provide for services such as homemaking, birth control, literacy development, and cultural opportunities; offer a maximum of flexibility to meet individual needs; assign to social workers case loads which do not exceed professional standards.

The Church must develop specialized ministries to the blind, the physically and mentally handicapped, unmarried expectant parents, the divorced, the social deviants, and other groups of special need. Face-to-face contacts between the socially privileged and the underprivileged are seriously needed.

3. *Aging.*—All aging persons should be able to enjoy the fruits of their labor and to contribute to society according to their abilities. The elderly must first be viewed as individuals and secondarily as those who may have the special needs characteristic of old age.

Public and private efforts must be stimulated to meet the needs of the aging for social, medical, housing, employment, and personal services. Care must be taken to help the aging to remain involved in the life of the community and to retain their self-respect. Programs should provide for continuing growth of the mind, the spirit, and service opportunities. Specialized care must be provided for those who are dependent.

4. *Crime and Delinquency.*—It is our Christian duty to help protect society from lawless behavior through improved methods of prevention, control, and treatment of crime and delinquency. We support all sound procedures which help persons to become responsible citizens. We do not believe an individual should be excused from his personal responsibility, but we

confess that all of us share responsibility for the social conditions which breed crime and delinquency. The judgment of God falls on all men.

We urge Methodists to work with other concerned citizens to improve law enforcement, judicial procedures, confinement and parole, and after-care systems. Specialized courts and treatment centers are often desirable, and deserve our full support.

The Methodist Church recognizes that most offenders can be rehabilitated. The redemptive fellowship and faith of the Church provide an essential resource for rehabilitation. We should study the factors which breed crime and delinquency, and be ready to accept children, youth, and adult offenders into our fellowship and to participate in face-to-face rehabilitative efforts.

5. *Gambling.*—Gambling as a means of seeking material gain only by chance is a menace to personal character and social morality. Gambling stimulates the desire to get something for nothing, to acquire wealth without honest labor. It encourages a primitive fatalistic faith in chance. Organized and commercial gambling is a menace to business, breeds crime and poverty, and is destructive of the interests of good government.

Legalized pari-mutuel betting has greatly increased gambling and stimulated illegal bookmaking. Dependence on gambling revenue has led many states to exploit the weaknesses of their own citizens. Public apathy and lack of awareness that petty gambling feeds organized crime have opened the door to the spread of legalized gambling. We support the strong enforcement of laws restricting gambling, the repeal of all laws legalizing gambling, and the rehabilitation of compulsive gamblers.

The Church has a key role in developing the spiritual health and moral maturity which frees persons from dependence on damaging social customs. All Methodist churches shall abstain from the use of raffles, lotteries, and games of chance for any purpose. Methodists should protest all forms of gambling practices carried on in their communities.

6. *Public Safety.*—We support all reasonable programs by public and private agencies which guard the safety of the public. We endorse driver-education classes in school systems, uniform traffic laws, the up-dating and strengthening of traffic courts and procedures, the requirement of seat belts for all new motor vehicles by law. Automobile manufacturers must take direct responsibility for designing cars with safety as a primary objective.

We urge passage of implied-consent laws, strict regulation of the drinking driver, and adequate legislation and enforcement to prohibit teen-age drinking. We recommend that The Methodist Church adopt a program emphasizing highway safety and driver responsibility.

7. *Mental Health.*—Mental illness is a major health problem in all parts of the world. The incidence may vary from country to country; so may the major underlying and associated factors. But the facts of mental illness are present and must be faced by Christians. Appropriate measures for the prevention, care, and rehabilitation of those afflicted should be a concern of the Christian Church in its world-wide ministry.

The spiritual resources of the Church can be a great asset in the healing process. We commend the co-operative efforts of ministers and physicians in the care of both the physically and the mentally ill.

We encourage our churches to work with other agencies to assure adequate facilities for the care of the mentally disturbed and the retarded of the community, to offer counseling services to those emotionally and spiritually distressed, and to co-operate intelligently with physicians and institutions of healing in the over-all care of the sick. We commend the development of pastoral counseling centers to give in-service training to ministers, counseling services to ministerial families, and referral services to the churches. We encourage mental health education through family life conferences, premarital counseling courses in sex education, and fellowship groups for young adults, those in middle life, and the aging.

8. *Medical Care.*—Christians have a direct concern for health and healing. The Church has through the years pioneered in the establishment of hospitals and specialized medical services. The growing co-operation between physicians and clergymen attests to the vital role of the Church and its ministry as members of the healing team.

The extension of highly specialized medical services to a growing population ought not to result in the depersonalization of medical care. All persons should be free to choose their own physician or medical service. The rapid expansion of efficient hospitals, clinics, and nursing homes, supported by federal and state as well as private funds, is needed. A continuing expansion of medical training facilities is required, as well as research facilities. Every church should counsel its young people on the Christian meaning of the healing professions.

Our national resources should be mobilized to furnish health services to those in need. The principle and use of prepayment health insurance is good. Subsidies and administrative co-ordination by private, federal, and state governmental agencies may be necessary to care for unmet needs.

9. *Drug Abuse.*—We express concern and alarm over the widespread abuse of drugs which stimulate, depress, or distort human perception and behavior. The use of such drugs for the self-medication of emotional problems or for social and recreational purposes is inflicting untold suffering on thousands of our citizens.

The Church should support carefully designed plans to control the traffic in narcotics and to rehabilitate the addict. We urge the reform of existing legal barriers for successful rehabilitation of the drug offender. Experimental programs of rehabilitation must be expanded, including those involving the administration of controlled amounts of drugs under strict medical supervision. Churches should assist in developing half-way houses and similar centers to provide a therapeutic and supportive community for addicts.

We call on our people to avoid easy indulgence in tranquilizers, psychic energizers, and barbiturates. Drugs should be used only under medical supervision and for purposes of health and well-being. We deplore the growing use of dangerous drugs which produce hallucinations, and condemn the exaggerated claims of their devotees that such drugs offer spiritual insight.

10. *Tobacco.*—Responsible medical authorities the world over have linked cigarette smoking with lung cancer, emphysema, chronic bronchitis, cardiovascular ailments, and a host of other maladies. The United States government health agencies officially warn that smoking is seriously injurious to health.

Our people should take seriously their obligation before God to be good stewards of their health, their resources, and their influence on others. It is deplorable that so many sincere Christians help to create the social climate of addiction through their example in this matter. We expect ministers of The Methodist Church to abstain from the use of tobacco and urge all lay members of the church to abstain as well.

We call upon churches to institute programs of education for youth and adults on health and smoking. There should be supportive groups in the churches for those who wish to quit smoking. We ask all Methodist agencies and institutions to remove smoking ads from their publications and tobacco vending machines from their premises. We urge government planning to decrease the dependence of large segments of our economy on the growing and processing of tobacco.

11. *Wholesome Attitudes Toward Sex.*—Our society is

caught up in a strange revolution in sex standards. The commercial exploitation and distortion of sex in novels, magazines, and films has become a distressing feature of our social life.

Youth and adults need the positive witness of the biblical perspective on human sexuality. God in creation purposed that man and woman would, within the bonds of matrimony, participate in the mysteries of procreation and know the joy of intimate companionship through sexual expression. The churches should lead out in programs of instruction on the biological, psychological, social, and theological dimensions of sex. Persons troubled and broken by sex problems must find forgiveness and redemption in our churches.

We call on our members to support responsible community action for the legal elimination of hard-core pornography. We urge parents and leaders to guide youth in good reading and recreational habits.

12. *Responsible Parenthood.*—We affirm the principle of responsible parenthood. Each married couple has the right and the duty prayerfully and responsibly to control conception according to the circumstances of their marriage. Married couples are free within the limits of Christian conscience to use those means of birth control which meet the approval of the medical profession. We find no moral distinction between periodic continence and the various types of contraception now available.

We call on the churches to counsel married couples and those approaching marriage on the principle of responsible parenthood. We urge the churches to support public policies which make available birth control advice and means to women on public welfare who wish to limit their offspring.

13. *Population Explosion.*—Over-population in vast areas of the earth has created a social crisis as threatening as the prospect of a third world war. World population, now approximately three billion people, will probably double before the end of this century. The ancient specters of poverty, famine, and war stalk the world.

We encourage the churches to urge participation by their governments in international programs of population control. We urge the United States to implement its avowed policy of offering to any country on request technical assistance for population control. We favor the expansion of public and private research programs on fertility and demography.

¶ 1823.   Peace and World Order

Contemporary man is engaged in a profound and fateful struggle to master the productive machinery he has created and to control the destructive forces he has unleashed. Confronted by human sinfulness, contemporary man is involved in a race against time as he seeks to find a basis for co-operation and community on which to build a more peaceful, just, and orderly world.

Armaments no longer hold hope of security, but only the threat of nuclear destruction. The developing and amassing of more awful weapons steadily undermines the foundations of civilization and progressively corrupts the souls of men.

Christians must consider the *spiritual, social,* and *economic* damage done to persons and societies gripped in the terror of the present arms race:

—When nations contemplate use of methods of warfare that would have been considered atrocity and genocide a few years ago, when lying, subversion, and starvation are considered viable instruments of policy and often unwittingly are concurred in by Christian people, the human spirit is becoming corrupted and calloused to an extent that should give grave concern to the Church.

—The world's underprivileged people are deprived of the good life that the miracles of modern science could make available to them if the world were not squandering its resources on arms, and if the crisis atmosphere did not inhibit needed social reforms in many countries.

—Spending for military purposes is a drain on the economy. It does not stimulate in the most constructive way the economies of the nation. It tends to distort research and deter expansion in the civilian sectors of most economies. It is wasteful of man's creative energies.

If man is not to destroy himself, the Church must use its unique and God-given opportunities with conviction and skill. We therefore address this message to the churches and to the nations of the world.

I. MESSAGE TO THE CHURCHES.—1. *The Basis for Our Concern.*—Let the Church remember that the basis for our concern is in biblical theology and Christian ethics. God's love in Christ has reconciled all men to himself and to each other. Through this reconciliation we acknowledge God as Father and all men as brothers. It is God's will that all men should live in intelligent good will with all others.

We have as our heritage the words of the prophets that the nations "shall beat their swords into plowshares, and their spears into pruning hooks," and that the nations shall not "learn war any more."

We who are called to be followers of the Prince of Peace should make the redemptive love that was in Jesus a dynamic and moving force within our society. Unless we are able to relate the deepest ethical insights of our religion to the task of making peace at this moment in history, and unless we are able to deal creatively with the forces that lead to war, then we will have failed God our Creator and Christ our Lord.

Therefore, let us open our lives to the influence of God's will, persistently explore the possibilities of moral force and spiritual power, and seek to become instruments for his peace-making purposes. Let us use ourselves and our resources of energy, influence, and treasure to establish the foundations of peace.

We call attention to the unique opportunities of the Church as an instrument of peace, and to the special responsibilities which these opportunities imply:

a) The Church can be objective, since it represents no particular nation, social class, economic theory, or political party.

b) The Church can be a means of communication, since it includes people of many nations and groups.

c) The Church can be a means of reconciliation and unity, since it holds forth a supreme loyalty greater than the lesser causes for which men fight.

d) The Church has, in the proclamations of the prophets, the standards of social righteousness without which peace is not secure.

e) The Church has, in the witness of Christ, the key to achieving needed change without violence.

f) The Church can hear and share the Spirit of the Eternal, in which contemporary passions may be seen in true perspective.

2. *The Failures of the Church.*—We must frankly face our past failures to be an effective peace-making instrument.

We have too frequently echoed the attitude of the secular institutions of our society instead of sharing God-given spiritual and ethical insights. We have sometimes been happy to follow, after others have demonstrated that it is safe to be for peace. We have allowed ourselves to become too adjusted to the idea of war and preparations to destroy our brothers. We have allowed our consciences to become so calloused that we have often accepted as justified nuclear, bacteriological, and chemical weapons of mass annihilation. We have often failed to seek reconciliation between estranged men and nations and to be the redemptive, suffering, serving fellowship that God has called us to be.

3. *The Peace-making Achievements of the Church.*—Despite its failures in effective peace-making, we rejoice that God has

nevertheless used the Church in the ministry of peace. The Church is by its nature a peace-maker. Its missionaries to every continent have been witnesses to a love that knows no boundary lines. In the midst of war it has supported a spiritual ministry to those involved in war. The Church has given support to those whose consciences have made them objectors to war and witnesses for what they believe to be "a more excellent way." Its humanitarian concern has meant sharing food, clothing, medicines, and technical assistance with needy people in every continent. The Church has participated by public pronouncement and witness in creating the atmosphere that has made it possible for governments to take more constructive steps in the direction of peace. Beyond this, the Church has witnessed to the need for international political order and the creation of responsible agencies of world cooperation.

4. *The Responsibility of a Churchman.*—Given our spiritual heritage and the frightening consequences if we fail to build lasting peace, it is our responsibility as churchmen today: (*a*) to declare that war is contrary to the will of God and a betrayal of the way of Jesus, (*b*) to be ready and eager to take calculated risks for peace, and (*c*) to be as diligent and sacrificial in the pursuit of peace as the nations have been in the prosecution of war.

II. MESSAGE TO THE NATIONS AND THE WORLD.—1. *Sovereignty.*—We remind the people and the leaders of all countries that no nation is ultimately sovereign. All nations and people are under the judgment of God. Scripture reminds us that in the eyes of God the welfare of the human race is more precious than the continued existence of any nation.

2. *Opposition to Materialistic Ideologies.*—The Christian religion stands in direct opposition to materialistic ideologies prevalent in many places in the world. These ideologies, with their disregard for human rights, their scorn for the dignity of the individual, and their failure to acknowledge the fatherhood of God and the brotherhood of man, are abhorrent to basic Christian principles.

We believe the best defense against these materialistic ideologies is found in the preservation and growth of democratic institutions and in the daily practice of the Christian way of life. We believe that such growth and practice provide powerful stimulus to the rapid elimination of: (*a*) racial and class distinctions; (*b*) economic conditions which cause hunger, disease, and ignorance for large segments of the human race; and (*c*) the political suppression of human rights.

We believe that Christian concern for the physical and

spiritual welfare of all people will promote unselfish sharing of essential goods and the values of life which God has so lavishly provided. Such sharing will give great impetus to the elimination of the basic causes of war.

3. *Disarmament.*—*a*) The use or threat of use of weapons which by their very nature are indiscriminate and difficult to control cannot be morally justified. The nations of the world should halt the immoral, futile, and suicidal quest for military supremacy. Every phase of a nation's foreign policy must be judged in part by whether it makes possible disarmament under law. There is no real substitute for world-wide safe-guarded disarmament under agreements that provide for adequate verification and enforcement.

b) We must be aware of the dynamic factors unrelated to foreign policy that keep an arms race going. For example, the military-industrial complex in some countries has developed into a powerful vested interest shared by business, labor, press, colleges and universities, and even entire communities to an extent which generates powerful pressures on political leaders.

We call on people involved in defense-related industry to continue to plan for conversion to civilian purposes, and to be willing to accept readjustments and even sacrifices in their lives, so that when safeguarded disarmament is possible the improvement of the world will not be impeded by what appears to be economic self-interest. We commend all present efforts, public and private, which contribute to this end.

c) A sense of stewardship should lead the nations to seek every reasonable opportunity to reduce the vast amounts of resources and manpower now devoted to the production of armaments. The people of most countries urgently need in-creased food production, decent housing, improved sanitary conditions, adequate medical services, literacy training, educa-tional opportunities, and essential consumer goods. The sub-stantial savings which can be achieved from significant reduc-tions in arms spending could and should be used, at least in part, to create social and economic conditions which contribute to the maintenance of peace with justice.

d) A concerted investigation of, and attack on, the roots of hate and violence and the factors of war psychology would be an important contribution to the search for secure disarma-ment.

4. *Peace-making Initiatives.*—The New Testament contains wise counsel to those interested in changing the enemy instead of destroying him. We encourage the leaders of all nations to seek out programs that can be executed on their own initiative, often without international agreements, and which could en-

courage conciliatory attitudes in others. Co-operative projects can also serve to relax tensions, increase understanding, and thus help to free the world from the threat of war.

5. *Civil Defense.*—Our urgent concern is for defense—the defense of all mankind from war. The development of nuclear, bacteriological, chemical, and other weapons of mass destruction and the rapid progress of scientific research leave little hope that civilian populations can be effectively protected in the event of a major war. Christians are under the moral imperative to declare this and to insist that our reliance is on efforts to obtain peace and protection through universal safeguarded disarmament rather than on the inadequate defenses available. Christians must always minister to victims of all kinds of disaster, but such willingness must not be interpreted to mean acceptance of the idea that civil defense programs offer protection against nuclear attack. Christians must also warn against subtle arguments and programs that seek to implant the idea that war is a rational and manageable alternative to the peaceful settlement of differences.

6. *Man's Struggle Toward Self-Government.*—Recent years have seen millions of people become independent under many new governments. We rejoice with these people in their pride in their new status. We also sympathize with them in the struggles and tribulations that are part of the early years of independence amid the confusions of today's world. We commend the United Nations for what it has been able to do in co-operation with these nations toward the establishment of useful economic and sound educational and social structures. We urge all nations to increase, in proportion to their ability to pay, their contributions to United Nations programs that will assist in the development of these nations. We also urge developed countries to give serious consideration to trade policies and other measures that will make it possible for developing countries to have access to markets for their commodities.

We are also deeply aware that all of the peoples who long for freedom and self-determination have not achieved it, and that many of them have, at this time, very little assurance that their status and condition will be changed in the foreseeable future. In a number of these territories our fellow churchmen are suffering repression and persecution. We commend the efforts of the United Nations to secure, through mediation, the effect of public opinion, and other peaceful measures, a change of policy by the countries controlling these territories. Such a change should provide for these peoples improved economic and social conditions and the opportunity to choose freely the governments under which they are to live. We urge all nations to give support to these efforts, so that suffering and denial of basic human rights can be halted and the danger of an explosion into violence which may threaten the peace of continents, if not the whole world, may be avoided.

7. *The United Nations.*—World understanding must be accompanied by concrete progress toward world order. One element of such progress is the strengthening of international organization by movement toward the goal of the membership of all nations in the United Nations. As provided in its Charter, "Membership in the United Nations is open to all other peace-loving states which accept the obligations contained in the present Charter and, in the judgment of the Organization, are able and willing to carry out these obligations." Approval of this participation does not necessarily involve endorsement of the form of government, the leaders, or the political practices of any member nation.

We commend the United Nations for its success in reconciling differences, promoting human rights, lifting the levels of health, education, and welfare, and advancing self-government among the nations. These accomplishments are in spite of a total budget that is currently less than one per cent of the United States military expenditures. It should become an increasingly useful instrument in the peaceful settlement of international disputes.

The erection of the Church Center for the United Nations during the past quadrennium and the presence of many denominations in that building are evidences of the strong support church bodies are giving to the United Nations. The work of the United Nations and its agencies can serve as an expression of the love of God for mankind. Its programs for human betterment are an extension of the kind of humanitarian work initiated by Christian missions, but on a scale greater than the churches could finance or administer.

We believe the United Nations and its agencies should be supported, strengthened, and improved. Moreover, if these facilities are to become most effective, the United Nations, with membership open to all nations which seek to join and which subscribe to its charter, must be given sufficient authority to enact, interpret, and enforce world law against aggression and war.

Meanwhile, the governments of all nations, and especially the great powers, should utilize to the fullest possible extent the avenues of the United Nations for the peaceful resolution of international conflicts.

All nations should give adequate financial support to the

United Nations and its peace-keeping operations and its specialized agencies. The charter provisions forbidding a nation whose financial support of the United Nations is in arrears to participate in voting should be enforced.

We urge the early ratification by all nations of the conventions on human rights developed and approved by the United Nations, including: The Convention on Genocide, The Supplementary Convention on the Abolition of Slavery, The Convention on the Political Rights of Women, The Convention on the Stateless Person, The Convention on the Abolition of Forced Labor.

We believe in the principle expressed in the United Nations Declaration of the Rights of a Child: "Mankind owes to the child the best that it has to give." We therefore commend the work of the United Nations Children's Fund (UNICEF), which has since 1947 served more than two hundred million children in more than one hundred countries through material aid to programs of supplemental food, disease control, nutrition, and maternal and child health.

We support the greater use of the International Court of Justice and urge the nations to remove any restrictions which they have adopted which impair the court's effective functioning.

8. *Re-examination of Policy Toward Mainland China, Cuba, and Other Countries.*—The Christian gospel involves reconciliation by encounter and by communication regardless of political considerations. Therefore we cannot accept the expression of hostility by any country, its policies, or its ideologies as excuses for the failure of Christians to press persistently, realistically, and creatively toward a growing understanding among the peoples of all countries.

It is our judgment that policies of isolation toward Mainland China and Cuba should be carefully re-examined to determine whether their continuance will not intensify bitterness, and imprison rather than free the people in those lands from hardships, repression, and authoritarian control. Accordingly, we commend the expressed willingness of the government of the United States to re-examine its policies, and we urge the United States and other nations to work toward improved cultural, economic, and political relations with those countries and with all countries.

9. *The Individual and Military Training and Service.*—*a*) We reaffirm the opposition of The Methodist Church to compulsory military training and service in peacetime. Efforts should be made to include the universal abolition of military conscription in any disarmament agreement the nations may

reach, so that all men and nations may be free from its harmful influence.

b) Regarding the duty of the individual Christian, opinions sincerely differ. Faced by the dilemma of participation in military service, he must decide prayerfully before God what is to be his course of action in relation thereto. What the Christian citizen may not do is to obey men rather than God, or overlook the degree of compromise in our best acts, or gloss over the sinfulness of war. The Church must hold within its fellowship persons who sincerely differ at this point of critical decision, call all to repentance, mediate to all God's mercy, minister to all in Christ's name.

We believe it is our obligation to render every assistance to the individual who conscientiously objects to service in the military forces. He should receive counsel concerning his rights in this respect, assistance in bringing his claim before the proper authorities, and support in securing recognition thereof.

Thousands of our sons and daughters have, with sincere Christian conscience, responded to the call for service in the military forces. We are obligated to provide pre-induction counseling and educational material prepared by the related agencies of the church. We believe particular emphasis should be directed to the serviceman's bearing a good witness for Christ, the Church, and the nation.

c) Christians cannot complacently accept rights or privileges accorded to them because of their religious views but denied to others equally sincere who do not meet a religious test. So long as military conscription legislation remains in effect, we believe that all sincere conscientious objectors should be granted recognition and assigned to appropriate civilian service regardless of whether they profess religious grounds as the basis of their stand.

10. *World Economic Development.*—The desperate unmet needs of people in this world are of grave concern to Christians. The economic gap between the rich nations and the poor nations is widening as time elapses. The population explosion further jeopardizes the stability and progress of many lands.

We believe that economic assistance, which seeks to make the benefits of scientific advance and industrial progress available for the improvement of underdeveloped areas, is an example of both Christian love and practical international brotherhood.

All programs of technical assistance and economic aid should be designed primarily to benefit the people of underdeveloped countries and their economies rather than to serve political or military purposes. For maximum effectiveness, it is important that these programs be on a long-range basis.

The provision of development assistance should be conditioned on the undertaking of land reform, equitable taxation, sound fiscal policies, and careful economic planning by the recipient countries. Strong encouragement should be given to the formation and growth of self-help institutions.

We endorse the principle of multilateral assistance, especially through the United Nations, and urge upon the nations wholehearted and generous participation in United Nations development programs. The Bible and the history of mankind contain ample warning to affluent peoples who will not share their abundance.

International trade is an important factor both in sound economic development and in friendly political relations. We affirm our support of efforts to reduce or eliminate barriers to the expansion of world trade and endorse the continuance and strengthening of the Reciprocal Trade Agreements program of the United States. Where such policies result in economic injury to workers, employees, and communities in certain sectors of the economy, we believe the national community should make provision for forms of temporary assistance which will alleviate this injury and facilitate conversion to other types of production.

11. *Immigration.*—Freedom to travel and to choose one's place of residence is a basic human right and a useful outlet for tensions that develop both within and between nations. We recommend a continual re-examination of the immigration laws of the nations in the light of this freedom. We condemn the provisions in such immigration laws which legalize racial and cultural discrimination and deny to persons desiring to enter a nation from other lands the respect and justice due to all men.

We affirm the duty of the church to provide pastoral care services to entering immigrants and refugees and in places where refugees and migrating peoples are assembled. We recognize the obligation of the Church to assist these people to find permanent residence, to help with their adjustment to the new environment, and to extend the fellowship of the local church with its pastoral ministry.

III. MESSAGE TO CHRISTIANS IN ALL LANDS.—*From Co-existence to Co-operation.*—The growing assertion of independent policies among the nations that make up both East and West may give concern to the leaders of the Soviet Union and the United States; but it also signals the loosening of alliances and an increase in cultural, economic, and political co-operation across ideological lines. This increasing diversity is contributing substantially to a relaxation of international tensions and readiness to seek agreement on outstanding issues, though no one would deny the important influence of nuclear weapons on national policies.

In several respects the churches may claim some share in the improvement which has occurred in the international atmosphere. The attitudes and expressions of national leaders regarding the present state of "co-existence" indicate the precarious balance of forces which currently prevails and the need to increase the momentum with which the world is moving toward a secure and just peace.

The Christian churches and their members have a special responsibility to press for a transformation of "co-existence" into "co-operation." The avoidance of major war coupled with ideological competition and based on mere toleration for the sake of mutual survival is not enough.

Churchmen should increase their contacts and fellowship with churchmen across national and ideological barriers. But they must do more. They must enter into communication and conversation with those who differ and who may be antagonistic to the Church. This requires careful preparation, patient dedication, and active imagination if Christians are to be faithful, responsible, and effective.

Those to whom Christ committed the gospel of reconciliation are now called to "speak truth to power" and to speak truth in love. Thus the redemptive and transforming power of God may flow into the lives of men and nations as Christians witness to their faith in word and deed.

¶ 1824. The Methodist Church and Race

A. *Principles.*—1. Our Lord Jesus Christ teaches that all men are brothers. His gospel makes no room for the arbitrary distinctions and expressions of racial or group prejudice. His followers early came to see that "God shows no partiality, but in every nation any one who fears him and does what is right is acceptable to him." (Acts 10:34-35.) "In Christ Jesus you are all sons of God, through faith. . . . There is neither Jew nor Greek, there is neither slave nor free, there is neither male nor female; for you are all one in Christ Jesus." (Gal. 3:26, 28.)

2. "The Church is the instrument of God's purpose. This is his Church. It is ours only as stewards under his lordship. The House of God must be open to the whole family of God. If we discriminate against any persons, we deny the essential

nature of the Church as a fellowship in Christ." (Message of the Dallas Conference on Human Relations, August 1959.)

3. The fundamental affirmations of The Methodist Church reflect the inclusive nature of the gospel's invitation. Christ's offering of himself was made "for all the sins of the whole world." (Article of Religion XX, ¶ 80.) Membership in The Methodist Church is open to "all persons seeking to be saved from their sins and sincerely desiring to be Christian in faith and practice." (¶ 107.) The invitation to Holy Communion is offered to those "that do truly and earnestly repent of [their] sins, and are in love and charity with [their] neighbors." (¶ 1715.) It is the duty of the local church "to seek out the unsaved and the unchurched in the community." (¶220, comprising specific instructions for the Commission on Membership and Evangelism.) To read a racial qualification into these statements is to ignore both the plain meaning of words as well as the plain meaning of the gospel.

4. Racial segregation has been expressed in the life and structure of The Methodist Church. The bishops of the church, meeting in council, have spoken sharply to the racial issue: "The Methodist Church stands for the equal rights of all racial, cultural, and religious groups. We confess with deep penitence that our performance as a church has not kept pace with our profession. . . . We urge our pastors, upon whom rests the responsibility of receiving persons into the Church, to receive all who are qualified and who desire to be received without regard to race, color, or national origin; and we individually and collectively pledge them our support as they do so. The Methodist Church is an inclusive church." (Detroit, Michigan, November 13, 1963.)

5. By biblical and theological precept, by the law of the church, by General Conference pronouncement, and by episcopal expression the matter is clear. With respect to race the aim of The Methodist Church is nothing less than an inclusive church in an inclusive society. The Methodist Church therefore calls upon all her people to perform those faithful deeds of love and justice in both church and community as will bring this aim into full reality.

B. *In the Church.*—1. We call on all pastors and church officials to maintain local church services and activities, and local church membership, open to persons of all races, with equal opportunity for all to participate fully in every aspect of local church life, including the appointment of ministers to the churches.

2. We call on all Methodist bodies, organizations, and officials to practice fair employment policies, and to render ser-

vices to the public without racial segregation or discrimination.

3. We call on all Methodist bodies, organizations, and individual church members to use their influence to secure fair employment practices and non-segregated services in the companies and concerns with which they do business.

4. We call on all Methodist bodies, organizations, and individual church members to use their influence to secure fair employment practices and non-segregated services in the corporations in which they hold investments.

5. We call on all Methodists always to address persons of all races with titles of courtesy and respect such as are proper to the particular occasion. Stories which bemean and belittle any persons should be avoided. Opprobrious and derogatory epithets or names should be repudiated as manifestations of prejudice.

C. *In the Community.*—1. The fact that Methodist churches and churchmen have often failed to work for racial justice in the past does not relieve us from a present obligation to end racial injustice in society as well as in the Church. The minimum requirements for justice in the social order include the recognition of equal rights and opportunities for all races in voting, law enforcement, education, employment, housing, public accommodations, and cultural advantages. We support the passage and enforcement of laws appropriate to every level of government for the establishment and maintenance of equal rights in each of these areas of our common life.

2. The right to vote is fundamental to the operation of democratic government. To deny the vote to any citizen solely because of race is to destroy a vital means for seeking a remedy to unjust treatment in that society. Churchmen should seek the removal of every racial barrier to voting.

3. Since we are from nations founded on respect for law, it is incredible that police conduct, jail conditions, and court procedures in many communities still grievously violate human dignity. It is the function of the Church and the Christian to call such violations to the attention of the community conscience and to work for their correction.

4. The Methodist Church insists that the benefits of public education be provided to all the people without reservation because of race. We affirm the potential social, cultural, and spiritual benefits of integrated education. Methodists should endeavor to eliminate racial segregation (including de facto segregation) in all public and Methodist schools everywhere.

5. A society that denies all but the most menial of jobs to a significant number of its minority-race members is wast-

ing its most precious resource—its people. A society which denies educational and employment opportunities to any of its members plants the seeds of unemployment, maladjustment, delinquency, and crime. We must now strive for fair employment practices in every section of the entire economy, with special efforts and investments in job retraining and special educational aid.

6. Christians must insist that all people have the freedom to reside wherever their economic means and their personal wishes permit. The local church should prepare its members to live in integrated neighborhoods and challenge them to help in creating fully inclusive communities.

7. Any business or institution open to the public is morally obligated to serve all the people without restrictions of race, color, or creed. Where community patterns of rejection are encountered in such public facilities as restaurants, hotels, motels, hospitals, and recreational areas, Christians should use all their influence to change those patterns.

8. "We affirm the legality and right of those minorities who are oppressed, anywhere in the world, to protest, to assemble in public, and to agitate 'for redress of grievances,' provided this is done in an orderly way." (Council of Bishops, Detroit, Michigan, November 13, 1963.) A public march or other demonstration as a dramatic petition for attention and justice is in line with the principles and practices of a free society. When such orderly protests are undertaken, the goal should be clearly identifiable.

When resort to orderly, responsible, non-violent public demonstrations by those engaged in the struggle for racial justice provokes violent retaliation on the part of police or onlookers, the blame for the violence should be placed on the violent, and not on the peaceable demonstrators. On the other hand, any demonstration that turns itself to violence takes to itself the same blame. Even peaceable demonstrations supporting entirely just causes must be restrained and limited by the recognition that no decent society can exist apart from the rule of just law and decent order. Thus limited, however, orderly and responsible demonstrations can serve to bring a better order into being.

There are certain circumstances when arbitrary authority is sought to be imposed under laws which are neither just nor valid as law. Even under such imposition the salutary principle of the rule of law requires that in all but the most extreme circumstances the individual confronting such authority must resort to legal processes for the redress of his grievances. However, Christians have long recognized that after exhausting every reasonable legal means for redress of grievances, the individual is faced with the moral and legal dilemma of whether or not his peculiar circumstances require obedience to "God rather than men." There are instances in the current struggle for racial justice when responsible Christians cannot avoid such a decision. Wherever legal recourse for the redress of grievances exists, the responsible Christian will obtain the best available legal and religious counsel for his dilemma. In rare instances, where legal recourse is unavailable or inadequate for redress of grievances from laws or their application that, on their face, are unjust or immoral, the Christian conscience will "obey God rather than men."

D. *Commitment to Prayer and Involvement.*—1. We recognize that in these days of tension and distress we need a deeper spiritual undergirding for the tasks that lie ahead. We therefore call our people to intense and continuing prayer for the guidance of the Holy Spirit as we seek in penitence to implement what we believe to be the will of God. We humbly request our fellow Methodists throughout the world to join in prayer for Methodism, especially that we retain unity in love while seeking to do the full will of God in all human relations.

2. We call on every Methodist to seek the rediscovery of a unique sense of joy in living in these days. We discern in the tensions of our times the stirrings of the kingdom of God, for which we pray in our Lord's Prayer.

We are called by our Lord, who in his coming to earth identified himself with our agony and need, to identify ourselves with the agony and need of all men. We rejoice to bear the name of one who bore in his body the sufferings of others. Let us now seek to follow him in taking into our own understanding and feeling the rejections experienced by so many of our brothers. By this means we shall come to a new sense of kinship with Christ which will yield us the joy of those who share his redeeming purpose.

¶ 1825.　　　　　　Renewal for Witnessing

The Church is of God and is the household of faith, but its spiritual energies ebb and flow. When the Church loses sight of its origin and destiny, the tide goes out. When its household duties obscure its mission, it stands in desperate need of renewal. The time for renewal has come. The call to mission is the hope of this renewal. In the recognition that "the Church exists for mission as a candle exists for burning" lies the promise of the resurrection of the Body of Christ in our time. Renewal is our most compelling imperative.

But renewal for renewal's sake is not enough. Renewal's

living counterpart is witnessing. Though life-giving water flows into the Dead Sea, the sea remains dead because there is no outlet. To live is to give, and to refuse to give is to die. Witnessing without renewal is shallow; renewal without witnessing is transitory. The next great movement of Methodism must be a witnessing movement.

Too long have we allowed ourselves to be content with nominal Christianity. Too long have we regarded the Church as a nice club for nice people. The time has come to "launch out into the deep." This calls for soul searching and new commitment. It calls for prophetic preaching. It calls for a rediscovery of the New Testament for millions of thinly veneered Christians. It calls for a willingness to grapple with basic theological questions on the part of rank-and-file church men and women. It calls for membership training "in depth" for both youth and adults.

The desire for renewal may lead us to a bold and dramatic mission to our nation and to all nations which must be big enough and daring enough to capture the imagination of the world. Such a mission must be conceived in devotion and planned with meticulous care, and it must utilize the preaching power of one or more of our ablest bishops, who could be released from presidential responsibilities for this purpose. Such a mission could sweep across the land and sea proclaiming the power of the living Christ to renew and to redeem with such force as to rock the world.

Renewal will awaken the desire to witness. If the Church is concerned only to win those who come to its worship services and enter its programs voluntarily, it leaves untouched a vast reservoir of persons who live as though the Church did not exist. Church members live next door to non-church members. Church members work alongside non-church members. Church members ride in the same car pool, attend the same PTA meetings and other community functions, and rub elbows daily with non-church members. There must be born among us a need and an urgency to witness to our neighbors on a person-to-person basis.

The desire to witness will bring renewal to families who have neglected to remember their Creator in daily worship. It will lead a local church to schedule multiple services of worship, not only on Sundays but during the week, to provide renewal opportunities for a fractured and fragmented society. It will lead to the creative use of commitment periods in the formal worship services whenever the living Word is preached. It will cause us to give wings to the N-1 (Neighborhood-1) Program suggested in the 1964-68 Quadrennial Program, which calls on church members to "pledge themselves to one year of voluntary service in helping to establish a new congregation, or working in a mission or outpost church school, or assisting other churches of the community." This desire to witness should lead to the use of a "lay staff" in many churches, utilizing the skills and services of able men and women who find time on their hands because of a shortened work week and early retirement regulations.

The compulsion to witness will take us to the beaches of the nation where thousands of young people converge for their Easter vacation. It will take us to drag-racing strips where people gather for thrills. It will take us to people not of our class, not of our race, not of our kind. It will take us to people wherever they are, whoever they are, and in whatever condition of life they may be. As John Wesley went to the fields and to the mine pits of England, renewal in our time will take us to all people for whom the Church seems irrelevant.

The renewal of the Church must lead us to the campuses of America and to the campuses across the seas. Here the future of the world is being formed. It has been said that the next great revolt will be a revolt against God. That revolt is grouping its forces on the college campuses of the world. To witness in intellectually sound and morally relevant ways to the young life now thronging the colleges and the universities is a dire necessity if the ethical principles of Jesus Christ are to govern world civilization.

The lay-directed program of The Twelve, convened to pray and dispersed to witness, the "gathered" and the "scattered" Church, gives promise of renewal for the Body of Christ and of life-transformation for many outside the Church.

Witnessing by words can be ignored. Men may close their ears to the spoken word, but they cannot close their eyes to the lived Word. Here is the ultimate in witnessing—a Christlike life—a life that is lived in obedience to the will of God. Renewal will be confirmed when the renewed life awakens a God-need in another life—without a word. The Word needs more than words; it needs a person who will incarnate it.

¶ 1826. Methodism and Town and Country Life

1. We recognize the necessity for improvement in the economic, social, and spiritual conditions of rural peoples throughout the world. Rapid changes are affecting town and country life. The world's hunger for food and dire need for clothing

and shelter speaks of a Christian world responsibility of our churches.

2. The provision of food and fiber needs is basic to the world economy and basic to our concept of Christian responsibility. The blessings of American agricultural abundance in contrast to the developing and underdeveloped areas of the world emphasize our obligation as Christians to share, to help, to serve. This has been implicit in Christian missions. Therefore we would co-operate with all groups and organizations that seek to fulfill these purposes.

3. We note the structural and social changes taking place in our town and country communities as some of them decline, others remain static, and still others expand rapidly. In these changing communities the Church must continue to concern itself with individual, family, and community redemption.

4. We register our concern about the rapidly growing world population. Greater attention on this issue must focus on at least two levels: Land, water, mineral, air, and nuclear energy resources must be accepted as a Christian stewardship for present and future generations. Our efforts to share our abundance with needy people must include family-planning information, assistance, and incentive in the utilization of their own resources and related educational programs.

5. We recognize that town and country life continues to offer more favorable environment for the maintenance of democratic institutions and for family stability in terms of home ownership and responsibility and of community participation. It offers, also, more opportunity for face-to-face relationships as well as freedom to speak and to be heard, all of which is necessary for the development of moral character and a more Christian society.

6. We would call attention to the economically disadvantaged everywhere, including the migrant laborers who are very essential in providing our nation's food. We pledge ourselves to the improvement of their conditions of life.

CHAPTER VI

TERRITORIES OF THE ANNUAL CONFERENCES

[Under the Constitution (¶ 29) the boundaries of Annual Conferences are determined by their respective Jurisdictional and Central Conferences, and accordingly their official delineations are recorded in the archives of the determining conferences. By order of the General Conference of 1960, renewed in 1964, unofficial condensed descriptions of the conference territories as they existed at the time of adjournment of the Jurisdictional Conferences are presented here for information. So that each territory may be quickly identified, the descriptions are expressed in terms of the features shown on any good map, without attempt to trace the lines across counties and around deviations and exceptions. To verify that a particular church or circuit is within a certain conference, the reader should consult the lists of appointments in the *General Minutes.*—Editors.]

¶ 1836. Conferences of the Northeastern Jurisdiction

1. This jurisdiction comprises the states of Maine, New Hampshire, Vermont, Massachusetts, Rhode Island, Connecticut, New York, New Jersey, Pennsylvania, Delaware, Maryland, West Virginia; the District of Columbia; Puerto Rico.

2. BALTIMORE: The District of Columbia; the western shore of Maryland through part of Garrett County; in West Virginia the counties of Jefferson, Berkeley, Morgan.

3. CENTRAL NEW YORK: In New York the counties of Madison (most), Onondaga, Cortland (most), Cayuga, Tompkins, Chemung, Schuyler, Seneca, Yates, Steuben (part), Ontario (part), Wayne (part).

4. CENTRAL PENNSYLVANIA: The part bounded by and included in the counties of Bedford, Cambria (part), Clearfield (most), Cameron, Potter, Tioga, Bradford (part), Sullivan, Luzerne (part); Columbia, Northumberland, Perry, Cumberland, York; also the city of Harrisburg.

5. DELAWARE: The former Central Jurisdiction churches in the eastern shore of Maryland, Pennsylvania east of the Susquehanna River (except towns thereon), Delaware, New Jersey, New York; after July 1, 1965, merged with the respective geographical conferences.

6. MAINE: The entire state.

7. NEW ENGLAND: Massachusetts except the part north of the Merrimack River and the part southeast from southeastern Norfolk County.

8. NEW ENGLAND SOUTHERN: Connecticut east of the Connecticut River; all Rhode Island; the part of Massachusetts southeast from southeastern Norfolk County.

9. NEW HAMPSHIRE: All New Hampshire; the part of Massachusetts north of the Merrimack River.

10. NEW YORK: In New York the counties of Westchester, Putnam, Duchess, Columbia, Greene, Delaware, Ulster, Sullivan (most), Orange (most), Rockland (part); New York City; Long Island; Connecticut west of the Connecticut River.

11. NORTHERN NEW JERSEY: Through the counties of Hunt-

erdon (most), Somerset (most), Middlesex (part) ; in New York the counties of Rockland (most), Orange (part), Sullivan (part).

12. NORTHERN NEW YORK: The counties of Franklin, St. Lawrence, Jefferson, Lewis, Oneida, Herkimer, Oswego, Madison (part), Otsego (part).

13. PENINSULA: All Delaware ; the eastern shore of Maryland.

14. PHILADELPHIA: Southeastern Pennsylvania through the counties of Lancaster, Dauphin (excluding Harrisburg), Schuylkill, Carbon, Monroe.

15. SOUTHERN NEW JERSEY: Through parts of the counties of Middesex, Somerset, Hunterdon.

16. TROY: All Vermont ; northeastern New York through the counties of Rensselaer, Albany, Schoharie, Montgomery, Fulton, Hamilton, Essex, Clinton.

17. WASHINGTON: The former Central Jurisdiction churches in the District of Columbia, the western shore of Maryland, Pennsylvania west of the Susquehanna River (including towns thereon), West Virginia ; after July 1, 1965, merged with the respective geographical conferences.

18. WEST VIRGINIA: All West Virginia except the counties of Jefferson, Berkeley, Morgan ; part of Garrett County, Maryland.

19. WESTERN NEW YORK: Through parts of the counties of Wayne, Ontario, Steuben.

20. WESTERN PENNSYLVANIA: Through the counties of McKean, Elk, Clearfield (part), Indiana, Cambria (part), Somerset.

21. WYOMING: In New York the counties of Otsego (most), Chenango, Broome, Tioga, Cortland (part) ; in Pennsylvania the counties of Pike, Wayne, Lackawanna, Luzerne (part), Wyoming, Bradford (part), Susquehanna.

22. PUERTO RICO PROVISIONAL: Puerto Rico and the adjacent islands, belonging to its civil juridiction, together with any work which may be established by The Methodist Church or come under its care in any of the islands known as the West Indies, except in Cuba.

¶ 1837. Conferences of the Southeastern Jurisdiction

1. This jurisdiction comprises the states of Virginia, North Carolina, South Carolina, Georgia, Florida, Alabama, Mississippi, Tennessee, Kentucky; also Cuba.

2. ALABAMA-WEST FLORIDA: Southern Alabama through the counties of Lee, Tallapoosa (part), Elmore, Chilton

(most), Bibb (part), Hale, Greene, Sumter (most) ; the part of Florida west of the Apalachicola River.

3. CUBA: The entire country. (*See* ¶ 1806.)

4. FLORIDA: All east of the Apalachicola River.

5. HOLSTON: Southwestern Virginia through the counties of Giles (part), Pulaski, Carroll; Dade County, Georgia; East Tennessee through the counties of Scott, Morgan, Roane, Rhea, Bledsoe, Sequatchie, Marion.

6. KENTUCKY: Eastern Kentucky through the counties of Trimble, Oldham (part), Shelby, Spencer, Nelson (part), Washington (most), Marion (part), Casey (part), Pulaski, McCreary (part).

7. LOUISVILLE: Central Kentucky from the Tennessee River eastward through the counties of Oldham (part), Jefferson, Bullitt, Nelson (part), Washington (part), Marion (most), Casey (part), Russell, Wayne, McCreary (part).

8. MEMPHIS: The parts of Tennessee and Kentucky west of the Tennessee River.

9. MISSISSIPPI: Southern Mississippi through the counties of Issaquena, Sharkey, Humphreys (part), Yazoo, Madison, Leake, Neshoba, Kemper.

10. NORTH ALABAMA: Through the counties of Sumter (part), Pickens, Tuscaloosa, Bibb (part), Chilton (part), Coosa, Tallapoosa (part), Chambers.

11. NORTH CAROLINA: Eastern North Carolina through the counties of Caswell, Alamance, Chatham, Montgomery (most), Richmond.

12. NORTH GEORGIA: Northern Georgia, except Dade County, through the counties of Troup, Merriwether, Upson, Monroe, Jones, Baldwin, Hancock, Warren, McDuffie, Richmond.

13. NORTH MISSISSIPPI: Through the counties of Washington, Humphreys (part), Holmes, Attala, Winston, Noxubee.

14. SOUTH CAROLINA: The entire state.

15. SOUTH GEORGIA: Through the counties of Harris, Talbot, Taylor, Crawford, Bibb, Twiggs, Wilkinson, Washington, Glascock, Jefferson, Burke.

16. TENNESSEE: Middle Tennessee from the Tennessee River eastward through the counties of Pickett, Fentress, Cumberland, Van Buren, Grundy, Franklin.

17. VIRGINIA: All east of and including the counties of Giles (part), Montgomery, Floyd, Patrick.

18. WESTERN NORTH CAROLINA: Through the counties of Rockingham, Guilford, Randolph, Montgomery (part), Stanly, Anson.

¶ 1838. Conferences of the Central Jurisdiction

1. This jurisdiction comprises the Negro Annual Conferences still to be transferred into the geographical jurisdictions.

2. CENTRAL ALABAMA: All Alabama; the part of Florida west of the Apalachicola River.

3. CENTRAL WEST: The state of Missouri.

4. FLORIDA: All east of the Apalachicola River.

5. GEORGIA: The entire state.

6. LOUISIANA: The entire state.

7. MISSISSIPPI: Southern Mississippi through the counties of Issaquena, Sharkey, Humphreys (part), Yazoo, Madison, Leake, Neshoba, Kemper.

8. NORTH CAROLINA–VIRGINIA: All North Carolina; most of Virginia, through the counties of Craig, Montgomery, Roanoke, Franklin, Patrick.

9. SOUTH CAROLINA: The entire state.

10. SOUTHWEST: All Arkansas and Oklahoma.

11. TENNESSEE–KENTUCKY: All Tennessee and Kentucky; southwestern Virginia through the counties of Giles, Pulaski, Floyd, Carroll.

12. TEXAS: Eastern Texas through the counties of Brazoria, Ft. Bend, Austin, Washington, Brazos, Madison, Leon, Anderson, Henderson, Kaufman, Rockwall, Hunt, Fannin.

13. UPPER MISSISSIPPI: Northern Mississippi through the counties of Washington, Humphreys, Holmes, Attala, Winston, Noxubee.

14. WEST TEXAS: Through the counties of Matagorda, Wharton, Colorado, Fayette, Lee, Burleson, Robertson, Limestone, Freestone, Navarro, Ellis, Dallas, Collin, Grayson.

¶ 1839. Conferences of the North Central Jurisdiction

1. This jurisdiction comprises the states of Ohio, Indiana, Illinois, Michigan, Wisconsin, Minnesota, Iowa, North Dakota, South Dakota.

2. CENTRAL ILLINOIS: Between and including, on the north, the counties of Whiteside (part), Bureau (part), Putnam, LaSalle (part), Grundy (part), Will (part), Kankakee and, on the south, the counties of Pike, Green (most), Macoupin (part), Montgomery (part), Shelby, Cumberland, Clark.

3. DETROIT: In Michigan the eastern part of the Lower Peninsula through the counties of Lenawee, Jackson (part), Ingham (part), Shiawassee, Saginaw, Midland (part), Gladwin (part), Roscommon, Crawford, Otsego, Cheboygan; all the Upper Peninsula.

4. INDIANA: Southern Indiana to U.S. Highway 40 (ex-

cluding Terre Haute, Richmond, and the northern part of Indianapolis).

5. MICHIGAN: The western part of the Lower Peninsula through the counties of Hillsdale, Jackson (part), Ingham (part), Clinton, Gratiot, Midland (part), Gladwin (part), Clare, Missaukee, Kalkaska, Antrim, Charlevoix, Emmet.

6. MINNESOTA: The entire state.

7. NORTH DAKOTA: The entire state.

8. NORTH INDIANA: North from U.S. Highway 40 and east from U.S. Highway 421, State Highways 29 and 25, U.S. Highway 31 (including Richmond and the northeastern part of Indianapolis and excluding South Bend).

9. NORTH IOWA: Through the counties of Monona, Crawford (part), Sac, Calhoun, Webster, Hamilton, Hardin, Marshall, Tama, Benton, Johnson (part), Muscatine (part), Scott (most).

10. NORTH-EAST OHIO: Through parts of the counties of Ottawa, Sandusky, Seneca, Wyandot, Marion, Delaware, Licking, Muskingum, Morgan, Washington.

11. NORTHWEST INDIANA: North from U.S. Highway 40 and west from U.S. Highway 421, State Highways 29 and 25, U.S. Highway 31 (including South Bend, Terre Haute, and the northwestern part of Indianapolis).

12. OHIO: Southwestern Ohio through parts of the counties of Ottawa, Sandusky, Seneca, Wyandot, Marion, Delaware, Licking, Muskingum, Morgan, Washington.

13. ROCK RIVER: Northern Illinois through parts of the counties of Whiteside, Bureau, LaSalle, Grundy, Will.

14. SOUTH DAKOTA: The entire state.

15. SOUTH IOWA: Through the counties of Harrison, Crawford (part), Carroll, Greene, Boone, Story, Jasper, Poweshiek, Iowa, Johnson (part), Muscatine (most), Scott (part).

16. SOUTHERN ILLINOIS: Through the counties of Calhoun, Greene (part), Macoupin (part), Montgomery (part), Fayette, Effingham, Jasper, Crawford.

17. WEST WISCONSIN: Through the counties of Green, Dane (part), Columbia (part), Marquette (most), Waushara (part), Wood (part), Marathon (part), Taylor, Price, Iron (most).

18. WISCONSIN: Eastern Wisconsin through the counties of Rock, Dane (part), Columbia (part), Marquette (part), Waushara (part), Wood (part), Marathon (most), Lincoln, Oneida, Vilas, Iron (part).

¶ 1840. Conferences of the South Central Jurisdiction

1. This jurisdiction comprises the states of Missouri, Ar-

kansas, Louisiana, Nebraska, Kansas, Oklahoma, Texas, New Mexico.

2. CENTRAL KANSAS: Western Kansas through the counties of Cowley, Butler, Marion, Dickinson, Clay, Washington.

3. CENTRAL TEXAS: The part bounded by and included in the counties of Williamson (most), Bell, Coryell, Hamilton, Milus, Brown, Coleman, Runnels (part), Eastland, Stephens, Young, Palo Pinto, Parker, Tarrant, Ellis, Navarro, Freestone (part), Limestone (part), McLennan.

4. KANSAS: Eastern Kansas through the counties of Chautauqua, Elk, Greenwood, Chase, Morris, Geary, Riley, Marshall.

5. LITTLE ROCK: Southern Arkansas through the counties of Polk, Montgomery, Garland, Saline, Pulaski (part), Lonoke (most), Prairie (most), Monroe (part), Arkansas.

6. LOUISIANA: The entire state.

7. MISSOURI EAST: Eastern Missouri through the counties of Schuyler, Adair, Macon, Randolph, Boone, Moniteau (part), Miller, Pulaski, Texas, Howell.

8. MISSOURI WEST: Western Missouri through the counties of Putnam, Sullivan, Linn, Chariton, Howard, Cooper, Moniteau (part), Morgan, Camden, Laclede, Wright, Douglas, Ozark.

9. NEBRASKA: The entire state.

10. NEW MEXICO: All New Mexico; southwestern Texas through the counties of Winkler, Ector, Crane, Pecos, Terrell, Val Verde (part).

11. NORTH ARKANSAS: Through the counties of Scott, Yell, Perry, Pulaski (part), Lonoke (part), White, Prairie (part), Monroe (most), Phillips, Desha (part).

12. NORTH TEXAS: Through the counties of Wichita, Archer, Jack, Wise, Denton, Dallas, Kaufman, Hunt, Hopkins, Franklin, Titus (part), Red River.

13. NORTHWEST TEXAS: Through the counties of Wilbarger, Baylor, Throckmorton, Shackleford, Callahan, Taylor, Nolan, Mitchell, Glasscock, Midland, Andrews.

14. OKLAHOMA: The entire state (excluding the Indian Mission).

15. RIO GRANDE: All Spanish-language work in Texas and New Mexico.

16. SOUTHWEST TEXAS: Southern Texas through the counties of Matagorda (part), Wharton (part), Colorado, Fayette, Bastrop, Travis, Williamson (part), Burnet, Lampasas, San Saba, McCulloch, Concho, Runnels (part), Coke, Sterling, Reagan, Upton, Crockett, Val Verde (most).

17. TEXAS: Eastern Texas through the counties of Mata-

gorda (part), Wharton (part), Austin, Washington, Lee, Milam, Falls, Limestone (part), Freestone (most), Henderson, Van Zandt. Rains, Camp, Titus, Bowie.

18. INDIAN MISSION: The Indian pastoral charges and missions in Oklahoma.

¶ 1841. Conferences of the Western Jurisdiction

1. This jurisdiction comprises the states of Washington, Idaho, Oregon, California, Nevada, Utah, Arizona, Montana, Wyoming, Colorado, Alaska, Hawaii.

2. CALIFORNIA–NEVADA: Northern California through the counties of Monterey, Kern (most), Tulare, Fresno, Mono; northwest Nevada through the counties of Elko, Eureka, Nye (most).

3. IDAHO: Southern Idaho through the counties of Adams, Valley, Custer, Butte, Clark; eastern Oregon through the counties of Harney, Grant, Union, Wallowa.

4. MONTANA: All Montana; Lemhi County, Idaho.

5. OREGON: Western Oregon through the counties of Lake, Deschutes, Crook, Wheeler, Umatilla.

6. PACIFIC NORTHWEST: All Washington; northern Idaho through Idaho County.

7. ROCKY MOUNTAIN: All Colorado, Utah, Wyoming; White Pine County, Nevada.

8. SOUTHERN CALIFORNIA–ARIZONA: All Arizona; in Nevada the counties of Lincoln, Clark, Nye (part); southern California through the counties of Inyo, Kern (part), San Bernardino, Los Angeles, Ventura, San Luis Obispo.

9. ALASKA MISSION: The entire state.

10. HAWAII MISSION: The entire state. (*See* ¶¶ 1808.2, 1810.1)

¶ 1842.   Conferences of Africa

AFRICA CENTRAL CONFERENCE comprises:

1. Angola Annual Conference.

2. Central Congo Annual Conference—Sankuru-Lomani region.

3. Rhodesia Annual Conference—Southern Rhodesia.

4. Southeast Africa Annual Conference—Portuguese East Africa (Mozambique); in the Transvaal work among people coming from Portuguese territories.

5. Southern Congo Annual Conference—Katanga region.

¶ 1843.   Conferences of Central and Southern Europe

CENTRAL AND SOUTHERN EUROPE CENTRAL CONFERENCE comprises:

1. Belgium Annual Conference—including Dunkirk, France.
2. Czechoslovakia Annual Conference.
3. Poland Annual Conference.
4. Switzerland Annual Conference—including German-speaking churches of France.
5. Austria Provisional Annual Conference.
6. Bulgaria Provisional Annual Conference.
7. Hungary Provisional Annual Conference.
8. North Africa Provisional Annual Conference—Algeria, Tunisia, and adjacent territory.
9. Yugoslavia Mission.

¶ 1844. Conferences of China

CHINA CENTRAL CONFERENCE comprises:

1. East China (formerly China) Annual Conference—the territory of the Wu dialects and Manchuria.
2. Foochow Annual Conference—Foochow Municipality, Futsing, Kutien, Linseng, Mintsing, Pintang Counties, except such portions as are included in the Hinghwa and Yenping Conferences.
3. Hinghwa Annual Conference—the counties of Putien and Sienyu and the adjoining territory where the Hinghwa dialect is spoken.
4. Kiangsi Annual Conference—the province of Kiangsi and that portion of Anhwei Province west of a line drawn north and south through the west wall of the city of Anking, the capital of the province, and also Hwangmei County in Hupeh Province.
5. Mid-China (formerly Central China) Annual Conference—Central China, with its central station at the city of Nanking, on the Yangtze River, excluding the Kiangsi Annual Conference.
6. North China Annual Conference—the northern part of the province of Hopei; the southern part of the province of Chahar.
7. Shantung Annual Conference—the counties of Tsinan, Taian, Szushui, Yenchow, Ningyang, Wensang, Chufu, Tsouhsien, Feicheng, Laiwu, Tungping, Tsining, Tunge in the central part of Shantung Province.
8. West China Annual Conference—the counties of Chengtu, Whayang, Gintang, Jienyang, Tsiyang, Tschung, Meikang, Lochi, Anyoh, Chungkiang, Bahsien, Kiangpeh, Pishan, Yungchwan, Jungchang, Hochwan, Wusheng, Tunknan, Suining.
9. Yenping Annual Conference—in Fukien the counties of Nanping, Sha, Yungan, Mingchi, Shunchang, Sanyuan, Yuki;

Kaotan of Chianglo County; Hsia-Shuan-keng of Kutien County.

10. Hong Kong Provisional Annual Conference—Hong Kong; but *see* ¶ 1805.3.

11. Kalgan Provisional Annual Conference—the city of Kalgan and contiguous territory of the Hopei Province and Inner Mongolia.

12. Taiwan Provisional Annual Conference—Taiwan (Formosa); but *see* ¶ 1805.3.

¶ 1845. Conferences of Germany

GERMANY CENTRAL CONFERENCE comprises:

1. Central Germany Annual Conference—Saxony and Thuringia, including the towns of Halle and Dessau.

2. Northeast Germany Annual Conference—bounded in the west by the Northwest Germany Conference, in the south by the Central Germany Conference, in the east by the boundary of Germany as of 1945. (*See* ¶ 1809.3.)

3. Northwest Germany Annual Conference—bounded in the east by the eleventh degree of longitude, in the south by the fifty-second degree of latitude to the boundary of the Southwest Germany Conference, in the west by the boundary of Germany as of 1945.

4. South Germany Annual Conference—Bavaria, except the Palatinate and Wuerttemberg.

5. Southwest Germany Annual Conference—bounded in the north by a line south of Lippe from Wesel to Hamm; in the east by a line from Hamm to Marburg, Geinhausen, Mosbach, Pforzheim to Lahr.

¶ 1846. Conferences of Latin America

LATIN AMERICA CENTRAL CONFERENCE comprises:

1. Argentina Annual Conference—northern Argentina through Mendoza, La Pampa, and Buenos Aires Province (most).

2. Bolivia Annual Conference.

3. Chile Annual Conference.

4. Uruguay Annual Conference.

5. Costa Rica Provisional Annual Conference. (*See* ¶ 1808.1.)

6. Panama Provisional Annual Conference.

7. Patagonia Provisional Annual Conference—southern Argentina through Neuquén, Río Negro, and the Bahía Blanca region of Buenos Aires Province.

8. Peru Provisional Annual Conference. (*See* ¶ 1808.1.)

¶ 1847. Conferences of Northern Europe

NORTHERN EUROPE CENTRAL CONFERENCE comprises:
1. Denmark Annual Conference.
2. Norway Annual Conference.
3. Sweden Annual Conference.
4. Baltic and Slavic Provisional Annual Conference—Estonia, Latvia, Lithuania.
5. Finland Provisional Annual Conference—Finland except as in § 6.
6. Finland-Swedish Provisional Annual Conference—the Swedish-speaking work in Finland.

¶ 1848. Conferences of Pakistan

PAKISTAN PROVISIONAL CENTRAL CONFERENCE (*see* ¶ 1806) comprises:
1. Indus River Annual Conference—in West Pakistan the Punjab and Bahawalpur Divisions.
2. Karachi Provisional Annual Conference—in West Pakistan the Karachi, Sind, and Baluchistan Divisions.

¶ 1849. Conferences of the Philippines

PHILIPPINES CENTRAL CONFERENCE comprises:
1. Middle Philippines Annual Conference—the provinces of Zambales, Tarlac (part), Nueva Ecija (part), Pampanga, Bulacan, Bataan.
2. Northern Philippines Annual Conference—the provinces of Batanes, Cagayan, Isabela, Nueva Vizcaya; the subprovinces Apayao, Kalinga, Ifugao of Mountain Province.
3. Northwest Philippines Annual Conference—the provinces of Ilocos Norte and Sur, Abra, La Union, Pangasinan, Tarlac (part), Nueva Ecija (part); the subprovinces Benguet and Bontoc of Mountain Province; the city of Baguio.
4. Philippines Annual Conference—the cities of Manila, Caloocan, Pasay, Naga; Quezon City; the provinces of Rizal, Batangas, Quezon, Camarines Norte and Sur; the islands of Masbate, Romblon, Mindoro, Catanduanes, Palawan.
5. Mindanao Provisional Annual Conference—the island of Mindanao and the Sulu Archipelago.

¶ 1850. Conferences of Southeastern Asia

SOUTHEASTERN ASIA CENTRAL CONFERENCE comprises:
1. Burma Annual Conference. (*See* ¶ 1806.)
2. Malaya Annual Conference—Malaya and Singapore, Malaysia, except as in § 3.
3. Malaysia Chinese Annual Conference—vernacular Chinese work in Malaya and Singapore, Malaysia.

701

4. Sarawak Annual Conference—Sarawak, Malaysia, except as in § 5.

5. Sarawak Iban Provisional Annual Conference—work among the Ibans of Sarawak, Malaysia.

¶ 1851.   Conferences of Southern Asia

SOUTHERN ASIA CENTRAL CONFERENCE comprises:

1. Agra Annual Conference—Agra, Aligarh, Bulandshahr, Mathura, Meerut, Muzaffarnagar, Roorkee, Dehra Dun, and Tehri Garhwal in Uttar Pradesh; Gwalior in Madhya Pradesh.

2. Bengal Annual Conference—all West Bengal; Pakaur, Birbhum, Dhanbad, and Gomoh in eastern Bihar; the Andaman Islands.

3. Bombay Annual Conference—all Maharashtra except the environs of Sironcha.

4. Delhi Annual Conference—Delhi, East Punjab, Himachal Pradesh, and Rajasthan.

5. Gujarat Annual Conference—the state of Gujarat.

6. Hyderabad Annual Conference—Andhra Pradesh; the environs of Sironcha in Maharashtra.

7. Lucknow Annual Conference—Lucknow, Allahabad, Kanpur, Gonda, Rae Bareli, Bahraich, Barabanki, and Ballia in Uttar Pradesh; Arrah, Buxar, and Patna in western Bihar.

8. Madhya Pradesh Annual Conference—all Madhya Pradesh except Gwalior.

9. Moradabad Annual Conference—Garhwal, Bijnor, Moradabad, Rampur, and parts of Bareilly and Budaun in Uttar Pradesh.

10. North India Annual Conference—Almora, Naini Tal, Pilibhit, Shahjahanpur, Sitapur, Hardoi, and parts of Bareilly and Budaun in Uttar Pradesh.

11. South India Annual Conference—the states of Mysore and Madras.

12. Nepal Mission—the work of The Methodist Church with the United Christian Mission in Nepal.

¶ 1852. Other Work Outside the United States

1. Liberia Annual Conference. (See ¶¶ 1806, 1807.1.)

2. Affiliated autonomous churches: The Methodist Church of Mexico, The Methodist Church of Brazil, Korean Methodist Church. United Church of Christ in Japan, The Church of Christ of Okinawa, The Methodist Church of Indonesia. (See ¶ 1806.)

GLOSSARY

This glossary, like the Index, is not part of the law of the church, but rather a guide to that law, arranged in alphabetical order for the convenience of readers. So far as possible the definitions are based on the Constitution and legislation, and use the Disciplinary language. Where there is no specific legislation, they are based on historical usage and accepted practice. For terms not defined here, see the Index, where paragraphs containing definitions or definitive information are indicated by boldface type.

Advance. The program for promoting special gifts to missionary causes over and above apportioned world service and conference benevolences. (¶¶ 756-61.)

Affiliate member. A person residing away from home for an extended period who is enrolled in a near-by church for fellowship, pastoral care, and participation in activities, but is still counted as a member of his home church. (¶ 116.) *See also* Associate member.

Affiliated autonomous church. A self-governing church in whose establishment The Methodist Church has assisted and with which it is co-operating through its Board of Missions. (¶¶ 600-7.)

Agency. A council, board, division, commission, committee, or other body established to carry out the work of the church. (¶¶ 8.8, 15.3, 19.3, 666-67, 1071-87.)

Appointment. The pastoral charge or other position in the church to which a preacher is assigned by a bishop or, between sessions of the Annual Conference, by a district superintendent. (¶ 362 .3, 431-33.)

Apportionment. An amount assigned to a local church or other Methodist body by proper church authority to be raised by that body as its share in some church fund.

Approved supply pastor. A local preacher who on recommendation of the Board of Ministerial Training and Qualifications has been approved by the Annual Conference as eligible for appointment during the ensuing year as a supply pastor of a charge. (¶¶ 314-20.) *See* Supply pastor.

Area, episcopal. The Annual Conference or Conferences assigned to a bishop for residential and presidential supervision. (¶¶ 37-38, 440.)

Associate member. A nominal member of another denomination, usually a state church, who under rules adopted by a Central Conference is permitted certain privileges and responsibilities of membership in a local Methodist church. (¶¶ 117, 562.) *See also* Affiliate member.

Bishop. A general superintendent of The Methodist Church. He is an elder who has been set apart after the manner prescribed in the Discipline for that office. (¶¶ 34-41, 47 i.)

Cabinet. The district superintendents of an Annual Conference acting together as a body under the presidency of the bishop.

Charge, pastoral. One or more churches which are organized under, and subject to, the Discipline, with a single pastoral-charge Quarterly Conference, and to which a minister is or may be duly appointed or appointable as preacher in charge. (¶ 105.1.)

Church, local. A connectional society of persons who have professed their faith in Christ, have been baptized, have assumed the vows of membership in The Methodist Church, and are associated in fellowship as a local Methodist church in order that they may hear the Word of God, receive the Sacraments, and carry forward the work which Christ has committed to his Church. Such a society of believers, being within The Methodist Church and subject to its Discipline, is also an inherent part of the Church Universal, which is composed of all who accept Jesus Christ as Lord and Saviour, and which in the Apostles' Creed we declare to be the holy catholic Church. (¶ 102.)

Church school. The program of the local church for instructing and guiding its entire constituency in Christian faith and living. It includes Sunday school, the Methodist Sunday Evening Fellowship, weekday activities, and home and extension service. (¶¶ 241-45.)

Circuit. Two or more local churches which are joined together for pastoral supervision, constituting one pastoral charge. (¶ 105.2.)

College of Bishops. All the bishops assigned to or elected by a Jurisdictional or Central Conference.

Conference, Annual. The basic administrative body in The Methodist Church, having supervision over the affairs of the church in a specific territory, as established by the Jurisdictional or Central Conference. (¶¶ 21-25, 47 x, 621-80.) Also, the territory administered by such a body.

Conference, Central. A representative body outside the United States of America comparable to a Jurisdictional Conference within the United States. (¶¶ 16-19, 47 ii, 541-81.)

Conference, Church. An assembly of the members of a charge or church for review and planning of the church's work, for action on matters requiring a vote of the church membership, and, when so authorized by the Quarterly Conference, for election of church officers. (¶¶ 33, 196-200.)

Conference, District. An assembly held annually in each district where authorized by the Annual Conference. It includes lay and ministerial representatives from each local church (¶ 687) and performs the duties assigned to it. (¶¶ 689-91, 695.)

Conference, General. The legislative body for the entire church, meeting every four years, and having full legislative powers over all connectional matters. It is composed of elected representatives, ministerial and lay, from all the Annual Conferences. (¶¶ 5-10, 47 vii, xi, 501-12.)

Conference, Jurisdictional. The representative body in the United States, established by the Plan of Union, composed of ministerial and lay delegates from the several Annual Conferences of a jurisdiction, and meeting every four years. It elects the bishops and certain members of the general boards of the church. (¶¶ 11-15, 47 iv, 516-35.)

Conference, Provisional Annual. A body similar to an Annual Conference but with powers limited because of insufficient membership. (¶¶ 608-14.)

Conference, Provisional Central. A body similar to a Central Conference but with powers limited because of insufficient membership. (¶¶ 586-90.)

Conference, Quarterly. The governing body of the pastoral charge. (¶¶ 31-32, 137-50.) A Church Quarterly Conference is a body similarly constituted in each local church of a circuit, with authority limited to control of the property of the local church. (¶¶ 152-54, 158.)

Connectional. Of or pertaining to the "connection," the general organization of The Methodist Church. (¶ 8; *see also* Judicial Council Decision 196.)

Council of Bishops. All the bishops of all the Jurisdictional and Central Conferences of the church. (¶ 36.)

Credentials. The official documents certifying to ministerial ordination.

Deacon. A preacher who, having fulfilled the requirements, has been elected to the order of deacon by an Annual Conference, has taken the vows prescribed, and has been duly ordained by the laying on of the hands of a bishop. (¶¶ 391-93.) A deacon may be either "local" or "traveling." *See* Preacher.

Deaconess. A woman who has been led by the Holy Spirit to devote herself to Christlike service under the direction of the Church, and who, having met the requirements, has been duly licensed, consecrated, and commissioned by a bishop. (¶ 1250.)

Director. On the staff of a world service agency, the head of a department (¶ 783.2*d*) ; in a local church, a layman certified as having full qualifications to lead the program of Christian education or of music (¶ 247).

Disciplinary. In accordance with the Constitution and laws of The Methodist Church, as set forth in the Discipline.

Discipline. The official and published statement of the Constitution and laws of The Methodist Church, its rules of organization and procedure, the description of administrative agencies and their functions, and the Ritual.

District. The major administrative subdivision of an Annual Conference, established by the Annual Conference and formed by the bishop. It comprises a number of pastoral charges and is under the supervision of a district superintendent. (¶ 431.3.)

District superintendent. A minister appointed by the bishop to travel through a district in order to preach and to oversee the spiritual and temporal affairs of the church. (¶¶ 361-62.)

Elder. A minister who, having fulfilled the requirements, has been elected to the order of elder by an Annual Conference, has taken the vows prescribed, and has been duly ordained by the laying on of the hands of a bishop and other elders. (¶¶ 401-3.)

This is the second and higher ministerial order in the church.

Itinerancy. The system by which The Methodist Church moves its ministers from church to church so that every preacher has a church and every church has a preacher.

Judicial Council. The final court of appeal in The Methodist Church, elected by the General Conference. It determines, on appeal, the constitutionality of any act of a General, Jurisdictional, or Central Conference, and exercises other judicial functions as set forth in the Discipline. (¶¶ 42-44, 901-18.)

Jurisdiction. A major division of The Methodist Church in the United States as established by the Plan of Union, composed of several Annual Conferences, and under the administration of a Jurisdictional Conference. (¶¶ 26, 28, 47 ix.) *See* Conference, Jurisdictional.

NOTE: When the organization into jurisdictions was introduced at the time of Unification in 1939, there was uncertainty whether such a division should be called a "jurisdiction" or a "Jurisdictional Conference." Some of the resulting inconsistencies are still found in the Constitution; but in 1944 all legislation was edited to conform to the popular usage which had by that time become established, to use the word "jurisdiction" except for the administrative body.

Lay speaker. A member of a local church certified by his Quarterly Conference as qualified to conduct services of worship and hold meetings for prayer and exhortation under the direction of his pastor or district superintendent. (¶ 293.)

Layman. A member of a local church. This term applies to a local preacher, even though ordained.

Location. The voluntary or involuntary termination of a minister's membership in an Annual Conference and return to the status of a local preacher. (¶¶ 374-79.)

Member, church. A person who has been baptized and has accepted the baptismal and membership vows, entering into solemn covenant with the members of the church, as provided in the Ritual. (¶¶ 106-17, 1713-14.)

Minister. Properly, an ordained traveling preacher. (*See* Order, ministerial; Preacher, traveling.) The term "minister" is generally used in place of "traveling preacher" as the alternative to "layman." It is sometimes loosely used of any ordained preacher, or of any pastor.

Minister on trial. One who, after meeting the conditions prescribed in the Discipline, has been received by vote of an Annual Conference as a probationary member of that body. (¶¶ 321-33.)

Minister in full connection. One who, having satisfactorily completed all the Disciplinary requirements, including the probationary period (except for those received on credentials), has been elected to full membership by an Annual Conference. (¶¶ 341-45.)

Minister in effective relation. One in full connection in an Annual Conference who is under appointment of a bishop.

Minister under special appointment (in detached service). One who has been appointed by a bishop to serve in some capacity other than as pastor or district superintendent. (¶ 432.4-.6.)

Minister, supernumerary. One who because of impaired health or other equally sufficient reason is temporarily unable to perform full work and has been granted this relation by vote of the Annual Conference. (¶ 365.)

Minister, retired (superannuated). One who has been placed in the retired relation by action of his Annual Conference or who has reached the age of seventy-two and therefore has automatically been placed in the retired relation. (¶¶ 367-71.)

Mission. The administrative body of a field of work outside any Annual Conference which is under the care of the Board of Missions and has not yet met the requirements of a Provisional Annual Conference. It exercises in a general way the functions of a District Conference. (¶¶ 1215, 1254.)

Missionary. A minister or layman who, on recommendation of the Joint Committee on Missionary Personnel, has been commissioned by the Board of Missions and assigned to some definite home or foreign field. (¶ 1209.)

Official Board. The administrative body of the local church, responsible to the Quarterly Conference. (¶¶ 206-16.)

Order, ministerial. The rank or status of a person in the Christian ministry. In The Methodist Church ministerial orders are of two classes: deacon's and elder's.

Ordination. The act of conferring ministerial orders. The ritual for ordination is set forth in the Discipline. (¶¶ 1720-21.)

Pastor. A preacher who, by appointment of the bishop or the district superintendent, is in charge of a station or circuit. (¶¶ 351-52.)

Preacher, local. A layman licensed to preach, or ordained, according to the laws of the church. He continues to be a lay member of a local church. (¶¶ 304-20.) *See note under* Preacher, traveling.

Preacher, traveling. One who is on trial or in full connection in an Annual Conference. (¶¶ 321-85.)

NOTE: This term has an interesting historical background. The minister, in early Methodism, who devoted his full time to the work of the ministry and was therefore subject to appointment in first one place, then another, was called a "traveling preacher," in distinction from the "local preacher," who, because he served only part time and earned his livelihood by other means, was tied to a local community and was unable to "travel" or "itinerate."

Reception on credentials. The process by which a minister coming from some other evangelical church is received into membership by an Annual Conference, on trial or in full connection, on presentation of his ministerial credentials. (¶¶ 411-13.)

Ritual. The rites and ceremonies which have been authorized for use in the administration of the Sacraments of the Lord's Supper and Baptism, in marriage, burial of the dead, ordination, and other offices for the conduct of public and private worship.

Secretary, associate. On the staff of a world service agency, an executive second in authority to a general secretary, who may be assigned authority to speak for the general secretary in his absence. (¶ 783.2*b*.)

Secretary, associate general. On the staff of a world service agency, the administrative head of a division within a board which has one general secretary. (¶ 783.2*b*.)

Secretary, executive. On the staff of a world service agency, the head of a section or of an interboard committee. (¶ 783.2*c*.)

Secretary, general. The chief executive of a major general agency. (¶ 783.2*a*.)

Section. In the structure of a world service agency, a broad subdivision of responsibility within a board or division. (¶ 783.1*b*.)

Special. A special gift to a specific benevolence cause, pledged and paid by a local church in addition to its apportioned benevolences. (¶¶ 745, 756-64.)

Steward. A layman charged with certain responsibilities; specifically, an elected or ex officio member of the Quarterly Conference and the Official Board in a local church. (¶¶ 208-11.)

Supply pastor. A preacher appointed to a pastoral charge as a substitute, either because of an emergency between sessions of the Annual Conference or because of a shortage of ministerial members of the conference.

World service. The basic general benevolences of The Methodist Church, approved by the General Conference and apportioned through the Annual Conferences to the local churches. The general agencies supported by world service funds are: the Board of Missions, the Board of Education, the schools of theology, the Board of Evangelism, the Board of Lay Activities, the Board of Christian Social Concerns, the Board of Hospitals and Homes, the Board of Pensions, the Television, Radio, and Film Commission, and the American Bible Society. (¶¶ 741-55.)

INDEX

The numbers refer to paragraphs (¶¶) and to subparagraphs, the subparagraphs being indicated by the figures following decimal points. The paragraphs are arranged according to the following plan:

Numbers in **bold-faced** type indicate main references or definitions.

A

Abandoned church property, 188, 354, 362.11-.12, 706

Abolition of the Central Jurisdiction, 47 ix, 48.5, 1813

Absentee church membership, 119-20, 127

Abstinence:
From alcoholic beverages, 95, 149.2, 207, 306.6, 322.5, 345 .16, 1536, 1820 III C.1, 1822 .1. *See also* Alcohol
From indulgences, 95, 306.6, 322.5, 345.16
From tobacco, 306.6, 322.5, 1535.1, 1820 III C.5, 1822.10

Acceptance of apportionment, 142.7, 147, 767, 795, 804

Accommodation admissions and ordinations, 651.33

Accounting:
Agencies, general, 737.6
Certified or recognized public accountant, 729, 737.2
Conference treasurer, 808
See also Auditing

Accreditation of schools, 1382, 1387. *See also* University Senate

Acuff's Chapel, 1591.6

Addresses:
Department of Records, 1106.2
Lay leaders, 362.10, 1504.3, 1508.2

Addresses, *cont'd:*
Members of local church, 127, 131-32, 352.25
Officers of local churches, 362.4, .10, .15e, 1106.2

Administration:
Director of organizational, 1531 .1
Errors of, 949
Fund, *See* General Administration Fund; Jurisdictional Administration Fund
Mission. *See* Mission

Administrative:
Agencies. See Agencies, administrative
Committee on the Methodist Youth Fund, 1414.2

Admission into church membership. *See* Reception into church membership

Admission of preachers, 22, 635
Accommodation arrangements, 651.33
Board of Ministerial Training and Qualifications, 669-74. *For details see* Conference Board of Ministerial Training and Qualifications
Department of Ministerial Education, 1371-77. *For details see* Department of Ministerial Education
District Committee on Ministerial Qualification, 695. *For details see* District Committee on Ministerial Qualifications

709

711

Apportionments, *cont'd:*
Committee on (circuit), 145.8
Conference Board of Education, 1450
Conference claimants, 147, 261, 651.11, 798, 822-23, 828, 1623-24
Determination of, 749, 767, 771, 778
District superintendents' support, 147, 261, 801-2, 822-23, 827.3-.5
Episcopal Fund, 147, 261, 738, 771, 799, 805, 822-23
General Administration Fund, 147, 738, 767, 800, 805
Interdenominational Co-operation Fund, 738, 778, 800, 805
Jurisdictional Conference, 795
Minimum salary fund, 651.9, 822-23, 826.3
Ministerial support, 798-99, 801-2, 826-28
Missionary society, city or district, 1232-33
Overpayments, 804-5
Pastor's salary, 145.8, 148, 215.2
Proportional payment (prorating), 267.8, 771, 802, 823, 1611.8, 1623-24, 1630.1
Special gifts not applied on, 745
Special offerings, credit for, 747
Sustentation fund, 828
To Annual Conferences, 651.12, 737.4, 738, 740, 767, 771, 778, 804-5
To districts, 795-97, 800-802, 822-23, 826-27
To local churches, 145.8, 147-48, 261, 740
To pastoral charges, 142.7, 147, 795-802, 822-23, 826-28, 1623-24
World Service Fund, 737.4, 738, 740, 749

Appropriations:
Board of Missions, 1180, 1189.4, 1200-1203, 1204.1*i*
Division of Higher Education, 1354-55, 1371.1, 1378
National Division, Board of Missions, 1229, 1243, 1246.3
Woman's Division, Board of Missions, 1201

Approved service (for pension credit), 1618.1-.5

Approved supply pastor, 8.2, 304.4, 307, **314-20,** 671, 695.3
Admission on trial, 325.3. *See also* Admission of preachers: On trial
Appointment, 309, 314-17, 362 .3, 432
Assistant pastor, 1631
Authority to administer Sacraments, etc., 318
Conference relation, 309, 314, 319-20, 325.3, 622, 630, 645, 651.39*b,* .43
Courses of study, 317-18, 1371.4, 1373
Definition, **314**
Discontinuance, 320, 672.2
Educational requirements, 306-7, 317-18, 1373
Evangelist, 353, 363
From other churches, 316
Full-time, 307.2, 317.2, 318.1, 651.21*b,* 827.1-.2, 1631.1, 1644.1
List of, 651.21
Membership, church, 309
Minimum salary, 317.2-.3, 1631.1
Ordination, 391-92, 393.3, 411.2
Part-time, 307.2, 317.3, 318.2, 651.21*c*
Pension, 651.22, 1623.5, **1631,** 1644.1
Relief, 1631.5
Retired, 651.43, 1631
Salary, 317.2-.3, 1631.1
Student, 307.1, 309.2, 316.1, 317.1, 318.1*b,* 651.21
Trial of, 945, 957-65, 1051-52
Widow of, 1631.7, .11
See also Local preacher; Pastor

Arbitration, Committee of (boundary changes), 534

Architecture:
Approval of plans, 180.4*b,* .7, 723, 1246.2, .9, 1248, 1299.6
Church-school facilities, 1401.1
Commission on Worship, 1569.2, 1571.3*e*
Counsel for local churches, 1248, 1401.1
Hospitals and homes, 1557.1, 1562.3
Interdenominational Bureau of,

712

Building, *cont'd:*
  Methodist Publishing House, 1085, 1156-57
  Metropolitan Area Planning Commission, 722.2, 1227
  Mortgage, 157.2, 171-73, 1246.6-.7
  National Division, Board of Missions, 1224, 1228, 1234, 1246-48, 1299.1, .6-.7
  Parking facilities, 722
  Parsonage, 145.7, 180-81, 183, 278.5, 723, 1246.4, .6, 1247.1, .5
  Purchase, 157.2, 167-70, 174, 180, 723-24, 1228, 1246-48
  Quarterly Conference authority, 157.2
  Remodeling, 157.2, 164.5, 180, 182, 723-24, 1246.4, 1247.1
  Sale, 157.2, 171-73, 175
  Site, 180.8, 722, 1248.5, 1299.1.
  Use of, 165, 233.6*h*
  See also Property; Trustees

Bulgaria Provisional Annual Conference, 1843.6

Bulletin, weekly church, 160, 168, 170, 171.1, 172.1, 180.3, .6, 196

Bureau:
  Architecture, Interdenominational, 1569.12
  Convention, 1109
  Personnel, 1557.5
  Definition, **783.1***d*

Burial of the dead:
  Duty of pastor, 352.2
  Report of, 312, 352.22*b*, 374
  Ritual, 1719

Burma, 1805.1, 1806, 1809.4, 1850.1

Business:
  Manager, church, 143.11, 209, 212.2, 262.2, 269, 1498.5
  Women, residences for, 1240

C

Cabinet:
  Agency membership, 675, 679, 755.2, 1253.3, 1302.1, 1452.2, 1502.1
  Appointment of preachers, 314, 432.1-.2, .4-.5
  Called session of Annual Conference, 627

Cabinet, *cont'd:*
  Consultation with, for nominations, 1296.1, 1301.1, 1302.4, 1452.1, 1479.2
  District boundaries, 431.3
  Election by, 675, 1295, 1453, 1455.1
  Emergency financial appeal, 810
  Location of minister, 378
  Missions and church extension, 1299.2-.3, 1301
  Nomination by, 669.1, 791, 1302.1, 1444, 1502.1
  Recommendation of preachers, 325.3, 393.4-.5

California-Nevada Annual Conference, 1841.2

Call to:
  Prayer and self-denial, 1208.1*f*
  Preach, 301-3, 322.5, 352.20, 362.15*g*, 671

Camp Activities, Commission on, 763, 1073, 1417.2, 1573, 1593.1

Campaign, financial. *See* Appeal, financial; Every-member visitation; Fund-raising agent

Camps and conferences:
  Conference Committee on, 1455, 1461.2
  Directors, 1461.2
  District Committee on, 1455, 1461
  Local church, 233.7*j*, 243
  Property, 1442.2-.3, 1455.2, 1461.3-.4
  Racial policies, 1401.4, 1813.5*e*
  Standards, 1401.4, 1442.1, .3, 1455.2, 1461.2-.4

Campus:
  Church Relations Committee, 1365.2-.3
  Ministry, 233.7*f*, 244.5, 1352.4, 1363-70, 1403, 1405, 1442.1, 1448.3. *See also* Methodist Student Movement; Wesley Foundation
  Religious Life, Committee on, 1365.2

Candidates:
  For church membership, 106-11, 114
  For deaconess, 146.2, 1253.4*b*

Central Conference, *cont'd:*
agencies
Ritual, 571
Rules, 547
Secretary, 445, 549, 560
Trials, 570, 930, 935
Woman's Work, Committee on, 568-69

Central Congo Annual Conference, 1842.2

Central Council (affiliated autonomous church), 602.3

Central Germany Annual Conference, 1845.1

Central Jurisdiction, 26, 47 ix
Abolition of, 47 ix, 48.5, 1813
Annual Conferences, 1838
Representation on general agencies, 1079
Temporary General Aid Fund, 732 note
Transfers from, 28, 47 ix, 532, 639, 651.18e, 680, 1079, 1813

Central Kansas Annual Conference, 1840.2

Central New York Annual Conference, 1836.3

Central Pennsylvania Annual Conference, 1836.4

Central promotional office, 750 .1, 752-54, 755.1, 761.3, 762.1. *See also* Commission on Promotion and Cultivation

Central Texas Annual Conference, 1840.3

Central treasury, 732, 735, 737 .1, 745-46, 759.3, 1595.3, 1596.4, *See also* Council on World Service and Finance: Treasurer

Central West Annual Conference, 1809.1, 1838.3

Certificate:
Baptism, 114.2
Bishop's resignation, 435.2
Election to General Conference, 501
Lay speaker, 293.3c

Certificate, *cont'd:*
Local preacher's official standing and dismissal, 308-9. *See also* License
Location, 374, 376
Medical, 1617.4, .6
Membership, 352.26, 950, 992. *See also* Certificate: Transfer
Organization of new local church, 642
Recognition from Board of Hospitals and Homes, 1566
Recognition of ministerial orders, 414-15
Supernumerary minister, 365
Transfer, 110-11, 114.4, 121-22, 155.3, 352.4, 602.1, *See also* Letter of notification
Withdrawal from membership, 124

Certification:
Council, 1557.3
Directors and ministers of Christian education and music, 247, 1401.2-.3, 1451.1

Certified public accountant, 729, 737.2, 739, 803

Chairman:
Board of:
Education, divisions of, 1327 .4, 1329.2
Publication, 1135, 1422
Commission (local church), 143.6, 144, 209, 221.1-.2, 232, 256, 262, 274.2, 276, 352.16, 362.10, 1106.2
Commission on:
Chaplains, 1572
Town and Country Work (Annual Conference), 1291, 1302.4
Worship, 1568.2
Committee (local church), 143 .6, 145.1, .3, .9, 262.5, 276.2, 278
Committee on:
Education and Cultivation, 1295
Family Life, General, 1417.2
Conference agency, 793
Conference Board of:
Evangelism, 1478.3, .4
Hospitals and Homes, 1561.3, 1565
Lay Activities. *See* Lay leader: Conference.
Ministerial Training and Qualifications, 675

Clearinghouse (pensions), 431.7, 1619, 1620.1, 1621.1, 1631.7, 1634.2-.3, 1636

Code of ethics (hospitals and homes), 1557.6

College:
Appointment to attend, 432.7
Campus-Church Relations Committee, 1365.2-.3
Classification, 1383.1, 1384, 1389, 1391.2
Committee on Campus Religious Life, 1365. 2
Department of College and University Religious Life, 1351.4, 1363, 1368-70
Educational requirements for ministry, 307.1, 309.2, 318.1, 323-25, 669-70, 673
Faculty Christian Movement, 1442.1
Financial support, 651.12*f*, 689 .5, 810, 1352.6-.9, 1354-55, 1385-86, 1391.2, 1450, 1452.1, .4
Interconference Commission on College and University Religious Life, 1370, 1448.3
Loan Fund, Student, 250.4, 1358
Methodist Student Movement, 1368-70. *For details see* Methodist Student Movement
Missionary education, 1208.1*g*, 1282.1
Promotion of enrollment, 149.1, 233.7*f*, 352.17, 362.15*e*, 689.5
Racial policies, 250.3, 1083, 1335, 1351.1, 1352.7, 1357, 1813.4*b*, 1824 B.2
Research studies, 1244
Scholarships. *See* Scholarships
Student religious work, 233.7*f*, 244.5, 1324, 1352.4, 1363-70, 1403, 1405, 1442.1, 1448.3
Trustees, 711.2, 728
Wesley Foundation, 1364-67. *For details see* Wesley Foundation
See also Educational institutions; School of theology

College of Bishops:
Called session, Jurisdictional or Central Conference, 523.2, 544-45
Disability of bishop, 435.3, 436 .4, 775

College of Bishops, *cont'd:*
Elections by, 1415.2, 1518-19, 1581.2
Nominations by 750.2, 1045, 1180.2, 1311, 1519, 1602.1
President, 436.3-.4, 775, 923-24
Retirement of bishop, 436.3-.4
Sabbatical leave of bishop, 426
Secretary, 436.3-.4, 924.6
Special assignment of bishop, 425
Transfer of bishop, 48.2
Vacancies, filled by, 750.3, 1082, 1091, 1311, 1552

Colored Methodist Episcopal Church, 46 iv. *See also* Christian: Methodist Episcopal Church

Comity agreement, 189.2, 578, 1285.3*d*

Commission:
Annual Conference, 651.4, .14, 666, 679, 1106.2, 1658. *See also* Agencies: Annual conference; Conference Commission on:
Chairman, local church, 143.6, 144, 209, 219.4, 221.1-.2, 232, 256, 262, 274.2, 276.2, 352.16, 362.10, 1106.2
General, 783.2*a*, 1071, 1106.2, 1658. *See also* Agencies, general. *For individual commissions see below* Commission on Camp Activities, etc.
Local church, 142-44, 155.7, 209, 219-77. *For individual commissions see below* Commission on Christian Social Concerns (local church), etc.
Optional, 219.1, 276-77
Quadrennial, 1812-15

Commission on Camp Activities, 763, 1073, 1417.2, 1573, 1593.1

Commission on Chaplains, 393.5, 403.4, 763, 1073, 1404 .2, 1415.2, 1417.2, 1476, **1572,** 1593.1, 1618.2*h*, 1671

Commission on Chaplains and Armed Forces Personnel, General, 778

Commission on Christian Higher Education (Confer-

743

Counsel, *cont'd:*
Legal, 1006-7, 1105.4
Premarital, 355-56

Counselor, audio-visual, 235

Courses of study, 1374
Admission:
Into full connection, 343-44, 635, 1373.1
On trial, 325.2-.3, 1373.1
Advanced, 1373.1
Approved supply pastors, 307.2, 317-18, 651.21, 1373
Board of Ministerial Training and Qualifications, 317, 325.2-.3, 330-32, 343-44, 393.2-.3, 403.2, **673-74,** 1373.3. *See also* Conference Board of Ministerial Training and Qualifications
Central Conferences, 333, 573
Continuing non-credit education, 1374
Correspondence study, 317.2, 331, 673, 674.2, 1373.4-.5
Credit for equivalent work, 327, 343.3
Deacon's orders, 393.2-.3
Department of Ministerial Education, 307.2, 317, 327, 343-44, 1371, 1373. *See also* Department of Ministerial Education
Discipline, 306.4
Elder's orders, 403.2
Four-year ministerial course, 307.2, 317-18, 325.3, 327, 332, 343, 393.2-.3, 403.2, 1373.1
Introductory studies for the ministry, 318, 325.2, 327, 393.3
License to preach, 306.4, 1373.1
Local preachers, 306-7, 312, 1373
Methodist history, polity, and doctrine, 342, 344, 411.3, 1373.2
Pastors' schools, 317.2, 331, 674.2, 1371.4, 1373.3
Records, 674.2
Special studies for minister without college degree, 343.2
Time limits, 307.2, 317-18, 332
Transfer to another conference, 431.7

Court:
Appellate, 1026-32, 1045-49, 1057-60

Court, *cont'd:*
Juvenile, 1228
Trial, 924-27, 935, 937, 959, 966, 973-74, 1057

Cox, Edward, House, 1591.6

Credentials:
Bishop, 435.2, 445
Deaconess, 1250.7, 1253.4b
Deprivation and restoration, 991-96. *See also* Credentials: Surrender
Issuance, 431.9
Minister from another church, 316.2, 411-15
Restoration, 695.3, 993, 995-96
Surrender, 311, 362.3, 380-82, 432.8, 636, 961, 992-93
See also Certificates; License to preach; Ordination

Credits:
Educational, 306-7, 317-18, 326-27, 344, 674
Income annuity, 1643.5-.7, 1646, 1647.2-.3, 1648.1, 1652.1, .3, 1656.4, .8-.9
Service annuity, 1624.3, 1643.4, .7, 1645.7-.8, .10, 1647.1, 1648.1, 1651.1b, 1652.1, .3, 1653.5c, 1656.3, .7-.9, .12b

Crime, 1535.1, 1820 III C.2, 1822.4

Crusade scholarships, 257.11, 760.1, .3, 1287

Cuba, 1805.1, 1806, 1809.4, 1823 II.8, 1837.3

Cultivation, Promotion, and Publication, Interagency Commission on, 1576-79

Current expenses, (local church), 148, 150.1, 173.1, 184, 261, 266-68

Curriculum:
Church school, responsibility, 233.3, 248.5
Committee, 233.3, 248.5, 1143, 1146-47, 1282.2, 1396, 1423-24, **1433**
Committee on Use of Methodist Curriculum Materials (Annual Conference), 1454
Materials, 1122, 1282.2, 1421-

Missions, *cont'd:*
District superintendent's duty, 362.15*d*
Pastor's duty, 257.5-.7, 352.16, .22*j*
School of, 257.2

Mississippi Annual Conference (C), 1838.7

Mississippi Annual Conference (SE), 1837.9

Missouri East Annual Conference, 1840.7

Missouri West Annual Conference, 1840.8

Montana Annual Conference, 1841.4

Moradabad Annual Conference, 1851.9

Mortgage, 157.2, **171-73,** 1246 .6-.7, *See also* Borrowing funds; Debt; Lien; Property

Motion pictures. *See* Audio-visual; Television, Radio, and Film Commission

Moving expenses, pastor, 148, 829

Mozambique, 1842.4

Music:
Assistant, 143.10, 247.2
Choirs, 233.3, 243, 278.4
Church school, 233.3, 247.2, 278.4
Commission on Worship:
Annual Conference, 1571.3*d, f*
General, 1569.2
Local church, 219.1, 276-77, 1569.1
Committee (local church), 143 .10, 247.2, 276.1, **278.4**
Director of, 143.10, 232.1, **247 .2,** 278.4, 1396, 1401.3, **1451**
Methodist Hymnal, The, 8.6, 1569.5, 1571.3*c*
Minister of, 232.1, **247.2,** 278.4, 1396, 1401.3, **1451**
National Fellowship of Methodist Musicians, 1401.3, 1571 .3*f*

N

N-1 Program, 1825

Name of church, 2, 701, 1618.8

Narcotics, 1535.1, 1820 III C.5, 1822.9

National Association of Methodist Hospitals and Homes, 1562.4, 1567

National Christian Council of Indonesia, 1810.2

National Conference:
Methodist Men, 1497.4, 1503.3
Methodist Student Movement, 1369, 1405
Methodist Youth Fellowship, 1180.5, 1326.4, **1404-5,** 1415 .2, 1458, 1468, 1518
Town and Country Work, 1238, 1285.2*b*

National Convocation on Christian Stewardship, 1498.7, 1503.3

National Council of Churches, 275.1, 760.3, 778, 1371.4, 1425-26, 1499.3, 1569.12, 1575, 1581.4*d*, .6, **1595**

National Division, Board of Missions, 1185, 1206, 1221-54
Administration of a Mission, 612-13, 615, 1254
Advance specials, 746.2, 756-59, 1189.2, 1202, 1206*e*, 1208 .1*i*. *For details see* Advance
Annuities, 1189.2, 1201, 1246.8
Appropriations, 1189.1, .4, 1201-3, 1222, 1229.5, 1239-43, 1246.3, 1260-61
Architecture, 1246.2, 1248, 1286
Assistant general secretaries, 1192.2, 1281
Associate general secretary, 1180.6, 1185.1, 1192.2, 1196, 1221, 1271, 1281, 1414.2, 1593.1
Authority, 1201
Bilingual work, 1228-29, 1254.5
Bishops, co-operation with, 1221
Buildings, church, 1224, 1228, 1234, 1246-48

Pension regulations, *cont'd:*

Fractional years of service, 1618 .2i

General Endowment Fund for Conference Claimants, 1608

General regulations, 1630

Group life insurance, 1630.10

Hospitalization and Medical Expense Program, 1681

Illinois Corporation, 1601

Incapacity of dependent child, 1621.2

Income annuity, 1643.5, .6, 1646 .1, .7, 1647.2, .3, 1648, 1652, 1656.4c, 8c-e

Initial reserve fund, 1654, 1656.7

Interest, regular, 1643.3

Investments, 1612.4, 1625.1b

Committee,, 1612.1

Funds, 1610.1

Printed in journal, 1612.7

Joint Contributory Annuity Fund, 1666

Joint Distributing Committee, 1609

Lay Employees Pension Fund, 1658-59

Liens on annuities, 1610.3, 1634

Life insurance company, 1630 .10

Loans from pension funds, 1612 .2, .3

Located person, 379, 1630.15

Maryland Corporation, 1601

Medical certificate, 1617.4, .6

Medical Expense Program, Hospitalization and, 1681

Merger of Annual Conferences, 1609

Methodist:

Church, The, definition, 1618 .8

Institutions, 1618.9, 1623.7

Publishing House, 9.5, 1124-25, 1625.1a

Ministerial support, 821, 1615

Ministers Reserve Pension, Fund, 1623.7, 1624.1-.3, 1642-55

Missionary, 1622, 1631.9. 1637

Missouri Corporation, 1601

Moneys for distribution, 1625

Partial Reserve Pension Fund, 1656

Payment of annuities, 1625

Penalty for defaults, 1630.5

Permanent funds, 1607-9, 1610 .1, .3

Preachers aid societies, 1610.1

Pension regulations, *cont'd:*

Proportional payment, 1611.8, **1624,** 1630.1, .5-.6

Real property, 1612.5

Refunds, 1652, 1656.11

Relief money, 1611.9-.10, 1625 .2, 1631.5

Relinquishment of claim, 1626, 1630.9

Remuneration of agency members, restriction on, 1612.2

Retired Ministers Day, 296.3b, 1610.6

Retirement, 367-69, 435-38, 559 .2, 774-77, 1614, 1617, 1619, 1631.2-.3, 1658.6, .8

Sabbatical leave, 1618.2f

Salary, 1610.4, 1618.6, 1623.2, 1624.1, .3, .6, 1631.1, .4, 1645.1, 1646.1, 1653.1, 1656 .4a

Schedule of payments, 1635.2, .4, 1646.1

Secretaries of bishops, 1659

Service annuity, 1643.4, 1647.1, 1648, 1651.1b, 1652, 1653.2, .5c, 1656.8a-d, .12b

Service Annuity Fund, 1653.1, .2

Service fee, 1635.3

Service records, 661, 1629

Special:

Appointment, 1644.1, 1645.8, .10, 1666, 1676

Claimant, 1631

Offerings, 1625.1e

Stabilization fund, 1611.13

Staff Pension Fund, 1676

Student, 1618.2e

Supernumerary ministers, 365, 1630.14

Support, 1643.2

Temporary General Aid Fund, 732 note, 1685

Term episcopacy, 559.2

Termination of employment, 1658.8

Transfers, 1656.3d, .4b

Widow, 435.2, 769-70, 772, 774, 777. 1614. 1618.2g, .3b, **1620,** 1627.4, 1630.12. .13, 1631.7, .11, 1648.1, 1652.4, 1656.8a, e. .9

Years of approved service, 777, 1618.1-.5

Pensions, Board of, 1601-6. *For details see* Board of Pensions

Per diem expenses, 602.3, 605

804

Race relations, *cont'd:*
322.5, 1813.4c, 1824 B.1
Methodist Social Creed, 1820 III D
Metropolitan Area Planning Commission, 722.2, 1227, 1299.1
Ministry, 322.5, 371, 432.1, 1813.4-.5, 1824 B
Missions among racial groups, 371, 1222, 1226.1, 1254
Participation in program of church, 106.1, 233.1, 322.5, 1813.5, 1824 B.1
Personnel policies, 1083, 1105.2 note, 1195, 1351.5-.6, 1813 .4b, 1824 B.2-.4, C.5
Reports to General Conference, 1105.2 note, 1813.2g, .9
Resolution of General Conference, 1824
Section of Christian Social Relations, 1813.2h
Sunday, 250.3, 275.3, 296.1b, 1335, 1357.3
Surveys, 1244, 1541.1, 1813.2
Temporary General Aid Fund, 732 note, 1685
Woman's Division, Board of Missions, 1813.2h

Radio. *See* Television, Radio, and Film Commission

Raffles, 272

Rally:
Day. *See* Christian: Education: Sunday
Missionary, 1307

Ratio distribution of funds:
Conference benevolences, 794-95, 804
Fellowship of Suffering and Service, 763
General Administration Fund, 766, 768
Local church, 267.8, 282.4, 771, 823, 1624
Methodist Youth Fund, 1414.1
Ministerial support, 771, 823, 1624
One Great Hour of Sharing, 760.3-.4
World service, 737.4, 742, 745, 748
World service and conference benevolences, 795, 804

Ratio of representation, 7, 12, 17, 47 ii, vii, 501, 517, 543. *See also* Delegates

Readmission, located minister, 376, 379, 432.8, 651.34, 993, 1630.15

Real estate. *See* Building; Property

Reception into Annual Conference. *See* Admission of preachers

Reception into church membership, 106-16, 1714
Affiliate, 116
All eligible for, 106.1, 107, 1714, 1820 III D.1, 1824 A.3-.5, B.1
Baptism, 102, 107, 111, 114, 1713. *See also* Baptism
Central Conference authority, 565
Certificate of, 352.26. *See also* Certificate: Membership; Certificate: Transfer
Chaplain, 108
Children, 114.4-.5, 1714
Congregation, presence of, 107-9, 1714
From other denominations, 111, 116
General Conference authority, 8.1
New local church, 155.3-.4
Preparatory, 114.2-.4
Profession of faith, 106.2, 107-8, 111, 114.5, 149.2, 155.4, 222.4, 352.4, .26
Qualifications for, 8.1, 94, 101-2, 107-9, 111, 114.5, 116, 565, 1714
Record of, 131, 352.23
Report of, 130, 149.2, 352.22b, .28
Restoral, 124, 127, 977
Ritual, 1714
Training for, 107, 114.5, 222.15, 233.7i, 241, 352.4, .22e, 1396, 1418
Transfer, 110-11, 114.4, 118-22, 128, 155.3, 308-9, 352.4, 602 .1, 1714
Visitation evangelism, 222.2
Vows, 102, 107-9, 111, 127, 1714

Recognized public accountant, 729